The Developmental Course of Marital Dysfunction

How do marriages become unhappy? How do marriages change? What theories and methods can best illuminate our understanding of marital development? As the first comprehensive volume to explore how marriages develop and deteriorate, *The Developmental Course of Marital Dysfunction* brings together leading scholars to present recent research on the longitudinal course of marriage. The chapters share a common focus on the early phases of marriage but address a diverse array of topics, including marital conflict, personality, social support, the transition to parenthood, violence, ethnicity, stress, alcohol use, commitment, and sexuality. Implications of this research for alleviating marital distress are also noted. The book concludes with six provocative analyses by prominent scholars in the areas of sociology, clinical psychology, social psychology, and developmental psychology.

By combining current theories, methods, and data, *The Developmental Course of Marital Dysfunction* serves as a valuable introduction to the longitudinal study of marriage.

Dr. Thomas Bradbury is Associate Professor of Psychology at the University of California, Los Angeles. He has earned numerous honors for his research, including the David Shakow Early Career Award from the Clinical Psychology Division of the American Psychological Association, the Reuben Hill Award from the National Council on Family Relations, and the Distinguished Scientific Award for Early Career Contribution to Psychology from the American Psychological Association.

Cambridge Studies in Social and Emotional Development

General Editor: Martin L. Hoffman, New York University

The Developmental Course
of Marital Dysfunction

Edited by
Thomas N. Bradbury

CAMBRIDGE
UNIVERSITY PRESS

CAMBRIDGE UNIVERSITY PRESS
Cambridge, New York, Melbourne, Madrid, Cape Town, Singapore, São Paulo

Cambridge University Press
The Edinburgh Building, Cambridge CB2 2RU, UK

Published in the United States of America by Cambridge University Press, New York

www.cambridge.org
Information on this title: www.cambridge.org/9780521451901

First published 1998
This digitally printed first paperback version 2006

A catalogue record for this publication is available from the British Library

Library of Congress Cataloguing in Publication data
The developmental course of marital dysfunction / edited by Thomas N.
Bradbury.
    p.   cm. – (Cambridge studies in social and emotional
development)
Includes bibliographical references and index.
ISBN 0-521-45190-6 (hc)
1. Marriage – Psychological aspects – Longitudinal studies.
2. Marital conflict – Longitudinal studies.   I. Bradbury, Thomas N.
II. Series.
HQ734.D527   1998
306.81 – dc21   97–29630
                                                           CIP

ISBN-13 978-0-521-45190-1 hardback
ISBN-10 0-521-45190-6 hardback

ISBN-13 978-0-521-02858-5 paperback
ISBN-10 0-521-02858-2 paperback

For all they have given me, I dedicate this book to the women in my life:

My grandmothers, Barbara Joyce Lynch Bradbury and Francess O'Neill Nelson Parr

My mother, Mary Elizabeth Nelson Bradbury

My sisters, Elizabeth O'Neill Carpenter, Susan Lynch Follett, and Barbara King Bradbury

My mother-in-law, Ruby Chung Yee

My wife, friend, companion, and colleague, Cindy May Yee-Bradbury

Contents

List of Contributors   *page* xii

Foreword   xv
Robert L. Weiss

Introduction: The Developmental Course
of Marital Dysfunction   1
Thomas N. Bradbury

Part I   Conceptual and Empirical Contributions

1   Communication in Early Marriage: Responses to Conflict,
    Nonverbal Accuracy, and Conversational Patterns   11
    Patricia Noller and Judith A. Feeney

2   Marital Aggression, Quality, and Stability in the First Year
    of Marriage: Findings from the Buffalo Newlywed Study   44
    Kenneth E. Leonard and Linda J. Roberts

3   Accommodation Processes During the Early Years
    of Marriage   74
    *Caryl E. Rusbult, Victor L. Bissonnette, Ximena B. Arriaga,
    and Chante L. Cox*

4   The Psychological Infrastructure of Courtship and Marriage:
    The Role of Personality and Compatibility in Romantic
    Relationships   114
    Ted L. Huston and Renate M. Houts

5   Happiness in Stable Marriages: The Early Years   152
    *Joseph Veroff, Elizabeth Douvan, Terri L. Orbuch,
    and Linda K. Acitelli*

ix

 6   Developmental Changes in Marital Satisfaction: A 6-Year
     Prospective Longitudinal Study of Newlywed Couples   180
     Lawrence A. Kurdek

 7   The Development of Marriage: A 9-Year Perspective   205
     Kristin Lindahl, Mari Clements, and Howard Markman

 8   Premarital Predictors of Relationship Outcomes:
     A 15-Year Follow-up of the Boston Couples Study   237
     Charles T. Hill and Letitia Anne Peplau

 9   Optimizing Longitudinal Research for Understanding
     and Preventing Marital Dysfunction   279
     Thomas N. Bradbury, Catherine L. Cohan,
     and Benjamin R. Karney

10   Socialization into Marital Roles: Testing a Contextual,
     Developmental Model of Marital Functioning   312
     Irv Tallman, Peter J. Burke, and Viktor Gecas

11   Physical Aggression in Marriage:
     A Developmental Analysis   343
     K. Daniel O'Leary and Michele Cascardi

Part II   Invited Commentaries

12   On Intervention and Relationship Events: A Marital
     Therapist Looks at Longitudinal Research on Marriage   377
     Andrew Christensen

13   A Developmentalist's Perspective on Marital Change   393
     Ross D. Parke

14   Couples, Gender, and Time: Comments on Method   410
     David A. Kenny

15   On the Etiology of Marital Decay and Its Consequences:
     Comments from a Clinical Psychologist   423
     John M. Gottman

16   Problems and Prospects in Longitudinal Research
     on Marriage: A Sociologist's Perspective   427
     Norval D. Glenn

17 A Social Psychological View of Marital Dysfunction
   and Stability   441
   Ellen Berscheid

   Author Index   461

   Subject Index   470

Contributors

Linda K. Acitelli
Department of Psychology
University of Houston
Houston, TX 77204-5341

Ximena B. Arriaga
Center for Organizational and
    Behavioral Sciences
The Claremont Graduate School
Claremont, CA 91711

Ellen Berscheid
Department of Psychology
University of Minnesota
Minneapolis, MN 55455

Victor L. Bissonnette
Department of Psychology
Southern Louisiana University
Hammond, LA 70402

Thomas N. Bradbury
Department of Psychology
University of California, Los Angeles
Los Angeles, CA 90095-1563

Peter J. Burke
Department of Sociology
Washington State University
Pullman, WA 99164-4020

Michele Cascardi
Dating Violence Prevention Project,
    Inc.
Bala-Cynwyd, PA 19004

Andrew Christensen
Department of Psychology
University of California, Los Angeles
Los Angeles, CA 90095-1563

Mari Clements
Department of Psychology
The Pennsylvania State University
University Park, PA 16820

Catherine L. Cohan
Department of Human Development
    and Family Studies
The Pennsylvania State University
University Park, PA 16820

Chante L. Cox
Department of Psychology
University of North Carolina at Chapel
    Hill
Chapel Hill, NC 27599-3270

Elizabeth Douvan
Institute for Social Research
The University of Michigan
Ann Arbor, MI 48106-1248

Judith A. Feeney
Department of Psychology
University of Queensland
Brisbane, Queensland, Australia 4072

Viktor Gecas
Department of Sociology
Washington State University
Pullman, WA 99164-4020

Norval D. Glenn
Department of Sociology
The University of Texas at Austin
Austin, TX 78712

John M. Gottman
Department of Psychology
University of Washington
Seattle, WA 98195

Charles T. Hill
Department of Psychology
Whittier College
Whittier, CA 90608

Renate M. Houts
Department of Human Ecology
The University of Texas at Austin
Austin, TX 78712

Ted L. Huston
Department of Human Ecology
The University of Texas at Austin
Austin, TX 78712

Benjamin R. Karney
Department of Psychology
University of Florida
Gainesville, FL 32610

David A. Kenny
Department of Psychology
University of Connecticut
Storrs, CT 06269-1020

Lawrence A. Kurdek
Department of Psychology
Wright State University
Dayton, OH 45435-0001

Kenneth E. Leonard
Research Institute on Addictions
1021 Main Street
Buffalo, NY 14203

Kirstin Lindahl
Department of Psychology
University of Miami
Coral Gables, FL 33124-2070

Howard Markman
Department of Psychology
University of Denver
Denver, CO 80208

Patricia Noller
Department of Psychology
University of Queensland
Brisbane, Queensland, Australia 4072

K. Daniel O'Leary
Department of Psychology
The University at Stony Brook
Stony Brook, NY 11794-2500

Terri L. Orbuch
Department of Sociology
The University of Michigan
Ann Arbor, MI 48109

Ross D. Parke
Department of Psychology
University of California, Riverside
Riverside, CA 92521

Letitia Anne Peplau
Department of Psychology
University of California, Los Angeles
Los Angeles, CA 90095-1563

Linda J. Roberts
Department of Child and Family
    Studies
University of Wisconsin
Madison, WI 53706

Caryl E. Rusbult
Department of Psychology
University of North Carolina at Chapel
    Hill
Chapel Hill, NC 27599-3270

Irv Tallman
Department of Sociology
Washington State University
Pullman, WA 99164-4020

Joseph Veroff
Institute for Social Research
The University of Michigan
Ann Arbor, MI 48106-1248

Robert L. Weiss
Department of Psychology
University of Oregon
Eugene, OR 97403

Foreword

Robert L. Weiss

In the back of every marital therapist's mind there is – or should be! – a gnawing doubt about values. As a professional, how does one know that a given marriage is "missing" something important? Clearly, therapists need to be informed about theories of adult intimacy. Familiarity with the myriad of piecemeal, cross-sectional studies showing this or that something about "basic" processes is also a good idea, albeit practically rather difficult. Over the years in my clinical work I have taken it as axiomatic that successful couples must achieve something unique to themselves and that they must be active! As a marital therapy supervisor, I confess to getting bored when a couple is boring, and I get even more bored when marital therapists allow their sessions to become boring. Isn't that just my own limited attention span masquerading as a "defining property" of all good marriages?

It was with unbridled glee that I read about "zest" – one of the variables Joseph Veroff, Elizabeth Douvan, Terri Orbuch, and Linda Acitelli included in their study of marital happiness in stable marriages in Chapter 5. I now feel less self-conscious insisting that spouses in good marriages should be active. "Zest!" That's my kind of construct.

Not every reader of this wide-ranging collection of studies is concerned with couples therapy. Nor has every reader shared my sinking feeling upon learning that some of our very best behavioral skills, those that we teach couples in distress, are not what the typical satisfied, nonclinical, couple does in real life. Yet I suspect that most readers of this volume will come away with a clear appreciation of the fundamental differences between longitudinal studies of marital development and cross-sectional studies that primarily serve to identify correlates of marital satisfaction. I also suspect that most readers will begin to reconsider the "special ingredient" that is missing from distressed marriages and perhaps the limited breadth of our existing models.

With this personal disclosure I hope to underscore the importance of longitudinal studies such as these in making important contributions to the processes of generating knowledge: Their very choice of constructs seems to do this. The vastness of adult human intimacy – as played out in the study of marriage – requires that we cast a big net into a very big ocean. The vastness of the enterprise becomes even more salient should we attempt to inventory possible determinants of marital accommodation. This volume is about *context,* and should there be any lingering doubt, Chapter 9, by Thomas Bradbury, Catherine Cohan, and Benjamin Karney, argues the case most forcibly on methodological grounds. It and the other chapters show that classes of variables, ranging from individual to social, may be necessary to describe adequately the influence of "contexts." The studies offered here represent work at various stages of completion, but all help to provide a fuller menu of the levels from which we can draw relevant variables for understanding marriage. The multidisciplinary focus of this volume, reflected both in the primary chapters and the high-level commentary, may be a glimpse of things to come.

Even a cursory reading of the journals indicates that knowledge about marriage has grown largely within each of our fairly restricted disciplines. There are numerous studies utilizing techniques of behavioral observation with distressed couples interacting in conflict-resolving tasks. For others, mainstream techniques involve survey research or lengthy in-depth interviews. Communication theories of marriage have spawned interesting approaches and numerous topologies. And certainly, clinical intervention techniques have been the basis of much empirical data. Yet my sense is that we have been working fairly independently of one another. There is no grand theory of human behavior (in the broadest sense of that term) that attempts to show how people succeed – or at least make a good struggle – with the vicissitudes of the marital life cycle. "Grand theory" has not been popular within psychology for many years. Freud attempted a grand theory (also a developmental theory). Considering the scope of the marital life cycle (i.e., the many factors that might account for change), I am inclined to ask whether the covert aim of this volume is to introduce "grand-scale" theorizing. Whatever the answer to this question, the present volume seeks to take us in this direction, and there can be little doubt that significant challenges await us.

Maybe just because of its potential for grandiosity, any developmental theory of marriage faces serious limitations. From the time of its inception, to the last day of data collection, longitudinal studies are muscle bound. As many of the contributors to this volume note, their starting constructs are quite dated when the study is prepared for dissemination. Planned analyses that made good sense at Time 1 are, in light of today's methodology, less pointed. The sample at the end of the study may be unlike the one initially planned for. Or, as we have seen in our own time, in studies over longer durations there may be significant cultural changes in how partners even define marriage. These are difficult problems to overcome. But because marital disruption and distress will likely transcend any longitudinal study, all evidence of progress should be evaluated and recognized.

Another limitation on developmental theorizing in this area is the choice of dependent variable. John Gottman once said that our task is to account for the variance in marital satisfaction. I now think this is only partly true. The choice of dependent variables has been restricted to "marital satisfaction" and "marital stability." In one sense, these are fixed-time, end-state variables. Certainly they are relevant to those of us who are interested in promoting prevention programs, or to those who have a vested interest in keeping families intact. Since the work presented addresses some of the basic issues in family science, it must be evaluated in terms of its theoretical contributions. For example, what difference does it make whether couples do or do not report marital satisfaction? How does "satisfaction" fit into a broader nomological net? By making satisfaction the major end-point variable, we may be able to discern predictors of the end state – as some of the authors here attempt to do. But we need to go further than this, and many of the chapters have moved in this direction (i.e., meeting the "so what" issue head on). Longitudinal studies will expose the manner in which "satisfaction" mediates other important aspects of personal and social adjustment. Studies of chronically stable marriages often remind me of newspaper "human interest" accounts of spouses celebrating their 50th wedding anniversary: They attribute "success" to factors ranging from "smoking a cigar every day" to "kissing good-night every night." Assuming there are sufficient numbers of 50-year couples available for study, and assuming they could actually articulate heuristically interesting reasons for staying together that long, how would we carry out prospective studies in this area? Satisfaction may be a useful weather balloon (i.e., a summary variable), but the action is going to be in the "doing." The sometimes awful ways people cope with their day-to-day existence (e.g., the economic vicissitudes they face) make one wonder about the significance of marital satisfaction in the lives of homeless families, drug-dependent persons, or people who barely manage their nonmarital lives. Satisfaction may just be the quintessential protean construct, and there is increasing evidence for this view from the longitudinal studies presented in this book.

One of the fascinating issues the authors address collectively is the relation between what people say and what they do publicly. A number of the present studies either will or do now provide data on these two channels. In an orderly world, we assume that subjective content (cognitions, sentiments) more or less mirrors overt actions when the stakes are high (i.e., intimate relationships). Yet there are many examples from the literature that highlight discrepancies between how spouses evaluate their relationship (sentiment) and the kinds of behaviors they engage in. For example, there is a poor numerical match between the percentage of spouses who answer survey questions about overall marital happiness (overwhelmingly positive) and the divorce rate. But then, historically, attitudes are not perfect predictors of behavior.

Finally, I applaud the authors' attempts to pull together what I would label theory fragments in order to frame their research questions. I suspect that this collection of essays dealing with developmental changes in the marital life cycle will be influential in shaping theory that deals even more broadly with how people cope, problem solve, and express themselves appetitively, and not just reactively.

Introduction: The Developmental Course of Marital Dysfunction

Thomas N. Bradbury

About 90% of all Americans will marry at some point in their life.

U.S. Bureau of the Census, 1992

1.2 million divorces, or about 23,000 per week, were granted in 1994.

De Vita, 1996

The likelihood that a first marriage will end in separation or divorce is now greater than the likelihood that it will continue.

Bumpass, 1990

More than 1 million children under age 18 saw their parents divorce in 1990.

Ahlburg & De Vita, 1992

Relationship problems are the primary reason why people seek counseling in the United States.

Veroff, Kulka, & Douvan, 1981

Sociodemographic facts such as the ones just cited have become well known to the public and are cited frequently by social scientists as justification for studying marriage. Since the 1970s scholars from a number of disciplines, building on the pioneering work of sociologists, have focused their attention on the diverse and complex phenomena associated with marriage – most commonly on the question of what makes marriages satisfying and stable – and their efforts have precipitated many important conceptual, methodological, and empirical advances. This work has gone through three fundamental transitions, and each has served to shape how marriage is conceived and examined.

Preparation of this chapter was supported by grant R29 MH48674 from the National Institute of Mental Health.

1

The First and Second Transitions: Studying Interpersonal and Intrapersonal Facets of Marriage

In the first transition, which began more than two decades ago, many family scientists rejected the prevailing views that (a) marriage could be understood by studying individual spouses rather than their relationship; and (b) spouses' self-reports, when collected in the absence of other forms of data, were particularly informative. This change is reflected in the classic work of Harold Raush and his colleagues (Raush, Barry, Hertel, & Swain, 1974), who maintained that "couples and families need to be studied as systems . . . [because] understanding a relationship requires knowledge of how the relationship functions" (p. 5) and that "studying what people say about themselves is no substitute for studying how they behave. . . . We need to look at what people do with one another" (p. 5).

Behaviorally oriented clinical psychologists who adopted this perspective in an effort to understand and modify dysfunctional patterns of interaction in couples and families (e.g., Patterson, Reid, Jones, & Conger, 1975; Stuart, 1969; Weiss, Hops, & Patterson, 1973) compiled a great deal of information in a laboratory setting on the observable behaviors that distinguished maritally distressed and nondistressed couples. Gottman's *Marital Interaction* (1979) is perhaps the best-known example of this line of work. Gradually, the notion that overt behavior is a key point of departure for understanding and altering marriage gained wide acceptance (for a review, see Weiss & Heyman, 1990), and it gave rise to a form of marital therapy known as behavioral marital therapy, which relied on behavioral principles to modify the rewarding and punishing exchanges of unhappy couples (see Jacobson & Margolin, 1979).

An important by-product of this orientation to marriage is that family scientists have become proficient in methods of quantifying dyadic interaction (e.g., Bakeman & Gottman, 1986) and of assessing the effects of marital therapy (e.g., Baucom & Hoffman, 1986). As the research and treatment in this tradition became increasingly sophisticated, however, investigators and therapists saw that the emphasis on observable *interpersonal* phenomena came at the expense of understanding complex *intrapersonal* variables and that the behaviors exchanged by spouses could not be understood without also examining associated thoughts and feelings (e.g., Berley & Jacobson, 1984; Epstein, 1982; Fincham & O'Leary, 1983; Levenson & Gottman, 1983; Margolin, 1983). Accordingly, a second transition is now occurring in which greater attention is being given to unobservable factors: the emotions that spouses experience in interaction and the physiological changes that accompany them (e.g., Gottman & Levenson, 1992), the association between the explanations or attributions that spouses offer for their relationship problems and the behaviors they display (e.g., Bradbury, Beach, Fincham, & Nelson, 1996), and spouses' divergent perspectives of interpersonal events (e.g., Christensen, Sullaway, & King, 1983), among others. Studies in this area have proliferated, and several books reflect this trend in research (e.g., Fletcher & Fincham, 1991; O'Leary, 1987). In turn, approaches to clinical intervention now tend to adopt a more encompassing view of marriage such that behavioral marital therapy has expanded into cognitive-behavioral marital therapy (e.g., see Baucom & Epstein, 1990) and has subsequently been transformed into integrative couples' therapy (e.g., Christensen, Jacobson, & Babcock, 1995), and an emotionally focused therapy for couples has been developed (e.g., Johnson & Greenberg, 1994).

The Third Transition: Studying the Development of Marital Dysfunction

As a result of these two transitions, investigators have made considerable progress in defining the domain of variables that may help them better understand marriage and establish methods and procedures for clarifying the interplay of these variables. Significant steps have also been taken to translate the research into clinical interventions. Despite these advances, however, many studies of marriage are limited because they are cross sectional in nature and are designed primarily to differentiate maritally distressed and nondistressed couples (see Bradbury & Karney, 1993; Robinson & Jacobson, 1987). Hence these studies reveal little about what causes marital distress and about how to prevent and treat it.

In the third transition, which is now beginning to unfold, several researchers are addressing this problem by collecting data from young couples at several points in their marriage. Although some attention was given to longitudinal change in marriage in the earlier research traditions (e.g., Markman, 1979; see also Kelly & Conley, 1987; Rusbult, 1983), only recently has it become possible to detect a notable shift in the field. Figure I.1 shows the dramatic rise in the number of published longitudinal studies of marriage. A total of 115 such studies had been published by 1995, with nearly 70% of them appearing since 1985. These longitudinal data collections, although building on the accomplishments of the two prior transitions in this area, have the potential to *explain* how marriages succeed and fail rather than simply *describe* the differences between couples who are already distressed and those who are not. This research is likely to have far-reaching

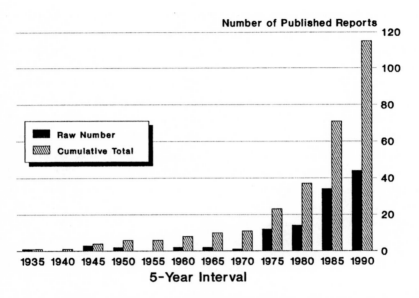

Figure I.1. Number of published longitudinal studies on marriage, from 1935–1940 to 1990–1995. This figure shows that a high proportion of all published longitudinal studies have been published since 1985, documenting the upsurge of interest in this topic. (Data for this figure were taken from Karney & Bradbury, 1995, Table 2.)

consequences because it will facilitate the development of marital therapies and educational prevention programs that are based on longitudinal data pertaining to the causes of marital dysfunction.

The Purpose of This Book: Fostering an Understanding of How Marriages Develop and Deteriorate

The purpose of this book is to facilitate the development of this third transition in the study of marriage. It does so in two ways. First, it presents in a single volume most of the known longitudinal studies that were under way in 1992 and that pertain specifically to the early years of marriage. The first 11 chapters are written by investigators who are actively working on such projects. The projects vary widely along a number of dimensions (e.g., when they were started, their theoretical orientation, the variables of primary interest, sample size, sample composition, and number and frequency of assessments), as do the chapters (e.g., the extent to which they emphasize theory versus data versus methods). Yet in each case the projects include (a) data on newlywed married couples, (b) data collected at more than one point in time, and (c) data on the quality or stability of the marriages.

Having these projects in a single volume makes it easier to identify replicable findings in this domain and thus to ensure that subsequent studies are built on a strong foundation and follow directly from what has already been learned. Despite the enormous benefits of conducting longitudinal studies of marriage, some scientific costs are also apparent: the time-consuming nature of this work sharply reduces our ability to replicate our own findings. Consequently, it is particularly important to focus on the findings in different laboratories in order to move more rapidly toward an understanding of marital development.

The decision to concentrate on the early years of marriage in this book requires a word of explanation. Although a large number of studies have examined longitudinal change in marriage (for a review, see Karney & Bradbury, 1995), most of them involve couples who vary widely in the duration of their marriage and their degree of marital satisfaction. As a result, these studies cannot distinguish readily between the *initial onset* of marital dissatisfaction and the *continuing course* of marital dissatisfaction; in a heterogeneous sample, an overall decline in satisfaction will reflect the onset of marital difficulties for some couples and further deterioration for other couples. It is only when we study samples that are relatively homogenous and high in satisfaction that we can investigate these two longitudinal effects separately. Couples in the early years of marriage, particularly newlyweds, provide a natural solution to this problem and permit investigation of the onset of marital dissatisfaction. The onset of marital dissatisfaction is of central interest to many researchers seeking to establish an empirical foundation for programs aimed at preventing marital discord and instability. It is far more difficult to learn about the onset of marital dissatisfaction and to clarify the origins of marital instability in a manner unconfounded by marital dissatisfaction when couples are already distressed at the beginning of data collection. Moreover, because the peak period for divorce is typically within the third year of marriage (see Fisher, 1992), and because a high proportion of all divorces occur within the first seven years of marriage, studies sampling a heterogenous group of couples will necessarily underrepresent those couples who have already ended their marriage in separation or divorce. Hence the samples will be biased. Again, newlywed couples provide a useful solution to this problem.

The second purpose of this book is to provide integrative commentaries on the work discussed in the first 11 chapters. Six prominent researchers – in the fields of marital therapy, developmental psychology, longitudinal methods, clinical psychology, sociology, and social psychology – were invited to expound on the completed chapters and their implications for subsequent research on marriage. These commentaries are both provocative and useful for looking backward and forward as we progress toward a better understanding of the developmental course of marital dysfunction.

Conclusion

As tempting and important as it is to speculate about the fourth transition in research on marital dysfunction, doing so probably underestimates the conceptual and methodological complexities surrounding the question of why marriages change, develop, and deteriorate. How does the high level of satisfaction experienced by newlywed spouses transform, as it does so often, into despair and discord? What are the early characteristics of marriages that will eventually end in permanent separation or divorce? The chapters in this book go far in revealing the complexity that underlies these questions and in suggesting steps that can be taken to resolve them.

References

Ahlburg, D. A., & De Vita, C. J. (1992). New realities of the American family. *Population Bulletin, 47,* 1–44.

Bakeman, R., & Gottman, J. M. (1986). *Observing interaction: An introduction to sequential analysis.* Cambridge University Press.

Baucom, D. H., & Epstein, N. (1990). *Cognitive-behavioral marital therapy.* New York: Brunner/Mazel.

Baucom, D. H., & Hoffman, J. A. (1986). The effectiveness of marital therapy: Current status and application to the clinical setting. In N. S. Jacobson & A. S. Gurman (Eds.), *Clinical handbook of marital therapy* (pp. 597–620). New York: Guilford.

Berley, R. A., & Jacobson, N. S. (1984). Causal attributions in intimate relationships: Toward a model of cognitive-behavioral marital therapy. In P. Kendall (Ed.), *Advances in cognitive-behavioral research and therapy* (Vol. 3, pp. 1–60). New York: Academic Press.

Bradbury, T. N., Beach, S. R. H., Fincham, F. D., & Nelson, G. M. (1996). Attributions and behavior in functional and dysfunctional marriages. *Journal of Consulting and Clinical Psychology, 64,* 569–576.

Bradbury, T. N., & Karney, B. R. (1993). Longitudinal study of marital interaction and dysfunction: Review and analysis. *Clinical Psychology Review, 13,* 15–27.

Bumpass, L. L. (1990). What's happening to the family? Interactions between demographic and institutional change. *Demography, 27,* 483–498.

Christensen, A., Jacobson, N. S., & Babcock, J. C. (1995). Integrative behavioral couple therapy. In N. S. Jacobson & A. S. Gurman (Eds.), *Clinical handbook of couple therapy* (pp. 31–64). New York: Guilford.

Christensen, A., Sullaway, M., & King, C. E. (1983). Systematic error in behavioral reports of dyadic interaction: Egocentric bias and content effects. *Behavioral Assessment, 5,* 129–140.

De Vita, C. J. (1996). The United States at mid-decade. *Population Bulletin, 50,* 1–44.

Epstein, N. (1982). Cognitive therapy with couples. *The American Journal of Family Therapy, 10,* 5–16.

Fincham, F. D., & O'Leary, K. D. (1983). Causal inferences for spouse behavior in maritally distressed and nondistressed couples. *Journal of Social and Clinical Psychology, 1,* 42–57.

Fisher, H. (1992). *Anatomy of love.* New York: Fawcett Columbine.

Fletcher, G. J. O., & Fincham, F. D. (Eds.) (1991). *Cognition in close relationships.* Hillsdale, NJ: Lawrence Erlbaum.

Gottman, J. M. (1979). *Marital interaction: Experimental investigations.* New York: Academic Press.

Gottman, J. M., & Levenson, R. W. (1992). Marital processes predictive of later dissolution: Behavior, physiology, and health. *Journal of Personality and Social Psychology, 63,* 221–233.

Jacobson, N. S., & Margolin, G. (1979). *Marital therapy: Strategies based on social learning and behavior exchange principles.* New York: Brunner/Mazel.

Johnson, S. M., & Greenberg, L. S. (1994). *The heart of the matter: Perspectives on emotion in marital therapy.* New York: Brunner/Mazel.

Karney, B. R., & Bradbury, T. N. (1995). The longitudinal course of marital quality and stability: A review of theory, method, and research. *Psychological Bulletin, 118,* 3–34.

Kelly, E. L., & Conley, J. J. (1987). Personality and compatibility: A prospective analysis of marital stability and marital satisfaction. *Journal of Personality and Social Psychology, 52,* 27–40.

Levenson, R. W., & Gottman, J. M. (1983). Marital interaction: Physiological linkage and affective exchange. *Journal of Personality and Social Psychology, 45,* 587–597.

Margolin, G. (1983). An interactional model for the behavioral assessment of marital relationships. *Behavioral Assessment, 5,* 103–127.

Markman, H. J. (1979). Application of a behavioral model of marriage in predicting relationship satisfaction of couples planning marriage. *Journal of Consulting and Clinical Psychology, 47,* 743–749.

O'Leary, K. D. (1987). *Assessment of marital discord.* Hillsdale, NJ: Lawrence Erlbaum.

Patterson, G. R., Reid, J. B., Jones, R. R., & Conger, R. E. (1975). *A social learning approach to family intervention.* Eugene, OR: Castalia.

Raush, H. L., Barry, W. A., Hertel, R. K., & Swain, M. A. (1974). *Communication, conflict, and marriage.* San Francisco: Jossey-Bass.

Robinson, E. A., & Jacobson, N. S. (1987). Social learning theory and family psychopathology: A Kantian model in behaviorism? In T. Jacob (Ed.), *Family interaction and psychopathology* (pp. 117–162). New York: Plenum.

Rusbult, C. E. (1983). A longitudinal test of the investment model: The development (and deterioration) of satisfaction and commitment in heterosexual involvements. *Journal of Personality and Social Psychology, 45,* 101–117.

Stuart, R. B. (1969). Operant-interpersonal treatment for marital discord. *Journal of Consulting and Clinical Psychology, 33,* 675–682.

U.S. Bureau of the Census. (1992, October). *Marriage, divorce, and remarriage in the 1990s* (Current Population Reports P23, No. 180: 4). Washington, DC: U.S. Government Printing Office.

Veroff, J., Kulka, R. A., & Douvan, E. (1981). *Mental health in America.* New York: Basic Books.

Weiss, R. L., & Heyman, R. E. (1990). Observation of marital interaction. In F. D. Fincham & T. N. Bradbury (Eds.), *The psychology of marriage* (pp. 87–117). New York: Guilford.

Weiss, R. L., Hops, H., & Patterson, G. R. (1973). A framework for conceptualizing marital conflict: A technology for altering it, some data for evaluating it. In L. A. Hamerlynck, L. C. Handy, & E. J. Mash (Eds.), *Behavior change: Methodology, concepts and practice* (pp. 309–342). Champaign, IL: Research Press.

PART I

Conceptual and Empirical Contributions

1 Communication in Early Marriage: Responses to Conflict, Nonverbal Accuracy, and Conversational Patterns

Patricia Noller and Judith A. Feeney

Although a clear relationship between marital satisfaction and marital communication has been established (for a review, see Noller & Fitzpatrick, 1990), little is known about the development of communication problems in marriage. In this chapter, we explore the development of couples' communication problems from the premarital stage through the first two years of marriage. We address three issues of theoretical and practical significance. First, what affects the stability of communication patterns and to what extent are problematic patterns of communication present before marriage? Second, to what extent are specific communication patterns related to concurrent and later satisfaction; in other words, are the communication patterns that are constructive in the short term also constructive in the long term? Third, in what direction does the link between communication and relationship satisfaction move; that is, do communication patterns drive relationship satisfaction, or does relationship satisfaction drive communication patterns? We address these issues in relation to three aspects of communication: responses to conflict, nonverbal accuracy, and conversational patterns.

Communication Problems and Relationship Satisfaction in Early Marriage

Development of Communication Problems

An important theoretical issue is whether the destructive communication patterns that lead to marital dissatisfaction are present premaritally, or whether such patterns develop over the course of marriage. Although a number of studies have looked at marital relationships longitudinally (Huston & Vangelisti, 1991; Markman, 1979, 1981, 1984; Smith, Vivian, & O'Leary, 1990), few have examined the extent to which communication behaviors change over time. Most studies, in fact, have measured communication

11

behaviors at only one point in time, although relationship satisfaction has been measured over a longer time span. Huston and Vangelisti (1991) are an exception, in that they measured socioemotional behaviors (using self-report via telephone calls) as well as satisfaction at all three waves of their study.

Although it has often been argued that communication behaviors are stable over the first few years of marriage (e.g., Markman, 1979, 1981, 1984), these claims have generally been based on indirect evidence, such as the extent to which communication measures at one point in time are able to predict relationship satisfaction at a later time. Similarly, Kelly, Huston, and Cate (1985) reported that communication behaviors remained stable over time, and that couples who experienced conflict before marriage continued to fight afterward. These researchers, however, collected their premarital data retrospectively and did not assess changes in mean levels over time. In contrast, we collected communication data at all phases of our study, in order to assess change over time and to explore the extent to which problematic communication patterns are present before marriage or develop later.

Links Between Communication and Concurrent and Later Satisfaction

Several longitudinal studies of marriage have examined the short-term versus long-term effects of particular communication behaviors. For example, Kelly et al. (1985) found that premarital conflict was not related to positivity of feelings for the partner at the time of the marriage but was the best predictor of conflict and dissatisfaction later in the marriage: the more premarital conflict, the less satisfaction couples reported with their relationships at the follow-up assessment and the less the wives reported being in love. The extent of maintenance (or working at the relationship) during the premarital period was also related to wives' love for their partners at follow-up. As already noted, a limitation of this study is that premarital variables were assessed retrospectively.

Several studies have demonstrated that negativity of affective expression covaries with lower levels of concurrent satisfaction (Gottman & Krokoff, 1989; Huston & Vangelisti, 1991; Smith, Vivian, & O'Leary, 1990). The question of the long-term effects of negativity, however, remains controversial. Longitudinal studies have variously shown negativity to be unrelated to later satisfaction (Smith et al., 1990), negatively related to later satisfaction for both spouses (Markman, 1981) or for wives only (Huston & Vangelisti,

1991), and positively related to later satisfaction (Gottman & Krokoff, 1989). It should be pointed out that subjects in the Gottman and Krokoff study had been married an average of 24 years, and that the effects of negativity may differ in these mature marriages.

One particular aspect of conflict that has been shown to predict later satisfaction is the extent to which couples engage in conflict rather than disengage from it. For example, Smith et al. (1990) found that disengagement at the premarital stage was negatively related to marital satisfaction after 18 and 30 months of marriage. In contrast, Gottman and Krokoff (1989) reported that conflict engagement (as indexed by disagreement and anger) had negative implications in the short term but was associated with increases in satisfaction in the long term. As Jacobson (1990) notes, this finding is highly provocative and much more work needs to be done before such a finding could be seen as established (for a discussion of this issue, see Woody & Costanzo, 1990; and Gottman & Krokoff, 1990). Note also that Gottman and Krokoff, like some others mentioned previously, measured communication at only one point in time.

In summary, longitudinal studies comparing premarital and later communication have provided evidence that premarital communication is related to later relationship satisfaction as much as to concurrent satisfaction. The methodology of some of these studies is problematic, however. The use of a longitudinal design in the present study will enable us to look at some of the issues raised by these studies.

Communication and Relationship Satisfaction: Direction of the Effects

A controversial issue in the literature is whether later communication behaviors are predicted by earlier relationship satisfaction, or whether later relationship satisfaction is predicted by earlier communication behaviors. In support of the position that earlier communication predicts later satisfaction, Markman (1979, 1981, 1984) found that the more positively partners rated their premarital communication, the more satisfied they were with their relationships 2½ and 5½ years later. These predictions were possible, even though there were no relationships at the time of the experimental session between evaluations of communication and relationship satisfaction.

In contrast, several studies have found evidence that later communication can be predicted from earlier satisfaction. In a longitudinal study, Huston and Vangelisti (1991) found that earlier satisfaction predicted later socioemotional behaviors over and above the effect of earlier behaviors, suggesting that high levels of satisfaction provide an atmosphere in which spouses are encouraged to behave positively. White (1983) found that the prediction of interaction from satisfaction was stronger than the reverse pattern, but she assessed the frequency rather than the quality of interaction and relied on cross-sectional data. It is clear that more research is needed to clarify the direction of these relationships. In addition, these issues need to be explored across a number of aspects of communication such as responses to conflict, nonverbal accuracy, and conversational patterns, as in the present study.

Key Aspects of Marital Communication

In designing our study, we assumed that at least three areas of communication are important to the development and maintenance of satisfying marital relationships. The first of these key areas is the way that couples deal with the inevitable conflicts that occur as they confront the lifestyle and relational issues connected with establishing their future together. The second is the extent to which they understand or misunderstand each other's communications, particularly the nonverbal aspects of messages. The third is the way couples handle their day-to-day conversations, including how frequently they talk, the extent to which they disclose their feelings and give recognition to each other's ideas, and the amount of conflict engendered by these conversations.

Responses to Conflict

There is considerable evidence that responses to conflict are related to marital satisfaction in important ways (Noller & Fitzpatrick, 1990). According to Cahn (1990), functional responses to conflict tend to be viewed more positively than destructive responses, are more likely to promote intimacy, and are more likely to result in the problem being resolved. Other theoretical and empirical work suggests that destructive conflict behaviors such as coercion, manipulation, and avoidance are likely to have negative effects on relationships (Fitzpatrick & Winke, 1979; Noller & White, 1990; Patterson, 1982).

Although researchers tend to agree about the negative effects of coercion and manipulation, they disagree about the relative merits of confronting versus avoiding conflict (Sillars & Weisberg, 1987). For example, there is empirical evidence that conflict avoidance may leave issues unresolved and cause feelings of resentment and anger (Roloff & Cloven, 1990). In addition, there is evidence that those in distressed marriages report more mutual avoidance and less use of conflict behaviors such as mutual expression and negotiation than those in more satisfied relationships (Noller & White, 1990). On the other hand, there are researchers who argue that confronting conflict may not fit with the relational style of some couples and may have negative consequences for relationships, to the point of making the situation worse (Fitzpatrick & Winke, 1979; Raush, Barry, Hertel, & Swain, 1974).

In some cases, the demand-withdraw pattern of marital interaction is negatively related to relationship satisfaction (Christensen, 1988). In this pattern of response to conflict, one spouse demands that the issue be resolved while the partner tries to withdraw from the conflict. The most common pattern is for the wife to demand and the husband to withdraw (Christensen, 1988; Gottman & Levenson, 1988), although this pattern is more likely to occur when the issue being discussed is one that has been raised by the wife (Christensen & Heavey, 1990).

Nonverbal Accuracy

The relationship between the ability to decode nonverbal messages from the partner and marital satisfaction has been consistently established through the standard content paradigm, which involves spouses sending and receiving a set of messages that can have different meanings, depending on how they are said (Gottman & Porterfield, 1981; Kahn, 1970; Noller, 1980). Noller (1980) found that the relation between marital satisfaction and nonverbal accuracy was stronger for husbands, and that wives were more accurate encoders than husbands, particularly for positive messages. In a later study (Noller, 1981), it became clear that spouses experiencing low marital satisfaction were less accurate decoders of their spouses' messages than they were of similar messages from strangers.

Although the connection between nonverbal accuracy and marital satisfaction is fairly well established, little is known about the development of nonverbal accuracy between partners. The present longitudinal study provides an opportunity to explore these questions in the context of early marriage. For partners having low relationship satisfaction, are decoding deficits present early in the relationship? Furthermore, do decreases in nonverbal accuracy lead to lower relationship satisfaction, or does lower relationship satisfaction lead to decreases in nonverbal accuracy?

Conversational Patterns

Diary studies of marital communication provide some indication of the frequency with which spouses talk to one another and the topics they discuss.

When Dickson-Markman and Markman (1988) asked spouses to record every interaction of 10 minutes or more over a 3-week period, they found an average of 1.24 interactions with each other per day, with an average duration of 2 hours. Couples reported spending very little time discussing their relationship, and most of their time discussing work, home maintenance, other family members, other relationships, conversations with others, and food. The relationship between time spent in interaction and marital satisfaction was shown in a diary study by Kirchler (1989), who found that happy couples reported being together about 2 hours longer per day than unhappy couples, and spending more time talking, more time discussing personal topics, and less time in conflict than other couples.

Dickson-Markman and Markman (1988) also showed that marital adjustment was related to the quality of interaction with the spouse. Couples high in marital adjustment reported more satisfying and higher-quality interactions with the spouse than did those low in marital adjustment. An important issue raised by this finding is what constitutes quality communication; for the present study, quality communication was assumed to involve self-disclosure, recognizing the partner's point of view, and being satisfied with the interaction. The importance of these variables is supported by other theorists, such as Montgomery (1981) and Reis and Shaver (1988). Montgomery includes openness and confirmation among her four characteristics of quality communication in marriage. She defines openness as being able to disclose one's feelings and being able to accept the disclosures that come from others, and confirmation as accepting the validity of the other person's position and his or her right to hold a different belief. Reis and Shaver (1988) also emphasized the importance of disclosure and of responses to disclosure that confirm and validate the partner's feelings. According to Hendrick (1981), competent marital communication includes the ability to disclose private thoughts and feelings to the spouse and is related to marital adjustment. In support of this position, Davidson and his colleagues (Davidson, Balswick, & Halverson, 1983) have demonstrated clear ties between self-reported disclosure and marital adjustment, although these results may be due, in part, to common method variance.

Methodological Issues

Data on the quantity and quality of interaction between partners can be collected in at least two ways: through self-report questionnaires or diaries. Self-report questionnaires provide information about the spouses' global perceptions of the frequency and quality of their interactions. Although such

Table 1.1. *Chronology of testing sessions*

Assessment phase	QMI	DAS	MCI	CPQ	Diary reports	Conflict task	Decoding task
Lab session (Time 1), 6 weeks before marriage	x		x	x		x	x
Diary study, 6 months after marriage					x		
Lab session (Time 2), 12 months after marriage	x	x	x	x		x	x
Lab session (Time 3), 21 months after marriage	x	x	x	x		x	x

Note: QMI = Quality Marriage Index; DAS = Dyadic Adjustment Scale; MCI = Marital Communication Inventory; CPQ = Communication Patterns Questionnaire.

measures yield valuable information that cannot be obtained in any other way, spouses' global perceptions are likely to be affected by factors such as memory and the mental arithmetic involved in averaging across interaction events (Huston & Robins, 1982). Diaries, on the other hand, require spouses to record their interactions and their perceptions of them on an event-by-event basis. Spouses do not need to remember the event for more than a few minutes, nor do they need to average across situations. Diaries, however, can be highly reactive, and spouses may increase their performance of the socially desirable behaviors being recorded (Noller & Guthrie, 1991).

The Present Study

In order to examine the development of communication patterns over the first 2 years of marriage and its implications for relationship satisfaction, we collected both questionnaire and interaction-based data in a longitudinal design. On three occasions over this time span (see Table 1.1), couples described their responses to conflict using a standard questionnaire and open-ended reports of strategies adopted in a videotaped problem-solving exercise. Couples also took part in a communication accuracy task that involved the standard content paradigm. Conversational patterns were assessed using a specially designed questionnaire and diaries in which spouses recorded information about conversations involving the partner. The study has a number of important and unique features: First, a number of aspects of communication were explored, including responses to conflict, nonverbal accuracy, and conversational patterns. Second, relationship satisfaction and communication variables were measured at all three points in time, allowing for the testing of predictive and reciprocal relations between communication and satisfaction. Third, communication was assessed using a range of both self-report and interaction-based methods. In addition, multiple measures of responses to conflict and conversational patterns were obtained.

Our aim in this chapter is to explore three major research questions that apply to all the aspects of communication assessed in this study:

1. Is there change over time in responses to conflict, nonverbal accuracy, and conversational patterns, or are couples' communication patterns established at the premarital stage?
2. To what extent are communication variables related to concurrent relationship satisfaction?
3. Do communication variables predict later relationship satisfaction, or does relationship satisfaction predict later communication?

Previously published findings for responses to conflict and nonverbal accuracy are reported briefly, but findings related to conversational patterns are the central concern. In a later section, we explore three other questions that relate specifically to conversational patterns and that were assessed by both questionnaire and diary methods.

Method

Subjects and Procedure

Subjects were couples recruited for a longitudinal study of communication in early marriage (Feeney, Noller, & Callan, 1994; Noller & Feeney, 1994; Noller, Feeney, Bonnell, & Callan, 1994). The sample at Time 1 consisted of 43 couples, with 35 providing data at Time 2, and 33 at Time 3. The work reported in this chapter is based on the 33 couples who completed all three sessions. (The most common reason for not continuing in the study was that couples moved out of the district.) Ages at the beginning of the study ranged from 17 to 34, with a mean of 23.7 years. The length of couples' relationships prior to marriage ranged from 5 to 101 months, with a mean of 32.9 months.

Couples were recruited about 6 weeks before marriage through newspaper advertisements and from marriage celebrants and premarriage courses and were paid $19.00 per session per couple for their participation. Subjects were assessed four times over a 2-year period. Three laboratory sessions were held about 6 weeks before marriage and again 12 months and 21 months later, and one interaction diary assessment 6 months after marriage. During the laboratory sessions, they independently completed questionnaire measures of relationship satisfaction and communication and other measures that will not be discussed in this chapter. Subjects also engaged in two communication-related tasks: a videotaped conflict and a communication accuracy task. The measures and tasks are described in detail below. See Table 1.1 for the timetable of sessions.

Measures

Relationship Satisfaction. Relationship satisfaction was assessed using the Dyadic Adjustment Scale (Spanier, 1976), which is a 32-item measure including both descriptive and evaluative items, and the Quality Marriage Index (Norton, 1983), which uses 6 evaluative items. Norton (1983) designed his measure to include only evaluative items because he argued that using descriptive items (involving communication, consensus, etc.) frequently created overlap between the dependent variables being studied and the measure of marital satisfaction. Because most of the couples were not cohabiting at Time 1, only the Quality Marriage Index was considered appropriate at this time. The Dyadic Adjustment Scale contains items (e.g., "How often did you or your partner leave the house after a fight?") not really suitable for couples not living in the same house. At Times 2 and 3, both measures were administered. Coefficient alpha was .88 for the Quality Marriage Index, and .93 for the Dyadic Adjustment Scale.

In order to compare the communication of happy and unhappy spouses, we categorized couples as high or low in satisfaction on the basis of a median split of scores on the Quality Marriage Index at Time 3, and this dichotomous measure of relationship satisfaction was used in later analyses. (Because the Quality Marriage Index was administered at all three times, it could be used to control for relationship satisfaction at Time 1, when appropriate; the categorization of couples as high or low in satisfaction was quite stable over the three measurement occasions.) The mean of the total sample on the Quality Marriage Index at Time 3 was 39.66, and the scores ranged from 26 to 41. The mean combined score for couples was 76.42, and the scores ranged from 64 to 82. The mean Quality Marriage Index score for the high adjustment group was 80.06, and the mean score for the low adjustment group was 72.56. Note that these latter scores do not fall into the dissatisfied range, although the two groups are significantly different.

Conflict Patterns. The Communication Patterns Questionnaire (Christensen & Sullaway, 1984b) is a self-report measure designed to assess the extent to which couples make use of various interaction strategies during conflict. The inventory is multidimensional (Noller & White, 1990), with four factors represented: Negativity or Coercion (blame, threat, and physical and verbal aggression), Mutuality (mutual discussion, understanding, and lack of mutual avoidance), Destructive Process (patterns of demand-withdraw, pressure-resist, etc.), and Postconflict Distress (guilt, hurt, withdrawal). The questionnaire possesses adequate reliability, and scores on the four factors clearly discriminate groups differing in marital adjustment (Noller & White, 1990).

Six scores were calculated from the Communication Patterns Questionnaire: three of these (Negativity, Destructive Process, and Postconflict distress) correspond to factors outlined by Noller and White (1990). In order to facilitate comparison with earlier studies (e.g., Smith et al., 1990), the Mutuality factor was subdivided into two scales: Positivity (including only the positive items) and Disengagement (including the negative items such as mutual avoidance and mutual withdrawal). Finally, we calculated a score on the Demand-Withdraw scale as detailed by Christensen (1988). These scales generally showed high internal consistency; alpha coefficients ranged from .74 for Demand-Withdraw to .85 for Destructive Process.

Conflict Interaction. Couples engaged in two videotaped conflict interactions. Husbands and wives were each asked to identify a problem that was currently salient in their relationship, and the couple was videotaped while discussing each of the issues for approximately 5 minutes. After each discussion, the spouse who had identified the issue was asked to work through the videotape, stopping the tape whenever he or she was aware of using a particular strategy in dealing with the partner. This spouse was asked to describe in his or her own words the strategy being used at that point. The descriptions of the strategies were audiotaped and transcribed for content coding. A six-category system was derived from the literature on compliance-gaining strategies and conflict resolution (e.g., Falbo & Peplau, 1980). The six strategies (reason, assertion, support of the partner, coercion, manipulation, and avoidance) are described in Table 1.2 and were chosen to represent a balance of positive and negative strategies and to cover both maintenance and influence strategies.

Spouses reported an average of 5.3 strategies at each of the three times. All but 4.3% of these strategies could be coded into the six-category system, with uncodable descriptions generally involving simple restatements

Table 1.2. *Definitions and examples of the six conflict strategy codes*

Strategy	Definition	Examples
Reason	Rational argument, problem solving (use of reason or logic; presenting alternatives or seeking solutions)	I use reason to back what I'm saying; I put forward options, being logical.
Assertion	Direct expression of opinions or wants (clear statement of one's position; redirecting conversation to topic; emphasis by gesture or eye contact)	I make a forthright statement of my points; I use repetition to emphasize my points; I face my partner directly.
Partner support	Acknowledgment of partner's views (active listening or questioning; supporting or agreeing with partner; compromise or concession)	I'm being a good listener; I try to understand his point of view; I look for areas of agreement.
Coercion	Seeking control through use of force (threat; blame; sarcasm; physical or verbal aggression)	A threat – warning her of the consequences; I attacked, without giving him a chance to talk; I used sarcasm because that really gets to him.
Manipulation	Attempts to gain compliance by indirect or false means (providing misleading information; attempts to make partner feel guilty/defensive; feigning of moods)	That was a bit of a con strategy; I used that as a real guilt trip; I try to sound sincere.
Avoidance	Physical/emotional retreat from the situation (changing or avoiding the topic; avoiding eye contact)	Joking because I can't deal with the topic; I look away; I'm nervous about broaching the subject.

of the partner's verbalization. Each of the six strategies was mentioned by at least 15% of the subjects. Transcripts were coded without prior knowledge of subjects' relationship satisfaction, and inter- and intrarater reliability were assessed on a randomly selected subsample of 20% of the transcripts. Cohen's Kappa for all six strategies reached acceptable levels and averaged .89 for intrarater reliability and .81 for interrater reliability. The number of strategies of a particular type reported by an individual was expressed as a proportion of the total number of strategies identified by that person.

Nonverbal Accuracy. In assessing nonverbal accuracy, we employed a standard content paradigm involving ambiguous messages designed in such a way that the verbal content could have a neutral, negative, or positive meaning, depending on the nonverbal communication that accompanied it.

For example, the verbal content of "What are you doing?" could be taken to mean either (a) I'm just interested in knowing what you are doing (neutral), or (b) How many times have I asked you not to do that? (negative), or (c) I'm really pleased to see you doing that (positive).

The materials and procedure for this task were based on the work of Noller (1980, 1984) as amended by Noller and Fitzpatrick (1987; see Fitzpatrick, 1988). Each subject sent a standard set of ambiguous messages to his/her spouse and decoded a similar set received from the spouse. Two sets of ambiguous messages were designed, one set for husbands to send and one for wives. Encoders were given a set of 30 cards, one for each communication, which contained a description of the situation in which the husband and wife were to imagine themselves, the intention to be communicated, and the words to be used. Each subject was asked to send 10 positive, 10 neutral, and 10 negative communications in randomized order after shuffling the cards. Encoders were asked to rate the clarity of each of their communications and to predict whether their partners would correctly decode each one. Decoders were also given a set of cards, one for each of the 10 messages; each card contained the situation and the three possible intentions for that item. Decoders were asked to decide which of the three alternative intentions their spouses had conveyed and to rate their own confidence in each of these decisions. In terms of nonverbal accuracy, an item was marked as correct when the decoder's response corresponded to the alternative the encoder was asked to send.

Marital Communication Inventory. This instrument was designed specifically for the present study, although it is based on an earlier instrument devised by Noller and Bagi (1985). The questionnaire assesses couples' perceptions of their communication across 6 dimensions and 12 topic areas. The dimensions assessed were frequency of discussion, frequency of initiation (assessed for both self and partner), recognition (self and partner), disclosure (self and partner), communication satisfaction (self and partner), and conflict. All dimensions were rated on 4-point scales. The topics covered included "likes, dislikes, and interests," "family members," "feelings about our relationship," "plans for the future," and "things that lead to anger or depression."

Interaction Diaries. Interaction diaries were sent to couples after about 6 months of marriage. Diaries were sent at this point to allow the couple time to settle down into married life and to obtain some between-session information about how the relationship was going. Completed diaries were returned by 27 couples, with an equal number of couples high and low in relationship satisfaction completing the task. Each subject was asked to keep a record of all interactions that involved the spouse and that lasted 10 minutes or more. Recordings were made over a week from Monday night to Sunday night, using a set of interaction records modeled after the Rochester Interaction Diary (Wheeler & Nezlek, 1977). Spouses were asked to record structural information about the interaction (date, time, length, who was present, topic, and who initiated) and to evaluate the interaction in terms of the levels of recognition, disclosure, conflict, and satisfaction. Ratings were provided for self and partner for all variables except conflict, using 6-point scales from 1 = very little to 6 = completely. The evaluative ratings were reduced to two scales to make the variables comparable with those from the Marital Communication Inventory: Quality, which included ratings of disclosure, recognition, and satisfaction (both self and partner); and Conflict.

Overview of Analyses

Effects for time were investigated using analyses of variance. These analyses also incorporated gender and relationship satisfaction as independent variables so that we could test for interactions of time with these variables. As noted earlier, relationship satisfaction was dichotomized in terms of couple scores on satisfaction at Time 3.

The links between the communication variables and relationship satisfaction were further explored using correlational analyses. These analyses examined concurrent and predictive relations between the constructs, with concurrent relations being assessed at all three times. The predictive analyses tested Time 1 communication as a predictor of Time 3 satisfaction (controlling for satisfaction at Time 1), and Time 1 satisfaction as a predictor of Time 3 communication (controlling for communication at Time 1). All analyses were carried out separately by gender.

Responses to Conflict: Time and Satisfaction Effects

Change over Time

There were no effects for time on the self-report measure of conflict (Communication Patterns Questionnaire), but there were some changes over time in the use of conflict strategies in the videotaped interaction. (For a full report of the findings for responses to conflict, see Noller, Feeney, Bonnell,

& Callan, 1994.) More specifically, there was an interaction of time and relationship satisfaction. That is, spouses low in satisfaction used less manipulation and less avoidance at Time 2 than at either of the other times; in addition, husbands low in satisfaction temporarily increased their use of reason at Time 2, and wives low in satisfaction temporarily increased their expressions of support for the partner. These findings suggest that these less happy couples make concerted attempts to improve their relationships during the first year but give up these efforts by the time of the third assessment. Perhaps these new behaviors are not reinforced by the partner and hence are not appropriately integrated into their behavioral repertoire.

Responses to the Communication Patterns Questionnaire indicated that spouses high in satisfaction after 2 years of marriage reported more Positivity and less Negativity, Disengagement, Destructive Process, and Demand-Withdraw across the three measurement occasions than those low in satisfaction. In other words, these high-satisfaction spouses were more likely than those low in satisfaction to engage in mutual discussion and negotiation and less likely to avoid dealing with the conflict, to behave coercively, and to engage in destructive patterns such as Demand-Withdraw.

Links with Concurrent Satisfaction

There were moderately strong associations between communication behaviors and concurrent satisfaction. The strongest evidence of concurrent relations between satisfaction and self-reported communication behaviors using the Communication Patterns Questionnaire was for wives at Time 1. Wives' satisfaction at Time 1 was directly related to reports of Positivity and inversely related to reports of Disengagement, Negativity, Destructive Process, Demand-Withdraw, and Postconflict distress. Positivity and Disengagement were also related to concurrent satisfaction for wives at Time 2. By contrast, concurrent relations for husbands were evident only at the later times, with satisfaction being directly related to Positivity, and inversely related to Disengagement, Destructive Process, and Demand-Withdraw. The interesting question raised by these findings is why the relation between satisfaction and communication is so strong for wives premaritally but weakens over time, whereas for husbands the relation between satisfaction and communication strengthens over time. Although the literature suggests that men are less sensitive to communication patterns generally (Tannen, 1990), it could be argued that the centrality of communication to married life may make them more conscious of the effects of communication on their satisfaction.

With regard to the conflict strategies identified from the videotapes, wives' use of avoidance was negatively related to their satisfaction at the same time, with wives low in satisfaction avoiding more. In line with the satisfaction by time interactions reported above, satisfaction at Time 2 was inversely related to wives' expressions of support for the partner, and to husbands' use of reason.

Direction of Effects

Communication behaviors predicted later satisfaction for wives only. Wives' reports of Negativity, Disengagement, and Destructive process at Time 1 predicted lower satisfaction at Time 2. In addition, wives' reports of Manipulation at Time 1 predicted lower satisfaction at Time 2. From these results and those reported earlier, it would seem that for wives, perceptions of premarital communication set the context of the relationship, at least for the first year. Further, the harmful effects of Negativity and Destructive process run counter to Gottman and Krokoff's (1989) claim that disagreement and anger are related to improvements in satisfaction over time.

Satisfaction also predicted later communication behaviors for both husbands and wives, with husbands' premarital satisfaction being inversely related to their reports of Disengagement and Demand-Withdraw at Time 2 and directly related to their reports of Positivity at both of the later times. With regard to conflict strategies, husbands' premarital satisfaction was inversely related to their reports of Reason at Time 2.

Wives' premarital satisfaction was inversely related to their reports of Negativity at Time 3, and positively related to their support of the partner. Wives' satisfaction at Time 2 predicted all later communication behaviors except Positivity, but husbands' satisfaction at Time 2 predicted only their reports of Disengagement at the later time. These results provide evidence that, for wives, earlier responses to conflict influence later satisfaction, but earlier satisfaction also influences later responses to conflict. The predominant pattern for husbands involves a link between premarital satisfaction and later responses to conflict.

Nonverbal Accuracy: Time and Satisfaction Effects

Change over Time

Nonverbal accuracy increased over time for all three message types: that is, positive, neutral, and negative. (A full report on the findings regarding nonverbal accuracy is presented in Noller & Feeney, 1994.) Although this finding suggests that nonverbal accuracy in newlyweds increases with increasing exposure to one another's communication, it is also possible that practice at the experimental task is a contributing factor, because subjects did the same task on three occasions. Several aspects of the data, however, suggest that factors other than practice effects were likely to be operating. First, improvement over time varied between message types, with accuracy increasing more for neutral and negative messages than for positive ones. Second, the time interval between testing sessions was long (at least 9 months), and hence it is unlikely that specific messages or behaviors would be remembered across this time frame. (This issue is discussed in more detail by Noller & Feeney, 1994.)

Accuracy was greater for wife-to-husband communication than for husband-to-wife communication, particularly on positive messages. This finding is similar to that of Noller (1980, 1984) who also found that positive messages from wives were more accurately decoded than those from husbands. Because the messages in her study were videotaped and decoded by outsiders as well as spouses, Noller was able to show that it was the superior encoding of the wives that contributed to this effect.

There was increased communication awareness over time for encoders only. Encoders became more accurate at predicting their partners' decoding, again suggesting increasing awareness of each other's nonverbal behavior. In addition, spouses' ratings of clarity discriminated more strongly between correct and incorrect messages at Time 2 than at Time 1, although this improvement was substantially lost by Time 3.

The only other findings for communication awareness involved interactions of gender and marital satisfaction. Specifically, husbands high in satisfaction were most likely to expect their partners to decode their communications correctly. With regard to decoders' confidence, all groups except wives in unhappy marriages were more confident on correct than incorrect messages.

Links with Concurrent Satisfaction

Links between nonverbal accuracy and concurrent relationship satisfaction occurred only for wife-to-husband accuracy; specifically, wife-to-husband accuracy for positive messages was related to husbands' concurrent satisfaction at Time 1, and wife-to-husband accuracy for neutral messages was related to husbands' concurrent satisfaction at Time 2, suggesting that husbands' decoding is affected by their concurrent satisfaction. Interpretation of this finding can be aided by that of Noller and Ruzzene (1991), who showed that the negativity that dissatisfied husbands attributed to their wives affected the accuracy of their decoding of their wives' emotional state. Overall, however, the link between nonverbal behavior and concurrent satisfaction appears to be weak, given that the results were specific to message type, gender, and time. In studies by Noller (1980) and Gottman and Porterfield (1981), in which measures of nonverbal accuracy were taken at only one point in time, effects were also limited by gender; husbands' accuracy at both encoding and decoding were related to marital satisfaction. Note that the methodology used in the present study does not permit us to separate accuracy at encoding and decoding.

Direction of Effects

There was no evidence that nonverbal accuracy predicted later satisfaction. By contrast, satisfaction predicted later accuracy, but mainly for husbands. Husbands' earlier satisfaction predicted wife-to-husband decoding at the later times, with husbands high in satisfaction being more accurate than other husbands for all message-types. This finding is consistent with White's (1983) finding that satisfaction predicted communication, rather than the other way around, although her measure of communication was frequency of interaction. Huston and Vangelisti (1991) also see satisfaction as providing a climate in which couples are likely to be more positive and less negative with one another. The present findings seem to suggest that satisfaction may also increase the likelihood of accurate understanding of one another's nonverbal messages.

Conversational Patterns: Time and Satisfaction Effects

Change over Time

We performed principal components analysis on the 10 scales of the Marital Communication Inventory summed across the 12 topics. This analysis was carried out on an expanded sample of 80 couples (i.e., 160 individuals). These additional couples were recruited from the community for another study and varied across the spectrum in terms of age and years married. Two major factors accounted for 68.8% of the total variance: Quantity and Quality of communication. The Quantity factor included frequency of talk and frequency of own and partner initiation; the Quality factor included recognition, disclosure, and satisfaction, for both self and partner. Scales were

Table 1.3. *Mean ratings over time of quantity, quality, and conflict for couples high and low in relationship satisfaction*

		Time		
Communication variable		1	2	3
Quantity	High satisfaction	2.43	2.43	2.46
	Low satisfaction	2.46	2.46	2.45
Quality	High satisfaction	3.13	3.19	3.27
	Low satisfaction	2.85	2.91	2.93
Conflict	High satisfaction	1.39	1.37	1.39
	Low satisfaction	1.78	1.74	1.73

formed to measure Quantity and Quality of Communication by summing scores across the relevant variables. Cronbach alphas ranged from .70 to .79 for Quantity and from .85 to .88 for Quality over the three times. The Conflict rating loaded equally (around 0.5) on both factors and was retained as a separate measure. Correlations of agreement between husbands and wives ranged from .06 (Quantity at Time 2) and .63 (Conflict at Time 1).

We carried out a MANOVA looking at the effects of relationship satisfaction, gender, and time on these three measures: Quantity, Quality, and Conflict (see Table 1.3 for means). Reports of communication tended to change over time $F(6, 26) = 2.04$, $p < .1$, with a significant effect for Quality only, $F(1, 31) = 8.27$, $p < .01$. Couples reported higher-quality communication at Time 3 than at Time 1. These findings suggest that the amount of talk and the amount of conflict remain relatively stable over the first 2 years of marriage, but that the perceived quality of the communication tends to increase. That is, spouses report more disclosure, more recognition, and more satisfaction for both themselves and their partners. Note that the measure of Conflict in the MCI reflects the extent to which husbands and wives hold different opinions on various topics, rather than the extent to which they fight over such issues. In other words, it is possible for Quality to increase without there being any decrease in the level of Conflict.

A significant multivariate effect was found for relationship satisfaction, $F(3, 29) = 7.12$, $p < .001$. This effect applied to both Quality and Conflict, with couples high in relationship satisfaction reporting higher-quality communication, $F(1, 31) = 10.16$, $p < .005$ and less conflict, $F(1, 31) = 17.51$, $p < .001$. In other words, there were no differences in the Quantity of communication between couples high and low in relationship satisfaction, but there were differences for Quality and Conflict. Although the couples in the low-satisfaction group do not fall into the distressed range on the

Table 1.4. *Correlations between conversational patterns and relationship satisfaction at each time*

Time	Quantity	Quality	Conflict
1			
Husbands	.02	.31*	−.38**
Wives	.36**	.58***	−.29*
2			
Husbands	−.08	.43**	−.53***
Wives	.01	.20	−.32*
3			
Husbands	−.08	.43**	−.46***
Wives	−.13	.33*	−.51***

$*p < .1.$ $**p < .05.$ $***p < .01.$

measures of relationship satisfaction, they are quite different from the high-satisfaction couples in terms of the quality of their communication and the amount of conflict they experience.

Links with Concurrent Satisfaction

In general, relationship satisfaction was positively related to Quality and negatively related to Conflict at each time and for both husbands and wives (see Table 1.4). The only exception was that the correlation between Quality and relationship satisfaction for wives at Time 2 failed to reach significance. This result is likely to be related to the finding reported with regard to conflict strategies where wives low in relationship satisfaction seemed to be engaging in more support for the partner at Time 2. If some of these wives were also tending to report higher-quality communication, the association between Quality and relationship satisfaction would be weakened at this time.

Direction of Effects

For husbands, the only communication variable related to later satisfaction was Conflict; Time 1 Conflict was negatively related to Time 3 satisfaction, controlling for satisfaction at the earlier time, $r(30) = -.56$, $p < .001$. Again this result provides no support for Gottman and Krokoff's proposition that disagreement has beneficial effects on long-term satisfaction. For wives, the communication variables at Time 1 were not significantly related to relationship satisfaction at Time 3.

For husbands, Time 1 satisfaction did not predict any of the three communication measures at Time 3, once the corresponding communication measure at Time 1 was controlled for. For wives, earlier satisfaction predicted only Conflict at the later time, $r(30) = -.40, p < .05$.

In summary, of the communication variables assessed using the MCI, only Conflict seems to be consistently related to satisfaction over time, but in different directions for husbands and wives. For husbands, high levels of conflict at Time 1 are related to lower satisfaction later on, and for wives high satisfaction at Time 1 was related to low levels of conflict at the later time.

When we compare these findings with those based on the Communication Patterns Questionnaire, it seems that early satisfaction may be a stronger predictor of later communication than early communication is of later satisfaction. Specifically, early satisfaction predicted how conflict is dealt with for husbands (those high in satisfaction report low negativity, high positivity, and low disengagement), even though it is not related to the amount of conflict at the later time. For wives, links between early satisfaction and later communication were evident for both the MCI and the Communication Patterns Questionnaire. Early satisfaction predicted low levels of conflict at the later time, as well as low levels of Demand-Withdraw interaction. The only evidence that communication influenced later satisfaction was for husbands, when Conflict was measured using the MCI.

Conversational Patterns: Effects of Topic

In this section, we explore the effects of topic of conversation on the quantity and quality of discussion, and the amount of conflict generated. We carried out three repeated measures ANOVAs, one on Quantity, one on Quality, and one on Conflict. The independent variables were relationship satisfaction, gender, time, and topic. (The 12 topics from the MCI formed the levels of the topic variable; see Table 1.5.) There was a main effect of topic for all three dependent variables: For Quantity, $F(11, 20) = 32.4$, $p < .001$; for Quality, $F(11, 20) = 7.83$, $p < .001$; for Conflict $F(11, 20) = 3.99$, $p < .005$. The topic variable did not interact with relationship satisfaction, gender, or time.

To further explore these effects, we performed Scheffe tests to assess differences between topics with regard to the three dependent variables. For Quantity, the three least discussed topics were "religious beliefs," "things that lead to anger or depression," and "world events and politics"; the most frequently discussed topics were "plans for the future," "likes, dislikes, and

Table 1.5. *Mean ratings of quantity, quality, and conflict across 12 topics*

Topic	Communication variable		
	Quantity	Quality	Conflict
Likes, dislikes, and interests	2.84	3.24	1.55
Finances and financial problems	2.74	3.16	1.77
Family members	2.60	3.16	1.62
Concerns about health/fitness	2.27	2.93	1.56
Feelings about our relationship	2.73	3.22	1.50
Religious beliefs	1.83	2.98	1.44
World events and politics	2.02	2.81	1.42
Plans for the future	3.05	3.30	1.52
Work and people at work	2.84	3.17	1.44
Feelings about appearance, personality, etc.	2.45	2.98	1.66
Things that lead to anger or depression	1.88	2.80	1.68
The worrying things about life	2.09	2.88	1.58

interests," "work and people at work," "finances and financial problems," and "feelings about the relationship." Interestingly, "feelings about the relationship" was one of the most frequently discussed topics, given that Dickson-Markman and Markman (1988) found in a diary study that there was little talk about the relationship, and that what talk did occur was mainly after a fight or after sexual intercourse.

The Quality of communication was rated lowest for "things that lead to anger or depression," "the worrying things about life," and "world events and politics." The topics rated as highest in quality were "plans for the future," "likes, dislikes, and interests," "feelings about the relationship," "work and people at work," and "family relationships." It is disturbing that when couples are trying to talk about the things that worry and depress them, the Quality of the communication is rated lowest, suggesting that spouses have trouble supporting one another through emotionally difficult experiences. Although it is not clear that the topics for which Quality was high were primarily positive in affective tone, two of the three topics rated low in Quality clearly involve negative affect.

Although there was a main effect of topic for Conflict, there were no significant differences between topics on Scheffe tests. This result suggests that there are no particular "hot topics" about which young couples have disagreements. Rather, differences occur across a whole range of topics. In addition, topics of conflict did not differ between couples high and low in relationship satisfaction, suggesting that high- and low-satisfaction couples have conflicts about similar topics. Peterson (1968) found that happy and unhappy couples had similar problems but that the happy couples were able to resolve them more effectively.

Conversational Patterns: Relations Between Quantity, Quality, and Conflict

A further question explored in this study was what pattern of relations emerged over time between communication quantity, quality, and amount of conflict? We reasoned that understanding the patterns of relations among these three communication variables was important in seeking to interpret our findings with regard to change over time and links between communication and satisfaction.

The links between the three communication variables were explored using correlational analyses. Again the purpose of these analyses was to examine both concurrent and predictive relations between the variables, with concurrent relations being assessed at all three times. The predictive analyses tested the extent to which each of the communication variables at Time 1 predicted the other variables at Time 3, controlling for the level of the outcome variable at Time 1. Again the analyses were carried out separately by gender.

Concurrent Relations

Quantity and Quality were generally unrelated, with the only significant correlation being for husbands at Time 1. Quality and Conflict were generally negatively correlated, with the relation reaching or approaching significance for all groups except husbands at Time 2. Quantity and Conflict were positively correlated for wives at Time 1 (trend only), for husbands and wives at Time 2, and for husbands at Time 3. Correlations are shown in Table 1.6.

It is clear from the relation between Quantity and Conflict that just talking a lot does not guarantee the resolution of conflict. In addition, the lack of relation between Quantity and Quality underlines the fact that not all talk is quality communication. This situation is not really surprising for three reasons. First, if relational conflicts are not being resolved, they are likely to surface repeatedly, even though they are being discussed (Peterson, 1968). Second, the measure of frequency in the Marital Communication Inventory includes not just amount of time spent talking about the issue but the number of times the issue is raised by either partner. Perceptions that one partner is pressuring the other to talk may lead to a high rating for initiation, even though little time has been spent on constructive discussion (or destructive discussion, for that matter). Third, high levels of initiation may

Table 1.6. *Correlations between measures of communication quantity, quality, and conflict at each time*

Time	Quantity/quality	Quality/conflict	Quantity/conflict
1			
Husbands	.35**	−.33*	−.07
Wives	.20	−.49***	.32*
2			
Husbands	.08	−.22	.37**
Wives	−.20	−.32*	.38**
3			
Husbands	.11	−.38**	.49***
Wives	.16	−.43**	.17

$*p < .01. **p < .05. ***p < .01.$

occur when one partner keeps refusing to talk about the issue, either because he or she is unwilling to deal with it or genuinely believes that the issue is best not discussed for the time being. Pressure to talk may be driven either by a desire to deal with the issue or by anxiety at leaving an issue unresolved, even in the short term.

Predictive Relations

As expected, husbands' ratings of Conflict at Time 1 predicted Quality at Time 3, $r(30) = -.39$, $p < .05$ (controlling for Time 1 Quality). Those who experienced considerable premarital conflict reported lower-quality communication after 2 years of marriage, suggesting that having a lot of disagreement in the early stages may have a negative effect on the development of quality communication (that is, communication high in disclosure, recognition, and satisfaction). This finding is in contrast to that for husbands' responses to conflict using the Communication Patterns Questionnaire, which did not predict later satisfaction. Although it is possible that the way these husbands deal with conflict premaritally has already led to a buildup of conflict issues by the time of the marriage, it seems that, at least for husbands, patterns of responding to conflict may not be as predictive as the amount of conflict. These findings contrast with those for wives: Quantity was not related to later Conflict for wives, and scores on the Communication Patterns Questionnaire (Disengagement, Negativity, and Destructive Process) were inversely related to satisfaction a year later.

For husbands also, Quantity at Time 1 predicted Conflict at Time 3, $r(30) = .70$, $p < .001$ (controlling for Time 1 Conflict). This finding that Quantity at Time 1 was so strongly related to Conflict at Time 3 for husbands was surprising, and it is important to note that this association was not present for wives. This gender difference may be partly explained by the fact that there was little agreement between the perceptions of husbands and wives for either of these variables: the agreement correlation at Time 1 for Quantity was .10 and that for Conflict at Time 3 was .18. In other words, husbands and wives are seeing these aspects of their communication quite differently. The pattern of correlations for the husbands' data would seem to suggest that those couples who are having a lot of conflict at Time 3 are talking to each other a lot premaritally, at least from the perspective of the husbands. In addition, given that Quality and Conflict are always negatively correlated, it seems likely that this early communication is of poor quality. This suggestion does not seem to fit, however, with the finding that for husbands at Time 1, Quantity and Quality were positively correlated. Also, Quantity and Quality were not correlated for any other group, or at any other time. One possible explanation for this association is that, at least before marriage, males may be less sophisticated than females in discriminating between communication of high and low quality and may tend to assume that if a lot of communication is occurring, it must be quality communication.

For wives, Quality at Time 1 predicted Conflict at Time 3, $r(30) = -.54$, $p < .001$, as hypothesized (controlling for Time 1 Conflict). This finding needs to be interpreted in the light of the fact that, for the sample as a whole, Quality increased over time, whereas Conflict stayed the same. What the present finding adds is that those wives who report increased conflict at Time 3 also reported lower communication quality premaritally. Perhaps couples who have low-quality communication early in their relationships have difficulty in dealing with conflict as it arises and are likely to have a buildup of unresolved issues over time.

The overall pattern of correlations would seem to suggest that young couples need to be taught not only the importance of communication but also the skills to make this communication helpful and constructive in terms of dealing with their conflict. The findings for husbands point to the fact that frequency of communication does not of itself guarantee that conflicts will be resolved, and the findings for wives further underline the importance of quality communication in reducing the potential for later conflict.

Conversational Patterns: Summary of Effects

There was a trend for change in conversational patterns over time, with significantly higher quality at Time 3 than at Time 1. Overall, there was clear evidence that concurrent relationship satisfaction was correlated with high Quality and low Conflict at all times. In other words, happy couples tended to report communication that was high in mutual disclosure, recognition, and satisfaction and low in Conflict. (However, the positive correlation for wives between Quality and satisfaction at Time 2 failed to reach significance.)

With regard to the direction of influence between communication and satisfaction, findings tended to be gender specific. For husbands and wives, however, Conflict was the only one of the three communication variables related to satisfaction over time. Specifically, Conflict predicted low satisfaction at the later time for husbands only, whereas for wives, earlier dissatisfaction predicted later Conflict.

There were some clear patterns of concurrent relations within the set of communication variables: Quantity and Quality were generally uncorrelated, and Quality and Conflict were generally negatively correlated. For wives, as would be expected, high Quality at Time 1 predicted low conflict at Time 3. For husbands, however, the prediction was again in the opposite direction, with low levels of premarital Conflict predicting high levels of Quality at the later time. Unexpectedly, high frequency of communication premaritally predicted higher Conflict later on for husbands.

Interaction Diaries

Our final research question was whether diary and questionnaire methods would yield similar results in terms of the association between conversational patterns and relationship satisfaction. In looking at the variables of interest for the diary study, we assessed quantity of communication using a set of structural variables that reflected the number and length of interactions involving the partner over the week of the data collection. In addition, as noted earlier, participant rating scales from husbands and wives were used to measure the quality of each interaction and the amount of conflict. These rating scales were then averaged across interactions.

Quantity of Communication

According to independent coders (who resolved discrepancies by discussion), about 30% of spouses' discussions were about the relationship, 27% were about friends and family, 16% were about work, 7% were about impersonal topics, and 20% were about miscellaneous topics. There were no relationship satisfaction or gender differences in terms of the topics discussed. In other words, husbands and wives agreed in their reports of the topics discussed, and happy and unhappy couples tended to discuss similar topics. These findings are similar to those using the MCI that were reported earlier, particularly in pointing to high levels of talk about the relationship. These findings are different, however, from those of Dickson-Markman and Markman (1988) who found little evidence of talk about the relationship among their sample of newlyweds.

The diary-based measures of quantity of communication included total number of interactions reported, length of interactions, proportion of interactions with partner alone, and proportion of interactions initiated by self. Spouses reported an average of 22.6 interactions over the week, with an average length of 34 minutes. Spouses indicated that 77% of these interactions occurred with the spouse alone, with initiation being equally divided between husbands and wives. The reliability of the diary data was assessed by calculating simple correlations between husbands' and wives' reports of the basic characteristics of the recorded interactions. Results generally indicated high correspondence between spouses' reports of the interactions (for more detail, see Feeney et al., 1994).

To assess the effects of relationship satisfaction and gender on the measures of communication quantity (total number of interactions reported, length of interactions, proportion of interactions with partner alone, and proportion of interactions initiated by self), we carried out four analyses of variance; relationship satisfaction varied between couples and gender varied within couple. In line with the findings for Quantity of communication using the Marital Communication Inventory, there were no significant effects for relationship satisfaction or gender in any of these analyses. Again, note that an effect for gender would only indicate a reporting difference, rather than an actual difference in husbands' and wives' behavior.

Qualitative Variables

To obtain a composite measure of communication quality comparable to that from the MCI, we averaged ratings across six scales: Recognition, Disclosure, and Satisfaction for self and partner. The Cronbach alpha for the composite scale was .91. The single rating of conflict was retained as a separate variable. A doubly repeated measures analysis of variance was performed to assess the effects of relationship satisfaction and gender on the two measures, Quality and Conflict.

There was a main effect of satisfaction, Fmult $(2, 24) = 5.48$, $p < .02$. This effect applied only to Conflict, $F(1, 25) = 4.8$, $p < .005$. Happy couples reported lower scores on Conflict (M = 1.90) than unhappy couples (M = 2.50). There were no effects for gender and no interactions.

These results suggest a reasonable amount of comparability across the two methodologies: the MCI and the diaries. Specifically, Conflict predicted later relationship satisfaction using both methods, and Quantity was unrelated to relationship satisfaction across the two methods. On the other hand, results for the link between relationship satisfaction and Quality were not consistent across methodologies: There were no differences between couples high and low in relationship satisfaction in terms of diary reports, but there was a difference at all three times when the MCI was used.

It could be argued that results based on questionnaires are more heavily influenced than diary methods by what Weiss (1984) has called "sentiment override." The idea here is that the overall evaluation of the relationship affects ratings of specific aspects of that relationship. It is important to keep in mind, however, that the MCI does not involve subjects making a global evaluation of the communication in their relationship (when the effects of "sentiment override" would be highest) but requires them to rate their communication on 10 dimensions and 12 topics.

Integrative Summary of Findings

Differences Related to Time

There were few effects for time across the study, and where there were changes, these tended to be in a positive direction. Nonverbal accuracy increased over time, as did communication awareness, with spouses becoming more accurate at predicting their partners' decoding. Communication Quality also tended to increase over time. By contrast, there was no significant change over time in Quantity of communication, amount of conflict, or specific responses to conflict.

Differences Between Happy and Unhappy Couples

Despite the fact that the low marital satisfaction group (as determined by a median split) were not in the clinically distressed range, there were clear differences in responses to conflict and in perceptions of conversations. Couples higher in satisfaction reported more positivity and higher-quality communication, and less negativity, disengagement, destructive process, and conflict. The two groups did not differ in nonverbal accuracy.

We could well expect interactions between satisfaction and time on the various communication measures used in this study, with the differences between couples high and low in satisfaction becoming more pronounced over time, but there was very little evidence of such interactions. The only interaction of relationship satisfaction and time occurred for conflict strategies. Couples lower in satisfaction decreased their use of negative strategies and increased their use of positive strategies in the first year of marriage, but they reverted to their earlier patterns less than a year later.

Concurrent Links with Satisfaction

Both conversational patterns and responses to conflict were related to concurrent satisfaction, as defined by scores on the continuous measure. At all times and for husbands and wives, satisfaction was positively related to quality of conversational patterns and negatively related to amount of conflict. With regard to responses to conflict, satisfaction tended to be associated with high levels of Positivity and low levels of Disengagement.

There were only scattered results for the conflict strategies. Wives who reported more conflict avoidance premaritally were less likely to be satisfied. On the other hand, after a year of marriage, less satisfied wives tended to report more support of the partner and less satisfied husbands tended to report more use of reason. The latter results may seem counterintuitive given that both of these behaviors are generally seen as positive. They are, however, consistent with the finding reported earlier, that husbands and wives low in satisfaction tended to temporarily increase their use of positive behaviors during the first year, although these efforts were not sustained during the second year.

Consistent with earlier research, links between concurrent satisfaction and nonverbal accuracy were limited to wife-to-husband communications. In addition, satisfaction was more clearly related to accuracy for positive and neutral messages than for negative messages.

Predicting Later Satisfaction

There was relatively weak prediction from earlier communication to later satisfaction and the results were gender specific. Only conversational patterns (extent of conflict) and responses to conflict were related to later satisfaction. Extent of conflict predicted later satisfaction for husbands only. With regard to responses to conflict, premarital levels of Manipulation, Negativity, Disengagement, and Positivity predicted wives' satisfaction after a year of marriage, even when earlier satisfaction was controlled.

Predicting Later Communication

Patterns of prediction from earlier satisfaction to later communication were also gender specific. Whereas amount of conflict predicted later satisfaction for husbands, low satisfaction predicted later conflict for wives. Similarly, the particular responses to conflict that predicted wives' later satisfaction were predicted by satisfaction for husbands. That is, for husbands, Negativity and Disengagement were related to lower satisfaction at the earlier time, and Positivity was related to higher satisfaction.

For wives, premarital satisfaction was negatively related to later reports of Demand-Withdraw, and positively related to later support of the partner. For husbands, premarital satisfaction was negatively related to use of reason after a year of marriage. Nonverbal accuracy was also predicted by earlier satisfaction, and this effect was consistent across message types.

Conclusions

Generally, there was little change over time on any of the measures used in this study. What change there was tended to be positive, with couples becoming more accurate at understanding each other's nonverbal behavior, and also reporting conversational patterns of higher quality after 2 years of marriage. These findings suggest that destructive patterns of communication that cause problems later in relationships develop premaritally. Given that most couples in this sample were not living together prior to marriage, it appears that their communication patterns, including their ways of dealing with conflict, are established before they have to handle the particular issues involved in setting up a home together. Although the failure to find substantial change over time could be attributed to a lack of statistical power because of the small sample size, inspection of the means indicates very little difference across time; hence it is unlikely that the differences would attain significance even with a large sample.

Despite the early stage of the marital relationship represented here and the relatively high scores overall in relationship satisfaction, couples high and low in satisfaction were clearly differentiated on almost all the variables assessed in this study. The exceptions were nonverbal accuracy, postconflict distress, and quantity of conversation. The pattern of differences between happy and unhappy couples was similar at all points in time, with no interaction between time and relationship satisfaction. That is, any differences between happy and unhappy couples that were evident after 2 years were also present at the time of marriage. Perhaps a longer time span would be needed for interactions between time and relationship satisfaction to emerge.

There were strong links between concurrent satisfaction and communication, particularly for perceived quality of conversation, extent of conflict, and habitual ways of dealing with conflict. Later satisfaction was related only to earlier conflict, specifically to the extent of conflict (for husbands) and to the ways couples dealt with conflict (for wives). Note that the effects of conflict were always negative, in the long and in the short term.

Although the literature has tended to emphasize the effect of communication on later relationship satisfaction, we found at least as much support for the proposition that relationship satisfaction affects later communication. For wives, low premarital satisfaction predicted high levels of conflict after 2 years of marriage; for husbands, high satisfaction predicted constructive ways of dealing with conflict.

This study, then, is an important addition to the literature on early marriage. It is unique in terms of the wide range of variables measured, the variety of methodologies employed, and the fact that both satisfaction and communication were assessed at all three times of the study. The study has pointed to the relative stability of communication patterns established premaritally, to the negative effects of conflict on marital relationships in both the long and short term, and to the reciprocal relations between communication and relationship satisfaction. These findings have implications for both theory and practice in the area of marital communication.

References

Cahn, D. (1990). Confrontation behaviors, perceived understanding and relationship growth. In D. Cahn (Ed.), *Intimates in Conflict.* Hillsdale, NJ: Lawrence Erlbaum.

Christensen, A. (1988). Dysfunctional interaction patterns in couples. In P. Noller & M. A. Fitzpatrick (Eds.), *Perspectives on marital interaction.* Philadelphia: Multilingual Matters.

Christensen, A., & Heavey, C. L. (1990). Gender, power and marital conflict. *Journal of Personality and Social Psychology, 59,* 73–81.

Christensen, A., & Sullaway, M. (1984a). Relationship Issues Questionnaire. Unpublished measure, University of California, Los Angeles.

Christensen, A., & Sullaway, M. (1984b). Communication Patterns Questionnaire. Unpublished measure, University of California, Los Angeles.

Davidson, B. J., Balswick, J., & Halverson, C. (1983). Affective self-disclosure and marital adjustment: A test of equity theory. *Journal of Marriage and the Family, 45,* 93–102.

Dickson-Markman, F., & Markman, H. (1988). The effects of others on marriage: Do they help or hurt? In P. Noller & M. A. Fitzpatrick (Eds.), *Perspectives on marital interaction* (pp. 294–322). Philadelphia: Multilingual Matters.

Falbo, T., & Peplau, L. A. (1980). Power strategies in intimate relationships. *Journal of Personality and Social Psychology, 38,* 618–628.

Feeney, J. A., Noller, P., & Callan, V. (1994). Attachment style, communication and satisfaction in the early years of marriage. In K. Bartholomew & D. Perlman (Eds.), *Advances in personal relationships.* London: Jessica Kingsley.

Fitzpatrick, M. A. (1988). *Between husbands and wives.* Newbury Park: Sage.

Fitzpatrick, M. A., & Winke, J. (1979). You always hurt the one you love: Strategies and tactics in interpersonal conflict. *Communication Quarterly, 27,* 3–11.

Gottman, J. M., & Krokoff, L. J. (1989). Marital interaction and marital satisfaction: A longitudinal view. *Journal of Consulting and Clinical Psychology, 57,* 47–52.

Gottman, J. M., & Krokoff, L. J. (1990). Complex statistics are not always clearer than simple statistics: A reply to Woody & Costanzo. *Journal of Consulting and Clinical Psychology, 58,* 502–505.

Gottman, J. M., & Levenson, R. W. (1988). The social psychophysiology of marriage. In P. Noller & M. A. Fitzpatrick (Eds.), *Perspectives on marital interaction.* Philadelphia: Multilingual Matters.

Gottman, J. M., & Porterfield, A. L. (1981). Communicative competence in the nonverbal behavior of married couples. *Journal of Marriage and the Family, 43,* 187–198.

Hendrick, S. S. (1981). Self-disclosure and marital satisfaction. *Journal of Personality and Social Psychology, 40,* 1150–1159.

Huston, T. L., & Robins, E. (1982). Conceptual and methodological issues in studying close relationships. *Journal of Marriage and the Family, 44,* 901–925.

Huston, T. L., & Vangelisti, A. (1991). Socioemotional behavior and satisfaction in marital relationships: A longitudinal study. *Journal of Personality and Social Psychology, 61,* 721–733.

Jacobson, N. S. (1990). Commentary: Contributions from psychology to an understanding of marriage. In F. D. Fincham & T. N. Bradbury (Eds.), *The psychology of marriage* (pp. 258–275). New York: Guilford.

Kahn, M. (1970). Nonverbal communication and marital satisfaction. *Family Process, 9,* 449–456.

Kelly, C., Huston, T., & Cate, R. (1985). Premarital relationship correlates of the erosion of satisfaction in marriage. *Journal of Social and Personal Relationships, 2,* 167–178.

Kirchler, E. (1989). Everyday life experiences at home: An interaction diary approach to assess marital relationships. *Journal of Family Psychology, 2,* 311–336.

Markman, H. (1979). The application of a behavioral model of marriage in predicting relationship satisfaction for couples planning marriage. *Journal of Consulting and Clinical Psychology, 4,* 743–749.

Markman, H. (1981). Prediction of marital distress: A 5-year follow-up. *Journal of Consulting and Clinical Psychology, 49,* 760–762.

Markman, H. (1984). The longitudinal study of couples' interactions: Implications for understanding and predicting the development of marital distress. In K. Hahlweg & N. Jacobson (Eds.), *Marital interaction: Analysis and modification* (pp. 253–281). New York: Guilford.

Montgomery, B. M. (1981). The form and function of quality communication in marriage. *Family Relations, 30,* 21–30.

Noller, P. (1980). Misunderstandings in marital communication: A study of couples' nonverbal communication. *Journal of Personality and Social Psychology, 39,* 1135–1148.

Noller, P. (1981). Gender and marital adjustment level differences in decoding messages from spouses and strangers. *Journal of Personality and Social Psychology, 41,* 272–278.

Noller, P. (1984). *Nonverbal communication and marital interaction.* Oxford: Pergamon Press.

Noller, P., & Bagi, S. (1985). Parent–adolescent communication. *Journal of Adolescence, 8,* 125–144.

Noller, P., & Feeney, J. A. (1994). Relationship satisfaction, attachment and nonverbal accuracy in early marriage. *Journal of Nonverbal Behavior, 18,* 199–221.

Noller, P., Feeney, J. A., Bonnell, D., & Callan, V. J. (1994). A longitudinal study of conflict in early marriage. *Journal of Social and Personal Relationships, 11,* 233–252.

Noller, P., & Fitzpatrick, M. A. (1987, August). Sending and receiving of specific emotional messages in marriage. In *International Conference on Language and Social Psychology.* Bristol.

Noller, P., & Fitzpatrick, M. A. (1990). Marital communication in the eighties. *Journal of Marriage and the Family, 52,* 832–843.

Noller, P., & Guthrie, D. M. (1991). Methodological issues in studying communication in close relationships. In W. H. Jones & D. M. Perlman (Eds.), *Advances in Personal Relationships.* London: Jessica Kingsley.

Noller, P., & Ruzzene, M. (1991). Communication in marriage: The influence of affect and cognition. In G. J. O. Fletcher & F. D. Fincham (Eds.), *Cognition in close relationships* (pp. 203–233). Hillsdale, NJ: Lawrence Erlbaum.

Noller, P., & White, A. (1990). The validity of the Communication Patterns Questionnaire. *Psychological Assessment: A Journal of Consulting and Clinical Psychology, 2,* 478–482.

Norton, R. (1983). Measuring marital quality: A critical look at the dependent variable. *Journal of Marriage and the Family, 45,* 141–151.

Patterson, G. R. (1982). Coercive family process: A social learning approach. Eugene, OR: Castalia.

Peterson, D. M. (1968). Husband–wife communication and family problems. *Sociology and Social Research, 53,* 375–384.

Raush, H. L., Barry, W. A., Hertel, R. K., & Swain, M. E. (1974). *Communication and conflict in marriage.* San Francisco: Jossey-Bass.

Reis, H., & Shaver, P. R. (1988). Intimacy as an interpersonal process. In S. Duck (Eds.), *Handbook of personal relationships* (pp. 367–389). New York: John Wiley & Sons.

Roloff, M., & Cloven, D. H. (1990). The chilling effect in interpersonal relationships. In D. Cahn (Ed.), *Intimates in conflict* (pp. 49–76). Hillsdale, NJ: Lawrence Erlbaum.

Sillars, A. L., & Weisberg, J. (1987). Conflict as a social skill. In M. E. Roloff & G. R. Miller (Eds.), *Interpersonal processes: New directions in communication research.* Newbury Park, CA: Sage.

Smith, D. A., Vivian, D., & O'Leary, K. D. (1990). Longitudinal prediction of marital discord from premarital expressions of affect. *Journal of Consulting and Clinical Psychology, 58,* 790–797.

Spanier, G. B. (1976). Measuring dyadic adjustment: New scales for assessing the quality of marriage and similar dyads. *Journal of Marriage and the Family, 38,* 15–28.

Tannen, D. (1990). *You just don't understand.* New York: Ballantine Books.

Weiss, R. L. (1984). Cognitive and behavioral measures of marital interaction. In K. Hahlweg & N. S. Jacobson (Eds.), *Marital interaction: Analysis and modification* (pp. 232–252). New York: Guilford.

Wheeler, L., & Nezlek, J. (1977). Sex differences in social participation. *Journal of Personality and Social Psychology, 35,* 742–754.

White, L. (1983). Determinants of spousal interaction: Marital structure or marital happiness. *Journal of Marriage and the Family, 45,* 511–520.

Woody, E. Z., & Costanzo, P. R. (1990). Does marital agony precede marital ecstasy? A comment on Gottman & Krokoff's "Marital interaction and satisfaction: A longitudinal view." *Journal of Consulting and Clinical Psychology, 58,* 499–501.

2 Marital Aggression, Quality, and Stability in the First Year of Marriage: Findings from the Buffalo Newlywed Study

Kenneth E. Leonard and Linda J. Roberts

Marriage represents one of the most important transition events in the course of individual development. When two individuals marry, it is likely to fundamentally alter their views of themselves and the social world, the nature of their interactions with friends and family, and their transactions with the broader social network (Boss, 1983; McGoldrick & Carter, 1982). Newlyweds are thus faced with a set of important and challenging tasks: they must negotiate a satisfactory division of roles and responsibilities; reestablish or redefine ties, both as individuals and as a couple, with each member's extended family and peer network; and learn ways to maintain and nurture their developing relationship. Although these tasks are often begun prior to marriage and continue throughout marriage, the early years of marriage are usually the time in which major conflicts are first revealed and confronted. For example, Suitor, Pillemer, and Straus (1990) report that marital conflict and verbal aggression within the marriage are negatively correlated with age (though this may represent either developmental declines or a winnowing effect of divorce). Consequently, the early years of marriage may represent the period in which marital conflict is the most frequent and most intense. Because a couple's ability to manage marital conflict and reconcile differences may be an important determinant of marital satisfaction and stability (e.g., Gottman, 1979; Markman, Floyd, Stanley, & Storaasli, 1988), the early years of marriage may represent a *critical phase* for the developmental course of the marriage.

Given the presumed frequency and intensity of disagreements and conflict during early marriage, it is perhaps not surprising that the prevalence of aggression during this period is also elevated in comparison with other times in the marriage. Data suggest that in a given year, approximately 15% of all married couples will experience some level of marital violence

This research was supported by NIAAA grants R01-AA07183 to Kenneth E. Leonard and 1K21-AA00149 to Linda J. Roberts.

(Straus, Gelles, & Steinmetz, 1980). Among couples in their early years of marriage, the prevalence is considerably higher. Suitor et al. (1990) reported that the rate of marital violence was 27% for men aged 18 to 29, 21% for men aged 30 to 39, and 8% or less for men 40 years and older. O'Leary, Barling, Arias, Rosenbaum, Malone, and Tyree (1989) indicated that 31% of the men in their newlywed sample acknowledged aggression in the year prior to marriage, 27% acknowledged aggression between 6 and 18 months of marriage, and 25% acknowledged aggression between 18 and 30 months of marriage. Thus, while the rate of marital aggression declines over the early years of marriage, it nonetheless remains elevated after 2½ years of marriage, in comparison with rates in the general population.

Studying how couples negotiate the early years of marriage, then, may be critical for understanding subsequent marital outcomes, including marital aggression, marital quality, and stability of the marital relationship. Focusing particularly on husband-to-wife marital aggression, we began a longitudinal study of early marriage in 1987. The Buffalo Newlywed Study (BNS) was designed specifically to contribute to our understanding of the causes and consequences of marital aggression, although other marital outcomes and their interrelationships with aggression were also of interest. The importance of understanding marital conflict and aggression in young married couples stems from several considerations. First, as noted above, marital conflict and its successful resolution, particularly in early marriage, are viewed as fundamental to the development of a stable, intimate marriage. Similarly, the rates of marital violence are highest among young married couples, and evidence suggests that the first instance of aggression is likely to occur within the first two years of marriage (Dobash & Dobash, 1979). Focusing on newly married couples enables us to examine the very early stages of marital aggression, perhaps before the patterns of marital aggression have become firmly entrenched or before the marriage has ended in divorce. Aggression in this early period may establish dominance and interactional patterns that have implications for later marital functioning, even in the absence of later physical aggression. Thus, understanding marital conflict and aggression in this early marital period would serve as a foundation for the development of preventive and early intervention approaches.

In addition to the central role of conflict behavior, the Buffalo Newlywed Study was designed to investigate the extent to which sociodemographic factors and individual difference factors (e.g., anger and hostility, depression, stress, masculinity, femininity, marital power beliefs, and the observation or experience of family violence during childhood) were related to aggression and other marital outcomes. Furthermore, we sought to examine in detail a specific factor that has been a consistent correlate of marital aggression and has also been linked to marital quality and stability, excessive alcohol use.

Excessive alcohol consumption has been frequently and consistently associated with marital violence in research spanning the past 20 years. Fcr example, Gelles (1974) reported that alcohol consumption accompanied marital violence in approximately 50% of the violent couples in this sample. Roy (1982) reported that 35% of 4,000 women who called an abuse hotline indicated that their husbands were "problem alcoholics." In addition to these clinical reports, several more systematic studies have found alcohol consumption, particularly episodic heavy drinking, to be related to the likelihood of marital violence (Kaufman-Kantor & Straus, 1990; Leonard, Bromet, Parkinson, Day, & Ryan, 1985; Pan, Neidig, & O'Leary, 1994).

Excessive alcohol use and alcoholism have also been linked to marital satisfaction (Brennan & Moos, 1990; Horwitz & White, 1991) and marital stability (Burns, 1984; McCrady, 1982; Power & Estaugh, 1990). Summarizing several studies, McCrady (1982) reported that alcoholics have rates of separation/divorce four to eight times greater than the rates in the general population. However, drinking behavior has often been overlooked as a predictor in large prospective studies of marital dissolution. As White (1990) notes: "Respondents' accounts of their own divorces illuminate several factors that receive little attention in the empirical literature . . . [including] alcoholism and drug abuse" (p. 908). Similarly, although there is a substantial body of literature documenting a concurrent association between poor marital functioning and problem drinking (e.g., Brennan & Moos, 1990), few longitudinal studies have addressed this issue, and the direction of causation is uncertain. Bidirectional effects are likely: Drinking may lead to marital distress, *and* marital distress may lead to problem drinking.

The rationale for studying alcohol use and alcohol problems in the Buffalo Newlywed Study stemmed from one other major factor: the prevalence of drinking and drinking problems among young adults. Frequent heavy drinking and alcohol problems reach their highest rate among men and women in their early 20s, decline somewhat in the late 20s, and decline markedly in the 30s and 40s (Hilton, 1991). Although marital researchers have generally not considered the role alcohol may play in determining marital outcomes, heavy drinking, by virtue of its prevalence among young adults and its empirical links to marital aggression and marital discord, may be a particularly important variable for researchers to address.

In what represents a return to historical roots in the field, a second type of individual difference variable is receiving increasing attention among researchers interested in marital outcomes: the personalities of the spouses. Although early attempts to relate personality constructs to marital adjustment met with only limited success, there is a growing recognition in the field that personality variables may influence marital outcomes and, in fact, may underlie some of the observed behavioral differences in couples' interactions (Bradbury & Fincham, 1988; Davis & Oathout, 1987). In the case of the three marital outcomes identified here (aggression, quality, and stability), two personality constructs have been found, with at least some consistency, to be potential risk factors: *Neuroticism,* that is, a propensity to experience negative affect, and *Gender Role,* that is, femininity and masculinity.

Neuroticism appears to have an effect on marital distress (Cole, Cole, & Dean, 1980; Kelly & Conley, 1987), and it is one of the few personality constructs found in more than one study to predict marital dissolution (Kelly & Conley, 1987; Kurdek, 1993). Although not labeled neuroticism, other variables that reflect a *propensity to experience negative affect* have also been identified as correlates or predictors of marital dysfunction. For example, hostility and irritability have been found to be associated with marital adjustment (Smith, Pope, Sanders, Allred, & O'Keefe, 1988; Smith, Sanders, & Alexander, 1990) and marital aggression (Hamberger & Hastings, 1991; Leonard & Blane, 1992; Maiuro, Cahn, Vitaliano, Wagner, & Zegree, 1988). Although gender role variables have not been systematically investigated as prospective predictors of marital outcomes, cross-sectional studies have reported that femininity is positively associated with marital adjustment (Antill, 1983; Baucom & Aiken, 1984; Bradbury & Fincham, 1988; Kurdek & Schmitt, 1986). Cross-sectional studies concerning marital aggression have implicated both masculinity and femininity (Bernard, Bernard, & Bernard, 1985; Boye-Beaman, Leonard, & Senchak, 1993; Burke, Stets, & Pirog-Good, 1989; Finn, 1986). Given the success demonstrated by these variables as correlates of marital outcomes, we sought to examine their utility as longitudinal predictors.

In summary, we view the early years of marriage as a critical period for the development of the conjugal bond and the future outcome of the marriage. Further, we have identified three variable domains that may be critical in determining these outcomes: conflict behavior, drinking behavior, and personality. Accordingly, we discuss changes in marital quality, stability, and aggression over the first year of marriage and examine the utility of variables from the three domains in the prospective prediction of these marital outcomes. Before presenting the results, we provide an overview of the study's design and procedures, highlighting the ways in which they may differ from other investigations of newlyweds.

Overview of the Buffalo Newlywed Study

Design and Procedures

The BNS is a three-wave longitudinal study of newly married couples conducted over the first three years of marriage. This chapter, however, focuses on the first two waves, T1 and T2. In developing this study, we endeavored to enhance generalizability by using a large representative sample of couples that could be assessed at the time of marriage. Although advertising for engaged couples or locating them through engagement announcements in newspapers would permit assessments at the time of marriage, these methods would introduce selection biases and thereby place serious restrictions on generalizability. In particular, couples who would be of most interest to the study (hostile, problem drinkers) might be the least likely to be identified through this method. Household or phone surveys would be hampered by the low percentages of individuals in the general population who would be planning to be married in the near future. The use of marriage license records would circumvent many of these problems, but identifying, locating, recruiting, and assessing these couples at a time close to their marriage date is a difficult task. Moreover, in our case, the confidential status of these records in New York State precluded this option.

Given these considerations and constraints, we decided on and, with the cooperation of the staff of the city clerk's office, implemented a marriage license bureau procedure that satisfied many of our concerns (see Figure 2.1). Two interviewers, one male and one female, were stationed at the city courthouse three days a week. These interviewers approached couples after they had applied for a marriage license. Couples who indicated that this was the first marriage for both husband and wife and that the husband was between the ages of 18 and 29 were requested to participate in a brief screening interview for which the couple would receive $5. If a couple indicated that they did not have the time, they were asked if they would be able to answer about 12 questions, for which they would still receive the $5. These couples were then interviewed separately by a same-gender interviewer concerning demographic and drinking variables. The purpose of the paid screening was threefold: (1) to provide couples with a context and motivation to remain at the office long enough for the research assistant to fully describe the longitudinal study; (2) to enhance our requests for their participation by allowing the couple to comply with a smaller request initially and by initiating a relationship between the interviewers and the couple; and (3) to provide some basic descriptive data for those who subsequently refused to participate in the longitudinal study. After the screening interview

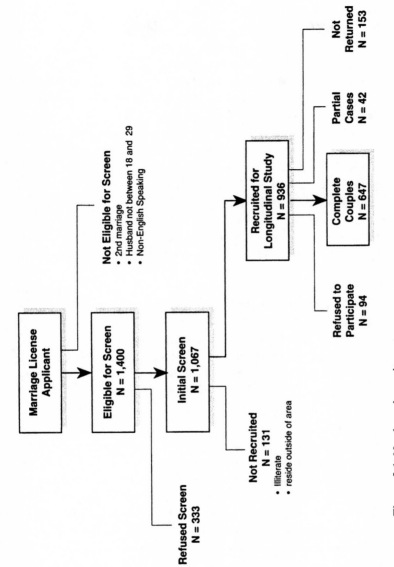

Figure 2.1. Newlywed recruitment.

was completed, the couples were recruited for the longitudinal study and informed that each would receive $25 for participating. They were asked for
their telephone numbers and addresses and the names, phone numbers, and
addresses of two individuals who would be able to contact them. Each member of the couple was given a questionnaire packet and a separate postage-
paid envelope to return the questionnaire and asked to complete it in private
and return it within two weeks.

The strengths of this methodological approach are many. First, all couples must apply in person for marriage licenses no more than 90 days prior
to their marriage. Thus, identifying and contacting a sample of first marriages is accomplished.[1] Further, this is accomplished shortly before marriage, allowing for assessment as close to the wedding as possible and minimizing delayed or canceled marriages.[2] By collecting information in the
screening interview, we can examine sample bias by comparing those couples who refused to participate or did not return the questionnaires with
couples who did return the questionnaires.

As shown in Figure 2.1, we approached 1,400 eligible couples and
screened 1,067 couples, or 76%. Among the screened subjects, 936 couples
were recruited for the longitudinal study. Only 94 (10%) refused to participate. Although 842 couples agreed to participate, not all of these couples
actually completed the questionnaires. Complete data were collected from
647 couples, or approximately 77% of the couples who agreed to participate. In 5% of the couples (42 couples), we have questionnaire data from at
least one member of the couple, usually the wife.

One of our primary concerns in developing this sample was the extent to
which the final sample reflects the overall population of newlywed couples
applying for marriage licenses. As seen in Figure 2.1, one reason a couple
may not appear in the final sample is that they refused to participate in the
screening interview or they did not complete the initial assessment of the
longitudinal study. We have no direct information concerning the characteristics of couples who declined to be interviewed. As noted earlier, however, couples who initially refused the full screening interview were offered
a brief screening interview. Comparisons between full-screen participants
and brief-screen participants suggested that the latter tended to have a
higher level of education and occupation, were more likely to be employed,
and were older. The magnitude of these differences was quite minimal. To
the extent that couples who refuse the screening interview are similar to
couples who agree to the short screen, our sample may slightly overrepre-
sent the young, lower socioeconomic status (SES) couples, but the degree
of that overrepresentation is not a serious limitation.

Couples also might not appear in the final participating sample because they did not complete the initial assessment (refused or never returned the questionnaire packets). There were some differences between couples who completed the premarital assessment and those who did not (see columns 1 and 2 of Table 2.1). African-American couples were less likely to complete the assessment than other racial/ethnic groups. Couples living together prior to marriage, couples with higher husband income, and couples in which the wife was unemployed were more likely to complete the assessment. Younger couples were more likely than older couples to complete the assessment. Once again, however, the impact of these biases is likely to be relatively small. There were many factors on which the complete and incomplete couples did not differ, including education, religion, length and trajectory of the couple's relationship, presence of children, premarital pregnancy, husband employment status, ratings of spouse consideration and communication, ratings of husband verbal and physical aggression according to both husband and wife, and husband and wife frequency of heavy drinking and smoking status.

The second data collection of the project involved the one-year follow-up assessment of couples (T2). This assessment involved separate interviews with husbands and wives as well as completion of the same questionnaire battery used at T1. Although we attempted to conduct intensive in-person interviews with all of the couples, in many cases (34%) we conducted a shorter telephone interview that assessed only the husband's verbal and physical aggression toward his wife and life events. These couples did, however, complete the questionnaire battery. Telephone interviews were used in three situations: (1) the couple did not reside within one hour of the Research Institute on Addictions; (2) the couple refused to participate, in which case the telephone interview was offered as a way of encouraging them to participate; and (3) the couple missed or canceled more than five appointments.

Of the 647 couples who participated at T1, at least one questionnaire or one interview was completed for 543 couples (84%), and questionnaires and interviews were completed for 494 couples (76%). Despite the relatively good rates of follow-up, certain subgroups manifested lower rates. In particular, follow-up rates were higher among older couples, white couples, and higher socioeconomic status couples. However, complete and incomplete couples at T2 did not differ with respect to premarital aggression, or husband or wife frequent heavy drinking.

Description of Sample

The couples successfully recruited for the Newlywed Study represent a large, heterogeneous sample (see Table 2.1). The average age of couples in

Table 2.1. *Subject characteristics: Comparison of screened couples, recruited couples, and completed couples (percentages)*

Characteristic	Recruited sample (N = 952)	T1 participants (N = 647)	T1 & T2 participants (N = 543)
Husband age			
18–21	17	18	18
22–25	47	48	47
26–29	35	34	35
Wife age			
17–21	33	34	31
22–25	45	45	47
26–29	17	16	17
30–40	5	5	4
Husband race			
White	67	71	73
African-American	28	25	22
Other	5	5	5
Wife race			
White	69	73	75
African-American	27	23	21
Other	4	4	4
Husband religion			
Catholic	50	51	52
Protestant, traditional	14	14	15
Protestant, conservative	25	23	21
Non-Christian	12	12	12
Wife religion			
Catholic	51	52	54
Protestant, traditional	15	15	15
Protestant, conservative	26	25	23
Non-Christian	8	8	8
Husband education			
Less than 12 years	12	11	10
High school grad or GED	33	31	29
Some college, associates degree, or trade school	32	34	35
College graduate	23	23	27
Wife education			
Less than 12 years	11	10	8
High school grad or GED	25	24	22
Some college, associates degree, or trade school	39	40	41
College graduate	25	26	28
Husband employed	81	80	80
Wife employed	59	56	58
Wife with children before marriage	31	32	29
Wife pregnant at time of marriage	14	14	13

the sample closely approximates the average age of couples at marriage nationally. Husbands were approximately 24 years old, and wives were one year younger. Reflecting the urban area in which the couples reside, approximately 70% of the sample are Caucasian, and approximately 25% are African-American. The sample is predominantly Catholic (approximately 50%) or Protestant (approximately 40%). Only 10% report no religious affiliation. The rates of other religions, including Judaism, are negligble in this sample. Approximately one third had completed high school or a General Educational Development test and 25% were college graduates. One of the most surprising statistics was that 32% of this sample of first marriages already had children and that 14% were currently pregnant. However, other representative samples of newlyweds have reported similar findings (Crohan & Veroff, 1989).

Measurements in the Buffalo Newlywed Study

The assessment battery used in the BNS reflects our interest in examining a broad range of hypotheses relevant to the substance abuse, aggression, and marriage fields. At each wave, we collected questionnaire and interview data concerning sociodemographic factors and each of four substantive domains; marital outcomes, marital conflict behavior, alcohol-related variables, and individual differences. In all instances, comparable measures were obtained from husbands and wives.

Marital Quality. We used three instruments to assess the multidimensional construct of marital quality: the Locke-Wallace Marital Adjustment Test (MAT; Locke & Wallace, 1959); the Family Assessment Measure (FAM; Skinner, Steinhauer, & Santa-Barbara, 1984); and the Miller Social Intimacy Scale (MSIS; Miller & Lefcourt, 1982). The FAM and MSIS were administered to subjects at both waves; the MAT was added after the study had begun. A modified version of the MAT was administered to most couples at T1,[3] but all subjects received the standard MAT at T2. The MSIS and FAM complement the focus on global satisfaction and marital "differences" assessed in the MAT. The FAM focuses on evaluations of the partner in a variety of marital tasks, while the MSIS assesses the overall degree of closeness, affection, and personal disclosure in the marriage.

These three scales were strongly intercorrelated at each assessment period. To reduce the number of measures while retaining a multidimensional assessment of the construct, we calculated a Marital Quality Index (MQI) that combines the three measures. Each measure was standardized, with the standardization being conducted separately for husband and wife scores. The mean of the three scales was then computed for each husband and wife. Finally, husband and wife scores were averaged to produce a single score reflecting the couple's evaluation of their current marital quality.

Premarital and Marital Aggression. Premarital aggression was assessed at T1 as part of the courthouse screening, and at T2 as part of the interview procedure. These assessments used a modified Conflict Tactics Scale (CTS; Straus, 1979). This scale consists of 18 items describing behaviors that the respondent may have displayed within a marital conflict situation. Although some of these behaviors are adaptive (i.e., "discussed the conflict calmly"), most describe different degrees of verbal and physical aggression (ranging from "argued heatedly but short of yelling" to "used a knife or gun"). For the T1 assessment of premarital aggression, an abbreviated version of the CTS was used to assess the husband's and wife's report of husband aggression. This brief version included two items, "push, grab, or shove" and "slap" and was used to minimize the time and increase the acceptability of the courthouse screen. The T2 assessments of marital aggression also employed the CTS, except that they omitted items concerning the use of weapons.

Marital Stability. Information regarding marital stability was collected in two ways. First, as part of the follow-up contacts, subjects often indicated that they were separated or divorced from their partner. In some cases, a contact person indicated that the couple was separated or divorced. This information was included only if we also had direct contact with at least one member of the couple and the information was not refuted. In addition to the follow-up contacts, divorce and separations due to marital problems were included in the list of life events completed by subjects who participated at T2. As with the other marital outcome measures, a report of separation or divorce by the husband or wife in either the contact information or in the interviews was viewed as definitive.

Drinking Behavior. Several important issues were addressed in the measurement of alcohol consumption patterns. First, quantity-frequency questions based on the work of Cahalan, Cisin, and Crossley (1969) were asked of couples with respect to the past year. These questions allowed us to compute the average daily consumption of alcohol. Although this index is useful, it is limited in that individuals with rather modest average daily consumption may also have fairly frequent episodes of heavy consumption. Thus additional questions assessing atypical heavy use were also asked of husbands and wives (frequency of drinking 6 or more drinks, 9 or more drinks, 12 or more drinks, and frequency of getting drunk). We also administered the Alcohol Dependency Scale (ADS; Skinner & Allen, 1982), which in clinical samples assesses the extent of physical and psychological dependence on alcohol. However, we have argued that among nonclinical samples, the ADS measures a risky drinking style marked by frequent episodes of very excessive consumption. A problem-drinking index was calculated that combines both the ADS score and items assessing frequent heavy drinking for each spouse.

Marital Conflict Behavior. The Conflict Inventory (CI; Margolin, 1980), a 26-item scale that measures typical behavioral responses to marital conflict, was administered at each time point. Each subject rated the frequency with which his/her partner engaged in various behaviors in the context of a "difference of opinion." Margolin has previously used 18 of the items to create three subscales: Problem Solving, Withdrawal, and Aggression. However, we omitted four of these items.[4] The remaining 14 items were subjected to principal component analyses separately for husbands and wives. A clean, interpretable three-factor solution was found that was essentially replicated across spouse and time (for further details see Roberts, Leonard, & Senchak, 1991). Exact factor scoring was used to create three measures of conflict behavior for each spouse: Problem Solving (e.g., "come up with helpful ideas or suggestions"); Anger Expression (e.g., "insult or call names"), and Avoidance (e.g., "give in to avoid an argument").

Personality. Three measures were used to assess neuroticism. The Perceived Stress Scale (PSS; Cohen, Kamarck, & Mermelstein, 1983) is a 14-item measure of the degree to which life situations are appraised as stressful. Although these items are influenced by stressful events, they appear to assess a more general disposition to overreact to stressful events. The Spielberger Trait Anger Scale (STAS) was employed as a measure of angry affect. This 10-item scale has extensive norms and excellent psychometric properties (Spielberger et al., 1979). Finally, the Center for Epidemiological Studies Depression Inventory (CES-D; Radloff, 1977) was used to assess dysphoric affect. These three scales evidenced moderate to high intercorrelations and were standardized and combined to reflect a disposition to experience negative affect, or Neuroticism. A measure of neuroticism (the NEO-PI; Costa & McCrae, 1985) was available on a subsample of couples, and this was highly correlated with the index we created (.63 for wives and .68 for husbands).

Gender role identity was assessed with the Personal Attributes Questionnaire (PAQ; Spence, Helmreich, & Stapp, 1974), which consists of two separate scales balanced for socially desirable items measuring Masculinity (M) and Femininity (F). The MF scale, which is made up of socially undesirable items, was not used.

Marital Outcomes in the First Year of Marriage

Rates of Premarital and Marital Aggression

Consistent with other research, the current sample shows marital aggression to be quite prevalent both before and after marriage. Over the course of their premarital relationship, 27% of the husbands and 28% of the wives reported at least one instance of husband aggression. Overall, 36% of the couples indicated at least one episode of husband-to-wife premarital aggression. In the first year of marriage, the rate of marital aggression was similar. At least one episode of husband marital aggression during the first year of marriage was reported by 29% of husbands and 30% of wives. These figures are comparable to the results of O'Leary et al. (1989), in which 31% of the men reported premarital aggression and 27% acknowledged marital aggression between 6 and 18 months of marriage. If we consider either the husband or wife report as definitive, 39% of the newlywed couples experienced at least one act of husband-to-wife aggression in the first year. The aggressive acts reported range from minor acts (push, grab, or shove) to more serious acts (hit with fist, beat up). Single episodes of minor violence (see Straus, 1990) were reported by 13% of the couples, while multiple episodes and/or severe episodes were reported by 26% of the couples.

Changes in Marital Quality

In general, couples' appraisals of the quality of their marriage dropped over the first year of marriage. A decline was evident for husbands and wives and on all three of the scales comprising the Marital Quality Index. For example, couples' average MAT scores were 119.34 (14.11) at T1 and 109.11 (22.21) at T2, indicating that on average, couples' marital satisfaction dropped approximately two thirds of a standard deviation. Of course, not all couples experienced this decrement. While 50% of the couples dropped at least one-half SD, 13% of the couples increased by the same amount. Overall, the couples' Marital Quality scores were fairly stable across time ($r = .57$). Other researchers have found drops in marital satisfaction of comparable magnitude by the first anniversary (Huston & Vangelisti, 1991; Smith, Vivian, & O'Leary, 1990), leaving little doubt that important negative effects on marriage occur very soon after the honeymoon is over.

Marital Instability

Among the 530 couples we successfully collected data from at their first anniversary, 8 (1.5%) were divorced or divorcing. If we broaden our definition of "unstable" couples to include all couples not living together at the time of contact owing to marital difficulties (which includes couples who did not indicate that they had initiated divorce proceedings, but who were nonetheless separated), 27 cases (5.1%) were identified. If we further broaden the definition of our outcome variable to include marital disruptions of any kind – that is, if we define "unstable" couples as those who report during the life events assessment that a "separation due to marital difficulties" occurred at some point in their first year of marriage – 72 cases (13.6%) are identified.

Prediction of Marital Aggression During the First Year of Marriage

Given the prevalence and variability of marital aggression, we focused our analysis on the extent and severity of marital aggression during the first year of marriage rather than the simple occurrence of aggression. Utilizing the weighted severity index described by Straus (1990), we employed the maximum score reported by husband or wife as the dependent measure in a hierarchical regression analysis. The regression analysis was conducted by entering sociodemographic factors at the first step and then assessing the unique variance associated with personality, conflict behavior, husband drinking, and wife drinking (Table 2.2).

Consistent with reports of the correlates of premarital aggression (McLaughlin, Leonard, & Senchak, 1992), the couples' age and minority status were predictors of marital aggression in the first year of marriage. Specifically, younger couples and couples in which at least one member was a minority had higher weighted aggression scores at T2. These effects could not be accounted for on the basis of socioeconomic status, which, while significant in the bivariate correlations, was not significant in the regression analysis.

Conflict behavior exhibited the strongest unique association with marital aggression, accounting for 7% of the variance. Four measures of conflict behavior were associated with marital aggression: husband and wife Anger

Table 2.2. *Prediction of marital aggression: Bivariate correlations and unique variance*

		Regression results	
Predictors	r	β	R^2 change
Entered at Step 1			
Sociodemographics			.12**
Age[a]	−.21**	−.14**	
Race[b]	.27**	.22**	
Relationship length[c]	−.08	−.04	
Presence of children[d]	.19**	.07	
SES[e]	−.23**	−.08	
Entered at last step (unique variance)			
Personality			.01
H Neuroticism	.21**	.00	
W Neuroticism	.25**	.08	
H Masculinity	.04	.06	
W Masculinity	−.05	−.01	
H Femininity	−.19**	−.09*	
W Femininity	−.07	−.01	
Conflict behavior			.07**
H Anger expression	.32**	.17**	
W Anger expression	.27**	.16**	
H Avoidance	.07	−.02	
W Avoidance	.07	−.02	
H Problem solving	.04	.11**	
W Problem solving	−.14**	−.09*	
Husband drinking behavior			.01*
Average daily consumption	.19**	.08	
Problem drinking	.20**	.05	
Wife drinking behavior			.02**
Average daily consumption	.02	−.14**	
Problem drinking	.19**	.18**	

Note: H = husband, W = wife; $N = 537$; final $R = .56$; final adjusted $R^2 = .28$. Severity weighted scale of the Conflict Tactics Scale (Straus, 1990).
[a]Calculated as mean age of partners.
[b]1 = Neither partner minority; 2 = at least one partner minority.
[c]Months known prior to marriage.
[d]0 = no children; 1 = at least one child.
[e]Hollingshead Index.
*$p < .05$. **$p < .01$.

Expression and husband and wife Problem Solving. Husband and wife Anger Expression were both positively associated with marital aggression. This finding is consistent with previous studies using self-report and observational methodologies (e.g., Margolin, John, & Gleberman, 1988).

Husband Problem Solving was positively associated with marital aggression, while wife Problem Solving was negatively associated with marital aggression. The finding with respect to husband Problem Solving is of particular interest. According to the wife report, high rates of husband problem-solving behaviors – behaviors that we typically view as facilitative (e.g., "starts discussion to tell you his point of view") – predict higher levels of aggression once the effect of Anger Expression has been entered. One plausible interpretation of this finding is that the problem-solving measure taps both facilitative behaviors and demanding/controlling behaviors, with these behaviors manifesting quite different associations with aggression. This interpretation would suggest that Anger Expression and husband domineering behaviors are independently associated with marital aggression.

Drinking behaviors at T1 by the husband and by the wife were unique predictors of marital aggression. Although neither husband average daily consumption nor problem drinking were unique predictors, these two variables were highly related to each other, $r = .72$. Consequently, neither was a unique predictor when they were entered as a block, but together, they uniquely predicted aggression. Thus heavy drinking, whether assessed in terms of average daily consumption or in terms of problem drinking, was predictive of first-year marital aggression.

Although previous studies have clearly established a relationship between excessive alcohol use and marital aggression, they have been uniformly cross-sectional. The present analyses suggest that the drinking characteristics of the husband before marriage predict marital aggression in the first year of marriage and that this effect is independent of conflict behavior and personality. Leonard (1993) has outlined several potential pathways by which excessive alcohol consumption, measured as a distal variable, as was done in this analysis, could have an impact on marital aggression. For example, heavy drinking may be associated with an unmeasured personality variable that facilitates aggression. However, a number of studies, including the present one, show that drinking patterns relate to marital aggression after controlling for likely personality characteristics. Alternatively, a husband's heavy drinking pattern could lead to increased marital discord and thereby provide more opportunities for aggressive conflict. Finally, a distal variable of heavy drinking can be thought of as a summary over time of the proximal variable of acute alcohol use. If acute alcohol consumption facilitates marital conflict and/or aggression, heavy drinkers might have more aggression because they have more instances of husband-wife interaction in which the husband has been drinking.

Although wives' drinking has been previously linked to marital aggression (e.g., Miller et al., 1990), in our previous analyses of predictors of premarital aggression (Leonard & Senchak, 1993), the drinking behavior of wives was unrelated to husband aggression. In the present analyses, however, wife drinking behavior at T1 was significantly associated with marital aggression, both in the simple correlations and in the regression analyses. This relationship uniquely accounted for 2% of the variance in marital aggression. Wife problem drinking was associated with higher levels of marital aggression, while wife daily consumption was related to lower levels of marital aggression. This pattern of results was precisely the same as the results with respect to changes in Marital Quality, as discussed in the next section.

Individual difference factors were related to marital aggression at the bivariate level. Both husband and wife Neuroticism predicted higher levels of aggression, and both husband and wife Femininity predicted lower levels of aggression (though the association between wife Femininity and aggression was only marginal). However, individual difference factors did not predict significant unique variance when entered as the last block of variables in the regression analysis. This raises the possibility that the relationship between individual difference factors and marital aggression may be mediated through the couple's conflict behavior.

Prediction of Changes in Marital Quality

What accounts for changes in marital quality over the first year of marriage? To address this question, we examined the relationship between the predictor variables and T2 Marital Quality, controlling for T1 Marital Quality. Table 2.3 displays the simple or zero order correlation for each predictor, the first order partial correlation, controlling for T1 Marital Quality, and the results of the regression analysis. As can be seen from Table 2.3, only four variables – relationship length, husband Masculinity, wife Femininity, and wife alcohol consumption – did *not* have a significant zero-order correlation with T2 quality. However, the pattern of results changes when T1 quality is controlled. The first-order correlations, displayed in the second column of the table, may be interpreted as reflecting the predictor's bivariate association with *change* in Marital Quality from the T1 to the T2 assessment. Because many of the predictor variables are intercorrelated, hierarchical regression analyses were undertaken to examine the unique contribution of each variable to the prediction of changes in Marital Quality. These results appear in the last columns of the table.

All of the sociodemographic variables were significant predictors of changes in Marital Quality, and all but age were unique predictors. A decline in Marital Quality over the first year was associated with minority

Table 2.3. *Prediction of changes in marital quality over the first year of marriage: Bivariate correlations, partial correlations, and unique variance*

Predictors	Correlations with T2 quality		Regression results	
	Zero order	T1 partialed	β	R^2 Change
Entered at step 1				
Time 1 marital quality	.57**	—	.57**	.32**
Entered at step 2				
Sociodemographics				.06**
Age[a]	.13**	.12**	.03	
Race[b]	−.26**	−.20**	−.12**	
Relationship length[c]	.03	.14**	.09*	
Presence of children[d]	−.23**	−.18**	−.08*	
SES[e]	.22**	.22**	.09*	
Entered at last step (unique variance)				
Personality				.02*
H Neuroticism	−.32**	−.12**	−.02	
W Neuroticism	−.36**	−.20**	−.12**	
H Masculinity	.06	.02	.03	
W Masculinity	.10*	−.01	.00	
H Femininity	.23**	.01	.01	
W Femininity	.08	−.07*	−.08*	
Conflict behavior				.01
H Anger expression	−.32**	−.12**	−.08+	
W Anger expression	−.27**	−.03	.00	
H Avoidance	−.19**	−.08*	−.04	
W Avoidance	−.11**	−.04	.01	
H Problem solving	.17**	−.08*	−.03	
W Problem solving	.20**	−.04	−.02	
Husband drinking behavior				.00
Average daily consumption	−.22**	−.09*	−.01	
Problem drinking	−.24**	−.10**	−.05	
Wife drinking behavior				.01**
Average daily consumption	−.02	.04	.14**	
Problem drinking	−.18**	−.12**	−.15**	

Note: H = husband, W = wife; $N = 526$; after controlling for T1 quality, predictors add 12% incremental variance.
[a]Calculated as mean age of partners.
[b]1 = neither partner minority; 2 = at least one partner minority.
[c]Months known prior to marriage.
[d]0 = no children; 1 = at least one child.
[e]Hollingshead Index.
+$p < .06$. *$p < .05$. **$p < .01$.

status, a shorter premarital relationship, the presence of at least one child, and lower SES. Taken together, the block of sociodemographics accounted for 6% of the variance in the residualized Marital Quality score. Although sociodemographic variables are recognized as strong correlates of marital satisfaction and important predictors of marital dissolution, they have not received sufficient attention from researchers investigating longitudinal predictors of changes in marital quality.

Together, the personality variables accounted for approximately 2% of unique variance in the residualized Marital Quality scores. Wife Neuroticism, but not husband Neuroticism, was related to a decline in Marital Quality. In addition, the commonly found positive association between Femininity and Marital Quality was replicated here in the zero-order correlations. However, husband's Femininity was not uniquely related to regressed change in Marital Quality, and while wife's Femininity was a significant predictor, its effects were in the reverse direction; high Femininity in wives led to a decline in Marital Quality. One explanation for this provocative finding is that femininity may be associated with a strong investment in interpersonal relationships and high expectations for the marital bond. When the pragmatic aspects of marriage are confronted and the "honeymoon is over," perhaps these individuals are the most disappointed. Admittedly, this is somewhat speculative, and this finding requires replication and further refinement.

Wife's problem drinking also was associated with drops in Marital Quality. However, after controlling for problem drinking, wives' alcohol consumption level was positively associated with Marital Quality. This finding is striking, not only because of the opposite effects of two highly correlated measures of drinking, but also because it replicates precisely the relationship between wives' drinking behavior and marital aggression. The results of these two analyses suggest that wife drinking, if it does not result in alcohol problems, tends to exert a positive influence on the marriage. Although there may be a number of different explanations of this finding, one possible interpretation is that given the fact that males generally drink more frequently than females, the frequent drinking of wives *matches* their husbands' drinking levels, and it is this congruence that contributes to marital harmony. Marital problems may be engendered when one partner drinks significantly less than the other. In such instances, the discrepancy between the partners' drinking behaviors may be the troublesome feature rather than the excessive drinking of one individual. As we have argued elsewhere (Roberts & Leonard, 1997), with marriage a *drinking partnership* is created; drinking is incorporated into the fabric of a marriage in diverse ways, and it may be this partnership rather than the independent effects of one partner's drinking that is critical to marital functioning. Recent research (Wilsnack & Wilsnack, 1990) provides some support for this more complex approach to the interrelationship of alcohol and marital functioning.

Surprisingly, conflict behavior did not predict unique variance in the change in Marital Quality. Only a handful of studies have attempted to predict changes in marital functioning on the basis of either observed or reported conflict behavior. In general, these studies have tended to find that negative conflict behaviors lead to either improvements (Gottman & Krokoff, 1989; Heavey, Layne, & Christensen, 1993) or no change in marital functioning (Markman, 1981; Smith et al., 1990). In contrast, conflict avoidance or withdrawal was detrimental across the three longitudinal studies that assessed it (Gottman & Krokoff, 1989; Heavey et al., 1993; Smith et al., 1990).

There are several potential explanations for the absence of a unique longitudinal effect for perception of conflict behavior in the present analyses. First, studies focusing on newlyweds (Markman, 1981; Smith et al., 1990), have found stronger effects in predicting satisfaction beyond the first year of marriage. Perhaps the pervasive drop in quality among nearly all couples represents a relatively uniform process reflecting a discrepancy between the romanticized expectations of marriage and the realistic tasks faced by the couples. Although conflict behavior did not provide unique information as a block, the contribution of husband Anger Expression approached significance in the final equation. It may be that acts of hostility specifically have a detrimental impact on marital quality in the first year of marriage rather than problem-solving or problem-engagement behaviors more generally. Second, our measure of Marital Quality is quite different from the Locke-Wallace Marital Adjustment Test (MAT) or a variant of this test that other investigators have used. Although it has been argued that the MAT is heavily influenced by global satisfaction (Fincham & Bradbury, 1987), most of the remaining items appear to assess the extent of conflict. Thus it may be that conflict-resolution behavior, such as negativity or withdrawal, predicts continued conflict, but not other aspects of marital quality. Our outcome measure consisted not only of the MAT, but also of the FAM, which represents an individual's evaluation of his/her partner in a variety of marital functions, and the MSIS, which assesses positive, intimate feelings toward the partner. Perhaps these latter aspects of quality are not as influenced by behavior, specifically in conflict settings, and are more influenced by less context-specific behavioral tendencies (e.g., personality). Clearly, further research is required to investigate these possibilities.

Prediction of Marital Disruption During the First Year of Marriage

What differentiates the 72 couples who experienced some kind of disruption during the first year of marriage from the 458 couples who experienced

Table 2.4. *Prediction of marital stability: Bivariate correlations and unique variance*

		Regression results	
Predictors	*r*	β	R^2 Change
Entered at step 1			
Sociodemographics			.10**
Age[a]	−.12**	−.06	
Race[b]	.27**	.23**	
Relationship length[c]	−.07	−.06	
Presence of children[d]	.18**	.10*	
SES[e]	−.18**	−.05	
Entered at last step (unique variance)			
Personality			.02**
H Neuroticism	.25**	.09*	
W Neuroticism	.19**	.06	
H Masculinity	−.05	−.04	
W Masculinity	.07*	.11*	
H Femininity	−.11**	−.02	
W Femininity	−.02	.00	
Conflict behavior			.03**
H Anger expression	.22**	.15**	
W Anger expression	.17**	.03	
H Avoidance	.13**	.08*	
W Avoidance	.05	−.02	
H Problem solving	−.09*	−.05	
W Problem solving	−.11*	−.05	
Husband drinking behavior			.02**
Average daily consumption	.23**	.15**	
Problem drinking	.18**	−.01	
Wife drinking behavior			.00
Average daily consumption	.02	−.06	
Problem drinking	.09*	.05	

Note: Marital Stability coded as 0 = no disruption; 1 = divorced, separated, or any marital disruption; H = husband; W = wife; $N = 537$; final $R = .47$; final adjusted $R^2 = .19$.
[a]Calculated as mean age of partners.
[b]1 = neither partner minority; 2 = at least one partner minority.
[c]Months known prior to marriage.
[d]0 = no children; 1 = at least one child.
[e]Hollingshead Index.
*$p < .05$. **$p < .01$.

no such disruption? We created a stability variable reflecting this variation in our sample by coding any marital disruption as 1 and no disruptions as 0; we then used the same analytic strategy as in the previous analyses to address this question.[5] Bivariate correlations and the regression results are reported in Table 2.4. With the exception of relationship length, husband Masculinity, wife Femininity, wife avoidance, and wife daily alcohol consumption, each variable evidenced a significant bivariate association with marital stability. However, the magnitude of these correlations is rather modest; none exceed .25. This relatively small effect is consistent with previous prospective analyses of marital dissolution (for a review, see Gottman, 1993a).

As a block, the sociodemographic variables account for 10% of the variance in stability. Race and SES are the only unique predictors; lower SES couples and couples in which at least one partner is of minority status are more likely to experience marital disruptions.

With the exception of the wife's drinking behavior, each block was significant when entered at the last step in the regression, contributing between 2% and 3% of unique variance. Taken together, the predictors examined here accounted for 22% of the variance in marital stability ($R = .47$; adjusted $R^2 = .19$). Overall, and in contrast to the results for Marital Quality, husband variables tended to be more predictive than wife variables. The more alcohol the husband consumed, at the time of marriage, the higher his Neuroticism score, the more his wife perceived him to express anger and to avoid or withdraw during problem-solving discussions, and the more likely the couple was to experience a marital disruption before their first anniversary. Gottman's (1993a, 1993b) recent work has also suggested that hostility and withdrawal in problem-solving interactions may be important risk factors for later marital dissolution. Interestingly, the only wife variable uniquely predictive of marital instability was Masculinity; the higher her self-reported Masculinity, the more likely was a dissolution. At least two alternate interpretations of this finding suggest themselves. Husbands may react negatively to wives high on Masculinity and this may lead to greater instability, or wives high on Masculinity may have the psychological and/or economic resources to initiate or sustain a separation in the presence of marital dysfunction. The later interpretation is more consistent with our findings for Marital Quality; wives' masculinity does not appear to erode marital quality, but only affects the likelihood of dissolution.

Summary and Future Directions

One of the main premises of the Buffalo Newlywed Study has been that the early years of marriage lay the groundwork for a successful marriage and that during this critical developmental period the couple must learn to successfully resolve conflicts and reconcile differences. Both avoiding marital conflicts and responding with anger or hostility seemed unlikely to produce positive marital outcomes. In contrast, we expected that engaging in problem-solving behaviors that are not accompanied by negative affect would enable couples to successfully manage the inevitable differences and conflicts they face in their first years of marriage. The results of our analyses, while generally supportive of the influential role of conflict behavior in marital outcomes, also suggest a more complicated picture. First, Anger Expression, particularly on the part of the husband as reported by the wife, was uniformly detrimental to the marriage. It was related to physical aggression and marital instability, and marginally related to declines in marital satisfaction. Second, each of the three marital outcomes was somewhat differentially influenced by the three conflict behavior scales, with marital aggression being the most strongly related and marital satisfaction being the least strongly related (probably because T1 satisfaction was controlled for). Avoidance was a significant predictor only of marital dissolution. Finally, problem-solving behavior did not necessarily exert a positive influence on the marriage. Although it was related univariately to marital stability and initial Marital Quality, it did not provide unique information to predict these variables over the first year. Further, while wife Problem Solving was related to lower levels of marital aggression, husband Problem Solving was related to higher levels of aggression. Perhaps high levels of husband Problem Solving reflect attempts to dominate and control the relationship.

Our approach to the measurement of marital conflict behaviors has several limitations. First, our measures reflect conflict behavior as *perceived* by the spouse. Hence the extent to which conflict behavior as opposed to the perception of conflict behavior is responsible for the observed marital problems is not clear. Second, our analyses focused only on the independent effects of each conflict behavior. There is a strong potential for interactions among the conflict behaviors exhibited by one spouse, as well as for interactions between a conflict behavior of husband and a conflict behavior of the wife. In other words, the specific configuration of husband and wife conflict behaviors may exert an effect over and above the independent effects of the conflict behaviors. Finally, although our measure includes the three most commonly assessed conflict behaviors, other ways of resolving differences may play equally important roles in maintaining the peace between spouses. In particular, we believe that in many instances conflicts are resolved without any specific verbal problem solving. Instead, spouses may become aware of differences with their partner and simply alter their own beliefs or behaviors in accord with their partner's. We refer to this process as *behavioral accommodation* and believe that it may be particularly characteristic of highly satisfied couples.

Our study supports the premise that conflict behavior plays an important role in the developmental course of a marriage, but we also found evidence to suggest that it is not the entire story. Personality and drinking factors exhibited unique associations with aggression, quality, and stability. In particular, both husband and wife Neuroticism were related to concurrent Marital Quality, and each was related to one of the other longitudinal outcomes. Although these findings replicate previous research on personality and marital outcomes, they also extend previous research in an important way. Heretofore, conflict behavior and personality have not been examined *together* as predictors of marital outcomes, and little is known about their unique effects on marital outcomes. Our results suggest that the effects of personality, particularly Neuroticism, are independent of conflict behavior. Similarly, both husband and wife drinking had important unique influences on marital outcomes, though the nature of these influences was not as uniformly detrimental as one might suspect. Again, these effects were not mediated through conflict behavior, nor were they artifacts of husband or wife personality. More detailed analyses of the effects of personality and drinking are necessary to understand the processes through which these factors have an impact. Further analyses might also examine whether personality, drinking, and conflict behavior interact to predict marital outcomes.

It is also important to point out the advantages of the approach we have adopted here in examining the unique contributions of variables to the prediction of marital outcomes. If we had reported only on the results of the bivariate correlations we calculated between our predictors and the outcome variables, a very different, and potentially misleading, picture of the developmental course of marital dysfunction would have emerged. We are particularly sensitive to the issue of unique variance, in part because of our interest in alcohol use and marital aggression. Within the marital aggression field, the association between heavy alcohol use and marital aggression is well known and often discounted as a spurious effect. Consequently, throughout our research we have been attendant to the possibility that sociodemographic and other individual or couple factors might account for an observed relationship between alcohol and marital aggression. It has been our observation that this unique variance approach is critical to further progress, but that it is currently underutilized in both longitudinal or cross-sectional studies of marital functioning.

It is also important to emphasize that our investigation of the longitudinal determinants of marital dysfunction is incomplete. Although we were able to describe the cross-sectional associations of marital aggression, quality, and stability, these three outcomes may have important and nonobvious longitudinal impacts on one another, and their interrelationships deserve further exploration. O'Leary et al. (1989), for example, have noted that marital aggression does not uniformly lead to declines in marital satisfaction. Similarly, in her decade-long review of research on divorce, White (1990) observes that "although a strong link between marital happiness and divorce seems simple and self-evident, empirical evidence is scant" (p. 907). Recently, however, Gottman and Levenson (1992) have found preliminary empirical support for a "cascade model" of marital dissolution in which sustained low marital quality is a precursor to separation and divorce. Additional longitudinal research that examines these issues is of critical importance to the field. Moreover, research is needed that goes beyond establishing empirical connections between these variables to specifying the *processes* that underlie their association. Longitudinal analyses that incorporate more than two time points are essential for this. As we complete data collection with our newlywed sample on their third anniversary, we hope to address some of these challenging issues in a more comprehensive fashion.

Notes

1. There are few constraints on the specific courthouse at which a couple may apply for a marriage license. Thus residents of the city could apply for their license in a suburb, and suburban residents could apply in the city. The population under study therefore includes urban and suburban residents.
2. Only 20 cases of canceled or significantly delayed marriages were discovered over the course of the study. These cases are not included in the figures presented here.
3. Several questions that presume that the couple is married were awkward to ask of couples who were about to be married.
4. Two items ("think about leaving the relationship altogether" and "feel closer to you at the end of a discussion than when it began") were dropped because they were not observable conflict behaviors. An item assessing physical aggression was omitted to avoid overlap with marital aggression. Finally, the item "repeat himself to make sure his point was understood" was omitted because preliminary analyses suggested that some subjects viewed it as "nagging," whereas others viewed it as problem solving.
5. We chose correlation and multiple regression as the analytic approaches to facilitate a comparison of the results in the previous two sets of analyses. Nonetheless, we also analyzed stability as a categorical variable using logistic regression, and we found essentially identical results. The only difference was that in the logistic regression results, the drinking behavior block fell short of significance.

References

Antill, J. K. (1983). Sex role complementarity versus similarity in married couples. *Journal of Personality and Social Psychology, 45,* 145–155.

Baucom, D. H., & Aiken, P. A. (1984). Sex role identity, marital satisfaction, and response to behavioral marital therapy. *Journal of Consulting and Clinical Psychology, 52,* 438–444.

Bernard, J. L., Bernard, S. L., & Bernard, M. L. (1985). Courtship violence and sex typing. *Family Relations, 34,* 573–576.

Boss, P. G. (1983). The marital relationship: Boundaries and ambiguities. In H. I. McCubbin & C. R. Figley (Eds.), *Stress and the family: Vol. 1. Coping with normative transitions* (pp. 26–40). New York: Brunner/Mazel.

Boye-Beaman, J., Leonard, K. E., & Senchak, M. (1993). Male premarital aggression and gender identity among black and white newlywed couples. *Journal of Marriage and the Family, 55,* 303–313.

Bradbury, T. N., & Fincham, F. D. (1988). Individual difference variables in close relationships: A contextual model of marriage as an integrative framework. *Journal of Personality and Social Psychology, 54*(4), 713–721.

Brennan, P. L., & Moos, R. H. (1990). Life stressors, social resources, and late-life problem drinking. *Psychology and Aging, 5,* 491–501.

Burke, P. J., Stets, J. E., & Pirog-Good, M. A. (1989). Gender identity, self-esteem, and physical and sexual abuse in dating relationships. In M. Pirog-Good & J. Stets (Eds.), *Violence in dating relationships* (pp. 72–91). New York: Praeger.

Burns, A. (1984). Perceived causes of marriage breakdown and conditions of life. *Journal of Marriage and the Family, 46,* 551–562.

Cahalan, D., Cisin, I. H., & Crossley, H. M. (1969). *American drinking practices: A national study of drinking behavior and attitudes.* New Brunswick, NJ: Rutgers Center of Alcohol Studies.

Cohen, S., Kamarck, T., & Mermelstein, R. (1983). A global measure of perceived stress. *Journal of Health and Social Behavior, 24,* 385–396.

Cole, C. L., Cole, A. L., & Dean, D. G. (1980). Emotional maturity and marital adjustment: A decade replication. *Journal of Marriage and the Family, 42,* 533–539.

Costa, P. T., Jr., & McCrae, R. R. (1985). *The NEO Personality Inventory manual.* Odessa, FL: Psychological Assessment Resources.

Crohan, S. E., & Veroff, J. (1989). Dimensions of marital well-being among white and black newlyweds. *Journal of Marriage and the Family, 51,* 373–383.

Davis, M. H., & Oathout, H. A. (1987). Maintenance of satisfaction in romantic relationships: Empathy and relational competence. *Journal of Personality and Social Psychology, 53*(2), 397–410.

Dobash, R. E., & Dobash, R. P. (1979). *Violence against wives.* New York: Free Press.

Fincham, F. D., & Bradbury, T. N. (1987). The assessment of marital quality: A reevaluation. *Journal of Marriage and the Family, 49,* 797–809.

Finn, J. (1986). The relationship between sex role attitudes and attitudes supporting marital violence. *Sex Roles, 14,* 235–244.

Gelles, R. (1974). *The violent home.* Beverly Hills, CA: Sage.

Gottman, J. M. (1979). *Marital interaction: Experimental investigations.* New York: Academic Press.

Gottman, J. M. (1993a). A theory of marital dissolution and stability. *Journal of Family Psychology, 1,* 57–75.

Gottman, J. M. (1993b). The roles of conflict engagement, escalation, or avoidance in marital interaction: A longitudinal view of five types of couples. *Journal of Consulting and Clinical Psychology, 61,* 6–15.

Gottman, J. M., & Krokoff, L. J. (1989). The relationship between marital interaction and marital satisfaction: A longitudinal view. *Journal of Consulting and Clinical Psychology, 57,* 47–52.

Gottman, J. M., & Levenson, R. W. (1992). Marital processes predictive of later dissolution: Behavior, Physiology, and Health. *Journal of Personality and Social Psychology, 63*(2), 221–233.

Hamberger, L. K., & Hastings, J. E. (1991). Personality correlates of men who batter and non-violent men: Some continuities and discontinuities. *Journal of Family Violence, 6,* 131–147.

Heavey, C. L., Layne, C., & Christensen, A. (1993). Gender and conflict structure in marital interaction: A replication and extension. *Journal of Consulting and Clinical Psychology, 61*(1), 16–27.

Hilton, M. E. (1991). The demographic distribution of drinking patterns in 1984. In W. B. Clark & M. E. Hilton (Eds.), *Alcohol in America: Drinking practices and problems* (pp. 73–86). Albany, NY: State University of New York Press.

Horwitz, A. V., & White, H. R. (1991). Becoming married, depression, and alcohol problems among young adults. *Journal of Health and Social Behavior, 32,* 221–237.

Huston, T. L., & Vangelisti, A. L. (1991). Socioemotional behavior and satisfaction in marital relationships: A longitudinal study. *Journal of Personality and Social Psychology, 61*(5), 721–733.

Kaufman-Kantor, K. G., & Straus, M. A. (1990). The "drunken bum" theory of wife beating. In M. A. Straus & R. J. Gelles (Eds.), *Physical violence in American families: Risk factors and adaptions to violence in 8,145 families* (pp. 203–224). New Brunswick, NJ: Transaction Books.

Kelly, E. L., & Conley, J. J. (1987). Personality and compatibility: A prospective analysis of marital stability and marital satisfaction. *Journal of Personality and Social Psychology, 52,* 27–40.

Kurdek, L. A. (1993). Predicting marital dissolution: A 5-year prospective longitudinal study of newlywed couples. *Journal of Personality and Social Psychology, 64*(2), 221–242.

Kurdek, L., & Schmitt, J. P. (1986). Interaction of sex role self-concept with relationship quality and relationship beliefs in married, heterosexual cohabiting, and gay and lesbian relationships. *Journal of Personality and Social Psychology, 51,* 365–370.

Leonard, K. E. (1993). Drinking patterns and intoxication in marital violence: Review, critique, and future directions for research. In National Institute on Alcohol Abuse and Alcoholism, *Alcohol and interpersonal violence: Fostering interdisciplinary research* (Research Monograph No. 25, NIH Pub. No. 93-3513). Rockville, MD: National Institute on Alcohol Abuse and Alcoholism.

Leonard, K. E., & Blane, H. T. (1992). Alcohol and marital aggression in a national sample of young men. *Journal of Interpersonal Violence, 7,* 19–30.

Leonard, K. E., Bromet, E. J., Parkinson, D. K., Day, N. L., & Ryan, C. M. (1985). Patterns of alcohol use and physically aggressive behavior. *Journal of Studies on Alcohol, 56,* 279–282.

Leonard, K. E., & Senchak, M. (1993). Alcohol and premarital aggression among newlywed couples. *Journal of Studies on Alcohol,* Supplement No. *11,* 96–108.

Locke, H. J., & Wallace, K. M. (1959). Short marital-adjustment and prediction tests: Their reliability and validity. *Marriage and Family Living, 21,* 251–255.

McCrady, B. S. (1982). Marital dysfunction: Alcohol and marriage. In E. M. Patterson & E. Kaufman (Eds.), *Encyclopedic handbook of alcoholism* (pp. 673–685). New York: Gardner Press.

McGoldrick, M., & Carter, E. A. (1982). The family life cycle. In F. Walsh (Ed.), *Normal family processes* (pp. 167–195). New York: Guilford Press.

McLaughlin, I. G., Leonard, K. E., & Senchak, M. (1992). Prevalence and distribution of premarital aggression among couples applying for a marriage license. *Journal of Family Violence, 7*(4), 61–71.

Maiuro, R. D., Cahn, T. S., Vitaliano, P. P., Wagner, B. C., & Zegree, J. B. (1988). Anger, hostility, and depression in domestically violent versus generally assaultive men and nonviolent control subjects. *Journal of Consulting and Clinical Psychology, 56,* 17–23.

Margolin, G. (1980). The Conflict Inventory. Unpublished manuscript.

Margolin, G., John, R., & Gleberman, L. (1988). Affective responses to conflictual discussions in violent and nonviolent couples. *Journal of Consulting and Clinical Psychology, 56*(1), 24–33.

Markman, H. J. (1981). Prediction of marital distress: A 5-year follow-up. *Journal of Consulting and Clinical Psychology, 49,* 743–749.

Markman, H. J., Floyd, F. J., Stanley, S. M., & Storaasli, R. D. (1988). Prevention of marital distress: A longitudinal investigation. *Journal of Consulting and Clinical Psychology, 56,* 210–217.

Miller, B. A., Nochajski, T. J., Leonard, K. E., Blane, H. T., Gondoli, D. M., & Bowers, P. M. (1990). Spousal violence and alcohol/drug problems among parolees and their spouses. *Women & Criminal Justice, 1*(2), 55–72.

Miller, R. S., & Lefcourt, H. M. (1982). The assessment of social intimacy. *Journal of Personality Assessment, 46,* 514–518.

O'Leary, D. K., Barling, J., Arias, I., Rosenbaum, A., Malone, J., & Tyree, A.

(1989). Prevalence and stability of physical aggression between spouses: A longitudinal analysis. *Journal of Consulting and Clinical Psychology, 57,* 263–268.

Pan, H. S., Neidig, P. H., & O'Leary, K. D. (1994). Predicting mild and severe husband-to-wife physical aggression. *Journal of Consulting and Clinical Psychology, 62,* 975–981.

Power, C., & Estaugh, V. (1990). The role of family formation and dissolution in shaping drinking behaviour in early adulthood. *British Journal of Addiction, 85,* 521–530.

Radloff, L. S. (1977). CES-D scale: A self-report depression scale for research in the general population. *Journal of Applied Psychological Measurement, 1,* 385–401.

Roberts, L. J., & Leonard, K. E. (1997). Gender differences and similarities in the alcohol and marriage relationship. In R. W. Wilsnack & S. C. Wilsnack (Eds.), *Gender and alcohol.* New Brunswick, NJ: Rutgers Center of Alcohol Studies.

Roberts, L. J., Leonard, K. E., & Senchak, M. (1991, August). Spousal perceptions of conflict behavior: Implications for marital functioning. Presentation at the annual convention of the American Psychological Association, San Francisco, CA.

Roy, M. (1982). Four thousand partners in violence: A trend analysis. In M. Roy (Ed.), *The abusive partner: An analysis of domestic battering.* New York: Worstrand Reinhold.

Skinner, H. A., & Allen, B. A. (1982). Alcohol dependence syndrome: Measurement and validation. *Journal of Abnormal Psychology, 91,* 199–209.

Skinner, H. A., Steinhauer, P. D., & Santa-Barbara, J. (1984). *The family assessment measure: Administration and interpretation guide.* Toronto, Ontario: Addiction Research Foundation.

Smith, D. A., Vivian, D., & O'Leary, K. D. (1990). Longitudinal prediction of marital discord from premarital expressions of affect. *Journal of Consulting and Clinical Psychology, 58*(6), 790–798.

Smith, T. W., Pope, M. K., Sanders, K. J. D., Allred, K. D., & O'Keefe, J. L. (1988). Cynical hostility at home and work: Psychosocial vulnerability across domains. *Journal of Research in Personality, 22,* 525–548.

Smith, T. W., Sanders, J. D., & Alexander, J. F. (1990). What does the Cook and Medley Hostility Scale measure? Affect, behavior, and attributions in the marital context. *Journal of Personality and Social Psychology, 58*(4), 699–708.

Spence, J. T., Helmreich, R. L., & Stapp, J. (1974). The personal attributes questionnaire: A measure of sex-role stereotypes and masculinity-femininity. *JSAS Catalog of Selected Documents in Psychology, 4,* 127.

Spielberger, C. R., Jacobs, G., Crane, R., Russell, S., Westberry, L., Baker, L., Johnson, E., Knight, J., & Marks, E. (1979). *Preliminary Manual for the State Trait Personality Inventory (STPI).* Tampa, FL: University of South Florida Human Resource Institute.

Straus, M. (1979). Measuring intrafamily conflict and violence: The Conflict Tactics (CT) Scales. *Journal of Marriage and the Family, 41,* 75–88.

Straus, M. (1990). New scoring methods for violence and new norms for the Conflict Tactics Scales. In M. A. Straus & R. J. Gelles (Eds.), *Physical violence in American families: Risk factors and adaptations to violence in 8,145 families* (pp. 535–559). New Brunswick, NJ: Transaction Publishers.

Straus, M. A., Gelles, R. J., & Steinmetz, S. K. (1980). *Behind closed doors: Violence in the American family.* Garden City, NY: Anchor Press/Doubleday.

Suitor, J. J., Pillemer, K., & Straus, M. A. (1990). Marital violence in a life course perspective. In M. A. Straus & R. J. Gelles (Eds.), *Physical violence in American families: Risk factors and adaptations to violence in 8,145 families* (pp. 305–320). New Brunswick, NJ: Transaction Publishers.

White, L. K. (1990). Determinants of divorce: A review of research in the eighties. *Journal of Marriage and the Family, 52,* 904–912.

Wilsnack, R. W., & Wilsnack, S. C. (1990, June). *Husbands and wives as drinking partners.* Paper presented at the 16th Annual Alcohol Epidemiology Symposium of the Kettil Bruun Society for Social and Epidemiological Research on Alcohol, Budapest, Hungary.

3   Accommodation Processes During the Early Years of Marriage

Caryl E. Rusbult, Victor L. Bissonnette,
Ximena B. Arriaga, and Chante L. Cox

Sometimes married life is blissful – intimacy and companionship are easy, feelings of trust and commitment are strong, partners treat one another with love and consideration, and the marriage seems indestructible. Unfortunately, many couples encounter periods when life is not so easy – times when intimacy and companionship are hard work at best, good times are a distant memory, trust and commitment are sorely strained, and the marriage verges on collapse. Much of married life unfolds in a middle ground between these extremes, in a state where good times are punctuated by dissatisfying incidents of greater or lesser intensity. The manner in which couples negotiate this intermediate state appears to be crucial to maintaining a long-term, enduring marriage. This chapter deals with one important feature of the "middle ground" of marriage by analyzing an interaction phenomenon termed *accommodation*. Interaction sequences involving accommodative behavior are initiated when one partner engages in a potentially destructive act, such as behaving in a thoughtless manner, saying hurtful things, yelling at the partner, or worse. Accommodation refers to an individual's willingness, when the partner has enacted a potentially destructive behavior, to (a) inhibit impulses to react destructively in turn and (b) instead behave in a constructive manner.

Our analysis of accommodative behavior is based on the principles of interdependence theory (Kelley, 1979; Kelley & Thibaut, 1978) and rests on the assumption that although accommodative behavior promotes couple well-being, such acts frequently are costly and effortful for the accommodating partner. To understand how couples sustain long-term, healthy functioning, we must explain how and why partners become willing to endure such costs and exert such effort, departing from their direct, self-interested

This research was supported by a grant from the National Institute of Mental Health (No. BSR-1-R01-MH-45417); preparation of this chapter was facilitated by a grant from the National Science Foundation (No. BNS-9023817).

74

preferences and coming to place greater value on pro-relationship behavior – behavior that solves the partners' interaction problem and promotes couple well-being. We begin by tracing the origins of our research program, describing the exit-voice-loyalty-neglect typology of responses to dissatisfaction (see Rusbult, Zembrodt, & Gunn, 1982). Then we present a conceptual analysis of accommodative behavior, suggesting that transformation of motivation lies at the heart of the process by which individuals come to forgo self-interested behavior for the good of a relationship. We outline a general model of commitment processes and relationship maintenance mechanisms that is designed to explain the variety of means, including accommodation, by which individuals sustain healthy relationships (see Rusbult & Buunk, 1993). This model suggests that commitment level is central to understanding how and why some relationships persist and thrive over time whereas others flounder and fail, proposing that pro-relationship transformation of motivation is promoted by feelings of commitment to a relationship. Finally, we present some early findings from an ongoing program of research that studies accommodation processes during the early years of marriage. The chapter closes with a discussion of fruitful directions for future research.

A Theory of Accommodation Processes

A Typology of Responses to Dissatisfaction: Exit, Voice, Loyalty, and Neglect

Interdependence theory assumes that our knowledge of interdependence phenomena must begin with an understanding of interaction processes. Accordingly, our model of accommodative behavior emerged from a program of research concerned with interaction during dissatisfying incidents. This work employs the exit, voice, loyalty, and neglect (EVLN) typology – a model of reactions to dissatisfying incidents that is based loosely on the writings of Hirschman (1970). Hirschman identified three primary reactions to decline in formal organizations: (a) *exit,* actively harming or terminating a relationship; (b) *voice,* actively and constructively attempting to improve conditions; and (c) *loyalty,* passively but optimistically waiting for conditions to improve. Research designed to assess the comprehensiveness of this typology not only demonstrated that these three categories characterize reactions to dissatisfaction in close relationships but also identified a fourth category of response: (d) *neglect,* passively allowing conditions to deteriorate (Rusbult & Zembrodt, 1983).

The EVLN response categories differ along two key dimensions. First, the responses differ in *constructiveness versus destructiveness.* Voice and loyalty are constructive reactions that serve to sustain or revive a relationship, whereas exit and neglect are relatively more destructive to a relationship's well-being. Here, we refer to a behavior's impact on the relationship and not to its impact on the individual. For example, exit might be healthy for an individual who is involved in a troubled relationship, but it is destructive to the relationship itself. The EVLN response categories also differ in *activity versus passivity.* Exit and voice involve direct action with respect to a problem (i.e., either solving the problem or making circumstances much worse), whereas neglect and loyalty are relatively more passive with regard to the problem at hand. Activity versus passivity refers to the impact of a response on the problem, not to the character of the response itself. For example, walking to a local bar so as to avoid an argument involves overt action, but this response is passively neglectful with regard to the couple's problem.

It is important to note that the EVLN category labels should not be interpreted literally, in that the categories are abstract constructs encompassing a broad range of related reactions. For example, "voice" represents all actively constructive reactions, many of which do not involve vocalization (e.g., changing one's behavior so as to solve a problem). Moreover, many acts involving vocalization do not fall in the voice category (e.g., screaming "I don't know why I married you!" represents exit, not voice). Also, the "exit" category includes taking action to end a relationship as well as other actively harmful acts such as hitting the partner or taking a lover. The following behaviors illustrate each response category:

> exit – separating, abusing the partner physically or emotionally, screaming at the partner, threatening to leave;
> voice – discussing problems, changing oneself so as to solve the problem (or urging the partner to change), seeking advice from a friend or therapist;
> loyalty – waiting and hoping that things will improve, supporting the partner in the face of criticism, praying for improvement; and
> neglect – refusing to deal with problems, ignoring the partner or spending less time together, criticizing the partner for unrelated problems, letting things fall apart.

Early research employing the EVLN typology sought to identify the predictors of each response category and demonstrated that response tendencies are shaped not only by broad qualities of interdependent relationships but also by individual-level dispositions (Rusbult, Johnson, & Morrow, 1986a; Rusbult, Morrow, & Johnson, 1987; Rusbult et al., 1982; Rusbult, Zembrodt, & Iwaniszek, 1986; for reviews, see Rusbult, 1987, 1993). Early work on the EVLN model also assessed the adaptive value of the four responses, examining their links with healthy couple functioning (Rusbult, Johnson, & Morrow, 1986b). This research revealed two important regularities, the first of which is termed the "good manners principle": Whereas destructive responses (exit and neglect) are exceptionally harmful to couple functioning, constructive responses (voice and loyalty) are not commensurately promotive of good health. These results are consistent with other research on couple distress and nondistress, which demonstrates that it is less important to engage in constructive acts than it is to scrupulously minimize the occurrence of destructive acts (e.g., Birchler, Weiss, & Vincent, 1975; Folger & Poole, 1984; Gottman, Markman, & Notarius, 1977; Jacobson, Follette, & McDonald, 1982; Markman, 1981).

Our research on couple functioning also revealed a second principle – one involving sequences of interdependent response. When an individual has behaved constructively (voice or loyalty), the partner's reaction is only weakly related to couple functioning. In contrast, when an individual has behaved destructively (exit or neglect), couple functioning is enhanced when partners inhibit their tendencies to react destructively and instead behave in a constructive manner; couple well-being is eroded to the degree that a destructive act is met with hostility or angry withdrawal. Over the course of an extended relationship, the well of trust and consideration is seriously depleted by reciprocal cycles involving repeated instances of destructive "payback in kind." Thus the second important principle identified in our work on EVLN processes is termed "accommodation," defined as the tendency – when an individual engages in a potentially destructive act (exit or neglect) – for the partner to (a) inhibit impulses to react destructively (inhibit exit and neglect) and (b) instead behave in a constructive manner (engage in voice or loyalty).

Other researchers studying couple functioning have observed similar phenomena, demonstrating that in comparison with nondistressed couples, distressed partners exhibit greater levels of "negative reciprocity" (e.g., Billings, 1979; Gottman et al., 1977; Gottman & Krokoff, 1989; Greenshaft, 1980; Margolin & Wampold, 1981). Unfortunately, little of this work has attempted to understand why couples sometimes accommodate yet at other times fail to do so. Prior research has tended to *describe* the behavior patterns associated with healthy functioning rather than attempting to understand *why* couples behave as they do. Thus, one important goal in our

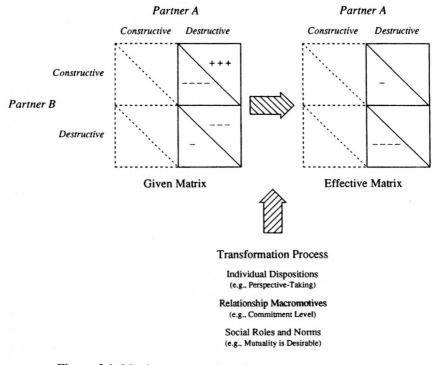

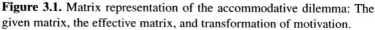

Figure 3.1. Matrix representation of the accommodative dilemma: The given matrix, the effective matrix, and transformation of motivation.

research program is to develop a theoretical understanding of the dynamics by which individuals come to accommodate rather than retaliate when a partner behaves poorly.

An Interdependence Analysis of Accommodation

Interdependence theory provides an ideal framework for examining marital phenomena because of its comprehensive analysis of interaction processes. Interactions between couple members involve at least a minimal level of interdependence – more typically, quite high levels of interdependence – in that the actions of one partner affect the options, preferences, and outcomes of the other. In accommodative dilemmas as well as other situations of interdependence, interacting partners' options and preferences can be represented by a 2×2 matrix in which one partner's actions are presented on the horizontal axis and the other's are presented on the vertical axis. For example, Figure 3.1 portrays a situation in which each partner can enact either a constructive or a destructive behavior. Partner A's feelings about each possible joint outcome are listed above the diagonal in each cell of the matrix; Partner B's feelings are listed below the diagonal. Because the accommodative dilemma is instigated by one partner's potentially destructive behavior, the Figure 3.1 matrices focus on the portion of the partners' response repertoires where Partner A has behaved destructively (the right-hand columns).

Partners' direct, self-centered feelings about various joint outcomes are termed *given matrix* preferences. As illustrated in the Figure 3.1 given matrix (see matrix on left), when Partner A enacts a destructive act – thereby moving the partners to the right-hand column of response options – Partner B's self-centered impulse to some degree favors reacting destructively rather than constructively (compare preferences for the upper and lower rows of the right-hand column): Partner A's destructive act may make Partner B feel angry, diminished, or otherwise distressed, and under these circumstances reacting constructively may seem more humiliating and less satisfying (upper row of the given matrix, – – – –) than retaliating (lower row of the given matrix, —). Note that this is a no-win situation for Partner B: Although retaliation (—) may seem preferable to humiliation (– – – –), the resultant consequences are by no means attractive in an absolute sense.

Of course, the temptation to retaliate will vary across interactions, and may be moderated by the severity of the destructive act, the importance of the problem situation, or the specific emotions and cognitions that accompany a given act (granted, some destructive acts are more hurtful or irritating than others). But given the pervasiveness of tendencies toward reciprocity and the contingent nature of inclinations to cooperate (Axelrod, 1984; Kelley & Stahelski, 1970) – and given that a partner's destructive act often arouses intense negative emotions – destructive acts on the part of one partner frequently engender impulses to react destructively in turn.

However, given matrix preferences do not directly guide behavior. In deciding how to deal with a specific problem of interdependence, individuals explicitly or implicitly "take account of broader considerations" such as long-term goals, social norms, or knowledge of and concern for a partner's outcomes. This process is termed *transformation of motivation*. The reconceptualized preferences resulting from the transformation process are termed the *effective matrix,* which represents partners' feelings about joint outcomes at the time they actually react to a particular problem of interdependence (see matrix on right in Figure 3.1). Transformation of motivation typically leads individuals to relinquish preferences based on immediate self-interest (i.e., to forgo that which might be desired in the given matrix) and instead act on the basis of broader interaction goals (i.e., to act in accord with the reconceptualized effective matrix). In the Figure 3.1 example, Partner B decides that for any of a number of reasons – for example, to promote a happy relationship, to avoid exacerbating the problem, or to show concern for A's well-being – reacting constructively (upper row of the effective matrix, —) seems preferable to reacting destructively (lower row of the effective matrix, – – – –). (This example illustrates pro-relationship transformation of motivation, in that Partner B has come to place greater value on behaving in such a manner as to maximize the partners' joint well-being.)

Is this characterization of the accommodative dilemma empirically supported? Research on nonclose interactions supports the distinction between the given matrix and effective matrix, providing evidence that is consistent with the transformation concept (e.g., Dehue, McClintock, & Liebrand, 1993; McClintock & Liebrand, 1988; Van Lange & Liebrand, 1991). But in the context of intimate involvement, is transformation of motivation necessary to yield pro-relationship behavior? It might be argued that close partners automatically take one another's interests into account, or that self-interest and partner-interest are inextricably merged. However, research on relationships suggests that these arguments are not entirely valid, in that: (a) individuals *do* perceive discrepancies between self-interest and the broader welfare of a relationship (i.e., self-interest and partner interest are not inextricably merged; e.g., Rusbult, Verette, Whitney, Slovik, & Lipkus, 1991); (b) individuals frequently *are* tempted to engage in behaviors that promote immediate self-interest, even at the expense of a partner's well-being (i.e., partners' immediate preferences frequently are self-oriented; e.g., Surra & Longstreth, 1990; Yovetich & Rusbult, 1994); and (c) transformation of motivation frequently *does* accompany pro-relationship behavior (i.e., taking a partner's interests into account is not necessarily automatic; e.g., Yovetich & Rusbult, 1994). In short, behaving well in an ongoing relationship is neither easy nor automatic, and self-sacrificial acts such as accommodation accordingly are noteworthy. Thus, it becomes important to identify the determinants and consequences of willingness to accommodate.

Commitment Processes and Relationship Maintenance Mechanisms

Our theoretical account of the determinants and consequences of accommodation is summarized in Figure 3.2. This theory parallels a general model of commitment processes that suggests that relationships are sustained through a variety of maintenance mechanisms, defined as the specific ac-

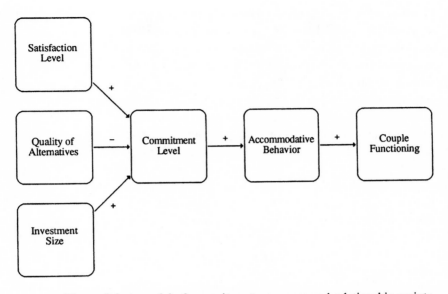

Figure 3.2. A model of commitment processes and relationship maintenance mechanisms in close relationships.

tivities through which individuals maintain or improve their relationships (Rusbult & Buunk, 1993). Previous research has examined maintenance phenomena such as derogation of attractive and tempting alternatives (Johnson & Rusbult, 1989; Simpson, Gangestad, & Lerma, 1990), willingness to sacrifice for the good of a relationship (Van Lange, Rusbult, Drigotas, Arriaga, Witcher, & Cox, 1997), and tendencies to perceive one's relationship as superior to other relationships (Rusbult, Van Lange, Verette, Yovetich, & Wildschut, 1997; Van Lange & Rusbult, 1995). We suggest that accommodation is yet another important maintenance mechanism. How so?

Specific patterns of interdependence such as the accommodative dilemma initially are experienced as unique problems to be solved. To resolve such dilemmas individuals may review their options, analyze the situation in light of surrounding circumstances, consider their goals for the relationship, and decide whether to accommodate or retaliate. Alternatively, individuals may impulsively act on the basis of immediate, given matrix preferences. In either event, the unique problem has been dealt with and experience has been acquired. Over time in a relationship, similar interdependence problems will be encountered with regularity and a relatively stable orientation to such situations may develop. Some individuals in some relationships may routinely engage in pro-relationship transformation, whereas other individuals may typically behave selfishly. According to

Holmes (1981), such stable transformational tendencies are guided by macromotives, which are the relatively enduring, internalized orientations that emerge in the context of a particular relationship and that guide behavior across the variety of interdependent situations that are encountered in the relationship.

Our model suggests that *commitment level* is a central motive in relationships – a motive that reliably influences willingness to accommodate. How can we explain the development of commitment to a relationship? Following Rusbult's (1980, 1983) investment model, we suggest that commitment level subjectively "summarizes" the net influence of three key features of interdependent relationships. Commitment is stronger when *satisfaction level* is high (i.e., an individual loves a partner and has positive feelings about a relationship), when *quality of alternatives* is judged to be poor (i.e., when specific alternative partners, the field of eligibles, and noninvolvement are relatively less attractive), and when *investment size* is large (i.e., when important resources are linked to a relationship and would be lost on termination). Thus Hypothesis 1 concerns the well-documented finding that high satisfaction, poor alternatives, and large investments are associated with enhanced commitment to a relationship (e.g., Felmlee, Sprecher, & Bassin, 1990; Lund, 1985; Rusbult, 1983; Rusbult, Johnson, & Morrow, 1986c; Rusbult et al., 1991; Simpson, 1987).

> *Hypothesis 1:* Feelings of marital commitment should be enhanced to the degree that (a) level of satisfaction with a relationship is high, (b) the quality of available alternatives is perceived to be poor, and (c) numerous important resources are directly or indirectly invested in the relationship.

Commitment is the internal representation of long-term orientation – the sense of being "linked" to a relationship, intending to maintain it for better or worse (Rusbult, 1980, 1983). Strong commitment should promote accommodation because: (a) long-term orientation should enhance the desire to sustain a healthy, enduring relationship, and thus should motivate a variety of pro-relationship maintenance behaviors; (b) in ongoing relationships, acts of accommodation may yield direct benefits on later occasions, when a partner feels inclined to reciprocate; and (c) accommodation may communicate the committed individual's cooperative, long-term orientation (Axelrod, 1984; Holmes, 1981; Kelley, 1979). Existing research provides indirect support for this prediction, in that strong commitment has been shown to be associated with maintenance mechanisms such as derogation of alternatives (Johnson & Rusbult, 1989), willingness to sacrifice (Van

Lange et al., 1997), and perceived relationship superiority (Rusbult et al., 1997).

> *Hypothesis 2:* The willingness to accommodate rather than retaliate when a partner behaves poorly should be enhanced to the degree that level of marital commitment is stronger.

Moreover, given that commitment level is assumed to stand in a hierarchical relationship with the investment model variables – representing not only the positive forces that draw one to a relationship (high satisfaction), but also the forces that bind one to a partner (high investments) or block one from leaving (poor alternatives) – we suggest that feelings of commitment typically mediate the effects of satisfaction, alternatives, and investments on tendencies to accommodate. Indeed, existing research regarding relationship maintenance mechanisms demonstrates that once the effects of commitment are accounted for, the impact of investment model variables tends to decline or drop to nonsignificance (e.g., in research on derogation of alternatives and willingness to sacrifice; Johnson & Rusbult, 1989; Van Lange et al., 1997).

> *Hypothesis 3:* The impact of satisfaction level, quality of alternatives, and investment size on willingness to accommodate should be mediated by feelings of commitment. Once the effects of commitment level are accounted for, the effects of satisfaction, alternatives, and investments will decline or drop to nonsignificance.

In addition to discussing the determinants of commitment and accommodation, our model also advances hypotheses regarding the correlates of healthy *couple functioning,* defined as the probability that a relationship will persist and display good adjustment (e.g., partners exhibit compatibility, express physical and verbal affection, engage in shared activities). How and why should the well-being of an ongoing relationship be influenced by partners' tendencies to accommodate? We suggest that accommodative dilemmas are potentially disruptive to a relationship for a variety of reasons. For example, partners may expend energy attempting to resolve such conflicts, they may become annoyed at one another's behavior, or they may feel betrayed in situations where one or both partners ignore the other's welfare in the pursuit of self-interest. By resolving such dilemmas through accommodation rather than retaliation, the accommodating partner (a) sidetracks escalation in destructiveness, (b) produces improved immediate outcomes for the partner, (c) motivates the partner to reciprocate this pro-relationship behavior in the future by creating for the partner a more congenial set of response options (a set of options in which reacting destructively is not necessarily a dominant response), and (d) communicates his or her long-term, pro-relationship orientation (i.e., because accommodation is contrary to immediate self-interest, such behavior is "informative"). Thus – and consistent with previous work on couple distress and nondistress (e.g., Gottman et al., 1977; Margolin & Wampold, 1981; Rusbult et al., 1986b) – our model suggests that greater accommodation will be associated with enhanced couple functioning.

> *Hypothesis 4:* Couple functioning should be enhanced to the degree that partners exhibit greater willingness to accommodate.

If commitment is indeed a central macromotive that promotes a wide range of maintenance mechanisms, commitment should exhibit links with couple functioning that parallel those of accommodation. That is, strong commitment, too, should be associated with healthier functioning.

> *Hypothesis 5:* Couple functioning should be enhanced to the degree that partners exhibit greater levels of marital commitment.

At the same time, given that accommodation is characterized as a mechanism through which committed individuals sustain or improve their relationships, accommodation should in part mediate the link between commitment and couple functioning. We did not anticipate complete mediation because only a portion of the variance through which commitment indirectly influences couple functioning is likely to be mediated through its link with accommodation (i.e., other variance is accounted for by alternative maintenance mechanisms).

> *Hypothesis 6:* The impact on couple functioning of commitment level – as well as satisfaction level, quality of alternatives, and investment size – should be partially mediated by willingness to accommodate. Once the effects of accommodation are accounted for, the impact of commitment and the investment model variables will decline or drop to nonsignificance.

The preceding analysis suggests that experience in a given relationship is cumulative, and that relationship-specific habits and orientations take on increased weight and potency over the course of development (Huston & Ashmore, 1986). How so? To begin with, whereas individuals initially experience events in their relationships as novel situations of interdependence with unique opportunities and constraints, over time specific patterns will be encountered with regularity and a relatively stable orientation to such situations will emerge. Moreover, over time in a relationship, stable orientations toward pattern-specific response tendencies increasingly come under the control of relationship-specific motives such as feelings of commitment. Thus, relationships develop unique histories of interdependence, and with the passage of time these histories – embodied in relationship-specific motives and response tendencies – should become increasingly powerful determinants of couple functioning.

> *Hypothesis 7:* Over time in a relationship, the impact on couple functioning of both willingness to accommodate and feelings of commitment will grow stronger.

The following sections of this chapter examine the empirical validity of our interdependence analysis of commitment processes and maintenance mechanisms. Each prediction outlined above is tested in the context of a longitudinal study of accommodation processes during the early years of marriage. Because the study was only partly completed at the time this chapter was written, we report preliminary findings from the project – findings relevant to a narrow range of the diverse phenomena that are investigated in the project, findings based on less than half of the data we will eventually obtain from study participants. Thus this chapter stands as an "interim report" of results from the University of North Carolina Marriage Study.

The University of North Carolina (UNC) Marriage Study: A Longitudinal Study of Accommodation

Subjects and Recruitment

One hundred twenty-three married couples participated (or are currently participating) in our ongoing longitudinal study of marital processes. Over the course of a 3-year recruitment period, the names of recently married couples were obtained from marriage license applications at the Orange County Office of Records and Deeds. Research assistants telephoned the first 230 couples applying for marriage licenses during the recruitment period, determining whether each couple wished to receive information about the study. Interested couples were mailed a letter describing the research project. The principal investigator subsequently telephoned each couple to solicit their participation. A total of 165 couples agreed to take part in the project, for a volunteer rate of 72%; 123 couples actually completed Time 1 research activities, for a participation rate of 75% (123 participants out of 165 volunteers) and a usable response rate of 53% (123 participants out of the sampling population of 230 couples). The analyses reported in this chapter are based on the first 57 couples to complete research activities at Times 1, 2, and 3.

At Time 1 subjects were 31.16 years old (32.43 for men, 29.91 for women) and had been married for about eight months. Thirty-four percent of the subjects had been married before and 21% had children from previous marriages; between Time 1 and Time 3, 19% of the couples had given birth to one or more children. At Time 1, all subjects had completed high school, and 92% had at least some college education. Their personal annual salary was around $25,000. The majority were Caucasian (96% Caucasian, 2% African-American, 2% Asian-American). Fifty percent were Protestant, 19% were Catholic, 5% were Jewish, and 27% had other religious or non-religious affiliations (e.g., Buddhist, atheist).

Research Design and Procedure

The study has a lagged longitudinal design. That is, couples began participating at different times, but over the course of the study they engaged in parallel activities at a parallel pace, completing research activities at approximately 6-month intervals. For example, if a couple completed Time 1 in February, Time 2 activities began 6 months later, in August; if a couple completed Time 1 in May, Time 2 activities began in November. We obtained data from each couple on six occasions – once every 6 to 8 months – over the course of a 3½-year period.

At Times 1, 3, and 5, each subject was mailed a copy of the UNC Marriage Study Questionnaire, an instrument that obtained self-report measures of each construct outlined in the introduction. Completed questionnaires were returned in prestamped, preaddressed envelopes. Partners were asked to complete their questionnaires independently, and not to speak to one another about their answers. Following Dillman's (1978) techniques for maximizing response rates, if subjects failed to return their questionnaires within 8 weeks, they were mailed reminder letters; 8 weeks later they were mailed a second reminder along with replacement questionnaires and return envelopes, followed by a third reminder 8 weeks later.

At Times 2, 4, and 6, couples participated in laboratory sessions, during which each subject completed: (a) the UNC Marriage Study Questionnaire; (b) the Participant Questionnaire, an instrument tapping interpersonal dispositions and individual well-being; and (c) additional specialized scales related to the specific activities associated with each research occasion. Also, couple interactions were videotaped, and these conversations were rated by trained coders so as to develop behavioral measures of accommodation. Our coding scheme was a modified version of the Rapid Couples Interaction Scoring System (Krokoff, Gottman, & Haas, 1989). Moreover, we employed a modified version of the dyadic interaction paradigm (Ickes, Bissonnette, Garcia, & Stinson, 1990) as a means of obtaining online reports of (a) each subject's own thoughts and feelings during the conversation, and (b) each subject's perceptions of the partner's thoughts and feelings during the conversation. (The behavioral measures of accommodation and data from the dyadic interaction paradigm were not yet ready for analysis at the time we prepared this chapter, so the procedures by which these data were gathered will not be described.)

At each research occasion throughout the study, subjects were assured that their responses would be confidential (i.e., their answers would be stored and coded by number rather than name, no one other than the principal investigator and her research assistants would view their data, and their partners would never be informed of their questionnaire responses). At the end of each research occasion couples were partly debriefed, reminded of upcoming activities, paid, and thanked for their assistance. At the outset of the study, project participants were paid $15 for mailed questionnaires and $25 for on-campus sessions; after obtaining federal funding for the project we were able to increase these rates to $25 for mailed questionnaires and $40 for laboratory sessions.

Questionnaires

In addition to the demographic information mentioned earlier, the UNC Marriage Study Questionnaires included measures of dyadic adjustment, own and partner's accommodative behavior, commitment level, satisfaction level, quality of alternatives, and investment size, along with measures tapping other features of their marriage (e.g., sacrifice, ideal-marriage/actual-marriage discrepancies). (Many of these variables are irrelevant to the goals of the current chapter; the procedures by which those variables were measured will not be described.) Following previous research on the investment model (Rusbult, 1983; Rusbult et al., 1991), the questionnaire included items to measure four key features of interdependent relationships: *Commitment Level* (five items; e.g., "To what degree do you feel committed to maintaining your marriage?" 0 = not very committed, 8 = completely committed); *Satisfaction Level* (four items; e.g., "How satisfied are you with your marriage?" 0 = not at all, 8 = completely); *Quality of Alternatives* (four items; e.g., "How appealing are the people other than your partner with whom you could become involved?" 0 = not very appealing, 8 = extremely appealing); and *Investment Size* (four items; e.g., "How much have you personally put into your marriage, e.g., time you've spent together, secrets you've disclosed to each other, memories you share?" 0 = very little, 8 = everything). A single measure of each variable was formed by averaging the items associated with that construct.

The questionnaire also measured subjects' perceptions of their own and their partners' tendencies to accommodate. Subjects were presented with four "stems" describing accommodative dilemmas – situations in which the partner enacted an exit or neglect behavior (e.g., "When my partner is upset and says something mean to me or snaps at me. . . ."). Each stem was followed by four items – one for each EVLN response category (e.g., "I talk to my partner about what's going on, trying to work out a solution," "I feel so angry that I want to walk right out the door"). Subjects reported the frequency with which they engaged in each of 16 responses (four responses for each of four stems; 0 = never, 8 = always). A parallel instrument measured perceptions of the partner's accommodation (e.g., "When I'm upset and say something mean to my partner or snap at him/her. . . ."; "My partner talks to me about what's going on, trying to work out a solution"). For both self and partner, a single measure of each response category (EVLN) was formed by averaging the items associated with that construct. We also developed measures of *Constructive Accommodation* (average of Voice and Loyalty), *Retaliative Behavior* (average of Exit and Neglect), and *Total Accommodation* (Constructive Accommodation minus Retaliative Behavior).

Couple functioning was measured using Spanier's (1976) 32-item Dyadic Adjustment Scale, which includes Likert-type, dichotomous, and checklist response formats. Given the breadth of items tapped by the Dyadic Adjustment Scale, it is not surprising that some scale items overlap with the features of interdependence that our work is designed to examine. To avoid studying couple functioning in such a manner as to include parallel information on the "determinants" and "consequences" sides of the equation, analyses examining the relationship between accommodation and couple functioning employed a conflict-purged adjustment scale (i.e., we dropped conflict-related items such as "How often do you and your partner quarrel?"), and analyses examining the relationship between commitment and couple functioning employed a commitment-and-satisfaction-purged adjustment scale (i.e., we dropped satisfaction- and commitment-related items such as "How often do you discuss or have you considered divorce, separation, or terminating your relationship?"). A single measure of *Dyadic Adjustment* – as well as conflict-purged and commitment-and-satisfaction-purged Dyadic Adjustment – was formed by summing all items associated with the construct.

Early Results from the Study

Reliability of Measures

As noted earlier, we calculated a single measure of each self-report variable for each subject at each time by combining the items associated with that construct. To ensure that this procedure was appropriate, we calculated reliability coefficients for each variable. The results of these analyses are displayed in Table 3.1 (see columns under "Reliability Coefficients"). These analyses revealed acceptable *alpha*s at Times 1, 2, and 3 for most self-report measures – for Dyadic Adjustment (total scores, conflict-purged scores, and commitment-and-satisfaction-purged scores), Commitment Level, and Satisfaction Level, as well as for perceptions of one's Own and the Partner's Constructive Accommodation, Retaliative Behavior, and Total Accommodation. However, reliability coefficients were low for Quality of Alternatives and Investment Size. Examination of the item-total statistics revealed that in neither case would deletion of an item substantially improve the reliabilities. These low values may be due to the multifaceted nature of the constructs themselves. The Quality of Alternatives items inquired about such diverse issues as the attractiveness of specific alternative partners, the broader field of eligibles, and the option of being single, and the Investment Size items inquired about the degree to which diverse qualities such as material resources, emotional resources, and important activities were linked to the marriage.

We also calculated test-retest correlations for each measure (see Table 3.1, columns under "Test-Retest Correlations"). Analyses evaluating Time 1–Time 2, Time 2–Time 3, and Time 1–Time 3 links among measures revealed significant correlations for most variables – for Dyadic Adjustment (total scores as well as both purged scales), Commitment Level, Quality of Alternatives, and Investment Size, as well as for perceptions of Own and Partner's Constructive Accommodation, Retaliative Behavior, and Total Accommodation. It appears that Satisfaction may be relatively more variable than other features of interdependent relationships: Although the Time 1–Time 2 correlation was significant, those for Time 2–Time 3 and Time 1–Time 3 were not. Because the *alpha*'s and test-retest correlations revealed mixed evidence for the reliability of our measures of Satisfaction, Alternatives, and Investments, we performed most analyses using not only these

Table 3.1. *Reliability coefficients, test-retest correlations, and correlations between partners' responses*

Response	Reliability coefficients			Test-retest correlations			Correlations between partners' responses		
	Time 1	Time 2	Time 3	Time 1–2	Time 2–3	Time 1–3	Time 1	Time 2	Time 3
Dyadic adjustment scale									
Total scores	.88	.92	.92	.80	.87	.70	.58	.66	.78
Conflict-purged	.81	.89	.89	.83	.85	.71	.60	.73	.74
Commitment/satisfaction-purged	.86	.91	.90	.76	.83	.66	.53	.60	.72
Qualities of interdependence									
Commitment level	.64	.81	.82	.77	.74	.63	.60	.55	.69
Satisfaction level	.95	.96	.97	.88	.10	.02	.73	.70	.79
Quality of alternatives	.57	.48	.53	.59	.66	.63	.37	.28	.41
Investment size	.36	.26	.40	.64	.55	.66	.38	.33	.26
Accommodative behavior									
Own constructive accommodation	.64	.72	.70	.67	.74	.63	.25	.21	.22
Own retaliative behavior	.79	.78	.79	.76	.80	.75	.68	.59	.62
Own total accommodation	.78	.83	.80	.81	.83	.74	.52	.54	.53
Partner's constructive accommodation	.78	.83	.82	.76	.85	.72	.24	.56	.42
Partner's retaliative behavior	.80	.84	.83	.82	.80	.79	.47	.43	.30
Partner's total accommodation	.84	.88	.86	.86	.86	.79	.43	.57	.43

Note: For test-retest correlations and correlations between partners' responses, for r's ranging from .23 to .25, $p < .10$; for r's from .26 to .33, $p < .05$; and for r's greater than .34, $p < .01$.

composite measures, but also the individual items that made up each composite measure. This strategy enabled us to determine whether the observed results were consistent across multiple indicators of a construct.

Validity of Measures

We also calculated correlations between partners' self-report measures (see Table 3.1, columns under "Correlations Between Partners' Responses"). Out of 39 analyses, 35 effects were statistically significant. How should these results be interpreted? The majority of these analyses are not relevant to assessing the validity of our self-report measures, in that accommodation and the investment model variables tap qualities that logically *can* differ for two partners in a given relationship (e.g., if husbands' and wives' reported Alternatives were uncorrelated, this could be because their alternatives really *do* differ in quality). Thus the majority of the partner correlations displayed in Table 3.1 simply reveal that typically, wives and husbands are mutually interdependent – for example, partners tend to be similarly committed to their marriage. At the same time, the statistics displayed for Dyadic Adjustment *are* relevant to assessing measure validity: Ratings of Dyadic Adjustment *should* be similar for partners in a given relationship, since this instrument asks both partners to rate the same construct – their *marriage* (e.g., if the marriage *is* in fact a poorly adjusted one, both partners should describe it as such). Indeed, partners exhibited good convergence for reports of total Dyadic Adjustment as well as for the conflict- and commitment-purged measures.

Since each subject described both his or her own *and* the partner's tendencies to accommodate, we were able to calculate correlations between each individual's report of his or her own accommodation and the partner's report of the individual's accommodation. In describing the husband's accommodative behavior, the wife's and the husband's reports were positively correlated for Time 1, 2, and 3 measures of Total Accommodation (respective r's = .63, .63, .60), Constructive Accommodation (r's = .35, .51, .42), and Retaliative Behavior (r's = .74, .61, .58); in describing the wife's behavior, the husband's and the wife's reports were positively correlated for Time 1, 2, and 3 measures of Total Accommodation (respective r's = .50, .57, .43), Constructive Accommodation (r's = .14, .33, .32), and Retaliative Behavior (r's = .57, .52, .45) (17 of 18 effects were significant; for r's ranging from .26 to .33, $p < .05$; for r's greater than .34, $p < .01$).

We also assessed the validity of the self-report measures of accommodation by examining their associations with behavioral measures obtained from codings of couples' videotaped interactions. These analyses are somewhat unreliable because they are based on a small sample (only a subset of the conversations were coded at the time we prepared this chapter). Nevertheless, these analyses revealed reasonable support for the validity of our self-report measures. Own Total Accommodation was positively correlated with a measure of total behavioral accommodation, as well as with the two subscales of this total score, speaker accommodation and listener accommodation (r's = .31, .27, .42); also Own Total Accommodation was positively correlated with coders' global ratings of each individual's level of accommodation (r = .47) (two of four effects were significant; for r's greater than .40, $p < .05$).

Subjects also answered questionnaire items in which they rated their own and the partner's relative levels of accommodation and relative levels of each investment model variable (e.g., "Who's more likely to smooth things over when you're having a fight?"; "Who's more committed to making your marriage last?"; 0 = my partner, 4 = we're equal, 8 = me). Although we do not employ these "mutuality" measures in the analyses reported in this chapter, these items can be used to evaluate the validity of subjects' self-reports. If some degree of "reality" underlies individuals' descriptions of their relationship, partners' reports should be negatively correlated (e.g., the husband circles "8," saying he is more committed; the wife circles "0," saying he is more committed). In support of the validity of subjects' self-report, correlational analyses revealed negative correlations between partners' reports of Relative Accommodation Level (r's = −.47, −.42, −.38), Relative Commitment Level (r's = −.46, −.37, −.45), Relative Satisfaction Level (r's = −.25, −.71, −.40), Relative Quality of Alternatives (r's = −.52, −.19, −.46), and Relative Investment Size (r's = −.34, −.34, −.22) (12 of 15 effects were significant; for r's ranging from .26 to .33, $p < .05$; for r's greater than .34, $p < .01$). The fact that partners to some degree exhibit awareness of which partner is more involved in their marriage suggests that their self-report measures to some extent tap an underlying "reality."

These analyses provide good support for the validity of our self-report measures. Granted, there appears to be some subjectivity in self-report – the above-reported statistics account for less than 100% of the variance in our measures. At the same time, the observed links between self-report and both (a) behavioral measures and (b) partner reports suggest that the self-report data to some extent reflect actual conditions in a relationship.

Tests of Model Predictions

To ensure that our findings are robust and reliable, we tested each hypothesis using a variety of analysis strategies. We performed multiple, conceptually parallel hypothesis tests using both (a) individual-level data (regressing individuals' self-reported criteria onto self-reported predictors) and (b) couple-level data (regressing the average of the partners' criteria onto the average of their predictors). We performed analyses (a) using a combined data set (combining data from both wives and husbands at all three research occasions), as well as (b) separately at each of three times (Times 1, 2, and 3) and (c) separately for wives and husbands. In addition, we performed both (a) concurrent analyses (regressing each criterion onto concurrent predictors) and (b) lagged analyses (regressing later criteria onto earlier predictors). It should be clear that many of these analyses involve nonindependent observations, in that a given analysis may include (a) data obtained from both partners in a given couple, and/or (b) data obtained from the same individual on numerous occasions. To deal with the nonindependence of multiple observations from a given couple, all analyses were replicated including *Couple Number* as a categorical variable (Cohen & Cohen, 1975). Thus our data were extensively analyzed so as to ensure that major findings are replicated.

Tables 3.2, 3, and 4 summarize the results of six separate tests of each hypothesis. For each hypothesis, we report the results of (a) concurrent analyses using individual-level data, (b) concurrent analyses using couple-level data, and (c) lagged analyses using individual-level data. All of these analyses employ a combined data set, including data for both wives and husbands at all three research occasions. Thus (a) concurrent analyses of individual-level data are based on 342 observations – data from three research occasions for two partners from 57 couples; (b) concurrent analyses of couple-level data are based on 171 observations – data from three research occasions for 57 couples; and (c) lagged analyses of individual-level data are based on 228 observations – data for two time lags (Time 1 predictors with Time 2 criteria, Time 2 predictors with Time 3 criteria) for two partners from 57 couples.

As noted above, each hypothesis was examined using both (a) unadjusted tests – analyses ignoring the nonindependence of partners' responses and (b) adjusted tests – analyses including Couple Number as a categorical variable, thus accounting for the nonindependence of multiple observations from a given couple. The adjusted tests are highly conservative, in that Couple Number controls for *all* variance shared by multiple observations from a given couple, and thus may "take away" variance that by rights should remain in the equation (Couple Number *alone* accounts for 67% to 79% of the variance in the criteria reported below). Also, this strategy seriously reduces degrees of freedom (one degree of freedom per couple, minus one). Moreover, the unadjusted and adjusted tests address slightly different questions.

For example, an unadjusted test might ask whether stronger commitment is associated with greater willingness to accommodate, within the context of a data set in which accommodation levels differ across couples, across individuals within each couple, and across time for each individual. In contrast, the parallel adjusted test "controls for" within-couple variance in accommodation, and asks whether *within a given couple,* stronger commitment is associated with greater willingness to accommodate (i.e., an intercept is calculated for each couple, and analyses examine deviations from this within-couple mean). Thus, in comparison to the unadjusted tests of each hypothesis, the adjusted analyses stand as inherently conservative tests of a highly specialized sort of research question. Accordingly, the "true" strength of association among variables lies somewhere between these two types of analysis. It is therefore important to examine all six analyses for a given hypothesis in order to evaluate the overall strength of support for each hypothesis.

Hypothesis 1: Do Satisfaction, Alternatives, and Investments Influence Feelings of Commitment? Hypothesis 1 of our model proposed that commitment would be positively associated with satisfaction level, negatively associated with quality of alternatives, and positively associated with investment size. To test this hypothesis we performed three-factor simultaneous regression analyses, regressing Commitment Level onto Satisfaction, Alternatives, and Investments. As can be seen in Table 3.2, all six tests revealed results congruent with the assertion that Satisfaction contributes unique variance to predicting Commitment (see analyses summarized under "Hypothesis 1"). The unadjusted and adjusted concurrent tests using individual-level data revealed that more satisfied individuals exhibit stronger concurrent commitment (see analyses labeled "Concurrent Prediction/ Individual-Level"; see columns under "Unadjusted Tests" and "Adjusted Tests; respective *betas* = .71 and .48). The unadjusted and adjusted concurrent tests using couple-level data revealed that couples with greater average levels of satisfaction exhibit stronger concurrent couple-level commitment (*betas* = .75 and .53). And the unadjusted and adjusted lagged tests using individual-level data revealed that individuals who are more satisfied on earlier occasions exhibit greater levels of commitment at later occasions (*betas* = .68 and .27).

However, the effects of alternative quality and investment size were less consistently observed. Quality of Alternatives was significantly predictive of Commitment in four of six tests, including the unadjusted and adjusted concurrent tests using both individual-level data (*betas* = −.16 and −.15) and

Table 3.2. *Regression analyses predicting commitment level, willingness to accommodate, and dyadic adjustment*

	Unadjusted tests			Adjusted tests		
		Overall model			Overall model	
Prediction	Beta	df	F	Beta	df	F
Hypothesis 1: Do high satisfaction, poor alternatives, and high investments enhance feelings of commitment?						
Concurrent prediction / individual level						
Satisfaction level	.71**	3,309	139.73**	.48**	58,254	14.08**
Quality of alternatives	−.16*			−.15*		
Investment size	.15*			.10*		
Concurrent prediction / couple level						
Satisfaction level	.75**	3,146	89.17**	.53**	58,91	14.02**
Quality of alternatives	−.15*			−.16*		
Investment size	.14*			.06		
Lagged prediction / individual level						
Satisfaction level	.68**	3,195	62.00**	.27**	56,142	7.75**
Quality of alternatives	−.03			.01		
Investment size	.06			.11		
Hypothesis 2: Does strong commitment enhance willingness to accommodate?						
Concurrent prediction / individual level						
Commitment level	.35**	1,310	42.33**	.19**	56,255	9.23**
Concurrent prediction / couple level						
Commitment level	.38**	1,144	24.54**	.14	55,90	12.72**
Lagged prediction / individual level						
Commitment level	.32**	1,196	21.90**	.03	55,142	5.95**
Hypothesis 4: Does the willingness to accommodate enhance dyadic adjustment?						
Concurrent prediction / individual level						
Own total accommodation	.49**	1,306	95.76**	.12*	56,251	12.03**
Concurrent prediction / couple level						
Own total accommodation	.61**	1,138	83.22**	.52**	56,83	12.71**
Lagged prediction / individual level						
Own total accommodation	.43**	1,189	42.37**	−.03	55,135	8.29**
Hypothesis 5: Does strong commitment enhance dyadic adjustment?						
Concurrent prediction / individual level						
Commitment level	.66**	1,311	241.93**	.36**	56,256	15.01**
Concurrent prediction / couple level						
Commitment level	.73**	1,145	161.70**	.41**	56,90	12.49**
Lagged prediction / individual level						
Commitment level	.57**	1,189	88.64**	.05	55,135	8.76**
Do both constructive accommodation and retaliative behavior influence dyadic adjustment?						
Concurrent prediction / individual level						
Own retaliative behavior	−.39**	2,305	49.35**	−.10	57,250	11.78**
Own constructive accommodation	.19**			.05		

Table 3.2. *(cont.)*

	Unadjusted tests			Adjusted tests		
		Overall model			Overall model	
Prediction	Beta	df	F	Beta	df	F
Concurrent prediction / couple level						
Own retaliative behavior	−.43**	2,137	41.33**	−.38**	57,82	12.35**
Own constructive accommodation	.29**			.24**		
Lagged prediction / individual level						
Own retaliative behavior	−.33**	2,188	21.48**	.04	56,134	8.08**
Own constructive accommodation	.17*			−.02		

Do both own accommodation and perceptions of the partner's accommodation influence dyadic adjustment?

Concurrent prediction / individual level						
Own total accommodation	.16**	2,295	93.62**	.02	57,240	13.65**
Partner's accommodation	.51**			.26**		
Concurrent prediction / couple level						
Own total accommodation	.12	2,129	67.27**	.28*	56,75	12.54**
Partner's accommodation	.62**			.46**		
Lagged prediction / individual level						
Own total accommodation	.08	2,182	50.12**	−.08	56,128	9.00**
Partner's accommodation	.54**			.25**		

Note: Statistics presented under "unadjusted tests" do not adjust for shared within-couple variance; statistics presented under "adjusted tests" account for shared within-couple variance by including as an additional predictor the categorical variable Couple Number. Statistics for "concurrent prediction" regress criteria onto predictor variables from the same time period; statistics for "lagged prediction" regress Time n criteria onto Time $n − 1$ predictor variables. Statistics for "individual level" list the results for analyses employing individual-level measures of each construct; statistics for "couple-level" analyses list the results for analyses employing averaged, couple-level measures of each construct.
*$p < .05$. **$p < .01$.

couple-level data (*betas* = −.15 and −.16). Investment Size was significantly predictive of Commitment in three of six tests, including the unadjusted and adjusted concurrent tests using individual-level data (*betas* = .15 and .10) and the unadjusted concurrent test using couple-level data (*beta* = .14). Neither Alternative Quality nor Investment Size contributed significant unique variance to predicting Commitment in the lagged regression analyses, although both variables exhibited significant zero-order lagged links with Commitment (respective *r*'s = −.26 and .24, both *p*'s < .05). Thus the most notable feature of these results is the finding that variations in satisfaction exert far more powerful effects on commitment than do variations in alternative quality or investment size.

Hypothesis 2: Does Commitment Level Influence Accommodation?

Hypothesis 2 asserted that commitment level is a central-relationship macromotive that reliably influences tendencies toward relationship maintenance activities, including tendencies to accommodate rather than retaliate when a partner behaves poorly. To test this prediction, we performed six analyses, regressing Own Total Accommodation onto Commitment Level. The results of these analyses are presented in Table 3.2 (see analyses summarized under "Hypothesis 2"). Consistent with model predictions, the association between Commitment and Accommodation was significant in four of six analyses. Individuals with stronger feelings of commitment to their marriage exhibit substantially greater concurrent tendencies to accommodate rather than retaliate (*betas* = .35 and .19). Moreover, the regression coefficients for commitment were significant in the unadjusted concurrent test using couple-level data and in the unadjusted lagged test using individual-level data: Couples with stronger commitment exhibit greater concurrent accommodation, and individuals who are more committed on earlier occasions exhibit greater levels of accommodation at later occasions (*betas* = .38 and .32). Given that the two nonsignificant effects were highly conservative adjusted tests, we assume that the Couple Number variable simply consumed too much of the variance in accommodation to allow for sensitive tests of this research question. Thus Hypothesis 2 received moderate support.

Hypothesis 4: Does Willingness to Accommodate Influence Dyadic Adjustment? Hypothesis 4 proposed that accommodation is a relationship maintenance activity, and that couple functioning accordingly would be enhanced to the degree that partners exhibited greater willingness to accommodate. To test this hypothesis, we regressed the conflict-purged measure of Dyadic Adjustment onto Own Total Accommodation. As can be seen in Table 3.2, the link between accommodation and dyadic adjustment was statistically significant in five of six analyses (see analyses summarized under "Hypothesis 4"). The only analysis that revealed nonsignificant results was the most conservative analysis – the adjusted lagged test employing individual-level data. Thus Hypothesis 4 received good support.

Hypothesis 5: Does Commitment Level Influence Dyadic Adjustment? Hypothesis 5 proposed that commitment is a key macromotive that promotes pro-relationship behavior across a wide range of situations. Accordingly, couple functioning should be enhanced to the degree that partners exhibit stronger commitment. To test this hypothesis we performed parallel sets of analyses, regressing the conflict- and commitment-purged measures of Dyadic Adjustment onto Commitment. These analyses revealed parallel findings; accordingly, Table 3.2 presents results for the commitment-purged measure. As can be seen in Table 3.2, the link between commitment and adjustment was significant in five of six analyses. The only analysis revealing nonsignificant results was the most conservative analysis – the adjusted lagged test using individual-level data. Thus Hypothesis 5 received good support.

Do Both Constructive Accommodation and Retaliative Behavior Influence Dyadic Adjustment? Table 3.2 presents analyses relevant to two additional questions, neither of which was embodied in formal model predictions. First, it is important to determine whether both constructive accommodation and retaliative behavior affect dyadic adjustment. To explore this issue we performed two-factor simultaneous regression analyses, regressing the conflict-purged measure of Dyadic Adjustment onto Own Constructive Accommodation and Own Retaliative Behavior. In two of the analyses displayed in Table 3.2, the regression coefficients were nonsignificant for both constructive accommodation *and* retaliative behavior. Given that both of these analyses were highly conservative adjusted tests, we assume that the Couple Number variable simply consumed too much of the variance in adjustment to allow for sensitive tests of this research question. In the remaining four tests, the analyses revealed that dyadic adjustment is enhanced by both inhibiting destructive impulses *and* enhancing constructive reactions. At the same time, the effects of inhibiting destructive impulses are descriptively larger than those for enhancing constructive reactions.

Do Both Own Accommodation and Perceptions of the Partner's Accommodation Influence Dyadic Adjustment? A final set of analyses presented in Table 3.2 asks whether individuals' reports of dyadic adjustment are influenced by both their own willingness to accommodate and their perceptions of the partner's willingness to accommodate. To explore this issue we performed two-factor simultaneous regression analyses, regressing the conflict-purged measure of Dyadic Adjustment onto Own Total Accommodation and Partner's Total Accommodation. The regression coefficient for Partner's Total Accommodation was significant in all six analyses. In contrast, the coefficient for Own Total Accommodation was significant in only two of six analyses. Thus it appears that reports of couple functioning are influenced more powerfully by judgments regarding the partner's willingness to accommodate than by individuals' own willingness to accommodate.

Hypothesis 3: Does Commitment Level Mediate the Effects of Investment Model Variables on Accommodation? Hypothesis 3 predicted that the impact of the investment model variables on willingness to accommodate would be mediated by feelings of commitment. Analyses relevant to testing this hypothesis are presented in Table 3.3. Consistent with the required preconditions for demonstrating mediation (Baron & Kenny, 1986), (a) the investment model variables are significantly predictive of commitment (see Table 3.2, analyses under "Hypothesis 1"), (b) the investment model variables are significantly predictive of accommodation (e.g., in unadjusted tests, R^2's ranged from .24 to .27; see Table 3.3, "Direct Effect of Investment Model Variables"), and (c) commitment level is significantly predictive of accommodation (in unadjusted tests, R^2's ranged from .10 to .15; see Table 3.3, "Direct Effect of Commitment Level").

We performed hierarchical regression analyses to evaluate the extent to which commitment mediates the effects of the investment model variables, regressing Own Accommodation onto Commitment Level in Step 1, and regressing the residuals from this analysis onto Satisfaction, Alternatives, and Investments in Step 2. As can be seen in Table 3.3, once the impact of Commitment Level was taken into consideration, Satisfaction, Alternatives, and Investments accounted for substantially reduced variance. Such effects are most readily interpreted in the unadjusted tests, in that we can examine the impact of model variables without complications involving variance due to Couple Number. Above and beyond the effects of Commitment, the investment model variables accounted for 8% to 11% of the variance in Own Accommodation (see "Indirect Effect"). These values are substantially lower than those observed in analyses regressing Accommodation directly onto the investment model variables – the discrepancy between the direct and mediated effects of the investment model variables was 18% in the concurrent test employing individual-level data, 14% in the concurrent test employing couple-level data, and 16% in the lagged test employing individual-level data (see "Discrepancy Between Direct and Mediated Effects"). These results suggest that commitment level partially mediates the effects of the investment model variables on willingness to accommodate.

Hypothesis 6: Does Willingness to Accommodate Mediate the Effects of Commitment on Dyadic Adjustment? Hypothesis 6 predicted that the effects on dyadic adjustment of commitment and the investment model variables would be partly mediated by willingness to accommodate. Analyses relevant to this hypothesis are presented in Table 3.3. Consistent with the required preconditions for demonstrating mediation, (a) both commitment

Table 3.3. *Causal modeling analyses predicting willingness to accommodate*

Prediction	Unadjusted tests			Adjusted tests		
		Overall model			Overall model	
	Beta	df	F	Beta	df	F

Hypothesis 3: Do feelings of commitment mediate the effects of investment model variables on willingness to accommodate?

Concurrent prediction / individual level

Step 1:	Commitment level	.35**	1,310	42.33**	.19**	56,255	9.23**
Step 2:	Satisfaction level	.28**	3,297	8.50**	.06	3,297	0.55
	Quality of alternatives	.04			.00		
	Investment size	−.08			−.05		

Direct effect of commitment level: $R^2 = .12**$ (unadjusted test).
Direct effect of investment model variables: $R^2 = .26**$ / indirect effect: $R^2 = .08**$ (unadjusted tests). Discrepancy between direct and mediated effects = .18.

Concurrent prediction / couple level

Step 1:	Commitment level	.38**	1,144	24.54**	.14	55,90	12.72**
Step 2:	Satisfaction level	.32**	3,136	5.01**	.08	3,136	0.97
	Quality of alternatives	−.06			−.10		
	Investment size	.01			−.04		

Direct effect of commitment level: $R^2 = .15**$ (unadjusted test).
Direct effect of investment model variables: $R^2 = .24**$ / indirect effect: $R^2 = .10**$ (unadjusted tests). Discrepancy between direct and mediated effects = .14.

Lagged prediction / individual level

Step 1:	Commitment level	.32**	1,196	21.90**	.03	55,142	5.95**
Step 2:	Satisfaction level	.32**	3,186	7.69**	.01	3,186	1.52
	Quality of alternatives	.15*			.15		
	Investment size	.03			.06		

Direct effect of commitment level: $R^2 = .10**$ (unadjusted test).
Direct effect of investment model variables: $R^2 = .27**$ / indirect effect: $R^2 = .11**$ (unadjusted tests). Discrepancy between direct and mediated effects = .16.

Hypothesis 6: Does willingness to accommodate mediate the effects of commitment and the investment model variables on dyadic adjustment?

Concurrent prediction / individual level

Step 1:	Own total accommodation	.49**	1,306	95.76**	.12*	56,251	12.03**
Step 2:	Commitment level	.58**	1,299	147.77**	.20**	1,299	12.91**
Step 3:	Satisfaction level	.32**	3,287	11.47**	.08	3,287	1.12
	Quality of alternatives	.07			−.05		
	Investment size	.05			.02		

Direct effect of own accommodation: $R^2 = .24**$ (unadjusted test).
Direct effect of commitment: $R^2 = .44**$ / indirect effect: $R^2 = .33**$ (unadjusted tests). Discrepancy between direct and mediated effects = .11.
Direct effect of investment model variables: $R^2 = .70**$ / indirect effect: $R^2 = .11**$ (unadjusted tests). Discrepancy between direct and mediated effects = .59.

Concurrent prediction / couple level

Step 1:	Own total accommodation	.61**	1,138	83.22**	.52**	56,83	12.71**
Step 2:	Commitment level	.63**	1,133	88.20**	.11	1,133	1.68

Table 3.3. *(cont.)*

| | | Unadjusted tests | | | Adjusted tests | | |
| | | | Overall model | | | Overall model | |
Prediction		Beta	df	F	Beta	df	F
Step 3:	Satisfaction level	.28**	3,126	4.45**	.08	3,126	0.32
	Quality of alternatives	.07			.05		
	Investment size	.20*			.01		

Direct effect of own accommodation: $R^2 = .38**$ (unadjusted test).
Direct effect of commitment: $R^2 = .53**$ / indirect effect: $R^2 = .40**$ (unadjusted tests). Discrepancy between direct and mediated effects = .13.
Direct effect of investment model variables: $R^2 = .80**$ / indirect effect: $R^2 = .10**$ (unadjusted tests). Discrepancy between direct and mediated effects = .70.

Lagged prediction / individual level

| | | Unadjusted tests | | | Adjusted tests | | |
		Beta	df	F	Beta	df	F
Step 1:	Own total accommodation	.43**	1,189	42.37**	−.05	55,135	8.29**
Step 2:	Commitment level	.48**	1,182	55.25**	.03	1,182	0.19
Step 3:	Satisfaction level	.28**	3,172	5.22**	.05	3,172	0.16
	Quality of alternatives	.11			.02		
	Investment size	.01			.01		

Direct effect of own accommodation: $R^2 = .18**$ (unadjusted test).
Direct effect of commitment: $R^2 = .32**$ / indirect effect: $R^2 = .23**$ (unadjusted tests). Discrepancy between direct and mediated effects = .09.
Direct effect of investment model variables: $R^2 = .53**$ / indirect effect: $R^2 = .08**$ (unadjusted tests). Discrepancy between direct and mediated effects = .45.

Note: Statistics under "Adjusted tests" account for shared within-couple variance by including as an additional predictor the categorical variable Couple Number. Statistics for "concurrent prediction" regress criteria onto predictor variables from the same time period; statistics for "Lagged prediction" regress Time *n* criteria onto Time *n* − 1 predictor variables. Statistics for "individual level" employ individual-level measures; statistics for "couple level" employ averaged, couple-level measures.
*$p < .05$. **$p < .01$.

and the investment model variables are significantly predictive of accommodation (see Table 3.3, analyses under "Hypothesis 3"), (b) both commitment and the investment model variables are significantly predictive of dyadic adjustment (e.g., in unadjusted tests, R^2's for Commitment ranged from .32 to .53, R^2's for the investment model variables ranged from .53 to .80; see Table 3.3, "Direct Effect of Commitment" and "Direct Effect of Investment model Variables"), and (c) willingness to accommodate is significantly predictive of dyadic adjustment (in unadjusted tests, R^2's ranged from .18 to .38; see Table 3.3, "Direct Effect of Own Accommodation").

We performed hierarchical regression analyses to evaluate the degree to which willingness to accommodate mediates the influence of commitment and the investment model variables, regressing Dyadic Adjustment onto

Own Accommodation in Step 1, regressing the residuals from this analysis onto Commitment Level in Step 2, and regressing the remaining residuals onto the three investment model variables in Step 3. As can be seen in Table 3.3, once the impact of Accommodation was taken into consideration, Commitment Level accounted for reduced but (typically) significant variance in Dyadic Adjustment. Once again, such effects are most readily interpreted in the unadjusted tests. Above and beyond the effects of Accommodation, Commitment accounted for 23% to 40% of the variance in Own Accommodation (see "Indirect Effect"). These values are somewhat lower than those observed in analyses regressing Adjustment directly onto Commitment Level – the discrepancy between the direct and mediated effects of Commitment was 11% in the concurrent test employing individual-level data, 13% in the concurrent test employing couple-level data, and 9% in the lagged test employing individual-level data (see "Discrepancy Between Direct and Mediated Effects"). These results suggest that willingness to accommodate only partly mediates the effects of commitment level on couple functioning.

Do accommodation and commitment mediate the influence of the investment model variables? As can be seen in Table 3.3, above and beyond the effects of Accommodation and Commitment, the investment model variables accounted for 8% to 11% of the variance in Dyadic Adjustment (see "Indirect Effect"). These values are substantially lower than those observed in analyses regressing Dyadic Adjustment directly onto the investment model variables – the discrepancy between the direct and mediated effects of the investment model variables was 59% in the concurrent test employing individual-level data, 70% in the concurrent test employing couple-level data, and 45% in the lagged test employing individual-level data (see "Discrepancy Between Direct and Mediated Effects"). These results suggest that commitment and willingness to accommodate largely mediate the effects of the investment model variables on couple functioning.

Hypothesis 7a: Does the Link between Accommodation and Dyadic Adjustment Grow Stronger over Time? Consistent with the assertion that relationship-specific habits and orientations take on increased potency over the course of a relationship, Hypothesis 7a predicted that over time, accommodation would exert increasingly powerful effects on couple functioning. To test this prediction, we performed regression analyses including main effects and interactions for Time (Time 1, 2, or 3). Such effects were explored using two strategies: (a) we included two dummy variables to represent the three-category Time variable, examining discrepancies between Times 1 and 2 with one dummy variable and examining discrepancies be-

Table 3.4. *Regression analyses examining the effects of time on links with dyadic adjustment*

| Prediction | Unadjusted tests | | | Adjusted tests | | |
| | Beta | Overall model | | Beta | Overall model | |
		df	F		df	F
Hypothesis 7a: Does the link between accommodation and dyadic adjustment change over time?						
Concurrent prediction / individual level						
Own total accommodation	.29**	3,304	34.79**	−.03	58,249	12.88**
Time	−.21**			−.20**		
Time * own total accommodation	.23+			.13		
Concurrent prediction / couple level						
Own total accommodation	.30+	3,136	30.03**	.23+	58,81	14.28**
Time	−.27*			−.24**		
Time * own total accommodation	.37+			.26*		
Lagged prediction / individual level						
Own total accommodation	.42**	3,294	20.92**	.16*	59,238	10.25**
Time	−.20*			−.15*		
Time * own total accommodation	.13			.03		
Hypothesis 7b: Does the link between commitment and dyadic adjustment change over time?						
Concurrent prediction / individual level						
Commitment level	.35**	3,297	70.74**	.11	58,242	13.00**
Time	−.64*			−.57**		
Time * commitment level	.63*			.52*		
Concurrent prediction / couple level						
Commitment level	.44*	3,131	47.18**	.14	57,77	11.24**
Time	−.66+			−.70*		
Time * commitment level	.64+			.62*		
Lagged prediction / individual level						
Commitment level	.45**	3,298	42.21**	.21*	59,242	12.47**
Time	−.75**			−.66**		
Time * commitment level	.68**			.55*		

Note: Statistics under "adjusted tests" account for shared within-couple variance by including as an additional predictor the categorical variable Couple Number. Statistics for "concurrent prediction" regress criteria onto predictor variables from the same time period; statistics for "lagged prediction" regress Time n criteria onto Time $n − 1$ predictor variables. Statistics for "individual level" employ individual-level measures; statistics for "couple level" employ averaged, couple-level measures.
$+ p < .10.$ $*p < .05.$ $**p < .01.$

tween Times 1 and 3 using a second dummy variable; (b) on the assumption that Time might exert linear effects, we included a single, three-level Time variable. The analyses employing two dummy variables revealed findings parallel to those for the single dummy variable (i.e., the effects of Time appear to be linear); since the single-variable analyses are simpler to interpret, we present the results of these analyses in Table 3.4.

As can be seen in Table 3.4 – and consistent with the Table 3.2 tests of Hypothesis 4 – five of six analyses revealed evidence of a positive association between Accommodation and Dyadic Adjustment (see main effects of "Own Total Accommodation"). Moreover, all six analyses revealed that levels of Dyadic Adjustment tend to decline over the early years of marriage (see main effects of "Time"). And consistent with Hypothesis 7a, three of six analyses revealed marginal or significant interactions of Time with Own Total Accommodation (see interactions of "Time * Own Total Accommodation"). The fact that the interaction *beta*s are positive means that the strength of association between accommodation and adjustment increases with time. Thus these analyses provide moderate support for Hypothesis 7a.

Hypothesis 7b: Does the Link between Commitment and Dyadic Adjustment Grow Stronger over Time? Hypothesis 7b predicted that over time, feelings of commitment would exert increasingly powerful effects on couple functioning. To test this prediction, we performed regression analyses including main effects and interactions for Time, following the strategy employed in tests of Hypothesis 7a. The analyses including two dummy variables revealed findings parallel to those for the single dummy variables (i.e., the effects of Time appear to be linear); since the single-variable analyses are simpler to interpret, we present these results in Table 3.4.

As can be seen in Table 3.4 – and consistent with the Table 3.2 tests of Hypothesis 5 – four of six analyses revealed evidence of a positive association between Commitment and Dyadic Adjustment (see main effects of "Commitment Level"). Moreover, all six analyses revealed that levels of Dyadic Adjustment tend to decline over the early years of marriage (see main effects of "Time"). And consistent with Hypothesis 7b, all six analyses revealed marginal or significant interactions of Time with Commitment Level (see interactions of "Time * Commitment Level"). The fact that the interaction *beta*s are positive means that the strength of association between commitment and adjustment increases over time. Thus these analyses provide good support for Hypothesis 7b.

Summary and Discussion

Hypothesis 1 of our model concerned the well-documented finding that commitment to a relationship is enhanced to the extent that feelings of satisfaction are strong, available alternatives are perceived to be poor, and numerous important resources have been invested in the relationship. The preliminary analyses reported above revealed good support for the link between satisfaction and commitment. However, the effects of alternative quality and investment size were somewhat weak and were inconsistently observed. These results suggest the existence of "sentiment override" (see Weiss, 1980): During the early years of marriage, the existence of positive versus negative "sentiment" (i.e., satisfaction) appears to be a considerably more potent determinant of commitment than other features of interdependence. In light of the broad support for investment model predictions observed in previous studies of commitment processes (for a review of this literature, see Rusbult & Buunk, 1993), the fact that the current results are weak would not seem to call for theory modification. At the same time, future research should attempt to determine whether the impact of each model variable is moderated by (a) type of relationship (e.g., dating relationship vs. marital relationship), (b) stage of relationship (e.g., early stages vs. later stages), or (c) level of relationship functioning (e.g., nondistressed vs. distressed, or voluntary vs. nonvoluntary).

Hypothesis 2 asked whether strong commitment promotes enhanced willingness to accommodate rather than retaliate when a partner behaves poorly. This prediction received moderate support, in that congruent evidence was revealed in four out of six analyses (i.e., in all analyses but the most conservative tests). Thus, and consistent with previous research, long-term orientation toward a relationship appears to promote a variety of pro-relationship behaviors – behaviors that communicate the individual's pro-relationship motives, induce reciprocal benevolent acts from the partner, and promote healthy functioning over the course of an extended relationship. Moreover, and consistent with Hypothesis 3, commitment partially mediates the effects on accommodation of the three investment model variables. Causal modeling analyses revealed that after accounting for the association between commitment and accommodation, the direct effect of the investment model variables was reduced by about 15% (i.e., their direct effect varied from .24 to .27, whereas their indirect effect varied from .08 to .11). These results are compatible with our representation of commitment as a broad, relationship-specific motive that "embodies" existing circumstances of interdependence, serving as the internal mediator of the effects of investment model variables.

Hypothesis 4 suggested that accommodation stands as one important mechanism by which committed individuals sustain healthy relationships. Indeed, in five of six analyses, self-reported willingness to accommodate was associated with enhanced dyadic adjustment. In previous research we have found that pro-relationship motivation is more powerfully linked with inhibiting destructive impulses (i.e., inhibiting exit and neglect) than with enhancing constructive reactions (i.e., enhancing voice and loyalty; e.g., Yovetich & Rusbult, 1994). Therefore, follow-up analyses split the measure of total accommodation into two components – constructive accommodation (voice and loyalty) versus retaliative behavior (exit and neglect) – to determine whether the components exert parallel effects on couple health. In the current work, both components of accommodation tended to exhibit significant links with couple functioning, although the ability to inhibit retaliative behavior was descriptively more impactful than was the inclination to enhance constructive reactions.

Previous research has also suggested that the sense of well-being in a relationship may be more powerfully linked to perceptions of the partner's motives and behavior than to perceptions of one's own motives and behavior (e.g., Rusbult et al., 1986b). Therefore a second set of follow-up analyses asked whether individual reports of couple functioning were more strongly influenced by the individual's own tendencies to accommodate or by the individual's perceptions of the partner's tendencies to accommodate. These analyses revealed substantially stronger effects for perceptions of the partner's accommodation, suggesting that during the early years of marriage – and perhaps over the entire course of a relationship – trust in the partner's benevolence and pro-relationship orientation may be a key to understanding couple functioning. Indeed, research examining the links among commitment, accommodation, and trust suggests that: (a) trust is enhanced by the perception that one's partner is willing to accommodate, or to depart from immediate self-interest for the good of the relationship; and (b) trust represents confidence in the strength and quality of the partner's commitment (Wieselquist, Rusbult, Foster, & Agnew, 1997).

Hypothesis 5 proposed that if commitment indeed stands as a central relationship-specific motive that promotes a wide range of pro-relationship behaviors, then strong commitment should be associated with enhanced dyadic adjustment. The analyses reported above provided good support for this prediction, in that the commitment-adjustment link was significant in five of six tests. Beyond this, Hypothesis 6 suggested that if accommodation stands as one of the specific mechanisms by which committed individuals sustain healthy ongoing relationships, willingness to accommodate should partially mediate the commitment-adjustment association. In support of this prediction, causal modeling analyses revealed that accommodation partially but not wholly mediates the effects of commitment: After accounting for the association between accommodation and adjustment, the direct effect of commitment was reduced by about 10% (i.e., the direct effect of commitment varied from .32 to .53, whereas its indirect effect varied from .23 to .40). Moreover, causal modeling analyses revealed that after accounting for the effects of both accommodation and commitment, the direct effect of the investment model variables was reduced by about 60% (i.e., their direct effect varied from .53 to .80, whereas their indirect effect varied from .08 to .11). These results are compatible with the portrayal of commitment as a central relationship-specific motive, and with the portrayal of accommodation as one of the specific mechanisms by which committed partners maintain ongoing relationships.

Hypothesis 7 predicted that experience in marriage is cumulative, and that over time, relationship-specific habits and motives should exert increasingly powerful effects on couple functioning. Consistent with this line of reasoning, analyses including interactions with time revealed moderate support for the prediction that over the course of the first few years of marriage, the accommodation-adjustment association becomes increasingly powerful. In addition, parallel analyses revealed good support for the prediction that over time, the commitment-adjustment link becomes increasingly powerful. Thus relationships indeed appear to develop unique histories that are embodied in relationship-specific motives and response tendencies. Over time, these motives and response tendencies become increasingly potent determinants of couple functioning.

What are the implications of these results for our knowledge of marital phenomena? What does an interdependence analysis contribute to our understanding of key processes in marriage? Several theoretical orientations have been advanced to provide a broad framework in which to understand behavior in relationships, including the attachment orientation (Hazan & Shaver, 1994), the evolutionary-biological orientation (Buss & Schmitt, 1993), the social-learning orientation (cf. Gottman, 1979; Patterson, 1982), and the social-cognitive orientation (Baldwin, 1992; Fletcher & Fincham, 1991). In what ways does the interdependence orientation (Kelley, 1979; Kelley & Thibaut, 1978) complement these approaches? First, whereas the attachment and evolutionary-biological orientations implicate individual-level factors in accounting for the course of an ongoing relationship (e.g., emphasizing acquired mental models of attachment), interdependence theory places relatively greater emphasis on dyad-level processes (e.g., emphasizing mutuality in levels of dependence). And second, although interdependence theory parallels the social learning, social-cognitive, and attachment orientations in suggesting that key marital processes are mediated by internal, cognitive events, interdependence theory places equal or greater emphasis on the "reality" of interdependence structure in shaping behavior in ongoing relationships. At the same time, it should be clear that (a) the attachment and evolutionary-biological orientations provide a more detailed account of the specific "concerns" that consciously or unconsciously guide behavior in marriage (e.g., genetic fitness), and (b) the social learning and social-cognitive orientations provide a more detailed account of the specific mechanisms by which relationship-specific motives shape marital processes (e.g., benevolent attributions regarding partner behavior during conflict).

Directions for Future Research

The analyses reported in this chapter clearly represent no more than a first, cursory analysis of the full range of issues that will ultimately be addressed using the data from our ongoing longitudinal study. To begin with, our analyses were based on early data from the study, and did not include data from Times 4 through 6. Also, our analyses were based on a subset of our larger sample – the first 57 couples to complete research activities at Times 1 through 3. In addition, at the time this chapter was prepared we had coded only a subset of the conversations from Time 2 laboratory sessions, so the analyses employing behavioral measures of accommodation were based on a very small sample of couples. Moreover, this chapter did not report analyses concerning an important criterion of couple health – breakup. Thus far, 13 of our couples have separated; we anticipate that we may have as many as 20 or so breakups by the end of the project. Although it is morbid to bemoan the low base rate of this key criterion variable, we nevertheless look forward to examining the predictors of this rather unambiguous indicator of relationship malfunctioning.

In addition, the range of theoretical issues addressed in this chapter was limited in several respects: First, the analyses only began to explore the dynamics of change over time in the links among model variables. Second, the analyses only began to take advantage of the fact that we have obtained data from both partners – we have only begun to examine truly *interdependent* aspects of marriage (e.g., mutuality of accommodation). Third, owing to limited space, this chapter presents no evidence regarding gender differences in either mean levels of the variables we have examined or in the strength of association among model variables. And fourth, there are scores of theoretical issues to be addressed in this project that we have not even begun to explore – issues such as the effects of accommodation on individual well-being, the role of emotional reactions and cognitive interpretations in promoting or inhibiting willingness to accommodate, the development of trust and the role of trust in promoting maintenance activities, and the role of dispositions in motivating maintenance activities. Such questions remain to be addressed in further analyses employing data from this project.

Conclusions

This work complements and extends previous studies of marital processes in several important respects. First, the early results of our study replicate previous researchers' observation that in comparison with poorly functioning relationships, partners in well-functioning relationships exhibit greater tendencies to accommodate – to inhibit the impulse to react destructively to a partner's potentially destructive act, instead behaving in a constructive manner. Second, our findings extend previous studies by asking *why* some partners are willing to accommodate whereas others are not. We have suggested that commitment level is a central relationship-specific motive, and that strong commitment to a marriage promotes greater willingness to accommodate. Our analyses not only provided support for this assertion, but also demonstrated the plausibility of a model in which commitment is assumed to mediate the effects on accommodation of other features of interdependence (e.g., perceived quality of alternatives, investments in a marriage). Third, given our analysis of relationship maintenance mechanisms, it becomes clear that accommodation stands as just one of several specific mechanisms through which committed individuals sustain their relationships – that is, the tendency to accommodate only partly mediates the link between commitment and dyadic adjustment. Thus we hope that this work begins to illuminate our understanding of both *how* and *why* some relationships persist and thrive, whereas other promising relationships do not.

References

Axelrod, R. (1984). *The evolution of cooperation.* New York: Basic Books.

Baldwin, M. W. (1992). Relational schemas and the processing of social information. *Psychological Bulletin, 112,* 461–484.

Baron, R. M., & Kenny, D. A. (1986). The moderator-mediator variable distinction in social psychological research: Conceptual, strategic, and statistical considerations. *Journal of Personality and Social Psychology, 51,* 1173–1182.

Billings, A. (1979). Conflict resolution in distressed and nondistressed married couples. *Journal of Consulting and Clinical Psychology, 47,* 368–376.

Birchler, G. R., Weiss, R. L., & Vincent, J. P. (1975). Multimethod analysis of social reinforcement exchange between maritally distressed and nondistressed spouse and stranger dyads. *Journal of Personality and Social Psychology, 31,* 349–360.

Buss, D. M., & Schmitt, D. P. (1993). Sexual strategies theory: An evolutionary perspective on human mating. *Psychological Review, 100,* 204–232.

Cohen, J., & Cohen, P. (1975). *Applied multiple regression/correlation analysis for the behavioral sciences.* New York: Wiley.

Dehue, F. M. J., McClintock, C. G., & Liebrand, W. B. G. (1993). Social value related response latencies: Unobtrusive evidence for individual differences in information processing. *European Journal of Social Psychology, 23,* 273–293.

Dillman, D. A. (1978). *Mail and telephone surveys: The total design method.* New York: Wiley.

Felmlee, D., Sprecher, S., & Bassin, E. (1990). The dissolution of intimate relationships: A hazard model. *Social Psychology Quarterly, 53,* 13–30.

Fletcher, G. J. O., & Fincham, F. D. (Eds.) (1991). *Cognition in close relationships.* Hillsdale, NJ: Erlbaum.

Folger, J. P., & Poole, M. S. (1984). *Working through conflict.* Glenview, IL: Scott, Foresman.

Gottman, J. M. (1979). *Marital interaction: Experimental investigations.* New York: Academic Press.

Gottman, J. M., & Krokoff, L. J. (1989). Marital interaction and satisfaction: A longitudinal view. *Journal of Consulting and Clinical Psychology, 57,* 47–52.

Gottman, J. G., Markman, H. J., & Notarius, C. I. (1977). The topography of marital conflict: A sequential analysis of verbal and nonverbal behavior. *Journal of Marriage and the Family, 39,* 461–478.

Greenshaft, J. L. (1980). Perceptual and defensive style variables in marital discord. *Social Behavior and Personality, 8,* 81–84.

Hazan, C., & Shaver, P. R. (1994). Attachment as an organizational framework for research on close relationships. *Psychological Inquiry, 5,* 1–22.

Hirschman, A. O. (1970). *Exit, voice, and loyalty: Responses to decline in firms, organizations, and states.* Cambridge, MA: Harvard University Press.

Holmes, J. G. (1981). The exchange process in close relationships: Microbehavior and macromotives. In M. J. Lerner and S. C. Lerner (Eds.), *The justice motive in social behavior* (pp. 261–284). New York: Plenum.

Huston, T. L., & Ashmore, R. D. (1986). Women and men in personal relationships. In R. D. Ashmore & F. K. Del Boca (Eds.), *The social psychology of female–male relations* (pp. 167–210). Orlando, FL: Academic Press.

Ickes, W., Bissonnette, V., Garcia, S., & Stinson, L. L. (1990). Implementing and using the dyadic interaction paradigm. In C. Hendrick & M. S. Clark (Eds.), *Review of personality and social psychology* (Vol. 11, pp. 16–44). Newbury Park, CA: Sage.

Jacobson, N. S., Follette, W. C., & McDonald, D. W. (1982). Reactivity to positive and negative behavior in distressed and nondistressed married couples. *Journal of Consulting and Clinical Psychology, 50,* 706–714.

Johnson, D. J., & Rusbult, C. E. (1989). Resisting temptation: Devaluation of alternative partners as a means of maintaining commitment in close relationships. *Journal of Personality and Social Psychology, 57,* 967–980.

Kelley, H. H. (1979). *Personal relationships: Their structures and processes.* Hillsdale, NJ: Erlbaum.

Kelley, H. H., & Stahelski, A. J. (1970). Social interaction basis of cooperators' and competitors' beliefs about others. *Journal of Personality and Social Psychology, 16,* 66–91.

Kelley, H. H., & Thibaut, J. W. (1978). *Interpersonal relations: A theory of interdependence.* New York: Wiley.

Krokoff, L. J., Gottman, J. M., & Haas, S. D. (1989). Validation of a global rapid couples interaction scoring system. *Behavioral Assessment, 11,* 65–79.

Lund, M. (1985). The development of investment and commitment scales for predicting continuity of personal relationships. *Journal of Social and Personal Relationships, 2,* 3–23.

McClintock, C. G., & Liebrand, W. B. G. (1988). The role of interdependence structure, individual value orientation and other's strategy in social decision making: A transformational analysis. *Journal of Personality and Social Psychology, 55,* 396–409.

Margolin, G., & Wampold, B. E. (1981). Sequential analysis of conflict and accord in distressed and nondistressed marital partners. *Journal of Consulting and Clinical Psychology, 49,* 554–567.

Markman, H. J. (1981). Prediction of marital distress: A five-year follow-up. *Journal of Consulting and Clinical Psychology, 49,* 760–762.

Patterson, G. R. (1982). *Coercive family process.* Eugene, OR: Castalia.

Rusbult, C. E. (1980). Commitment and satisfaction in romantic associations: A test of the investment model. *Journal of Experimental Social Psychology, 16,* 172–186.

Rusbult, C. E. (1983). A longitudinal test of the investment model: The development (and deterioration) of satisfaction and commitment in heterosexual involvements. *Journal of Personality and Social Psychology, 45,* 101–117.

Rusbult, C. E. (1987). Responses to dissatisfaction in close relationships: The exit-voice-loyalty-neglect model. In D. Perlman & S. Duck (Eds.), *Intimate relationships: Development, dynamics, and deterioration* (pp. 209–237). Newbury Park, CA: Sage.

Rusbult, C. E. (1993). Understanding responses to dissatisfaction in close relationships: The exit-voice-loyalty-neglect model. In S. Worchel & J. A. Simpson (Eds.), *Conflict between people and groups: Causes, processes, and resolutions* (pp. 30–59). Chicago: Nelson-Hall.

Rusbult, C. E., & Buunk, B. P. (1993). Commitment processes in close relationships: An interdependence analysis. *Journal of Social and Personal Relationships, 10,* 175–204.

Rusbult, C. E., Johnson, D. J., & Morrow, G. D. (1986a). Determinants and consequences of exit, voice, loyalty, and neglect: Responses to dissatisfaction in adult romantic involvements. *Human Relations, 39,* 45–63.

Rusbult, C. E., Johnson, D. J., & Morrow, G. D. (1986b). Impact of couple patterns of problem solving on distress and nondistress in dating relationships. *Journal of Personality and Social Psychology, 50,* 744–753.

Rusbult, C. E., Johnson, D. J., & Morrow, G. D. (1986c). Predicting satisfaction and commitment in adult romantic involvements: An assessment of the generalizability of the investment model. *Social Psychology Quarterly, 49,* 81–89.

Rusbult, C. E., Morrow, G. D., & Johnson, D. J. (1987). Self-esteem and problem solving behavior in close relationships. *British Journal of Social Psychology, 26,* 293–303.

Rusbult, C. E., Van Lange, P. A. M., Verette, J., Yovetich, N. A., & Wildschut, R. T. (1997). A functional analysis of perceived superiority in close relationships. Unpublished manuscript, University of North Carolina at Chapel Hill.

Rusbult, C. E., Verette, J., Whitney, G. A., Slovik, L. F., & Lipkus, I. (1991). Accommodation processes in close relationships: Theory and preliminary empirical evidence. *Journal of Personality and Social Psychology, 60,* 53–78.

Rusbult, C. E., & Zembrodt, I. M. (1983). Responses to dissatisfaction in romantic involvements: A multidimensional scaling analysis. *Journal of Experimental Social Psychology, 19,* 274–293.

Rusbult, C. E., Zembrodt, I. M., & Gunn, L. K. (1982). Exit, voice, loyalty, and neglect: Responses to dissatisfaction in romantic involvements. *Journal of Personality and Social Psychology, 43,* 1230–1242.

Rusbult, C. E., Zembrodt, I. M., & Iwaniszek, J. (1986). The impact of gender and sex-role orientation on responses to dissatisfaction in close relationships. *Sex Roles, 15,* 1–20.

Simpson, J. A. (1987). The dissolution of romantic relationships: Factors involved in relationship stability and emotional distress. *Journal of Personality and Social Psychology, 53,* 683–692.

Simpson, J. A., Gangestad, S. W., & Lerma, M. (1990). Perception of physical attractiveness: Mechanisms involved in the maintenance of romantic relationships. *Journal of Personality and Social Psychology, 59,* 1192–1201.

Spanier, G. B. (1976). Measuring dyadic adjustment: New scales for assessing the quality of marriage and similar dyads. *Journal of Marriage and the Family, 38,* 15–28.

Surra, C. A., & Longstreth, M. (1990). Similarity of outcomes, interdependence, and conflict in dating relationships. *Journal of Personality and Social Psychology, 59,* 501–516.

Van Lange, P. A. M., & Liebrand, W. B. G. (1991). Social value orientation and intelligence: A test of the goal-prescribes-rationality principle. *European Journal of Social Psychology, 21,* 273–292.

Van Lange, P. A. M., & Rusbult, C. E. (1995). My relationship is better than – and not as bad as – yours is: The perception of superiority in close relationships. *Personality and Social Psychology Bulletin, 21,* 32–44.

Van Lange, P. A. M., Rusbult, C. E., Drigotas, S. M., Arriaga, X. B., Witcher, B. S.,

& Cox, C. L. (1997). Willingness to sacrifice in close relationships. *Journal of Personality and Social Psychology, 72,* 1373–1395.

Weiss, R. L. (1980). Strategic behavioral marital therapy: Toward a model for assessment and intervention. In J. P. Vincent (Ed.), *Advances in family intervention, assessment and theory* (Vol. 1, pp. 229–271). Greenwich, CT: JAI Press.

Wieselquist, J., Rusbult, C. E., Foster, C. A., & Agnew, C. R. (1997). Commitment and trust in close relationships. Unpublished manuscript, University of North Carolina at Chapel Hill.

Yovetich, N. A., & Rusbult, C. E. (1994). Accommodative behavior in close relationships: Exploring transformation of motivation. *Journal of Experimental Social Psychology, 30,* 138–164.

4 The Psychological Infrastructure of Courtship and Marriage: The Role of Personality and Compatibility in Romantic Relationships

Ted L. Huston and Renate M. Houts

This chapter examines the extent to which relationships are structured in particular ways by the partners' personality characteristics and their compatibility. Three models pertaining to the psychological and interpersonal roots of the development and deterioration of intimate relationships have been proposed by social scientists. (1) The *disillusionment* model portrays lovers as driven to put their best foot forward and as inattentive to each other's – and the relationship's – shortcomings until after the wedding knot is tied (Huston, 1994; Swann, De La Ronde, & Hixon, 1994; Waller, 1938). (2) The *perpetual problems* model, in contrast, suggests that the interplay between the partners' dispositions gets played out during courtship and that, as a consequence, the partners develop feelings and views about each other that reflect the underlying, relatively stable, psychological infrastructure of the relationship (Burgess & Wallin, 1953; Heaton, Albrecht, & Martin, 1985; Huston, 1994; Surra, 1990). (3) The *accommodation* model posits that when problematic dispositions or incompatible desires surface in a relationship they initially create disappointments and antagonisms; over time, however, partners who remain together maintain a satisfactory bond by adapting their expectations or otherwise coming to terms with their situation (Bernard, 1964; Heaton et al., 1985; Rusbult, Verette, Whitney, Slovik, & Lipkus, 1991).

Figure 4.1a depicts the disillusionment model, a model that proposes that during courtship potentially troublesome aspects of personality are put out of view and that couples are inclined to seek out common ground, rather than test their compatibility. When problems or incompatibilities appear during courtship, partners are disposed to redefine them as less threatening

The authors would like to thank John Caughlin, Gilbert Geis, Marika Ripke, and Laura Shebilske for helpful comments on an earlier draft of this manuscript. Work on this chapter was supported by grants from the National Science Foundation (SBR-9311845) and the National Institute of Mental Health (MH33938).

114

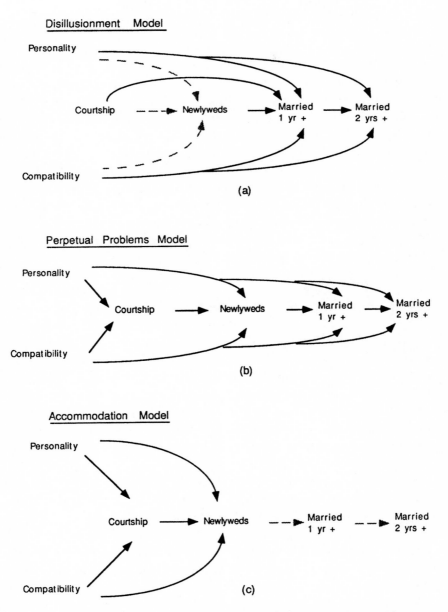

Figure 4.1. Models for conceptualizing the psychological and interpersonal roots of the development and deterioration of relationships.

(cf. Murray & Holmes, 1993; Waller, 1938). Premarital partners who fail to withhold vexatious behavior, or who focus on it unduly when it surfaces, are likely to become disillusioned and break off the relationship. The idea that courting partners on their way to the altar feel a sense of euphoria and suppress behavior and thoughts that might puncture their romance suggests that personality and compatibility issues will not have much of an impact on relationships during courtship. That courting partners carefully monitor their behavior and filter events through rose-colored glasses is reflected in the absence of arrows in Figure 4.1a linking personality and compatibility to courtship.

The problematic personality dispositions and incompatibilities that lurk beneath the surface like an undetected virus during courtship are thought to become increasingly evident in marriage. The arrow that bypasses the new-lywed period to link courtship to marriage after one year illustrates this idea. With commitment, according to Waller (1938), idealized images give way to more realistic ones because the intimacy of marriage forces hidden elements of each partner's personality into the open. (Had Waller been writing today, he undoubtedly would have recognized the greater difficulty couples who live together before marriage would have in maintaining idealized images.)

The increasing strength of the connections between personality and com-patibility during marriage is shown in Figure 4.1a by the dotted line linking personality and compatibility to marriage when couples are newlyweds, fol-lowed by solid lines linking personality and compatibility to marriage there-after. Because the partners' behavior in marriage ought to increasingly re-flect their personality, relationships ought to stabilize over time and spouses ought to improve in their ability to separate the wheat (enduring qualities) from the chaff (images that are fictional).

The perpetual problems model (Burgess & Wallin, 1953; Huston, 1994), shown in Figure 4.1b, takes the view that courting couples behave much as they do after they are married and suggests that the problems that surface during courtship often persist into marriage. This model also assumes that once individuals' psychological dispositions surface in the relationship, the partners' feelings of love and satisfaction are affected regardless of whether couples are courting or married. Moreover, problems that surface during courtship are thought to persist and continue to erode partners' feelings to-ward one another into marriage. Proponents of this early determinism view (e.g., Burgess & Wallin, 1953) argue that courting couples enter marriage with their eyes open to each other's character strengths and flaws. Most peo-ple, they point out, are aware that in order to marry a real person instead of a fantasized mate they must compromise their ideals. The idea that problems associated with personality and compatibility surface during courtship and persist into marriage is illustrated in Figure 4.1b by the solid lines throughout the diagram.

The accommodation model (Bernard, 1964; Heaton et al., 1985; Waller, 1938), shown in Figure 4.1c, suggests that partners adapt to problems that surface in the relationship. The Norwegian dramatist Henrik Ibsen (1959), in *The Wild Duck,* suggests that a marriage based on complete confidence, unqualified frankness on both sides, and no dissimulation is a marriage in which the spouses have "an agreement for the mutual forgiveness of sin" (p. 283). The accommodation model portrayed in Figure 4.1c illustrates this general idea by showing that personality and compatibility affect relationships during courtship and early in marriage but, with time, personality and compatibility issues recede into the background. The timing of the initial intrusion of personality problems or incompatibilities may be earlier or later than shown in Figure 4.1c. A version of the accommodation model could be rendered, for example, in which personality and compatibility issues do not arise until after couples become married.

The disillusionment and perpetual problems models are similar in that problems are seen to persist once they surface, whereas the accommodation model suggests that the impact of problems that are worked through fades in time. This adaptation can take several forms: People married to moody spouses may learn to take with a grain of salt what their partner says when in a bad mood; couples who experience a high degree of conflict early in marriage may learn to avoid certain issues or may spend less time together, so as to maintain a sense of equanimity.

Personality as a Root Cause of Marital Happiness and Distress

The idea that relational happiness and distress can be traced to the psychological makeup of the partners has a long history in the social sciences. More than 50 years ago, Terman and his colleagues (1938) proposed that "in a large proportion of unsuccessful marriages it is possible to discover either in the husband or the wife, or perhaps both, numerous elements of the unhappy temperament and evidence that these elements have played a causal role" (pp. 110–111). Terman et al. (1938) found that unhappily married men and women exhibit characteristics very similar to a component of personality known as *negative affectivity* (Watson & Clark, 1984). Negative affectivity reflects a tendency to be anxious and emotionally labile. Individuals high in negative affectivity are more inclined to report distress or discomfort, more likely to be introspective and honest with themselves, and more inclined to dwell on their own and other people's shortcomings (Watson & Clark, 1984). Recent studies have shown that negative affectivity captures much of what scales measuring "neuroticism," "anxiety," and "emotional stability" capture (Noller, Law, & Comrey, 1987; Watson & Clark, 1984). "Neuroticism," for example, has been found in several studies to relate to a person's inability to create a self-satisfying and enduring marriage (e.g., Bentler & Newcomb, 1978; Burgess & Wallin, 1953; Kelly & Conley, 1987).

Few efforts have been mounted to explore the causal pathways linking personality to relationship functioning. Buss (1991) has shown that husbands' and wives' personality – particularly "emotional instability" and "agreeableness" – is linked to their tendency to complain that their spouse acts in a moody, jealous, or dependent manner, or otherwise upsets them by being condescending or self-centered. However, Buss (1991) did not explore directly whether the complaints were merited by the partner's behavior, or if they reflected a predisposition on the part of the reporting spouse to see the partner in negative terms. Buss (1992) also has explored connections between one spouse's personality and the other's view of their behavior. Husbands and wives low in agreeableness, compared with those who were high in agreeableness, were seen by their spouses as more self-centered. Agreeableness was implicated in a broader array of behavior for the husbands than for the wives. Husbands low in agreeableness were also seen by their wives as more condescending, dependent, neglecting, moody, and sexually aggressive. Buss (1992) also found that the more emotionally unstable and less agreeable spouses are, the more they reportedly use coercive strategies to get their way.

A recent study (Karney, Bradbury, Fincham, & Sullivan, 1994) of married couples, however, found no connections between spouses' negative affectivity and their partners' tendency to see their behavior as caused by global, stable, negatively valenced dispositions. This presumed lack of a connection may reflect a tendency of people to see qualities such as moodiness and emotional lability as situationally anchored rather than as enduring dispositions. Husbands and wives high in negative affectivity in the Karney et al. (1994) study, however, tended to make more negative attributions for their partners' behavior. Husbands' level of negative affectivity and their tendency to view their partners' negative behavior as reflective of negatively valenced dispositions was related to both their own and their wives' marital satisfaction. Wives' negative affectivity, in contrast, was related only to their own marital satisfaction and then only insofar as it was reflected in their tendency to make negative attributions about their husbands' behavior.

The focus on personality characteristics that undermine intimate relationships provides only a partial view of how such characteristics may affect courtship, marriage, and other intimate relationships. A communal orientation to others, as indexed by "expressiveness" (Spence, Helmreich, & Stapp, 1974) may be a key "protective" personality quality that should enhance marital satisfaction (Antill, 1983; Bradbury, Campbell, & Fincham, 1995; Lamke, 1989; Lamke, Sollie, Durbin, & Fitzpatrick, 1995). The self-descriptive adjectives and phrases that define expressiveness include "kind," "gentle," "aware of others' feelings," "able to devote self to others," "helpful," "warm," and "emotional," all of which might reduce conflict in relationships. People high in "psychological femininity," or expressiveness, are more likely to respond constructively when an intimate partner has behaved poorly (Rusbult, et al., 1991), less likely to communicate negative feelings, and more inclined to express positive feelings during interaction (Burger & Jacobson, 1979). Since responsiveness tends to be reciprocated (Kelley, 1979; Rusbult et al., 1991), it serves to build up positive feelings. Among happily married couples, husbands' and wives' psychological femininity is unrelated to how affectionately spouses behaved toward each other. Among less than happily married couples, however, psychological femininity was strongly associated with the expression of affection (Huston & Geis, 1993). Husbands' psychological femininity also relates to the extent to which spouses occupy a central place in each other's day-to-day leisure activities and husbands' proportional involvement in household work (Huston & Geis, 1993).

Compatibility, Courtship, and Marriage

Compatibility theories of mate selection and marriage contend that individuals who are matched in specified characteristics have an increased likelihood of forming harmonious and mutually satisfying relationships (Levinger & Rands, 1985). The empirical work on marital compatibility has focused almost exclusively on the extent to which partners who marry have similar social, psychological, and physical characteristics (Kerckhoff, 1974; Surra, 1990) and whether such similarity, when it prevails, covaries with marital satisfaction (e.g., Heaton & Pratt, 1990; Crohan, 1992) and marital stability (e.g., Hill, Rubin, & Peplau, 1976; Kurdek, 1993). Causal linkages between compatibility, defined in terms of combinations of partner attributes, and the interpersonal processes through which compatibility affects mate selection, marital satisfaction, and marital stability have yet to be explored.

The compatibility between partners' preferences and predilections presumably influences the likelihood that the couple will agree or disagree about various matters. Courting and married couples determine what to do with their free time, whether to spend it together or apart, and they come to create an understanding of what it means to be the man or the woman in their particular relationship. The extent to which couples have leisure interests in common and role preferences that mesh ought to be related to how much they enjoy each other's company, how well they get along, and how they feel about each other and their relationship. Courting partners and spouses experience the consequences of each other's attitudes and preferences. If, for example, a man and woman have few leisure interests in common, or if the man believes that women should care for the house and the woman believes that the responsibility for household work should be shared, many arguments may ensue. The less well matched partners are, the more negativity they are likely to express toward each other, the more ambivalence they are likely to feel about their relationship, and the more turbulent their relationship is likely to be. Couples who are well matched, in contrast, presumably will be more affectionate and engaged in the relationship.

Our data show that newly married couples are significantly more likely to be matched in leisure interests and role preferences than they would be if they were randomly paired with others in our sample (Houts, Robins, & Huston, 1996). Nonetheless, considerable variation exists among the couples with regard to their overall compatibility. The average person could expect to match with a bit less than 60% of the people of the opposite sex with regard to their liking for any one, average, leisure activity (59%), or in the role preferences regarding who should perform any average family task (56%). Given the small and nonsignificant correlations between the likelihood that people can find a match with regard to leisure interests and the likelihood that they can find a match in role performance preferences, we can treat them as independent assessments. Therefore, it is reasonable to illustrate the conjoint probability of being matched with any particular person in the pool of potential spouses by multiplying the probabilities of being matched on each particular attribute.

Given that the probabilities of finding a partner whose preferences match one's own on any one leisure interest or role performance preference are 59% and 56%, respectively, the conjoint probability of finding a compatible partner with regard to *both* leisure interests and role preferences is 33%. In addition, if there is a third independent area in which the average probability of finding a compatible partner is 50%, the conjoint probability of finding a compatible mate on *all three* dimensions is decreased to approximately 17%. It is clear that as the number of independent dimensions a person considers when choosing a mate increases, the likelihood of finding a spouse who meets *all* the criteria decreases considerably. The average person will be matched on *all three* dimensions with only 1 out of every 6 people he or she dates. Since the average person in our sample reported dating only five people more than casually, on average, achieving multidimensional compatibility is a lofty, and often unrealistic, goal for most individuals (see Cate & Lloyd, 1992). Most married couples are compatible in some areas and incompatible in others. Thus particular areas of compatibility will have only weak associations at best with relationship processes and outcomes. Moreover, as the accommodation model suggests, spouses in relationships that endure may learn to work around their differences.

Our data pertain to *personality* and *compatibility* as they are linked to (a) couples' courtship experiences; (b) their marital behavior patterns; (c) the spouses' feelings about each other and their marriage, and (d) the spouses' characterizations of each other's personality qualities. The project described below includes data on both partners' personality; the development of their relationship during courtship; patterns of socioemotional behavior in marriage (i.e., affectional expression and negativity); and both spouses' feelings of love, ambivalence, and marital satisfaction. The chapter summarizes research on how the qualities partners bring to their premarital and marital relationship shape the course of the relationship. We focus on partners' personality qualities and their level of compatibility in connection with the evolution of their romantic relationships.

Overview of the PAIR Project

The PAIR Project, a longitudinal study that traces romantic relationships back into courtship and forward into the early years of marriage, was designed to identify the extent to which the course of marriage can be foreseen from data gathered about the courtship when couples were newlyweds (see Huston, 1994).[1] Marriage license records maintained in a four-county area in central Pennsylvania were used to identify potential participants. Prospective participants (couples in which neither partner had previously married) were contacted and asked to participate. The 168 couples who agreed (42% of the eligible pool) did not differ from couples who declined to participate in terms of their age, educational background, or father's occupational status, as determined by information contained on the marriage licenses (Robins, 1985). The average participant was white, young (wives' average age at marriage = 21.1 years; husbands' average age = 23.6 years), had a high school diploma, and was raised in a working-class family. Nonetheless, the sample included participants from a broad range of educational levels and social backgrounds.

Data Collection Plan

The study was initiated in 1981, with each couple being interviewed 2 months after they were wed and at yearly intervals over the following 2 years. At each phase, couples were first interviewed by a pair of trained interviewers, the husband by a man and the wife by a woman. The interviews lasted about 3 hours and took place wherever the couple preferred, usually in their home. After the face-to-face interviews, couples were telephoned nine times, over a 2- to 3-week period, and asked to provide information about their participation in leisure and household activities and their marital interactions over the 24-hour period ending shortly before the call (for more complete information about the data collection procedures, see Huston, 1994; Huston, McHale, Crouter, 1986). Of the 168 couples, 129 stayed married for the duration of the study and participated in at least the face-to-face interview throughout the course of the study. Thirteen of the original 168 couples (7.7%) were known to have divorced prior to what would have been their second anniversary; a group of 12 and an additional group of 14 did not participate in the second and third interviews, respectively. Only a handful of couples who participated as newlyweds (Phase 1) declined to continue with the study, although each year some participants chose not to take part in the more time-consuming sequence of telephone interviews.

Measures

Table 4.1 provides a summary of the measures relevant to the present chapter, organized according to the proposed causal flow of the models shown in Figure 4.1. The table shows how each construct was measured, how reliable the measures were, and when the data were gathered.

Stable/General Attributes. The personality constructs (Section A of Table 4.1) were measured with paper-and-pencil instruments administered individually to the partners when they were newlyweds. Previous research on the impact of personality on marriage led us to focus on two personality constructs: "anxiety" (Cattell, Eber, & Tatsuoka, 1970) and "expressiveness" (Spence et al., 1974). Anxiety, as measured by Cattell's IGPF (IPAT Staff, 1986) aptly describes a personality disposition that others have termed emotional stability (John, 1990), neuroticism (Conley, 1985; Mc-Crae & Costa, 1985), and negative affectivity (Watson & Clark, 1984). The expressiveness scale developed by Spence and her colleagues (1974) captures key elements of "psychological femininity." The scale does not assess body type, looks, dress, leisure interests, and sexuality, however, all of which are part of the cultural meaning of femininity (Spence, 1984).

It is theorized that anxiety undermines marital relationships (Bentler & Newcomb, 1978; Kelly & Conley, 1987), whereas expressiveness, or "psychological femininity" enhances marriage (Antill, 1983; Lamke, 1989; Lamke et al., 1995). These personality traits are placed antecedent to courtship and marital patterns because they are seen as measuring stable, general dispositions and because a body of evidence shows that personality traits are generally stable during the adult years (Caspi & Bem, 1990; Conley, 1984; Costa & McCrae, 1988).

Compatibility. As noted earlier, two types of compatibility (Section B of Table 4.1) – similarity in leisure interests and marital role preferences – seem particularly germane to the development of commitment during courtship and early marriage (Houts et al., 1996; Levinger & Rands, 1985). To assess leisure preferences, partners were individually asked each time we interviewed them to sort 50 cards, each card identifying a specific leisure activity, into seven piles representing the degree to which they liked or disliked the activity. We recategorized the responses into three broad categories reflecting how much the activities were liked or disliked (liked, neutral, disliked). Compatibility was operationalized as the proportion of the activities both partners jointly liked, felt neutral about, or disliked. With regard to role preferences, partners were individually given a set of cards, each of which listed a household task, and asked to place each card in one of four piles indicating whom they would prefer to do the task all or most of the time: (a) the husband, (b) the wife, (c) the spouses together, or (d) the spouses apart (but with the responsibility equally shared). Because the third and fourth options indicate a preference for equal responsibility, these choices were collapsed. Compatibility in marital role preferences was indexed by the proportion of the 26 tasks the partners assigned to the same category. Couples' compatibility with regard to both leisure interests and role preferences is generally stable across time: Leisure interests – Phases 1→2 r = .53, Phases 2→3 r = .58; Role preferences – Phases 1→2 r = .31, Phases 2→3 r = .45.

Table 4.1. *Summary of measures used*

Type of construct	Description of measure	When measured	Interview type
A. Stable/general attributes			
Personality			
Anxiety	Anxiety (Cattell et al., 1970), a second-order factor in the 16PF Questionnaire, was used to measure a propensity toward moodiness and emotional distress. Test-retest reliability ranges from .78 to .92 (Cattell et al., 1970).	Phase 1	Face-to-face
Expressiveness	The extent to which people ascribe to themselves stereotypical feminine qualities (e.g., kind, helpful to others, aware of others' feelings). Alpha = .82 (Spence et al., 1974).	Phase 1	Face-to-face
B. Compatibility			
Leisure interests	Extent to which leisure preferences and aversions were similar.	Phases 1, 2, & 3	Face-to-face
Role preferences	Extent to which partners were in agreement concerning responsibility for performing of household tasks.	Phases 1, 2, & 3	Face-to-face
C. Properties of relationships			
Features of Courtship			
Hesitancy of commitment	Time in months to move from 25% to 75% probability of marriage (graphing procedure; see Huston, 1994).	Phase 1	Face-to-face
Turbulence	Number of times during the courtship that the probability of marriage declined (graphing procedure; see Huston, 1994).	Phase 1	Face-to-face
Socioemotional behavior			
Conflict	The extent of anger and disagreement reported in the relationship (Braiker & Kelley, 1979). Alphas ranged from .68 to .81[a]	Phases 1 (courtship & marriage), 2, & 3	Face-to-face
Negativity	The number of times each partner enacted 6 negative interpersonal acts each day over 9 days each year, as reported by his or her spouse. Alphas ranged from .78 to .91 (see Huston & Vangelisti, 1991).[a]	Phases 1, 2, & 3	Telephone
Affectional expression	The number of times each partner enacted 7 positive interpersonal acts each day over 9 days each year, as reported by his or her spouse. Alphas ranged from .78 to .84 (see Huston & Vangelisti, 1991).[a]	Phases 1, 2, & 3	Telephone
Maintenance	Efforts to improve the relationship or to resolve problems (Braiker & Kelley, 1979). Alphas ranged from .52 to .76[a]	Phases 1 (courtship & marriage)	Face-to-face

D. Attitudes and dispositions toward the partner

Attraction and satisfaction

Love	Feelings of belonging, closeness, and attachment (Braiker & Kelley, 1979). Alphas ranged from .78 to .91.[a]	Phases 1 (courtship & marriage), 2, & 3	Face-to-face
Ambivalence	Confusion about the partner, anxiety about commitment, concern about loss of independence (Braiker & Kelley, 1979). Alphas ranged from .73 to .83.[a]	Phase 1 (courtship & marriage), 2, & 3	Face-to-face
Marital satisfaction	A global rating of marital satisfaction and ratings of the marriage in terms of a series of bipolar adjectives (e.g., rewarding–disappointing, miserable–enjoyable) (Campbell, Converse, & Rodgers, 1976; Huston & Vangelisti, 1991). Alphas ranged from .63 to .80.[a]	Phases 1, 2, & 3	Face-to-face

Beliefs about partner's personality

| Perceived level of contrariness | The extent to which spouses ascribe to their partner trait adjectives such as hot-tempered, domineering, jealous, stubborn, fault-finding, moody, nosey, and possessive. Alphas ranged from .77 to .84[a] | Phases 1, 2, & 3 | Face-to-face |
| Perceived level of responsiveness | The extent to which spouses ascribe to their partner trait adjectives such as friendly, enthusiastic, polite, cooperative, easygoing, amusing, forgiving, sincere, generous, and energetic. Alphas ranged from .81 to .88.[a] | Phases 1, 2, & 3 | Face-to-face |

[a]Separate alphas were calculated for men and women at each phase of data collection.

Courtship and Marriage. The data we gathered about courtship and marriage can be divided into two broad categories of information. The first category, *Properties of relationships* (Table 4.1, Section C), includes data pertaining to the development of partners' commitment during courtship and how they reportedly got along, both before and after they were married. The second category of information refers to the *attitudes and dispositions* that partners develop toward each other and their relationship (Table 4.1, Section D). The extent to which partners' personality dispositions and their compatibility covary with relationship properties and the partners' feelings toward and their beliefs about each other's psychological makeup at different stages of their involvement has bearing on the tenability of the three models outlined at the outset of this chapter.

The courtship data were gathered through a structured interview procedure whereby the partners, independently, and with the help of an interviewer, reconstructed the development of their commitment to marriage from when they first paired off to when they were married (see Cate, Huston, & Nesselroade, 1986; Huston, 1994; Huston, Surra, Fitzgerald, & Cate, 1981; Surra, 1985). Each spouse constructed a graph depicting changes in the perceived likelihood of marriage over the course of the courtship. The horizontal axis represented "time," with each division corresponding to one month; the vertical axis represented the "chance of marrying the partner."

To prime their memory, participants were first asked to designate along the baseline significant events that occurred during their courtship. They were requested to think about the beginning of their relationship and to indicate with a dot on the graph the chance of marrying their partner, taking into account their own ideas and the feelings they sensed the partner had. They then were asked to identify when they believed the likelihood of marriage had changed and what the probability of marriage was at that point. A dot was marked at the appropriate place on the graph. The interviewees were shown various ways in which the two dots on the graphs could be connected (e.g., by a straight or curved line). Participants then indicated how to draw the line between the points to provide the best representation of the pattern of change over time. They subsequently indicated what led them to believe the chance of marriage had changed. The overall trajectory of the courtship was constructed, from transition to transition, until the progression of change in chance of marriage to the wedding day was complete.

Figure 4.2 shows the shape of several graphs. The graphs created by partners usually were roughly parallel; the collection of graphs created by the various couples, however, shows considerable diversity (Huston, 1994). Much of that diversity can be captured by two measures derived from the

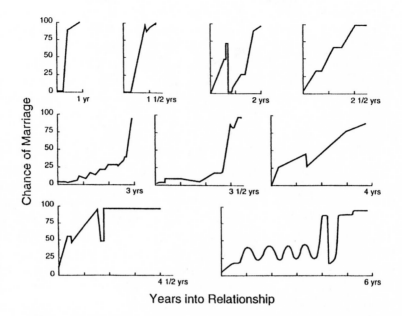

Figure 4.2. Examples of patterns of change in courtship graphs (adapted from Huston, 1994).

graphs: (a) "hesitancy to commit," as indicated by the number of months it took to move from a low (25%) to a high (75%) chance of marriage, and (b) "turbulence," as indicated by the number of times the chance of marriage declined over the course of the courtship. The graph in the upper left-hand corner of Figure 4.2 portrays a courtship in which commitment was fast and smooth; the graph in the lower right-hand corner portrays a slow, rocky courtship, while the other graphs show varying degrees of hesitancy and turbulence.

After finishing the graph, participants were asked to indicate on its baseline the periods during which they were casually dating, regularly dating (with no clear understanding they were a pair), seen by themselves and others as a couple, and committed to marriage. Next, the interviewer pointed to the time period when the participant indicated the two of them considered themselves "a couple" and reminded the person of the events that they had previously said took place during that period. The participants then filled out a questionnaire developed by Braiker and Kelley (1979) designed to assess (a) the amount of *conflict* and negativity in the relationship, (b) the extent to which the partners made efforts to resolve problems or improve the relationship (i.e., *maintenance*), (c) the amount of *love* the partners felt as reflected in feelings of belonging, closeness, and attachment), and (d) the degree of *ambivalence* they felt about the relationship and the anxiety they felt about their loss of independence. Conflict and maintenance are listed in Table 4.1, Section C, as *Properties of Relationships* because they reflect the nature of the partners' overt behavior. Love and ambivalence, however, refer to psychological rather than behavioral phenomena. Therefore they are placed in the section of the table listing *Attitudes and dispositions toward the partner* (Table 4.1, Section D).

Each year the spouses again filled out the Braiker and Kelley (1979) questionnaire, using the previous two months of their marriage as a point of reference. The information about how the partners treat each other, as indexed by the conflict and maintenance items on the Braiker and Kelley (1979) questionnaire, was supplemented by telephone diary data gathered each year from the husbands and wives regarding the extent to which their partners behaved negatively toward them and expressed affection. A series of nine telephone interviews was conducted in each phase during which the spouses independently reported the number of times, if any, their partners enacted six negative behaviors (negativity) and seven positive behaviors (affectional behavior). The six negative behaviors were criticizing or complaining, showing anger or impatience, interrupting, seeming bored or uninterested, dominating conversation, failing to follow through on promises, and doing things known to create annoyance. The positive behaviors included offering approval or compliments, sharing emotions, feelings, or problems and saying "I love you."

The reference point for each telephone interview was always the same 24-hour period for both spouses, typically from 5 p.m. one evening to 5 p.m. the evening of the call. Calls were usually made every other day over a 2- to 3-week period and generally took between 8 and 15 minutes per spouse. The data are aggregated across the telephone interviews to provide a portrait of the affect each partner expressed. The global estimates of conflict provided by the Braiker and Kelley (1979) measure (which is based on spousal ratings on scales using a 2-month period as a reference point) and telephone reports of negativity are significantly correlated, as expected (rs range from .24 to .37). Maintenance and affectional expression are also (with one exception) significantly correlated (rs range from .19 to .34). The telephone diary procedure yields highly reliable and valid data about marital behavior patterns (for further information about the procedure, see Huston & Robins, 1982; Huston, Robins, Atkinson, & McHale, 1987; Huston & Vangelisti, 1991).

The measures of love and ambivalence used to gather information about partners' feelings during courtship were carried into marriage and supplemented with a measure of marital satisfaction (Campbell, Converse, & Rodgers, 1976; Huston & Vangelisti, 1991). The measure requires spouses to evaluate the satisfactoriness of their marriage and, unlike the Locke and Wallace (1959) and Spanier (1976) scales, clearly separates spouses' feelings about their marriage from their ideas concerning what might properly be viewed as the antecedents or behavioral consequences of feeling satisfied (Fincham & Bradbury, 1987; Huston et al., 1986).

Finally, the partners were asked to characterize each other's personality by sorting a set of cards, each containing a different adjective trait, into seven piles forming a Likert-type scale with "1" being not at all like their partner and "7" being very much like their partner. The adjectives were drawn from a more encompassing list of personality-trait words – half of those chosen were likable traits; the other half were disagreeable traits (Anderson, 1968). Based on the assumption that the adjectives captured two broadly based personality dispositions, confirmatory principle components analyses were performed with oblique rotations with the data gathered during each year. Items that loaded .40 or more on the same factor each year and were more strongly loaded on that factor than the other factor were retained. The resulting scales reflect the extent to which the partner is seen as "responsive," on the one hand, and having a "contrary" personality, on the other. Items making up the responsiveness scale included qualities such as pleasant, friendly, cooperative, amusing, forgiving, sincere, and generous. People seen as possessing contrary characteristics are viewed as hot-tempered, domineering, jealous, stubborn, fault-finding, moody, and possessive.

Data Analysis

The data are presented as a collection of bivariate, cross-sectional correlations, organized into a series of tables. This approach was preferred over more complex data analytic strategies, such as those that begin by reducing the data by combining variables, those that use the longitudinal data to try to tease out reciprocal causal processes, or those that attempt to partial out covariance among predictor variables. First, the variables "upstream" in the causal system – gender, personality, and compatibility – are either immutable (gender), known to be highly stable at least over the short-run (personality), or found in preliminary analyses to be reasonably stable (compatibility) (see Houts et al., 1996). Second, the two measures of personality – anxiety and expressiveness – are not correlated with each other or with either measure of compatibility. The two indices of compatibility – leisure interests and role preferences – are also uncorrelated with one another. Moreover, spouses' personality characteristics do not covary significantly with the exception that wives who are relatively more expressive tend to marry men who are lower in anxiety. The correlation is low enough ($r = .21$) that interpretive caution is called for only in cases where either variable is marginally correlated with another variable.

Third, the competing theoretical orientations focus on (a) the stability of the features of relationships across time, (b) whether personality and compatibility ought to first come into play in relationships during courtship, and (c) the strength and stability of the covariation between personality and compatibility, on the one hand, and features of relationships and spouses' views of each other's personality, on the other. At the conclusion of the chapter, we consider the ramifications of the pattern of correlations for the three models discussed earlier and make some proposals regarding the causal pathways through which personality and compatibility affect marriage relationships.

Stability and Change in Relationships over Time

This section uses data gathered from the PAIR project to examine a series of issues pertaining to stability and change in relationships that bear upon the explanatory value of the three models. Stability and change can be examined in terms of (a) constancy or change in the amount of an attribute (absolute stability), (b) consistency of differences within a sample of individuals over time (differential stability), and (c) the persistence of correlational patterns among a set of variables across time (structural stability) (Caspi & Bem, 1990).

Absolute Stability

The disillusionment model suggests that communal forces (e.g., affection, love) weaken and agonistic forces (e.g., negativism, ambivalence) become stronger with marriage. Lord Byron (1975) wrote Anne Isabella Milbanke in December 1814, a month before their wedding, "I have great hopes that we shall love each other all our lives as much as if we had never married at all" (p. 239). Byron anticipated the difficulty he and Anne Isabella would have of carrying their mutual enchantment into marriage; she left him after a year. Waller (1938) must have had love affairs like Byron's in mind when he suggested that marriage brings with it a certain disillusionment.

Our data support the adage that lovers are more loving and less antagonistic during courtship and as newlyweds than after they are married a year or two. Men and women report falling in love more deeply as they move from being a "couple" to being newlyweds and that love abates somewhat during the first two years of marriage ($F = 77.33$, $p < .01$). Reported marital satisfaction also declines over the first two years of marriage ($F = 39.63$, $p < .01$), as does the pattern of growth and decline in mutual attentiveness, as indexed by the "maintenance" subscale of the Braiker and Kelley (1979) measure ($F = 11.84$, $p < .01$), and in the expression of affection in marriage ($F = 69.82$, $p < .01$), as reflected in the diary reports.

Ambivalence declines from courtship into marriage and only increases over the first 2 years of marriage ($F = 52.19$, $p < .01$). Conflict, which is low during courtship and shortly after couples wed, increases during the first year of marriage and remains relatively higher into the second year ($F = 10.36$, $p < .01$). Husbands' and wives' negativity toward each other remain relatively low and stable through the first two years of marriage ($F = .62$, *ns*).

In summary, a small yet reliable change in the intensity and hedonic tone of relationships appears to take place early in marriage. Declines in love, satisfaction, affection, and maintenance, coupled with increases in ambivalence and conflict are consistent with Waller's (1938) view that a "psychic honeymoon" begins in courtship and ends early in marriage.

Differential Stability

Even though relationships, on average, become less romantic and more conflicted as couples move from courtship into marriage, differences among couples with regard to the intensity of their feelings and how well they get along with one another may persist across time. The perpetual problems model of marital distress presumes that cracks in cohesion that surface during courtship – perhaps in muted form – continue and widen over time. The disillusionment model, in contrast, argues that courting couples and newlyweds ought to be highly and nearly uniformly enchanted with one another and not readily differentiable in terms of conflict. The PAIR Project couples proved to be more homogeneous with regard to their behavior patterns and their feelings about each other during courtship and as newlyweds than they were 2 years later. Nonetheless, the stability coefficients across time were remarkably strong ($p < .001$) with regard to all measures: affectional behavior (*r*s from .75 to .80), maintenance behavior (*r*s from .47 to .65), negativity (*r*s from .61 to .89), conflict (*r*s from .58 to .69), love (*r*s from .45 to .74), ambivalence (*r*s from .45 to .74), and marital satisfaction (*r*s .56 to .59). Spouses' views of each other's personality as responsive and contrary were also highly stable across each successive year of marriage (*r*s from .68 to .81).

Relationships appeared to stabilize over time. Consistent with the perpetual problems model, couples who reportedly had trouble getting along while they were courting were more likely to experience relatively greater levels of conflict at each successive year of their marriage. Findings reported in a previous discussion (Huston, 1994) have shown, in addition, that premarital conflict and ambivalence both foretell how satisfied and how much in love spouses report that they are with one another two years into marriage. These data, when considered together, provide strong support for the perpetual problems model of the roots of marital distress.

Structural Stability

"Structural stability refers to the persistence of correlational patterns among a set of variables across time" (Caspi & Bem, 1990, p. 551). The three theoretical models differ with regard to their ideas about the likely temporal stability of the correlations between how well partners get along and both the feelings and beliefs partners have about each other and their relationship. The perpetual problems model suggests that a highly stable pattern of correlations ought to prevail: problems surface early and are immediately and consistently reflected in how partners feel and think about each other. The disillusionment model, in contrast, argues that partners put their best foot forward during courtship and that they are loath to entertain negative thoughts about each other and their relationship. The accommodation model, like the disillusionment model, maintains that such matters will change over time. Whereas the disillusionment model predicts that attitudes (e.g., ambivalence, dissatisfaction) and problematic behavior (e.g., conflict) are apt to be minimally correlated during courtship but become increasingly intertwined in marriage, the accommodation model predicts that attitudes and problematic behavior become less well integrated. According to the accommodation model, if spouses do not make allowances for each other, problems that surface in the relationship may cause them to distance themselves from one another and, perhaps, terminate the relationship.

Behavior and Partners' Feelings about Each Other and the Relationship. Table 4.2 displays the cross-sectional correlations between reports of interpersonal behavior patterns and the partners' feelings about each other premaritally (P), as newlyweds (N), and after they have been married 1 and 2 years (1 & 2). The behavior patterns constitute the rows of the table; the

Table 4.2. *Cross-sectional correlations between marital behavior and spouses' attitudes about their partner and their relationship*

	Men's attitudes about partner and the relationship												Women's attitudes about partner and the relationship											
	Love				Marital satisfaction				Ambivalence				Love				Marital satisfaction				Ambivalence			
Partners' behavior	P	N	1	2	P	N	1	2	P	N	1	2	P	N	1	2	P	N	1	2	P	N	1	2
Communal																								
Affectional expression[a]	—	.41**	.45**	.47**	—	.27**	.33**	.37**	—	-.31**	-.29**	-.32**	—	.27	.16	.28**	—	.27**	.11	.31**	—	-.12	-.06	-.23**
Maintenance[b]	.09	.37**	.17*	.36**	-.07	.18*	.12	.29**	.02	-.17*	-.06	.17*	.08	.08	.05	.18*	.03	-.03	-.06	.20**	.03	.03	.08	-.08
Agonistic																								
Negativity[a]	—	.03	-.06	-.24**	—	-.15	-.22	-.25**	—	.18*	.25**	.25**	—	-.21**	-.38**	-.41**	—	-.40**	-.43**	-.48**	—	.35**	.35**	.37**
Conflict[b]	.16	-.22**	-.23**	-.42**	.35**	-.28**	-.29**	-.35**	.17**	.29**	.29**	.45**	.17**	-.30**	-.38**	-.38**	.33**	-.37**	-.46**	-.42**	.33**	.24**	.31**	.30**

Note. Data regarding levels of conflict and maintenance provided by one partner were correlated with the other's attitudes about the partner (love) and the relationship (satisfaction, ambivalence). Data on partner's affectional expression and negativity were gathered via the telephone diary interviews. P = premarital; N = newlywed; 1 = married 1 year; 2 = married 2 years.

[a] $N = 100$.

[b] $N = 168$ for data pertaining to courtship; $N = 121$ for data pertaining to marriage.

*$p < .05$. **$p < .01$.

data pertaining to how each type of behavior correlated with participants' evaluations of their mate (love) and their feelings about the relationship (satisfaction, ambivalence) are displayed in columns. The three stages of involvement (P→N→1→2) are nested within each of the three types of evaluations. Men's and women's evaluations are displayed side-by-side in Table 4.2.

The data shown in the columns labeled "P" (premarital), suggest, consistent with the perpetual problems model, that conflict may weaken romantic love and increase ambivalence during courtship. Thus, at least to some extent, problems that surface in their relationship affect how courting partners view each other and their relationship. The combination of declining love, increasing ambivalence, and greater conflict, coupled with the fact that relationships are relatively consistently ordered with regard to both their communal (maintenance, affection) and agonistic features (negativity, conflict), suggests that spouses' feelings about their relationship (love, satisfaction, ambivalence) and their images of each other's personality (their responsiveness, contrariness) ought to become increasingly integrated with time. The pattern displayed in Table 4.2 is consistent with the idea that feelings of love are increasingly difficult to sustain in the face of negativity and conflict. Although love consistently covaries with partners' expressions of affection through the first two years of marriage, the correlations between spouses' love and both measures of agonistic behavior were significantly higher (with one exception) after couples had been married 2 years compared with when they were courting or when they were newlyweds.[2] Partners' negativity and partners' reports of conflict are strongly, and inversely, correlated with both husbands' and wives' reported love after they have been married two years. These data fit the disillusionment model well and provide striking support for the idea that love and conflict are more apt to coexist in relationships during courtship and early in marriage than after couples have been married two years (see Braiker & Kelley, 1979).

The same conclusion does not hold, however, when we examine how patterns of communal and agonistic behavior covary with ambivalence and marital satisfaction. Negativity and conflict are significantly and about equally related to satisfaction and ambivalence, regardless of the stage of the couples' relationship. Why would the pattern of correlations differ for love but not for satisfaction and ambivalence? Marital satisfaction and ambivalence, as we have measured them, probably reflect the affect generated by the relationship, whereas the intensity of love may reflect psychological dispositions (e.g., romanticism) or be more broadly anchored in relationship patterns.

Table 4.3. *Courtship and spouses' perceptions of each other's personality as newlyweds*

Feature of courtship[a]	Husbands' beliefs about wives' personality		Wives' beliefs about husbands' personality	
	Responsiveness	Contrariness	Responsiveness	Contrariness
Partners' communal behavior and attitudes				
Love	.09	−.10	.23**	−.05
Maintenance	.12	.01	.13	.03
Partners' agonistic behavior and attitudes				
Hesitancy to commit	−.12	.20**	−.13	.02
Turbulence	−.16*	.18**	−.11	.06
Conflict	−.24**	.44**	−.26**	.25**
Ambivalence	−.16*	.19**	−.16*	.08

[a]Husbands' reports about the courtship were correlated with wives' perceptions of the husbands' personality; wives' reports of courtship were correlated with husbands' perceptions of wives' personality.
*$p < .05$. **$p < .01$.

The weak associations between conflict and love for the premarital period of relationships, when coupled with the modest degree to which ambivalence and love are correlated ($r = -.40$ for women, and $r = -.58$ for men), no doubt is partly related to the sense of angst many premarital partners report. By the time couples have been married two years, however, husbands and wives who are highly in love experience relatively little conflict and feel only minimally ambivalent about their marriage ($r = -.73$ $p < .01$ for women, $r = -.68, p < .01$ for men). Conjugal love, when it persists, typically takes on a more comfortable aura.

Behavior and Spouses' Views of Each Other's Personality. The perpetual problems model and the disillusionment model differ in their view of the extent to which courtship experiences are apt to be reflected in newlyweds' perceptions of each other's personality traits. The relevant correlations appear in Table 4.3. In order to control for response biases, we correlated data gathered from one spouse about the courtship with the other's view of the first partner's personality. The data shown in Table 4.3 show, as predicted by the perpetual problems model, that courtship processes are reflected in the images partners have of each other (as either having "responsive" or "contrary" personality characteristics) as newlyweds. Particularly notable are two patterns of correlations. First, when wives are more agonistic during courtship, their husbands see their personality as less responsive and as more contrary. Second, conflict in courtship is reflected in newlyweds' views of their spouses' personality as being both less responsive and more contrary. When considered along with the data briefly summarized earlier in this chapter pertaining to the significance of premarital conflict for marital satisfaction and love, the overall pattern of data provides strong support for the idea that what happens during courtship has an important bearing on the subsequent marriage relationship.

Table 4.4 shows correlations between spouses' agonistic and communal behavior in marriage and their views of each other's personality. The strong correlations between marital behavior patterns and the spouses' views of each other's personality qualities as newlyweds suggest that even at the beginning of a marriage the spouses' views of each other covary with how they behave toward one another. Husbands and wives married to mates who are affectionate see their spouses as having a "responsive" personality. People who are married to people who are negative, or who report relatively high levels of conflict, in contrast, see their partners as being both less responsive and as more contrary. The consistency of the pattern of these correlations, coupled with those shown in Table 4.3 between courtship patterns and spouses' perceptions of each other's personality, suggests that views of each other's personality traits develop early in the history of the relationship and reflect the extent to which the relationship has agonistic and communal properties.

The Impact of Personality on Premarital and Marital Relationships

Interpersonal theories of personality (e.g., Carson, 1969) suggest that people create relationships in their own image. Accordingly, people who have "expressive" personalities ought to create highly affectionate, open, and satisfying relationships; those who are anxious, or high in negative affectivity ought to create relationships in which the partners are critical of each other and unhappy. Waller (1938) suggests that during courtship partners may be disinclined to introduce and attend to psychological qualities that might puncture the romance. The disillusionment model leads to the expectation that expressiveness and anxiety should have little impact on how partners behave and feel about each other during courtship and as newlyweds. The perpetual problems model, in contrast, proposes that personality qualities surface in interaction early in the relationship and erode attraction even during courtship. The accommodation view leads to the expectation that the impact of spouses' personality qualities on relationships will emerge and then dissipate with time as the spouses adapt to each other.

Table 4.4. *Cross-sectional correlations between marital behavior and spouses' beliefs about each other's personality*

	Husbands' beliefs about wives' personality						Wives' beliefs about husbands' personality					
	Responsiveness			Contrariness			Responsiveness			Contrariness		
Partners' behavior	N	1	2	N	1	2	N	1	2	N	1	2
Communal												
Affectional expression[a]	.32**	.31**	.34**	-.15	-.13	-.12	.36**	.30**	.28**	-.12	-.02	-.07
Maintenance[b]	.10	.10	.21*	-.05	-.12	-.03	.02	-.00	-.04	.11	.10	.10
Agonistic												
Negativity[a]	-.09	-.16	-.24**	.27**	.38**	.44**	-.21*	-.39**	-.36**	.35**	.30**	.41**
Conflict[b]	-.30**	-.17*	-.33**	.40**	.35**	.23**	-.34**	-.37**	-.31**	.23*	.34**	.33**

Note: Data regarding levels of conflict and maintenance provided by one partner were correlated with the other's beliefs about personality. Data on partner's affectional expression and negativity were gathered via the telephone diary interviews. N = newlywed; 1 = married 1 year; 2 = married 2 years.

[a]N = 100.

[b]N = 168 for data pertaining to courtship; N = 121 for data pertaining to marriage.

*p < .05. **p < .01.

Table 4.5. Correlations between spouses' personality and courtship

| | Evidence of problems in the premarital relationship | | | | | | Communal/problem-solving behavior | | Feelings about the partner and the relationship | | | |
| | Hesitancy to commit | | Turbulence | | Conflict | | Maintenance behavior | | Love | | Ambivalence | |
Personality	Own	Partner	Own	Partner	Own	Partner	Own	Partner	Own	Partner	Own	Partner
Men's												
Anxiety	-.15	.01	.06	-.02	.18*	.14*	.02	.10	-.08	-.08	.17*	.15*
Expressiveness	-.04	-.20**	-.28**	-.03	-.09	-.08	.27**	.10	.23**	.01	-.27**	-.08
Women's												
Anxiety	.03	-.07	.22**	.07	.18*	.17*	.05	.05	-.03	-.08	.17*	.10
Expressiveness	-.22**	.03	-.08	-.11	-.23**	-.18**	.14*	-.01	.30**	.11	-.33**	-.04

$N = 161$.
*$p < .05$. **$p < .01$.

The data summarized in Tables 4.5 and 4.6 show the connections between the spouses' anxiety and expressiveness and (a) the development of relationships during courtship (Table 4.5) and (b) the character of the subsequent marriage relationship the couple creates together (Table 4.6). We focus our discussion of the role of personality in courtship and marriage on patterns of significant correlations rather than on individual correlations, except when a correlation is of particular theoretical interest.

Personality and Courtship

Personality characteristics are generally weakly correlated with features of courtship, but the pattern is strong enough to provide some support for the perpetual problems model. Expressiveness draws couples toward each other (as indexed by greater love and lower ambivalence), hastens commitment, and eases conflict. Anxiety, in contrast, creates conflict and increases ambivalence. The data in Table 4.5 show, as would be expected, that men's and women's personality characteristics are more consistently associated with variables based on their own characterization of the courtship rather than their partner's characterization.

Problems in courtship are positively associated with both men's and women's anxiety and inversely associated with their expressiveness. Women high in anxiety report more turbulence (downturns in commitment). Men's and women's anxiety and women's expressiveness covary in expected ways with both partners' reports of premarital conflict. The correlations between personality and conflict, although weak, are consistent with the pattern found in marriage (see Table 4.6). Men and women who are high in anxiety are also more ambivalent about their relationship. In addition, women paired with men who are high in anxiety are more ambivalent. The latter correlation, although barely reaching statistical significance, may be of importance because men's anxiety (as discussed below) and women's premarital ambivalence both foreshadow lower levels of love and satisfaction once the partners are married (see Huston, 1994). The connection during courtship between men's anxiety and women's ambivalence may thus account, at least in part, for the predictive significance of women's premarital ambivalence for both men's and women's marital satisfaction and love.

Men high in expressiveness portray their courtship as having less turbulence (as shown by fewer downturns in their graphs); moreover, their wives created graphs with a more rapid progression from low to high commitment to marriage. Expressiveness in women also was reflected in how quickly

Table 4.6. *Cross-sectional correlations between personality, marital behavior, and the spouses' feelings toward each other and the relationship*

A. Communal behavior and attitudes

	Focal partner's own														
	Behavior						Feelings about the partner and relationship						Beliefs about partner's personality		
Focal spouse's personality	Affectional expression[b1]			Maintenance[a2]			Love[a2]			Satisfaction[a2]			Responsiveness[a2]		
	N	1	2	N	1	2	N	1	2	N	1	2	N	1	2
Husbands'															
Anxiety	-.13	-.14	-.21*	-.09	-.01	.00	-.17*	-.18*	-.17*	-.23**	-.23**	-.17*	-.14	-.11	-.27**
Expressiveness	.24**	.28**	.18*	.43**	.44**	.33**	.45**	.44**	.39**	.32**	.31**	.33**	.30**	.25**	.25**
Wives'															
Anxiety	.03	-.02	.10	-.10	-.20*	-.08	-.19*	-.22*	-.08	-.20*	-.25**	-.18*	-.19*	-.20*	-.14
Expressiveness	.23*	.17*	.12	.16*	.15*	.21*	.34**	.27**	.23**	.37**	.32**	.19*	.35**	.16*	.14

B. Agonistic behavior and attitudes

	Focal partner's own												
	Behavior						Feelings about the partner and relationship			Beliefs about partner's personality		
	Negativity[b1]			Conflict[a2]			Ambivalence[a2]			Contrariness[a2]		
	N	1	2	N	1	2	N	1	2	N	1	2
Husbands'												
Anxiety	.20**	.24**	.22*	.25**	.27**	.16*	.18*	.19*	.22*	.16*	.21**	.21*
Expressiveness	-.04	.03	-.07	-.22**	-.26**	-.14	-.37**	-.32**	-.33**	-.08	-.06	-.09
Wives'												
Anxiety	.11	.18*	.12	.33**	.35**	.22*	.24**	.31**	.19*	.28**	.22**	.17*
Expressiveness	-.07	.00	.10	-.28**	-.21**	-.13	-.20*	-.09	.01	-.06	-.00	-.07

Note: P = premarital; N = newlywed; 1 = married 1 year; 2 = married 2 years.
[a]N = 119.
[b]N = 102.
[1]Partner report.
[2]Own report.
*p < .05. **p < .01.

they showed commitment progressing during courtship. Significant correlations were found between expressiveness and both men's and women's reports of their own level of maintenance. Women and men having expressive personalities tend to be more in love and less ambivalent about their relationship during courtship. Expressiveness in men and women, however, is not significantly related to how much in love their partners were with them, or with their partners' feelings of ambivalence during courtship.

Personality and Marriage

The data summarized in Table 4.6 show substantial and consistent correlations between both men's and women's personality characteristics and the

						Other partner's								
	Behavior					Feelings about the focal spouse and the relationship						Other beliefs about the focal spouse's personality		
Affectional expression[b1]			Maintenance[a1]			Love[a1]			Satisfaction[a1]			Responsiveness[a1]		
N	1	2	N	1	2	N	1	2	N	1	2	N	1	2
-.14	-.17*	-.16*	-.11	-.02	-.12	-.14	-.26**	-.26**	-.14	-.18*	-.21*	-.14	-.27**	-.30**
.22*	.34**	.32**	.33**	.10	.18*	.21*	-.05	.08	.13	.02	.12	.17*	.09	.07
.06	.05	.09	.07	.01	.05	-.09	-.19*	-.10	-.15*	-.23**	.03	-.29**	-.30**	-.25**
.27**	.18*	.10	.09	-.08	.08	.14	.11	.12	.07	.14	-.13*	.25**	.16*	.12

						Other partner's					
	Other behavior					Other feelings about the focal spouse and the relationship			Beliefs about the focal spouse's personality		
Negativity[b2]			Conflict[a1]			Ambivalence[a1]			Contrariness[a1]		
N	1	2	N	1	2	N	1	2	N	1	2
.05	.22*	.15	.07	.16*	.08	.12	.22**	.15	.21**	.23**	.26**
.09	.14	.08	-.11	.02	.03	-.11	.05	-.09	-.03	-.02	-.00
.31**	.26**	.29**	.16*	.27**	.15	.07	.18*	.12	.23**	.27**	.23**
-.09	-.07	-.10	-.29**	-.19*	-.26**	-.08	-.08	-.08	-.15	-.23**	-.18*

spouse's behavior in marriage, their feelings about each other and the relationship, and the beliefs they have about each other's personality characteristics. The correlations were almost always in the expected direction (88%), with more than half (53%) statistically reliable (p < .05). The table breaks down into a 2 × 2 matrix: the top and bottom halves show correlations between each spouses' personality characteristics and the communal (top) and agonistic (bottom) elements of the marriage; the left and right halves of the table show the correlations between a person's personality and his or her own behavior, feelings, and beliefs (to the left), and the partner's behavior, feelings, and beliefs (to the right).

The pattern of correlations does not support the view that personality increasingly comes into play within marriage as the wedding day recedes.

This generalization holds regardless of what personality quality is scruti-
nized and whether personality is examined in connection with spouses' own
or their mate's behavior, feelings, or beliefs concerning the other's personality. Contrary to Waller's (1938) analysis, the impact of personality on marriage is as strongly evident when couples are newlyweds as it is later in
marriage. It is important to realize, however, that correlations between personality and marital behavior at years 1 and 2 are likely to be attenuated
somewhat by the fact that personality was measured only when couples
were newlyweds, but as we noted earlier, the stability coefficients for all the
features of marriage were generally quite strong. We would expect that the
more partners' personality characteristics deviate from the midpoint of
the relevant scales, the more stable is the connection between personality
and marital processes. To simplify the following discussion of personality
and marriage, we averaged data concerning each aspect of marriage across
the three phases and then correlated the personality traits with these averaged scores. The significant overall correlations in Table 4.6 are shown by
shaded background across the three years of marriage. The next section focuses on features of marriage that were significantly correlated, overall,
with either the husbands' or wives' personality. It should be noted that we
find no evidence of assortative mating with regard to either anxiety or expressiveness.

The Role of Anxiety in Marriage. The greater the husbands' anxiety, the
more they show anger or impatience, the more they complain, and the more
they express negative feelings by failing to make good on promises. Husbands high in anxiety are more ambivalent about their relationship and see
more conflict in the marriage; they are also less in love with their wives and
less satisfied with their marriage. Husbands high in anxiety see their partners as possessing a less responsive and more contrary personality. It is not
surprising, given the range of ways husbands' anxiety is reflected in their
attitudes and behavior, that women married to men relatively high in anxiety are less affectionate, less in love, less satisfied with their marriage, and
more ambivalent. Husbands high in anxiety are seen by their wives as possessing a less responsive and a more contrary personality.

Wives' anxiety is unrelated to their own negative behavior in marriage
but is consistently related to how negatively their husbands treat them, how
much conflict they and their husbands see in their marriage, how much ambivalence they feel, the level of love they have for their partner, and how satisfied they are with their marriage. Wives high in anxiety see their spouse
as less responsive and more contrary and are seen by their spouses in sim-

ilar ways. Given that husbands' and wives' levels of anxiety are themselves uncorrelated, the overall pattern suggests that anxiety, regardless of whether it is possessed by the husband or the wife, creates an atmosphere that encourages husbands to behave negatively toward their wives.

The Role of Expressiveness in Marriage. Husbands and wives who have expressive personalities are more affectionate, engage in more maintenance, report lower levels of marital conflict, and are more in love and satisfied with their marriage. Expressive men are seen by their wives as engaging in more maintenance behavior; husbands married to expressive women see less conflict in their marriage. Expressiveness is also related to the spouses' inclinations to view their partner as having more responsive and less contrary personalities. The linkage between spouses' expressiveness and their mate's sense of their personality is reflected in the fact that expressive men and women are seen by their partners as more responsive and less contrary. There was no connection, however, between the expressiveness of one partner and the other's feelings of love, satisfaction, or ambivalence. Considered together, the analyses suggest that personality characteristics affect relationships early in their history and set in motion a series of interpersonal processes that create an emotional climate in marriage that reinforces the partners' personality dispositions.

The Impact of Compatibility on Premarital and Marital Relationships

Compatibility theories presume that certain combinations of psychological qualities are more conducive than others to forming and maintaining harmonious and mutually satisfying relationships. Combining compatibility theory with the models of relationship development presented earlier leads to specific expectations regarding similarity between partners in leisure interests and role preferences. The disillusionment model suggests that early in a relationship, partners are not attuned to issues of compatibility and may actually present themselves in a manner that is inconsistent with their actual preferences. However, once the honeymoon is over and partners begin presenting their true selves, the issues of compatibility are likely to become salient. In contrast, the perpetual problems model suggests that couples are aware of incompatibilities as they arise during courtship, and the impact of areas of difference continues as couples establish their marriages. Finally, the accommodation model suggests that when areas of incompatibility arise, partners work through their differences, and the effects are negated

Table 4.7. *Cross-sectional correlations between compatibility, marital behavior, and the spouses' feelings toward each other and the relationship*

A. *Communal behavior and attitudes*

								Husbands										
		Behavior							Feelings about the partner and relationship							Beliefs about wive's personality		
	Affectional expression[b]			Maintenance[a]				Love[a]				Satisfaction[a]			Responsiveness[a]			
Compatibility in	N	1	2	P	N	1	2	P	N	1	2	N	1	2	N	1	2
Leisure interests	.15	.28**	.19*	.23**	.12	.04	.02	.19*	.18*	.18*	.18*	.13	.16*	.22*	.16	.10	.26**
Role preferences	.10	-.07	-.09	-.00	-.14	-.05	.11	-.03	.04	.06	.17*	.13	-.09	-.15	.08	-.08	-.07

B. *Agonistic behavior and attitudes*

								Husbands									
		Behavior							Feelings about partner and relationship				Beliefs about wive's personality		
	Negativity[b]			Conflict[a]					Ambivalence[a]				Contrariness[a]		
Compatibility in	N	1	2	P	N	1	2	P	N	1	2	N	1	2
Leisure interests	.12	-.05	-.07	.07	-.09	-.17*	-.09	-.08	-.15	-.09	-.16*	.02	-.05	-.02
Role preferences	-.03	.00	-.12	-.25**	-.19*	.05	-.04	-.10	-.12	-.04	-.20*	-.01	-.03	.02

Note: P = premarital; N = newlywed; 1 = married 1 year; 2 = married 2 years.
[a]N = 168 for data pertaining to courtship; N = 108 for data pertaining to marriage.
[b]N = 92.
*p < .05. **p < .01.

once this process is completed. Although no one model received overwhelming support from our data with regard to compatibility, all three models were somewhat supported.

Table 4.7 shows the correlations between compatibility in leisure interests and role preferences as they relate to relationship development during courtship and marriage. Data regarding individuals' perceptions of their partner's behavior and personality characteristics are presented. Cohesive forces are grouped at the top of each person's reports, while agonistic forces are grouped at the bottom.

The persistent and stable correlations between compatibility in leisure interests and men's love provides support for the perpetual problems model of relationship development. Men appear to be aware, from courtship into marriage, whether their leisure interests and their partners' leisure preferences match, and the less well-matched the partners are, the less men feel in love. The connection between compatibility in leisure interests and women's reports, however, best fits the disillusionment model of relationship development. During courtship and early in marriage, compatibility in

		Wives														
Behavior							Feelings about the partner and relationship						Beliefs about husband's personality			
Affectional expression[b]			Maintenance[a]				Love[a]				Satisfaction[a]			Responsiveness[a]		
N	1	2	P	N	1	2	P	N	1	2	N	1	2	N	1	2
.11	.28**	.19*	.05	.20*	.08	.08	−.04	.11	.22**	.21*	.06	.26**	.25**	.25**	.28**	.15
.07	−.05	−.01	.01	.03	−.01	.07	.10	.08	.06	.20*	.10	−.03	.12	−.01	.04	.15

		Wives												
Behavior							Feelings about partner and relationship				Beliefs about husband's personality			
Negativity[b]			Conflict[a]				Ambivalence[a]				Contrariness[a]			
N	1	2	P	N	1	2	P	N	1	2	N	1	2	
.19*	.12	−.04	.05	−.03	−.26**	−.22*	.09	−.12	−.08	−.14	.08	−.08	−.06	
−.22*	−.05	−.12	−.25**	−.10	.01	−.13	−.22**	.05	−.09	−.18*	−.22*	−.02	−.24**	

leisure interests is not related to women's reports of conflict, love, or satisfaction. However, significant correlations between incompatibility and these three variables emerge after 1 year of marriage, and persist over the next year, suggesting that such incompatibility may become increasingly important for women. Compatibility in leisure interests appears especially relevant to wives as they enter the second year of marriage. When compatibility in leisure interests is higher, wives report more love, more satisfaction, more affectional expression from their husbands, less conflict, and view their husbands as more responsive.

The emergence of significant correlations between similarity in role preferences and women's reports of love, ambivalence, and their perception of their husbands as contrary 2 years into marriage suggests a disillusionment process that occurs somewhat later than Waller (1938) predicted. It is possible that this disillusionment results from the fact that many of our couples experienced the transition to parenthood between the first and second anniversary. With this transition, renegotiation of who should be doing which household tasks may reemerge as salient for many of the women.

A lack of consensus about roles is reflected during courtship and early marriage in higher levels of reported conflict and negativity; in addition, role dissensus during courtship is reflected in women's ambivalence. The connection between role dissensus and conflict, however, does not persist over time, suggesting that some behavioral or mental adjustments may take place over the first two years of marriage. Role dissensus after two years of marriage is related to both spouses' ambivalence about the marriage and, for wives, to their believing their husband possesses a contrary, or antagonistic personality.

Conclusion

The perpetual problems model – with its suggestion that problems surface in relationships relatively early, continue to persist, and have similarly strong connections with how partners feel and think about each other from courtship into early marriage – was strongly supported in the present longitudinal study. Conflict, love, and ambivalence were intercorrelated during courtship, although not as strongly as they were later in marriage. Even as newlyweds, the bride and groom have images of each other's personality that reflect their courtship experiences and that remain relatively stable over the first 2 years of their marriage. The images they develop also reflect the personality qualities that both spouses bring to marriage, their compatibility, and their life together as a couple.

Nonetheless, consistent with the disillusionment model, relationships do change over the first 2 years of marriage, both behaviorally and with regard to their affective tone. Love, satisfaction, affection, and maintenance, in particular, show significant declines. Conflict increases over the first year of marriage and then levels off. Perhaps the strongest support for the disillusionment model, however, comes from the increasingly strong inverse correlations between love and both negativity and conflict. These findings suggest that men and women in love may not fully assimilate their experiences into their attitudes and their feelings about their partner. Accommodation, to the extent that it occurs, may reflect an adaptation that takes place only after spouses discover, through extensive experience, that their mate is inflexible or unwilling to change.

Finally, it is clear that anxiety and incompatibility appear to produce fissures in the rock of marriage that weaken their ability to endure. Whether these fissures widen, crack, and break the rock apart, or otherwise leave the marriage vulnerable to erosion, may depend on the kinds of stresses and strains couples face over the ensuing years and how well they learn to work around their difficulties (see Conger & Elder, 1994). Marriages may be particularly at risk when personality vulnerabilities and incompatibilities are combined with unemployment, illness, or other stressors. However, the psychological qualities people bring to marriage, such as expressiveness and various kinds of competencies, may help partners fend off the potentially corrosive effects that stress may otherwise have on marriage – at least for a while. We have recently gathered data that allow us to track how the marriages studied in the report have fared over the past decade. Because we are a few months away from being in a position to report our findings, we hope – as Charles Dickens must have hoped when leaving readers hanging at the end of each installment of his serial novels – to have whetted the reader's appetite for the next chapter of this unfolding story of the course of romantic relationships.

Notes

1. PAIR stands for Processes of Adaptation in Intimate Relationships. The acronym captures our focus on the marital pair and our interest in tracking how individuals and their relationships change over time.

2. Steiger's (1980) formula was used to compare the strength of the correlations between love and agonistic behaviors during courtship, early in marriage, and 2 years into marriage. For both men and women, their love was more strongly associated with their partners' reports of conflict 2 years into marriage as opposed to when the spouses were courting (men's love with women's reports of conflict, $z = 4.10$, $p < .01$; women's love and men's reports of conflict, $z = 3.18$, $p < .01$). Similarly, the correlations between one spouse's love and the other's agonistic behavior was stronger 2 years into marriage as opposed to when couples were newlyweds (husbands' love with wives' reports of conflict, $z = 3.15$, $p < .01$; husbands' love with wives' negativity, $z = 3.15$, $p < .01$; wives' love with husbands' reports of conflict, $z = 1.04$, *ns;* wives' love with husbands' negativity, $z = 2.75$, $p < .05$).

References

Anderson, N. H. (1968). Likableness ratings of 555 personality-trait words. *Journal of Personality and Social Psychology, 9,* 272–279.

Antill, J. K. (1983). Sex role complementarity versus similarity in married couples. *Journal of Personality and Social Psychology, 43,* 145–154.

Bentler, P. M., & Newcomb, M. D. (1978). Longitudinal study of marital success and failure. *Journal of Consulting and Clinical Psychology, 46,* 1053–1070.

Bernard, J. (1964). The adjustments of married mates. In H. T. Christensen (Ed.), *Handbook of marriage and the family* (pp. 675–739). Chicago: Rand McNally.

Bradbury, T. N., Campbell, S. M., & Fincham, F. D. (1995). Longitudinal and behavioral analysis of masculinity and femininity in marriage. *Journal of Personality and Social Psychology, 68,* 328–341.

Braiker, H. B., & Kelley, H. H. (1979). Conflict in the development of close relationships. In R. L. Burgess & T. L. Huston (Eds.), *Social exchange in developing relationships* (pp. 135–168). New York: Academic Press.

Burger, A. L., & Jacobson, N. S. (1979). The relationship between sex role characteristics, couple satisfaction, and couple problem-solving skills. *American Journal of Family Therapy, 7,* 52–60.

Burgess, E. W., & Wallin, P. (1953). *Engagement and marriage.* Philadelphia: Lippincott.

Buss, D. M. (1991). Conflict in married couples: Personality predictors of anger and upset. *Journal of Personality, 59,* 663–688.

Buss, D. M. (1992). Manipulation in close relationships: Five personality factors in interactional context. *Journal of Personality, 60,* 477–499.

Byron, G. C. (Lord) (1975). *Byron's letters and journals* (Vol. 4; Leslie A. Marchand, Ed.). Cambridge, MA: Harvard University Press.

Campbell, A., Converse, P., & Rodgers, W. L. (1976). *The quality of American life: Perceptions, evaluations, and satisfactions.* New York: Russell Sage.

Carson, R. C. (1969). *Interaction concepts of personality.* Chicago: Aldine.

Caspi, A., & Bem, D. (1990). Personality continuity and change across the life course. In L. Pervin (Ed.), *Handbook of personality: Theory and research* (pp. 549–575). New York: Guilford.

Cate, R., Huston, T. L., & Nesselroade, J. R. (1986). Premarital relationships: Toward the identification of alternative pathways to marriage. *Journal of Social and Clinical Psychology, 4,* 3–22.

Cate, R., & Lloyd, S. (1992). *Courtship.* Newbury Park, CA: Sage.

Cattell, R. B., Eber, H. W., & Tatsuoka, M. M. (1970). *Handbook for the sixteen personality factor questionnaire (16PF).* Champaign, IL: Institute for Personality and Ability Testing.

Conger, R., & Elder, G. (1994). *Families in troubled times: Adapting to change in rural America.* New York: Aldine deGruyter.

Conley, J. J. (1984). The hierarchy of consistency: A review and model of longitudinal findings on adult individual differences in intelligence, personality, and self-opinion. *Personality and Individual Differences, 5,* 11–25.

Conley, J. J. (1985). Longitudinal stability of personality traits: A multitrait-multimethod-multioccasion analysis. *Journal of Personality and Social Psychology, 49,* 1266–1282.

Costa, P. T., & McCrae, R. R. (1988). Personality in adulthood: A six-year longitudinal study of self-reports and spouse ratings on the NEO personality inventory. *Journal of Personality and Social Psychology, 54,* 853–863.

Crohan, S. E. (1992). Marital happiness and spousal consensus on beliefs about marital conflict: A longitudinal analysis. *Journal of Social and Personal Relationships, 9,* 89–92.

Fincham, F. D., & Bradbury, T. (1987). The assessment of marital quality: A reevaluation. *Journal of Marriage and the Family, 49,* 797–809.

Heaton, T., & Pratt, E. (1990). The effects of religious homogamy on marital satisfaction and stability. *Journal of Family Issues, 11,* 191–207.

Heaton, T., Albrecht, S. L., & Martin, T. K. (1985). The timing of divorce. *Journal of Marriage and the Family, 47,* 631–639.

Hill, C. T., Rubin, Z., & Peplau, L. A. (1976). Break-ups before marriage: The end of 103 affairs. In G. Levinger & O. Moles (Eds.), *Divorce and separation: Context, causes, and consequences* (pp. 64–82). New York: Basic Books.

Houts, R. N., Robins, E. R., & Huston, T. L. (1996). Compatibility and the development of premarital relationships. *Journal of Marriage and the Family, 58,* 7–20.

Huston, T. L. (1994). Courtship antecedents of marital satisfaction and love. In R. Erber & S. Duck (Eds.), *Theoretical frameworks for personal relationships* (pp. 43–65). Hillsdale, NJ: Erlbaum.

Huston, T. L., & Geis, G. (1993). In what ways do gender-related attributes and beliefs affect marriage? *Journal of Social Issues, 49,* 87–106.

Huston, T. L., McHale, S., & Crouter, A. (1986). When the honeymoon's over: Changes in the marriage relationship over the first year. In R. Gilmour & S. Duck (Eds.), *The emerging field of personal relationships* (pp. 109–132). Hillsdale, NJ: Erlbaum.

Huston, T. L., & Robins, E. R. (1982). Conceptual and methodological issues in studying close relationships. *Journal of Marriage and the Family, 44,* 901–925.

Huston, T. L., Robins, E., Atkinson, J., & McHale, S. (1987). Surveying the landscape of marital behavior: A behavioral self-report approach to studying marriage. In S. Oskamp (Ed.), *Family processes and problems: Social psychological aspects* (pp. 46–71). Beverly Hills, CA: Sage.

Huston, T. L., Surra, C. A., Fitzgerald, N., & Cate, R. (1981). From courtship to marriage: Mate selection as an interpersonal process. In S. Duck & R. Gilmour (Eds.), *Personal relationships* (Vol. 2, pp. 53–88). London: Academic Press.

Huston, T. L., & Vangelisti, A. (1991). Socioemotional behavior and satisfaction in marital relationships: A longitudinal study. *Journal of Personality and Social Psychology, 41,* 721–733.

Ibsen, H. (1959). *Four great plays by Henrik Ibsen: A Doll's House, Ghosts, An Enemy of the People, The Wild Duck* (R. F. Sharp, Trans.). New York: Bantam Books.

IPAT Staff. (1986). *Administrator's manual for the 16PF.* Chicago, IL: Institute for Personality and Ability Testing.

John, O. P. (1990). The "Big Five" factor taxonomy: Dimensions of personality in the natural language and in questionnaires. In L. Pervin (Ed.), *Handbook of personality: Theory and research* (pp. 66–100). New York: Guilford.

Karney, B. R., Bradbury, T., Fincham, F. D., & Sullivan, K. T. (1994). The role of negative affectivity in the association between attributions and marital satisfaction. *Journal of Personality and Social Psychology, 66,* 413–424.

Kelley, H. H. (1979). *Personal relationships: Their structures and processes.* Hillsdale, NJ: Erlbaum.

Kelly, E. L., & Conley, J. J. (1987). Personality and compatibility: A prospective analysis of marital stability and marital satisfaction. *Journal of Personality and Social Psychology, 52,* 27–40.

Kerckhoff, A. C. (1974). The social context of interpersonal attraction. In T. L. Huston (Ed.), *Foundations of interpersonal attraction* (pp. 61–78). New York: Academic Press.

Kurdek, L. (1993). Predicting marital dissolution: A 5-year prospective study of newlywed couples. *Journal of Personality and Social Psychology, 64,* 221–242.

Lamke, L. K. (1989). Marital adjustment among rural couples: The role of expressiveness. *Sex Roles, 21,* 579–590.

Lamke, L. K., Sollie, D. L., Durbin, R. G., & Fitzpatrick, J. A. (1995). Masculinity, femininity, and relationship satisfaction: The mediating role of interpersonal competence. *Journal of Social and Personal Relationships, 11,* 535–554.

Levinger, G., & Rands, M. (1985). Compatibility in marriage and other close relationships. In W. Ickes (Ed.), *Compatible and incompatible relationships* (pp. 309–331). New York: Springer-Verlag.

Locke, H. J., & Wallace, K. M. (1959). Short marital-adjustment and prediction tests: Their reliability and validity. *Marriage and Family Living, 21,* 251–255.

McCrae, R. R., & Costa, P. T. (1985). Updating Norman's "adequate taxonomy": Intelligence and personality dimensions in natural language and in questionnaires. *Journal of Personality and Social Psychology, 49,* 710–721.

Murray, S. L., & Holmes, J. G. (1993). Seeing virtues in faults: Negativity and the transformation of interpersonal narratives in close relationships. *Journal of Personality and Social Psychology, 65,* 707–722.

Noller, P., Law, H., & Comrey, A. L. (1987). Cattell, Comrey, & Eysenck personality factors compared: More evidence for the five robust factors? *Journal of Personality and Social Psychology, 53,* 775–782.

Robins, E. R. (1985). *An empirical test of the compatibility model of marital choice.* Unpublished doctoral dissertation, Pennsylvania State University.

Rusbult, C., Verette, J., Whitney, G. A., Slovik, L. F., & Lipkus, I. (1991). Accommodation processes in close relationships: Theory and preliminary empirical evidence. *Journal of Personality and Social Psychology, 60,* 53–78.

Spanier, G. B. (1976). Measuring dyadic adjustment: New scales for assessing the quality of marriage and similar dyads. *Journal of Marriage and the Family, 38,* 15–28.

Spence, J. T. (1984). Masculinity, femininity, and gender-related traits: A conceptual analysis and critique of current research. In B. Maher (Ed.), *Progress in experimental personality research* (Vol. 13, pp. 2–66). New York: Academic Press.

Spence, J. T., Helmreich, R. L., & Stapp, J. (1974). The Personal Attributes Questionnaire: A measure of sex-role stereotypes and masculinity-femininity. *JSAS Catalog of Selected Documents in Psychology, 4,* 127.

Steiger, J. H. (1980). Tests for comparing elements of a correlation matrix. *Psychological Bulletin, 87,* 245–251.

Surra, C. A. (1985). Courtship types: Variations in interdependence between partners and social networks. *Journal of Personality and Social Psychology, 49,* 357–375.

Surra, C. A. (1990). Research and theory on mate selection and premarital relationships. *Journal of Marriage and the Family, 52,* 844–865.

Swann, W. B., Jr., De La Ronde, C., & Hixon, J. G. (1994). Authenticity and positivity strivings in marriage and courtship. *Journal of Personality and Social Psychology, 66,* 857–869.

Terman, L. M., Buttenwieser, P., Ferguson, L. W., Johnson, W. B., & Wilson, D. P. (1938). *Psychological factors in marital happiness.* New York: McGraw-Hill, 1938.

Waller, W. (1938). *The family: A dynamic interpretation.* New York: Cordon.

Watson, D., & Clark, L. A. (1984). Negative affectivity: The disposition to experience aversive emotional states. *Psychological Bulletin, 96,* 465–490.

5   Happiness in Stable Marriages: The Early Years

Joseph Veroff, Elizabeth Douvan, Terri L. Orbuch, and Linda K. Acitelli

With so many marriages ending in divorce, researchers studying marriage have focused their attention on factors that contribute to marital stability or breakup. Some of these factors have been structural (Kitson, 1992; Teachman & Polonko, 1990), some have been psychological (Gottman & Levenson, 1988), and some interpersonal (Gottman & Krokoff, 1989; Levinger, 1965). Hatchett, Veroff, and Douvan (1996) have dealt with all these levels of analysis simultaneously. But whether such factors are indeed responsible for especially happy marriages is yet another question. Cuber and Harroff (1965) long ago made an important distinction among types of marriages in which husbands and wives may have no question about maintaining loyalties to their spouses and the future of their bonds: Some reflected vital satisfying interdependent relationships while others did not. Among those committed to each other but less satisfied were couples who maintained highly independent life spheres in which husbands and wives had little to do with each other as well as couples whose daily interactive lives were devoid of any vital core of gratifying experience.

What accounts for satisfying marriages among those couples who are unquestionably committed to each other? That is the topic of the current chapter. Having a satisfying marriage is more than just remaining married to someone; it is more than just living by commitments to stay together until "death do us part." It demands a harmonious sharing of lives that each partner finds fulfilling. Such satisfactions go a long way in underscoring men and women's positive mental health (Ryff, 1989).

How does that harmony come about? How do couples in the early years of marriage move beyond simply feeling that their marriages are important to maintain and experience their marriage as a major gratifying part of their lives? These are questions we asked in the research reported in this paper. We looked only at couples who have never thought about separating from their partners. We considered these couples to be clearly committed to the

152

marriage. Then we asked which ones of them are especially happy and which ones are not. At that point we searched for factors associated with this differential marital happiness.

What makes this analysis unique is that in most studies of stability or marital happiness, these aspects of marital quality are intertwined. Corresponding to the distinctions that have been drawn by several researchers (Cuber & Harroff, 1965; Kelley, 1983; Rusbult & Buunk, 1993), Crohan and Veroff (1989) posited that stability and happiness would emerge as separate factors in a factor analysis of a variety of measures of marital well-being among newlyweds. Instead they found that questions asked specifically about the stability of the marriage cluster on the same dimension as questions asked specifically about happiness and satisfaction. Heaton and Albrecht (1991) have analyzed responses of married couples to identify the factors that promote stability in unhappily married couples. This chapter answers a reversed question: What are the factors involved in marital happiness among couples who are in stable relationships? So often feelings that a marriage is stable and feelings that a marriage is satisfying are indistinguishable in marital research. We wish to differentiate these phenomena.

Although we examine couples only in the early years of marriage, it stands to reason that the patterns for marital well-being are established in most cases during the early years when couples first establish ways of being with one another. Transitions during later stages, especially as couples move out of family-building periods and into coping with adolescent children, the empty nest, and aging, may present new issues for satisfying relationships. In this study we concentrate only on the first 4 years of marriage.

Theoretical Issues

We use three general conceptual frameworks in considering factors that are correlated with especially gratifying marriages among couples who are committed to being in stable marriages. The first depends on the importance of fulfilling gender role expectations for socially constructing the bases of marital happiness. The second depends on there being an affective balance in the marriage weighted toward positive rather than negative experiences. The third depends on the assumption that a balance between obtaining individual gratification and relational gratification, often in dialectical tension with each other, is the basis for satisfying marriage. We discuss each in turn.

Social Construction of Marital Happiness

Discovering sources of human happiness has been an elusive theoretical quest. The most reasonable theoretical position that social psychologists have offered is that happiness is socially constructed, that one's role, culture, gender, ethnicity, and class carry with them prescriptions and expectations that help the person establish the dimensions on which happiness should be evaluated and anchors for evaluating each dimension (see Veroff, Douvan, & Kulka, 1981, chap. 2). Thus the individual evaluates his/her marriage according to the expectations of the groups with whom he/she identifies. "Should marriage be important to my happiness?" and "How happy is my marriage?" are questions that each individual answers with the polyphony that comes from the voices of each of his/her major reference groups. That polyphony can be discordant or relatively harmonious. Indeed, it may not turn out to be polyphony at all if all the reference groups speak in unison.

We can also ask whether some reference groups are more potent than others in affecting evaluations of marital happiness either with regard to the dimensions used or the evaluations made. We believe that one's gender identity represents a powerful grouping for determining affective responses to this all-important heterosexual bonding.

Expectations about marriage for husbands as "men" and for wives as "women" or expectations based on any important social identity must in turn affect marital evaluations. If expectations are high, disappointments may be even greater. If expectations are meager, disappointments may not be so critical. In *The Inner American* (Veroff, Douvan, & Kulka, 1981), we suggested that a relationship paradigm that asks individuals to evaluate the quality of their intimate relationships rather than their performance in roles places an undue burden on contemporary Americans, perhaps especially as it applies to marriage. High expectations can only lead to disappointments. If the authors of *Habits of the Heart* (Bellah et al., 1985) were polled they would no doubt also speak of the difficulties that men and women in the culture have with regard to marital commitment because it is antithetical to another long-standing American value of independence and autonomy. Men and women have been trained differently with regard to which of these two opposing forces should be emphasized in their lives and moral judgments (Chodorow, 1978; Gilligan, 1982). The gender differentiation appears to be stronger among working-class people than it is among the more affluent classes. Indeed, *Worlds of Pain* (Rubin, 1976) has alerted us to ways in which expectations about what should take place in the marriage might be very different for working-class as opposed to middle-class couples.

Expectations about marriage may also differ among ethnic groups. The familism value in Latino culture, for example, is different from the values of white majority cultural groups (Vega, 1990).

At the heart of the differential expectations for marriage is the orientation to gender roles. What are men and women expected to do in the culture generally and as married husbands and wives specifically? In our analyses of marriage we focus primarily on potentially different meanings that gender roles in marriage have for black couples as compared with white couples in modern urban American society.

Affective Balance and Marital Happiness

Regardless of the bases for evaluating one's marriage, we can still assume that evaluations will take place. An important theoretical conception of what takes place in deriving these evaluations comes from Bradburn's (1969) research on affective balance. In Bradburn's conceptualization, general and marital well-being both depend on taking account of both the positive aspects of well-being, what one enjoys and finds fulfilling, and the negative aspects of well-being, what one finds frustrating and difficult. General or marital well-being thus depends on the balance of pluses and minuses. The absence of a minus is not the same as the presence of a plus, and the absence of a plus is not the same as the presence of a minus; instead pluses and minuses have to be assessed separately before the overall balance is calculated.

Achieving affective balance is a very important idea, the root of which stems from general theories of motivation. In midcentury there was a raging controversy about whether human motivation rested solely on the deprivation-tension model that seemed to underlie both psychoanalytic theory of dynamics and learning theory based on human survival needs. The capacity for pleasure per se was not considered. This view of motivation has been modified considerably, especially as neuropsychology began to identify pleasure centers (Olds, 1956) and ego psychologists began to incorporate ideas of mastery and competence as positive goals in human experience. Maslow's (1954) motivation hierarchy became a popular way to distinguish tension or negative goals from growth or positive goals.

Much the same reasoning applies to topics such as marital well-being. We can certainly expect negative tensions to exist in any marital relationship and suggest that marriages will be happy where such tension is minimal. But we can also identify marital pleasures independent of the absence of tension, including such pleasures as companionate interaction, passionate sexual interaction, a warm sense of togetherness with one's partner, a sense of connection and caring. Like Bradburn's model, these positive and negative feelings can be assessed separately and can differentially affect people's evaluations of their marriage.

Furthermore, we can argue that husbands' and wives' affective dispositions affect the quality of the marriage. We can assume that zestful or agreeable spouses are likely to generate zestful and agreeable marriages and anxious and irritable spouses are likely to develop tense marriages. Thus in our analyses we will try to account for not only positive and negative interpersonal styles in marriage but also positive and negative individual styles, as they may contribute to well-being in marriage.

Dialectical Views of Happiness

Ever since Bakan (1966) offered a dialectical theory of motivation positing that humans face a motivational tension between two often incompatible tendencies of agency, or an individuated mastery of one's experience, and communion, or a relational connection with others, theorists and researchers have sought ways to tap this dialectic in human activity. The marital experience is no exception. Malley (1989) and Malley and Veroff (1990) have suggested that a balance between these two orientations in marriage is what lies behind marital well-being. To experience a loving connection in marriage is fine, but not as gratifying as experiencing it along with a sense of one's self in that relationship. An absence of a sense of self in marriage could decrease the fulfillment experienced in a loving marital relationship. Perhaps being in a loving relationship and having little self-fulfillment are in fact a contradiction in terms. A person may not feel that he/she is in a loving relationship without at the same time experiencing a solid sense of self. If we can measure the extent to which the individual feels validated as a person within the marital relationship, we could test ideas proposed by Malley and Veroff that a balance between individuated and more relational gratifications experienced in a marriage is diagnostic of highly gratifying marriages.

Analysis Plan

These three conceptual orientations guide and inform the work we report in this chapter. We studied a representative group of couples from their 1st year through their 4th year of marriage. Many different analyses have emerged from this longitudinal investigation (see Veroff, Douvan, & Hatchett, 1995; Veroff, Sutherland, Chadiha, & Ortega, 1993). Most of the research has focused on identifying variables that are associated with marital well-being and stability. In this chapter we focus on one particular aspect of well-being: What is associated with especially satisfying marriages? We identify a group of couples whose marriages we know to be stable and then explore a variety of factors that may affect their expressed happiness or satisfaction about their marriages.

For the analysis, we select measures from Year 3 of the study that can be interpreted to reflect the contribution of each of the three frameworks we have enumerated and analyze the degree to which each is associated with marital well-being or satisfaction in Year 4. Then we present multivariate analyses to highlight particularly strong factors in each framework, and to suggest the comparative usefulness of each framework. In all the multivariate analyses we also enter as predictors premarital parenthood, cohabitation, and household income, because these factors were significantly different in the black couples compared with the white couples. Black couples were more likely than white couples to have cohabited before marriage, to have entered marriage as parents, and to start marriage with lower household incomes. With these structural factors controlled as predictors, we can have more confidence that psychological factors emerging as statistically significant predictors can be interpreted equally meaningfully for the two groups. We then repeat each multivariate analysis with an additional control: 3rd-year marital happiness. These additional analyses permit us to examine whether certain third year marital factors may be potentially *causally* related to changes in marital happiness from the third to the fourth years. While we will not emphasize these more refined multivariate analyses, they do yield important information.[1]

The Study

The Early Years of Marriage Study (Veroff, Douvan, & Hatchett, 1992) was designed to describe the first 4 years of marriage in a representative urban sample of black and white couples. One hundred ninety-nine black and 174 white couples agreed to participate after having been contacted through a sampling of marriage license applications in Wayne County, Michigan, during the period of April–June 1986. This was a 65% response rate. To be eligible, both spouses had to be starting their first marriages, and the wife had to be 35 years or younger in age. During the 1st and 3rd years of the study, couples participated in 90-minute individual face-to-face interviews and in a couple interview that lasted about an hour. Brief telephone interviews were conducted in Years 2 and 4. An eclectic array of assessments was used.

In Year 4, 255 marriages (145 white; 110 black) remained intact. We will note the procedures for assessments in the text as the measures are systematically presented.

Defining Marital Stability and Happiness

To obtain only stable couples for the analysis, we selected only those couples that were intact after four years, and then from among them selected only those in which the wife and the husband in Year 4 both answered, "Never" to the question, "In the last few months, how often have you considered leaving your wife/husband? (often, sometimes, rarely, never)." For these couples we measured Marital Happiness separately for the husband and the wife by normalizing and totaling their responses to the following three items asked in the fourth year of marriage (alpha = .84):

1. "Taking things all together, how would you describe your marriage? Would you say your marriage is very happy, a little happier than average, just about average, or not too happy?" (4 = very happy; 3 = a little happier than average; 2 = just about average; 1 = not too happy)
2. "All in all, how satisfied are you with your marriage? Would you say you are very satisfied, somewhat satisfied, somewhat dissatisfied, or very dissatisfied?" (4 = very satisfied; 3 = somewhat satisfied; 2 = somewhat dissatisfied; 1 = very dissatisfied)
3. "When you think about your marriage – what each of you puts into it and gets out of it – how happy do you feel? Would you say very happy, fairly happy, not too happy, or not at all happy?" (4 = very happy; 3 = fairly happy; 2 = not too happy; 1 = not at all happy)

The first two items, which derive from Veroff, Douvan, and Kulka (1981), have considerable construct validity from analyses of various demographic differences (e.g., higher-income spouses are happier in marriage than lower-income spouses) as well as relationships with other aspects of marital functioning. The third item is derived from Austin's (1974) scale assessing marital equity. Research using the equity scale has obtained results compatible with equity reasoning about personal relationships. All three items are part of an overall "happiness" scale coming from Crohan and Veroff's (1989) analyses. The means and standard deviations on this measure for the four groups we will be considering (white wives; white husbands; black wives; black husbands) are presented in Table 5.1. It should be noted that in selecting only stable couples we are dealing with a limited range of very high

Table 5.1. *Mean marital happiness in Year 4 (by race × gender)*

Race and gender	(N)	Mean	SD	Range
White "stable couples"				
Wives	(100)	11.14	1.32	7–12
Husbands	(98)	11.14	1.56	6–12
Black "stable couples"				
Wives	(53)	10.79	1.31	7–12
Husbands	(52)	10.98	1.1	8–12
All couples (stable + unstable)				
Wives	(244)	10.15	2.11	3–12
Husbands	(233)	10.40	1.81	4–12

marital happiness scores. If we had included all couples in this analysis (stable and unstable), the mean scores would have been lower, and the range greater, as noted in the table. It is for this reason that we consider that we are analyzing the dynamics of especially happy marriages.

The Social Construction of Happy Marriages Through Gender Role Expectations

Measures

The following eight measures were selected to examine gender role expectations in marriage:[2]

Role-Sharing Orientation. This 10-item index (alpha = .64) summarizes a couples' attitudes and behaviors about whether they should (and do) share equally in a series of household tasks. Orbuch (1994) has found that differentiating distinctions between attitudes and behaviors regarding role sharing does not significantly change results using this scale and actually produces less reliability.

Accommodation. In Year 1 and Year 3, each spouse was asked to use a series of 12 descriptors to report his/her ideal and actual self, and his/her ideal and actual spouse. Ruvolo (1990) investigated the degree to which each spouse changed the ratings of his/her actual self on each of these descriptors from Year 1 to Year 3 in the direction of his/her partner's ideals for him/her in Year 1.[3] Veroff (1992) has called this a type of accommodation to the spouse. Since social norms would predict that women accommodate in this way more than men, these measures could implicate gender role expectations. We used these two measures: (1) the Wife's Accommodation to the husbands' ideals for her; and (2) the Husband's Accommodation to his wife's ideals for him.

Job Achievement. Three measures of job achievement were used: *Wife's Personal Income* earned; the ratio of the wife's income to the husband's income (*F/M income*); and whether or not the person thought of his/her job as a very important part of his life or just a way of earning money (*Career Orientation*).

Equity. Couples were asked whether each spouse had an equal say in important matters. An index was created based on each spouse's response to this question. This index assesses perceptions of differential power in decision making within the couple.

Parental Status. Whether the couple had a child by the 4th year was also considered an important reflection of the concerns that men and women have about their sex role adequacies and fulfillments. Having a child is often perceived as the demonstration of womanhood and manhood.

Results

Table 5.2 and subsequent tables summarizes results from three sets of analyses for each Race × Gender group. The first column is devoted to zero-order correlations between a variable and 4th-year marital happiness; a second is devoted to the correlation between the variable and 4th-year marital happiness, partialling out in linear multiple regressions the variance attributable to all other variables in the set under scrutiny, plus the three structural variables (premarital parenthood, cohabitation, and household income in the 1st year); a third column is identical to the second but also includes 3rd-year marital happiness as an additional predictor.

What do we learn from Table 5.2 about factors in gender role construction that contribute to satisfying marriages? For all but the black husbands we find a very important result, one that defies common sense: For all wives and white husbands, the more the husband changes in his self-perceptions by the 3rd year in the direction of the ideals that his wife sets for him in the 1st year of marriage, the *less* satisfying are these people's marriages. These results are disturbing. They suggest that when men accommodate in this way they are probably responding to general problems in their marriage and that the problems are not reduced by the change but may even become

Table 5.2. *Predicting 4th-year marital happiness among stable couples with gender role construction factors assessed in the 3rd year (by race × gender)*

	White couples						Black couples						
	Wives (N = 100)			Husbands (N = 98)			Wives (N = 53)			Husbands (N = 52)		
		Partial r Yr 3 control[a]			Partial r Yr 3 control[a]			Partial r Yr 3 control[a]			Partial r Yr 3 control[a]	
Gender role construction factors	r	No	Yes	r	No	Yes	r	No	Yes	r	No	Yes
Role-sharing orientation	19	09	14	−05	−13	−10	06	−01	−06	32**	35**	25*
W's accommodation	−09	−05	−10	−15	−11	−10	−44***	−03	−05	−06	21	09
H's accommodation	−34***	−28**	−18*	−26**	−20**	−12	−28***	−17	−15	−07	06	−07
W's personal income	16	−02	00	11	−01	−05	18	09	03	00	03	−08
Ratio W/H income	−01	−07	−05	09	08	12	−03	−12	−08	10	00	04
W's career orientation	−10	−02	−05	−02	04	05	04	−18	−14	−03	−10	−12
H's career orientation	−19	−08	−05	−08	−01	02	−20	00	04	−10	−19	−06
Equity in power	03	−09	−20*	20	10	00	28**	17	05	29**	27*	05
Parental status	−08	−01	01	−12	00	−05	−23	10	05	18	32**	30*

Note: Partial r computed from regression analyses that include all gender role construction factors, and three control variables (Cohabitation, Premarital Parental Status, 1st-Year Household Income).
[a] For marital happiness Year 3.
*p < .10. **p < .05. ***p < .001.

exacerbated. The need for this kind of accommodation probably stems from a marriage that is not working. From the man's point of view this might mean giving up his power to determine what he is going to be, a kind of emasculation, in order to please a wife, who ends up being displeased anyway. This is a vicious circle that no doubt reflects the kind of peculiar enmeshments husbands and wives get into when they try to change core aspects of themselves that their spouse finds unlikable. Indeed, some of the accommodation we are measuring may be only perceived changes that do not translate into any actual behavioral changes modified by men's wives.

The most revealing results for black husbands is that their commitment to role sharing, equity, and being a parent are especially associated with their marital well-being. Such is not the case with any other group, but only in the case of the black husbands compared with the white husbands are the differences in partial correlations statistically significant. One has the impression that black men who do not experience marital breakup (and many black marriages collapsed in the first 4 years) are men who are especially gratified by the family commitments in marriage. Emasculation is not a problem for them. Quite the contrary. We need to look more closely at these men to see what lies behind this more androgynous gender role orientation.

Controlling for 3rd-Year Marital Happiness. As we would expect, introducing 3rd-year marital happiness as another predictor in the regression models had the general effect of reducing the impact of the gender role construction factors on 4th-year marital happiness. It would be difficult to argue for any potentially causal predictive power from this set of variables. Indeed, the one variable that remained significant at $p < .05$ was parental status for black men, which was assessed in the 4th year.

Affective Balance: Positive Versus Negative Factors Contributing to Happy Marriages

Measures

Two different types of measures of positive and negative affective factors in marriages were used: Measures of personal style and measures of interactive style. Two of the measures of personal style were directed specifically toward affect, *Anxiety* (sum of 3 negative symptoms of distress, such as nervousness (alpha = .73); see Veroff, Douvan, & Kulka, 1981) and *Zest* (sum of 4 items about feeling positive about life, such as feeling useful and needed (alpha = .74); also found in Veroff et al., 1981). The other two measures of personal affective style derive from self-reports that the respondents gave of their personalities: one being their *Agreeableness* (sum of 5 items, such as how considerate they are, in Year 1 and Year 3, making it a 10-item scale (alpha = .77)); and the other being their *Abrasiveness* (sum of 4 items such as how stubborn and moody they are, in Year 1 and Year 3, making it an 8-item scale (alpha = .80)). These scales derived from cluster analyses that Young, Franz, Veroff, and Frieband (1993) have made of 12 such self-descriptions. To assure us that these were relatively stable personal characteristics, we summed the parallel measures from the 1st year with these 3rd-year scores.

The other measures are more specific to affective dimensions of the couple's interactions with each other. On the positive side, these include: *Positive Sexual Interaction*, the product[4] of 2 indices that included each spouse's report of having "joyful and exciting" sex with each other and each spouse's report of how he/she thought his/her spouse feels about this (4 items; alpha = .86); *Companionateness*, the product of each spouse's report about their overlapping interests and hobbies (2 items, alpha = .60); *Shared Leisure*, the product of each spouse's report about spending their leisure together (2 items, alpha = .74); and *Constructive Conflict Style*, each spouse's report of handling conflicts constructively such as taking the spouse's point of view (4 items, alpha = .70). On the negative side are: *Negative Sexual Interaction*, the product of 2 indices that included each spouse's report of feeling upset about his/her sex life with each other and each spouse's report of how he/she thought his/her spouse feels about this (4 items, alpha = .78); *Frequency of Conflict*, the product of each spouse's report about the frequency of conflict in the marriage (alpha = .59); *Absence of Support*, each spouse's report of finding it easier to talk to someone other than his/her spouse (1 item); and *Destructive Conflict Style*, each spouse's report of handling conflict destructively, such as yelling and insulting (3 items, alpha = .65).

Results

Affective Balance in Personal Style. The importance of women's optimistic style (*Zest*) for both herself and her husband's marital happiness is apparent in Table 5.3's results for white couples. This factor is also apparent for black husbands but absent in the results for black wives. It should be noted, however, that no significant finding for any group about how *Zest* or any other personal styles relate to happiness produced results in one group that were significantly different from the parallel results in the other groups. The impact of other aspects of positive personal style can be found in the

Table 5.3. *Predicting 4th-year marital happiness among stable couples with positive versus negative personal factors assessed in the 3rd year (by race × gender)*

	White couples						Black couples					
	Wives (N = 100)			Husbands (N = 98)			Wives (N = 53)			Husbands (N = 52)		
		Partial r Yr 3 control[a]			Partial r Yr 3 control[a]			Partial r Yr 3 control[a]			Partial r Yr 3 control[a]	
Positive vs. negative personal factors	r	No	Yes	r	No	Yes	r	No	Yes	r	No	Yes
W's zest	40***	32***	21**	29**	18*	11	03	22	08	21	33**	25
H's zest	10	−07	−04	23***	06	00	−12	−11	−13*	09	13	−14
W's agreeableness	20	11	10	32***	32***	28***	14	26*	22	00	01	−10
H's agreeableness	09	04	03	05	16	18	04	−26*	−25*	−13	−18	−09
W's abrasiveness	−04	01	01	01	−01	−01	−26*	−21	−15	−14	−30**	−09
H's abrasiveness	−03	00	13	26*	12	14	−17	−11	−11	−11	−06	−08
W's anxiety	−15	−04	08	05	20**	22**	−01	11	06	06	26*	12
H's anxiety	−15	−19	−13	17	−09	−03	−23	−33**	−28*	−05	−14	11

Note: Partial r computed from regression analyses that include all positive versus negative personal factors, and three control variables (Cohabitation, Premarital Parental Status, 1st-Year Household Income).

[a] For marital happiness Year 3.

*p < .10. **p < .05. ***p < .01.

results for white husbands who are positively affected by their own optimistic style and their wives' agreeableness. Thus for white husbands more than for anyone else, we have results indicating that their spouses' being zestful and agreeable through their cooperative and considerate ways (two of the items on the Agreeableness scale) contributes to the husbands' having particularly satisfying marriages.

With regard to negative characteristics of spouses that affect a person's experience of an especially satisfying marriage, a curious pattern emerges for black couples. Black wives' anxious styles have a *positive* impact on satisfying marriages of their husbands (as it does for white wives), but black husbands' anxious styles have a *negative* impact on their wives' marriages. We expected that the presence of negative characteristics would adversely affect spouses' marriage. We have further evidence for such an expectation in the negative impact that black wives' *Abrasiveness* has on both wives' and husbands' marriages.

Results that need closer attention are those suggesting that wives' *Anxiety* has a positive effect on their husbands' satisfaction with the marriages. Why is this so? Anxiety may reflect and reinforce the young wife's concern about playing the spouse role adequately – that is, pleasing her husband. We can speculate that her anxiety also may feed into men's protective concerns. When wives are anxious, men can be the caretakers. The reverse does not happen. Indeed, black husbands who are anxious have a negative effect on their wives' satisfaction with their marriages.

In sum, agreeableness and zest appear to have positive payoffs for marriages, and abrasiveness has negative payoffs. Anxiety can have either negative or positive consequences depending on whether a man or woman exhibits such a style, respectively. Furthermore, it will be important to see in overall multivariate analysis in the later sections whether these personal styles, either positive or negative, are associated with certain kinds of interactive patterns, which in turn help explain how these styles have their impact on marital happiness.

Controlling for 3rd-Year Marital Happiness. Again the predictors tended to be considerably dampened when 3rd-year marital happiness was entered into the regression models for positive–negative personal factors that predict 4th-year marital happiness. However, two results remain strong – the effect of white wives' *Agreeableness* and *Anxiety* on the marital happiness of their husbands. This suggests that these characteristics in white women have considerable generative power in producing satisfied husbands. Following traditional "feminine" characteristics may be just what white males need to maintain their sense of satisfaction in marriage over time in these early years.

Affective Balance in Interactive Style. In Table 5.4, a number of interactive factors distinguish the happy from unhappy marriages in our group of stable marriages. Sharing leisure activities and time together, the frequency and style of conflict, the partners' supportiveness of each other, and positive and negative sex all bear reliable relationships to happiness in at least one of our analysis groups.

Companionateness with spouse tends to be related to marital happiness for wives, but is clearly related for black husbands. Among the black husbands, the relationship holds up in the multiple regression analysis. For the black men, *Companionateness* with their partners is a powerful predictor of well-being in stable marriages when other predictors and controls are entered in the analysis.

The other item closely related to *Companionateness* is *Shared Leisure* with one's spouse. In this case, we get first-order relationships to marital happiness in three of our four groups (white wives and both husbands and wives in the black sample), and for white wives the relationship holds up in the multiple regression analysis. Only the white husbands seem impervious to the amount of time or leisure they spend with their wives – impervious in that it does not affect their marital happiness one way or the other.

The factor that appears to have the greatest impact on the happiness of white husbands is sex. White husbands who rate their marital sex positively also report that they are very happy in their marriages. If they say that their sex life is not so good, they also indicate that their marriages are not so happy. *Positive Sexual Interaction* shows a zero-order relationship to happiness for wives of both racial groups, and for white wives it remains significant when we proceed to the multivariate analysis. Black wives also show a zero-order relationship of *Negative Sexual Interaction* and lowered marital happiness. Thus black wives who say that their marital sex is problematic also indicate that their marriages are not as happy as they might be.

Only the black husbands – who seem to depend on the time and activity with their partners as a basis of their marital happiness, as noted in the preceding results – do not seem to depend on the role of sex in having especially happy marriages. The partial correlation between *Positive Sexual Interaction* and marital happiness is significantly lower in black husbands than it is in white husbands. The affection implied in spending time and sharing leisure activities together is apparently more crucial to black husbands' experience of marital happiness. In fact, *Companionateness* was

Table 5.4. *Predicting 4th-year marital happiness among stable couples with positive versus negative interactive factors assessed in the 3rd year (by race × gender)*

	White couples						Black couples					
	Wives (N = 100)			Husbands (N = 98)			Wives (N = 53)			Husbands (N = 52)		
		Partial r Yr 3 control[a]			Partial r Yr 3 control[a]			Partial r Yr 3 control[a]			Partial r Yr 3 control[a]	
Positive vs. negative interactive factors	r	No	Yes	r	No	Yes	r	No	Yes	r	No	Yes
Companionateness	21**	01	02	08	03	06	27*	00	02	52***	43***	44***
Positive sexual interaction	27**	31***	26**	22**	34***	35***	37***	11	01	14	-17	-26*
Negative sexual interaction	-18	10	08	-09	20**	22**	-30**	05	-01	-11	-12	-18
Frequency of conflict	-17	-09	-05	-08	-13	-21*	-54***	-37***	-30*	-26*	11	25
Shared leisure	-36***	-30***	-22**	00	07	15	-29*	03	03	-32**	-20	-29
W's destructive conflict style	-07	05	02	-07	00	01	00	-19	-18	-18	-25*	-06
H's destructive conflict style	-11	-06	05	03	15	27**	02	01	-09	-02	12	03
W's constructive conflict style	-05	-14	-16	05	-01	-03	24	14	20	-24*	-27*	-21
H's constructive conflict style	02	06	01	13	16	18*	-04	-31**	-36**	28*	17	21
Absence of H's support	-29**	-28***	-19	-04	-02	00	-21	-16	-10	-13	20	26*
Absence of W's support	-13	21**	21**	03	06	12	-34**	-16	-15	-42***	-37***	-20

Note: Partial r computed from regression analyses that include all positive versus negative interactive factors, and three control variables (Cohabitation, Premarital Parental Status, 1st-Year Household Income).

[a]For marital happiness Year 3.

*p < .10. **p < .05. ***p < .01.

significantly higher in its prediction of marital happiness in black husbands than it was for any other group.

As predicted, the absence of support on the part of a spouse is a negative factor for the marital happiness of white wives and black husbands. While the results for black wives are not significant, the trend is in the right direction. The most curious finding is that white husbands were not influenced by a spouse's absence of support. This finding is consistent with a study conducted with older, predominantly white, couples by Acitelli and Antonucci (1994). They found that spouses' social support predicted the marital satisfaction of wives only.

Further, in the multivariate analyses, the absence of support on the part of wives was a positive predictor of white wives' happiness and not related to white husbands' happiness. It may be the case that when white husbands take their concerns elsewhere, wives are happier in their marriages.

In addition, conflict plays a somehow more significant role in the happiness (or unhappiness) of young black couples than it does for white couples. For the black wives, the frequency of conflict they report is negatively related to their marital happiness. This shows up as a correlation, remains significant in the multiple regression, and is significantly higher for them than it is for their husbands. Further, style of conflict behavior is also significantly related to black couples' marital happiness. It is somewhat puzzling at first glance. For the young black wives, their husbands' constructive conflict style (i.e., responding to conflict with reasonable conciliatory, problem-solving actions) has a *negative* effect on their happiness. In this case, the effect is apparently suppressed by other variables and only appears in the multiple regression. Similarly, for the young black husbands, their wives' constructive conflict style has a negative effect on their happiness. This effect is true for both the zero-order correlation and the multiple regression.

The finding that more conflict should lead to more unhappiness in the marriage seems on its face a reasonable outcome. The question arises: Why does this relationship appear so prominently among black wives, at least in comparison with their husbands? And while *Destructive Conflict Style* seemed reasonably related to lower marital happiness, why should a constructive style also have negative effects on marital happiness? Kochman (1981) has observed that conflict style in the black community may be different from the dominant white style. For many blacks, being more open and expressive may mean less fear that conflict will inevitably lead to violence or disruption of relationships. Under these normative conditions, partners may become particularly susceptible to overinterpreting constructive conflict gestures as condescending, withdrawing, less engaged, or involved, perhaps causes for suspicion.

Controlling for 3rd-Year Marital Happiness. Most of the 3rd-year inter-active positive versus negative factors that were found to be related to 4th-year marital happiness continue to be significantly related even when 3rd-year marital happiness is entered into the regression model. In fact, a number of predictors become significant after being suppressed in the pre-vious regression models. These results are important because they suggest that affective balance regarding marital interaction can have a causal con-nection to later marital well-being. The aftereffects of interactive styles may be more long lasting and cumulative and not quickly translated into marital quality.

Dialectical Tension of Affirmation of Self Versus Relational Gratification in Happy Marriages

Measures

We explored four measures that reflect different ways of thinking about the affirmation of self found in dialectical balance with relational gratification in marriage. The first, *Affective Affirmation,* is derived from Oggins, Veroff, and Leber's (1993) factor analysis of perceived marital interactions; it is a sum of four items (alpha = .80) indicating in one way or another that the spouse makes the person feel good about himself/herself in the relationship. One item in this scale, for example, asks whether the person's spouse makes the person "feel good about the kind of person you are." The second mea-sure is a single item asking the person whether he/she feels his/her spouse does not understand him/her (*Lack of understanding*). The third three-item measure (alpha = .50), *Competence,* assesses how competent the person feels in the marital relationship (i.e., feelings of inadequacy as a spouse). The last, *Control* (alpha = .63), is a two-item measure that assesses the per-ceived control that the person has in affecting well-being for his/her spouse (i.e., being able to make a distressed spouse feel better). The latter two mea-sures are derived from Crohan and Veroff's (1989) factor analyses of di-mensions of marital well-being. Each of the four measures assesses ways that a husband and wife might feel good about themselves within their mar-ital relationship and hence find some balance between self and relational needs that may be in dialectical tension.

Results

The results are reported in Table 5.5. For all men and women, the measure of *Affective Affirmation* is positively linked to having particularly satisfying marriages. This is as expected. What was not expected is how important this measure is for predicting men's well-being in comparison with women's. We find that in the multivariate treatment of the variables that *Affective Affirmation* is not significant for women. On the other hand, the measure seems to be a primary issue for men's feelings of happiness in these stable marriages. While the correlation between the measure of affirmation and marital well-being is not significantly higher in white men compared with white women, it is significantly different in black men compared with black women. We thus tentatively conclude that being affirmed by one's spouse plays a more prominent role in men's marital happiness than it does in women's.

The measure of affirmation of the self in marriage that has the largest effect on women's well-being is the husband's *Lack of Understanding*. This factor survives multivariate treatment of the various measures of affirmation, for both white and black women; the greater lack of understanding by husbands, the less happiness in wives.

How is *Lack of Understanding* different from *Affective Affirmation*? In a certain sense, understanding entails appreciating the position or role that a person is in while affirmation goes one step further because it entails appreciating that particular person in the role. One would have thought that affirmation would be critical for women, but if women feel that the greatest obstacle to their satisfaction in marriage is their relegation to an inferior role status, their lack of power, then maybe the greatest concern for satisfaction *is* understanding. Can there be women who feel affirmed by their husbands but feel their husbands do not understand them? Understanding is a necessary condition for affirmation. One might guess that some women feel appreciated as sex objects, or feel that their husbands are passionately involved with them and their ideas, or are very dependent upon them for support and comfort, who nevertheless still feel that their husbands do not understand their position as wives.

In the multivariate treatment only one other trend occurs among the affirmation variables predicting the well-being of couples. For black wives, their own *Competence* emerged as a suppressed variable and is negatively related to their own well-being, a finding that is significantly different from the parallel comparison for white wives. It may very well be that black women have taken on as part of their marital role assignment the cultiva-

Table 5.5. *Predicting 4th-year marital happiness among stable couples with self-affirmation factors assessed in the 3rd year (by race × gender)*

	White couples						Black couples					
	Wives (N = 100)			Husbands (N = 98)			Wives (N = 53)			Husbands (N = 52)		
		Partial r Yr 3 control[a]			Partial r Yr 3 control[a]			Partial r Yr 3 control[a]			Partial r Yr 3 control[a]	
Self-affirmation factors	r	No	Yes	r	No	Yes	r	No	Yes	r	No	Yes
W's affective affirmation	33***	15	10	18	05	-02	44***	-03	-10	16	-10	-04
H's affective affirmation	28**	-10	-11	26**	20**	11	36**	23	20	41***	46***	10
W's lack of understanding	-09	01	04	-15	-09	-04	32**	-12	-11	-04	17	19
H's lack of understanding	-47***	-30***	-24**	-13	02	00	-47***	-41***	-37**	-09	-11	-07
W's competence	24**	14	00	-03	-13	-15	04	-24*	-30*	-08	-20	-26*
H's competence	19	16*	15	-01	-08	-10	27*	23	28*	07	16	04
W's control	36**	13	10	20	14	17	27	08	08	06	-06	02
H's control	18	02	00	20	10	06	06	-07	-03	17	23	10

Note: Partial *r* computed from regression analyses that include all self-affirmation factors, and three control variables (Cohabitation, Premarital Parental Status, 1st-Year Household Income).

[a] For marital happiness Year 3.

p < .10. **p* < .05. ***p* < .01.

tion of their husbands' sense of adequacy in marriage and all that entails. Indeed, husbands' sense of competence tends to be correlated with wives' well-being. With cards stacked against black men's capacities to be good providers in the way that the larger culture demands of men, marriage can induce a considerable threat to black husbands' sense of adequacy. When that is not the case, when black husbands feel competent about being adequate husbands and those feelings are apparent to their wives, then their wives may feel particularly comfortable about their marriage. The wives' own competence may thus be problematic for their marital well-being because it may imply social inadequacy in their husband. There are other significant effects in Table 5.5, either individual correlations with the well-being measures or suppressed effects. All but one of these have to do with measures of control, but they fade in comparison with the measures of *Affective Affirmation* and *Lack of Understanding*.

Controlling for 3rd-Year Marital Happiness. The effect of *Affective Affirmation* for both black and white husbands was dampened when the 3rd-year marital happiness was entered into the equation. Yet, interestingly enough, we find that most of the significant predictors of happiness for wives (husbands' lack of understanding and wives' competence for black wives) continue to remain significant when 3rd-year happiness is entered in the model. For both black and white wives, husbands' lack of understanding may have accumulative effects over time.

Integration of Perspectives

We have clear evidence for each of the theoretical frameworks with which we began in thinking about happiness in stable marriages. Aspects of how couples deal with their gender roles are associated with marital satisfaction; some contribution of both positive and negative feelings about the person and the relational interactions enter into marital satisfaction; and indeed some affirmation of self in the relationship seems to be critical to marital satisfaction. All of this is independent of the contribution of certain control variables. While we find that the Year 1 Household Income positively predicts marital well-being for white wives and Premarital Parental Status predicts marital *un*happiness for black wives, these factors do not wash out the significance of the psychological variables we have been discussing.

The question that remains, however, is whether there is any reason to think that one of the three formulations has more explanatory power than the others. This question can be approached by combining the strong pre-

Table 5.6. *Predicting 4th-year marital happiness among stable white couples with all significant (p < .05) predictions from previous analyses*

	Partial r	
	Yr 3[a] control	
Significant previous predictions	No	Yes
Wives ($N = 100$)		
Husband's accommodation	−22**	−17
Wife's zest	17*	14
Positive sexual interaction	22*	19*
Shared leisure	−14	−10
Husband's absence of support	−19*	−13
Husband's lack of understanding	−21**	−16
Husbands ($N = 98$)		
Husband's accommodation	−15	−11
Wife's zest	12	07
Wife's agreeableness	29***	24**
Positive sexual interaction	25**	25**
Negative sexual interaction	15	14
Husband's affective affirmation	07	−02

Note: Partial r computed from multiple-regression analyses that include all prior significant ($p < .05$) factors and three control variables (Cohabitation, Premarital Parental Status, 1st-Year Household Income).
[a]For marital happiness.
*$p < .10$. **$p < .05$. ***$p < .01$.

dictors from each set in a high-order regression analysis to see which variables emerge as particularly potent ones in comparison with the others. We ran four separate regression analyses for the 4 Race × Gender groups, each with the variables from the previous analyses that were significant at the .05 level or better in the multivariate analyses. These results are summarized in Tables 5.6 and 5.7 for the white couples and the black couples, respectively.

Tables 5.6 and 5.7 indicate that our understanding of well-being in stable marriages receives the most explanatory power from the variables focusing on issues of affective balance, followed closely by variables focusing on issues of self-affirmation. Role-construction concerns are less powerful in the array of predictors we have selected except for black husbands. Furthermore, most of the affective balance variables that remain important in predicting especially satisfying marriages in the analyses reported in Tables 5.6 and 5.7 derive from assessments of the nature of marital interaction. Most of the affective balance measures deriving from personal

Table 5.7. *Predicting 4th-year marital happiness among stable black couples with all significant (p < .05) predictors from previous analyses*

| | Partial *r* | |
| | Yr 3[a] control | |
Significant previous predictors	No	Yes
Wives (*N* = 53)		
Frequency of conflict	−29**	−25*
Husband's lack of understanding	−41***	−35**
Husband's constructive conflict style	−30**	−31**
Husband's anxiety	−30**	−29**
Husbands (*N* = 52)		
Role-sharing orientation	19	22
Parental status	34**	32**
Companionateness	32**	22
Wife's lack of support	−09	−03
Husband's affective affirmation	32**	04
Wife's zest	20	23
Wife's abrasiveness	−07	−08

Note: Partial *r* computed from multiple regression analyses that include all significant (*p* < .05) variables from previous analyses and three control variables (Cohabitation, Premarital Parental Status, 1st-Year Household Income).
[a]For Marital Happiness.
*$p < .10$. **$p < .05$. ***$p < .01$.

qualities of the spouses pale, except for two instances: for white husbands, their wives' *Agreeableness* is still a significant predictor; for black wives, their husbands' *Anxiety* remains a significant predictor, independent of other factors. Although wife's *Zest* had important and significant effects within the analyses about positive and negative personal characteristics for the white couples (see Table 5.3), it is no longer a significant ($p < .05$) predictor for these couples in Table 5.6, although it remains a trend for white wives. With regard to the affective balance interactive factors, we are once again struck by how critical positive sexual interactions are for the white couples, especially husbands. It suggests that within the dominant white culture today, experiencing pleasure through sexuality is a strong component of marital happiness for both men and women. This clearly is not prominent in its association with marital happiness for black couples. Differential socialization factors in these groups could account for this difference. Once more, the results suggest that black husbands implicitly focus more on companionateness, and black wives focus more on the absence of conflict, when evaluating their marriages.

We should note that measures of both positive and negative interaction are important, but generally only positive sources of interaction are significant for black and white men, while negative sources are significant for black and white women. Men accentuate the presence of positive in their feelings of well-being, and women tend to emphasize the absence of the negative in their feelings. Thus in thinking about affective interactive balances we cannot rule out the importance of either the positive or the negative side in general, but we must emphasize one or the other when we think about the meaning of marriage for husbands and wives separately.

The importance of affirmation of self in marriage as a basis for well-being in stable marriages is well supported in this overall analysis. Husband's *Lack of Understanding* remains a significant predictor for both black women and white women. Husband's *Affective Affirmation* also remains a significant predictor for black men. Only in the case of white men did the major affirmation of self variable (*Husband's Affective Affirmation*) disappear in the overall regression analysis. It is important to realize that for white men the strong predictor *Positive Sexual Interaction* was significantly correlated with Husband's *Affective Affirmation* ($r = .52$). This suggests that a major source of affirmation white husbands experience is a gratifying sex life with their wives. The causal connections cannot be presumed, but perhaps causal models over the 4 years could be attempted to test the hypothesis that there is a causal link between gratifying sex and feeling affirmed for white husbands.

It is interesting to realize that there is a parallel between the gender differences we obtained in considering affirmation variables and the gender differences noted above with regard to interaction variables. Women accentuate the absence of negative experiences with regard to affirmation, and men – at least the black men – emphasize the positive affirmation of self. Jesse Bernard long ago said in *The Future of Marriage* (1972) that men generally have a good deal in marriage, and women have all the burdens. If that is the case, then men might be expected to focus on their pleasures and women on minimizing their burdens as they evaluate their married life.

Limitations of the Study. Although this study has several strengths (a relatively representative urban sample of couples; data from both members of each couple; oversampling of black couples; a wide variety of psychological and interpersonal aspects of marriage), some of its limitations should be mentioned. These couples represent a subset of marriages in the United States. All of the couples in the sample have been married for 4 years, and all are in stable marriages. Thus we do not examine how the various factors affect longer-term marriages, unstable couples, or those that have already divorced. But we chose to study this subset of couples for important reasons.

First, we wanted to follow a sample of married couples from the time they first married through the early years of marriage. The young couple's transition to marriage is an important developmental stage in the lives of many young adults and may be pivotal to the survival of the marriage. Second, we wanted to focus on what makes marriages work, rather than factors that lead to divorce. Thus we chose to limit our sample to those couples who were very stable and focused on factors that predicted their happiness. It should be noted, however, that with such a sample there is a restricted range on scores of marital happiness. Thus our results could be underestimating the connections between variables because of the difficulty of obtaining significant effects with attenuated distributions.

A concern with the many different analyses that were performed in the study is that we may have been capitalizing on chance findings. However, our reliance on patterns of findings, rather than any single correlation, guards against overinterpretation of any single or chance finding.

Another characteristic of the study that could be perceived as a limitation is its reliance on self-report and the shared variance that might occur as a result of similar methods being used to assess various factors. Moreover, variables that are considered interactive are not really observed interactions, but rather spouses' perceptions or impressions of how they interact as a couple. However, one of the main goals of this project is to discover how partners create a marital relationship by mentally constructing the norms that govern it. We believe the best way to shed light on that mental construction is to ask respondents to report on their own thoughts and feelings about the relationship.

Conclusion

What can we say about what makes for especially satisfying marriage, once we filter out the marriages in which there is some clear element of instability? It is hard to draw a general conclusion without specifying whether we are talking about a man or a woman, a black couple or a white couple. This is perhaps as it should be because gender and ethnicity can have important effects in setting norms for smooth functioning in marriage and for evaluating whether gratification is occurring in one's relationship. We tried to examine gender role norms with the measures of gender role construction, but using these particular measures did not have great payoffs. Few of the analyses revealed that gender considerations had differential implications for happiness in stable marriages. And those variables that were significant worked differently for the different groups. The different ways that men and women structure their marriages emerge in more subtle ways. And the ways that black couples and white couples structure their marriages are also quite different, again in quite subtle ways.

Nevertheless, we can conclude that for all groups, the affective consequences of some aspects of marital interaction as well as the sense of self affirmation in the marital relationship in one way or another are the major issues that husbands and wives consider in evaluating their marital happiness. We must remember, however, that the interaction of race and gender affect which aspect of interaction, and which basis of self-affirmation, are prominent in creating a gratifying marriage.

Notes

1. We resisted focusing on these multivariate analyses with 3rd-year marital happiness as an additional predictor because results emerging from them will point to what predictors are related to *changes* in marital happiness from Year 3 to Year 4. They undermine our understanding of the general correlational hypotheses of how factors in marital experience are connected to marital happiness. Overcontrolling for 3rd-year marital happiness could hide the dynamic interplay that must exist between marital experiences and the evaluation of marital well-being. There is every reason to think that these factors are constantly related to well-being over time, without necessarily being causally connected to further change. Nevertheless, we will present results from these more refined analyses to underscore factors that do have potential causal linkages to changes in marital well-being from the 3rd to the 4th year.

2. In this and subsequent sections describing the measures used, the measures are based on responses to the individual face-to-face interviews in the 3rd year of marriage, unless otherwise indicated.

3. The accommodation score was the sum across all the descriptors of the difference between two discrepancies: the discrepancy for the actual self from Year 1 to Year 3, and the discrepancy between the spouse's ideal and actual judgments about him/her.

4. The product rather than the sum of items was arbitrarily used in a number of instances to give more weight to those couples who agreed on the presence or absence of a given type of interactive style or marital experience in their lives.

References

Acitelli, L. K., & Antonucci, T. C. (1994). Gender differences in the link between marital support and satisfaction in older couples. *Journal of Personality and Social Psychology, 67,* 688–698.

Austin, W. G. (1974). *Studies in "equity with the world": A new application of equity theory.* Unpublished doctoral dissertation. University of Wisconsin.

Bakan, D. (1966). *The duality of human existence.* Boston: Beacon Press.

Bellah, R. N., Madsen, R., Sullivan, W. M., Swidler, A., & Tipton, S. M. (1985). *Habits of the heart.* Berkeley, CA: University of California Press.

Bernard, J. (1972). *The future of marriage.* New York: World.

Bradburn, N. (1969). *The structure of psychological well-being.* Chicago: Aldine.

Chodorow, N. (1978). *The reproduction of mothering: Psychoanalysis and the sociology of gender.* Berkeley, CA: University of California Press.

Crohan, S. E., & Veroff, J. (1989). Dimensions of marital well-being among white and black newlyweds. *Journal of Marriage and the Family, 51,* 373–384.

Cuber, J. F., & Harroff, P. B. (1965). *The significant Americans.* New York: Appleton Century Crofts.

Gilligan, C. (1982). *In a different voice: Psychological theory and women's development.* Cambridge, MA: Harvard University Press.

Gottman, J. M., & Krokoff, L. J. (1989). Marital interaction and satisfaction: A longitudinal view. *Journal of Consulting and Clinical Psychology, 57,* 47–52.

Gottman, J. M., & Levenson, R. W. (1988). The social psychophysiology of marriage. In P. Noller & M. A. Fitzpatrick (Eds.), *Perspectives on marital interaction* (pp. 182–200). Levedon, England: Multilingual Matters.

Hatchett, S., Veroff, J., & Douvan, E. (1996). Marital instability among newlywed black and white couples. In B. Tucker & C. Mitchell Kernan (Eds.), *The crisis in black marriages.* New York: Russell Sage.

Heaton, T. B., & Albrecht, S. L. (1991). Stable unhappy marriages. *Journal of Marriage and the Family, 53,* 747–758.

Kelley, H. H. (1983). Love and commitment. In H. H. Kelley, E. Berscheid, A. Christensen, J. H. Harvey, T. L. Huston, E. McClintock, L. A. Peplau, & D. Peterson (Eds.), *Close relationships* (pp. 265–314). New York: W. H. Freeman.

Kitson, G. (1992). *Portrait of divorce: Adjustment to marital breakdown.* New York: Guilford.

Kochman, T. (1981). *Black and white styles of conflict.* Chicago: University of Chicago Press.

Levinger, G. (1965). Marital cohesiveness and dissolution: An integrative review. *Journal of Marriage and Family, 17,* 19–28.

Malley, J. C. (1989). *The balance of agency and communion: Adjustment and adaptation in single parents.* Unpublished doctoral dissertation. Boston University.

Malley, J. C., & Veroff, J. (1990). *Agency and communion in black and white newlywed couples.* Unpublished manuscript.

Maslow, A. (1954). *Motivation and personality.* New York: Harper and Row.

Oggins, J., Veroff, J., & Leber, D. (1993). Perceptions in interaction among black and white newlyweds. *Journal of Personality and Social Psychology, 65,* 494–511.

Olds, J. (1956). Pleasure centers in the brain. *Scientific American, 195,* 105–116.

Orbuch, T. (1994). *Rolesharing and marital well-being in black couples and white couples.* Unpublished manuscript.

Rubin, L. (1976). *Worlds of pain.* New York: Basic Books.

Rusbult, C. E., & Buunk, B. P. (1993). Commitment processes in close relationships: An interdependence analysis. *Journal of Social and Personal Relationships, 10,* 175–204.

Ruvolo, A. (1990). *Interpersonal ideals and personal change in newlyweds: A longitudinal analysis.* Unpublished doctoral dissertation. University of Michigan.

Ryff, C. C. (1989). Happiness is everything, or is it? Explorations on the meaning of psychological well-being. *Journal of Personality and Social Psychology, 57,* 1069–1081.

Teachman, J. D., & Polonko, K. A. (1990). Cohabitation and marital stability in the United States. *Social Forces, 69,* 207–220.

Vega, W. A. (1990). Hispanic families in the 1980s: A decade of research. *Journal of Marriage and the Family, 52,* 1015–1024.

Veroff, J. (1992, July). *Early marriage in black and white.* Paper presented at the International Society for the Study of Personal Relationships. Orono, Maine.

Veroff, J., Douvan, E., & Hatchett, S. (1993). Marital interaction and marital quality in the first year of marriage. In W. Jones & D. Perlman (Eds.), *Advances in personal relationships, 4,* 103–137.

Veroff, J., Douvan, E., & Hatchett, S. (1995). *Marital instability.* Westport, CT: Praeger.

Veroff, J., Douvan, E., & Kulka, R. (1981). *The inner American.* New York: Basic Books.

Veroff, J., Sutherland, L., Chadiha, L., & Ortega, R. (1993). Newlyweds tell their stories. *Journal of Social and Personal Relationships, 10,* 437–457.

Young, A., Franz, C., Veroff, J., & Frieband, D. (1993). *Cluster analyses of the stability of self and other perceptions over time.* Unpublished paper.

6 Developmental Changes in Marital Satisfaction: A 6-Year Prospective Longitudinal Study of Newlywed Couples

Lawrence A. Kurdek

Although the early years of marriage are critical for marital stability (National Center for Health Statistics, 1991), little is known about the processes that maintain marital happiness in stable couples (Dindia & Canary, 1993). The lack of information in this area is unfortunate in light of evidence that even spouses in stable relationships can be dissatisfied with their marriages (Heaton & Albrecht, 1991) and that marital dissatisfaction is linked to physical and psychological problems (Bloom, Asher, & White, 1978).

The relative neglect of what maintains marital happiness may be due to the scarcity of longitudinal studies in the early years of marriage. There are longitudinal data (e.g., Belsky & Rovine, 1990; Cowan et al., 1985; Hackel & Ruble, 1992; MacDermid, Huston, & McHale, 1990; Markman & Hahlweg, 1993) consistent with the view that marital quality declines over the first few years of marriage as spouses negotiate issues regarding conflict, control, and power (Kovacs, 1983). However, most of this information comes from studies of spouses during the transition to first-time parenthood. Without a comparison group of spouses not experiencing this transition, normative changes in marital interactions are confounded with those resulting from parenthood (see Chapter 7 in this volume).

Consequently, longitudinal studies involving newlywed couples who do and do not become parents are needed to chart the developmental course of marital well-being. However, even such studies would not do justice to the variety of couples now entering new marriages. Because remarriage rates have paralleled divorce rates (Wilson & Clarke, 1992), and because about 16% of remarried couples have at least one stepchild (Moorman & Hernandez, 1989), a comprehensive study of change in marital well-being also

I would like to thank the couples who participated in this study; David Arnold, Glenna Darnell-Goetschel, and Pete McConnell for their assistance in subject recruitment and data entry; and Mark Fine and Tom Bradbury for comments on an earlier version of the paper.

180

needs to include remarried persons with and without stepchildren. This chapter presents findings from a longitudinal study of newlywed husbands and wives, some of whom were in first marriages and eventually had children and some of whom were in remarriages with stepchildren. Spouses were first assessed shortly after marriage (Year 1) and then again at five annual follow-ups (Year 2 through Year 6).[1]

The first purpose of this study was to describe patterns of change in marital satisfaction over the first 6 years of marriage. Marital satisfaction was of interest because it figures prominently in theories of relationship commitment and relationship stability. For example, Rusbult (1983) postulated that low relationship satisfaction is the joint effect of perceiving few rewards from the relationship, perceiving many costs to being in the relationship, and perceiving the relationship as falling short of an internalized standard of what a "good" relationship should be. On the basis of previous models of marital change (e.g., Kovacs, 1983) as well as previous empirical evidence (e.g., Markman & Hahlweg, 1993), it was predicted that marital satisfaction for husbands and wives would show a linear decrease over time, with a particularly noticeable drop occurring after the first year of marriage (a "honeymoon is over" effect).

The second purpose of this study was to identify Year 1 risk factors that predicted both low marital satisfaction at Year 6 and the rate at which marital satisfaction declined over the 6-year period. Given current interest in the prevention of marital distress (Markman & Hahlweg, 1993), documentation of such risk variables has practical significance. The risk variables of interest in this study come from four conceptual approaches guiding much of the current study of marital well-being. These are demographic, individual differences, interdependence, and spousal discrepancy approaches.[2] The specific risk variables of interest from each set as well as the way in which these variables may be linked to low marital satisfaction (i.e., few rewards, many costs, and an unmet standard) are discussed in turn.

The major premise of the *demographic approach* is that negative marital well-being is linked to personal demographic variables, relationship demographic variables, and child-related variables (Raschke, 1987). Persons who are young, not well educated, and unemployed or poorly paid – the personal demographic risk variables of interest – may perceive few rewards from their marriage, perceive many costs to their marriage, and generate unattainable standards for their marriage because they are ill-equipped to perform marital roles and because cumulative stressful changes are imminent in their marriages (Crohan & Veroff, 1989; Morgan & Rindfuss, 1985). The relationship demographic risk variables of interest were divorce history, length of acquaintance, and whether finances were pooled. Persons who re-marry after divorce may have high thresholds for marital rewards and low thresholds for marital costs (Booth & Edwards, 1992); persons who marry after brief courtships are likely to incur high costs to being in their marriage as they gradually discover negative characteristics of their spouses and be-latedly experience ineffectual strategies for resolving conflict (Raschke, 1987); and couples who do not pool finances may perceive fewer rewards from their marriages than those who do because the lack of joint income lowers the amount of marital-specific capital (e.g., home ownership; Green-stein, 1990). Finally, whereas children born postmaritally may be costly because they decrease the leisure time both spouses have for each other (MacDermid et al., 1990), stepchildren may be costly because of tensions surrounding the ambiguity of the stepparent role (Giles-Sims, 1987).

The *individual differences approach* to the study of marital well-being posits that certain personality traits predispose a partner to distort relation-ship events or to overreact to negative relationship events (Baucom & Ep-stein, 1990; Bradbury & Fincham, 1991). These risk traits may bias a spouse to perceive few rewards and many costs in the marriage, and to see the cur-rent marriage as falling short of an internalized standard (Kurdek, 1991b). Although the "divorce-prone" personality has long been of interest (e.g., Kelly, 1939), recent studies collectively provide support for four facets of this personality that were of interest in this study. These are dispositions to experience negative affect, to be low in expressivity, to endorse dysfunc-tional beliefs regarding relationships, and to be dissatisfied with perceived social support (Bradbury & Fincham, 1988; Kelly & Conley, 1987; Kurdek & Schmitt, 1986).

The *interdependence approach* to marital well-being posits that per-ceiving few rewards and many costs in the relationship, and perceiving the relationship as falling short of one's ideal relationship results in low levels of dependence on the relationship. On the basis of previous work, low de-pendence was operationalized as low confidence and security (i.e., faith) in the partner and the relationship (Rempel, Holmes, & Zanna, 1985), a low value on attachment in the relationship (Cochran & Peplau, 1985; Kur-dek & Schmitt, 1986), a high value on autonomy in the relationship (Kur-dek, 1992), weak intrinsic motives for being in the relationship (Blais, Sabourin, Boucher, & Vallerand, 1990; Rempel et al., 1985), and strong extrinsic motives for being in the relationship (Blais et al., 1990; Rempel et al., 1985).

Finally, the *spousal discrepancy approach* to the study of relationship well-being predicts that large differences between partners on individual differences variables or on level of interdependence are risk factors for relationship distress (Bentler & Newcomb, 1978; Larsen & Olson, 1989). Partners with large discrepancies on individual differences scores may experience difficulties because they appraise relationship events from incompatible vantage points (Cowan et al., 1985). Partners who vary in their levels of interdependence may experience distress because one or both of them lack the investment in the relationship to work on communicating constructively about critical relationship problems (Christensen & Shenk, 1991). In either case, these discrepancies are likely to decrease the rewards and increase the costs of being in the relationship.

Generalizing from past studies of concurrent correlates of marital satisfaction, low marital satisfaction at Year 6 for each spouse was expected to be related to high levels of risk for Year 1 demographic scores (young age, few years of education, low income, the couple's not pooling finances, the couple's having been acquainted few months, each spouse having been divorced, and the presence of stepchildren); Year 1 individual differences scores (high negative affectivity, low expressivity, many dysfunctional beliefs about relationships, and low satisfaction with perceived social support); Year 1 interdependence scores (low faith in the marriage, high value on autonomy, low value on attachment, weak intrinsic motives for being married, and strong extrinsic motives for being married); and Year 1 spousal discrepancy scores (large interspouse differences on the individual differences and interdependence scores).

However, it was unclear how well the set of Year 1 risk variables would predict the rate of change in marital satisfaction from Year 1 to Year 6. Given that the individual differences, interdependence, and spousal discrepancy risk variables themselves are likely to change over time (Markman & Hahlweg, 1993), it seemed plausible that the rate of change in marital satisfaction would be more strongly linked to the rate of change in these three sets of scores than to their Year 1 values. Although data from Years 1 through 6 were not available for the individual differences, interdependence, and spousal discrepancy scores of interest in this study, they were available for Years 1 through 4.

Finally, because the presence of children was the only demographic score that showed appreciable change over the entire 6-year period of study, the link between the rate at which children were present in the household and the rate of change in marital satisfaction was also examined. Previous work on the transition to parenthood (e.g., MacDermid et al., 1990) suggests that the rate of decrease in marital satisfaction should be highest for couples having children early in their marriage.

Method

Subjects in the Year 1 Phase of Study and Attrition Rates

Subjects were recruited from the marriage licenses published in the *Dayton Daily News* from May 1986 through January 1988. Generally, licenses appeared 1 month after the marriage. Each couple was sent a letter that described the study as an examination of factors contributing to marital happiness. If both spouses were interested in participating in the study, they returned their names and address in a postage-paid envelope. Of the 7,899 couples who received the letter, 1,407 indicated an interest in the study. This response rate of 18% is similar to that obtained from other studies recruiting subjects from public records (e.g., 17% by Spanier, 1976). Completed surveys were mailed in by 538 couples at Year 1 for a return rate of 38%.

Follow-up mailed data were obtained at Years 2, 3, 4, 5, and 6 from 402, 319, 272, 241, and 205 couples, respectively. The loss of 333 couples over the 6 years was due to separation/divorce ($n = 71$), voluntary withdrawal from the study ($n = 86$), not responding to the surveys ($n = 166$), inability to locate ($n = 7$), and death of spouse ($n = 3$). Because of their small numbers, couples with 6 years of data in which a spouse was remarried after death of a spouse, couples experiencing premarital pregnancy, and couples in which the wife was a residential stepmother were excluded, leaving a final sample of 186 stably married couples. Bias among the couples in this sample is addressed later by comparing them with couples in the withdraw and no-response groups who were not excluded by the above criteria.

Measure of Year 1 Through Year 6 Marital Satisfaction

Marital satisfaction from Year 1 through Year 6 was assessed by the 10-item Dyadic Satisfaction score of the Dyadic Adjustment Scale (Spanier, 1976). This score has been found to be an independent dimension of marital quality, to account for a large portion of the variance in other marital quality scores, and to predict relationship dissolution (Kurdek, 1993c; Sabourin, Lussier, Laplante, & Wright, 1990; Spanier, 1976).[3] The range of Cronbach's alphas for the Year 1 through Year 6 scores was .75 to .88 for husbands and .75 to .87 for wives.

Information on degree of linear change in marital satisfaction was conveyed by the slope derived from ipsative regressions in which each subject's marital satisfaction score was regressed on the year of assessment (1 through 6) to model the nature of intraindividual change (Bryk & Raudenbush, 1987).[4] The linear slope value derived from these regressions captured information about the extent to which marital satisfaction across the six annual assessments declined linearly over time (a negative slope), showed no systematic linear change over time (a slope close to 0), or increased linearly over time (a positive slope).

Measures of Risk Variables from the Demographic Approach

Subjects provided information regarding age, education, and annual personal income. The highest level of formal education completed was represented by 8 intervals ranging from completion of less than seventh grade to the award of a doctorate. Personal income was represented by 12 intervals ranging from $5,000 or less to $50,000 or more.

Subjects also provided information regarding divorce history, the number of months they and their spouse have known each other, whether finances were pooled (i.e., whether the couple had a joint savings or a joint checking account), and the presence of residential children and stepchildren. Following Booth and Edwards (1992), the couple's joint divorce history was assessed by a three-level variable (0 if both spouses were in a first marriage, 1 if one of the spouses was in a remarriage after divorce, and 2 if both spouses were in a remarriage after divorce).

By Year 6, of the 109 couples in which both spouses were married for the first time, 62 had children. Of the 42 couples in which one of the spouses was remarried after divorce, 26 had their own children and 9 involved a husband with stepchildren. Of the 35 couples in which both spouses were remarried after divorce, 7 had children of their own and 12 involved a husband with stepchildren. The mean Year 6 age of children was 2.11 years whereas that for stepchildren was 12.99 years.

The number of couples making the transition to first parenthood at Year 2, Year 3, Year 4, Year 5, and Year 6 was 15, 26, 25, 23, and 6, respectively. To take into account the timing of parenthood, a weighted presence of children score was computed. Couples not having children received a 0 on this score, whereas those making the transition at Years 6, 5, 4, 3, and 2 received scores of 1, 2, 3, 4, and 5, respectively. Thus couples living with children the longest time received the highest score.

Measures of Risk Variables from the Individual Differences Approach

Negative Affectivity. Negative affectivity was assessed by the anxiety, depression, interpersonal sensitivity, and hostility scores from the Symptom

Checklist 90-R (Derogatis, 1983). These scores reflect the dimensions of negative affectivity identified by McCrae and Costa (1987). Subjects indicated how much discomfort (0 = *not at all*, 4 = *extremely*) each of 38 problems (e.g., nervousness or shakiness inside, feeling blue, feeling that other people are unfriendly or dislike you, and temper outbursts that you could not control) caused them during the past 7 days. Cronbach's alpha for the summed composite score over Years 1 through 4 ranged from .92 to .93 for husbands and from .94 to .95 for wives.

Expressiveness. Expressiveness was assessed by the Femininity score of the Bem Sex Role Inventory (Bem, 1974). Respondents indicated how true (1 = *never or almost never true*, 7 = *always or almost always true*) each of 20 items (e.g., helpful, sympathetic, sensitive to the needs of others, understanding, and compassionate) was of them. Cronbach's alpha for the summed composite score over Years 1 through 4 ranged from .73 to .75 for husbands and from .73 to .78 for wives.

Dysfunctional Beliefs About Relationships. Dysfunctional beliefs regarding relationships were assessed by the Relationship Beliefs Inventory (Eidelson & Epstein, 1982). Respondents indicated how false or true (0 = *very false*, 5 = *very true*) each of 32 items was for them. Beliefs included that disagreement was destructive to relationships, that mindreading is expected, that partners cannot change, and that sexual perfection is expected. (Items from the original measure that tapped beliefs that men and women were different were deleted owing to questionable evidence regarding the validity of this scale, Eidelson & Epstein, 1982). Cronbach's alpha for the summed composite score over Years 1 through 4 ranged from .80 to .86 for husbands and from .85 to .88 for wives.

Satisfaction with Social Support. Respondents first read each of 6 items from the short form of the Social Support Scale (Sarason, Sarason, Shearin, & Pierce, 1987) that described ways in which people give help or support (e.g., "Think of the people you can count on to be dependable when you need help."). They then rated how satisfied (1 = *very dissatisfied*, 6 = *very satisfied*) they were with the support they received in each area. Cronbach's alpha for the summed composite score over Years 1 through 4 ranged from .87 to .92 for husbands and from .88 to .90 for wives.

Pearson correlations indicated that the eight Year 1 individual differences scores (4 for husbands, 4 for wives) did not overlap extensively. The absolute value of Pearson *r*'s ranged from .00 to .40, with a mean of .12. Consequently, each score was retained. Information regarding degree of linear change in each individual differences score over Years 1 through 4 was obtained from slopes derived from ipsative regressions.

Measures of Risk Variables from the Interdependence Approach

Faith in the Marriage. Faith in the marriage was assessed by the 6-item Faith score derived from Rempel et al.'s (1985) Trust scale. Subjects indicated the level of agreement (1 = *strongly disagree, 7 = strongly agree*) with each item (e.g., "Though times may change and the future is uncertain, I have faith that my partner will always be ready and willing to offer me strength and support, come what may."). Cronbach's alpha for the summed composite score over Years 1 through 4 ranged from .71 to .86 for husbands and from .71 to .84 for wives.

Value of Autonomy and Attachment. The value placed on autonomy and the value placed on attachment were separately assessed by Peplau and Cochran's (1981) Survey of Relationship Values. Respondents indicated how important (1 = *not important, 9 = very important*) each of 13 aspects of their relationship was to them. There were 7 items for attachment (e.g., "Living together.") and 6 items for autonomy (e.g., "Having major interests of my own outside of the relationship."). Cronbach's alpha for the summed composite autonomy score over Years 1 through 4 ranged from .63 to .69 for husbands and from .65 to .75 for wives. For the summed composite attachment score, corresponding ranges were .67 to .74 and .61 to .63.

Intrinsic and Extrinsic Motives to Be in the Marriage. Motives for being in the marriage were assessed by Rempel et al.'s (1985) Motivation Scale. Respondents indicated how much of a role (0 = *plays no role at all,* 8 = *plays a major role*) each of 14 items played in forming the basis for their relationship. Two scores were derived that reflected intrinsic (6 items, e.g., "We are close and intimate.") or extrinsic (8 items, e.g., "He/she is someone my parents would approve of.") motives. Cronbach's alpha for the summed composite intrinsic score over Years 1 through 4 ranged from .67 to .73 for husbands and from .56 to .73 for wives. Corresponding ranges for the summed composite extrinsic score was .80 to .84 and .81 to .84.

Pearson correlations indicated that the ten Year 1 interdependence scores (5 for husbands, 5 for wives) did not overlap extensively. The absolute value of Pearson r's ranged from .00 to .41, with a mean of .17. Consequently, each score was retained. Information regarding degree of linear change in each interdependence score over Years 1 through 4 was obtained from slopes derived from ipsative regressions.

Measures of Risk Variables from the Spousal Discrepancy Approach

Variables from the spousal discrepancy approach were the absolute value of the difference between spouse's individual differences scores as well as the absolute value of the difference between their interdependence scores; absolute values were used because directional differences were not of interest. Pearson correlations indicated that the nine Year 1 spousal discrepancy scores (4 individual differences scores and 5 interdependence scores) did not overlap extensively. The absolute value of Pearson r's ranged from .00 to .21, with a mean of .09. Consequently, each score was retained. Information regarding degree of linear change in each spousal discrepancy score over Years 1 through 4 was obtained from slopes derived from ipsative regressions.

Results

Bias in the Stably Married Sample

To assess bias in the longitudinal sample, the 186 stably married couples were compared with the 76 intact couples who voluntarily withdrew from the study and the 145 intact couples who did not respond to the follow-up letters on the following scores: husbands' Year 1 personal demographic and marital satisfaction variables, wives' Year 1 personal demographic and marital satisfaction scores, and Year 1 relationship demographic scores. Because most of the sample was white at each annual assessment (95% to 96% for husbands and 95% to 98% for wives) and variability limited, race was not considered. Relevant means and standard deviations are presented in Table 6.1. A one-way (follow-up status) MANOVA on these twelve Year 1 scores yielded a significant effect, $F(24, 788) = 3.45, p < .0001$. The results of subsequent one-way (follow-up status) ANOVAs and Student Newman-Keuls comparisons are also shown in Table 6.1.

Relative to couples who withdrew or did not respond, those who remained in the study were older (wives only), were better educated (husbands and wives), had higher incomes (husbands and wives), and were less likely to involve a stepfather. Although husbands from the three follow-up groups did not differ on Year 1 marital satisfaction, wives did. Specifically, wives in the longitudinal sample reported higher marital satisfaction at Year

Table 6.1. *Means and standard deviations for Year 1 demographic and marital satisfaction scores for longitudinal, withdraw, and no-response samples*

Score	Longitudinal ($n = 186$)		Withdraw ($n = 76$)		No response ($n = 145$)		$F(2,404)$
	M	SD	M	SD	M	SD	
Husband							
Age	29.49	7.97	29.86	7.77	27.84	7.38	2.46
Education	5.55^a	1.07	5.11^b	1.04	4.93^b	1.13	13.96**
Income	6.48^a	2.65	5.56^b	2.20	5.33^b	2.65	8.83**
Proportion stepfather	0.15^a	0.35	$0.19^{a,b}$	0.40	0.26^b	0.44	3.59*
Satisfaction	42.78	3.57	41.92	4.25	42.47	4.06	1.34
Wife							
Age	27.65^a	7.08	28.57^a	6.41	25.90^b	6.85	4.50**
Education	5.54^a	0.95	5.34^a	1.04	4.93^b	1.00	15.76**
Income	4.56^a	2.34	4.64^a	2.12	3.53^b	2.38	9.71**
Satisfaction	43.22^a	3.28	$41.94^{a,b}$	4.45	42.12^b	4.49	4.32**
Couple							
Divorce history	0.59	0.78	0.80	0.84	0.62	0.82	1.83
Months known	45.66	45.10	49.60	63.00	36.11	37.99	2.63
Proportion pooled finances	0.63	0.40	0.56	0.45	0.53	0.41	2.46

Notes: Maximum values for education and income were 8 and 12, respectively. Means with different superscripts differ from each other, $p < .05$.
*$p < .05$. **$p < .01$.

1 than did wives in the no-response group but reported levels of Year 1 marital satisfaction that were equivalent to those in the withdraw group. Because of the low response rate in the original sample and because of the above-noted biases in the longitudinal sample, the findings of this study may not be representative of all stably married couples.

The Nature of Change in Marital Satisfaction from Year 1 to Year 6

To test the hypothesis that marital satisfaction would decline over the 6-year period, and to see if this decline was moderated by spouse, husbands' and wives' Dyadic Satisfaction scores for each of the 6 years were submitted to a 6 (Year) × 2 (Spouse) multivariate analysis of variance. Year and spouse were repeated measures factors. The degrees of freedom for the Year effect were decomposed into three single-degree-of-freedom trend effects. The first effect tested a linear trend, the second effect tested a curvilinear trend, and the third tested for deviations from the linear and curvilinear trends. Means are plotted by year for husbands and wives in Figure 6.1 (standard deviations are also presented).

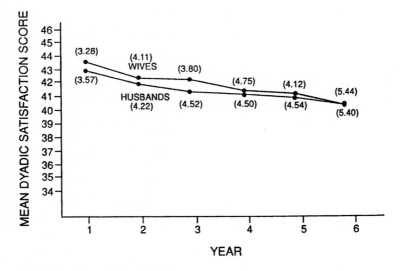

Figure 6.1. Mean Dyadic Satisfaction scores by year of assessment for husbands and wives (standard deviations in parentheses).

The only significant effects were the three trend effects. The linear trend effect was largest, $F(1, 185) = 91.83, p < .001$, followed by the curvilinear effect, $F(1, 185) = 4.29, p < .05$, and the deviations from the linear/curvilinear effects, $F(3, 183) = 3.14, p < .05$. As expected, and as shown in Figure 6.1, the change in marital satisfaction for husbands and wives showed the same pattern: a gradual decline over the 6-year period, with the steepest drop (accounting for the curvilinear effect) between Years 1 and 2. As also shown in Figure 6.1, standard deviations tended to increase across the 6 years of study.

Consistent with the linear trend effects just reported, the mean linear slope value derived from ipsative regressions on marital satisfaction was significantly negative for husbands, slope = $-0.48, t(185) = -7.74, p < .001$, and for wives, slope = $-0.59, t(185) = -9.17, p < .001$. More important, there was appreciable variability in the rate of linear change for both spouses. As shown in Figure 6.2, slopes for husbands ranged from -4.08 to 1.57. As shown in Figure 6.3, slopes for wives ranged from -5.08 to 1.34.

Predicting Year 6 Marital Satisfaction from Year 1 Risk Scores

To assess whether any of the four sets of Year 1 risk scores predicted Year 6 marital satisfaction for husbands and wives, multiple regressions were conducted for each spouse. To identify more easily patterns of findings, bivariate correlations for individual risk scores within a set were interpreted

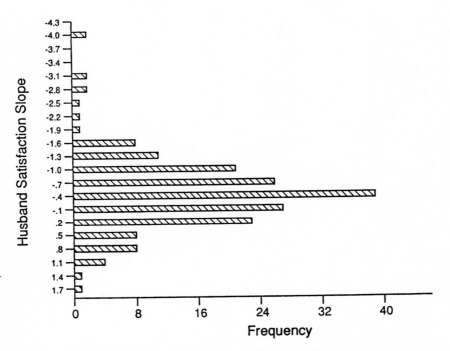

Figure 6.2. Frequency distribution of husband's linear slopes for change in marital satisfaction from Year 1 through Year 6.

only when the R^2 associated with the entire set of risk scores was significant. Because the focus here was on the predictive information of each risk score rather than the unique information provided by each risk score in relation to the information provided by the entire set of risk scores, bivariate correlations rather than beta weights were of interest.[5]

For baseline purposes, Pearson correlations and multiple R^2 values are presented first between each spouse's Year 1 marital satisfaction and the set of Year 1 demographic, individual differences, interdependence, and spousal discrepancy risk scores. Values for husbands are shown in column 1 of Table 6.2, whereas those for wives are shown in column 2. All R^2's except that involving the demographic risk scores and husbands' marital satisfaction were significant.[6]

Of key interest in the next set of analyses was whether the sets of risk variables retained their predictive value at Year 6. As shown by the R^2 values in column 3 of Table 6.2, for husbands, only the set of Year 1 interdependence risk variables maintained its predictive value, although at a much lower level. R^2 was .43 for Year 1 marital satisfaction versus .15 for Year 6

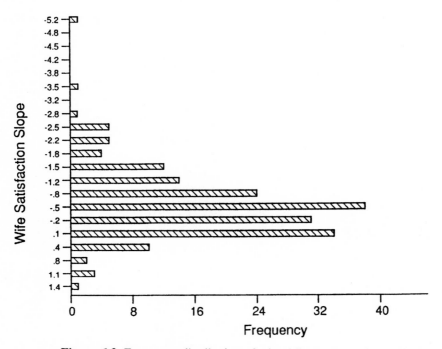

Figure 6.3. Frequency distribution of wives' linear slopes for change in marital satisfaction from Year 1 through Year 6.

marital satisfaction. Specifically, husbands' low marital satisfaction at Year 6 was related to their own low faith, low attachment, and low intrinsic motives at Year 1 and to their wives' low faith, high autonomy, and high extrinsic motives at Year 1.

For wives, as shown by the R^2 values in column 4 of Table 6.2, the set of Year 1 individual differences, interdependence, and spousal discrepancy risk scores retained their predictive value, although (as for husbands) at diminished levels. R^2 values for Year 1 marital satisfaction and R^2 values for Year 6 marital satisfaction were .28 versus .12 for the individual differences risk scores; .49 versus .22 for the interdependence risk scores; and .13 versus .10 for the spousal discrepancy risk scores.

Specifically, wives' low marital satisfaction at Year 6 was related to the following profile of Year 1 scores: to their husbands' high negative affectivity; to their own high negative affectivity, high dysfunctional beliefs, and low social support (individual differences variables); to their husbands' low faith; to their own low faith, high autonomy, weak intrinsic motives, and strong extrinsic motives (interdependence variables); and to large discrep-

Table 6.2. *Correlations between sets of predictors and marital satisfaction indices*

Index	Y1 predictor, Y1 satisfaction H 1	Y1 predictor, Y1 satisfaction W 2	Y1 predictor, Y6 satisfaction H 3	Y1 predictor, Y6 satisfaction W 4	Y1 predictor, slope satisfaction H 5	Y1 predictor, slope satisfaction W 6	Slope predictor, slope satisfaction H 7	Slope predictor, slope satisfaction W 8
Demographic								
Husband								
Age	.04	.12*	.09	.12*	.02	.04	—	—
Education	.00	−.29**	.03	−.01	.00	.13*	—	—
Income	−.04	−.12*	.08	.09	.09	.16*	—	—
Wife								
Age	.05	.11	.05	.15*	−.03	.06	—	—
Education	.03	−.19**	.04	.00	.00	.13*	—	—
Income	.05	−.05	.11	.18**	.05	.20**	—	—
Couple								
Divorce history	.07	.19**	.01	.06	−.08	−.03	—	—
Pooled finances	.11	.05	.11	.02	.03	.01	—	—
Months known	−.14*	−.18**	.06	.02	.19**	.14**	—	—
Stepchildren	.08	.13*	.05	−.01	.00	−.04	—	—
Children	—	—	—	—	—	—	−.15*	−.19**
R^2	.06	.17**	.05	.06	.07	.07	—	—
Individual differences								
Husband								
Negative affectivity	−.23**	−.07	−.20**	−.13*	−.07	−.09	−.02	.06
Expressivity	.29**	.23**	.12*	.06	−.08	−.09	.11	.09
Dysfunctional beliefs	−.17**	−.01	−.07	−.06	.02	−.05	−.14*	−.07
Social support	.28**	.14*	.14*	−.06	−.06	−.15*	.17*	.22**
Wife								
Negative affectivity	−.31**	−.32**	−.10	−.17**	.11	.00	−.20**	−.14*
Expressivity	.01	.10	−.04	.01	−.04	−.01	.07	.06
Dysfunctional beliefs	−.27**	−.34**	−.05	−.23**	.15*	−.03	−.15*	−.25**
Social support	.16*	.40**	.09	.24**	.00	.02	.14*	.24**
R^2	.26**	.28**	.07	.12**	.05	.05	.10**	.17**
Interdependence								
Husband								
Faith	.47**	.24**	.29**	.18**	−.07	.02	.47**	.26**
Autonomy	.00	.04	−.01	.04	−.01	.06	−.17**	−.12
Attachment	.43**	.24**	.17**	.05	−.17*	−.09	.34**	.27**
Intrinsic	.43**	.30**	.17**	.08	−.12*	−.06	.35**	.28**
Extrinsic	.00	.07	−.03	−.01	−.03	−.05	.10	.14*
Wife								
Faith	.30**	.53**	.17**	.25**	−.04	−.04	.31**	.45**
Autonomy	−.22**	−.18**	−.21**	−.20**	−.05	−.05	−.06	−.06
Attachment	.01	.19**	.01	−.01	.01	−.13*	.16*	.24**
Intrinsic	.24**	.46**	.07	.20**	−.07	.00	.20**	.21**
Extrinsic	−.24**	−.14*	−.22**	−.29**	.00	−.18**	.00	.09
R^2	.43**	.49**	.15**	.22**	.05	.08	.35**	.31**

Table 6.2. *(cont.)*

Index	Y1 predictor, Y1 satisfaction		Y1 predictor, Y6 satisfaction		Y1 predictor, slope satisfaction		Slope predictor, slope satisfaction	
	H 1	W 2	H 3	W 4	H 5	W 6	H 7	W 8
Spousal discrepancy								
Negative affectivity	−.21**	−.16*	−.11	−.15*	−.02	−.03	−.06	−.02
Expressivity	−.27**	−.25**	−.21**	−.13*	−.04	.00	.09	.06
Dysfunctional beliefs	.11	.11	.08	.00	−.01	−.09	.04	.11
Social support	−.10	−.09	.01	.05	.07	.10	−.02	−.10
Faith	−.02	−.11	−.05	−.12*	.01	−.04	−.20**	−.02
Autonomy	−.08	−.05	−.10	−.17**	−.08	−.14*	−.16*	−.13*
Attachment	−.24**	−.18**	−.08	−.05	.05	.06	−.09	−.05
Intrinsic	−.19**	−.20**	−.13*	−.12*	.01	.01	−.07	−.16*
Extrinsic	−.02	.00	.00	−.07	.02	−.06	−.01	−.07
R^2	.16**	.13**	.08	.10*	.02	.06	.08	.08

Note: Y1 = Year 1; Y6 = Year 6; H = husband; and W = wife. Slope refers to the rate of linear change. Columns 1 and 2 provide information on the relationship between the Year 1 risk scores and Year 1 marital satisfaction. Columns 3 and 4 provide information on the relationship between the Year 1 risk scores and Year 6 marital satisfaction. Columns 5 and 6 provide information on the relationship between the Year 1 risk scores and the rate of linear change in marital satisfaction from Years 1 through 6. Columns 7 and 8 provide information on the relationship between the rate of linear change in the risk scores from Years 1 through 4 and the rate of linear change in marital satisfaction from Years 1 through 6.
$*p < .05. **p < .01.$

ancies on negative affectivity, expressivity, faith, autonomy, and intrinsic motives (spousal discrepancy variables).

Predicting Rate of Linear Change in Marital Satisfaction over Years 1 Through 6 from Year 1 Risk Scores

Of interest here was whether the rate of linear change in marital satisfaction was predicted by any set of Year 1 risk scores. Only linear change was of interest given the sizable linear trend effect reported earlier. As shown by the R^2 values in column 5 of Table 6.2 for husbands and in column 6 of Table 6.2 for wives, neither husbands' nor wives' rate of linear change in marital satisfaction was predicted by any set of Year 1 risk variables.

Predicting Rate of Linear Change in Marital Satisfaction over Years 1 Through 6 from the Cumulative Presence of Children and from Linear Change in Risk Scores over Years 1 Through 4

The focus of the last set of analyses was to see if the rate of linear change in marital satisfaction over Years 1 through 6 was related to the weighted presence of children score and to the rates of linear change in the individual differences, interdependence, and spousal discrepancy risk scores over Years 1 through 4. As shown in column 7 of Table 6.2 for husbands and in column 8 of Table 6.2 for wives, the rate of linear change in marital satisfaction for both husbands and wives was linked to the weighted presence of children score, to the rates of linear change in the individual differences risk scores, and especially to the rates of linear change in the interdependence risk scores.

For both spouses, decreases in marital satisfaction were linked to the presence of children early in the marriage; to decreases in husbands' and wives' satisfaction with social support; to increases in wives' negative affectivity and dysfunctional beliefs about relationships; and to decreases in husbands' and wives' faith in the marriage, value placed on attachment, and strength of intrinsic motives for being in the marriage. In addition, decreases in husbands' marital satisfaction were linked to increases in their dysfunctional relationship beliefs and in their wives' value on autonomy. Hierarchical multiple regressions indicated that with controls for Year 1 individual differences and interdependence scores, the rate of linear change in both sets of scores over Years 1 through 4 accounted for a significant additional 34% of the variance in husbands' rate of change in marital satisfaction and 32% of the variance in wives' rate of change in marital satisfaction.

Discussion

The Nature of Change in Marital Satisfaction from Year 1 to Year 6

As expected, and consistent with the findings of Markman and Hahlweg (1993), marital satisfaction for husbands and wives decreased over the first 6 years of marriage, with the steepest drop occurring between Years 1 and 2. These descriptive findings indicate that declines in marital satisfaction over the early years of marriage are typical (Kovacs, 1983).

Predicting Year 6 Marital Satisfaction from Year 1 Risk Variables

In contrast to findings regarding the concurrent link between Year 1 risk variables and Year 1 marital satisfaction, the strength of the predictive link between Year 1 risk variables and Year 6 marital satisfaction was attenuated. For husbands, only the set of interdependence risk variables retained predictive value, whereas for wives, the sets of individual differences, interdependence, and spousal discrepancy risk scores retained predictive value.

The obtained pattern of findings had four striking features. First, although wives who were in marriages in which both they and their husbands were remarried tended to report high marital satisfaction at Year 1, the relation between the couple's divorce history and either spouse's marital satisfaction at Year 6 was nonsignificant. Second, although wives who brought children to their remarriages tended to report high marital satisfaction at Year 1, the relation between the presence of stepchildren and either spouse's marital satisfaction at Year 6 was nonsignificant. Third, of the four sets of Year 1 risk variables, the predictive information provided by the set of interdependence risk scores was most robust. Finally, of the interdependence risk scores, both spouses' long-term low marital satisfaction was predicted by husbands' and wives' low Year 1 faith in the marriage, wives' high Year 1 autonomy, and wives' high Year 1 extrinsic motives for being married.

The loss of predictive information for both divorce history and the presence of children (i.e., husbands' stepchildren) with regard to wives' marital satisfaction may be due to habituation effects. Remarried wives and wives who bring children to their new marriages may be prone to report high marital satisfaction at the start of their marriages because remarriage brings some relief to divorce-related financial and childcare stresses (Raschke, 1987).

The longitudinal salience of both spouses' faith in the marriage at Year 1 is of note because Rempel et al. (1985) conceptualized faith as being rooted not in past experiences but rather in positive expectations regarding future, unknown events. Further, they argued that such expectations were linked to patterns of caring and responsiveness that fostered confidence and emotional security in the face of future uncertainty. These notions form the basis for speculating that spouses with low faith at the start of the marriage may report low marital satisfaction 6 years later because they lack the motivation or the skill to engage in the kinds of relationship maintenance behaviors that maintain high, stable levels of satisfaction (e.g., accommodating during conflict, derogating attractive alternative partners, managing jealousy, and willingness to sacrifice; see Rusbult & Buunk, 1993).

If women indeed do the bulk of relationship repair and relationship maintenance work (Bradbury & Karney, 1993; Thompson & Walker, 1989), then the finding that long-term low marital satisfaction for *both* spouses was predicted by high Time 1 levels of autonomy and extrinsic motives for being married for wives but not for husbands is especially noteworthy. Neither of these dispositions makes it likely that the wife would assume the primary role of relationship expert. If anything, they make it likely that the wife will depend less on the marriage and eventually find more appealing alternatives to an unhappy marriage (Rusbult & Buunk, 1993).[7]

Predicting Rate of Linear Change in Marital Satisfaction

The major finding from this study was that variability in the rate of change in marital satisfaction over the first 6 years of marriage was accounted for by information based on patterns of change over Years 1 through 4 in both spouses' risk scores – particularly the interdependence risk scores – rather than by the levels of risk variables assessed at the time of marriage. This finding is entirely consistent with a relational dialectics perspective that asserts that change is at the heart of marital developmental processes, and that sustaining a relationship involves adjusting to the tensions of relational forces such as autonomy versus connection and novelty versus predictability (Montgomery, 1993).

These forces are plausibly reflected in the changes in both spouses' faith, attachment, and intrinsic motives for being married that predicted change in husbands' and wives' marital satisfaction. The tension between autonomy and connection can be operationalized as changes in the value placed on attachment as well as changes in the perceptions that both spouses are motivated to be in the marriage because it is a value in and of itself, whereas the tension between novelty and predictability can be operationalized as changes in how much faith one has in future marital events (Rempel et al., 1985). The exact mechanisms by which changes in wives' negative affectivity and relationship beliefs feed into these tensions is unclear, although – as argued earlier – they may affect wives' willingness to play the role of relationship expert.

These polarized tensions might also explain why the rate of decline in marital satisfaction was particularly high for couples having their own children relatively early in their marriage. The transition from the marital dyad to the family system introduces new roles and complex dynamics in the relationship maintenance process. Personal autonomy might be even more frequently sacrificed by the demands of a young child, and novelty might be hard to find in the course of routine childcare. Together, these tensions regarding autonomy and novelty may violate romantic expectations about how parenthood enhances marital bliss (Hackel & Ruble, 1992).

Implications for Prevention

Although the current study is limited by a biased sample, an exclusive reliance on self-report methods, and the lack of information regarding the rate of change in the individual differences, interdependence, and spousal discrepancy risk variables in Years 5 and 6, its findings provide the basis for concluding that the prevention of marital distress would benefit from a relational dialectic perspective. Because decreases in marital satisfaction have been linked to violations of expectations about what typical marriages are like (Baucom & Epstein, 1990; Hackel & Ruble, 1992; Rusbult, 1983), prevention efforts might be geared toward normalizing the decrease in marital satisfaction over the early years of marriage so that realistic expectations for long-term marital functioning are constructed. Although most current prevention programs target communication and problem-solving behaviors (e.g., Markman & Hahlweg, 1993), they provide little or no structured opportunity for learning how to deal with normative relationship change, unrest, inconsistency, and fluctuations in interdependence. Such opportunities may come from cognitive-behavioral interventions that are based on cognitive factors that include selective perceptions of what spouses do, assumptions about the nature of spouses and marriage, attributions about the causes of negative marital events, and expectancies about what marital events will occur in the future (Baucom & Epstein, 1990).

A Personal Note on Conducting This Study

As a developmental psychologist, I am keenly aware that longitudinal data are needed to address issues regarding change. Accordingly, I have been involved in several longitudinal studies in the course of my career, but they usually involved only one follow-up assessment. In contrast, one of the exciting features of the newlywed project was the possibility of modeling change over multiple time points. Eight years into this project, I can look back over the design of this study and recognize that I did some things right and many things wrong.

Perhaps the best thing I did was to recruit a large Year 1 sample. I hasten to add, however, that this did occur at some cost. I came to dread reading the Wednesday issue of the *Dayton Daily News* because the number of marriage licenses published therein dictated the incredibly tedious nature of my research-related activities for the next few days. Nonetheless, once the initial sample was recruited, its size enabled me to address sorely understudied issues such as the prediction of marital dissolution (Kurdek, 1993b) with more statistical power than has usually been the case (Gottman, 1994).

Although longitudinal data form the essence of the study of change, psychological science as a whole is somewhat unkind to researchers involved in extensive longitudinal studies. Particularly in the field of close relationships, there has been major developmental growth in how we think about and how we study close relationships. Consequently, the theories and methodologies that formed the basis of the design of this study are now somewhat outdated. If I were to design the Year 1 phase of this study again, I would do so with a different set of questions and with a different set of measures. Perhaps the major conceptual oversight of the initial project was not including conflict resolution and marital commitment as key elements of relational maintenance (Gottman, 1994; Rusbult & Buunk, 1993). Although measures of these variables have been included since the Year 5 data collection, information on these variables during the early phases of marriage cannot be retrieved.

Furthermore, although I remain convinced of the importance of interdependence variables and individual differences variables, more refined measures are now available for critical interdependence variables, such as rewards, costs, comparison level, barriers, alternatives, and investments (Kurdek, 1995), and individual differences variables, such as marital attributions (Fincham & Bradbury, 1992). Finally, I regret that I was not able to compensate the participants in this project for their time and interest. Their continuing interest in this project – although raising issues of sample bias – has been nothing short of inspirational.

Notes

1. Previous reports based on this data set that may be of interest to readers of this volume have described concurrent correlates of marital quality shortly after marriage (Kurdek, 1989), predictors of increases in marital distress over the first three years of marriage (Kurdek, 1991a), predictors of change in marital quality for first-married husbands and wives who did and who did not make the transition to parenthood over the first four years of marriage (Kurdek, 1993a), and predictors of divorce over the first five years of marriage (Kurdek, 1993b).
2. There is a large literature on how marital well-being is affected by communication and problem-solving skills (e.g., Markman & Hahlweg, 1993). Because these skills were not assessed in this study, this approach was not considered.
3. It is worth noting that at Year 6, the Dyadic Satisfaction score was strongly related to the Kansas Marital Satisfaction Scale (Schumm et al., 1986), a relatively "pure" measure of satisfaction. For husbands, $r = .82$; for wives; $r = .84$, $ps < .001$.
4. Bryk, Raudenbush, Seltzer, and Congdon (1989) note that the use of ordinary least squares (OLS) regression slopes as outcome variables has some technical difficulties and recommend a hierarchical linear model (HLM) approach that allows for explicit modeling of effects that are adjusted for both individual level and group level influences on outcome.

However, because the HLM approach yielded the same pattern of findings as the OLS approach, only findings from the more widely used OLS approach are presented.

5. In multiple regression analyses not reported here, the information provided by interactions between husbands' and wives' risk scores was assessed. No significant findings were obtained.

6. To determine if the strength of the correlations involving marital satisfaction and any of the four sets of scores differed between husbands and wives, structural equation modeling using LISREL VII (Joreskog & Sorbom, 1989) was employed to test the hypothesis that each set of correlations was equivalent for husbands and wives (see Green, 1992). The hypothesis of equivalence between husbands and wives was rejected if the Comparative Fit Index (CFI) was less than .90 (Bentler, 1990). Resulting CFIs for all sets of scores shown in Table 6.2 exceeded .91, indicating that correlations were equivalent for husbands and wives.

7. More formal support for this notion was obtained by two 2-step hierarchical multiple regressions. In the first regression, husbands' Year 6 marital satisfaction was the dependent variable. At step 1, the set of husbands' Year 1 interdependence scores was entered whereas at step 2, the set of wives' Year 1 interdependence scores was entered. In the second regression, wives' Year 6 marital satisfaction was the dependent variable. At step 1, the set of wives' Year 1 interdependence scores was entered whereas at step 2, the set of husbands' Year 1 interdependence scores was entered. In line with the position that wives' interdependence at the beginning of the marriage is more important for husbands' long-term marital satisfaction than husband' interdependence at the beginning of the marriage is for wives' long-term marital satisfaction, the change in R^2 associated with step 2 was significant for the first regression but not for the second.

References

Baucom, D. H., & Epstein, N. (1990). *Cognitive-behavioral marital therapy.* New York: Brunner/Mazel.

Belsky, J., & Rovine, M. (1990). Patterns of marital change across the transition to parenthood: Pregnancy to three years postpartum. *Journal of Marriage and the Family, 52,* 5–20.

Bem, S. L. (1974). The measurement of psychological androgyny. *Journal of Consulting and Clinical Psychology, 47,* 155–162.

Bentler, P. M. (1990). Comparative fit indexes in structural models. *Psychological Bulletin, 107,* 238–246.

Bentler, P. M., & Newcomb, M. D. (1978). Longitudinal study of marital success and failure. *Journal of Consulting and Clinical Psychology, 46,* 1053–1070.

Blais, M. R., Sabourin, S., Boucher, C., & Vallerand, R. J. (1990). Toward a motivational model of couple happiness. *Journal of Personality and Social Psychology, 59,* 1021–1031.

Bloom, B. L., Asher, S. J., & White, S. W. (1978). Marital disruption as a stressor. *Psychological Bulletin, 85,* 867–894.

Booth, A., & Edwards, J. N. (1992). Starting over: Why remarriages are more unstable. *Journal of Family Issues, 13,* 179–194.

Bradbury, T. N. & Fincham, F. D. (1988). Individual difference variables in close relationships: A contextual model of marriage as an integrative framework. *Journal of Personality and Social Psychology, 54,* 713–721.

Bradbury, T. N., & Fincham, F. D. (1991). A contextual model for advancing the study of marital interaction. In G. J. O. Fletcher & F. D. Fincham (Eds.), *Cognition in close relationships* (pp. 127–147). Hillsdale, NJ: Erlbaum.

Bradbury, T. N., & Karney, B. R. (1993). Longitudinal study of marital interaction and dysfunction: Review and analysis. *Clinical Psychology Review, 13,* 15–28.

Bryk, A. S., & Raudenbush, S. W. (1987). Application of hierarchical linear models to assessing change. *Psychological Bulletin, 101,* 147–158.

Bryk, A. S., Raudenbush, S. W., Seltzer, M., & Congdon, R. T. (1989). *An introduction to HLM: Computer program and user's guide.* Chicago, IL: Scientific Software.

Christensen, A., & Shenk, J. L. (1991). Communication, conflict, and psychological distance in nondistressed, clinic, and divorcing couples. *Journal of Consulting and Clinical Psychology, 59,* 458–463.

Cochran, S. D., & Peplau, L. A. (1985). Value orientations in heterosexual relationships. *Psychology of Women Quarterly, 9,* 477–488.

Cowan, C. P., Cowan, P. A., Heming, G., Garrett, E., Coysh, W. S., Curtis-Boles, H., & Boles, A. J. (1985). Transitions to parenthood. *Journal of Family Issues, 6,* 451–481.

Crohan, S. E., & Veroff, J. (1989). Dimensions of marital well-being among white and black newlyweds. *Journal of Marriage and the Family, 51,* 373–383.

Derogatis, L. (1983). *SCL 90-R: Administration, scoring, and procedures manual.* Towson, MD: Clinical Psychometric Research.

Dindia, K., & Canary, D. J. (1993). Definitions and theoretical perspectives on maintaining relationships. *Journal of Social and Personal Relationships, 10,* 163–174.

Eidelson, R. J., & Epstein, N. (1982). Cognition and relationship maladjustment: Development of a measure of relationship beliefs. *Journal of Consulting and Clinical Psychology, 50,* 715–720.

Fincham, F. D., & Bradbury, T. N. (1992). Assessing attributions in marriage: The relationship attribution measure. *Journal of Personality and Social Psychology, 62,* 457–468.

Giles-Sims, J. (1987). Social exchange in remarried families. In K. Pasley & M. Ihinger-Tallman (Eds.), *Remarriage and stepparenting: Current research and theory* (pp. 141–163). New York: Guilford.

Gottman, J. M. (1994). *What predicts divorce? The relationship between marital processes and marital outcomes.* Hillsdale, NJ: Erlbaum.

Green, J. A. (1992). Testing whether correlation matrices are different from each other. *Developmental Psychology, 28,* 215–224.

Greenstein, T. N. (1990). Marital disruption and the employment of married women. *Journal of Marriage and the Family, 52,* 657–676.

Hackel, L. S., & Ruble, D. N. (1992). Changes in marital relationship after the first baby is born: Predicting the impact of expectancy disconfirmation. *Journal of Personality and Social Psychology, 62,* 944–957.

Heaton, T. B., & Albrecht, S. L. (1991). Stable unhappy marriages. *Journal of Marriage and the Family, 53,* 747–758.

Joreskog, K. G., & Sorbom, D. (1989). *LISREL VII: User's reference guide.* Mooresville, IN: Scientific Software.

Kelly, E. L. (1939). Concerning the validity of Terman's weights for predicting marital happiness. *Psychological Bulletin, 36,* 202–203.

Kelly, E. L., & Conley, J. J. (1987). Personality and compatibility: A prospective analysis of marital stability and marital satisfaction. *Journal of Personality and Social Psychology, 52,* 27–40.

Kovacs, L. (1983). A conceptualization of marital development. *Family Therapy, 10,* 183–210.

Kurdek, L. A. (1989). Relationship quality for newly married husbands and wives: Marital history, stepchildren, and individual-difference predictors. *Journal of Marriage and the Family, 51,* 1053–1064.

Kurdek, L. A. (1991a). Predictors of increases in marital distress in newlywed couples: A 3-year prospective longitudinal study. *Developmental Psychology, 27,* 627–636.

Kurdek, L. A. (1991b). Correlates of relationship satisfaction in cohabiting gay and lesbian couples: Integration of contextual, investment, and problem-solving models. *Journal of Personality and Social Psychology, 61,* 910–922.

Kurdek, L. A. (1992). Relationship stability and relationship satisfaction in cohabiting gay and lesbian couples: A prospective longitudinal test of the contextual and interdependence models. *Journal of Social and Personal Relationships, 9,* 125–142.

Kurdek, L. A. (1993a). Nature and prediction of changes in marital quality for first-time parent and nonparent husbands and wives. *Journal of Family Psychology, 6,* 255–265.

Kurdek, L. A. (1993b). Predicting marital dissolution: A 5-year prospective longitudinal study of newlywed couples. *Journal of Personality and Social Psychology, 64,* 221–242.

Kurdek, L. A. (1993c). Dimensionality of the Dyadic Adjustment Scale: Evidence from heterosexual and homosexual couples. *Journal of Family Psychology, 6,* 22–35.

Kurdek, L. A. (1995). Assessing multiple determinants of relationship commitment in cohabiting gay, cohabiting lesbian, dating heterosexual, and married heterosexual couples. *Family Relations, 44,* 261–266.

Kurdek, L. A., & Schmitt, J. P. (1986). Relationship quality of partners in heterosexual married, heterosexual cohabiting, gay and lesbian relationships. *Journal of Personality and Social Psychology, 51,* 711–720.

Larsen, A. S., & Olson, D. H. (1989). Predicting marital satisfaction using PREPARE: A replication study. *Journal of Marital and Family Therapy, 15,* 311–322.

McCrae, R. R., & Costa, P. T. (1987). Validation of the five-factor model of personality across instruments and observers. *Journal of Personality and Social Psychology, 52,* 81–90.

MacDermid, S. M., Huston, T. L., & McHale, S. M. (1990). Changes in marriage associated with the transition to parenthood: Individual differences as a function of sex-role attitudes and changes in the division of household labor. *Journal of Marriage and the Family, 52,* 475–486.

Markman, H. J., & Hahlweg, K. (1993). The prediction and prevention of marital distress: An international perspective. *Clinical Psychology Review, 13,* 29–43.

Montgomery, B. M. (1993). Relationship maintenance versus relationship change: A dialectical dilemma. *Journal of Social and Personal Relationships, 10,* 205–223.

Moorman, J. E., & Hernandez, D. J. (1989). Married-couple families with step, adopted, and biological children. *Demography, 26,* 267–277.

Morgan, S. P., & Rindfuss, R. R. (1985). Marital disruption: Structural and temporal dimensions. *American Journal of Sociology, 90,* 1055–1077.

National Center for Health Statistics (1991). Advance report of final marriage statistics, 1988. *Monthly Vital Statistics Report.* Vol. 39, No. 12, suppl. 2. Hyattsville, MD, Public Health Service.

Peplau, L. A., & Cochran, S. D. (1981). Value orientations in intimate relationships of gay men. *Journal of Homosexuality, 6,* 1–9.

Raschke, H. J. (1987). Divorce. In M. B. Sussman & S. K. Steinmetz (Eds.), *Handbook of marriage and the family* (pp. 597–624). New York: Plenum.

Rempel, J. K., Holmes, J. G., & Zanna, M. (1985). Trust in close relationships. *Journal of Personality and Social Psychology, 49,* 95–112.

Rusbult, C. E. (1983). A longitudinal test of the investment model: The development (and deterioration) of satisfaction and commitment in heterosexual involvements. *Journal of Personality and Social Psychology, 45,* 101–117.

Rusbult, C. E., & Buunk, B. P. (1993). Commitment processes in close relationships: An interdependence analysis. *Journal of Social and Personal Relationships, 10,* 175–204.

Sabourin, S., Lussier, Y., Laplante, B., & Wright, J. (1990). Unidimensional and multidimensional models of dyadic adjustment: A reconciliation. *Psychological Assessment, 2,* 333–337.

Sarason, I. G., Sarason, B. R., Shearin, E. N., & Pierce, G. R. (1987). A brief measure of social support: Practical and theoretical implications. *Journal of Social and Personal Relationships, 7,* 495–506.

Schumm, W. R., Paff-Bergen, L. A., Hatch, R. C., Obiorah, F. C., Copeland, J., Meens, L. D., & Bugaighis, M. A. (1986). Concurrent and discriminant validity of the Kansas Marital Satisfaction Scale. *Journal of Marriage and the Family, 48,* 381–387.

Spanier, G. B. (1976). Measuring dyadic adjustment. *Journal of Marriage and the Family, 38,* 15–28.

Thompson, L., & Walker, A. J. (1989). Gender in families: Women and men in marriage, work, and parenthood. *Journal of Marriage and the Family, 51,* 845–872.

Wilson, B. F., & Clarke, S. C. (1992). Remarriages: A demographic profile. *Journal of Family Issues, 13,* 123–141.

7   The Development of Marriage: A 9-Year Perspective

*Kristin Lindahl, Mari Clements,
and Howard Markman*

In the past decade significant progress has been made in furthering our understanding of how marriages change over time. Much of this progress can be attributed to the availability of increasingly sophisticated theoretical models and the development of methodological strategies to test them. The relatively recent empirical shift from cross-sectional, descriptive studies to longitudinal studies, in addition to the increasing emphasis on the observational study of dyadic interaction, have brought the study of marital relationships to a new level (Bradbury & Karney, 1993; Notarius & Markman, 1981). Clearly, the most significant advantage of using longitudinal data is that they permit a more stringent examination of causal hypotheses. In addition, by observing and analyzing couples' interactions, rather than relying on their self-reports, questions about the processes or mechanisms of change can be examined more carefully.

In the Denver Family Development Project, originated in 1981 by Howard Markman at the University of Denver, we studied how relationship quality in a group of satisfied and committed premarital couples changed over time over the first decade of their marriages. We sought to discover what individual or relationship characteristics ultimately lead to distress, divorce, or continued happiness. In this chapter, we present some of the results of the first 9 years of our longitudinal study and discuss our successes and failures while meeting the challenges of longitudinal work.

One of the more obvious changes for the couples in our study was that many of them began having children. This provided the unique opportunity to examine the impact of children on marriage, as well as the marital factors that predict parenting behavior. As the children in our study grew older, we adjusted to their developmental shifts by studying attachment, self-concept, and peer relationships. Throughout the study, however, our central focus has been on negative affect and its regulation. We have postulated that effective management of conflict and negative emotions is a critical task for any relationship, most notably for marital and parent–child relationships (Lindahl

& Markman, 1990). Negative affect regulation is defined as the ability to express one's own negative emotions constructively, as well as to validate negative affect expressed by one's partner or child.

Although the primary purpose of this chapter is to review the results from the Denver Family Development Project regarding the developmental course of marriage and early family life, it is also important to note that some of the couples completed an intervention program designed to improve couples' communication skills. The program, the Prevention and Relationship Enhancement Program (PREP) (Markman, Renick, Floyd, Stanley, & Clements, 1993; Renick, Blumberg, & Markman, 1992) was designed to enhance or modify those dimensions of couples' relationships that have been found through theory and empirical research to be linked to effective marital functioning (e.g., communication and problem-solving skills). Results of the prevention program are summarized in detail elsewhere (Markman, 1981; Markman, Floyd, Stanley, & Lewis, 1986; Markman, Floyd, Stanley, & Storaasli, 1988; Markman & Hahlweg, 1993; Markman, Renick, Floyd, Stanley, & Clements, 1993).

The chapter opens with a brief description of the goals and features of the Denver Family Development Project. The evolution of the couples' relationships is described next, with the emphasis on changes in satisfaction and negative affect regulation in the context of couples' communication. The effects of the transition to parenthood on marital satisfaction and negative affect regulation are then examined, followed by the implications of marital quality for the development of attachment, self-concept, the nature of parent–child interaction, and peer relations. The chapter concludes with a word about our experience with some of the inherent difficulties of doing longitudinal research.

Goals and Overview of the Denver Family Development Project

One of the primary objectives of our project was to identify the premarital factors, particularly those related to how couples' manage conflict, that predict not only the quality of their relationships years later and their adjustment to becoming parents, but also the quality of the parent–child relationships and important dimensions of child development in the context of marital relationships such as attachment, self-esteem, and peer relations. We assume that most couples encounter problems and disagreements, and that the couple's ability to handle differences, and not the differences themselves, is the critical factor in determining future marital success (Markman,

Floyd, & Dickson-Markman, 1982; Storaasli & Markman, 1990). Although there has been a recent increase in the number of longitudinal studies of marriage that have assessed the predictive power of marital interaction and related constructs, the Denver Family Development Project differs in that it (a) started before marriage and before the conception and birth of any children and assessed predistress relationship functioning; (b) continues through the primary risk period for divorce, enabling marriage specialists to predict divorce as well as marital satisfaction; and (c) assesses communication annually to detect changes in important dimensions of marital interaction (Markman, 1979; Markman, 1981).

Subjects

We recruited couples who had made a commitment to marry to participate in a longitudinal study of marriage and family development. For over a decade we annually have chronicled shifts in the quality of couples' relationship, especially with regard to satisfaction, conflict, and communication. The subjects were 135 couples planning their first marriage, 99 of whom actually married later. The majority of the sample was engaged (59.8%), while the remainder were planning marriage but were not formally engaged. None of the couples had or were expecting children. To date, data have been collected at 10 time points, the first 9 of which are summarized in this chapter: Time 1 (the initial data-collection period), Time 2 (post-PREP intervention assessment, 11 weeks after Time 1), and at seven subsequent follow-up sessions (Times 3 through 9). Follow-up sessions occurred at 1 to 1½-year intervals. After Time 1 data collection, couples were matched on four variables: (a) engaged versus planning marriage, (b) relationship satisfaction, (c) their own ratings of the impact of their communication on one another, and (d) confidence in getting married. From the matched sets, couples were randomly selected to participate in the Premarital Relationship Enhancement Program (PREP) (Markman & Floyd, 1980). PREP, which teaches communication and conflict-resolution skills extrapolated from behavioral marital therapy (BMT; Markman, 1991), was offered to 85 of the 135 couples in the sample. Thirty-three couples (24% of the sample) completed the program, 9 (7%) completed it in part, 43 (32%) declined, and 50 (37%) served as controls. As noted above, intervention data comparing these groups of couples can be found elsewhere (e.g., Markman et al., 1993).

At Time 1, the partners had known each other an average of 28.5 months (range = 2 months to 7.5 years; sd = 19.59 months) and had been dating an average of 21.8 months (range = 1.5 months to 6.25 years; sd = 15.8 months). The women's average age was 23.2 years (range = 16–35 years; sd = 4.14 years) and the men's average age was 24.1 years (range = 16–35 years; sd = 3.88 years). On average, subjects had completed 15.3 years of education (range = 9–38 years; sd = 2.63 years), and the median personal income level was between $5,000 and $10,000 (range = $0 to more than $20,000). As for other couples planning marriage (Markman & Hahlweg, 1993), the average relationship satisfaction score on a modified version of the Locke-Wallace Marital Adjustment Test (Locke & Wallace, 1959) was in the highly satisfied range (male mean = 122.15, sd = 16.61; female mean = 123.09, sd = 15.93). By the follow-up 7 assessment (9 years after the study began), couples reported a median combined income of over $40,000 per year and had been married an average of 8.1 years.

Self-Report Measures

The Marital Adjustment Test (MAT; Locke & Wallace, 1959) is a 15-item self-report measure assessing such domains of marital functioning as areas of disagreement, perceived communication quality, leisure-time activities, and regrets about having married a spouse. The MAT is one of the most frequently used measures of marital satisfaction and has excellent reliability and validity for discriminating between distressed and satisfied couples (Gottman, Markman, & Notarius, 1977).

The Conflict Tactics Scale (CTS; Straus, 1979) is a widely used self-report measure that assesses strategies used in handling marital conflict. Respondents are asked to report the frequency with which they use various methods, ranging from discussing the issue calmly, to shouting at the partner, to threatening the partner with a knife or a gun. This measure has demonstrated adequate reliability and validity.

The Relationship Problem Inventory (RPI; Knox, 1970) and the Marital Agendas Protocol (MAP; Notarius & Vanzetti, 1984) require each partner to rate the perceived intensity of each of 10 commonly experienced problem areas in marriage (e.g., sex, money, communication, children). In addition, couples are asked to write in any problems that they feel are salient in their relationship that have not been included in this list. For both the RPI and the MAP, the areas rated and the order of presentation are identical. The MAP also asks each partner to estimate the number of arguments out of every 10 on each issue that are resolved to the couple's mutual satisfaction. Finally, the MAP asks each partner who is responsible for unresolved arguments: self, partner, or both. For all the analyses presented in this chapter, only partners' report of problem intensity, or the level of unresolved conflict, is used. Ratings of problem intensity were calculated by summing partners' intensity ratings of the 10 common problem areas for relationships.

The RPI and the MAP have demonstrated adequate levels of reliability and discriminate between distressed and nondistressed couples (Gottman, Notarius, Markman, Banks, Yoppi, & Rubin, 1976; Notarius & Vanzetti, 1984). In the current study, the RPI was used for Time 1 through Time 5 data-collection points. The MAP has been used for subsequent follow-ups.

The Attachment Behavior Q-Set (Waters & Deane, 1985) was used to assess parents' perception of their child with respect to attachment and sociability. The Q-set is a list of 100 descriptive items that parents are asked to sort into piles ranging from least to most descriptive of their child. The parental sorts are correlated with a standardization sort developed on the basis of experts' descriptions of security, sociability, and dependency for the appropriate age group.

The Pictorial Scale of Perceived Competence and Social Acceptance for Young Children (Harter & Pike, 1984) was used to assess children's self-concept. This 24-item measure contains four subscales: Cognitive Competence, Physical Competence, Peer Acceptance, and Maternal Acceptance. The internal consistency, reliability, and predictive validity of these domains have been found to be acceptable (Harter, 1989; Harter & Pike, 1984).

Communication Measures

The Interactional Dimensions Coding System (IDCS; Julien, Markman, & Lindahl, 1989) was developed to assess the constructs of conflict management and intimacy in couples' interactions, constructs that have emerged as key interactional dimensions associated with marital distress from studies using microanalytic coding systems. The IDCS is a global interaction coding system that assesses four positive and five negative dimensions of communication. The positive dimensions are communication skills, support/validation, problem solving, and positive affect. The negative dimensions are withdrawal, denial, conflict, dominance, and negative affect. In addition, the IDCS taps two dyadic aspects of communication that assess the partners as an interactive unit: negative and positive escalation. An entire (10- to 15-minute) interaction is used as the unit of observation for the nine individual and two dyadic dimensions. The dimensions are scored on a scale from 1 to 9, with a score of 1 indicating no evidence of the communication behavior occurring, and 9 indicating high behavioral frequencies. Cohen's kappas for the individual codes comprising this measure average .60 and alphas for the positive and negative summary codes are .87 and .90, respectively. The codes discriminate between distressed and nondistressed couples (Julien et al., 1989).

The Couple Interaction Scoring System (CISS; Gottman, 1979; Notarius & Markman, 1981) is a microanalytic behavioral observation system for couples that uses 36 verbal (content) codes and 3 nonverbal (affect) codes to analyze each unit of an interaction (i.e., a grammatical clause). Each unit receives a verbal and a nonverbal code. The content and affect codes are combined to form four summary codes: problem-solving facilitation, problem-solving inhibition, emotional validation, and emotional invalidation (Notarius & Pellegrini, 1987). Cohen's kappas average .91 for content codes and .72 for affect codes (Gottman, 1979; Notarius & Markman, 1981).

A more recently developed coding system, the System for Coding Affect Regulation in the Family (SCARF; Lindahl & Markman, 1991; 1993), was developed as part of the Denver Family Development Project to assess how parents and their children modulate negative affect when interacting with one another. Separate sets of codes were developed for dyadic and triadic interactions so that both parent–child and mother–father–child systems could be analyzed. Sixteen parent and 7 child codes that collapse into 4 summary codes, assess negative affect regulation in dyadic parent–child interactions. The two parent summary codes, invalidation and emotional support, refer to a parent's response to a child's affective display, and also indicate to what extent a parent's reaction to his or her child is generally negative or positive. The 2 child summary codes, escalation and negative affect regulation, refer to how well a child modulates feelings of anger and frustration. Intercoder Pearson correlation coefficients have been found to be satisfactory; the average reliability coefficient was .82 (Lindahl & Markman, 1991).

To assess negative affect regulation in triadic mother–father–child interactions, four types of codes were developed from the SCARF, varying by unit of analysis, including: family codes (tension, warmth), a couple code (couple cohesiveness), parenting codes (invalidation, emotional support, triangulation), and child codes (negative affect, positive affect, support seeking, self-triangulation). Adequate levels of reliability were established; the average reliability coefficient was .85 (Lindahl & Markman, 1993).

The work of Gottman and his colleagues (Gottman, 1986; Gottman & Katz, 1989) was used to develop a behavioral coding system to assess children's peer interactions. The coding system was used during a 30-minute observation of subjects at free play with their peers in their school or day care setting. This observation was coded live and thus several aspects of the original coding systems were omitted or streamlined for purposes of analyses. The adapted coding system assesses level of play (solitary to interactive fantasy play), assesses specific behaviors reflecting positive and negative affect, and provides four global codes: positive attention received from peer group, positive attention given peers, negative attention given peers, and negative escalation. Cohen's kappas for the four domains averaged .72.

Procedure

Although couples have participated in 10 research sessions in total, only the data pertaining to the first 9 are reported here. The current chapter covers assessments up to Time 9 (the seventh follow-up visit following Time 1), which occurred 9 years after the beginning of the study. Across all time periods, data collection emphasized the following constructs: marital satisfaction and negative affect regulation, especially in the context of conflict, conflict management, and communication.

Time 1. Couples participated in two 2-hour research sessions that were scheduled 1 week apart. During these sessions, couples were interviewed, completed questionnaires, and participated in two 10- to 15-minute videotaped problem-solving interaction tasks. Questionnaires administered included the MAT, a measure of marital satisfaction, and the RPI, a measure of problem intensity and unresolved conflict. Couples' communication was assessed during six problem-solving tasks. The first four involved discussions of a vignette from the Inventory of Marital Conflicts (Olson & Ryder, 1970) and are not presented here. For the latter two discussions, couples were instructed to discuss two of their top three relationship problem areas (chosen from the RPI or MAP). This task was completed once using a procedure in which partners rated the emotional impact of each other's communication, and once without this procedure. In order to create more stable and reliable codes for analysis, observations of couples' communication, using the IDCS and the CISS, were summarized across these two discussions. The relationship problem discussion task was chosen for its ecological validity and prevalence in the marital interaction literature (Markman & Notarius, 1987). Following the Time 1 session, couples assigned to the intervention group were invited to participate in PREP (Markman & Floyd, 1980). Couples assigned to the control group were not informed about the intervention program but were scheduled for the Time 2 assessment session 11 weeks later.

Time 2 and Subsequent Follow-ups. At Time 2, couples completed the same set of questionnaires and interaction tasks as at Time 1. Follow-up sessions were conducted on an approximately yearly basis thereafter. Although slight modifications were made in the assessment protocol at some of the subsequent follow-ups, a core set of questionnaires (MAT, RPI/MAP, CTS) and interaction tasks (problem discussions) remained constant. Couples who could not attend the sessions because they had moved from the area completed questionnaire measures and returned them by mail.

Changes in Satisfaction and Communication

Given the number of years that couples have been involved in the study, the project is well suited to answer basic questions about the development of marital relationships over time. This section discusses the major developmental trends that have emerged for the sample as a whole. Unless otherwise noted, subjects are included in analyses only if they participated in all nine data-collection points. Thirty-six of the 90 couples who married met this criteria. These 36 couples did not differ from the larger sample in terms of premarital satisfaction, relationship problems, or positivity of communication. They did, however, display significantly lower levels of negative communication.

In general, MAT scores declined over the early years of the relationship, before plateauing at Time 4. As can be seen in Figure 7.1, significant declines were present from Time 1 to Time 2 (F (1, 35) = 14.17, $p < .001$), Time 2 to Time 3 ($F(1, 35) = 10.10$, $p < .003$), and Time 3 to Time 4 ($F(1, 35) = 4.82$, $p < .04$). By Time 4 (approximately 3¼ years after the original Time 1 session), marital satisfaction appeared to stabilize, and no further significant declines over time have been noted. In addition, although declines over time were significant (F (8, 28) = 4.82, $p < .03$; Wilks' Lambda = 58), it is important to note that the sample mean is still well within the nondistressed range on the MAT at the 9-year follow-up (for husbands, mean MAT = 117.70, sd = 14.03; for wives, mean MAT = 118.59, sd = 16.51). In contrast to several other studies of marriage (e.g., Gottman, 1979; Spanier, Lewis, & Cole, 1975), wives in this sample reported higher marital satisfaction overall than did husbands ($F(1, 35) = 6.58$, $p < .02$). A complete listing of MAT means for husbands and wives is presented in Table 7.1. Our findings may mirror changes in society that have brought increased opportunities to women to pursue careers and hence reduced dependence on their marriage. In addition, the roles of men and women have changed, with men contributing more to household chores and childrearing than was

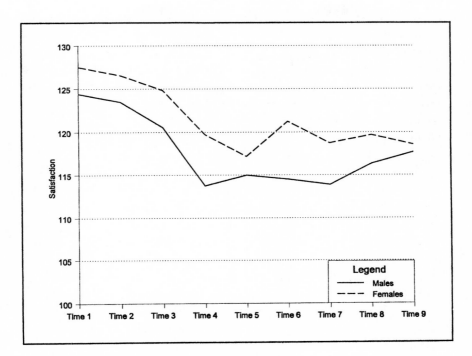

Figure 7.1. Marital satisfaction over time.

Table 7.1. *MAT means and standard deviations (in parentheses) over time*

Time period	Male	Female
Time 1	124.40	127.50
	(15.30)	(13.60)
Time 2	123.48	126.52
	(12.70)	(15.05)
Time 3	120.56	124.81
	(17.20)	(16.30)
Time 4	113.73	119.74
	(21.83)	(15.56)
Time 5	114.99	117.20
	(19.14)	(19.97)
Time 6	114.49	121.26
	(17.07)	(12.81)
Time 7	113.86	118.75
	(15.50)	(17.94)
Time 8	116.35	119.69
	(12.94)	(15.77)
Time 9	117.70	118.59
	(14.03)	(16.51)

previously the case. These added contributions to the functioning of the couple may have enabled women to feel more satisfied in their relationship than was true in the past.

As one might expect, marital satisfaction has significantly eroded for some of the couples in the study, and approximately 20% have decided to divorce or separate. Given our interest in predicting marital outcome, we planned a set of analyses assessing the extent to which premarital communication and self-report variables would discriminate between couples who remained married and those who decided to end their marriage. On the basis of premarital indices of communication, problem ratings, satisfaction, and demographics, a discriminant analysis of the total sample of couples who married correctly classified over 90% of the couples as either married or divorcing (for details, see Clements, Stanley, & Markman, 1998). A variety of communication and conflict-related variables were important in this prediction, suggesting that it is not only the static demographic factors such as age at marriage that predict marital success or failure. The importance of the dynamic, communication variables in the obtained prediction highlights the need for spouses to adequately regulate their own and their partners' negative affect (e.g., feelings of anger, frustration, mistrust, and resentment) arising from conflict in their relationships.

Further, it is important to note that the majority of couples misclassified in this analysis were couples predicted to divorce who were still married. As the lifetime divorce rate hovers around 50%, it is likely that the number of divorced couples in the sample will rise over time.

A second observed developmental trend has been the decrease in intensity of reported problems over time on the RPI and MAP ($F(2, 28) = 3.66$, $p < .005$; Wilks' Lambda = .49). As can be seen in Figure 7.2, the mean problem intensity peaked by Time 4 and declined over time. Consistent with the satisfaction results, wives tended to report lower problem intensities than did husbands ($F(1, 35) = 3.51, p < .07$).

The strategies couples report using to handle conflict have shown improvement over time. As may be seen in Figure 7.3, the levels of reported withdrawal and verbal aggression on the CTS have declined over time (withdrawal: $F(5, 29) = 7.51$, $p < .001$, Wilks' Lambda = .44; verbal aggression; $F(5, 29) = 6.77, p < .001$, Wilks' Lambda = .54). For both of these variables, the reported levels are highest at Time 4 (the first time this measure was administered) and dropped significantly from Time 4 to Time 5 (withdrawal: $F(1, 33) = 9.75, p < .004$; verbal aggression: $F(1, 33) = 11.50$, $p < .002$) and again from Time 5 to Time 6 (withdrawal: $F(1, 33) = 24.68$, $p < .001$; verbal aggression: $F(1, 33) = 17.52, p < .001$). Men and women

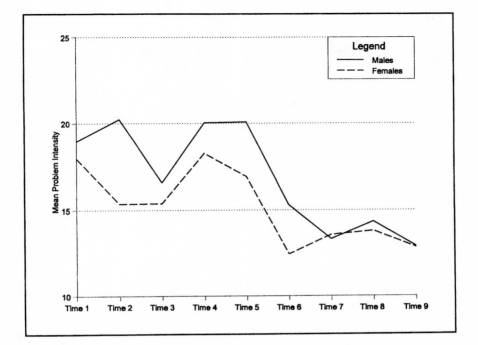

Figure 7.2. Mean problem intensities over time.

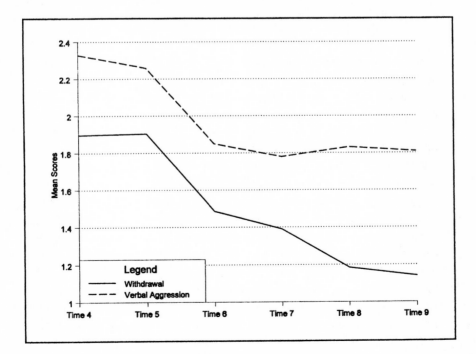

Figure 7.3. Withdrawal and verbal aggression over time.

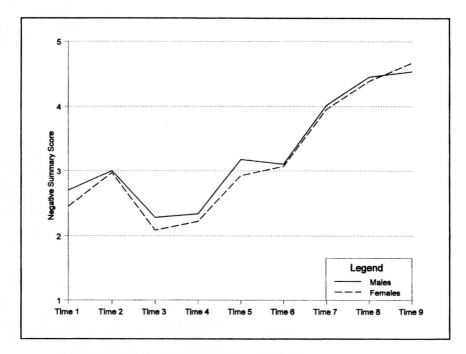

Figure 7.4. IDCS negative summary score over time.

did not differ on either withdrawal ($F(1, 33) = .32$, $p = .57$) or verbal aggression ($F(1, 33) = .14$, $p = .71$). Thus for the sake of parsimony in the graph, data for both genders are combined in Figure 7.3. As these analyses were conducted on the intact couples, they shed light on marital success.

In terms of observer-rated communication, both the negative and the positive summary scores from the IDCS have shown significant increases over time ($F(8, 8) = 13.06$, $p < .001$, Wilks' Lambda = .07). The negative communication summary score represents the overt display of conflict, negative affect, and in general, a person's inability to constructively contribute to a marital problem discussion. As illustrated in Figure 7.4, the increase in negativity was observed for both men and women, and across all time periods except two (Time 2 to Time 3 and Time 8 to Time 9) (see Table 7.2 for actual means). No gender differences were noted ($F(1, 15) = 1.69$, $p = .21$).

Interestingly, positive communication, the use of supportive, clear, and reinforcing communication and body language, has also significantly increased over time ($F(8, 8) = 4.59$, $p < .02$, Wilks' Lambda = .18). As seen in Figure 7.5, positive, or constructive, communication generally increased over the years, despite leveling off between Time 4 and Time 5, and across

Table 7.2. *Increases in negative communication over time*

| Time period | Mean (and standard deviation) | | Significance of change from preceding time | |
	Male	Female	F (1,15)	p
Time 1	2.46 (.63)	2.35 (.52)	—	—
Time 2	2.74 (.53)	2.63 (.53)	48.71	<.001
Time 3	2.23 (.67)	2.26 (.72)	28.47	<.001
Time 4	2.52 (1.07)	2.35 (1.46)	88.69	<.001
Time 5	3.33 (.87)	3.14 (1.29)	29.18	<.001
Time 6	3.07 (1.06)	3.09 (1.16)	12.00	<.003
Time 7	3.93 (.91)	3.84 (1.29)	32.25	<.001
Time 8	4.42 (.89)	4.28 (.89)	4.40	<.05
Time 9	4.99 (1.01)	4.66 (1.37)	.83	.38

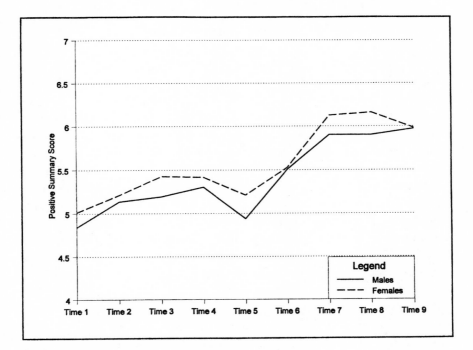

Figure 7.5. IDCS positive summary score over time.

Table 7.3. *Increases in positive communication over time*

Time period	Mean (and standard deviation)		Significance of change from preceding time	
	Male	Female	F (1,15)	p
Time 1	5.00 (1.29)	5.16 (1.20)	—	—
Time 2	5.19 (.53)	5.45 (.53)	3.29	<.09
Time 3	5.28 (.67)	5.13 (.72)	2.20	.16
Time 4	5.34 (1.07)	5.42 (1.46)	7.91	<.01
Time 5	4.84 (.87)	5.20 (1.29)	1.56	.23
Time 6	5.56 (1.06)	5.48 (1.16)	18.24	<.001
Time 7	6.03 (.79)	6.19 (.97)	8.42	<.01
Time 8	5.91 (.89)	6.02 (.89)	.10	.76
Time 9	6.03 (.95	6.17 (1.19)	.22	.64

Times 7 through 9 (see Table 7.3 for actual means). Men and women were not found to differ with respect to their use of the positive elements of communication ($F(1, 15) = 1.58$, $p = .23$). Thus, although the overall level of negative communication has increased over time, this is in the context of increases in positive communication and decreases in withdrawal from conflict, verbal aggression, and level of unresolved conflict. These data suggest that as successful relationships evolve over time, partners remove the "rose-colored glasses" of early relationship bliss, and there is an initial decrease in marital satisfaction. Without the positive bias, what remains is a marriage in which partners have a more realistic appraisal of their relationship. In a comfortable, predictable, and familiar partnership, individuals are more likely to vocalize complaints. At the same time, partners also become more adept at resolving disagreements effectively and constructively.

Marital Development over the Transition to Parenthood

A great deal of attention has focused on the effects of having a child shortly after getting married. Both scientific research and the popular press have examined this issue, and with good reason. Because approximately 90% of married couples in America eventually have children (Houseknecht, 1987), it is important to understand what effects, if any, the birth of the first child has on marriages and marital satisfaction. An opportunity to examine this question arose as couples in this study began to have children. Although the current sample cannot be regarded as nationally representative, the abundance of longitudinal data provides an excellent opportunity for a clinical outcome study of the transition to parenthood complete with a childless comparison group.

The current study was not designed to evaluate specifically the effects of the transition to parenthood on marriage. Actual studies of the transition to parenthood typically recruit couples when they are expecting their first child and follow them for up to a year or more after the birth of the child. The current study, in contrast, recruited couples before marriage and followed them through the first 9 years of marriage. Some of these couples have had children and some have not, but a great deal of information is available about all parents before and after birth and about all childless couples over the same period.

Although the current study design has some disadvantages for addressing the transition to parenthood, it also yields some benefits. In particular, the study was not originally designed to answer questions about the transition to parenthood, and thus some measures of interest (e.g., attitudes toward childrearing, infertility, and childbirth preparation) were not collected. In addition, couples had children at vastly different time points both in their marriage and in the study. The timing of the research sessions was in no way related to birth of the first child: Research sessions occurred within weeks of the birth to within a year of the birth. For this reason, acute reactions to the birth of a child are not measured. Finally, the current sample is probably functioning at a level higher than the population in general in that they have continued to participate in research sessions for a number of years (Bradbury, 1994; Rubin & Mitchell, 1976).

On the other hand, the current study does have at least two distinct advantages over previous investigations. First, because the marital development of the couples has been studied for 9 years, a great deal of information is available about the marital relationship before the child's conception. Thus we are in the position to build on the important contributions of several key studies of transition to parenthood in which couples were recruited during pregnancy (e.g., Belsky, 1985; Cowan et al., 1985). Second, the current study involves a childless comparison group that has been married the same length of time. This allows for separation of the effects of having a child from developmental changes in marriage that occur as a function of the passage of time. This enables us to build on previous studies that have only assessed changes in marriage due to the transition to parenthood based only on assessment of couples before and after birth (e.g., Belsky, 1985; Markman & Kadushin, 1986; Wallace & Gotlib, 1990; Wilkie & Ames, 1986). Without the use of a childless comparison group, it is not possible to state with certainty that these effects are due to the birth of the child. It is also possible that, as has been noted above, marital satisfaction normatively tends to decline over the course of the marriage, and assessments made before and after the birth of a child reflect two points on this trajectory as opposed to a distinct decline due to the birth of a child.

Couples who had children and childless couples were matched on length of time married, premarital satisfaction, engagement status, quality of communication, and ratings of partners' communication (Clements & Markman, 1998; Markman, Clements, & Wright, 1991). For the analyses reported here, data were collected from 31 couples who became parents and 28 childless couples. This was the entire sample for whom complete laboratory data were available (1) immediately preceding marriage, (2) immediately before the birth of the first child for parents (or the same length of time after marriage for childless couples), and (3) at the subsequent follow-up.

In contrast to many other studies in the literature (Belsky, 1985; Belsky, Lang, & Rovine, 1985; Belsky & Rovine, 1990; Cowan et al., 1985; Cowan, Cowan, Heming, & Miller, 1991; Wallace & Gotlib, 1990; Wilkie & Ames, 1986), the current study has not generally found having a child to be associated with declines in reported romantic love and marital satisfaction or with increases in marital conflict and reported marital problems. When childless couples and parents who had been married the same length of time were examined in a repeated measures ANOVA, declines in marital satisfaction across groups did not differ. It was revealed that MAT scores examined at three time points (before marriage, the follow-up before the birth of the first child or the equivalent length of time for childless couples, and the follow-up after the birth of the first child) were indistinguishable for parents and childless couples. Significant declines were noted from Time 1 to Time 2 ($F(1, 36) = 11.00$, $p < .01$) and from Time 2 to Time 3 ($F(1, 36) = 4.22$, $p < .05$), but these declines did not differentiate the two groups.

A similar picture was revealed for level of reported marital problems as assessed by the RPI and MAP at the same three time points. No differences between parents and childless couples were observed in either problem totals (the sum of ratings of all problem areas) or for ratings of individual problem areas with the exception of alcohol and drugs; childless couples rated alcohol and drugs as more of a problem in their relationship than did parents ($F(1, 35) = 6.82, p < .05$).

Taken together, these results suggest that the transition to parenthood may not be the traumatic experience for marriage that the recent press and research studies have suggested. Having children is a salient point on the general marital developmental trajectory for the lay public and researchers alike. It is comparatively easy to identify periods before and after a discrete event such as childbirth. This may encourage attribution of cause to the event as opposed to the greater context surrounding the event. In other words, when comparisons are made before and after the birth of a child, significant differences may well be apparent; however, these declines may be due to a general developmental trend as opposed to parenthood.

Marital and Family Functioning

As noted earlier, we hypothesized that the parents' ability to handle negative affect is one of the key mechanisms linking marital quality and child functioning. We based this hypothesis on the growing body of literature implicating a causal link between marital quality and child functioning and the quality of the parent–child relationship (e.g., Emery, 1982; Goldberg & Easterbrooks, 1984; Gottman & Katz, 1989; Grych & Fincham, 1990). Marital distress has been shown to be a risk factor for a variety of forms of psychopathology for both adults (e.g., depression) and children (e.g., conduct disorder) (Crockenberg & Covey, 1991). Though most of the empirical work is correlational rather than causal, most theories suggest a causal relationship between marital distress and children's adjustment. Consequently, as the couples in our study started having children, we were interested in exploring the effect of marital distress on child development and parent–child relationships.

Attachment

When a cohort of the children were toddlers (1–3 years old), we invited parents to participate in a study of the relationship between marital functioning and the quality of the early parent–child relationship (Howes & Markman, 1989). Attachment between caregiver and child was assessed because it represented the quality of the interactional history between parent and child in general, and how well the child handles negative affect in particular.

As indicated above, we had assessed dimensions of the marital relationship associated with managing negative affect at annual follow-up sessions, starting before the couples were married. By starting with the couples before the child was born, we were able to examine the effects of the marriage on the child separately from the effects of the child on the marriage. The Attachment Behavior Q-Set (Waters & Deane, 1985) was used to assess parents' perception of their child with respect to attachment and sociability. The availability of the longitudinal data allowed us to ascertain whether there was a relationship between couples' early relationship quality and the quality of the attachment relationship 3 to 5 years later. The results below summarize across the domains of marital satisfaction and level of marital conflict.

Predictive associations were found between mothers' premarital relationship quality and later child security of attachment and sociability and between fathers' premarital relationship quality and child dependency. More specifically, children of premaritally dissatisfied mothers tended to be insecurely attached ($r = .49$, $p < .10$) and less sociable ($r = .39$, $p < .10$), while fathers' premarital reports of conflict were associated with more dependency in parent–child relationships ($r = .49$, $p < .05$). Thus, compared with their less satisfied counterparts, more maritally satisfied mothers may facilitate attachment, and fathers' perception of low conflict in the marriage may facilitate autonomy. These results suggest that the ability of parents to handle differences in their relationship through appropriate conflict management and communication skills contributes to their child's well-being. Consistent with other studies (e.g., Easterbrooks & Emde, 1988), mothers' data were associated more with child outcomes than were fathers' data. This makes sense in light of the greater quantity of time mothers spend with their children than do fathers.

Self-Concept

Self-concept was chosen as a measure of child functioning for several reasons. First, it is central to human development and has been associated with many areas of functioning (Wylie, 1979). It is feelings of worth, effectiveness, and self-satisfaction that allow an individual to develop new skills and to achieve independent, internally regulated functioning (Coopersmith, 1967). Self-concept has been found to be highly influenced by parental factors in early development (Harter, 1989) and therefore would be likely to be sensitive to the stresses of marital conflict and distress. In fact, Coopersmith (1967) found that boys with low self-esteem had parents whose marital history was more likely to include previous marriages and greater tension and conflict than boys with high self-esteem.

While young children (4–7) are not able to self-report on global self-esteem, they have been found to be able to self-report on specific domains of the self-concept if these are presented in terms of concrete observable behaviors (Damon & Hart, 1982; Harter, 1983, 1986; Montemayor & Eisen, 1977). Using pictorial stimuli, we were able to obtain children's self-reports on their perception of their behavior or conduct and on their affective experience of their family (with higher scores indicating more happiness or satisfaction with their family). In addition, children also reported on the domains of parental acceptance, peer acceptance, and cognitive competence (Dunn & Markman, 1994).

Of all the marital variables assessed in the study, it has been the marital interaction variables rather than marital satisfaction that have accounted for the most variance in children's self-concept. This highlights the importance of considering specific mechanisms when studying the impact of marital factors on child functioning. Specifically, couples' negative escalation, support and validation, and withdrawal within the marital interaction were all particularly important in predicting child self-concept. Aspects of children's self-concept were predicted by the quality of marital interaction both premaritally and at the transition to parenthood.

We found that wives' marital interaction variables before marriage, especially how emotionally supportive and validating they were with their husbands, predicted higher levels of positive experiences with the family ($r = .44$, $p < .05$), parental acceptance ($r = .39$, $p < .10$), satisfaction with their own behavior ($r = .43$, $p < .10$), and cognitive competence ($r = .37$, $p < .10$) in children 5 years later. Fathers' premarital behavior was not predictive of children's self-concept.

During the transition to parenthood (mean = 9 months before birth of child), however, we found that both positive and negative communication predicted child outcomes for both husbands and wives. After partialling out premarital interaction quality, it was found that a high level of negative escalation in the marriage was associated with children perceiving their conduct more negatively (husbands: $r = -.62$, $p < .01$; wives: $r = -.67$, $p < .01$) and reporting less happiness with their family (husbands: $r = -.56$, $p < .01$; wives: $r = -.57$, $p < .01$). Wives' negative escalation during the transition to parenthood was also predictive of children's report of less peer acceptance ($r = -.44$, $p < .05$). On the other hand, a high level of supportive interaction was associated with children perceiving their behavior more positively (husbands: $r = .53$, $p < .05$; wives: $r = .44$, $p < .05$). Wives' appeasement of their husbands during the marital interactions at the transition to parenthood was predictive of children reporting less positive or happy experiences with their family ($r = -.48$, $p < .05$) and perceiving their behavior in a more negative light ($r = -.41$, $p < .05$). It was initially surprising to find that mothers' avoidance of or withdrawal from marital conflict was related to children reporting more positive feelings about their family ($r = .54$, $p < .05$). However, because direct exposure to marital conflict has been found to be detrimental to child development (Hetherington, Cox, & Cox, 1985; Emery, 1982; Fincham & Osborne, 1993), avoidance of conflict may result in a family atmosphere that is less conflictual and thus more conducive to the development of a healthy self-concept in children.

Parent–Child Affect Regulation

Data indicate that a distressed marriage is associated with less sensitive and more negative parenting, whereas a satisfying marriage is associated with warm, engaged parenting (e.g., Goldberg & Easterbrooks, 1984; Gottman & Katz, 1989; Jouriles, Pfiffner, & O'Leary, 1988). We suggest that the parent–child relationship, especially with regard to how negative affect is regulated in parent–child interactions, is a potentially fruitful avenue to explore in more fully explicating the link between marital conflict and child development. Given our longitudinal interest in how couples manage negative affect and conflict with each other, we became interested in how marital quality affects child development and how affect regulation occurs in parent–child relationships. We hypothesized that spouses' ability to handle or regulate negative affect (e.g., the ability to avoid negative escalation cycles and to handle conflict and disagreements constructively) in their marriage would be related to how they handled negative affect with their children (Lindahl & Markman, 1990). We hypothesized that deficiencies in the marital dyad's ability to regulate negative affect would lead to affect regulation problems in the family which, in turn, would be expressed ultimately in the child's own inability to effectively regulate negative interaction in relevant interpersonal situations. Thus a major objective of this study was to test the hypothesis that the negative effects of marital discord on children involves the transmission of problems in affect regulation to children through parent–child interactions.

A couple of hypotheses were tested. First, it was hypothesized that marital satisfaction, both at the transition to parenthood and currently, would be related to how negative affect is managed within families. Negative affect regulation was assessed in both dyadic (parent–child) and triadic (mother–father–child) interactions to test for influences on both the separate relationships a child has with each parent as well as family functioning overall. Second, it was expected that the tendency of parents to triangulate their child into an ongoing marital problem discussion would be associated with higher levels of dysregulated negative affect (i.e., tension, conflict) within the family.

Thus far, 25 families (13 boys, 12 girls) from the longitudinal study have participated in the family functioning assessment. Couples were invited to participate when their child was approximately 5 years old (mean = 5 years, 2 months, sd = 7 months). Families participated in four negative affect regulation interaction tasks, three of which are reported here. Families completed two dyadic tasks, one for each parent. Each parent–child pair was assigned a complex task that was meant to be above the developmental level of the children in order to elicit mild levels of frustration for the parents and children. For the third negative affect regulation task, the triadic task, couples discussed one of the top problem areas in their marriage while their child was in the room. This task was chosen both for its ecological validity, as it represents a developmental task facing many young couples, and for its potential for frustration.

Dyadic Parent–Child Interactions. Only concurrent marital variables (rather than premarital or transition to parenthood marital factors) were consistently related to parents' behavior in the parent–child tasks. Husbands' marital satisfaction was related to how fathers responded to their child's frustration during the dyadic parent–child tasks. Marital satisfaction was inversely related to fathers' invalidation ($r = -.44$, $p < .05$) and positively associated with fathers' emotional support ($r = .49$, $p < .05$) with their child. As predicted, wives who reported a higher level of problem intensity in the marriage were more invalidating ($r = .50$, $p < .05$) and less emotionally supportive ($r = -.64$, $p < .01$) with their children. Couples' communication was related in predicted directions to parenting behavior. When husbands were positive and supportive with their wives, they were also supportive with their children ($r = .49$, $p < .05$). Wives' conflict and negative affect with their spouses was associated with invalidation with their children ($r = .59$, $p < .01$).

Triadic Family Interactions. Results indicate that marital satisfaction before a child is born is predictive of how negative affect is managed in the family years later. Couples' marital satisfaction at the transition to parenthood was correlated with the SCARF family, couple, and parenting codes from the triadic interaction. Specifically, when husbands were happier with their marriage before parenthood, the family expressed more warmth with each other ($r = .45$, $p < .05$), and parents appeared more cohesive as a couple ($r = .41$, $p < .05$) years later during a marital problem discussion witnessed by their child. Likewise, wives' marital satisfaction before parenthood was predictive of families' expression of higher levels of warmth ($r = .40, p < .05$) and less tension ($r = -.45, p < .05$) with each other 5 years later during the triadic discussion.

Similar results were found for current levels of marital satisfaction. For both parents, marital satisfaction was associated with more warmth (husbands: $r = .38, p < .10$; wives: $r = .41, p < .05$) and less tension (husbands: $r = -.48, p < .01$; wives: $r = .58, p < .01$) between family members, and greater couple cohesiveness (husbands: $r = .42, p < .05$; wives: $r = .38, p < .10$). In addition, for both parents, marital satisfaction was negatively associated with parents triangulating their children into the marital discussion during the triadic task (husbands: $r = -.50, p < .01$; wives: $r = -.43, p < .05$). Furthermore, parental triangulation of the child, in an apparent effort to regulate negative affect emanating from the marriage, was strongly related to family affect and couple functioning. Triangulation of the child into the marital conflict was highly associated with the level of tension in the family (husbands: $r = .62, p < .01$; wives: $r = .78, p < .001$) and was inversely related to positive family affect (husbands: $r = -.40, p < .05$; wives: $r = -.52, p < .01$), and couple cohesiveness (husbands: $r = -.65, p < .001$; wives: $r = -.42, p < .05$). Interestingly, it was also found that when fathers incorporated their children in the marital discussion, children engaged in higher levels of support seeking from their mothers ($r = .40, p < .05$).

Wives' satisfaction was also linked with their parenting behavior during the marital discussion with their child present. When wives were more content with their marriage, they were more emotionally supportive ($r = .40, p < .05$) and less conflictual ($r = -.50, p < .01$) with their children during the triadic interaction.

In sum, the preliminary results reported here suggest that current levels of family functioning can be predicted to some extent by marital satisfaction before the child is born. When parents reported higher satisfaction with their marriages before their children were born, they were more likely later to set a tone of warmth, supportiveness, and appropriate regulation of negative affect in a family interaction 5 years later. Current level of marital satisfaction was also highly associated with the affective tone of the family and how family members interacted with one another. Thus it would appear that couples with more satisfying marriages are more likely to balance the needs of their marriages and their children and are less likely to let marital problems interfere with parenting, at least in this type of family interaction. Though the families reported here are by no means a clinically distressed sample, these results suggest that even mildly dissatisfied couples tend to triangulate their children and set a tone that is tense and conflictual in family interactions. These data suggest that poorly regulated negative affect, which has been shown to be a strong predictor of marital distress, is also associated with distress at a family level and may be passed on to subsequent generations through dyadic and triadic interactions in the family.

Peer Relationships

We expected children from families with lower marital satisfaction to demonstrate more difficulty in regulating negative affect with their peers. This hypothesis was generally not supported. In fact, marital satisfaction was found to be related to receiving more negative attention from peers. This association was present with both the father's marital satisfaction ($r = .62, p < .01$) and the mother's satisfaction ($r = .53, p < .05$). However, when parental conflict behaviors, as opposed to overall satisfaction, were examined, a different picture emerged.

Mother's reported use of negative conflict resolution strategies before the child's birth were strongly related to negative behaviors on the part of the child. In particular, there were strong relationships between children's negative escalation in the peer setting and the wives' reports of violence ($r = .71, p < .05$) and physical aggression ($r = .69, p < .05$). In addition, verbal aggression in the marriage was found to be associated with more isolative play ($r = .78, p < .01$). These results, indicating a link between couples' anger management strategies *before* the child was born and children's display of negative affect escalation with their peers 5 years later, are among the first from this study to implicate a causal link between marital functioning and children's emotional functioning outside the family.

Concluding Comments and Discussion of Longitudinal Issues

In this section we offer some observations and advice to fellow researchers concerning issues conducting longitudinal studies with couples and families.

When to Start the Study?

Before embarking on a longitudinal study of couples or families, researchers must decide at what developmental point to start recruiting the sample. Although this decision largely depends on the research questions being asked, even when we decided to predict marital distress, a number of important choices that we made affected the course of the study. For example, we decided to recruit young couples when they were planning marriage in order to start our prediction and prevention work with couples before distress set in. However, we did not pin the recruitment to any particular point in development, such as the date of first marriage or having a first child. As seen in this chapter, couples reached these developmental milestones at different rates, thus affecting statistical analyses and interpretation of results. Many other studies of young couples start in the first year of marriage so that all the couples are at the same developmental point. However, even these studies eventually encounter similar issues. For example, couples have children at different points in time.

Sample Size

There are many issues for recruiting a sample in any study; this is no less true for a longitudinal project. Researchers struggle between selecting an epidemiologically sound sample that requires large numbers from diverse populations and a smaller sample that should be studied more extensively and frequently with observational methods. Large sample size studies of families are going to be imperative as the field moves on, in order to assess differential effects of fathers and mothers on boys and girls. Most longitudinal studies in the family development field, including ours, simply do not have the power to adequately address such questions. It is going to be critically important to address such questions as a number of studies have indicated differential effects of mothers on sons versus mothers on daughters, and fathers on sons versus fathers on daughters. On the other hand, there is also a value in relatively small sample size studies in which the results are replicated and extended within and across research laboratories.

We believe there is a place in the marital and family psychology area for both kinds of studies, and we hope to see more studies that blend both designs. For example, subpopulations from large-scale studies could be selected for more intensive study through methods such as observational coding.

Sample Retention

Once the sample has been recruited, retaining the sample over time becomes a critical issue in longitudinal research. Dropouts from groups or subgroups clearly threaten the validity of a study. In our work, we have been very successful in retaining our sample. Perhaps the most important factor in our retention rate is that subjects have generally felt respected by our research staff and have felt they were contributing to an important scientific enterprise. In fact, the reason given by many in our sample for participating in our study was to further science.

Paying subjects for their time has also been helpful in retaining the sample. We were able to pay our subjects relatively small amounts early on but have steadily increased our payments such that we now pay them $50 for a two-hour follow-up session. In addition to scientific credibility and payment, the third factor that seems important in retention is keeping in touch with the subjects on a regular basis. We do this through a newsletter that is mailed to the subjects on an ongoing basis without threatening the basic hypotheses of the investigation.

Measure Decay

In longitudinal research, subjects are often administered the same measures and the same procedures over and over again. This leads to potential problems in interpreting the data over time, particularly if the subjects develop response sets. In addition, feelings of boredom may generate a hesitancy among subjects not to return for follow-up sessions. While it is critical for longitudinal investigators to use the same measures over time, in our investigation we have also tried to change at least one aspect of the follow-up sessions so that subjects could look forward to doing something new as well as something familiar. We have tried to be as creative as possible in generating tasks for subjects that are relevant to the developmental stage of the study. For example, for one of our recent follow-up visits, subjects reviewed a portion of their premarital interaction task and were videotaped while discussing how their communication and conflict management skills had changed over time.

The Impact of Couples Research on the Subjects

Rubin and Mitchell (1976) were among the first to acknowledge the possibility that research participation could affect subjects' close relationships. In terms of couples research, they suggested that just receiving attention on a regular, ongoing basis could be helpful. Recently, Bradbury (1994) found empirical evidence to support this conclusion. In a series of studies, Bradbury (1994) found that a high proportion of newlywed couples reported that participating in marital research had had an impact on their relationship. For the vast majority, the impact had been positive in that it heightened awareness and appreciation of the relationship.

Involvement in research has also been shown to positively affect the quality of couples' communication, at least in the context of the research session, if not the long term. Talking about difficult relationship issues within the structure of a videotaped research setting is likely to produce interactions that are more positive than similar interactions at home. For example, in our work we have found that when couples use a "communication box" to rate each other's communication in a counterbalanced design controlling for the order of problem intensity, they dramatically and significantly increase positive communication and decrease negative communication, in comparison to speaking without such structure in place. Similarly, in an unpublished study (conducted in the days prior to today's rigorous ethical standards) examining the impact of videotaping on couples' communication, we found that couples communicated more positively when they were aware they were being videotaped than when they thought they were not being videotaped. Thus participating in research that includes an interactional component seems to help couples improve their communication at least for the duration of the laboratory session. However, as many marital therapists are likely to attest, it is unlikely that without further intervention such changes will generalize to the home and other environments. In addition, it is not the goal of observational marital research to replicate the exact nature of the communication that occurs in the home. Rather, the goal is to compare distressed and nondistressed couples in similar interactional situations. What we tend to find is that even though the overall levels of positivity and negativity may change across settings, the actual sequencing and patterning of interactions tends to be similar.

Seeking and Keeping Funding for Longitudinal Studies

One of the biggest issues facing researchers interested in collecting longitudinal data is that these studies are very expensive and federal resources are steadily shrinking. Most longitudinal investigations supported by the National Institute of Mental Health are initially funded for a 3-, 4-, or 5-year period. Most investigators submitting such grants clearly intend to continue the study beyond the first funding period. Because of the enormous effort required to initiate a longitudinal project and the length of time required for data collection and analysis (especially if observational methods are included), many researchers find that the initial funding period is inadequate to carefully answer the questions that the study set out to examine. Before the first funding period is complete, researchers are put in the position of needing to submit a second grant application. In turn, grant reviewers are faced with evaluating requests for subsequent money that may contain inadequate early data, and thus the request for additional funds may seem unsubstantiated. Grant review committee members are often in a bind at this point. On the one hand, they feel that they have made an investment in the study, and it would be interesting to know the results beyond the earlier period of funding. On the other hand, new cross-sectional and longitudinal applications are coming in as well as other longitudinal studies that are already in their second to fourth stage and making similar arguments. Furthermore, when the proposal is resubmitted for additional funding, it is likely that the grant review committee will have substantially changed and a different set of reviewers will review the application.

There are no easy answers to the above issues. One suggestion is that when designing a longitudinal study, the investigator clearly articulates when the study is intended to stop. Often studies only stop when funding runs out or energy is directed to another research endeavor. Of course, determining the termination date in advance carries liabilities with it as well. In many cases, the initial data that are generated lead to new discoveries or new questions that need further investigation. This was certainly the case in our study. Although the original goals were to study the prevention and prediction of marital distress, the study has been expanded to examine the effects of premarital and marital interaction on children and parenting.

Conclusion

In conclusion, we hope that this last section of the chapter has served as an abbreviated user's guide for thinking about issues in conducting longitudinal research. We hope these comments will be useful to young investigators as they move on in their careers. Unfortunately, there are not enough young investigators in the area of marital interaction, or more generally. For example, NIMH reports that there has been a sharp decline in the number of R01 grants submitted by investigators under age 36, and the section of NIMH that funds marital and family process research reports that it is receiving very few applications from young investigators at this time. Longitudinal research is almost by definition for younger researchers, as studies are intended to continue over generations. We hope that this guide has been particularly useful to our young colleagues.

References

Belsky, J. (1985). Exploring individual differences in marital change across the transition to parenthood: The role of violated expectations. *Journal of Marriage and the Family, 47,* 1037–1044.

Belsky, J., Lang, M. E., & Rovine, M. (1985). Stability and change in marriage across the transition to parenthood: A second study. *Journal of Marriage and the Family, 47,* 855–865.

Belsky, J., & Rovine, M. (1990). Patterns of marital change across the transition to parenthood: Pregnancy to three years postpartum. *Journal of Marriage and the Family, 52,* 5–19.

Bradbury, T. N. (1994). Unintended effects of marital research on marital relationships. *Journal of Family Psychology, 8,* 187–201.

Bradbury, T. N., & Karney, B. R. (1993). Longitudinal study of marital interaction and dysfunction: Review and analysis. *Clinical Psychology Review, 13,* 15–27.

Clements, M., & Markman, H. J. (1996). The transition to parenthood: Is having children hazardous to your marriage? In N. Vanzetti & S. Duck (Eds.), *A lifetime of relationships* (pp. 290–310). Pacific Grove, CA: Brooks/Cole.

Clements, M., & Markman, H. J. (1998). *Declines in marital functioning over the transition to parenthood: Can we blame the marriage and not the child?* Manuscript in preparation, Pennsylvania State University.

Clements, M. L., Stanley, S. M., & Markman, H. J. (1998). *Prediction of marital distress and divorce: A discriminant analysis approach.* Manuscript submitted for publication.

Coopersmith, S. (1967). *The antecedents of self-esteem.* San Francisco, CA: Freeman.

Cowan, C. P., Cowan, P. A., Heming, G., Garrett, E., Coysh, W. S., Curtis-Boles, H., & Boles, A. J. (1985). Transitions to parenthood: His, hers, theirs. *Journal of Family Issues, 6,* 451–481.

Cowan, C. P., Cowan, P. A., Heming, G., & Miller, N. B. (1991). Becoming a family: Marriage, parenting, and child development. In P. A. Cowan & M. Hetherington (Eds.), *Family transitions* (pp. 79–109). Hillsdale, NJ: Lawrence Erlbaum.

Crockenberg, S., & Covey, S. L. (1991). Marital conflict and externalizing behavior in children. In D. Cicchetti & S. Toth (Eds.), *Models and integrations: Rochester Symposium on Developmental Psychopathology* (Vol. 3, pp. 235–260). Rochester, NY: University of Rochester Press.

Damon, W., & Hart, D. (1982). The development of self-understanding from infancy through adolescence. *Child Development, 53,* 841–854.

Dunn, A., & Markman, H. J. (1994). *The effects of marital communication and conflict management on children's perceptions of self and of the family.* Manuscript in preparation, University of Denver.

Easterbrooks, M. A., & Emde, R. (1988). Marital and parent–child relationships:

The role of affect in the family system. In R. Hinde & J. Stevenson-Hinde (Eds.), *Relationships within families: Mutual influences* (pp. 104–141). Oxford: Oxford University Press.

Emery, R. E. (1982). Interparental conflict and the children of discord and divorce. *Psychological Bulletin, 92,* 310–330.

Fincham, F. D., & Osborne, L. N. (1993). Marital conflict and children: Retrospect and prospect. *Clinical Psychology Review, 13,* 75–88.

Goldberg, W. A., & Easterbrooks, M. A. (1984). The role of marital quality in toddler development. *Child Development, 20,* 504–515.

Gottman, J. M. (1979). *Marital interaction: Experimental investigations.* New York: Academic Press.

Gottman, J. M. (1986). The world of coordinated play: Same and cross-sex friendship in young children. In J. Gottman & J. Parker (Eds.), *Conversations of friends.* New York: Cambridge University Press.

Gottman, J. M., & Katz, L. F. (1989). Effects of marital discord on young children's peer interaction and health. *Developmental Psychology, 25,* 373–381.

Gottman, J. M., Markman, H. J., & Notarius, C. I. (1977). The topography of marital conflict: A sequential analysis of verbal and nonverbal behavior. *Journal of Marriage and the Family, 39,* 461–477.

Gottman, J. M., Notarius, C. I., Markman, H. J., Banks, D., Yoppi, B., & Rubin, M. E. (1976). Behavior exchange theory and marital decision making. *Journal of Personality and Social Psychology, 34,* 14–23.

Grych, J. H. & Fincham, F. D. (1990). Marital conflict and children's adjustment: A cognitive-contextual framework. *Psychological Bulletin, 108,* 267–290.

Harter, S. (1983). Developmental perspectives on the self-system. In M. Hetherington (Ed.), *Handbook of child psychology: Vol. 4. Socialization, personality, and social development* (pp. 275–386). New York: Wiley.

Harter, S. (1986). Processes underlying the construction, maintenance, and enhancement of self-concept in children. In J. Suls & A. G. Greenwald (Eds.), *Psychological perspectives on the self* (pp. 137–181). Hillsdale, NJ: Lawrence Erlbaum.

Harter, S. (1989). Causes, correlates and the functional role of global self-worth: A life-span perspective. In J. Kolligian & R. Sternberg (Eds.), *Perceptions of competence and incompetence across the life-span* (pp. 67–97). New Haven, CT: Yale University Press.

Harter, S., & Pike, R. (1984). The pictorial perceived competence scale for young children. *Child Development, 55,* 1969–1982.

Hetherington, E. M., Cox, M., & Cox, R. (1985). Long-term effects of divorce and remarriage on the adjustment of children. *Journal of the American Academy of Child Psychiatry, 24,* 518–530.

Houseknecht, S. K. (1987). Voluntary childlessness. In M. B. Sussman & S. K. Steinmetz (Eds.), *Handbook of marriage and the family* (pp. 369–395). New York: Plenum.

Howes, P., & Markman, H. J. (1989). Marital quality and child functioning: A longitudinal investigation. *Child Development, 60,* 1044–1051.

Jouriles, E. N., Pfiffner, L. J., & O'Leary, K. D. (1988). Marital conflict, parenting, toddler conduct problems. *Journal of Abnormal Child Psychology, 16,* 197–206.

Julien, D., Markman, H. J., & Lindahl, K. L. (1989). A comparison of a global and a microanalytic coding system: Implications for future trends in studying interactions. *Behavioral Assessment, 11,* 81–100.

Knox, D. (1970). *Marriage happiness.* Champaign, IL: Research Press.

Lindahl, K. M., & Markman, H. J. (1990). Communication and negative affect regulation in the family. In E. A. Blechman (Ed.), *Emotions and the family: For better or for worse* (pp. 99–115). Hillsdale, NJ: Lawrence Erlbaum.

Lindahl, K. M., & Markman, H. J. (1991, November). *System for Coding Affect Regulation in the Family (SCARF): A global coding system for dyadic interactions.* Paper presented at the annual meeting of the Association for Advancement of Behavior Therapy, New York, NY.

Lindahl, K. M., & Markman, H. J. (1993, April). *Regulating negative affect in the family: Implications for dyadic and triadic family interactions.* Paper presented at the biennial meetings of the Society for Research in Child Development, New Orleans, LA.

Locke, H. J., & Wallace, K. M. (1959). Short-term marital adjustment and prediction tests: Their reliability and validity. *Marriage and Family Living, 21,* 251–255.

Markman, H. J. (1979). Application of a behavioral model of marriage in predicting relationship satisfaction in couples planning marriage. *Journal of Consulting and Clinical Psychology, 47,* 743–749.

Markman, H. J. (1981). Prediction of marital distress: A five-year follow-up. *Journal of Consulting and Clinical Psychology, 49,* 760–762.

Markman, H. J. (1991). Backwards into the future of couples therapy and couples therapy research: A comment on Jacobson. *Journal of Family Psychology, 4,* 416–425.

Markman, H. J., Clements, M., & Wright, R. (1991, April). *Why father's pre-birth negativity and a first-born daughter predict marital problems: Results from a ten-year investigation.* Symposium presented at biannual meeting of the Society for Research in Child Development, Seattle.

Markman, H. J., & Floyd, F. (1980). Possibilities for the prevention of marital discord: A behavioral perspective. *American Journal of Family Therapy, 8,* 29–48.

Markman, H. J., Floyd, F., & Dickson-Markman, F. (1982). Toward a model of the prediction and prevention of marital and family distress and dissolution. In S. Duck (Ed.), *Personal relationships 4: Dissolving personal relationships* (pp. 223–261). London: Academic Press.

Markman, H. J., Floyd, F., Stanley, S., & Lewis, H. (1986). Prevention. In N. Jacobson & A. Gurman (Eds.), *Clinical handbook of marital therapy* (pp. 173–195). New York: Guilford.

Markman, H. J., Floyd, F., Stanley, S. M., & Storaasli, R. (1988). The prevention of marital distress: A longitudinal investigation. *Journal of Consulting and Clinical Psychology, 56,* 210–217.

Markman, H. J., & Hahlweg, K. (1993). The prediction and prevention of marital distress: An international perspective. *Clinical Psychology Review, 13,* 29–43.

Markman, H. J., & Kadushin, F. S. (1986). Preventive effects of Lamaze training for first-time parents: A short-term longitudinal study. *Journal of Consulting and Clinical Psychology, 54,* 872–874.

Markman, H. J., & Notarius, C. I. (1987). Coding marital and family interaction: Current status. In T. Jacob (Ed.), *Family interaction and psychopathology* (pp. 329–390). New York: Plenum Press.

Markman, H. J., Renick, M. J., Floyd, F. J., Stanley, S. M., & Clements, M. (1993). Preventing marital distress through communication and conflict management training: A 4- and 5-year follow-up. *Journal of Consulting and Clinical Psychology, 61,* 70–77.

Montemayor, R., & Eisen, M. (1977). The development of self-conceptions from childhood to adolescence. *Developmental Psychology, 13,* 314–319.

Notarius, C. I., & Markman, H. J. (1981). The Couples' Interaction Scoring System. In E. Filsinger & R. Lewis (Eds.), *Assessing marriage: New behavioral approaches* (pp. 117–136). Beverly Hills, CA: Sage.

Notarius, C. I., & Pellegrini, D. P. (1987). Differences between husbands and wives: Implications for understanding marital discord. In K. Hahlweg & M. Goldstein (Eds.), *Understanding major mental disorders: The contribution of family interaction research* (pp. 231–239). New York: Family Process.

Notarius, C. I., & Vanzetti, N. (1984). The marital agenda protocol. In E. Filsinger (Ed.), *Marital and family assessment* (pp. 209–227). Beverly Hills, CA: Sage.

Olson, D. H., & Ryder, R. G. (1970). Inventory of marital conflicts (IMC): An experimental interaction procedure. *Journal of Marriage and Family Living, 32,* 433–448.

Renick, M. J., Blumberg, S. L., & Markman, H. J. (1992). The Prevention and Relationship Enhancement Program (PREP): An empirically based preventive intervention program for couples. *Family Relations, 41,* 141–147.

Rubin, Z., & Mitchell, C. (1976). Couples research as couples counselling: Some unintended effects of studying close relationships. *American Psychologist, 31,* 36–46.

Spanier, G. B., Lewis, R. A., & Cole, C. L. (1975). Marital adjustment over the family life cycle: The issues of curvilinearity. *Journal of Marriage and the Family, 37,* 263–275.

Storaasli, R. D., & Markman, H. J. (1990). Relationship problems in the premarital and early stages of marriage: A test of family development theory. *Journal of Family Psychology, 2,* 80–98.

Straus, M. (1979). Measuring intra-family conflict and violence: The Conflict Tactics (CT) scales. *Journal of Marriage and the Family, 41,* 75–88.

Wallace, P. M., & Gotlib, I. H. (1990). Marital adjustment during the transition to parenthood: Stability and predictors of change. *Journal of Marriage and the Family, 52,* 21–29.

Waters, E., & Deane, K. E. (1985). Defining and assessing individual differences in attachment relationships: Q-methodology and the organization of behavior in infancy and early childhood. In I. Bretherton & E. Waters (Eds.), *Growing points of attachment theory and research: Monographs of the Society for Research in Child Development, 50* (1–2, Serial No. 209).

Wilkie, C. F., & Ames, E. W. (1986). The relationship of infant crying to parental stress in the transition to parenthood. *Journal of Marriage and the Family, 48,* 545–550.

Wylie, R. (1979). *The self-concept: Vol. 2. Theory and research on selected topics.* Lincoln: University of Nebraska Press.

8   Premarital Predictors of Relationship Outcomes: A 15-Year Follow-up of the Boston Couples Study

Charles T. Hill and Letitia Anne Peplau

Selecting a mate is one of life's most important decisions. In our fiercely independent culture, young people place a premium on personal choice in matters of the heart. Unfortunately, current divorce statistics suggest that many Americans are not making good marital choices. At present, empirical research offers few guidelines for detecting which dating relationships are likely to develop into successful marriages. Although there is abundant research on factors such as good looks and attitude similarity that foster initial interpersonal attraction, we know little about the long-term importance of these factors in continuing relationships. There is also a growing literature using information about marital patterns at one point in time to predict later marital success (e.g., Bentler & Newcomb, 1978; Bradbury & Fincham, 1990; Gottman, 1994; Kurdek, 1993). Although such information assists in identifying existing marriages at risk for misery and dissolution, it may not help young lovers to avoid unhappy marriages.

Prospective studies of the premarital predictors of marital success are rare. In a pioneering study, Burgess and Wallin (1953) followed 666 couples from the time of their engagement in the late 1930s to a few years after their marriage. Burgess and Wallin concluded that successful marriage was more likely when individuals had been reared by happily married parents, were self-confident, showed sexual restraint before marriage, had a longer courtship, and endorsed the traditional belief that the husband should be head of the family and the wife should stay home. They reported a significant correlation between a composite measure of these premarital

The original data collection was supported by National Science Foundation grant GS27422 to Zick Rubin. Collection of the 15-year follow-up data was supported by grants to Charles T. Hill from the Haynes Foundation and Whittier College, and by a University Research Grant from UCLA to Anne Peplau. We are grateful to John Graham for assistance with data analysis. This chapter has greatly benefited from the insightful comments of Thomas Bradbury, Khanh-Van T. Bui, Sheri De-Bro, Ben Karney, and Paula Vincent.

237

predictors and marital success three to five years later ($r = .31$ for husbands and .27 for wives).

In another prospective study, Kelly followed 300 couples from their engagements in the 1930s until 1980 (Kelly & Conley, 1987). Eventually, 278 of these engaged couples were married and 50 later divorced. Divorce was more likely among participants who, before marriage, were rated high on neuroticism and had a history of more extensive premarital sexual activity. For men, low impulse control and less conventional attitudes about family life were also predictive of marital instability. On the basis of their long-term follow-up, Kelly and Conley categorized couples as divorced, stable but unhappy, or happily married. This "marital compatibility" measure was significantly correlated with three premarital personality measures: the husband's neuroticism, the husband's impulse control, and the wife's neuroticism (multiple $R = .38$). The prediction of marital success was improved (multiple $R = .49$) by adding 14 other premarital measures, including attitudes about marriage, sexual history, and childhood family background. These two studies of couples from the 1930s found that sexual restraint, traditional beliefs about marriage, and positive parental models contributed to marital success. How applicable these patterns are to contemporary young couples is an open question.

More recently, Olson and his colleagues have used PREPARE, a 125-item premarital inventory, to predict marital success (Fowers & Olson, 1986; Larsen & Olson, 1989; cf. Holman, Larson, & Harmer, 1994). The PREPARE questionnaire assesses 14 areas of relationship functioning. Discriminant analyses indicated that PREPARE scores obtained premaritally correctly differentiated couples who later had satisfying marriages from those who did not (i.e., who divorced or who were maritally dissatisfied) with at least 80% accuracy. Couples who, before marriage, had more realistic expectations about their relationship, felt good about the personality of their partner and the way they resolved conflicts, enjoyed communicating with their partner, and agreed on their religious values were more likely to have a happy marriage a few years later. Olson's ability to predict marital success is impressive, but several limitations of his studies raise concerns about the generalizability of his findings. All participants initially took the PREPARE instrument as part of a counseling program for engaged couples, usually offered by their church. Virtually all couples were Caucasian and Christian. For the postmarriage follow-up, couples were nominated by clergy and then contacted by the researchers to complete a questionnaire. Response rates were low: 49% in the Fowers and Olson (1986) study and 38% for the married sample in the Larsen and Olson

(1989) study. In analyzing data from the married couples, the researchers used extreme groups.

Two small longitudinal studies (Filsinger & Thoma, 1988; Markman, 1981) have attempted to link the premarital behavior of couples in a laboratory setting to relationship status or satisfaction several years later. Both studies suggest that premarital communication patterns may set the stage for later problems in a relationship. At present, however, various limitations of these studies raise questions about the generalizability of their findings (for a critique, see Bradbury & Karney, 1993).

The scarcity of prospective longitudinal studies makes it difficult to assess the potential importance of premarital predictors of marital outcomes. Indeed, researchers have come to opposite conclusions. Some argue for the premarital determinism of marital success. Olson (1990, p. 404) asserted that "the core of the marriage is formed during the premarital period, and . . . self-reported relationship characteristics are predictive of ultimate marital success or failure." In contrast, Whyte (1990, p. 247) concluded from a study of wives' retrospective reports that "most measures of dating and other premarital experiences have little impact on marital success." The research presented here investigates this issue. Before describing this study, however, consider two young couples we interviewed in the early 1970s when they were in college. (Their names have been changed.)

> *Ross and Betsy met during the second week of freshman year. At first, they spent endless hours talking to each other. After Christmas it was "just understood" that they wouldn't date anyone else, and in February they told each other, "I love you." Soon after, they became sexually intimate. Although Betsy had slept with her high school boyfriend, Ross had never had intercourse before. Ross described sex with Betsy as "a bond, an entrusting thing, a sharing – an outward sign of cementing our relationship." When conflicts arose, Betsy was more often the one to initiate a reconciliation. They agreed that the main sources of conflict were "external to the relationship," things outside their control – like Ross's mother. They both expected to go to graduate school – Ross in astrophysics and Betsy in dentistry. They planned to apply to more than a dozen graduate programs, hoping that they'd both be accepted in the same city.*
>
> *When Diane and Alan first met, they found each other boring. Later, they met again in Diane's dorm, where Alan had come to visit a female friend and smoke a joint of marijuana. Diane declined to*

share the joint, explaining that she was "very antidrug." But later
that evening they began to talk and eventually a relationship de-
veloped. At first, Diane explained, "There were all those unveilings
of self that go on for a couple of months until we got to know each
other and felt comfortable with each other." Both agreed they were
"in love," but whereas Diane was very open in expressing affec-
tion, Alan was more reticent and logical. Both were concerned
about traditional versus nontraditional life styles. Diane did vol-
unteer work for the Women's Yellow Pages, a feminist group in
Boston. Alan suggested that our interview questions were too con-
servative because they emphasized dating and traditional mar-
riage. He thought social scientists had an obligation to study al-
ternative life styles, "like people in communal relationships and
people in long-distance commuter relationships." Alan believed
that "in general, marriage is not something to do until it becomes
necessary" – that is, in order to have children. Both Alan and Di-
ane told us that their relationship was very egalitarian. Diane and
Alan were intellectual and introspective; she planned on a Ph.D.
in English literature and he on a career in law.

In considering what might have happened to these young couples over
time, we wondered if there were clues in their attitudes and descriptions of
their relationships that would enable us to predict their future together. In
more formal terms, our primary goal was to determine whether or not comprehensive premarital assessments of dating couples can predict relationship outcomes 2 and even 15 years later. In pursuing this goal, we also considered more specific questions. Were there warning signs that a dating
couple was headed for a breakup? Could we distinguish dating couples who
eventually got married from those who broke up? Were there premarital predictors about which of these married couples would get divorced? Would
the same factors that contributed to dating satisfaction affect marital success years later?

The Boston Couples Study

This chapter presents findings from the Boston Couples Study, a project begun in 1972 by Zick Rubin, Letitia Anne Peplau, and Charles T. Hill. Details of recruitment and sample characteristics are described more fully in
Hill, Rubin, Peplau, and Willard (1979). Members of 231 college-age dating couples were recruited by letters mailed to a random sample of sopho-

mores and juniors at four colleges in Boston, and by advertising at one of the schools. The colleges included a large private university, a small private university, a Catholic university, and a state college enrolling commuter students. Reflecting the religious composition of these colleges, 44% of respondents were Catholic, 26% were Protestant, and 25% were Jewish. Most participants (97%) were white. The modal couple was a 20-year-old sophomore woman dating a 21-year-old junior man; they had been dating for a median of 8 months.

In 1972, both members of each couple independently completed a 38-page questionnaire about themselves and their dating relationship. Periodic follow-ups were conducted, and response rates were relatively high. In 1974, 80% of the individuals who initially participated returned a mailed questionnaire (Hill, Rubin, & Peplau, 1976). Since the relationship status (together versus broken up) of a couple could be ascertained from the report of only one partner, these responses provided information about the current status of 95% of the original couples.

In 1987, fifteen years after the initial data collection, a brief follow-up was conducted by mail. This assessed the person's history of education, employment, marriage, and childrearing. These questionnaires were completed by 70% of the original participants, representing 87% of the original couples. Of the 138 questionnaires not completed, 81 (59%) were undeliverable because of invalid addresses. Our response rate compares favorably with other longitudinal studies. For example, the 15-year response rates of the National Longitudinal Surveys of Labor Market Experience were 69% for young women and 65% for young men (Center for Human Resource Research, 1987). We investigated whether individuals who responded to the 15-year follow-up differed systematically from nonrespondents on the many characteristics assessed in 1972. Only one significant difference was found. This concerned the few participants who were not college students in 1972, but were recruited through a dating partner who was in college. These individuals were less likely to participate in the 15-year follow-up, usually because we could not obtain their current mailing addresses from a college alumni office. No other differences were found in the background characteristics, attitudes, or relationship experiences of respondents versus nonrespondents.

By the time of the 15-year follow-up, participants were in their mid-30s and most were married with children. Of the original 231 dating couples, 4% had an unknown marital outcome (based on reports from 1974 and 1987). Among the rest, 67% had broken up before marriage and 33% had married their college partner. Among those who never married their college partner, 77% of women and 78% of men were known to have married someone else.

A few limitations of our sample and measures are noteworthy. Virtually all participants were white college students drawn from a single metropolitan area. Participants were bright, with mean combined SAT scores just under 1200. These couples attended college during the turbulent early 1970s, a time when many aspects of male–female relationships were being reexamined. Their experiences are undoubtedly different from those of other historical cohorts. Like all longitudinal studies, our analyses rely on measures created many years ago. Therefore, some topics of current interest such as adult attachment and interpersonal trust could not be addressed. Furthermore, the quality of the available measures varies from highly reliable multi-item scales to single-item ratings. Our pattern of findings may be affected by these differences in the types of measures. Finally, most of our measures are paper-and-pencil self-reports, and all premarital predictors were assessed at the same testing session. The intercorrelations found among premarital predictor variables may be affected by common method variance; this should be less problematic for associations between premarital predictors and reports of relationship status obtained 2 and 15 years later.

The Boston Couples data have many strengths. They provide prospective, longitudinal information about the long-term outcomes of dating relationships initially studied in considerable depth. The size of the initial sample was relatively large, involving 231 dating couples that led to 73 marriages. Compared with other research on premarital predictors that has studied engaged couples or newlyweds, participants in this research were first contacted at an earlier stage in their relationship, when only 10% of couples were engaged to be married. We were able to investigate five relationship outcomes: initial dating satisfaction, the stability of the dating relationship over a 2-year period, whether or not the dating partners eventually married each other, whether these marriages continued or ended in divorce, and the marital satisfaction of those couples still together at our 15-year follow-up. Another advantage of our research is the availability of extensive information about the premarital attitudes and dating experiences of participants. This enabled us to conduct a comprehensive analysis of a range of premarital predictors including partners' feelings of love and intimacy and their perceptions of the rewards and costs of their relationship. We also have information about each individual's background and attitudes, personal goals, and social network.

In the sections that follow, we describe our measures of relationship outcomes, consider how well dating couples were able to predict the future of their own relationship, and then examine how well our various premarital measures predicted the developmental course of the young couples in the Boston Couples Study.

Assessing Relationship Outcomes

Five different relationship outcomes were considered. Of particular interest was the possibility that different factors may predict immediate versus long-range outcomes of a relationship. First, we used participants' reported satisfaction with their dating relationship in 1972 at the time of initial testing. Each partner responded on a 9-point scale to the question: "All in all, how satisfied would you say you are with your relationship with (_____)?" On average, participants were quite satisfied (mean = 7.3, sd = 1.4 for women; mean = 7.4, sd = 1.4 for men). Second, we assessed the short-term stability of relationships by comparing the 103 couples who had broken up by 1974 to the 117 couples who were still together. This measure will be referred to in tables as "Together 2 Years Later," with a high score indicating stability. There was a modest but significant correlation between dating satisfaction and staying together for 2 years (point-biserial $r(219) = .23$, $p < .001$ for women; $r(219) = .31$, $p < .001$ for men).

The 15-year follow-up questionnaire provided three measures of long-term relationship outcomes. To assess stability, we compared the 73 dating couples who were known to have married their college partner with the 149 couples who were known to have broken up before marriage. This measure will be referred to as "Ever Married P" (with a high score indicating that the couple was married). We also compared the 50 couples who were known to still be married to their college partner in 1987 with the 15 couples whose marriage to their college partner had ended in divorce. This measure will be referred to as "Stayed Married to P" (with a high score indicating the couple was still married). Finally, a single item 9-point rating of marital satisfaction was available for 48 women and 44 men who were still married to their college partner at the time of our 15-year follow-up and completed our questionnaire. In general, these respondents were highly satisfied with their marriage (mean = 7.5, sd = 1.5 for women; mean = 7.5, sd = 1.6 for men) and had been married for an average of 12.8 years. Initial dating satisfaction was significantly correlated with marrying one's college partner (point-biserial $r(221) = .23$, $p < .001$ for women; $r(220) = .27$, $p < .001$ for men), but not with divorcing the partner or with marital satisfaction 15 years later.

Forecasting the Future

Burgess and Wallin (1953) noted that when a couple contemplates marriage, friends and family as well as the couple often use their knowledge and intuition to forecast the future, declaring, "This is a marriage made in heaven" or "You two will never be happy." At the time of our initial testing, participants estimated the likelihood that they and their dating partner would eventually marry each other. Estimates ranged from virtually no chance of marriage to certainty of marriage, with mean estimates of roughly 50% for both sexes.

How accurately did respondents forecast the future? Marriage probability estimates correlated significantly with staying together over a 2-year period (point-biserial $r(217) = .30$, $p < .001$ for women; $r(216) = .32$, $p < .001$ for men). They also correlated with whether or not the couple ever married ($r(218) = .39$, $p < .001$ for women; $r(218) = .45$, $p < .001$ for men). For example, when the man estimated the likelihood of marriage as 80% or better, 66% of couples eventually married, whereas when his estimate was below 40%, only 14% of couples married. So, to some extent, students were able to foresee the future accurately. But it is also clear that their forecasts were not foolproof – people who did not initially expect to marry changed their views, and some of those who expected to wed chose not to do so. Initial estimates of marriage likelihood were not correlated with whether or not a couple stayed married or got divorced, nor with marital satisfaction 15 years later.

Predicting Relationship Outcomes

To provide a comprehensive examination of factors affecting the developmental course of dating relationships, we investigated eight classes of premarital predictors. Our presentation of results begins with measures of intimacy and dyadic interdependence – a view of the "psychological interior" of a relationship. We then consider the partners' personal goals and attitudes, including their plans for combining marriage with paid employment. We then move beyond the circle of the couple to consider social networks and family background. We conclude with the issue of partner similarity.

The general analysis strategy for each class of predictors was the same. First, we examined the bivariate correlations between predictor variables in that class and each of five outcome measures. For the two continuous outcome measures (dating and marital satisfaction), Pearson correlations were used. For the three dichotomous outcome measures of relationship status, correlations were point-biserial. As will be readily apparent in Tables 8.1 to 8.8, a great many correlations were computed, and therefore some statistically significant correlations may have occurred by chance. Consequently, we can have more confidence in a consistent pattern of findings than in any one isolated correlation and in the general findings for a class of predictors rather than for one individual measure.

Once bivariate associations were identified, we conducted stepwise multiple regression analyses to assess the predictive strength of each *class* of predictors for each of the five outcome measures. Predictive strength was determined by the percentage of variance in the outcome measure (multiple R squared) explained by the class of predictors. Since the predictor variables in each class were intercorrelated with each other, it would be difficult to interpret the unique contribution of any one variable in the absence of a causal model relating them. Furthermore, we often had many measures within a class (e.g., 9 intimacy measures; 14 interdependence measures). Including all possible measures in a given regression analysis would have increased subject loss due to listwise deletion of missing cases. Consequently, only those predictors with statistically significant bivariate correlations were used as independent variables in stepwise multiple regression analyses. These multiple regressions were then repeated using only variables that met standard statistical criteria for inclusion in the final regression equation; these analyses are presented in Tables 8.1 to 8.8.

In each table, the columns on the left present correlations between women's scores on the predictor variables and each outcome. The columns on the right present correlations for men's scores. Outcomes are arranged from most immediate (dating satisfaction assessed at the same time as the predictors) to more long-term measures of staying together over time. For those couples who were married to their college partner at the 15-year follow-up, a measure of marital satisfaction was also available.

Intimacy

Many young Americans believe that love is the sine qua non for a happy relationship (e.g., Simpson, Campbell, & Berscheid, 1986). Theories of relationship stability also include positive attractions to the partner as a key ingredient (e.g., Levinger, 1979; Rusbult & Buunk, 1993). Several studies have shown that love and intimacy contribute to the short-term stability of dating relationships (e.g., Berg & McQuinn, 1986; Rubin, 1970).

However, research linking premarital love to long-term outcomes is scant and contradictory. In a study of 459 wives in Detroit, Whyte (1990) found that retrospective reports of premarital love correlated significantly with marital stability (together versus divorced, $r = .29, p < .05$) and marital quality ($r = .30, p < .05$). Whyte correctly observed, however, that retrospective accounts of premarital love do not provide clear evidence about the causal connections involved. Kelly, Huston, and Cate (1985) correlated newlyweds' retrospective reports of premarital love with reports by the same couples two years later. They found no significant association between retrospective accounts of premarital love and marital love, satisfaction, or dyadic adjustment. Similarly, Olson (1990, p. 404) reported, without presenting specific data, that "surprisingly, love was not a significant predictor of marital success in our studies, possibly because all of these premarital couples were in love." Our prospective study may help to clarify these inconsistent findings.

Our questionnaire contained many measures of intimacy. When asked directly "Are you and (_____) in love?" 70% of respondents said yes. Responses to Rubin's (1970) Love Scale were generally high (with a maximum score of 9, the mean = 7.1, sd = 1.4 for women; the mean = 7.0, sd = 1.4 for men). Participants also completed Rubin's Liking Scale and rated on 9-point scales how close they felt to their partner and how well they knew their partner. Two 17-item scales assessed self-disclosure given to and received from the partner. All these intimacy measures were significantly intercorrelated, with correlations ranging from .3 to .7. We also asked participants about cohabitation and sexuality. At the time of our first testing, only 23% of respondents reported that they and their partner were living together most or all of the time. In contrast, 80% of the couples had had sexual intercourse with their current partner, and these respondents were asked to rate their sexual satisfaction. Couples who had not had intercourse were asked to rate on 9-point scales how interested they would be in having intercourse and how this might affect the closeness of their relationship.

As shown in Table 8.1, virtually all intimacy measures were significantly correlated with dating satisfaction. For women only, cohabitation and having had sexual intercourse were also associated with greater dating satisfaction. Multiple regressions showed that intimacy measures accounted for 41% of the variance in women's dating satisfaction and 48% of the variance for men. In interpreting these and later results for dating satisfaction, it should be kept in mind that all predictor measures and the measure of dating satisfaction were based on self-reports obtained at the same testing session.

Next we considered the association between initial intimacy and later relationship outcomes. For both sexes, several intimacy measures predicted

Table 8.1. *Predicting relationship outcomes from premarital intimacy*

Intimacy measures	Predicting from women's measures					Predicting from men's measures				
	Her dating satisfaction	Together 2 years later	Ever married college partner	Stayed married to college partner	Her marital satisfaction	His dating satisfaction	Together 2 years later	Ever married college partner	Stayed married to college partner	His marital satisfaction
Rubin's Love Scale	.55**	.32**	.21**	.35**	-.23	.46**	.18**	.23**	.03	.08
Rubin's Liking Scale	.51**	.15*	.12*	.16	-.12	.49**	.11	.09	.04	.14
You & P in love?[a]	.45**	.29**	.21**	-.02	-.10	.45**	.28**	.25**	-.06	-.07
Closeness rating	.55**	.25**	.20**	-.02	-.05	.63**	.28**	.28**	-.10	.13
How well I know P	.45**	.13	.10	-.05	-.09	.40**	.19**	.20**	-.01	.11
Disclosure to P	.31**	.16*	.07	.05	.06	.28**	.08	.08	-.10	-.21
P's disclosure to me	.31**	.12	.08	.10	.01	.19**	.09	.06	-.07	-.18
Sex with P[a]	.19**	.04	-.02	-.06	.11	.09	.00	-.05	.01	-.07
Live with P	.15*	.07	.02	-.28*	-.21	.11	.04	.03	-.19	-.10
Multiple R	.64**	.32**	.21**	.46**	n.s.[b]	.69**	.28**	.28**	n.s.	n.s.
R^2 (variance explained)	.41	.10	.04	.21	n.s.	.48	.08	.08	n.s.	n.s.
If had sex with P, sexual satisfaction with P	.41**	.08	.06	-.25	.18	.35**	.11	.15	-.25	-.07
If had not had sex with P:										
Interest in having sex	.31*	.34*	.36*	-.43	.28	-.07	.29	.43**	-.36	-.18
Expected closeness	.18	.34*	.46**	-.22	.19	.04	.21	.19	-.18	.46

Note: In this and subsequent tables, the maximum N for zero-order correlations varies. The maximum N for dating satisfaction = 231, for together in 2 years = 220, for ever married = 222, for stayed married = 65, and for marital satisfaction = 48 for women and 44 for men. Sexual variables for "if had sex" and "if had not had sex" were not included in regression analyses because of reduced sample size.

[a]High value indicates "yes" response.

[b]n.s. indicates nonsignificant.

*$p < .05$. **$p < .01$.

relationship stability. Those young people in closer, more loving relationships were significantly more likely to be together two years later and ultimately to marry each other. In contrast, whether or not a couple had had sexual intercourse or lived together at the time of our initial testing was unrelated to staying together for two years or getting married. However, for those more sexually conservative couples who had not had intercourse with their dating partner, strong sexual attraction was predictive of relationship stability and marriage, especially for women. Although our study included multi-item measures of self-disclosure given and received, we found few associations between disclosure and long-term relationship outcomes. Taken together, premarital intimacy measures accounted for 21% of the variance in women's marital stability but were unrelated to marital stability for men or to marital satisfaction 15 years later. Two findings deserve special comment.

Love. Lay people often assume that the more "in love" dating partners are, the higher the likelihood that they will have a happy marriage. Previous studies (Kelly et al., 1985; Olson, 1990) failed to identify premarital love as a significant predictor of marital experiences. In contrast, our results, based on a 9-item Love Scale administered to dating partners, demonstrated the importance of love. We found that premarital love was a significant predictor not only of staying together for 2 years but also of marriage. Fifteen years later, women's initial love for their boyfriends predicted whether a couple was still together or had divorced. Love was a stronger predictor of relationship outcomes than either liking (feelings of affection and respect for a partner) or sexual intimacy. Yet premarital love was not related to marital satisfaction 15 years later. This lack of association may reflect the generally high level of marital satisfaction among the couples who avoided breakups and divorce to stay together for 15 years, as well as the ups and downs in feelings of love that may take place in relationships that endure many years.

Sexual Restraint. In the 1930s, premarital sexual restraint was associated with marital success (Burgess & Wallin, 1953; Kelly & Conley, 1987). The dating couples we studied came of age in a time of increasing sexual permissiveness, spurred by the availability of reliable contraceptives and the so-called "sexual revolution" of the era. We found that whether or not dating partners had sexual intercourse was unrelated to future relationship outcomes, perhaps because 80% of couples had already had intercourse by the time of our first testing and many of the rest may have done so later in their dating relationship. For women, however, premarital cohabitation – a living arrangement typically understood to imply sexual intimacy between partners – was associated with an increased likelihood of divorce. Women who married their college partner were less likely to stay married if they had lived with him while dating. We can speculate that cohabitation was characteristic of less traditional women who were less committed to the institution of marriage. Indeed, there was a weak but significant negative association between cohabitation and sex-role traditionalism ($r(225) = -.16$, $p < .02$ for women; $r(219) = -.25$, $p < .001$ for men). In a review of other studies linking premarital cohabitation to higher probability of divorce, White (1990, p. 906) noted that a common interpretation is that "the kinds of people who choose to flout convention by cohabiting are the same kinds of people who flout normative marital behavior, have lower commitment to marriage as an institution, and disregard the stigma of divorce." In a later section, we will see that permissive sexual attitudes also correlated with relationship instability (Table 8.4).

Interdependence and Social Exchange

Theorists suggest that relationship happiness and stability depend on the rewards and costs a person obtains in a relationship, as well as the currently available alternatives to the relationship (e.g., Rusbult & Buunk, 1993; Sabatelli & Shehan, 1993). Exchange theory also emphasizes the balance between partners in their relative involvement in the relationship (e.g., Blau, 1964). Our questionnaire assessed these constructs (see Table 8.2).

Rewards and Costs. To the extent that a partner provides many rewards, an individual should be satisfied and seek to continue the relationship. In our study, respondents used 9-point scales to rate their partner on such qualities as physical attractiveness, intelligence, and desirability as a marriage partner (see Table 8.2). For both sexes, positive evaluations of the partner were significantly correlated with dating satisfaction, perhaps because attractive partners create satisfying relationships or because the glow of a good dating relationship favorably colors perceptions of the partner's looks. In contrast, partner ratings were generally not correlated with long-term outcomes. The exception was rating the partner as a desirable mate, which correlated with continuing to date and marrying the college partner.

Relationships can entail many costs, both material and psychological. Perceiving low costs should be associated with higher satisfaction and greater relationship stability. One type of cost involves relational problems,

Table 8.2. *Predicting relationship outcomes from premarital interdependence*

Interdependence measures	Predicting from women's measures						Predicting from men's measures			
	Her dating satisfaction	Together 2 years later	Ever married college partner	Stayed married to college partner	Her marital satisfaction	His dating satisfaction	Together 2 years later	Ever married college partner	Stayed married to college partner	His marital satisfaction
Rewards										
My ratings of P										
Creativity	.24**	.04	–.00	–.22	–.11	.24**	.05	–.07	–.10	–.15
Physical attractiveness	.22**	.05	.03	–.06	.13	.23**	.03	.09	–.08	–.11
Intelligence	.34**	.08	.10	–.17	.08	.24**	–.04	–.06	–.26*	.18
Self-confidence	.15*	.03	.01	–.11	.13	.16*	–.04	–.01	–.01	.32*
Desirable date	.56**	.18**	.09	.00	.13	.37**	.06	.04	–.06	–.05
Desirable mate	.54**	.25**	.30**	.16	–.12	.50**	.25**	.25**	.14	.15
Costs										
Problem index	–.30**	–.14*	–.14*	–.04	–.04	–.42**	–.22**	–.27**	–.10	–.12
We argue a lot	–.29**	–.23**	–.17*	–.25*	–.06	–.21**	–.10	–.11	–.15	–.09
We can argue without harming relationship	.41**	.22**	.10	–.18	–.15	.36**	.12	.09	–.11	–.06
Alternatives[a]										
Date other now	–.26**	–.31**	–.24**	–.01	.07	–.17*	–.21**	–.23**	.07	–.05
Other I could date	–.22**	–.10	–.08	.07	.10	–.17*	–.08	–.15*	–.24	.28
Sex with another	–.26**	–.18**	–.23**	.07	–.15	–.15*	–.15*	–.13	–.08	.04
Prefer *not* to be single	.06	.13	.19**	.28**	.09	.13	.13	.18*	.17	.51**
Balance of involvement	.42**	.17*	.18*	.10	.14	.41**	.20**	.25**	.13	.25
Multiple *R*	.73**	.41**	.36**	.25*	n.s.[b]	.66**	.27*	.31*	.26*	.51**
R² (variance explained)	.53	.17	.13	.08	n.s.	.44	.07	.10	.07	.26

[a]High value indicates "yes" response.
[b]n.s. indicates nonsignificant.
*p < .05. **p < .01.

such as differing sexual attitudes, differing interests, boredom, or a partner's desire for independence. Our initial questionnaire assessed 14 specific problem areas. Table 8.2 presents a scale constructed by summing responses across these 14 problems. There is no necessary reason why reporting one type of problem should necessarily be associated with reporting other types of problems. Nonetheless, scale reliability was moderate (alpha = .72 for women and .69 for men). For both sexes, a higher level of problems was associated with lowered dating satisfaction, a greater likelihood of breakup, and a lower probability of marriage.

Another cost is conflict, and there is growing evidence that premarital conflict can set the stage for a troubled marriage. For example, Larsen and Olson (1989) found that self-reports of poor conflict resolution before marriage predicted marital dissatisfaction and divorce. Using retrospective reports of premarital experiences, Kelly, Huston, and Cate (1985) found that premarital conflict did not covary with partners' love for one another during courtship but did predict subsequent conflict and dissatisfaction 2 years after marriage. These researchers suggested that although partners may ignore conflict during courtship, it erodes positive feelings over time.

Participants in our study rated on a 9-point scale how "true" it was that "(_____) and I argue a great deal of the time." As shown in Table 8.2, reports of frequent arguments were associated with less dating satisfaction. This finding differs from that of Kelly et al., who found no immediate links between conflict and premarital love. To pursue this matter, we also examined correlations between frequent arguments and respondents' scores on the Love Scale, a measure more similar to that used by Kelly et al. (1985). Frequency of arguing was *not* related to love, nor to estimates of the likelihood of marrying the partner. In sum, we found that frequent arguments were associated with lower dating satisfaction, but not with lower love or poorer marriage prospects. Would we, like Kelly et al. (1985), find long-term effects of premarital conflict? For women only, frequent arguing during courtship was significantly linked to ending the relationship rather than marrying this partner. In those cases where partners did marry, women's reports of frequent premarital conflict increased the likelihood of divorce.

Why does conflict not detract from love or provide a stronger warning to young lovers that marriage may be risky? A possible explanation is provided by responses to another statement, that "(_____) and I can have arguments without hurting our relationship." Scores on this measure were not correlated with frequency of arguments ($r(227) = -.11$, ns for women; $r(229) = -.03$, ns for men). Some partners who argued constantly believed that conflict was harmless, as did some partners who seldom argued. However, the more a person loved the partner, the stronger their belief that conflict is not detrimental ($r(227) = .42$, $p < .001$ for women; $r(226) = .39$, $p < .001$ for men). Similarly, the more they believed they would marry this partner, the stronger their conviction that arguments cause no harm ($r(224) = .27$, $p < .001$ for women; $r(222) = .24$, $p < .001$ for men). In short, although empirical studies indicate that premarital conflict can increase the chances of a troubled marriage, some young adults believe that arguments are harmless. As a result, they may not use conflict as a sign of possible long-term relationship problems.

Alternatives. An interdependence perspective suggests that the availability of more attractive alternatives can reduce relationship satisfaction. Alternatives should also affect the stability of relationships, with greater access to alternatives decreasing one's dependence on a particular partner. Several measures of the quality of a person's alternatives were used. We assessed the exclusivity of the current dating relationship by asking, "Do you currently date or go out with anyone other than (_____)?" About 18% of women and 14% of men said they were dating others. A second question asked, "Is there a particular other person whom you might be going with, if you were not currently going with (_____)?" To this question, 32% of women and 31% of men said "yes." As shown in Table 8.2, exclusive dating was associated with greater dating satisfaction, with staying together for 2 years, and with marriage. Similar but weaker trends were found for the question about a potential alternative partner. A third question asked about sexual exclusivity: "During the past two months, have you had sexual intercourse with anyone other than (_____)?" Only 15% of women and 14% of men said "yes." As before, exclusivity was associated with higher dating satisfaction and a greater likelihood of staying together over time. It is unclear from these correlational data whether dissatisfied individuals seek alternative partners, or whether the existence of alternatives diminishes satisfaction with a current partner.

Finally, another possible alternative to a romantic relationship is to remain "unattached." A person who does not want to be single rejects this alternative and hence should be more committed to continuing a current relationship. We asked partners to rank four life styles, including being single. For women, a rejection of being single correlated with getting married and staying married to the college partner. For men, rejection of being single correlated with marrying the college partner and with marital satisfaction (see Table 8.2).

Relative Involvement. On the basis of their research, Burgess and Wallin (1953) listed "unequal attachment" as a factor underlying breakups. The hypothesis that equal involvement facilitates the continuation of a relationship was spelled out by Blau (1964, p. 84): "Commitments must stay abreast for a love relationship to develop into a lasting mutual attachment." We asked participants which partner is "more involved in your relationship" on a 5-point scale, and recoded responses so that high scores indicated equal involvement. Slightly less than half the participants (49% of women and 43% of men) reported equal involvement. As shown in Table 8.2, equal involvement was significantly correlated with dating satisfaction, staying together for 2 years, and marrying one's partner. For example, among women who reported equal involvement, 41% married their boyfriend compared to 25% of those who perceived unequal involvement (χ^2 (1) = 6.2, $p < .02$). Among men reporting equal involvement, 45% married their partner compared with 24% in unequal relationships (χ^2 (1) = 10.4, $p < .002$).

For both sexes, multiple regressions showed that interdependence measures were strong and significant predictors of dating satisfaction, accounting for close to half the variance. Although the strength of association between interdependence measures and outcomes decreased over time, the multiple Rs were significant in 9 of 10 analyses. One surprising finding was that although premarital measures of interdependence did not affect women's marital satisfaction, they accounted for 26% of the variance in men's marital satisfaction 15 years later.

Personal Goals

Young adulthood is a time when people clarify their life goals and take steps to accomplish these goals. When our study began in the early 1970s, many young people were questioning traditional roles for women and men. The women's movement urged educated women to consider full-time careers and challenged the view that marriage and childrearing should be the defining activities in a woman's life. Virtually all participants in our study expected that they would eventually marry someone, not necessarily their college dating partner. However, participants varied considerably in their educational goals, their preferences for combining marriage and paid employment, and their plans about having children.

Educational Plans. In our study, some individuals expected to complete their education with a college degree. Others, 47% of women and 58% of men, planned to go to graduate school. We anticipated that plans for advanced education might have different effects on the relationship outcomes of men and women. In the 1970s, graduate training usually increased a man's desirability as a mate by improving his ability to be a good provider. In contrast, for women, graduate training was still less conventional. Models of couples trying to coordinate their graduate school acceptances were scarce, and women's plans for graduate school might be less compatible with the stability of a college romance. As shown in Table 8.3, men's educational plans were unrelated to relationship outcomes. Women's educational plans were unrelated to dating satisfaction, but women who sought advanced degrees were less likely to marry their college dating partner. (Other analyses indicate, however, that they were no less likely than other women to marry someone else.)

Combining Marriage and Career. Participants were asked their preferences among four options for combining marriage and a career 15 years in the future. A majority of women (65%) ranked as their first choice being a married career woman, 22% preferred to be a homemaker with a part-time job, 7% preferred to be a full-time homemaker, and 6% preferred to be a single career woman. As shown in Table 8.3, women's preferences about combining work and marriage were unrelated to dating satisfaction or to maintaining a relationship with their college partner. However, women who preferred to be full-time homemakers and who married their college partner were less likely to get divorced.

Men were asked a parallel question about preferences for their future wife. Many men (49%) preferred a career wife, 23% preferred a full-time homemaker, 22% preferred a homemaker with a part-time job, and 6% preferred to remain single. Men who wanted their wife to stay home full-time were more likely to marry their college partner, to stay married, and to be maritally satisfied.

Children. Respondents indicated how many children they would ideally like to have (mean = 2.4, sd = 1.3 for women; mean = 2.4, sd = 1.1 for men). They also used a 9-point scale to rate how important having children was to them personally. These future-oriented beliefs about children had no impact on respondents' dating relationships or likelihood of marrying their college partner. However, among women who married their college partner, wanting more children was associated with greater marital stability. Among men who married their college partner, giving greater importance to having children was associated with greater marital satisfaction.

Table 8.3. *Predicting relationship outcomes from premarital personal goals*

	Predicting from women's measures					Predicting from men's measures				
Goal measures	Her dating satisfaction	Together 2 years later	Ever married college partner	Stayed married to college partner	Her marital satisfaction	His dating satisfaction	Together 2 years later	Ever married college partner	Stayed married to college partner	His marital satisfaction
Prefer full-time home-maker in 15 years[a]	-.02	.09	.11	.32*	.27	.01	.07	.19**	.31*	.38*
Number kids I want	-.06	.08	-.01	.30*	.24	-.03	.06	.09	.08	.20
Importance of kids	.05	.10	.05	.24	.06	.05	.08	.07	-.10	.32*
Year in school	.09	.07	.19*	.16	.06	.03	.02	.17*	-.14	.05
Plan graduate school[a]	-.06	-.15*	-.23**	-.21	-.12	-.01	-.05	-.05	-.09	.25
Multiple R	n.s.[b]	.15*	.31**	.32*	n.s.	n.s.	n.s.	.19**	.31*	.38*
R^2 (variance explained)	n.s.	.02	.10	.10	n.s.	n.s.	n.s.	.04	.10	.14

[a]High value indicates "yes" response.
[b]n.s. indicates nonsignificant.
*$p < .05$. **$p < .01$.

In summary, multiple regression analyses (see Table 8.3) indicated that personal goals were generally unrelated to dating satisfaction and short-term stability but were modest predictors of marital outcomes. Individuals who preferred a more traditional family orientation (emphasizing the home-maker role for women and the importance of children) were more likely to marry their college partner and to stay married.

Individual Attitudes and Experiences

As mentioned earlier the young adults we studied went to college during a time of changing values. The topics of the day included the new women's movement and the "sexual revolution." As we will see, the participants in our research varied substantially in their adherence to traditional beliefs about love, sex, gender roles, and religion – and these differences affected the outcomes of their relationships.

Romanticism. The questionnaire included a six-item Romanticism Scale, assessing adherence to a romantic, "love conquers all" ideology about intimate relationships (Rubin, Peplau, & Hill, 1981). For both men and women, higher romanticism scores were correlated with greater dating satisfaction. For women only, romanticism also predicted staying married to one's college partner many years later. In an earlier study of dating couples, Rubin (1970) reported that love scores were predictive of progress toward a more intense relationship 6 months later, but only for couples who were high in romanticism. We tested this hypothesis, but found no evidence that love was more predictive of staying together among high romantics than among low romantics.

Sexual Permissiveness. In their early study, Burgess and Wallin (1953) reported that marital success was associated with premarital sexual restraint. For instance, individuals who had sexual intercourse with fewer partners before their spouse reported greater marital happiness. Would a similar pattern emerge in the more sexually "liberated" 1970s? The answer for our participants who married a college partner appears to be yes. For example, we asked participants to rate on a 9-point scale the acceptability of casual sex for an unmarried woman (mean = 3.9, sd = 2.8 for women; mean = 5.1, sd = 2.7 for men). As shown in Table 8.4, greater sexual permissiveness was associated with a greater likelihood of divorce.

We also asked participants if they had ever had sexual intercourse with someone other than their current partner and, if so, with how many partners.

Table 8.4. *Predicting relationship outcomes from premarital individual attitudes*

Attitude measures	Predicting from women's measures						Predicting from men's measures			
	Her dating satisfaction	Together 2 years later	Ever married college partner	Stayed married to college partner	Her marital satisfaction	His dating satisfaction	Together 2 years later	Ever married college partner	Stayed married to college partner	His marital satisfaction
Romanticism	.17*	.11	.03	.35**	.09	.17**	.04	.05	.14	.23
Casual sex for women	-.06	-.08	-.07	-.29*	-.12	-.17**	-.07	-.06	-.26*	-.13
No. other sex partners	-.06	-.15*	-.18*	-.05	-.14	.03	-.12	-.11	-.22	.11
Sex-role traditionalism	.08	.06	.09	.46**	.24	-.01	.00	.09	.28*	.43**
Religiosity	-.06	-.05	-.02	.22	.16	.16*	.01	.03	.27*	.13
Multiple R	.17*	.15*	.18*	.54*	n.s.ᵃ	.23*	n.s.	n.s.	.27*	.43**
R^2 (variance explained)	.03	.02	.03	.29	n.s.	.05	n.s.	n.s.	.07	.17

[a] n.s. indicates nonsignificant.
*p < .05. **p < .01.

Approximately 37% of women and 25% of men had no previous sex partners when they began to date their current partner. At the other extreme, about 18% of women and 27% of men reported having had "6 or more" other sex partners. Women with more sexual partners were more likely than other women to break up with their dating partner. We also found that age of first intercourse, while not affecting short-term outcomes, did affect marital stability. A later age of first sex was associated with a greater likelihood of staying married to one's college partner ($r(50) = .31$, $p < .03$ for women; $r(60) = .26$, $p < .04$ for men). Although the magnitude of these correlations is relatively small, the pattern of findings suggests that for some respondents, sexual restraint was correlated with relationship stability.

Sex-role Traditionalism. Previous studies about the links between gender attitudes and relationship outcomes have been inconsistent. For example, Fowers and Olson (1986) found no association between the "egalitarian roles" scale of their premarital inventory and later marital outcomes. In a subsequent study using the same inventory, Larsen and Olson (1989) reported that couples with more egalitarian or flexible beliefs about roles were more likely to have happy, stable marriages. In contrast, Whyte (1990) found that women with more liberal or feminist attitudes about women's roles tended to report poorer marital quality and a higher incidence of divorce.

Our questionnaire included a 10-item Sex-Role Traditionalism Scale (Peplau, Hill, & Rubin, 1993). It assessed respondents' agreement or disagreement with such statements as "If both husband and wife work full-time, her career should be just as important as his in determining where the family lives" and "When a couple is going somewhere by car, it's better for the man to do most of the driving." As shown in Table 8.4, sex-role attitudes were not associated with dating satisfaction or the likelihood of marrying one's college partner. However, for both men and women who married their college partner, greater traditionalism was significantly associated with staying married rather than getting divorced. For men, traditionalism also correlated with marital satisfaction.

Religiosity. Participants were asked to rate "How religious a person would you say you are?" on a 9-point scale. There was considerable variation on this measure (mean = 4.1, sd = 2.4 for women; mean = 3.9, sd = 2.5 for men). In general, religiousness was not associated with relationship satisfaction or stability. The one exception was that, for men only, greater religiosity was associated with greater dating satisfaction and lesser tendency to divorce. In a later section, we will consider the effects of particular religious affiliations.

In summary, dating satisfaction and short-term stability were only weakly linked to partners' attitudes. In contrast, over time a trend emerged for conservative attitudes to foster relationship stability and, in particular, staying married to a college partner rather than getting divorced. Among women who married their college partner, divorce was less likely if the woman held a romantic view of love, had less permissive attitudes about premarital sex, and had more traditional attitudes about gender roles. As we saw earlier in Table 8.3, divorce was also less likely among women who evaluated being a homemaker more highly and wanted a larger number of children. Among men who married their college partner, divorce was less likely if the man had more conservative attitudes about premarital sex, had more traditional sex-role attitudes, was more religious, and preferred a homemaker wife. Traditionalism also affected men's marital happiness. Men's marital satisfaction was significantly higher when men held traditional sex-role attitudes, wanted to have a homemaker wife, and gave greater importance to children (Table 8.3).

In interpreting these findings, it is important to remember that the married couples we studied were a highly selected group who had followed a fairly conventional life style of finding a mate in college. For this group of college graduates, traditional attitudes were associated with marital stability. It is possible, however, that traditionalism has different effects in couples who pursue other life patterns. We will return to this issue later in the chapter.

Self-Evaluations

Respondents rated themselves on six personal qualities such as physical attractiveness and intelligence. They also rated how satisfied they were with themselves. As shown in Table 8.5, multiple regressions indicated that self evaluations were significantly associated with 7 of 10 relationship outcomes, although the magnitude of these associations was often modest. Positive self-evaluations were associated with greater dating satisfaction for both sexes. The causal direction of this pattern is unclear: does a positive self-image foster good dating relationships or does a satisfying dating relationship enhance self-perceptions? Over time, different links between self-evaluations and long-term marital outcomes emerged for women and for men.

For men, higher self-ratings on physical attractiveness, desirability as a date, and "satisfaction with self" were significantly related to greater marital satisfaction 15 years later, accounting for 27% of the variance. Men with a positive self-view who married their college partner tended to find their

Table 8.5. *Predicting relationship outcomes from premarital self-evaluations*

Self-evaluation measures	Predicting from women's measures						Predicting from men's measures			
	Her dating satisfaction	Together 2 years later	Ever married college partner	Stayed married to college partner	Her marital satisfaction	His dating satisfaction	Together 2 years later	Ever married college partner	Stayed married to college partner	His marital satisfaction
Self-ratings										
Creativity	.04	-.09	-.13	-.12	.04	.03	-.04	-.07	-.18	-.21
Physical attractiveness	-.03	-.14*	-.14*	-.30*	.07	.13*	.03	.05	.02	.34*
Intelligence	-.04	-.16*	-.16*	-.39**	-.21	.03	-.07	-.01	-.13	-.05
Self-confidence	.09	-.13	-.10	-.09	.19	.22**	.01	-.01	-.12	.29
Desirable date	.19*	-.13	-.13*	-.03	.27	.22*	.08	.05	.02	.39**
Desirable mate	.24**	.00	.01	.13	.17	.17*	.13	.18**	.06	.20
Satisfied with self	.18**	-.14*	-.10	.08	.22	.26**	.05	.01	-.09	.40**
Multiple R	.24**	.16*	.16*	.39*	n.s.[a]	.26**	n.s.	.18**	n.s.	.52**
R² (variance explained)	.06	.03	.03	.15	n.s.	.07	n.s.	.03	n.s.	.27

[a] n.s. indicates nonsignificant.
*p < .05. **p < .01.

marriage rewarding. In contrast, for women, higher self-ratings on physical attractiveness and intelligence were associated with relationship *instability*. Women who viewed themselves positively on these two qualities were more likely to break up with their college boyfriend in the next two years, less likely to marry their college partner, and if they did marry, were more likely to divorce. These self-evaluations accounted for 15% of the variance in women's marital stability. Perhaps these women felt more confident about attracting alternate partners or being successful in a career.

Social Networks

What impact do social networks have on the progress of romantic relationships? In a longitudinal study of dating relationships, Sprecher and Felmlee (1992) found that perceived support from family and friends correlated with current relationship satisfaction, love, and commitment and also predicted relationship quality 18 months later. For women only, support from family and friends was also associated with relationship stability: the less support women reported receiving, the more likely their relationship was to end and the sooner the breakup occurred. Leslie, Huston, and Johnson (1986) make the further point that dating partners are often selective in what they tell their parents about a relationship: the more involved and committed a person is to a relationship, the more likely he or she is to inform parents about it and try to influence their opinions. However, Leslie et al. found that the amount of support provided by parents did not predict change in the premarital relationship over time. We were able to investigate several aspects of social networks.

Parents. Participants indicated on a 9-point scale how well their parents knew their partner. As shown in Table 8.6, parental knowledge was positively correlated with dating satisfaction only for men, but was predictive of staying together for 2 years and getting married for both sexes. Other questions (using 9-point rating scales) asked if the parents approved of the partner as someone to date and as someone to marry. Parental approval was correlated with greater dating satisfaction, with staying together, and with marriage. For women, parental approval of the college dating partner was also a significant predictor of marital satisfaction 15 years later.

Living at Home. Another index of a young person's social connection to their family is their place of residence. When our study began, 24% of respondents lived at home with parents or relatives. The rest lived on campus

Table 8.6. *Predicting relationship outcomes from premarital social networks*

Social network measures	Predicting from women's measures						Predicting from men's measures			
	Her dating satisfaction	Together 2 years later	Ever married college partner	Stayed married to college partner	Her marital satisfaction	His dating satisfaction	Together 2 years later	Ever married college partner	Stayed married to college partner	His marital satisfaction
Parents know P	.10	.21**	.28**	.15	.20	.15*	.19**	.23**	-.05	.09
Parents approve of P as date	.22**	.17*	.23**	.11	.29*	.26**	.14**	.22**	.06	.07
Parents approve of P as mate	.22*	.13*	.25*	.04	.13	.26**	.12	.21**	.04	-.01
I live at home[a]	.04	.15*	.24*	.13	.35*	.12	.18**	.27**	.25*	.20
My friends like P	.32**	.10	.06	.23	.10	.33**	.14*	.11	.16	.08
P likes my friends	.16*	.10	.10	.34**	.06	.32**	.08	.07	.15	.01
P knows my friends	.12	.16*	.13*	.23	.25	.16*	.14*	.06	-.03	.07
No. best friends who are male (of 4)	.00	.05	.03	-.28*	-.14	.03	.03	.03	.09	-.21
Someone introduced me to P	.03	.04	.06	.23	-.14	.04	-.00	.02	.37**	-.19
Multiple R	.36**	.21**	.31**	.44**	.35*	.38**	.19*	.33**	.44**	n.s.[b]
R^2 (variance explained)	.13	.04	.10	.19	.12	.14	.04	.11	.19	n.s.

[a]High value indicates "yes" response.
[b]n.s. indicates nonsignificant.
*p < .05. **p < .01.

in dorms, in fraternities or sororities, or in apartments. Place of residence was not related to dating satisfaction, but was significantly associated with later relationship outcomes (see Table 8.6). For instance, the percentage of women who married their college partner was 53% among those living at home compared to 27% among those living elsewhere (χ^2 (1) = 12.4, $p <$ .001). For men, the comparable figures were 55% versus 25% (χ^2 (1) = 16.1, $p <$ .000). For women only, living at home during college was significantly associated with marital satisfaction 15 years later (mean of 8.2 for those who lived at home versus 7.1 for others, $t(46) = 2.88$, $p < .01$). Divorce was also linked to college residence. Among men who married their college partner, only 11% of those who had lived at home got a divorce, compared to 32% of those who lived away from home (χ^2 (1) = 4.0, $p < .04$). For women the comparable figures were 16% versus 28%, a difference that was not statistically significant. One interpretation is that students who were more closely tied to their parents tended to be more marriage-oriented. Those living at home were significantly more traditional in their sex-role attitudes ($t(222) = 2.0$, $p < .05$ for women; $t(217) = 2.4$, $p < .02$ for men) and were more often Catholic (83% of women and 64% of men compared to 33% of women and 34% of men who did not live at home).

Friends. Respondents indicated on 9-point scales how much their friends liked the partner, and how much the partner liked these friends. As shown in Table 8.6, both liking measures were correlated with dating satisfaction. For women only, the partner's liking for the friends was related to staying married 15 years later. We also asked how well the partner knew the respondent's four best friends (shown in Table 8.6 as "P knows my friends"). For women, this measure predicted breakup and marriage, albeit weakly. The better the partner knew the friends, the more likely the couple was to stay together and to get married. For men, this measure predicted dating satisfaction and staying together during the 2-year period. Another measure was the number of the respondent's four best friends who were men (ranging from zero to four men). For women who married their college partner only, reporting a high number of male best friends was associated with a greater likelihood of divorce. A last question asked how the partners had met. About 45% of respondents had initially been introduced to their partner by someone. Personal introductions by a third party may indicate that a couple is more involved in a shared social network. For men who married their college partner, being introduced was significantly associated with marital stability.

Finally, Table 8.6 presents multiple regressions using social network variables to predict each relationship outcome. With the exception of men's marital satisfaction, all multiple Rs were significant and accounted for nearly 10% of the variance in marrying one's college partner and even more of the variance in staying married to that partner.

Background Characteristics

Summarizing evidence available in the mid-1950s, Burgess and Wallin (1953, p. 513) asserted that "a young person has better than an average chance of marital success if he has been reared in a home of education and culture where the parents are happily mated, where they have close and affectionate relations with their children." We were able to test many of these ideas. The participants in our study had fairly diverse family backgrounds. Their parents' educational levels were varied: 49% of fathers had not completed college, 26% had college degrees, and 25% had graduate degrees. Mothers had less education, with 70% attaining less than a college degree, 18% having a college degree, and 12% holding a graduate degree. Many mothers had stayed home full-time with their children: 46% of respondents said that their mother did not work for pay at any time during their childhood. Only 22% of women and 18% of men said their mothers had worked when they were very young. The majority of respondents (84%) came from intact marriages. When parents were not living together, death and divorce were equally common reasons. There was also variability in respondents' ratings of their parents' marital satisfaction, their own closeness to their mother and father, and how similar their partner was to their parent of the same sex. Despite the range of backgrounds in our sample, virtually no aspect of family background was associated with any measure of relationship success. As shown in Table 8.7, the sole exception was the mother's education, which had inconsistent links to relationship stability with lower maternal education predicting staying together.

We also investigated various background characteristics of the individual such as birth order but found no associations with relational outcomes. The one exception concerned religion. Religion was unrelated to measures of relationship satisfaction, either during dating or marriage. However, there was a tendency for Catholic women to marry their college partner and for Catholic men to stay married. In contrast, Jewish women were less likely to marry their college partner (but no less likely than other women to get married to someone).

Multiple regressions indicate that background predictors had limited associations with relationship outcomes. Only 4 of 10 multiple Rs were

Table 8.7. *Predicting relationship outcomes from premarital background characteristics*

Background measures	Predicting from women's measures						Predicting from men's measures			
	Her dating satisfaction	Together 2 years later	Ever married college partner	Stayed married to college partner	Her marital satisfaction	His dating satisfaction	Together 2 years later	Ever married college partner	Stayed married to college partner	His marital satisfaction
Parents										
Father's education	-.07	-.08	-.08	-.08	.06	.11	.01	.03	-.21	-.02
Mother's education	-.13	-.14*	-.11	-.07	.01	.08	-.01	-.03	-.28*	.05
Extent of mother's work in childhood	.06	.06	.06	.11	.26	.12	.09	.02	.13	.11
Marital satisfaction	-.05	-.03	-.01	.22	.18	.03	-.04	.03	.15	-.01
Similarity of P to parent of P's sex	-.04	-.03	.02	.17	.02	.12	.08	.01	.13	.21
Self										
Birth order	.04	.04	.05	-.12	.17	-.06	.04	.04	.12	.18
Catholic vs. other[a]	.02	.13	.21*	.02	-.00	.05	.14*	.05	.25*	.06
Jewish vs. other[b]	.03	-.17*	-.19*	.14	-.04	-.03	-.07	-.11	-.24	.14
Multiple R	n.s.[c]	.17*	.21*	n.s.	n.s.	n.s.	.14*	n.s.	.38*	n.s.
R² (variance explained)	n.s.	.03	.04	n.s.	n.s.	n.s.	.02	n.s.	.14	n.s.

[a]High score indicates Catholic.
[b]High score indicates Jewish.
[c]n.s. indicates nonsignificant.
*p < .05. **p < .01.

significant, and these primarily reflected the influence of religion, a topic we will explore further later in this report. Although our study found little evidence for the importance of background characteristics, we believe caution is warranted in generalizing these findings. For example, demographic studies using more representative samples amply demonstrate that the probability of divorce is increased by such factors as parental divorce, young age at marriage, low education, low income, premarital pregnancy, and race (e.g., Raschke, 1987; White, 1990). In a recent 5-year prospective study of newlyweds, Kurdek (1993) found that personal demographic factors including education and length of courtship predicted marital stability as well or better than social-psychological factors such as interdependence and spousal discrepancy variables.

Similarity and Agreement

It is an axiom of research on interpersonal attraction that similarity leads to liking, and empirical studies demonstrate that intimate relationships tend to be homogamous. According to a review by Buss (1985), age, education, race, and religion show the strongest similarity effects, followed by attitudes, cognitive abilities, socioeconomic status, and personality. Some of these patterns of demographic homogamy could not be tested meaningfully in our sample, because virtually all couples were similar in education and race. When our study began, dating partners had already been together for several months and were significantly matched in many ways. For example, when both partners were currently enrolled in college, 69% of couples attended the same school. They tended to be similar in their previous sexual experience: in 68% of couples both partners were sexually experienced or both were virgins when their relationship began. Partners were significantly matched in such diverse ways as religiosity ($r(226) = .37$, $p < .001$), SAT scores ($r(186) = .23$, $p < .01$), height ($r(230) = .21$, $p < .01$), and desired number of children ($r(227) = .51$, $p < .001$). There was also some consensus in partners' views of their relationship, for instance in reports of how often they argued ($r(230) = .50$, $p < .001$) and the likelihood that they would marry each other ($r(223) = .80$, $p < .001$) (Hill, Peplau, & Rubin, 1981). Would couple differences in the *degree* of similarity and agreement affect relationship outcomes?

We used as our measure of similarity the absolute difference between the responses of dating partners. These scores were then reversed so that high scores indicate greater similarity or agreement. Note that unlike the previous analyses in which we used women's measures to predict women's outcomes and men's measures to predict men's outcomes, these analyses use information from both partners (difference scores) to predict outcomes. Table 8.8 presents the strongest predictors uncovered in our systematic investigation.

Intimacy. We investigated agreement in participants' assessment of intimacy in their relationship. In general, partners tended to give similar reports of their love for their partner ($r(230) = .40, p < .001$), liking ($r(230) = .15$, $p < .03$), and feelings of closeness ($r(230) = .55, p < .001$). These correlations reflect the degree of mutuality or balance of intimacy in the relationship. As shown in Table 8.8, there is some evidence that more similar levels of premarital intimacy were associated with greater dating satisfaction, but did not predict long-term marital outcomes.

Attitudes. Partners tended to have similar attitudes about romanticism ($r(230) = .20, p < .002$), premarital sex among acquaintances ($r(225) = .25$, $p < .001$), sex-role traditionalism ($r(213) = .46, p < .001$), their personal preference concerning marriage and women's work (for example, $r(202) =$ $.25, p < .01$ for wife with career), and their preference for being (or not being) single ($r(188) = .45, p < .001$). Perhaps as a result, the degree of similarity for most attitudes was unrelated to relationship outcomes. Two significant findings emerged, however, concerning partners' preferences for combining work and marriage. Specifically, greater agreement about being (or rejecting being) single was correlated with greater dating and marital satisfaction for men. In addition, partners who married were more likely to stay married if they had similar preferences about the wife's having (or not having) a career.

Background. A final set of analyses concerns the association between similarity in partners' background characteristics and relational outcomes. We found no significant correlation between partners in our sample with respect to parents' education, mother's work history, or perception of parents' marital satisfaction. In general, degree of background similarity was not correlated with relationship outcomes, with a few notable exceptions. Women's marital satisfaction was higher when the fathers had similar educations and when both sets of parents were perceived as similar in marital satisfaction. Men's marital satisfaction was higher when both mothers had similar histories of work outside the home.

As shown in Table 8.8, couples of the same religion were no more or less likely than other couples to marry. Overall, 45% of the dating couples were

Table 8.8. *Predicting relationship outcomes from premarital similarity and agreement*

Similarity measures	Her dating satisfaction	His dating satisfaction	Together 2 years later	Ever married college partner	Stayed married to college partner	Her marital satisfaction	His marital satisfaction
Intimacy							
Rubin's Love Scale	.19**	.18**	-.04	.04	.14	-.20	-.21
Rubin's Liking Scale	.10	.32**	.04	.05	-.21	-.12	-.02
Closeness rating	.23**	.34**	.19**	.13	.06	.08	.07
Attitudes and goals							
Romanticism	-.08	.02	.10	.00	.01	-.12	-.05
Sexual permissiveness	-.07	-.03	.00	-.07	-.05	.02	.00
Sex-role traditionalism	.08	.06	.10	.03	.07	-.20	-.09
Prefer *not* to be single	.13	.28**	.10	.11	.24	.12	.48**
Prefer career wife	.03	-.01	.06	.01	.30*	.04	.19
Background							
Father's education	.02	.09	.01	.04	.10	.34*	-.27
Mother's education	.14*	.12	.10	.16*	.07	-.02	-.11
Extent of mother's work in childhood	-.02	.04	.10	.12	.21	.06	.40*
Parents' marriage satisfaction	.03	.16*	.11	.11	.06	.35*	.05
Own age	.00	.11	.08	.05	-.06	.11	-.25
Religion	-.09	-.05	.00	-.01	.29*	.07	.08
Photo rating	.22**	-.07	.10	.06	.02	.12	.36*
Multiple *R*	.31*	.43**	.19**	.16*	.30*	.35**	.64*
*R*² (variance explained)	.10	.18	.04	.03	.09	.12	.41

Note: Correlations are based on difference scores (the absolute difference of the woman's response minus her boyfriend's response), recoded so that high scores indicate greater similarity or agreement between partners.
*p < .05. **p < .01.

of the same religion, as were 45% of those who got married. However, religious similarity did affect the likelihood of divorce: Only 10% of same-religion marriages ended in divorce compared with 35% of couples of different religions (χ^2 (1) = 5.4, $p < .02$). Although this pattern held for Protestant, Jewish, and Catholic couples, it should be noted that in our sample, 79% of the same-religion marriages were Catholic. Finally, partners tended to be similar in physical attractiveness as rated by judges from photos ($r(174) = .24$, $p < .001$). Degree of similarity in attractiveness was associated with greater dating satisfaction for women and greater marital satisfaction for men.

Multiple regressions indicated that similarity was a significant predictor of all relationship outcomes, with multiple Rs ranging from .16 to .64. The strongest findings were for men's marital satisfaction. Here, similar attitudes about married life (not being single) and similar maternal work histories accounted for 41% of the variance in men's marital satisfaction.

A final measure, not included in the multiple regressions, was each person's own rating of how similar he or she was to the partner. On this 9-point scale, the mean similarity rating was 5.6 (sd 2.2) for women and 5.7 (sd 2.4) for men. For both sexes, this subjective measure of similarity was significantly correlated with dating satisfaction ($r(230) = .30$, $p < .001$ for women; $r(228) = .33$, $p < .001$ for men) and with marrying the college partner ($r(221) = .13$, $p < .05$ for women; $r(220) = .15$, $p < .03$ for men).

These data suggest that matching on background characteristics and attitudes may occur relatively early in the development of a relationship. We found considerable similarity between partners, who had typically been dating for 8 months. Despite the general homogeneity of the sample and their initial matching, differences in the degree of similarity still had some significant but modest associations with relationship outcomes.

Assessing Premarital Predictors of Relationship Outcomes

After this long journey through eight classes of premarital predictors of five relationship outcomes, it is time to take stock. How well have we done in our primary goal of predicting relationship outcomes from premarital measures? Table 8.9 summarizes the results of multiple regressions for each class of predictor and then presents a final set of regressions based on all classes of predictors combined. As in previous tables, we use only women's measures to predict women's satisfaction and only men's measures to predict men's satisfaction, with the exception of similarity scores that are a composite measure. Unlike earlier tables, however, we use premarital measures

Table 8.9. *Multiple regressions predicting relationship outcomes from eight classes of premarital measures*

Predictor measures	Her dating satisfaction	His dating satisfaction	Together 2 years later	Ever married college partner	Stayed married to college partner	Her marital satisfaction	His marital satisfaction
Intimacy	.64	.69	.35	.28	.46	n.s.	n.s.
Interdependence	.73	.66	.41	.41	.39	n.s.	.51
Personal goals	n.s.	.15	.15	.35	.32	n.s.	.38
Individual attitudes	.17	.23	.15	.18	.54	n.s.	.43
Self-evaluations	.24	.26	.16	.24	.39	n.s.	.52
Social network	.36	.38	.21	.37	.52	.35	n.s.
Background	n.s.	n.s.	.17	.21	.38	n.s.	n.s.
Similarity	.36	.43	.19	.16	.30	.35	.64
All predictors $R =$	.73	.79	.43	.41	.60	.35	.70
R^2 (variance explained)	.53	.55	.17	.17	.36	.12	.49

Note: Multiple regressions use only women's variables to predict women's satisfaction and men's variables to predict men's satisfaction. Both men's and women's variables are used to predict dyadic outcome measures. For all outcomes, "similarity" measures are based on the absolute difference between men's and women's responses. All R's presented in this table are statistically significant at $p < .05$ or less.

from both partners to predict the three dyadic outcomes of staying together or not.

Not surprisingly, Table 8.9 shows that premarital measures were significant and sizable predictors of concurrent dating satisfaction, accounting for more than half the variance in men's and women's reports. More important, premarital measures were predictive of subsequent relationship outcomes, both 2 years and 15 years later. Our premarital measures accounted for 17% of the variance in staying together versus breaking up during a 2-year period, 17% of the variance in whether or not a couple eventually married, and 36% of the variance in whether a married couple stayed together or divorced. Finally, for those individuals who married their college partner, premarital measures also predicted marital satisfaction 15 years later, accounting for 12% of the variance in women's marital satisfaction and 49% of men's marital satisfaction. In this study, information about dating partners and their premarital relationships was significantly predictive of relationship outcomes 2 and 15 years later.

Another approach to assessing the usefulness of multiple predictors is to ask how well they enable us to categorize couples into various outcome groups. In two studies described earlier, Olson and his colleagues used scores on a premarital self-report inventory to predict marital outcomes (Fowers & Olson, 1986; Larsen & Olson, 1989). Using discriminant analyses, they correctly differentiated engaged couples who became satisfied spouses from those who divorced, or from those who became unhappy spouses, with an accuracy of 80% or better. We also used discriminant function analyses to predict our three measures of relationship stability. Specifically, like Olson and his colleagues, we performed stepwise discriminant function analyses utilizing Rao's V to maximize the distance between groups for optimal classification.

First, we compared those couples who stayed together for 2 years versus those who broke up, successfully classifying 70% of these couples correctly. A second analysis predicted which couples would eventually marry each other versus breakup: 75% of couples were categorized correctly. A final analysis predicted which of those married couples who had been college partners would stay married versus divorce: 94% of couples were classified correctly. In each analysis, approximately 12 predictor variables provided the best possible prediction, and these predictors ranged across the various classes of premarital measures described earlier in this chapter. (For a comparison with research involving already married couples, see Buehlman, Gottman, & Katz, 1992; or Kurdek, 1993.)

To interpret these results, it is necessary to compare our predictions with the base rates for each relationship outcome. Two years after our initial testing, 53% of couples for whom information was available were still together. Knowing this base rate and predicting that all couples continued their relationship would have led to successful classification of 53% of couples. The discriminant analysis using premarital predictors substantially improved this success rate, enabling us to classify 70% of couples correctly. At our 15-year follow-up, 67% of couples for whom information was available had ended their dating relationship and 33% married each other. Our empirically based discriminant analysis enabled us to classify 75% of couples correctly, a modest improvement over guessing that everyone had broken up. Finally, our success rate for predicting continuing marriage versus divorce was 94%; this compares favorably with the 77% base rate for continuing marriages. In short, the assessment of premarital features of partners and relationships did improve our ability to predict short-term and long-term relationship outcomes, but these predictions also benefited from unequal base rates of continuing versus ending relationships.

Final Comments

Our results provide clear evidence that premarital attitudes and experiences can make a difference in marital outcomes. Although space limitations did not permit us to examine each class of premarital predictors in detail, several general patterns emerged from our analyses. First, although love was not enough to guarantee a happy, long-lasting relationship, it did make a difference. Measures of premarital intimacy were significant predictors of whether a couple married and stayed married. Second, measures derived from interdependence theories were also important predictors of long-term outcomes. Premarital relationships that were relatively rewarding, had few alternatives, and were balanced in involvement tended to endure over time (see also Bui, Peplau, & Hill, 1996). Third, young adults' personal goals and attitudes about work and family affected the outcome of their dating relationships. For example, women who planned to attend graduate school were less likely to marry their college partner. Men who preferred a traditional homemaking role for their future wife were more likely to marry their college partner and to stay married. Evidence was also found for associations between relationship outcomes and social networks, background factors, and partners' similarity and agreement.

Sleeper Effects. Our analyses uncovered several "sleeper effects," instances in which a premarital measure was not related to concurrent dating satisfaction or to early breakups but did affect marital outcomes years later. Two examples illustrate this point. Sex-role traditionalism was unrelated to dating satisfaction or to marrying the college partner. Over time, however, significant effects of premarital traditionalism emerged for those married couples who had been college partners (see Table 8.4). Individuals with more traditional attitudes were less likely to get divorced, and more traditional men reported greater marital satisfaction. To rule out the possibility that this pattern reflected differences between the initial sample of 231 couples and the subsample of 73 couples who eventually married, we recalculated all correlations separately for the subsample of couples who married each other. The same "sleeper effects" were found. A second example concerns attitudes about children – how many children a person would like to have and the importance given to having children (see Table 8.3). Premarital beliefs about children were unrelated to dating satisfaction or to selecting the college partner as a spouse. However, women who wanted more children were less likely to divorce, and men who gave greater importance to having children reported greater marital satisfaction. Again, when these correlations were repeated for the 73 couples who married each other, an identical pattern was found.

These examples demonstrate that some premarital attitudes can have long-term consequences that are independent of their impact on initial dating satisfaction. Attitudes about gender roles and children may not be salient when young adults assess the quality of a dating relationship, but these attitudes may gain greater prominence once a couple marries and begins to coordinate their family life. For those interested in fostering successful marriages, "sleeper effects" help to identify issues that young couples might profitably consider prior to marriage.

"Early Nesters" Versus "Later Nesters." Our study of college romances began with a broad sample of student couples, but the subsample of couples who eventually married each other was more restricted. Our discussion of marriage and divorce has been based on partners who met early in college and married their college partner, usually soon after graduation. We might call these couples "early nesters" because they selected a marital partner at a relatively early age compared with their college student peers. Only one third of our initial respondents are represented in this married-couple subsample. The majority of participants in our study broke up with their college partner but eventually married someone else. We might call these individuals "later nesters." Our strategy of beginning with dating couples and following those who remained together over time has the advantage of allowing long-term prospective analyses. But this strategy may inadvertently have resulted in a relatively conventional sample of married couples.

Results for our "early nesters" suggest that sex-role traditionalism, conservative attitudes about premarital sex, and an emphasis on women's role as homemaker were associated with more stable, happier marriages. This is perhaps not surprising, since young adults who marry shortly after college can be seen as following a fairly conventional lifestyle that might be more congruent with traditional attitudes and values. Would we find similar attitudinal correlates of marital stability and satisfaction among "later nesters" who followed a somewhat different life trajectory? Analyses (reported in more detail in Peplau & Hill, 1995) clearly show that we would not. For men and women who married a later partner, there were no significant correlations between sex-role traditionalism, attitudes about premarital sex, or views about homemakers and either marital stability or satisfaction. In short, the attitudinal correlates of happy marriages differed significantly for early versus later nesters.

These findings highlight the importance of thinking carefully about the generalizability of research findings. It was obvious to us from the start that our white, well-educated Bostonians were not representative of all young dating couples. But we were initially less sensitive to the more subtle ways in which our strategy of following couples who remained together over time might introduce further restrictions to the generalizability of some of our findings.

The two couples described earlier illustrate several of our findings. Ross and Betsy followed an "early nester" pattern. They were married a year after graduating from college. Ross went on to obtain a Ph.D. and Betsy a master's degree. At the time of our follow-up, they were happily married and had one child. Diane and Alan followed a "later nester" pattern. They broke up shortly after graduation; the breakup was precipitated by their divergent plans for graduate study. Alan moved to Pennsylvania to attend graduate school; Diane stayed in Boston to earn a master's degree. Whereas Ross and Betsy married soon after college, Alan and Diane each waited nearly 5 years after college to get married. Alan and Diane are now married to new partners, and both report high levels of marital satisfaction. Neither had children at the time of our follow-up, although both said they hoped to have children in the future.

Theory in Relationship Research. Our goal in this chapter has been straightforward – to investigate whether features of individuals and couples measured premaritally can predict later relationship outcomes. We believe that our data provide strong support for the importance of premarital predictors.

At the same time, many questions about our couples remain unanswered. We have said little about which premarital factors are the "best" or strongest predictors of relationship outcomes, and deliberately so. Many of our premarital measures were intercorrelated. For example, women who were Catholic (background factor) were more likely to live at home (social network factor). Women who lived at home tended to have traditional sex-role attitudes (individual difference factor). Each of these variables was associated with relationship outcomes. To determine which factor was "more important" would require a theory or causal model about relationships – a way to assert the primacy of one variable over another and therefore to know which variables to "control" so that we could test the effects of others. Theories enable researchers to bring meaningful order to the massive web of interconnections among people's relationship attitudes and experiences. In other papers, we have used data from the Boston Couples Study in this theory-driven way, for instance to test Rusbult's model of relationship commitment and stability (Bui, Peplau, & Hill, 1996). In this chapter, however, our goal has been to be as inclusive of potential predictors as possible, casting a broad net to see which empirical associations emerged and how well a comprehensive set of predictors could accomplish the goal of predicting relationship outcomes.

Although our analyses have identified links between premarital attitudes and experiences and subsequent relationship outcomes, our data cannot address the processes by which these associations occur. How, for instance, are traditional sex-role attitudes linked to marital stability among early nesters? Do such attitudes set the stage for a gender-based division of labor which limits conflict between spouses? Or do traditional attitudes cause individuals to value the institution of marriage more and so work harder to preserve their relationship? Or do enduring traditional attitudes make divorce a less attractive alternative? Research focusing on the processes through which premarital factors influence later relationship outcomes will provide answers to important questions such as these. Ultimately, efforts to combine long-term predictive studies and fine-grained process analyses will provide a more comprehensive understanding of the development of intimate relationships.

References

Bentler, P. M., & Newcomb, M. D. (1978). Longitudinal study of marital success and failure. *Journal of Consulting and Clinical Psychology, 46,* 1053–1070.

Berg, J. H., & McQuinn, R. D. (1986). Attraction and exchange in continuing and noncontinuing dating relationships. *Journal of Personality and Social Psychology, 50,* 942–952.

Blau, P. M. (1964). *Exchange and power in social life.* New York: Wiley.

Bradbury, T. N., & Fincham, F. D. (1990). Preventing marital dysfunction: Review and analysis. In F. D. Fincham & T. N. Bradbury (Eds.), *The psychology of marriage* (pp. 375–401). New York: Guilford.

Bradbury, T. N., & Karney, B. R. (1993). Longitudinal study of marital interaction and dysfunction: Review and analysis. *Clinical Psychology Review, 13,* 15–27.

Buehlman, K. T., Gottman, J. M., & Katz, L. F. (1992). How a couple views their past predicts their future: Predicting divorce from an oral history interview. *Journal of Family Psychology, 5,* 295–318.

Bui, K-V. T., Peplau, L. A., & Hill, C. T. (1996). Testing the Rusbult model of relationship commitment and stability in a 15-year study of heterosexual couples. *Personality and Social Psychology Bulletin, 22,* 1244–1257.

Burgess, E. W., & Wallin, P. (1953). *Engagement and marriage.* New York: J. B. Lippincott.

Buss, D. M. (1985). Human mate selection. *American Scientist, 73,* 47–51.

Center for Human Resource Research. (1987). *NLS Handbook.* Columbus, OH: Ohio State University.

Filsinger, E. E., & Thoma, S. J. (1988). Behavioral antecedents of relationship stability and adjustment: A five-year longitudinal study. *Journal of Marriage and the Family, 50,* 785–795.

Fowers, B. J., & Olson, D. H. (1986). Predicting marital success with PREPARE: A predictive validity study. *Journal of Marital and Family Therapy, 12,* 403–413.

Gottman, J. M. (1994). *What predicts divorce? The relationship between marital processes and marital outcomes.* Hillsdale, NJ: Erlbaum.

Hill, C. T., Peplau, L. A., & Rubin, Z. (1981). Differing perceptions in dating couples. *Psychology of Women Quarterly, 5*(3), 418–434.

Hill, C. T., Rubin, Z., & Peplau, L. A. (1976). Breakups before marriage: The end of 103 affairs. *Journal of Social Issues, 32*(1), 147–168.

Hill, C. T., Rubin, Z., Peplau, L. A., & Willard, S. (1979). The volunteer couple: Sex differences, couple commitment, and participation in research on interpersonal relationships. *Social Psychology Quarterly, 42,* 415–420.

Holman, T. B., Larson, J. H., & Harmer, S. L. (1994). The development and predictive validity of a new premarital assessment instrument. *Family Relations, 43,* 46–52.

Kelly, C., Huston, T. L., & Cate, R. M. (1985). Premarital relationship correlates of the erosion of satisfaction in marriage. *Journal of Social and Personal Relationships, 2,* 167–178.

Kelly, E. L., & Conley, J. J. (1987). Personality and compatibility: A prospective analysis of marital stability and marital satisfaction. *Journal of Personality and Social Psychology, 52,* 27–40.

Kurdek, L. A. (1993). Predicting marital dissolution: A 5-year prospective longitudinal study of newlywed couples. *Journal of Personality and Social Psychology, 64,* 221–242.

Larsen, A. S., & Olson, D. (1989). Predicting marital satisfaction using PREPARE. *Journal of Marital and Family Therapy, 15,* 311–22.

Leslie, L. A., Huston, T. L., & Johnson, M. P. (1986). Parental reactions to dating relationships: Do they make a difference? *Journal of Marriage and the Family, 48,* 57–66.

Levinger, G. A. (1979). A social exchange view on the dissolution of pair relationships. In R. L. Burgess & T. L. Huston (Eds.), *Social exchange in developing relationships* (pp. 169–193). New York: Academic Press.

Markman, H. J. (1981). Prediction of marital distress: A five-year follow-up. *Journal of Consulting and Clinical Psychology, 49,* 760–762.

Olson, D. H. (1990). Commentary: Marriage in perspective. In F. D. Fincham & T. N. Bradbury (Eds.), *The psychology of marriage* (pp. 402–420). New York: Guilford.

Peplau, L. A., & Hill, C. T. (1995, March 31). *Meant for each other? Premarital predictors of marital success.* Paper presented at the annual meeting of the Western Psychological Association, Los Angeles, CA.

Peplau, L. A., Hill, C. T., & Rubin, Z. (1993). Sex-role attitudes in dating and marriage: A 15-year followup of the Boston Couples Study. *Journal of Social Issues, 40*(3), 31–52.

Raschke, H. J. (1987). Divorce. In M. B. Sussman & S. K. Steinmetz (Eds.), *Handbook of marriage and the family* (pp. 597–624). New York: Plenum.

Renick, M. J., Blumberg, S. L., & Markman, H. J. (1992). The Prevention and Relationship Enhancement Program (PREP): An empirically based preventive intervention program for couples. *Family Relations, 41,* 141–147.

Rubin, Z. (1970). Measurement of romantic love. *Journal of Personality and Social Psychology, 16,* 265–273.

Rubin, Z., Peplau, L. A., & Hill, C. T. (1981). Loving and leaving: Sex differences in romantic attachments. *Sex Roles, 7,* 821–835.

Rusbult, C. E., & Buunk, B. P. (1993). Commitment processes in close relationships: An interdependence analysis. *Journal of Social and Personal Relationships, 10,* 175–204.

Sabatelli, R. M., & Shehan, C. L. (1993). Exchange and resource theories. In P. G. Boss, W. J. Doherty, R. LaRossa, W. R. Schumm, & S. K. Steinmetz (Eds.), *Sourcebook of family theories and methods: A contextual approach* (pp. 385–411). New York: Plenum.

Simpson, J. A., Campbell, B., & Berscheid, E. (1986). The association between romantic love and marriage: Kephart (1967) twice revisited. *Personality and Social Psychology Bulletin, 12,* 363–372.

Sprecher, S., & Felmlee, D. (1992). The influence of parents and friends on the quality and stability of romantic relationships: A three-wave longitudinal investigation. *Journal of Marriage and the Family, 54,* 888–900.

White, L. K. (1990). Determinants of divorce: A review of research in the eighties. *Journal of Marriage and the Family, 52*(4), 904–912.

Whyte, K. M. (1990). *Dating, mating, and marriage.* New York: Aldine de Gruyter.

9 Optimizing Longitudinal Research for Understanding and Preventing Marital Dysfunction

Thomas N. Bradbury, Catherine L. Cohan, and Benjamin R. Karney

The longitudinal literature on marriage, which consists of 115 studies, some 68 independent samples, and more than 45,000 marriages (Karney & Bradbury, 1995a), provides many important clues about how marriages succeed and fail, but it also contains many valuable lessons about how research in this domain can be improved. For example, whereas replicable associations between various marital processes and marital outcomes are beginning to emerge, conceptual frameworks for evaluating and integrating these findings remain to be developed. Whereas extensive progress has been made in assessing key independent variables, a number of methodological factors – such as specifying the samples and the dependent variables that are maximally informative for clarifying how marriages change – await further refinement. And whereas this literature already holds considerable promise for understanding and preventing marital dysfunction, its limitations have undermined its impact, and much of its promise therefore remains unfulfilled. Thus, despite its size and scope, this body of research has been overlooked (e.g., Hinde, 1995, p. 3, notes that longitudinal studies are "sadly neglected except in cases of parent–child relationships and studies of the effects of therapy or social support") and underestimated (e.g., Gottman & Levenson, 1992, p. 221, note that "we know of only four prospective longitudinal studies that have attempted to predict future separation and divorce").

These observations highlight the need to scrutinize prevailing concepts and methods in longitudinal research on marriage so that better answers to fundamental questions can be attained. The purpose of this chapter is to

Preparation of this chapter was supported by grant R29 MH48674 awarded by the National Institute of Mental Health to Thomas N. Bradbury, by grant F31 MH10779 awarded by the National Institute of Mental Health to Catherine L. Cohan, and by a dissertation year fellowship awarded by the UCLA Graduate Division to Benjamin R. Karney.

279

identify what we perceive to be some of the important barriers to progress in understanding the longitudinal course of marriage, and to offer some suggestions for how these barriers can be overcome or understood more fully. We organize our discussion first around conceptual issues and then around methodological issues, and in both cases we refer to efforts designed to prevent marital dysfunction and to our ongoing studies of newlywed marriage to address limitations and ambiguities in the larger longitudinal literature.

Implications of a Social-Learning Approach for Understanding and Altering the Longitudinal Course of Marriage

A social-learning or behavioral model (e.g., Jacobson & Margolin, 1979; O'Leary & Turkewitz, 1978; Weiss, 1978) and various extensions of it (e.g., Bradbury & Fincham, 1987; Margolin, 1983) have served as the foundation for much of the psychological research on marriage and marital intervention over the past 2 decades, and it is probably the best perspective from which to begin conceptualizing how marriages change (Karney & Bradbury, 1995a). Although there is no single, coherent theory of marital distress within this broad framework, there is probably some consensus for the premise that "distress, in this model, is assumed to be a function of couples' interaction patterns. Inevitably, couples have wants and needs that conflict. Distress results from couples' aversive and ineffectual response to conflict" (Koerner & Jacobson, 1994, p. 208). This orientation originated with the belief that the application of behavioral and social exchange principles could aid in the treatment of distressed marriages (e.g., Stuart, 1969), and it has proven to be remarkably useful for this purpose (see Alexander, Holtzworth-Munroe, & Jameson, 1994).

The social learning view of marriage can be interpreted and expanded to accommodate a wide range of phenomena that arise in clinical settings and in basic research. This breadth and flexibility accounts for the longevity of the model, but it also makes the model difficult to specify, critique, and refute. In the present context, this is particularly unfortunate because the original reason for developing this approach – to improve the marriages of distressed couples – appears to have constrained theorizing about the longitudinal course of marriage and about the etiology of marital discord. Specifically, with its strong focus on behavior and behavioral exchange as determinants of marital dissatisfaction, this model is limited to phenomena that, at least in principle, can be changed. Phenomena that are unlikely to change (e.g., family history of divorce) or change to any significant degree (e.g., spouses' personalities, socioeconomic status) are generally outside the scope of this model, regardless of any association they may have with the longitudinal course of marriage. This may be an appropriate and desirable constraint when the goal is to specify how discordant couples can be transformed with clinical interventions to become more maritally satisfied, but it may prove unduly restrictive when the goal is to understand how satisfied marriages become distressed or unstable, or how distressed couples deteriorate further or improve naturally.

We now consider some of the major conceptual problems that arise as a consequence of this emphasis on potentially changeable phenomena. To define the target of our analysis, we focus on the core behavioral premise outlined earlier, namely, that marital distress results from the behaviors that spouses exchange when attempting to reconcile their differing needs and desires. We offer this analysis with the view that any successful model of marital change is likely to place great emphasis on the behaviors exchanged by spouses, but with the added assumption that any such model is probably at a disadvantage in explaining marital change if it is limited to interpersonal behavior and closely related phenomena.

Limitations of the Social-Learning Approach

Inability to Explain the Changing Divorce Rate. One reason for the assumption that an interactional model is incomplete is that fluctuations in the divorce rate (i.e., the rapid rise in divorce from 1960 to 1980, the stabilization from 1980 to 1990; see Cherlin, 1992), which are presumably a rough index of prevailing levels of marital distress, are difficult to explain with the behavioral premise alone. Changes in conflict-resolution behavior are unlikely to account for these shifts and, even if they could, the question of what gave rise to these behavioral changes would have to be answered. Although it might be reasonable to assert that spouses' changing wants and needs or numerous sociodemographic factors have changed in this period, with a corresponding increase in poorly resolved marital conflicts, these factors and their association with observable behavior have received relatively little attention within the behavioral model. Even if this model provided a valid portrayal of the behavioral antecedents of marital failure, it would be incomplete because it fails to explain why more or fewer marriages fail at one point in time than at another point in time.

Undue Emphasis on Conflict. A second reason for questioning the limited scope of the behavioral premise is that it emphasizes conflict and responses to conflict as the cause of marital distress while downplaying the possible role of behaviors displayed in other domains. Thus this approach appears to assume that two equally satisfied newlywed couples with very similar capacities for conflict resolution would be similar in their marital quality and marital stability over time, even if the spouses in one of the couples were very poor or very skillful at, for example, providing support and comfort to each other. Although this hypothesis has not been tested directly, there is evidence that the social support behaviors newlywed spouses display, in an interaction where one spouse is instructed to "respond as you normally would" as the partner talks about a personal issue that he or she would like to change, are associated with marital outcomes 24 months later after controlling for initial levels of marital satisfaction (Pasch & Bradbury, in press). This finding, along with the finding that marital satisfaction covaries concurrently with reciprocation of negative behaviors in this task – long viewed as the hallmark of maladaptive behavior in marital conflict discussions – suggests a behavioral deficit in marriage that extends beyond the domain of conflict. The behavioral premise, because it arose in part from clinical observations of overt conflict displayed by discordant married couples, may overestimate the role of conflict as a cause of marital dysfunction. Consequently, researchers have overlooked the possibility that deficits in some behavioral domains may precede mismanaged conflict and the onset of marital distress.

Lack of Attention to External Stressors. Third, according to the behavioral premise, marital distress arises from poor handling of conflict, and in many instances the conflict arises from or is a reflection of discrepant needs and wants. As a result of this primary focus on the interpersonal consequences of intrapersonal states, the possible contributions of a wide range of extradyadic factors on interpersonal functioning tend to be minimized. Although there is some recognition in the social learning model that "for some couples the antecedents of distress stem from changes which occur outside the relationship, which have little directly to do with anything that has transpired within the dyad itself" (Jacobson & Margolin, 1979, p. 26) and that "external stresses can disrupt marital stability despite the initial absence of interactional difficulties" (Robinson & Jacobson, 1987, p. 150), the interior of marriage receives far more attention than the exterior, and little is known about the interplay between the stressful events that couples encounter, their interactional tendencies, and the longitudinal course of marriage.

In a study designed to address this problem, Cohan and Bradbury (1997) asked newlywed spouses to complete a checklist of stressful life events that occurred in the previous 6 months and also observed them attempting to resolve a marital difficulty. Results revealed that to the extent they reported more life events, husbands reported more symptoms of depression and displayed more anger and less sadness during the problem-solving discussion. Wives reporting more life events were less maritally satisfied shortly after marriage, and they displayed less positive and more negative verbal behavior. Longitudinal analyses, linking life events variables to marital outcomes 18 months later, showed that the association between life events and marital satisfaction was moderated by observed problem-solving behavior. For example, among wives who displayed higher levels of anger during problem solving, reports of more life events predicted increases (or smaller decreases) in satisfaction. Among wives displaying lower levels of anger, in contrast, more life events were related to decreases in satisfaction (for details, see Cohan & Bradbury, 1997). In addition to showing that anger is not routinely detrimental to marriage, these findings demonstrate more generally the importance of investigating the events, circumstances, and transitions that couples encounter and their relation to marital behavior.

Lack of Attention to Individual Differences. Fourth, with the behavioral approach to marriage, individual differences and personality variables are generally assumed to be unimportant (see Robinson & Jacobson, 1987), and there is a sense with this model that "all spouses are created equal" when it comes to the association between behavior and the course of marriage. Again, clarifications or exceptions to this view can be found (e.g., from Jacobson & Margolin, 1979, p. 28, "Although we have been emphasizing environmental antecedents of relationship distress, it is also possible that individual differences between partners can lead to substantial difficulties"), but few steps have been taken to integrate interpersonal and individual differences views of marriage or to demonstrate that individual differences do not add to behavioral variables when explaining the longitudinal course of marriage. The need to confront this issue was heightened with the publication of a 45-year longitudinal study of 278 marriages (Kelly & Conley, 1987), which demonstrated, for example, that marital incompatibility was related to higher levels of husbands' and wives' neuroticism and to husbands' lower levels of impulsivity; these data were provided by spouses' acquaintances early in marriage.

Although the relatively global level at which these data were collected prohibits a clear interpretation of how individual difference variables might affect the course of marriage, the Kelly and Conley (1987) study probably should not be dismissed for this reason alone. Defined as a tendency for individuals "to focus differentially on the negative aspects of themselves, other people, and the world in general" (Watson & Clark, 1994), neuroticism is among the strongest and most consistent predictors of marital instability and dissatisfaction (effect sizes computed with six or more studies range from −.13 to −.22; see Karney & Bradbury, 1995a), and as a reliable indicator of these outcomes neuroticism may suggest useful hypotheses about how behavioral mechanisms operate. For example, the degree of negativity or pessimism that spouses bring to their marital interactions may affect the sorts of behaviors they then display or the conclusions they later draw from the interactions about their partner and marriage, and either pattern could presumably contribute to declines in marriage over time (see Bradbury & Fincham, 1991). Not all spouses high in neuroticism may do this, and not all spouses who do this may be high in neuroticism, but a trait-like propensity toward negativity could potentiate interactional mechanisms that operate to varying degrees in all marriages. Possibilities such as these, along with evidence that masculinity and femininity covary with behavior in marriage and predict change in marital satisfaction independent of behavior (Bradbury, Campbell, & Fincham, 1995), highlight the benefits that can arise when the behavioral premise is reconceptualized in terms of individual difference variables.

Reliance on Null Model Tests. Finally, the hypothesis that problem-solving behavior in marriage causes marital distress is usually tested against the null hypothesis, which maintains that no such association will be obtained. As a consequence, we can learn only whether or not behavior predicts change in marital satisfaction and not whether behavior predicts change better than some other variable, whether the effects of behavior are moderated by some other variable, and whether the effects of behavior are mediated by some other variable. Null model tests can contribute to refinements in understanding the relative strength of prediction afforded by different behaviors and how behavior-satisfaction associations vary with gender, but they provide no information about the strength of behavioral prediction in relation to other variables, about the means by which behavior exerts its effect, and about the boundary conditions for the prediction.

A better alternative would involve strategic comparisons between the behavioral premise and other credible explanatory frameworks, thereby emphasizing discriminant validity over convergent validity. This would permit more rapid progress toward understanding what does and does not contribute to marital change. Even if these comparative tests failed, of course, our confidence in the behavioral approach would be enhanced if the basic premise were replicated.

Summary. Because it was introduced into the marital domain as a framework for alleviating marital discord, the social-learning model places great emphasis on aspects of marriage – particularly behaviors enacted during conflict-resolution interactions – that are likely to change with clinical interventions. However, there are several reasons to question whether the contributions of this approach to marital therapy can be matched when the model is extended to investigate how marriages naturally succeed and fail. For example, it remains to be shown that the behavioral premise can fully account for the longitudinal course of marriage without reference to the ecological niches that couples inhabit (and the stressful events and circumstances that accompany them) or to the individual differences and life experiences that spouses bring to marriage. These factors may not change much naturally and they may not be particularly amenable to change, yet they may contribute to variation in the behaviors that spouses display and to variation in marital outcomes.

The behavioral premise also seems to be limited in that it cannot easily account for fluctuations in the divorce rate, it overlooks the behaviors that spouses exchange outside the context of marital conflict, and it tends to constrain hypothesis testing to tests against the null model, which yield data that provide little direction for theoretical refinements. Although the social-learning approach to marriage is sufficiently flexible to generate significant counterarguments to these observations, they nevertheless highlight some key concerns with the more specific behavioral premise that has been the focus of this analysis. Recognizing the limitations of this premise is valuable because longitudinal investigations of the more inclusive social-learning approach typically begin with studies of the specific behavioral premise, as is the case with Gottman and Krokoff (1989), Filsinger and Thoma (1988), and Smith, Vivian, and O'Leary (1990).

Applied Consequences of a Restricted View of Marriage

We have argued that a focus on the changeable elements of marriage is unduly restrictive for understanding the longitudinal course of marriage, yet we have also observed that this focus may be viable as a foundation for clinical interventions designed to alleviate marital dysfunction. It is important to recognize that this latter observation probably does not generalize to programs designed to prevent marital dysfunction, which stems from the fact that marital therapies and prevention programs have different links to basic research on marriage. Whereas innovations in treatment are more likely to give rise to basic research than vice versa (e.g., the primary resource for cognitive-behavioral marital therapy, by Baucom and Epstein, 1990, was published at the same time that basic research findings were beginning to accumulate, not after those findings were established; see Bradbury & Fincham, 1990a), prevention programs are in a much better position to be shaped by and benefit from basic longitudinal research on marriage. This difference may arise because marital therapies must attend not only to the factors that may have caused marital distress but also to the diverse and complex consequences that the distress has had within the marriage (e.g., feelings of frustration, mistrust, depression), whereas prevention programs have the ostensibly more straightforward goal of intervening in a manner that decreases the likelihood that the causes of marital distress operate.

One key task that must be accomplished in order to reach this goal is to identify putative causal mechanisms so that empirically based interventions can be devised (see Bradbury & Fincham, 1990b). Although "most prevention programs for couples have been based on clinical intuition and common sense" (Hahlweg, Baucom, & Markman, 1988, p. 422), Markman and his colleagues developed the Premarital Relationship Enhancement Program (PREP) based on research supporting the behavioral premise outlined earlier. As Markman, Floyd, Stanley, and Lewis (1986, p. 178) note, "We have based the content of our program on the [family life cycle model] and empirical foundations laid by cross-sectional and longitudinal research on relationships. . . . These findings indicate that dysfunctional interaction patterns precede the development of relationship dissatisfaction and that early signs of impending distress are potentially recognizable in premarital interactions, independent of the couples' premarital relationship satisfaction and problems." PREP, the resulting program, consists of five 3-hour sessions devoted to training couples in communication and problem-solving skills, clarification of marital expectations, and principles of sexual functioning.

The long-term follow-up data on PREP reveal the power of basing a prevention program on changeable elements of marriage as well as the boundaries that are imposed when doing so. Thus, on one hand, couples participating in PREP compared with a no-treatment control group maintain their early levels of marital quality over 36 months (Markman, Floyd, Stanley, & Storaasli, 1988) and, at least for husbands, over 60 months (Markman, Renick, Floyd, Stanley, & Clements, 1993). These data support the view that a relatively brief premarital intervention can affect marital satisfaction, and they represent a major step toward an empirically based approach to the prevention of marital dysfunction.

On the other hand, these data also point to one of the refinements that is needed in the next generation of outcome research on prevention and how recognition of marital variables that do not change much can improve preventive interventions. Specifically, the Markman et al. (1988, 1993) studies show that (a) the average level of relationship satisfaction remained in the nondistressed range of marital functioning after 60 months even among couples who did not receive the intervention (on the MAT (Locke & Wallace, 1959), where scores above 100 are viewed as indicative of satisfying marriages, husbands in the control and decline groups averaged 108.4 (sd = 23.1) and 110.01 (sd = 21.1), respectively, and wives in these groups averaged 115.1 (sd = 21.2) and 120.4 (sd = 14.5); see Markman et al., 1993), and (b) the rate of marital instability in this sample appears to be lower than that in the general population (according to Markman & Hahlweg, 1993, only 17% of the married couples separated or divorced by 72 months).

Thus it appears that these couples were not at particularly high risk for eventual marital difficulties, and as a consequence inferences about the impact of this intervention cannot be as strong as they would be if the control group had a lower level of satisfaction over time or if the rate of instability in the sample were higher. How could at-risk couples be identified, even early in their marriage? From our perspective, the longitudinal literature has developed to the point where risk factors for later marital dissatisfaction and instability are now identifiable (e.g., age at marriage, neuroticism, education, income, unhappy childhood, parental divorce; see Karney & Bradbury, 1995a). Most of these factors cannot change or are unlikely to change a great deal and hence are outside the usual scope of the behavioral literature, but they could be used in the future to ensure that at-risk samples are studied and that interventions are targeted to those couples most in need of them.

Summary. We conclude that prevention programs will be maximally *effective* – that is, participating couples are likely to benefit over significant spans of time in contrast to couples who do not participate – if they are based on changeable elements of marriage that are shown to be important in longitudinal studies. More relevant to the purposes of this chapter, however, is the conclusion that prevention programs will have a significant *impact* – that is, participating couples are likely to remain maritally satisfied whereas the couples who do not participate will become maritally distressed or divorced – if stable indicators of risk are used to determine which couples are to receive the interventions. Failure to screen on the basis of risk will result in limited treatment resources being expended on many couples who may have satisfying marriages even without premarital counseling (see Sullivan & Bradbury, 1997). In short, in the same manner that a strong focus on marital conflict behavior as a cause of marital distress may preclude a complete understanding of how marriages naturally succeed and fail, this focus may also impede progress in developing programs that prevent poor marital outcomes.

Developing an Alternative View of How Marriages Change

The social-learning approach to marriage draws our attention to the consequences of behaviors that spouses display when their needs and interests conflict and, indeed, it is difficult to conceive of a model of marital change without acknowledging the significance of this behavioral domain. The foregoing critique suggests that in some respects this approach does not assign enough importance to marital behavior in explaining how marriages change, whereas in other respects it relies too heavily on behavior to accomplish this goal. In the paragraphs below we outline a model that overcomes these limitations and that provides a blueprint for future research on the longitudinal course of marriage. This model is designed as a general framework for studying marital change rather than as a specific theory that explains how marriages succeed and fail, yet it does suggest some specific research agendas which, if explored, would shed light on the form that a more specific theory might take. The model invokes three inclusive constructs – which we refer to as adaptive processes, stressful events, and enduring vulnerabilities – to account for variation in marital dysfunction. A brief rationale for each of these constructs is presented next, followed by a discussion of how they interrelate.

Generalizing the Behavioral Premise to Adaptive Processes. Early social-learning analyses of marriage adopted a rather broad concept of marital behavior. For example, in a well-known exchange about the merits of behavioral marital therapy, Jacobson and Weiss (1978, p. 152) wrote:

> Marriage produces an incredible array of mutual interdependencies that are controlled by ideological factors, the operational necessities of daily life, and the stage of the life cycle. Conceptualizing these as relationship tasks makes it possible to ask how well a given couple is *accomplishing* these tasks. . . . The opportunities for trial-and-error learning to occur are enormous in such relationships . . . as are the opportunities for failure to match outcome with expectation. It is understanding the consequences of these *attempts* at mastery that preoccupy the behavioral marriage therapist. The consequences lead to patterned ways of resolving "problems" (in the broadest sense of that term).

Despite this view, in subsequent research on marital interaction the subtleties of a broad task-based analysis of marriage were relinquished in favor of in-depth analysis of the skills that spouses display in problem-solving interactions.

One consequence of this shift away from the inclusive view of marital interaction is that our understanding of behavior as it relates to change in marriage is limited almost exclusively to behavior in marital problem-solving discussions. Although this literature has proven to be informative (for reviews, see Bradbury & Karney, 1993; and Weiss & Heyman, 1990), data on other marital tasks have been collected only rarely (e.g., Levenson & Gottman, 1983, observed couples at the end of the work day), and as a consequence it is difficult to determine whether the behavioral effects that have been observed are unique to the problem-solving domain or whether they reflect other interpersonal deficits. Similarly, the possibility that there are diverse behavioral deficits that contribute to distress in different marriages remains untested, as does the possibility that difficulties in marital problem-solving arise from shortcomings in the accomplishment of other central tasks.

Particularly lacking in this regard is behavioral data on the capacity of spouses to provide support and understanding to each other. Weiss (1978) identified this as one of four basic relationship accomplishments that couples must successfully resolve in order to have a satisfying marriage (along with objectification, problem-solving, and behavior change) and, as noted earlier, we have collected some promising longitudinal data on this important interpersonal domain (Pasch & Bradbury, in press; see also Cutrona & Suhr, 1994). In the same manner that the effects of negative behavior appear to be offset by positive behavior in the course of a marital problem-solving discussion (see Gottman, 1994), it is quite plausible that the likelihood of overt conflict is reduced in marriages where the quality of social support is high or increased in marriages where the quality of social support is low. Moreover, the longitudinal impact of conflict behaviors on marriage might be lessened in the context of an otherwise supportive marriage but heightened when spouses are particularly poor at providing this support.

Thus, whereas early social-learning formulations of marriage favored a broad conception of the different behaviors that spouses might exchange in the course of accomplishing a variety of basic marital tasks, empirical tests conducted within this tradition have come to focus almost exclusively on marital conflict resolution as the key behavioral domain in marriage. The relative importance of marital conflict has been assumed rather than demonstrated, and as a consequence we believe that the behavioral literature rests on a narrow and incomplete foundation. Accordingly, as a first step toward developing an alternative view of how marriages change, we propose a modification of the behavioral premise so that it is replaced with the more inclusive concept of adaptive processes. We define this as the manner in which individuals and couples contend with differences of opinion and individual and marital difficulties and transitions. Adaptation therefore refers to how spouses regulate, manage, or sustain their marriage generally and in response to marital and nonmarital events, and we propose that it is particularly likely to be expressed in problem-solving behavior, support-giving behavior, and the affective and cognitive concomitants of these exchanges. Although we believe it is very important to highlight the limited manner in which marital behavior has been studied within the behavioral tradition, it is at least as important to recognize that simply returning to the earlier, broader conceptualization of behavior is likely to prove inadequate for understanding the longitudinal course of marriage. Two additional directions for expansion are considered next.

Incorporating Stressful Events and Individual Differences. The above discussion implies that couples displaying better skills in adaptation will have better marital outcomes. We have argued, however, that spouses and couples probably vary widely with respect to the stressful events that they encounter and the individual differences and life experiences that they bring to marriage. These sorts of variables have received only passing interest within the social-learning tradition, but there is ample research to suggest that marriage in general, and adaptive processes in particular, are affected by the ecological niche that couples inhabit and the background and unique experiences that a spouse would bring to any relationship.

With regard to the role of stress in marriage, maritally distressed spouses report more negative life events and higher levels of stress than nondistressed spouses (e.g., Whiffen & Gotlib, 1989), spouses receiving marital therapy report a higher number of life events over the past year compared to those not receiving therapy (Frederickson, 1977), and the benefits of marital therapy last longer to the extent that spouses report fewer negative life events (Jacobson, Schmaling, & Holtzworth-Munroe, 1987). Spouses' interpersonal exchanges also appear to be associated with the stressors they encounter, particularly in the workplace. Days described by spouses as stressful appear to give rise to relatively negative marital interactions (Bolger, DeLongis, Kessler, & Wethington, 1989), and higher daily workloads of air traffic controllers, for example, are associated with more reported negativity in marital interaction (Repetti, 1989). Direct observational data add to this picture by showing that husbands in blue-collar occupations display more negative affect in marital interaction than husbands in white-collar occupations (Krokoff, Gottman, & Roy, 1988), and that husbands experiencing higher levels of economic strain display more hostile behavior and less positive behavior, which in turn covaries with wives' marital instability (Conger et al., 1990). These data indicate that a necessary second step in developing an alternative model of marital change is to include the full range of stressful events and circumstances that spouses and couples encounter in their marriage.

Finally, the third component of the proposed model involves the demographic, historical, individual-difference, and experiential factors that individuals bring to their marriage. These are the characteristics that a spouse would bring to any marriage, and because they are expected to be relatively stable and to "set the stage" for the ensuing adaptive processes and stressful events, they are referred to as enduring vulnerabilities. In addition to the Kelly and Conley (1987) study noted earlier, which links acquaintance ratings of neuroticism and impulsivity to marital outcomes, considerable research suggests that all marriages do not begin on an equal footing and that attention to spousal characteristics may be important for understanding how a marriage evolves. Cross-sectional studies demonstrate an association between personality traits and the occurrence and experience of negative life events (e.g., Poulton & Andrews, 1992; and Marco & Suls, 1993, respectively), and life-span studies demonstrate that early personality is associated with level of accomplishment in adulthood (e.g., Caspi, Bem, & Elder, 1989). Together with data that show that (a) adults from divorced family backgrounds tend to fare worse than those from intact families on a number of dimensions of well-being (e.g., psychological adjustment, educational attainment, marital quality, likelihood of divorce; for a review see Amato & Keith, 1991), and (b) various indices of marital interaction and social skills are associated with spouses' reports of their family of origin (e.g., Franz, McClelland, & Weinberger, 1991), with education (Griffin, 1993), and with neuroticism (McGonagle, Kessler, & Schilling, 1992), there appears to be sufficient evidence to suggest that enduring vulnerabilities may indeed be pertinent to understanding the course of marriage.

Research on stressful events and enduring vulnerabilities is important, because it can suggest explanations for variations in the divorce rate. For example, it is reasonable to infer that the increased rate at which married women have joined the labor force has created new dynamics within the family, and that these dynamics can contribute to the deterioration of marriages that otherwise would remain intact (see Greenstein, 1990). Similarly, the likelihood of a newly married spouse having divorced parents is far greater now than it was 30 years ago; with evidence for the intergenerational transmission of divorce (Amato & Keith, 1991), this suggests that present-day marriages will perpetuate the divorce rate until some other factor (e.g., an increase in the age at marriage; see Ahlburg & DeVita, 1992) helps to override this mechanism.

Integrating Adaptive Processes, Stressful Events, and Enduring Vulnerabilities. A model showing the interrelationships among the three main components of the model, and their association with marital quality and marital stability, is shown in Figure 9.1. Four of the paths in this model already have been mentioned (i.e., path f, between adaptive processes and marital quality; path a, between stressful events and adaptive processes; path c, between enduring vulnerabilities and stressful events; and path b, between enduring vulnerabilities and adaptive processes), to which we add a link between marital quality and marital stability (path h; for further discussion of this path, see Karney & Bradbury, 1995a), the possibility that stressful events are caused by chance factors (via path d), and reciprocal links from marital quality to adaptive processes (path g) and from adaptive processes to stressful events (path e).

According to this model, spouses and couples encounter a variety of stressful or challenging events to which they must adapt or adjust (path a). The capacity for adaptation will be influenced in part by enduring vulnerabilities and strengths that individuals possess (path b). These vulnerabilities themselves can contribute to the occurrence of stressful events (path c), as can chance factors (via path d). Poor adaptation may allow stressful events to perpetuate or worsen, whereas adequate adaptation will help to alleviate them (path e). Spouses will base their judgments about the quality of the marriage on their accumulated experiences with adaptation (path f). A negative evaluation of the adaptive processes will lead to lowered marital quality, while a positive evaluation will lead to no change or to an increase in marital quality; these judgments will feed back to either diminish or enhance, respectively, the couples' capacity to adapt to subsequent stressful events (path g). With repeated failures in adaptation, marital quality is likely to continue to decline, and the probability of marital instability will increase accordingly (path h).

As an example of how this framework might reflect change in marriage, consider a husband who is laid off, either because of his low level of education (path c) or because of chance factors (path d). An impulsive, unsupportive wife may hinder the couple's adjustment to this (path b), which will contribute to marital conflict and make it difficult to resolve the problem (path e). A series of such adaptive failures could lead the husband to conclude that

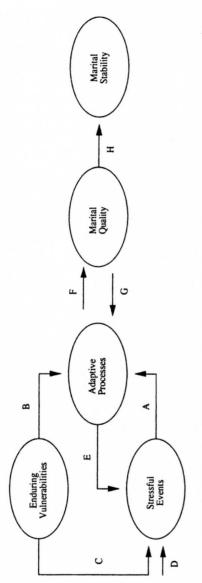

Figure 9.1. A vulnerability-stress-adaptation model of marital outcomes (from Karney & Bradbury, 1995a).

he is not happy with the marriage (path f), which will further reduce the couple's capacity to manage stressful events (path g). Over time the quality of the marriage might erode further because of this reduced capacity and the manner in which couples evaluate it (path f). Separation or divorce may follow (path h).

This framework suggests that a couple with effective adaptive processes who encounter relatively few stressful events and have few enduring vulnerabilities are expected to experience a satisfying and stable marriage. In contrast, a couple with ineffective adaptive processes who encounter many stressful events and have many enduring vulnerabilities are expected to be unhappily married, separated, or divorced. Couples falling at other points along the three basic dimensions of the model are expected to fall between these two extreme outcomes. These hypotheses are represented in Figure 9.2, for couples with poor, average, and good adaptive processes. Following the basic logic of vulnerability-stress models (e.g., Monroe & Simons, 1991; Zubin & Spring, 1977), in all three cases poor marital outcomes are expected when the degree of enduring vulnerabilities and stressful events is high, and good marital outcomes are expected when enduring vulnerabilities and stressful events are low. However, the relative distribution of good and poor marital outcomes is expected to be moderated by the quality of couples' adaptive processes. Specifically, all else being equal, a higher proportion of good outcomes is likely among couples who are skillful in adapting to difficulties and change, and a lower proportion of good outcomes is likely among couples less skillful in their adaptive processes.

The model is distinguished from the social-learning view in general, and from the behavioral premise in particular, by the relative emphasis it places on interaction. Whereas the behavioral premise treats the quality of problem-solving interactions as a critical determinant of marital outcomes, in the present model interaction is viewed more generally in terms of adaptive processes and more functionally in terms of its role in enabling couples to adapt to the circumstances that they create and confront. Consequently, adaptive processes are not expected to correspond directly with marital outcomes. As Figure 9.2 indicates, couples with effective skills in adaptation may have dissatisfying or unstable marriages if vulnerabilities and stressors are high, and couples who are very poor in adaptation may not experience marital discord and instability if vulnerabilities and stressors are low.

Summary.   At the start of most marriages, spouses are very satisfied and have high hopes for a successful and enduring relationship. What factors account for the differing degrees of satisfaction and stability that these marriages attain and the fluctuations in marital quality that these spouses experience?

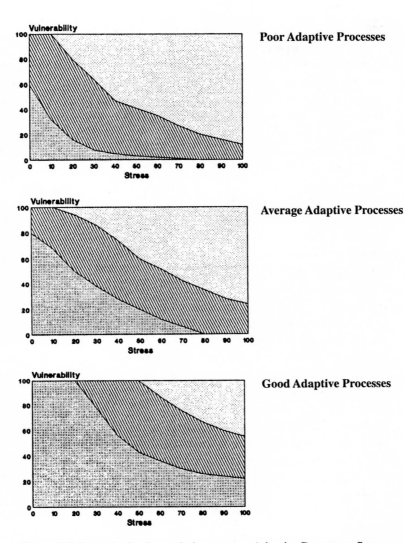

Figure 9.2. Hypothesized associations among Adaptive Processes, Stressful Events, Enduring Vulnerabilities, and Marital Outcomes. The proportion of maritally satisfied couples is represented in the lower left corner of each panel, the proportion of separated and divorced couples is represented in the upper right of each panel, and the proportion of discordant couples is shown between these two groups in each panel. At any level of adaptive processes, good marital outcomes are more likely when enduring vulnerabilities and stress are low, and poor marital outcomes are more likely when enduring vulnerabilities and stress are high. However, level of adaptive processes is hypothesized to moderate these associations, such that a couple with an average level of enduring vulnerabilities and an average level of stress could be unstable if adaptive processes were poor, discordant if adaptive processes were also average, or maritally satisfied if adaptive processes were good.

A central premise of the influential social-learning view of marriage holds that these outcomes are determined by how couples resolve the conflicts that arise between them. Drawing from our earlier critique of this view, we outlined an alternative model of marital change that recognizes the important role of marital conflict while also emphasizing that the effect of conflict behaviors on marriage can itself be affected by other classes of interpersonal behavior, such as social support. We argued further that the effects of interpersonal behavior (which we label as adaptive processes) on marriage cannot be understood without reference to the stressful events and circumstances to which couples must adapt, and to the enduring traits, characteristics, and experiences that spouses bring to their marriage. The expected associations among stressors, enduring vulnerabilities, and marital outcomes were described, along with the observation that this association should vary as a function of the quality of couples' adaptive processes.

In its present form, this model emphasizes the role of a few inclusive constructs rather than which of the many elements within these constructs are important for marital functioning. A major disadvantage of this model is that it overlooks many differences that could prove important (e.g., acute versus chronic stressors; controllable versus uncontrollable stressors; gender differences in particular paths; the role of spousal discrepancies on particular variables). On the other hand, the model recognizes the potential role of many diverse phenomena, organizes findings from diverse literatures, and acknowledges that associations among variables within the inclusive constructs will prove less informative than associations among variables between constructs.

Methodological Considerations in Longitudinal Research on Marriage

Although longitudinal studies of marriage have been appearing in the literature since the 1930s, more than half of the 115 studies identified by Karney and Bradbury (1995a) have been published since about 1980. And although this rapid increase in longitudinal data holds great potential for understanding how marriages succeed and fail, a wide array of methodological issues must be confronted if this potential is to be fully realized. Next we discuss two methodological topics that are important to consider in conducting and evaluating longitudinal research with married couples, regardless of the theoretical orientation that is adopted.

Refining Samples and Sampling

The Problem of Heterogeneity in Marital Duration. Several problems arise when longitudinal studies are conducted with samples in which the couples vary widely in marital duration at the time of the initial data collection. First, any effort to obtain a reasonably representative sample of these marriages will be unsuccessful because many marriages already will have ended in separation or divorce. As Glenn (1990, p. 820) notes, "The population of married persons is not approximately closed, and the tendency to move out of it is rather highly correlated with marital quality. Since the influences that tend to lower marital quality also tend to drive persons out of the married population, the effects of those influences will tend to be underestimated, or not studied at all, in studies of persons in intact marriages."

Second, a sample of this sort is likely to yield a fairly high degree of variation in marital satisfaction. Of course, this is often the intended purpose of the sampling in cross-sectional studies of marriage, but in longitudinal research it means that the couples may be starting the study at rather different points in the cycle of their relationship. As a consequence, equivalent amounts of change in their marriage cannot be interpreted the same way. For example, it would not be uncommon for a sample to include very satisfied, somewhat satisfied, and dissatisfied couples at Time 1. If all couples declined the same amount on a standard index of marital satisfaction from Time 1 to Time 2, then some couples would remain satisfied, some would begin to experience marital discord, and some would continue to deteriorate. Efforts to predict change in marital satisfaction from some other variable collected at Time 1 would overlook these different kinds of change, and a variable uniquely related to the onset of marital discord (compared with further deterioration, for example) might be overlooked because this subsample was combined with the other subsamples. These interpretive problems are compounded when the couples are at different stages in the marriage (for example, some couples might be newlyweds, others might be undergoing the transition to parenthood, others might be retired) or, in view of evidence that the likelihood of divorce is greater in the early years of remarriage than over the same time in first marriages (see Cherlin, 1992), when some couples in the sample have been married previously.

Recruiting couples shortly after their marriage is a first step to solving these problems, because most couples will be maritally satisfied and at a similar stage of marriage. Further steps can be taken to screen out newlywed couples who are maritally distressed or who have been married previously.

Although the resulting increase in sample homogeneity has other important ramifications (e.g., spouses still can vary widely in age; couples can vary in whether or not they gave birth to or conceived a child premaritally), it would seem that these problems are outweighed by the benefits and that in any case this type of sample would permit stronger inferences about marital change than samples of couples varying widely in marital duration. In view of the evidence that the likelihood of divorce is highest in the first few years of marriage (National Center for Health Statistics, 1990), perhaps the most important reason for conducting longitudinal research with young, satisfied newlywed couples is that their data will be of greatest relevance to preventing declines in satisfaction through this period of high risk.

The Effects of Different Sampling Procedures. Once the decision to study newlywed couples has been made, does the manner in which they are recruited affect the final samples that are obtained? Because there has been surprisingly little attention to sampling issues in the marital literature (Kitson et al., 1982), we conducted a study to address this question by recruiting 60 couples from newspaper advertisements and 60 couples from public records (Karney et al., 1995). In both samples, couples were eligible to participate if this was the first marriage for both spouses, neither spouse had children, both spouses were 18 or older and wives were 35 or younger (so that all couples might undergo the transition to parenthood), both spouses spoke English and had received at least a 10th-grade education, and the couple had no immediate plans to move from the area.

In the first set of analyses, spouses recruited with the two methods were compared on demographic measures, premarital experiences, personality variables, and marital quality. These comparisons indicated that couples recruited with newspaper advertisements were at greater risk for marital dysfunction than couples recruited through public records. Effect size r values computed to quantify the magnitude of the between-group effects demonstrated, for example, that spouses in the newspaper sample were younger ($r = .25$ for wives; .23 for husbands), had lower incomes ($r = .24$ for wives; .25 for husbands), were more likely to have cohabited premaritally ($r = .32$ for wives; .38 for husbands), were less likely to have received premarital counseling ($r = .40$ for wives; .37 for husbands), reported more symptoms of depression ($r = .24$ for wives; .32 for husbands), had higher neuroticism scores ($r = .28$ for wives; .22 for husbands), and were less maritally satisfied (modal $r = .32$ for wives; .24 for husbands). In sum, across a variety of measures there were consistent differences between the two sampling methods, which we interpret as suggesting that some of the couples responding to newspaper advertisements may have been seeking some guidance or experience that would enable them to strengthen their marriage.

These results indicate that there are mean differences between the samples recruited with different sampling methods. A second set of analyses was conducted to determine whether the relationships among variables differed across the two methods. To do this we computed the 55 nonredundant correlations that were possible for husbands and for wives in each of the samples, and we determined the proportion of correlations that were statistically significant in one sample, both samples, and in neither sample. For husbands, the two methods yielded different results in 20% of the correlations. For wives, the two methods yielded different results in 27% of the correlations. Although the direct relevance of these data to longitudinal associations is limited, they nonetheless suggest that different methods of sampling married couples may affect inferences about relationships between variables about one time in four. Thus, studies recruiting subjects in different ways may not be directly comparable, and replication across sampling methods is very important.

Finally, in a third set of analyses we compared the 637 couples in the public records data base who responded to an invitation to participate in a longitudinal study with the 2,928 couples in the data base who did not respond to our invitation; the dependent measures were the variables available on the marriage licenses for all couples. These comparisons indicated, for example, that responding couples had more years of education (effect size $r = .29$ for wives; .18 for husbands) and higher occupational status ($r = .18$ for wives; .20 for husbands) than the couples that did not respond. Responding couples were more likely to have cohabited premaritally ($r = .11$), responding husbands were more likely to be students ($r = .13$), and responding wives were less likely to be housewives ($r = .12$). Overall, then, responding couples appeared to be less traditional and of a higher status than those not responding. These data are important because, in addition to demonstrating the value of using public records to quantify the magnitude of any response bias that might be observed, they show that response biases can arise even when the entire population of interest is given the opportunity to participate in a longitudinal study. They also show that the effects of self-selection are generally of a smaller magnitude than the effects that arise when comparing samples obtained using public records versus newspaper advertisements.

Clarifying the Dependent Variable

Limitations of Two-Wave Designs. Analysis of the dependent variable in cross-sectional research is usually straightforward: assess marital satisfaction with a standard instrument and correlate scores on this instrument with other variables of interest. In contrast, in a typical longitudinal study, marital satisfaction is assessed twice, and the investigator is confronted with the question of how to extract change from these assessments. Should we predict Time 2 satisfaction from the Time 1 variable of interest, after controlling for Time 1 satisfaction (e.g., Fincham & Bradbury, 1993)? If so, should Time 1 satisfaction be partialled from the Time 1 variable of interest (i.e., a semipartial correlation), or should Time 1 satisfaction be partialled from the Time 1 variable and from Time 2 satisfaction (i.e., a partial correlation)? Should we compute difference scores by subtracting Time 1 satisfaction from Time 2 satisfaction and then predict these scores from the Time 1 variable of interest (e.g., Gottman & Krokoff, 1989)? Or should we compute difference scores and then predict these scores from the Time 1 variable of interest only after partialling Time 1 satisfaction (e.g., Levenson & Gottman, 1985)?

It is essential to determine how to study change under these conditions because most longitudinal studies are two-wave designs or are at least analyzed as such; an evaluation of the methods used to assess change in these studies can clarify how much weight we can assign to them when designing future studies. Furthermore, future studies probably will use this design, and, as is evident from the few examples cited earlier, there is surprising diversity among the approaches that can be taken to estimate the association between a theoretically relevant variable at Time 1 and change in marital satisfaction from Time 1 to Time 2. Prompted to a large degree by the counterintuitive findings of Gottman and Krokoff (1989) – for example, wives' positive verbal behavior was found to covary directly with their marital satisfaction concurrently but inversely with their longitudinal change in satisfaction – there has been extensive discussion in the marital literature on how to interpret longitudinal findings of this sort and on the optimal methods for assessing change with two waves of data (e.g., Gottman & Krokoff, 1990; Jacobson, 1990; Smith, Vivian, & O'Leary, 1991; Weiss & Heyman, 1990).

Although this discussion has proven useful in several respects, the best solution to the problem of how to analyze two waves of data may be to redefine the problem in terms of the broader goals of longitudinal research on marriage. Two factors motivate such a redefinition. First, whereas the merits of the different approaches have been argued (e.g., Gottman & Krokoff,

1990, favor difference scores but maintain that the methods should yield similar findings; Woody & Costanzo, 1990, favor residualized change scores but note that other methods could produce paradoxical reversals in the direction of associations), there is now evidence that all such methods yield similar findings and that they are adequate only under unusual conditions.

Specifically, in a simulation study, Bradbury and Karney (1995) manipulated the population values representing the three possible associations among Time 1 satisfaction, a Time 1 variable of theoretical interest, and Time 2 satisfaction. Each of the three associations was allowed to take one of three values, yielding 27 possible population configurations. Within the constraints of these parameters, 100 random data sets of 180 subjects each were defined for each of the 27 possible configurations. A difference score was computed for each subject in each data set. Each of the 2,700 data sets was analyzed using the difference score method, the partial correlation method, and the semipartial correlation method, and the results of these analyses were then compared across the manipulated conditions.

These comparisons showed that all three methods of analysis yielded the same basic findings. The three methods were most accurate in reproducing the population value representing the association between the Time 1 variable of interest and Time 2 Satisfaction (i.e., the path of greatest theoretical interest) when the stability of marital satisfaction was low, and when the cross-sectional correlation between the variable of interest and marital satisfaction was low. In most research in this area, both of these associations tend to be *high;* our results show that these conditions produce unambiguous inverses in estimates of the path of greatest interest (particularly when the population value of this path is low), which is what attracted attention to this problem initially (see Woody & Costanzo, 1990). In short, Gottman and Krokoff (1990) appear to be correct in asserting that the different approaches to assessing change tend to yield equivalent results, and Woody and Costanzo (1990) appear to be correct in asserting that some of these methods can be expected to yield paradoxical inverse findings. This study extends these arguments by demonstrating the pervasive tendency of the most commonly used methods to provide inaccurate estimates of the association between the Time 1 variable of interest and Time 2 marital satisfaction.

Two solutions to this problem are evident. First, these analyses indicate that any of the three methods can be used when the stability of marital satisfaction is low (e.g., when marriages are followed over long time periods) and, more important, when the Time 1 variable of interest has a weak association with marital satisfaction cross-sectionally. However, because most longitudinal research in this area fails to satisfy these criteria (and, in fact, longitudinal studies are often undertaken only after cross-sectional associations between the variable of interest and marital satisfaction are demonstrated to be strong), this is unlikely to be a practical solution. A second solution would be to collect Time 1 data from subjects who are highly homogeneous in their level of marital satisfaction (e.g., very satisfied newlywed spouses), so that there is little need to control for Time 1 satisfaction differences when predicting satisfaction at later intervals. This solution is more promising than the first, yet it is also limited because a sample of uniformly satisfied couples might be expensive to obtain and might not be representative of the larger population of newlyweds.

Of far greater importance, however, is the fact that two waves of data, collected across any interval in any sample, can provide very little information about marital change (see Rogosa, Brant, & Zimowski, 1982). Although we recognize that there may be conditions and questions for which two-wave designs are appropriate, use of these designs is unlikely to be optimal or advantageous. The inadequacy of two-wave designs is the second factor that, in our opinion, motivates the need to redefine the nature of the dependent variable in longitudinal research on marriage.

Defining Marital Change in Terms of Trajectories. We propose that the trajectories defined by multiwave assessments of marital satisfaction can serve as a valuable starting point for this task. Data collected in this manner can reveal the diverse trajectories that spouses follow in their marriage and can suggest an alternate view of one of the key variables we are trying to explain in longitudinal research on marriage. For example, the data shown in Figure 9.3 are the MAT scores reported by six spouses over the first five assessment intervals in one of our ongoing studies of marriage; these spouses were within 6 months of their wedding at Time 1, and they provided MAT data at approximately 6-month intervals. As a rough index, MAT scores above 100 can be interpreted as being in the maritally satisfied range, whereas scores below 100 can be considered in the maritally distressed range.

This figure illustrates that the developmental course of marriage can involve, for example, an initially high level of satisfaction that remains high over time (spouse 1; see numbers on the right-hand side of Figure 9.3), an initially high level of satisfaction that deteriorates gradually but remains well within the satisfied range of functioning (spouse 2), a moderately high level of satisfaction early in marriage, followed by a marked onset of dissatisfaction and then a gradual increase in satisfaction but still within the

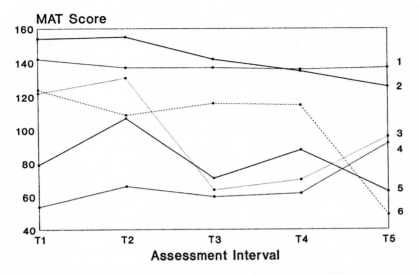

Figure 9.3. Marital Adjustment Test (MAT) scores of six spouses over five 6-month assessment intervals. Spouse numbers are shown on the right side.

distressed range of functioning (spouse 3), a very low level of marital satisfaction that remains stable but then shows a modest increase within the distressed range (spouse 4), a moderately low level of satisfaction followed by a rise into the nondistressed range and then upward and downward fluctuations in the distressed range (spouse 5), and, finally, a moderately high level of satisfaction that persists over three intervals before dropping sharply into the distressed range (spouse 6).

The trajectories shown in Figure 9.3, which are derived from only 5% of the sample, are not necessarily representative of all such trajectories. Instead they are intended to illustrate the richness and complexity of the developmental course of marriage and marital dysfunction. Viewing marriage from this perspective has a number of noteworthy implications. First, a great deal of information can be lost when the longitudinal course of marriage is reduced to two data points. For example, spouse 3 shows increases in satisfaction from Time 3 to Time 4 and from Time 4 to Time 5, but if this trajectory were reduced to two time points – Time 1 and Time 5 – it would appear to be a modest decline into the distressed range. Second, a great deal of information is concealed when sample means are used to represent satisfaction data for any assessment interval. The means across-assessment intervals in Figure 9.3, for example, are 112.5, 117.5, 98.3, 101, and 93.8, thus suggesting only a modest mean change in satisfaction over the 2-year period.

Means of this sort can be very informative, certainly, but it is important to recognize that they often are rather poor approximations of actual marriages.

Third, at the risk of stating the obvious, longer follow-up periods are to be preferred over shorter ones. For example, the marital satisfaction reported by spouses 3 and 4 increases by about 30 points between Time 4 and Time 5, which would seem to alter dramatically the impression we would form of their marriages on the basis of data collected from Time 1 to Time 4. Indeed, data collected at Time 6 or Time 7 could change how we view the six spouses shown in Figure 9.3. Fourth, describing trajectories can suggest hypotheses about how marriages fail. For example, whether an exclusively behavioral model could account for the trajectory shown for spouse 6 is arguable. In view of the relatively stable level of satisfaction reported from Time 1 to Time 4, it seems unlikely that the precipitous decline in satisfaction between Time 4 and Time 5 is due solely to the behaviors that spouses exchange; instead this decline suggests the possibility that some highly stressful event (e.g., a serious illness, loss of a job, an extramarital affair) has occurred to overwhelm this couple's otherwise adequate adaptive processes.

Representing the longitudinal course of marriage in this way brings us back to the question of how best to assess change. Although the optimal method for assessing change may vary widely, depending on the particular hypothesis being studied, there is increasing interest in the use of growth-curve analysis for this purpose. Presentation of this method is beyond the scope of this chapter (for general introductions, see Bryk & Raudenbush, 1992, and Willett, 1988; for overviews of this method applied to marriage, see Karney & Bradbury, 1995b, and Raudenbush, Brennan, & Barnett, 1995; for empirical examples in the marital and family domain see Belsky & Rovine, 1990, Karney & Bradbury, 1977, and Kurdek, 1995), but here it would involve (a) specifying some linear or nonlinear model of change in marital satisfaction, (b) estimating the parameters that describe the line formed by the five waves of data (i.e., the slope, the Y-intercept, the error), (c) evaluating these parameter estimates in various ways (e.g., describing their variability, assessing their reliability, examining their intercorrelations), and (d) treating these estimated individual parameters as dependent variables and, accordingly, relating them to other variables of theoretical interest.

One of the advantages of this approach is that it uses all waves of marital data simultaneously to create the dependent variable, rather than just two waves. This leads to a more precise method for characterizing the longitudinal course of a marriage, and it leads to the recognition that trajectories can have high intercepts with low error and either flat or negative slopes (spouse 1 and 2, respectively), high intercepts with negative slopes and high error (spouse 3), low intercepts with relatively flat slopes and high error (spouse 5), and so on. More generally, the point is that the parameters can combine in different ways when they are used to capture the longitudinal course of marital satisfaction.

A second advantage is that this method permits tests of relatively specific hypotheses about marital change. For example, an independent variable such as neuroticism or maladaptive attributions or negative reciprocity assessed at Time 1 can be examined in terms of whether it is associated with the initial level of satisfaction in the marriage (i.e., the Y-intercept), or with the rate at which satisfaction changes (i.e., the slope), or with some combination of these parameters. Although the method is not without limitations (e.g., it was developed to model individual change rather than dyadic change; it is designed for continuous dependent processes and thus may not be adequate for categorical outcomes such as divorce; it must be used cautiously when the independent variable is changing substantially less than the outcome of interest; for further discussion, see Karney & Bradbury, 1995b), it holds great promise as an analytic tool that can help illuminate the longitudinal course of marriage.

Summary

Several significant methodological challenges must be recognized and resolved before the inferential benefits of longitudinal research on marriage can be reaped. In this section we discussed problems that arise when collecting data from couples who vary widely in marital duration, and we emphasized that different procedures used to recruit newlywed couples can affect the samples and data that are obtained. We also discussed a simulation study that demonstrates the serious limitations of common approaches to analyzing two-wave longitudinal designs, and, in an effort to identify a better alternative, we outlined the merits of studying the trajectories that spouses follow over the early years of their marriage. The topics addressed in this section are no more important than the myriad topics that were not examined, such as contending with attrition, determining when data collection should start in longitudinal studies of marriage, judging the frequency with which marriages should be assessed in longitudinal designs, and specifying how the continuous variable of satisfaction can be examined at the same time as the categorical variables of separation and divorce. Nonetheless, this discussion demonstrates that developmental research on marriage involves far more than adding a longitudinal component to cross-sectional designs and that data can help resolve important methodological problems that arise when such research is undertaken.

Conclusion

Three prerequisites for advancing our understanding of the longitudinal course of marriage should be evident from this chapter. First, conceptual frameworks are likely to prove most useful to the extent that interpersonal behavior is assigned a central but not exclusive role in determining marital outcomes. Whereas social learning models of marriage have emphasized marital behavior in this regard, particularly behavior during problem-solving discussions, this focus arose largely for the purpose of designing clinical interventions, and it is probably incapable of fully explaining how marriages succeed and fail. To address this problem, we presented a model of marital outcomes that adopts a broader view of the behavioral domains relevant to marriage and that acknowledges how the course of marriage can be affected by the enduring personal characteristics that spouses bring to marriage and the stressful events and circumstances that couples encounter.

Second, the significance of future studies will depend to a large degree on the nature of our samples and the way we obtain them. Samples consisting of couples who vary widely in marital duration pose a number of interpretive problems, and a variety of benefits accrue from the study of newlywed marriage. We outlined one such benefit – the ability to use public records for sample recruitment, which permits quantification of sample bias – and we noted that couples recruited in this manner differ systematically from those recruited via media advertisements.

Third, progress in explaining the longitudinal course of marriage will be facilitated by data that describe the longitudinal course of marriage and by analytic methods that extract information about change from these data. Two waves of data are inadequate for clarifying the developmental course of marriage, and common methods for assessing change with two waves of data often produce misleading results. Multiwave assessments are necessary for measuring the dependent variable in longitudinal studies of marriage, and growth-curve modeling shows promise for analyzing data collected in this manner.

Fourth, the quality of efforts to prevent marital dysfunction depends on our understanding of the longitudinal course of marriage. Although applied issues were not the major focus of our analysis, we adopted the view that an emphasis on interpersonal behavior in marriage will direct attention toward the content of prevention programs, whereas consideration of elements of marriage that cannot be changed and that are related to long-term outcomes (such as certain personality traits, age at marriage, education level, and so forth) can direct attention toward the at-risk couples who are most in need of early intervention. Explanations for how marriages succeed and fail certainly can be put forth without concern for their applied value, but the social costs of marital dysfunction add to the urgency of conducting conceptually clear, methodologically rigorous research that will help solve this problem.

References

Alexander, J. F., Holtzworth-Munroe, A., & Jameson, P. (1994). The process and outcome of marital and family therapy: Research review and evaluation. In A. E. Bergin & S. L. Garfield (Eds.), *Handbook of psychotherapy and behavior change* (pp. 595–630). New York: Wiley.

Amato, P. R., & Keith, B. (1991). Parental divorce and adult well-being: A meta-analysis. *Journal of Marriage and the Family, 53,* 43–58.

Baucom, D. H., & Epstein, N. (1990). *Cognitive-behavioral marital therapy.* New York: Brunner/Mazel.

Belsky, J., & Rovine, M. (1990). Patterns of marital change across the transition to parenthood: Pregnancy to three years postpartum. *Journal of Marriage and the Family, 52,* 5–19.

Bolger, N., DeLongis, A., Kessler, R. C., & Wethington, E. (1989). The contagion of stress across multiple roles. *Journal of Marriage and the Family, 51,* 175–183.

Bradbury, T. N., Campbell, S. M., & Fincham, F. D. (1995). Longitudinal and behavioral analysis of sex role identity in marriage. *Journal of Personality and Social Psychology, 68,* 328–341.

Bradbury, T. N., & Fincham, F. D. (1987). Affect and cognition in close relationships: Towards an integrative model. *Cognition and Emotion, 1,* 59–87.

Bradbury, T. N., & Fincham, F. D. (1990a). Attributions in marriage: Review and critique. *Psychological Bulletin, 107,* 3–33.

Bradbury, T. N., & Fincham, F. D. (1990b). Preventing marital dysfunction: Review and analysis. In F. D. Fincham & T. N. Bradbury (Eds.), *The psychology of marriage: Basic issues and applications* (pp. 375–401). New York: Guilford.

Bradbury, T. N., & Fincham, F. D. (1991). A contextual model for advancing the study of marital interaction. In G. J. O. Fletcher & F. D. Fincham (Eds.), *Cognition in close relationships* (pp. 127–147). Hillsdale, NJ: Erlbaum.

Bradbury, T. N., & Karney, B. R. (1993). Longitudinal studies of marital interaction and dysfunction: Review and analysis. *Clinical Psychology Review, 13,* 15–27.

Bradbury, T. N., & Karney, B. R. (1995). *Assessing longitudinal effects in marital research: A simulation study comparing three approaches.* Unpublished manuscript.

Bryk, A. S., & Raudenbush, S. W. (1992). *Hierarchical linear models: Applications and data analysis methods.* Newbury Park, CA: Sage.

Caspi, A., Bem, D. J., & Elder, G. H. (1989). Continuities and consequences of interactional styles across the life course. *Journal of Personality, 57,* 376–406.

Cherlin, A. J. (1992). *Marriage, divorce, remarriage* (rev. ed.). Cambridge, MA: Harvard University Press.

Cohan, C. L., & Bradbury, T. N. (1997). Negative life events, marital interaction, and the longitudinal course of newlywed marriage. *Journal of Personality and Social Psychology, 73,* 114–128.

Conger, R. D., Elder, G. H., Lorenz, F. O., Conger, K. J., Simons, R. L., Whitbeck, L. B., Huck, S., & Melby, J. N. (1990). Linking economic hardship to marital quality and instability. *Journal of Marriage and the Family, 52,* 643–656.

Cutrona, C. E., & Suhr, J. A. (1994). Social support communication in the context of marriage: An analysis of couples' supportive interactions. In B. Burleson, T. Albrecht, & I. Sarason (Eds.), *The communication of social support: Messages, interactions, and community* (pp. 113–135). Thousand Oaks, CA: Sage.

Filsinger, E. E., & Thoma, S. J. (1988). Behavioral antecedents of relationship stability and adjustment: A five-year longitudinal study. *Journal of Marriage and the Family, 50,* 785–795.

Fincham, F. D., & Bradbury, T. N. (1993). Marital satisfaction, depression, and attributions: A longitudinal analysis. *Journal of Personality and Social Psychology, 64,* 442–452.

Franz, C. E., McClelland, D. C., & Weinberger, J. (1991). Childhood antecedents of conventional social accomplishment in midlife adults: A 36-year prospective study. *Journal of Personality and Social Psychology, 60,* 586–595.

Frederickson, C. G. (1977). Life stress and marital conflict: A pilot study. *Journal of Marriage and Family Counseling, 3,* 41–47.

Glenn, N. D. (1990). Quantitative research on marital quality in the 1980s: A critical review. *Journal of Marriage and the Family, 52,* 818–831.

Gottman, J. M. (1994). *What predicts divorce?* Hillsdale, NJ: Erlbaum.

Gottman, J. M., & Krokoff, L. J. (1989). Marital interaction and satisfaction: A longitudinal view. *Journal of Consulting and Clinical Psychology, 57,* 47–52.

Gottman, J. M., & Krokoff, L. J. (1990). Complex statistics are not always clearer than simple statistics: A reply to Woody and Costanzo. *Journal of Consulting and Clinical Psychology, 58,* 502–505.

Gottman, J. M., & Levenson, R. W. (1992). Marital processes predictive of later dissolution: Behavior, physiology, and health. *Journal of Personality and Social Psychology, 63,* 221–233.

Greenstein, T. N. (1990). Marital disruption and the employment of married women. *Journal of Marriage and the Family, 52,* 657–676.

Griffin, W. A. (1993). Transitions from negative affect during marital interaction: Husband and wife differences. *Journal of Family Psychology, 6,* 230–244.

Hahlweg, K., Baucom, D. H., & Markman, H. J. (1988). Recent advances in therapy and prevention. In I. R. H. Faloon (Ed.), *Handbook of behavioral family therapy* (pp. 413–448). New York: Guilford.

Hinde, R. A. (1995). A suggested structure for a science of relationships. *Personal Relationships, 2,* 1–15.

Jacobson, N. S. (1990). Contributions from psychology to an understanding of marriage. In F. D. Fincham & T. N. Bradbury (Eds.), *The psychology of marriage: Basic issues and applications* (pp. 258–275). New York: Guilford.

Jacobson, N. S., & Margolin, G. (1979). *Marital therapy: Strategies based on social learning and behavior exchange principles.* New York: Brunner/Mazel.

Jacobson, N. S., Schmaling, K. B., & Holtzworth-Munroe, A. (1987). Component analysis of behavioral marital therapy: 2-year follow-up and prediction of relapse. *Journal of Marriage and Family Therapy, 13,* 187–195.

Jacobson, N. S., & Weiss, R. L. (1978). Behavior marriage therapy: III. The contents of Gurman et al. may be hazardous to our health. *Family Process, 17,* 149–163.

Karney, B. R., & Bradbury, T. N. (1995a). The longitudinal course of marital quality and stability: A review of theory, method, and research. *Psychological Bulletin, 118,* 3–34.

Karney, B. R., & Bradbury, T. N. (1995b). Assessing longitudinal change in marriage: An introduction to the analysis of growth curves. *Journal of Marriage and the Family, 57,* 1091–1108.

Karney, B. R., & Bradbury, T. N. (1997). Neuroticism, marital interaction, and the trajectory of marital satisfaction. *Journal of Personality and Social Psychology, 72,* 1075–1092.

Karney, B. R., Davila, J., Cohan, C. L., Sullivan, K. T., Johnson, M. D., & Bradbury, T. N. (1995). An empirical investigation of sampling strategies in marital research. *Journal of Marriage and the Family, 57,* 909–920.

Kelly, E. L., & Conley, J. J. (1987). Personality and compatibility: A prospective analysis of marital stability and marital satisfaction. *Journal of Personality and Social Psychology, 52,* 27–40.

Kitson, G. C., Sussman, M. B., Williams, G. K., Zeehandelaar, R. B., Shickmanter, B. K., & Steinberger, J. L. (1982). Sampling issues in family research. *Journal of Marriage and the Family, 44,* 965–981.

Koerner, K., & Jacobson, N. S. (1994). Emotion and behavioral couple therapy. In S. M. Johnson & L. S. Greenberg (Eds.), *The heart of the matter: Perspectives on emotion in marital therapy* (pp. 207–226). New York: Brunner/Mazel.

Krokoff, L. J., Gottman, J. M., & Roy, A. K. (1988). Blue-collar and white-collar marital interaction and communication orientation. *Journal of Social and Personal Relationships, 5,* 201–221.

Kurdek, L. A. (1995). Predicting change in marital dissatisfaction from husbands' and wives' conflict resolution styles. *Journal of Marriage and the Family, 57,* 153–164.

Levenson, R. W., & Gottman, J. M. (1983). Marital interaction: Physiological linkage and affective exchange. *Journal of Personality and Social Psychology, 45,* 587–597.

Levenson, R. W., & Gottman, J. M. (1985). Physiological and affective predictors of change in relationship satisfaction. *Journal of Personality and Social Psychology, 49,* 85–94.

Locke, H. J., & Wallace, K. (1959). Short marital-adjustment and prediction tests: Their reliability and validity. *Marriage and Family Living, 21,* 251–255.

McGonagle, K. A., Kessler, R. C., & Schilling, E. A. (1992). The frequency and determinants of marital disagreements in a community sample. *Journal of Social and Personal Relationships, 9,* 507–524.

Marco, C. A., & Suls, J. (1993). Daily stress and the trajectory of mood: Spillover, response assimilation contrast, and chronic negative affectivity. *Journal of Personality and Social Psychology, 64,* 1053–1063.

Margolin, G. (1983). An interactional model for the assessment of marital relationships. *Behavioral Assessment, 5,* 103–127.

Markman, H. J., Floyd, F. J., Stanley, S. M., & Lewis, H. C. (1986). Prevention. In N. S. Jacobson & A. S. Gurman (Eds.), *Clinical handbook of marital therapy* (pp. 173–195). New York: Guilford.

Markman, H. J., Floyd, F. J., Stanley, S. M., & Storaasli, R. D. (1988). Prevention of marital distress: A longitudinal investigation. *Journal of Consulting and Clinical Psychology, 56,* 210–217.

Markman, H. J., & Hahlweg, K. (1993). The prediction and prevention of marital distress: An international perspective. *Clinical Psychology Review, 13,* 29–43.

Markman, H. J., Renick, M. J., Floyd, F. J., Stanley, S. M., & Clements, M. (1993). Preventing marital distress through communication and conflict management training: A 4- and 5-year follow-up. *Journal of Consulting and Clinical Psychology, 61,* 70–77.

Monroe, S. M., & Simons, A. D. (1991). Diathesis-stress theories in the context of life stress research: Implications for the depressive disorders. *Psychological Bulletin, 110,* 406–425.

National Center for Health Statistics (1990). Advance report of final divorce statistics, 1987. *Monthly vital statistics report* (Vol. 38, No. 12, Suppl. 2). Hyattsville, MD: Public Health Service.

O'Leary, K. D., & Turkewitz, H. (1978). Marital therapy from a behavioral perspective. In T. J. Paolino and B. S. McCrady (Eds.), *Marriage and marital therapy: Psychoanalytic, behavioral and systems theory perspectives* (pp. 240–297). New York: Brunner/Mazel.

Pasch, L. A., & Bradbury, T. N. (in press). Social support, conflict, and the development of marital dysfunction. *Journal of Consulting and Clinical Psychology.*

Poulton, R. G., & Andrews, G. (1992). Personality as a cause of adverse life events. *Acta Psychiatrica Scandanavica, 85,* 35–38.

Raudenbush, S. W., Brennan, R. T., & Barnett, R. C. (1995). A multivariate hierarchical model for studying psychological change within married couples. *Journal of Family Psychology, 9,* 161–174.

Repetti, R. L. (1989). Effects of daily workload on subsequent behavior during marital interaction: The roles of social withdrawal and spouse support. *Journal of Personality and Social Psychology, 57,* 651–659.

Robinson, E. A., & Jacobson, N. S. (1987). Social learning theory and family psychopathology: A Kantian model in behaviorism? In T. Jacob (Ed.), *Family interaction and psychopathology* (pp. 117–162). New York: Plenum.

Rogosa, D., Brant, D., & Zimowski, M. (1982). A slow growth curve approach to the measurement of change. *Psychological Bulletin, 92,* 726–748.

Smith, D. A., Vivian, D., & O'Leary, K. D. (1990). Longitudinal prediction of marital discord from premarital expressions of affect. *Journal of Consulting and Clinical Psychology, 58,* 790–798.

Smith, D. A., Vivian, D., & O'Leary, K. D. (1991). The misnomer proposition: A critical reappraisal of the longitudinal status of "negativity" in marital communication. *Behavioral Assessment, 13,* 7–24.

Stuart, R. B. (1969). Operant interpersonal treatment for marital discord. *Journal of Consulting and Clinical Psychology, 33,* 675–682.

Sullivan, K. T., & Bradbury, T. N. (1997). Are premarital prevention programs reaching couples at risk for marital dysfunction? *Journal of Consulting and Clinical Psychology, 65,* 24–30.

Watson, D., & Clark, L. A. (1984). Negative affectivity: The disposition to experience aversive emotional states. *Psychological Bulletin, 96,* 465–490.

Weiss, R. L. (1978). The conceptualization of marriage from a behavioral perspective. In T. J. Paolino and B. S. McCrady (Eds.), *Marriage and marital therapy: Psychoanalytic, behavioral and systems theory perspectives* (pp. 165–239). New York: Brunner/Mazel.

Weiss, R. L., & Heyman, R. E. (1990). Observation of marital interaction. In F. D. Fincham & T. N. Bradbury (Eds.), *The psychology of marriage* (pp. 87–117). New York: Guilford.

Whiffen, V. E., & Gotlib, I. H. (1989). Stress and coping in maritally distressed and nondistressed couples. *Journal of Social and Personal Relationships, 6,* 327–344.

Willett, J. B. (1988). Questions and answers in the measurement of change. In E. Z. Rothkopf (Ed.), *Review of research in education* (Vol. 15, pp. 345–422). Washington, DC: American Educational Research Association.

Woody, E. Z., & Costanzo, P. R. (1990). Does marital agony precede marital ecstasy? A comment on Gottman and Krokoff's "Marital interaction and satisfaction: A longitudinal view." *Journal of Consulting and Clinical Psychology, 58,* 499–501.

Zubin, J., & Spring, B. (1977). Vulnerability – A new view of schizophrenia. *Journal of Abnormal Psychology, 86,* 103–126.

10 Socialization into Marital Roles: Testing a Contextual, Developmental Model of Marital Functioning

Irv Tallman, Peter J. Burke, and Viktor Gecas

Theory and research in marital and family relations have produced notable advances in recent years. It is now possible to identify with considerable accuracy patterns of couple interaction that lead to emotional distress, marital unhappiness, and divorce (Bradbury & Karney, 1993; Gottman, 1990; Larsen & Olson, 1989). There is also a growing body of knowledge about the conditions under which families and their members either withstand or collapse under the onslaught of externally and/or internally induced stressors (Conger et al., 1990, 1992; Elder, 1974; Elder, Liker, and Cross, 1984).

These accomplishments seem all the more remarkable considering the rapid changes that are occurring in family life in the United States and throughout the world. Fundamental to these changes is the increasing proportion of married women in the labor force (Bielby, 1992). As women seek and obtain expanded opportunities and greater choices in education and jobs, it is inevitable that their roles as wives and mothers must change. For the majority of American families, traditional family roles and behavioral patterns are becoming anachronistic (cf. Gerson, 1985; Turner, 1990). As a result, established norms governing the intrafamily division of labor, the allocation of resources, and the distribution of authority among family members are being challenged and reassessed. New norms are probably being developed but, in the process, men and women are confronted with novel and varied choices – with very little experience to assist them in making these choices. The result is a growing diversity of family forms and structures (Tepperman & Wilson, 1993).

Ironically, this period of change and uncertainty may have contributed indirectly to the breakthroughs in our knowledge about marital relationships. New family forms and behavioral patterns upset the established order, contributing to social discord among a large segment of the population. The increase in cohabitation as a precursor to or a substitute for marriage, the high rate of divorce, the growing acceptance of serial marriages, the decline in marriage rates, and the increased visibility of wife and child

312

abuse have aroused public interest and concern about what is happening to the family. Thus the shroud of secrecy that traditionally surrounded marriage and family life and insulated it from the prying eyes of researchers is gradually being lifted.

Family scholars have taken good advantage of this window of opportunity. The types of affect, attributions, attitudes, physiological responses, and behavioral interaction patterns leading to marital unhappiness and divorce have been identified with increasing precision and reliability. The result is that patterns of marital interaction that lead to divorce can be predicted with a level of accuracy never before attained (Buehlman, Gottman, & Katz, 1992; Gottman, 1990; Larsen & Olson, 1989). Perhaps even more important, some of these studies may have tapped basic behavioral processes that are sufficiently generalizable to transcend a specific time, place, or culture. There are patterns of emotional withdrawal, combined with negative evaluations of the partner and ineffective or "chaotic" communication that may predict the dissolution of long-standing intimate relationships regardless of how and when they occur. There is also a large and growing body of research that demonstrates how aversive interactions produce negative emotional arousal, which, in turn, generates defensive, "hypervigilant," regressive, rigid, and, consequently, maladaptive responses (e.g., Gottman, 1979; Gottman & Levenson, 1988; Patterson, 1982). It seems feasible that the processes of spiraling disaffection, anger, and withdrawal identified by these researchers would inhibit the efficient functioning of any human interactive system.

Like many breakthroughs, these findings seem intuitively apparent once they are revealed. Given this knowledge, the inevitable question becomes how do couples get themselves into this state of affairs? To explore this question, we must broaden the scope of our investigation. We want to know what conditions increase the chances that a marital relationship will evolve into the morass of negative feelings, frustration, and ineffective communications that predict so well marital unhappiness and dissolution. Conversely, we must ask whether it is possible to identify unique conditions, not necessarily the obverse of those leading to conflict and distress, that assist couples in maintaining positive relationships.

In this chapter we describe a research program that seeks to address these questions. The research is designed to investigate the processes through which couples are socialized into marital roles and the influence of these socialization processes on the quality of the couple relationship as well as on the mental and physical health of each spouse. Couple interaction patterns are considered an integral, but not the only, part of this socialization process. In the following section we provide a brief overview of the project and the model we are testing. We then discuss the theoretical and empirical work that has led us to include various elements in the model. This will be followed by a more complete explication of the model that drives this research. We conclude with the presentation of some relevant preliminary findings.

Overview

We are in the initial stages of a 5-year, three-wave, panel study of newly-wed couples. Our study sample consists of 313 couples who have not been married previously. The sample was drawn from a pool of randomly selected marriage license applications in two middle-size metropolitan communities in the state of Washington. Fifty-nine percent of the eligible couples contacted agreed to participate in the study.

In each of the three waves, husbands and wives were interviewed separately. Subsequently, couples were asked to fill out a daily diary for four weeks. When the diaries were completed, they came to a university facility located in their city where, after a brief interview, they participated in a videotaped discussion focused on resolving some of their major disagreements. The interval between the date of marriage and the initial interview ranged from 2 days to 3 months. The mean time between the wedding and this interview was 50 days.

We also drew two control samples. The first control group consisted of 55 couples selected in the same way as the study sample. These couples participated in a much briefer interview and will be contacted by telephone on a yearly basis to assess their marital stability and happiness. Fifty percent of the control couples contacted agreed to participate. The second control group of 25 couples will be contacted only at the end of the project to determine their current marital status. Both control groups are used to determine the possible confounding effects of the extensive interventions involved in this research (for a detailed discussion of such unintended biases, see Bradbury, 1994; and Veroff, Hatchett, & Douvan, 1992). The first control group allows us to match the couples on key variables and to assess the degree to which external events influence marital relationships. The second control group allows for a rudimentary assessment of the impact of even minimal intervention on the course of the marital relationship.

The research is designed to test a four-phase general process model depicted in Figure 10.1. Much of the remainder of the chapter is devoted to explicating this model and indicating how we go about testing its various

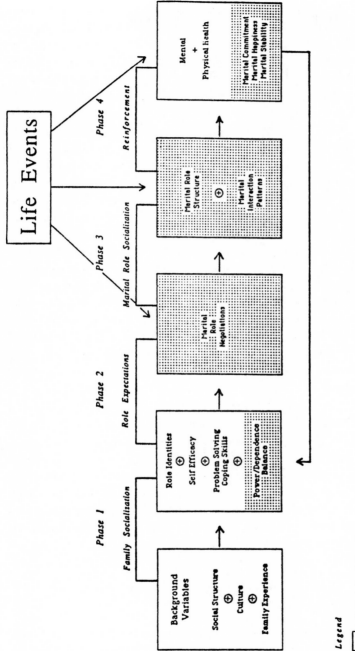

Figure 10.1. General causal process model depicting socialization into marital roles and key outcomes.

elements and predicted relationships. The model is designed to link four sequential phases in the development of couple relationships. The first phase, which we term family socialization, identifies the early experiences that influence the behavioral expectations spouses hold for themselves and their partners. These role expectations are thought to determine the nature of the couple's initial role negotiations (phase 2). In the process of these negotiations, we expect the couples' role expectations for one another to be further altered or modified. The outcome of these negotiations, in combination with external life events, determine the marital role structure (i.e., division of labor, distribution of resources, and authority patterns) and set the couple on particular patterns of interaction that are either effective or ineffective in dealing with their daily life events (phase 3). Phase 4 reinforces these patterns and links them with the individuals' mental and physical health and the state of the couples' marital relationships. The model also directs attention to the reciprocal, feedback, and crossed lagged influences that occur over the three waves of the study. For example, the indicators of marital quality and individual well-being designated as outcome variables are also considered potential influences on the behaviors and self-assessments depicted in phases 2, 3, and 4. As indicated in Figure 10.1 we anticipate that the individual spouse's mental and physical health as well as the couple's marital commitment and marital stability assessed during the first wave of the study will effect the partners' role expectations during the second wave. Changing role expectations, in turn, affect the role negotiation process and therefore the marital role structure and marital interaction patterns. All of this further modifies the individual partner's mental and physical health and the quality of the couple's marital relationship. Thus we envision an ongoing process, modifiable by early socialization and life events, in which marital role behaviors, individual mental and physical health characteristics, and the quality of the couples' relationship function as reciprocal influences. With this overview in mind, we turn now to an exposition of the theoretical and methodological perspectives that were used in developing the model.

Theoretical, Conceptual, and Methodological Principles Underlying the Model

The centrality of couple role negotiations in the model presented in Figure 10.1 highlights the importance of the sequential microanalysis of couple interactions in our research. The principles underlying such analyses derive in large part from social learning theory (Bandura, 1977; Gottman, 1979;

Patterson, 1982, 1984). An essential proposition of this theory holds that people internalize patterns of behavior that have been positively reinforced and avoid behaviors that have been costly or punishing.

This principle is an integral component of the conceptual framework guiding our research. We propose that virtually all behavior is based on choosing or deciding between alternative courses of action (including the choice of nonaction), and that such choices or decisions are based on the person's estimate of the chances that a given course of action will have rewarding or costly outcomes. We assume that such estimates occur as a result of prior learning in the same or similar situations. It follows that if we wish to explain why destructive (or positive) interaction patterns develop in some married couples and not in others, it will be useful to explore the prior (premarital) and current couple life experiences that relate to how the individual partners develop expectations about marital relationships. To investigate these life experiences, we need to introduce two additional ideas, each representing a different research and theoretical perspective. The first concerns the social and cultural *contexts* in which spouses' values and expectations are forged; the second the development and consequences of the key social roles and the role identities to which the partners are committed.

The Social and Cultural Contexts of Marital Relations

Too often, reference to "contexts" in marital or family research has implied simply setting parameters that are thought to constrain couple interaction and communication. We believe this conception is too limiting for two important reasons. First, it fails to recognize the processes of mutual influence by which couples and families affect and are affected by the larger culture and social structure. Second, it does not consider the numerous ways in which culture and social structure are manifest and modified in daily interactions and relationships.

The term *social* as used here is synonymous with social structure. *Social structure* is defined as a network of social relationships in which actors hold positions that determine the form and type of interaction they have with one another.[1] Such networks are usually characterized by an unequal distribution of valued resources across various positions and by unequal access between actors holding positions in the network. Thus an individual's or couple's position in the social structure can determine in large part the resources they control and their opportunities to obtain or transfer resources. Both are essential for people to achieve their life goals.

Culture refers here to the shared sets of meanings attached to material and nonmaterial symbols and objects in a given social system. Culture and social structure combine to establish the macrosystem in which couples function and thus play an important part in determining the kinds of problems they will face.

The available evidence suggests that the interplay between external events and intracouple or intrafamily relationships is intricate, often subtle, and virtually continuous. Studies of the effects of chronic and acute economic hardship on family relationships and family functioning illustrate the importance of external events and internal family resources in accounting for family resilience and effectiveness in crisis situations (Conger et al., 1990, 1992; Elder, 1974; Elder et al., 1984; Liker & Elder, 1983). Although no family, whatever its internal strengths, seems able to avoid completely the distress and disorganization produced by extreme economic hardship (Liker & Elder, 1983; for a review, see Menaghan, 1991), some are better able than others to reorganize themselves in the face of such onslaughts. The voluminous research literature on the mental health effects of social and economic crises has yielded evidence that families differ in their abilities to withstand externally induced stressful events (Angell, 1965; Elder, 1974; Garmezy, Musten, and Tellyen, 1984; Kelvin & Jarrett, 1985; Liker & Elder, 1983; Patterson, 1982).

Research by Conger and his colleagues (1990, 1992) on economically distressed farm families illustrates the corrosive effects of income loss. They identify a process of deteriorating marital relationships in which increased hostility by husbands erodes wives' marital satisfaction, increases marital conflict, and thus adversely affects marital quality. At the same time, there is evidence suggesting that certain precrisis personality characteristics such as the husband's irritability, explosiveness, and tenseness contribute to setting this process in motion (Caspi & Elder, 1988; Liem & Liem, 1990). Moreover, Elder and his colleagues have shown that these negative personality characteristics are transmitted from generation to generation (Caspi & Elder, 1988; Elder, Caspi, & Downey, 1986). It appears that the more chronic such conditions are, the greater their debilitating effect on family relationships. In general the data seem to suggest that those at the lower end of the socioeconomic ladder are least able to deal with new crises (Liem & Liem, 1978; McLeod & Shanahan, 1993; for a review, see Aneshensel, 1992).

The harsh reality is that married couples in the United States and elsewhere are not all provided with the resources or opportunities necessary to confront either their mundane day-to-day problems or catastrophic events (Pearlin, 1989). Some couples are bombarded constantly with external threats to their well-being, whereas others experience such threats only on rare occasions (Aneshensel, 1992).

Although economic hardship has received the most attention from researchers in recent years, it is not the only external problem that has been shown to have an aversive impact on couples and families. Wars and separation (Hill, 1949), illness and death, difficulties with the criminal justice and legal systems, problems at work (Bolger, DeLongis, Kessler, & Wethington, 1989), and "role overload" (Rosenfield, 1989) have all been found to produce family disorganization.

Marital partners who are currently experiencing or have a history of experiencing social and economic hardship tend to be under greater stress than those who live under more benign conditions. Such stress is likely to produce negative affect, which can impede the individual's ability to function effectively. Gottman and Levenson (1988) claim that negative affect releases stress-related hormones that interfere with cognitive functions. This, in turn, results in inflexible behavior patterns that impede effective problem solving. Given the data indicating that economic and social hardship increase stress, it is reasonable to infer that those people who grew up in, or are currently living under such conditions are more likely to display inflexible behaviors. Thus couples with low socioeconomic status should be more likely than those who are better off to exhibit coercive, chaotic, and, eventually rigid, negative, and uncooperative interaction patterns. Such patterns, in turn, should lead to greater couple hostility and psychological withdrawal resulting in marital unhappiness and dissolution.[2]

Clearly not all distressed couples suffer from economic and social hardships. Moreover, such hardships are not the primary source of marital distress for many couples. The failure of partners to meet each other's expectations (or their expectations for themselves), value conflicts, developing disagreements about life styles, jealousies, and extramarital demands all are potential contributors to marital discord.

It is also possible for marital difficulties to create conditions that contribute to economic hardship or social isolation. For example, marital conflict may increase depression and anxiety in an individual, which may then be manifest in poor job performance or community conflicts, thus producing problems for the couple in the external world (for evidence of such "spillover" effects, see Bolger et al., 1989). The most accurate depiction of the impact of external and internal factors on marital relationships would be to consider them so tightly interwoven in the daily fabric of the marital relationship as to require meticulous care in unraveling the causal sequences (Bolger et al., 1989).

Marital Roles and Role Identity

The literature on marital roles and stress often contains an implicit (and sometimes explicit) assumption that variability in emotional responses to the demands of various roles is best explained by the meaning of the roles for peoples' self-concepts (Thoits, 1983, 1986; Kessler & McLeod, 1984; Kessler & McRae, 1982). Thoits, in particular, has stressed the utility of "role identities" for understanding the emotional responses of husbands and wives to a variety of roles. She has used the concept to clarify ambiguous findings about the contribution of multiple roles to psychological well-being for husbands and wives.

Role identities represent the cognitive and emotional meanings an individual attaches to a given social role and the application of such meanings to his/her self-concept (Burke, 1980; Burke & Reitzes, 1981; McCall & Simmons, 1978; Stryker, 1980). Role identities are structured hierarchically by their salience or importance (Stryker & Serpe, 1982; Thoits, 1983). It follows that if a spouse places greater value on the marital role and less value on occupational, friendship, or filial roles, then success or failure in the marital role will have a greater effect on his or her self-concept. On the other hand, if he or she places relatively equal weight on several roles, then failure in one of these roles should be less stressful. Thus the salience of a role for the individual's identity may be a critical factor in determining his or her commitment to the role.

The relevance of role identities in marital relationships has been given considerable research attention in recent years primarily because of the growing commitment of wives to occupational roles. Wives in the labor force, especially newlywed wives, are not a new phenomenon. What seems to be changing is the salience of their occupational role identities. This is manifest in the *expectations* of both partners that wives' participation on the job is both important and permanent. These changes are of concern in the study of marital relationships because they influence the commitment each partner makes to his or her work roles as opposed to marital roles and because they add additional sources of stress by increasing the partners' workloads and role obligations.

The available evidence suggests that wives tend to be slightly more committed to family and family roles, whereas husbands are somewhat more inclined to invest in work roles (see Bielby, 1992). However, these trends seem to be gradually changing. A large body of research suggests that work that allows for initiative and self-direction is more highly valued and is personally more rewarding than housework for both men and women (see Menaghan, 1991).

We expect that in the first wave of data collection both husbands and wives will tend to have higher levels of commitment to the marriage than to work, but this pattern is likely to change over the course of the study. This prediction is based on the evidence that the strongest expressions of marital happiness and satisfaction occur in the initial phases of the family life cycle (Spanier, Lewis, & Cole, 1975), whereas job involvement is relatively unstable in the first phase of work careers and grows more stable over the course of one's career (Lorence & Mortimer, 1985).

Couple differences in commitment to the marital role and the relative salience of marital versus work roles should have a discernible effect on interaction patterns. Other things being equal, we expect that partners who share similar levels of commitment to the marriage will have fewer negative interactions than those in which one partner is more committed than the other. The key issue is the relative symmetry of the level of commitment. Couples who share a greater commitment to work than to their marriage may not have a high level of marital commitment but they are also less likely to become highly distressed because of marital issues.

Although wives generally *evidence* more emotional distress than husbands, the data suggest that employed wives are less subject to such distress than housewives (Aneshensel, 1992; Kessler & McRae, 1984). This seems to be true despite the fact that working increases the role demands on wives more than on their husbands (Kessler & McRae, 1984; Pleck, 1984). Although some data show an association between wives' employment and husbands' emotional disorders (Rosenfield, 1989), in general investigators have not been able to identify any set of concepts or variables that provide causal links between wives' employment and the quality of marital relationships. Thus Aneshensel (1992, p. 32) concludes, "The impact of work and home maker roles is not universally positive or negative, but depends upon role-related experiences."

Such "role-related experiences" are best understood by examining the systemic and reciprocal nature of roles in the marital relationship. For example, Kessler and McLeod (1984) report that wives' nurturant roles tend to increase their dependence on external social support networks. Because wives tend to take responsibility for providing their husbands with emotional support, husbands are less needful of such support from outside sources. Thus they can remain relatively independent of outside networks and relatively free of anxieties associated with social approval or disapproval.

It is an open question whether the increasing number of wives who are making serious commitments to work outside of the home will change this pattern. In some areas changes that might be reasonably expected are inordinately slow. One such area is housework. Although husbands of employed wives do more housework than those whose wives are not employed, the discrepancy remains great – working wives continue to do most of the housework (Coverman, 1985; Robinson, 1988). This slow rate of change is incommensurate with changing role expectations and economic conditions (Brines, 1993). We expect this discrepancy between role expectations and the actual household division of labor to be one of the most salient topics in the initial couple role negotiations.

Summary

We have reviewed the research for three main reasons. First, we wanted to introduce a dynamic conception of social and cultural context and illustrate the reciprocal relationships that exist between couples' interpersonal interactions and their interactions in the outer world. Second, we wanted to introduce the concepts of role identity, role salience, and role structure, which provide a means for linking the sometimes subtle interface between the couple and the social structure. Third, we hoped to identify key aspects of the current sociohistoric conditions in which our current research is taking place. These conditions pertain to fundamental changes in the marital and work activities of husbands and wives in current society. They combine to provide focus in our attempt to explain why some couples find themselves in interaction patterns that lead to failed marriages whereas others merely survive and still others succeed in having satisfying relationships.

Explicating the Model

Marital distress, as evidenced in coercive rigid interaction patterns, is assumed to be the consequence of the couple's failure to resolve its interpersonal problems.[3] The components of the model shown in Figure 10.1 may be understood as depicting the conditions and behavioral processes pertaining to the individual and joint resources spouses bring to the marriage and the problems that develop in the marriage. The model is also designed to identify sources of problems and the conditions under which events may be interpreted as problems.

We assume that no couple, however endowed with material and personal resources, can live their lives free of problems. We also assume that the basis for couples' abilities to cope or solve problems lies in the peculiar mix of background, socialization, material resources, and personality traits created by the union. What is important is the combination of experiences, resources, and traits that enable some to solve their internally or externally induced problems while others succumb to, or passively endure, unhappy and unstable relationships. The model is designed to specify key connections between the experiences, resources, and traits that affect the couples' abilities to deal with their problems.

The Four Phases

Figure 10.1 depicts the marital relationship as a continual learning process. Each of the four phases pertains to different learning experiences. For purposes of clarity, the discussion concentrates on the type of data gathered in the first wave of the study. Phase 1, family socialization, is a preparatory phase in which individuals develop their conceptions of who they are and how they will behave in marriage. During this phase they also develop conceptions of how their spouse should behave. The data pertaining to these learning processes consist of respondents' memories and evaluations of the significant people in their childhoods and their marital relationships. Data for phase 1 are gathered only in the first wave of the study; data for phases 2, 3, and 4 will be gathered in all three waves.

Phases 2, 3, and 4 portray ongoing learning experiences that are expected to modify spouses' initial self-evaluations and role expectations for themselves and their partners. These changes are thought to occur in the process of the couples' confronting their internal or external problems. As indicated in Figure 10.1, we will be collecting both individual and couple-level data. Both levels of analysis are used because we assume that they combine to effect the developing marital relationship. For example, couple-level successes or failures in obtaining material goods, maintaining the home, communicating effectively, performing compatible roles, and resolving shared problems all are hypothesized to have direct and indirect influences on the individuals' mental health. Conversely, emotional distress, psychopathology, lack of commitment, and disinterest on the part of an individual marriage partner can affect the couple's functioning as a unit.

In summary, the model indicates that structural and cultural conditions combined with childhood experiences are prime contributors to the material, social, and psychological resources each partner brings to the marriage (phase 1). These resources combine with life events to determine the initial role negotiations that take place in phase 2. Role negotiations then determine the couples' role structures and set couples on particular patterns of interaction. The resulting patterns, in combination with the couple role structure, determine the couples' motivation and capacity to cope with or resolve their day-to-day problems, many of which result from changing life events (phase 3). The effectiveness with which couples deal with their internal and external problems should, in turn, affect the mental health of the individual partners and the couples' mutual commitment, marital happiness, and marital stability. These latter outcome variables, in combination with life events, are then thought to influence the individuals' role identities, sense of efficacy, and power/dependence balance and thus set the whole process in motion again (phase 4). If the initial process results in extremely low levels of marital commitment or unhappiness, the couple is likely to engage in the kinds of interactions that will result in the dissolution of the marriage.

Given these hypothesized general processes, we now examine more precisely how specific variables are expected to combine to produce the conditions that determine positive or destructive couple interactions. Owing to limitations of space, we are unable to explicate the entire model. The discussion that follows is limited to only the first two phases.

Phase 1: Family Socialization

Socialization has been defined as, "*A process in which individuals living in a given social context learn, through interactions with each other, the particular identities extant within their social context and the ways to establish, maintain, and transform such identities*" (Tallman, Marotz-Baden, & Pindas, 1983, p. 25; see also Gecas, 1981). Establishing, maintaining, or changing identities requires knowing the roles appropriate for such identities and the ability to perform those roles. In new situations, such as when couples are in the early stages of a marriage, there is likely to be ambiguity about the appropriate roles for each partner. Thus we expect that most marriages will require some period of role negotiation. This is especially true in an era of social change, when many view traditional gender-linked family roles as anachronistic. The process of role negotiation is itself a learning experience and thus is considered an aspect of the couple's socialization into marital roles. Consequently, phase 1 is concerned with socialization that takes place within two contexts: the individuals' families of origin and the couples' early functioning as married partners.

The Family of Origin

Most people form their initial identities as children through interactions within their family and by interacting or observing other family members interacting with segments of the larger society. The key elements in this larger system are the social structure and the culture as manifest and interpreted in the family. Let us first consider the impact of the social structure.

a. Social Structure. We noted that families suffering from economic or social deprivation will probably be faced with more problems (both external and internal) than families who are better off. For convenience, we shall refer to an individual's or couple's social and economic condition as SES (i.e., socioeconomic status). The relevant question for us is how growing up in families of varying social statuses affects the material, social, and psychological resources individuals bring to the marriage. We anticipate that those who grow up in families from higher SES families are likely to have more education and better-paying jobs than those from lower SES families. The available research also suggests that they will tend to have higher self-esteem and a better sense of self-efficacy (Gecas & Seff, 1989, 1990; McLeod & Shanahan, 1993). We have less knowledge about the degree to which family SES is associated with the identification process, particularly the use of parents as role models. We anticipate that the more closely individuals identify with a particular parent, the more likely their expectations about marriage and their commitment to the marital role will be associated with that parent's marital experiences.

b. Culture. The important cultural variables in this research are the salience of respondents' ethnic and religious identities. We expect that strong ethnic identities will imply close ties to the family of origin and traditional beliefs about marital roles and childrearing. Thus ethnic identities may be associated with traditional gender-linked marital role identities. They may also influence interaction styles. For example, some cultural groups are more likely than others to adhere to aggressive and conflictual interaction styles. It is important, therefore, to distinguish between styles of interaction and the meanings couples attach to specific behavioral acts or patterns.

We shall also explore the extent to which cultural homogamy/heterogamy influences the content and style of marital role negotiations. We anticipate that heterogamy will result in more pervasive negotiation problems, but we have no prediction as to the outcome of such negotiations.

Persons who grow up in families with strong conventional religious beliefs are likely to develop traditional gender and marital role identities but *only if* they experienced their family life as happy and identify with a parent who holds these beliefs.[4] Such people should also be strongly committed to their marriage. Bellah and his colleagues suggest that people with strong beliefs in God as eternal and unchanging develop rationales for maintaining marital stability even in the face of vicissitudes and misfortune (Bellah et al., 1985). We expect persons with strong traditional religious beliefs, especially if they are consistent with the beliefs of their own parents, to tend to view marital relationships in positive terms. Such views, we predict, should carry over into couple interactions. More generally, we hypothesize that those couples who are constrained by beliefs or loyalties to family and community from considering divorce as an available option will tend to avoid negative or coercive statements in their marital interactions.[5]

c. Family Experiences. One of the principal mechanisms of socialization into role identities is the process of identification (Gecas, 1981; Tallman et al., 1983). It is a process that is akin to modeling in which the child attaches him- or herself to a person, usually a parent, and adopts key aspects of that person's identity. In our study, we ask respondents to indicate who among the persons they lived with while growing up they felt closest to and who they felt they were most like. Respondents also complete a trait checklist for these models and for themselves. These data provide indications of the respondents' perceptions of the role models' strength and efficacy. The vast majority of the role models in our study are respondents' natural parents. Others most often included are siblings and grandparents. We are also gathering data on the respondents' assessment of the quality of their parents' marital relationship, parents' conceptions of appropriate gender and marital roles, and perceived family power structure. We expect individuals who have strong identifications with either of their parents (as opposed to siblings or others in the household) to report relatively positive family experiences. It should follow that individuals with strong commitments to their marital role identities are more likely to come from intact families in which the parents are perceived as happy and competent.

Some data suggest that persons who grow up in families in which the parents are considered to be happily married are more likely to be optimistic about the state of marriage (Carnelley & Janoff-Bulman, 1992). There is also evidence that parents who are happily married have more influence on some of the ways their offspring interact in their marriages (Van Lear, 1992). Finally, the research of Ross and Mirowski (1988) and others suggests that couples who do not adhere to traditional views of a gender-linked household division of labor have more positive conceptions of married life than more traditional couples. These three sets of findings lead to the hypothesis that those respondents in our sample who grow up in families in which their parents are viewed as happily married and hold egalitarian values regarding marital roles will be most likely to identify with their parents and have strong commitments to their marital roles. It also should follow that partners who have open, nonrigid, and egalitarian expectations regarding the household division of labor are more likely to have a strong commitment to the marital role. Because these behaviors are associated with effective problem solving in family groups (Tallman & Miller, 1974) we predict that if both partners share such expectations, initial marital role negotiations will be marked by positive, flexible interactions with a strong emphasis on problem solving.

The Couple: Factors Influencing Initial Interactions

a. Role Identities, Self-Efficacy, and Problem Solving. If, as we have asserted, role identities are formed and altered in the process of interpersonal interactions, then individuals' most salient role identities must require frequent validation by significant others in their daily lives (Burke, 1991; Swann, 1983). It seems likely, therefore, that for newly married couples initial role negotiations will focus on issues pertaining to validating each partner's key role identities. For most couples, these negotiations can be expected to revolve around their marital role identities during the first months of their marriage. Thus early role negotiations should center on household activities, particularly the household division of labor, or on the conflict between marital roles and other role commitments.

Whereas the desire to validate salient role identities is expected to be a primary determinant of the *content* of early role negotiations, participants' appraisal of personal efficacy should contribute to the *length* and *quality* of the negotiations. *Efficacy* is defined as the individual's assessment of his or her ability to accomplish specific goals. We expect that the study participants who identify with parents who are perceived as competent are likely to have a positive sense of their personal efficacy (Gecas, 1989). Bandura (1986) notes that the family is the source of the initial efficacy experiences for most people. Tallman et al. (1983) found that the sons of parents who had recently experienced problem-solving success were more likely to exhibit appropriate risk-taking behaviors in a problem-solving situation than those sons whose parents experienced persistent failures.

Self-efficacy should influence the self-assurance partners bring to the negotiation process. It also contributes to persistence in efforts to attain satisfactory outcomes (Bandura, 1986). Thus if partner A's self-efficacy is greater than B's, other things being equal, A may be more likely than B to persist until his or her goals in role negotiations are achieved. If both partners have high self-efficacy, negotiations may be longer lasting than for those whose appraisals are lower. Self-efficacy has also been linked to effective problem solving and the actor's readiness to engage in problem-solving activities. Tallman, Leik, Gray, and Stafford (1993) hypothesized that people who have a history of problem-solving success in a particular arena will not only view themselves as efficacious but they will be more likely to identify and attempt to solve new problems as they arise.

It is important to draw a distinction here between problem solving and coping behaviors (for a more complete discussion of this distinction, see Tallman, 1988; and Tallman et al., 1993). Problem-solving behaviors in couple interactions entail positive suggestions for changing a given situation. Coping attempts are more likely to involve reassuring, supporting statements that facilitate adjustment but do not necessarily bring about change. Consider, for example, a situation in which one partner's work schedule makes it difficult for him or her to do the dishes after dinner. A problem-solving focus might involve suggestions by a partner to move the dinner time up, use paper plates, provide comparable household work in another area, and so forth. A coping response would be a statement by a partner (usually the one who feels victimized) that conveys understanding and sympathy for the other's position or behavior (e.g., "I know it's hard given the pressure you have been under"), indications that the problem "was not that bad," or statements that others put up with worse situations (e.g., "Other wives [husbands] have to put up with a lot more than I do"). The use of either or both coping and problem-solving behavior should help release tension and produce positive feelings for both partners. The difference is that if problem solving is effective the problem will not return. With the advantage of longitudinal research, we will be able to observe the extent to which the same interpersonal problems keep recurring and whether problem-solving or coping behaviors have any direct effect on such reoccurrences. We anticipate that most couples will use both problem-solving and coping behaviors in their interactions. Our interest will be in the proportion of each that is used and their consequences for marital stability and happiness.

b. Power/Dependence Balance. Our attempt to develop an indicator of power/dependence (hereafter referred to as P/D) balance is an effort to assess the power potential of each partner in the context of the couple's relationship. Power potential refers to the degree to which an individual can (or is perceived as being able to) control another's outcomes. In our view, efforts to study power in interpersonal relationships have been ineffective primarily because they failed to explore sufficiently the conditions under which an individual is *ready or willing* to comply with stated or unstated directives from another individual. If A has a predisposition to comply with B, then B has to do very little if anything to exercise his or her power (Molm, 1987, 1990). The readiness of A to comply with B should be a direct function of A's dependence on B for resources A believes B controls. The more important these resources are to A, the greater B's potential power over A.

Tallman, Gray, and Leik (1991) propose that in relationships such as marriage, virtually all known resources are exchanged, thereby creating very high levels of interdependency. Moreover, as partners increase their commitments to one another, they give up alternative resource opportunities, thus further increasing their dependence on one another. When a relationship is going well, the dependence of one partner on the other is mutual and P/D is balanced. If one partner is more dependent than the other, the system is unbalanced. In unbalanced relationships a partner may or may not use his/her power advantage, but the weaker partner is always vulnerable. Under such conditions, it is possible that the weaker partner may engage in anticipatory compliance in which he or she seeks to meet the partner's wishes or needs before they are expressed; our preliminary observations of videotaped couple interactions suggest that the weaker partner often talks most and is the most demanding (albeit unsuccessfully). In general, we expect the P/D imbalance to produce a strain and conflict in the relationship most often manifest by efforts of the weaker person to reestablish balance (for a discussion of the consequences of power/dependence balance/imbalance, see Emerson, 1972).

Assessment of P/D balance will employ indicators of material, social, and psychological dependencies. We will gather data on the financial, educational, and occupational status each partner brings to the marriage. We will also obtain respondents' scores on scales measuring their love and liking of their partner; their perceptions of their own and their partner's physical appearance, intelligence, social skills, and friendliness; and the level of their commitment to the marriage. Finally, because dependency is reduced if alternative sources for valued resources are available, we include a measure of the extent of social support and assistance (other than by the spouse) used by the respondent during times of need. The comparison of the differences between spouse scores on these indicators provides us with our measure of P/D balance/imbalance.

The types of dependencies partners have on one another and the P/D balance are likely to change over the course of the study as life events effect the couple's state of affairs. For example, the birth of the first child typically alters the P/D balance for most couples, especially if the new mother decides to stay home with the child. In that case, the wife will become more dependent on the husband for income, and the husband may or may not increase his dependence on the wife for child care and homemaking. Even if the wife continues to work, the P/D balance is likely to change with the introduction of a new person requiring love, time, and attention from one or both partners.

Phase II: Role Expectations and Marital Role Negotiations

The socialization process is ongoing. Family experiences influence the development of initial role identities and role expectations, but these are amenable to change as a function of subsequent life experiences. The model depicted in Figure 10.1 suggests that initial marital role negotiations are another essential socializing experience for married people. Such negotiations are likely to be affected by the partners' self-efficacy, coping, and/or problem-solving skills and their collective power/dependence balance. It should also be affected by other personality traits such as a predisposition to depression, anger, anxiety, and so forth.

Marital Role Negotiations

In this study, we are investigating both the content of the couple's role negotiations and the structure or patterns of interactions developed by such negotiations. By *content* we mean the issues couples identify and choose to discuss when seeking to resolve their disagreements. By *interaction* we mean the moment-to-moment reciprocal verbal and nonverbal communication exchanges that take place between spouses. We hypothesize that the primary issues discussed will pertain to the partners' most salient role identities. An important consideration here is the extent to which these role identities are either shared or complementary.[6] Couples whose role identities are not compatible should be less able to focus on a collective or "we" perspective in attempting to resolve their interpersonal problems. As noted earlier, coding the content of couple negotiations at one point in time provides a means for determining whether the couple is able to overcome problems as opposed to persevering on the same issues over the three waves of data collection.

From the available evidence, we expect the microanalysis of couple interactions to provide the best single predictor of marital unhappiness and marital dissolution (Bradbury & Karney, 1993). We also believe it will be the best predictor of the couples' abilities to deal effectively with their marital problems. The essential element in the analysis and the primary reason that the predictions seem to hold is the assessment of the emotional quality of the exchanges. There is mounting evidence that excessive negative affect increases couple distress and inhibits effective problem solving (Gottman, 1979; Forgatch, 1989; Patterson, 1982). This is largely because angry, critical, and disparaging comments are not only painful to the recipient but they tend to elicit predictable negative responses from the partner. The persistent use of anger, criticism, or disgust in couple interaction thus narrows the range of possible responses and escalates the partners' feelings of sadness, hostility, and withdrawal (Gottman, 1991; Gottman & Levenson, 1986). The more predictable these patterns are, the more limited the range of behaviors available to the couples to deal with unanticipated events or developing interpersonal problems.

The basic coding scheme we use in our assessment of couple interaction is a slightly revised version of Gottman's Rapid Couples Interaction Scoring System (RCISS). We shall use lag sequential analysis techniques for determining the interaction structure that develops for each couple (Bakeman & Gottman, 1986; Gottman, 1979; Sackett, 1979). The method allows us to determine whether certain events elicit predictable response patterns. On the basis of the research of Gottman (1979) and Patterson (1982), we expect initial interaction patterns to set couples on interaction trajectories that will influence their potential to solve future problems. We will attempt to identify four interaction dimensions: rigid-flexible, competitive-cooperative, coercive-compliant, and positive-negative. We anticipate that flexible, cooperative, and positive interactions will be most predictive of couples capable of solving their daily problems. We also expect interaction styles that are neither overly coercive or overly compliant to produce the most effective problem-solvers. Finally, we will explore the extent to which couples approach their problems as a unit or as competing individuals seeking to maximize personal outcomes. These differences, we believe, will be manifest in the type of strategies the partners use in their role negotiations. The strategies used will depend, in part, on whether the couple has a shared universe of discourse; that is, whether their discussions are based on the same or differing assumptions. Do they understand each other's meanings or are they talking "past" each other? Strategies will also depend on the goals each partner desires. Is the desired outcome the couple's well-being or personal benefit? For example, accusations of unfairness may focus on procedural matters concerned with the collective outcomes ("You don't do the dishes even when you have time") or the distribution of the outcomes themselves ("You spend so much money on clothes there is nothing left for me if I want to have some fun"). Finally, strategies may focus on seeking compliance, consensus or submission. The latter is most frequently characterized by the use of ultimatums or declarations of intent designed to end conversations. In general, we expect strategies that emphasize collective benefits and focus on establishing and validating facts to be most successful in contributing to the development of cohesive and flexible marital role structures.[7]

Life Events

Many events that occur outside the marriage can have an independent effect on couple interactions. We have already discussed "spillover" effects in which frustrations on the job carry over into couple interactions. Similarly, neighborhood quarrels, conflicts with parents, family illnesses, or close involvements with friends may demand the couples' attention and energy. External events also have indirect influences on the interaction processes by affecting role identities, self-efficacy, problem-solving/coping strategies, and the P/D balance. This is because such events affect the couple's collective and individual allocations of time, effort, and material resources. The birth of a child, the loss of a job, a promotion, or graduation from school are among the more common life events that may alter the partners' self-concepts, their opportunity structure, their collective goals, the problems they consider salient, and their relative dependency on one another. All are factors that can influence the content and patterns of couple's interactions.

Our research design allows us to study the influence of external events as they occur in the couples' lives. We should also be able to study the effects of major or minor crises on couple interaction patterns. This will allow us to measure problem-solving activities as they occur or within some close approximation of when they occur. We hope this procedure will enable us to better understand the development of couple distress and identify the antecedent conditions that lead to such distress.

The Research Design

As we noted in the beginning of this chapter, data will be collected over three waves, each wave separated by a year. We employ three different data-collecting methods for each wave: a face-to-face interview conducted separately with each spouse in the couples' residence; a daily diary completed by each spouse over a four-week period; and a videotaped couple interaction that focuses on resolving current disagreements.

The Interview

The initial interview in the first wave is designed, in part, to provide a retrospective family history and elicit data about the respondent's socialization into gender, marital, and occupational identities. This part of the interview is not repeated in the second and third waves of the study.

The following information will be gathered in each wave of the study:

1. Structural conditions that provide data about the respondents' (and couples') changing socioeconomic conditions, work and/or academic history, and sources for expressive and material support at times of need.
2. Respondents' physical and mental health.
3. Respondents' feelings for their spouse. This includes love and liking, trust of partner, dependence on partner for material and emotional support, and perceptions of the spouse regarding such attributes as intelligence, physical attraction, likability, friendliness, and understanding.
4. Role identities and marital-role performance. This includes assessments of the relative salience of respondents' marital, occupational, filial, friendship, recreational, and religious roles, and the respondents' commitments to marital, occupational, and familial role identities. Finally, we measure marital identities in terms of the meanings attached to the various activities that make up the marital role. This involves obtaining respondents' evaluations of 10 distinct behaviors attached to marital roles. These are provider, cook, housekeeper, yardworker, sexual partner, recreational partner, therapist, childrearer, participant with spouse's family, and participant with own family.
5. Measures of spousal role expectations. We assess spouses' aspirations and expectations for their own occupational careers. We also measure the respondents' expectations for self and spouse about carrying out the various marital roles discussed under (4).
6. Assessments of the amount of time each partner spends on each of the activities presented in (4) and the respondents' satisfaction with the time they spend on these activities provide the basis for assessing couple role structure.
7. We use multiple indicators of global measures of self-concepts such as self-esteem, self-worth, and self-efficacy.

The Daily Diary

The daily diary is a short questionnaire designed to assess daily stress, mood changes, expressive and instrumental family role activities, types of problems the couple confronts, and coping and problem-solving responses to these problems. Despite the fact that the diary takes between 5 and 10 minutes a night to complete, it is the most onerous part of the research for the participating couples. As a consequence, an as yet unknown percentage of the respondents have failed to complete all four weeks of the diaries. At the same time, our preliminary analysis suggests that this is a remarkably rich data source that amplifies the videotaped interaction data.

Videotaped Observations of Marital Interaction

Each spouse is asked to fill out a revised version of Gottman's "Areas of Disagreement Form," which asks spouses to indicate the severity and duration of 14 possible sources of disagreement. A member of the interviewing team, using both spouses' responses on this form, identifies key areas of disagreement and then asks the couple to discuss these areas with the idea of trying to resolve the difficulty. Once the discussion is under way, the facilitator leaves the room promising to return in 15 minutes. This 15-minute videotaped session provides the basic data for our interaction analysis.

Preliminary Data

Control Group Comparisons

This study requires participants to invest a considerable amount of time and effort over a 3-year period. It is conceivable that this experience may have some effect on the outcomes of the study. Participants may be more committed to their marriages than would be the case otherwise, either because of the effort they put into the project or the insights they gain from participation. Conversely, they may become sensitized to problems that they might have ignored if they were not exposed to the issues raised in the various data-gathering techniques; such awareness could lead to marital dissolution. The control samples were drawn to provide a means for determining whether such contingencies did in fact occur.

To provide an adequate test of whether the research methods influenced outcome variables, we drew two control samples. One sample was given an initial interview to determine how well it matched the study sample on variables that might conceivably effect such outcomes as marital happiness and marital stability. We found no significant differences between the control and study samples on all indicators of socioeconomic status, parents' marital status, religion, or marital happiness. In fact, none of our comparisons between the control and study groups were statistically significant.

In general, our sample represents a group of newlyweds from a broad range of ethnic and socioeconomic backgrounds who tend to feel extremely happy about their marriage and who describe themselves as very close to their partners. This provides an appropriate point of departure for attempting to understand the interplay of the variables depicted in Figure 10.1 on the couple's ability to deal with their developing problems.

Initial Areas of Disagreement

We stated earlier that, given the changing role of women in the labor force, traditional marital roles are likely to be challenged and we expected the primary source of early couple disagreements to reflect such changes and confusion about such roles. Evidence of such changes might be disagreements about the household division of labor. One indicator of such disagreements is the form couples fill out prior to engaging in their videotaped interaction. This form provides subjects with a list of 14 possible areas of disagreement with the option to write in other disagreements. Respondents are asked to indicate on a 0 to 100 scale the degree to which a particular issue is problematic to them.

Table 10.1 provides a comparison of the importance of areas of disagreements by gender. As indicated in the table, husbands and wives display considerable agreement in their overall rankings of the issues they find most problematic. The most important disagreements for both partners tend to be about money, followed by disputes about who does what around the house, communication, and the amount of time the couple is able to spend together. We shall be able to develop more sensitive measures of the impact of different types of disagreement when we analyze the content of videotaped interactions. These data do suggest, however, that early disagreements focus on the allocation of resources and the division of labor within the household. They provide tentative support for the idea that couples getting married today are more likely than those in earlier eras to challenge traditional role allocations. Other evidence of such changes comes from data indicating that more than 60% of both the study and control samples reported living together before their marriage. This is a larger proportion than reported in previous studies of married couples (see Sweet & Bumpass, 1987).

Table 10.1. *Mean magnitude (0–100) of disagreement by area of disagreement and marital gender role*

Area of disagreement	Husbands		Wives	
	Mean	SD	Mean	SD
Who does what around the house?	24.05	27.00	24.94	27.63
Time spent together	17.69	22.86	18.14	25.16
Time with friends	16.47	22.6	12.17	20.01
Time spent at work	14.57	22.43	11.85	20.95
Money	30.97	28.68	31.35	30.29
Communication	20.71	24.48	22.00	25.76
In-laws	15.71	22.13	14.33	22.68
Sex	15.19	21.05	13.21	20.16
Religion	9.34	19.96	8.81	19.94
Recreation	16.27	21.00	12.47	19.27
Friends	14.46	21.82	10.96	19.33
Alcohol & drugs	9.88	20.11	9.91	22.09
Children	8.09	17.56	7.04	17.13
Jealousy	11.37	19.49	11.86	20.07

Conclusions

The model described in this chapter and the research designed to test it are intended to amplify and extend the scope of current explanations for the causes of marital unhappiness and dissolution. To this end, we have attempted to integrate principles drawn from social learning theory, social exchange theory, symbolic interaction theory, role theory, and the life course perspective. We have also attempted to integrate a variety of research methods to provide data on the often subtle interplay between the structural and cultural context in which couples live their day-to-day lives and go about solving their problems through interpersonal interactions.

Any attempt to integrate principles and concepts from different perspectives into a single process model runs the risk of simply adding to the complexity of earlier explanations without contributing to their predictive power or scope. This is obviously not our intention. We may not improve on the predictions of divorce resulting from the observations of couple interactions, but we think it is possible to provide more complete, yet parsimonious explanations for these outcomes. Our goal then is to expand the *scope* of previous explanations of marital unhappiness and dissolution without losing their explanatory power. As noted at beginning of the chapter, we want to build on the body of work that has successfully identified specific patterns of couple interaction that lead to marital breakdown. Given this knowledge, the question we address is how couples find themselves in this state of spiraling miscommunication, hostility, and emotional withdrawal. Our model identifies a four-phase process through which social and psychological experiences contribute to the partner's role identities, self-efficacy, coping and problem-solving skills, and the couple's power/dependency balance. These factors combine with life events to produce patterns of interaction that either adjust to or alleviate the problems couples must confront, or they contribute to increasing alienation, which leads to marital breakdowns.

The ongoing nature of human relationships and socialization processes make any time point for testing causal models with natural groups somewhat arbitrary. However, by beginning this research with never-before married couples who are in the initial stages of forming their families, we may be in a better position to investigate how people become socialized into these critical new role sets. By exploring the couple relationship as a developing process, it may be possible to identify the patterning of events or interactions that set couples on trajectories that bind them together or tear them apart.

Notes

1. The term "actor" is used to refer to any entity capable of taking action as a single unit. Thus it may be an individual, a group, an organization, a nation, and so forth.
2. Bradbury and Fincham (1990) report that distressed couples rarely attribute their problems to external sources. The foregoing is not intended to dispute that conclusion. Our point is simply that if people live in a social context that keeps them under high levels of stress, there is likely to be a spillover effect that increases the probabilities that their frustration and anger will be expressed in negative feelings toward one another.
3. A problem is defined as "a situation in which there is a barrier that interferes with an actor attaining a desired goal and in which some uncertainty exists as to whether the barrier can be overcome" (Tallman et al., 1993).
4. The available data do not demonstrate a high correlation between membership in fundamentalist or conservative Protestant denominations and marital stability (Glenn & Supancic, 1984). This may be because many members of the fundamentalist sects come from unhappy households and "convert" to fundamentalist denominations in the hope of finding miracle solutions to personal problems (see Chi & Houseknecht, 1985).
5. This notion is similar to Reiss's conception of normative inputs leading to dyadic commitment (Reiss, 1980).
6. In an application of Chaos Theory to family relationships, Gottman (1991) draws the distinction between the family as a regulated system and the family as a chaotic system. A regulated system has a fixed point whereas

a chaotic system has no fixed point. Fixed point systems, Gottman suggests, are energy restoring and energy conserving whereas systems without fixed points are likely to be energy dissipating. It is possible that role identities may be one way of conceptualizing couples with fixed points from those without such anchors. Couples with compatible role identities are likely to have shared goals and either have a shared value hierarchy or a tolerance for their value difference.

7. Space does not allow us to explain the reasoning behind these hypotheses or an extensive discussion of role structures. Suffice it to say that rigid role structures are those in which the incumbents of given positions (e.g., wife) adhere to designated roles and cannot easily or willingly conceive of performing different or reciprocal roles. We hypothesize that couples with such rigid role structures will find it more difficult than couples in flexible role structures to adapt to changing conditions and life events.

References

Aneshensel, C. S. (1992). Social stress: Theory and research. In J. Blake & J. Hagan (Eds.), *Annual Review of Sociology, 18,* 15–38.

Angell, R. C. (1965). *The family encounters the depression.* Gloucester, MA: Charles Scribner.

Bakeman, R., & Gottman, J. M. (1986). *Observing interaction: An introduction to sequential analysis.* Cambridge: Cambridge University Press.

Bandura, A. (1977). *Social Learning Theory.* Englewood Cliffs, NJ: Prentice-Hall.

Bellah, R. N., Madsen, R., Sullivan, W. M., Swidler, A., & Tipton, S. M. (1985). *Habits of the heart: Individualism and commitment in American life.* New York: Harper & Row.

Bielby, D. D. (1992). Commitment to work and family. *Annual Review of Sociology, 18,* 281–302.

Bolger, N., DeLongis, A., Kessler, R. C., & Wethington, E. (1989). The contagion of stress across multiple roles. *Journal of Marriage and the Family, 55,* 175–183.

Bradbury, T. N. (1994). Unintended effects of marital research on marital relationships. *Journal of Family Psychology, 8,* 187–201.

Bradbury, T. N., & Fincham, F. D. (1990). Attributions in marriage: Review and critique. *Psychological Bulletin, 103,* 3–33.

Bradbury, T. N., & Karney, B. R. (1993). Longitudinal study of marital interaction and dysfunction. *Review and Analysis, 13,* 15–27.

Brines, J. (1993). The exchange value of housework. *Rationality and Society, 5,* 302–340.

Buehlman, K. T., Gottman, J. M., & Katz, L. F. (1992). How couples view their past predicts their future: Predicting divorce from an oral history interview. *Journal of Family Psychology, 5,* 295–318.

Burke, P. J. (1980). The self: Measurement requirements from an interactionist perspective. *Social Psychology Quarterly, 43,* 18–29.

Burke, P. J. (1991). Identity processes and social stress. *American Sociological Review, 56,* 836–849.

Burke, P. J., & Reitzes, D. (1981). The link between identity and role performance. *Social Psychology Quarterly, 44,* 83–92.

Carnelley, K. B., & Janoff-Bulman, R. (1992). Optimism about love relationships: General vs. specific lessons from one's personal experiences. *Journal of Social and Personal Relationships, 9,* 5–20.

Caspi, A., & Elder, G. H., Jr. (1988). Emergent family patterns: The intergenerational construction of problem behavior and relationships. In R. A. Hinde & J. Stevenson-Hinde (Eds.), *Relationships within families* (pp. 218–40). Oxford: Clarendon.

Chi, S. K., & Houseknecht, S. K. (1985). Protestant fundamentalism and marital success: A comparative approach. *Sociology and Social Research, 69,* 351–375.

Conger, R., Conger, K. J., Elder, G. H., Jr., Lorenz, F. O., Simons, R. L., & Whitbeck, L. B. (1992). A family process model of economic hardship and adjustment of early adolescent boys. *Child Development, 631,* 526–541.

Conger, R., Elder, G., Lorenz, F., Conger, K., Simons, R., Whitbeck, L., Huck, S., & Melby, J. (1990). Linking economic hardship to marital quality and instability. *Journal of Marriage and the Family, 52,* 643–656.

Coverman, S. (1985). Explaining husband's participation in domestic labor. *Sociological Quarterly, 26,* 81–97.

Elder, G. H., Jr. (1974). *Children of the Great Depression.* Chicago: University of Chicago Press.

Elder, G. H., Jr., Caspi, A., & Downey, G. (1986). Problem behavior and family relationships: Life course and intergenerational themes. In A. B. Sorenson, F. E. Weinert, & L. R. Sherrod (Eds.), *Human development and the life course: Multidisciplinary perspectives* (pp. 293–340). Hillsdale, NJ: Lawrence Erlbaum.

Elder, G. H., Jr., Liker, J. K., & Cross, C. E. (1984). Parent–child behavior in the Great Depression: Life course and intergenerational influences. In P. B. Baltes & O. G. Brim, Jr. (Eds.), *Life span development and behavior* (Vol. 6, pp. 108–158). New York: Academic Press.

Emerson, R. M. (1972). Exchange theory, parts I and II. In J. Berger, M. Zelditch, Jr., & B. Anderson (Eds.), *Sociological theories in progress.* Boston: Houghton, Mifflin.

Forgatch, M. S. (1989). Patterns and outcome in problem solving: The disruptive effect of negative emotion. *Journal of Marriage and the Family, 51,* 115–124.

Garmezy, N., Masten, A. S., & Tellegen, A. (1984). The study of stress and competence in children: A building block for the study of developmental psychopathology. *Child Development, 55,* 97–111.

Gecas, V. (1981). Contexts of socialization. In M. Rosenberg & R. Turner (Eds.), *Sociological perspectives in social psychology.* New York: Basic Books.

Gecas, V. (1989). The social psychology of self-efficacy. *Annual Review of Sociology, 15,* 291–316.

Gecas, V., & Seff, M. A. (1989). Social class, occupational conditions, and self-esteem. *Sociological Perspectives, 32,* 352–365.

Gecas, V., & Seff, M. A. (1990). Social class and self-esteem: Psychological centrality, compensation, and the relative effects of work and home. *Social Psychology Quarterly, 53,* 165–173.

Gerson, K. (1985). *Hard choices: How women decide about work, career, and motherhood.* Berkeley: University of California Press.

Glenn, N. D., & Supancic, M. (1984). The social and demographic correlates of divorce and separation in the United States: An update and reconsideration. *Journal of Marriage and the Family, 46,* 563–575.

Gottman, J. M. (1979). *Marital interaction: Experimental investigations.* New York: Academic Press.

Gottman, J. M. (1990). How marriages change. In G. R. Patterson (Ed.), *Depression and aggression in family interaction.* Hillsdale, NJ: Lawrence Erlbaum.

Gottman, J. M. (1991). Chaos and regulated change in families – A metaphor for the study of transitions. In P. A. Cowan & M. Hetherington (Eds.), *Family transitions* (pp. 247–272). Hillsdale, NJ: Lawrence Erlbaum.

Gottman, J. M., & Levenson, R. W. (1986). Assessing the role of emotion in marriage. *Behavior Assessment, 8,* 31–46.

Gottman, J. M., & Levenson, R. W. (1988). The social psychophysiology of marriage. In P. Noller & M. A. Fitzpatrick (Eds.), *Perspectives on marital interaction.* Clevedon: Multilingual Matters.

Hill, R. (1949). *Families under stress.* New York: Harper & Row.

Kelvin, P., & Jarrett, J. E. (1985). *Unemployment: Its social psychological effects.* New York: Cambridge University Press.

Kessler, R. C., & McLeod, J. (1984). Sex differences in vulnerability to undesirable life events. *American Sociological Review, 49,* 620–631.

Kessler, R. C., & McRae, J. A., Jr. (1982). The effects of wife's unemployment on the mental health of married men and women. *American Sociological Review, 47,* 216–227.

Larsen, A. S., & Olson, D. H. (1989). Predicting marital satisfaction using PREPARE: A replication study. *Journal of Marital and Family Therapy, 15,* 311–322.

Liem, J. H., & Liem, G. R. (1990). Understanding the individual and family effects of unemployment. In J. Eckenrode & S. Gore (Eds.), *Stress between work and family* (pp. 175–204). New York: Plenum.

Liker, J. K., & Elder, G. H., Jr. (1983). Economic hardship and marital relations in the 1930's. *American Sociological Review, 48,* 343–359.

Lorence, J., & Mortimer, J. (1985). Job involvement through the life course: A panel study of three age groups. *American Sociological Review, 50,* 18–38.

McCall, G. J., & Simmons, J. L. (1978). *Identities and interactions* (2d ed.). New York: The Free Press.

McLeod, J. D., & Shanahan, M. J. (1993). Poverty, parenting and children's mental health. *American Sociological Review, 58,* 351–366.

Menaghan, E. G. (1991). Work experiences and family interaction: The long reach of the job? In W. R. Scott & J. Blake (Eds.), *Annual Review of Sociology, 17,* 419–44.

Molm, L. (1987). Linking power structure and power use. In K. S. Cook (Ed.), *Social exchange theory* (pp. 101–129). Beverly Hills, CA: Sage.

Molm, L. (1990). The dynamics of power in social exchange. *American Sociological Review, 57,* 427–447.

Patterson, G. R. (1982). *Coercive family process.* Eugene, OR: Castalia.

Patterson, G. R. (1984). Microsocial analysis: A view from the boundary. In J. C. Masters and K. Yarkin-Levin (Eds.), *Boundary areas in social and developmental psychology,* New York: Academic Press.

Pearlin, L. I. (1989). The sociological study of stress. *Journal of Health and Social Behavior, 30,* 241–256.

Pleck, J. H. (1984). The work–family role system. In P. Voydanoff (Ed.), *Work and family.* Palo Alto, CA: Mayfield.

Reiss, I. L. (1980). *Family systems in America* (3rd ed.). New York: Holt, Rinehart, & Winston.

Robinson, J. P. (1988). Who's doing the housework? *American Demographics, 10,* 24–28.

Rosenfield, S. (1989). The effects of wives' employment: Personal control and sex differences in mental health. *Journal of Health and Social Behavior, 30,* 77–91.

Ross, G. E., & Mirowsky, J. (1988). Child care and emotional adjustment to wives' employment. *Journal of Health and Social Behavior, 29,* 127–138.

Sackett, G. P. (1979). The lag sequential analysis of contingency and cyclicity in behavioral interaction research. In J. Osofsky (Ed.), *Handbook of infant development.* New York: Wiley.

Spanier, G. P., Lewis, R. A., & Cole, C. L. (1975). Marital adjustment over the family life cycle: The issue of curvilinearity. *Journal of Marriage and the Family, 37,* 263–275.

Stryker, S. (1980). *Symbolic interactionism.* Menlo Park, CA.: Benjamin/Cummings.

Stryker, S., & Serpe, R. T. (1982). Commitment, identity, salience, and role behavior. In W. Ickes & E. S. Knowles (Eds.) *Personality, roles and social behavior.* New York: Springer-Verlag.

Swann, W. B., Jr. (1983). Self-verification: Bringing social reality into harmony with the self. In J. Suls & A. Greenwald (Eds.), *Psychological perspectives on the self* (pp. 33–66). Hillsdale, NJ: Lawrence Erlbaum.

Sweet, J. A., & Bumpass, L. L. (1987). *American families and households.* New York: Russell Sage.

Tallman, I. (1988). Problem solving in families: A revisionist view. In D. M. Klein & J. Aldous (Eds.), *Social stress and family development.* New York: Guilford Press.

Tallman, I., Gray, L. N., & Leik, R. K. (1991). Decision, dependency, and commitment: An exchange based theory of group formation. In E. J. Lawler, B. Markowsky, C. Ridgeway, & H. A. Walker (Eds.), *Advances in Group Processes, 8,* 227–257.

Tallman, I., Marotz-Baden, R., & Pindas, P. (1983). *Adolescent socialization in cross-cultural perspective.* New York: Academic Press.

Tallman, I., & Miller, G. (1974). Class differences in family problem solving: The effects of verbal ability, hierarchical structure, and role expectations. *Sociometry, 37,* 13–37.

Tallman, I., Leik, R. K., Gray, L. N., & Stafford, M. C. (1993). A theory of problem solving behavior. *Social Psychology Quarterly, 56,* 157–177.

Tepperman, L., & Wilson, S. J. (1993). *Next of kin.* Englewood Cliffs, NJ: Prentice-Hall.

Thoits, P. (1983). Multiple identities and psychological well-being: A reformulation and test of the social isolation hypothesis. *American Sociological Review, 48,* 174–187.

Thoits, P. (1986). Multiple identities: Examining gender and marital status differences in distress. *American Sociological Review, 51,* 259–272.

Turner, R. H. (1990). Role change. In W. R. Scott & J. Blake (Eds.), *Annual Review of Sociology, 16,* 87–110.

Van Lear, C. A. (1992). Marital communication across the generations: Learning and rebellion, continuity and change. *Journal of Social and Personal Relationships, 9,* 103–123.

Veroff, J., Hatchett, S., & Douvan, E. (1992). Consequences of participating in a longitudinal study of marriage. *Public Opinion Quarterly, 56,* 315–327.

11   Physical Aggression in Marriage: A Developmental Analysis

K. Daniel O'Leary and Michele Cascardi

In June 1994, O. J. Simpson was accused of murdering his former wife, Nicole Brown Simpson, and her friend Ronald Goldman. Since that time, attention has been riveted on the problem of spouse abuse. Indeed, matters in the wife abuse area have not been the same since these brutal murders. For those who work in shelters and treat abused women daily, as reflected in many media accounts, there was much open dismay about the acquittal of Simpson in October 1995. Nonetheless, it remains the hope that the media attention focused on this case for over a year will bring needed changes in service delivery and financial support to this long-neglected problem.

Spouse abuse received little attention from mental health professionals until the late 1980s and early 1990s, when federal agencies such as the Centers for Disease Control and the National Institute of Mental Health (NIMH) and professional organizations such as the American Psychological Association began to encourage research on its etiology, prevention, and treatment. This neglect provides a context for understanding the slow and fragmented development of this field, although it is only one reason for the slow growth. Social reasons such as stigmatization and/or minimization of the problem by abusive men and their wives are also to blame. This chapter examines some of the reasons for this neglect and then reviews psychological and biological factors that psychologists found to have an influence on physical aggression in intimate relationships.

Reasons for Neglect of the Area

Psychology's neglect of wife abuse as a substantive area of study stands in marked contrast to the tremendous attention it has given aggression in general for years. The reasons for this neglect can be viewed from a cultural, religious, or legal perspective (for comprehensive analyses, see Dobash & Dobash, 1979; Pagelow, 1984; Pleck, 1987). The central thrust of these analyses is that societal mores supported men's domination of women and

343

the use of physical aggression against their wives and children. The initial interest in spouse abuse grew out of the volunteer efforts of women outside the established professions in the 1970s to establish shelters for abused women. Legal actions such as orders of protection and mandatory arrests of abusers became common in the 1980s. Psychologists, however, were slow to acknowledge the significant presence of wife abuse.

Both social and professional reasons contributed to this neglect. Although the social and professional reasons are interrelated, we have broadly classified them under these two headings.

Social Reasons

Stigma of Abuse. Physical aggression in marriage is not a problem that people have wanted to discuss openly. Abused women have long felt ashamed or afraid to seek treatment for their problems, and abusive men often feel the stigma of the disapproval of friends and family. Even if the problem is treated successfully, few men are willing to reveal to a national audience that they were abusive. In contrast, scores of well-known individuals who have suffered depression chronicle their coping with such a problem (Cronkite, 1994). The stigmatization of wife abuse is well illustrated in Charlotte Fedders's autobiography, *Shattered Dreams* (Fedders & Elliot, 1987). This book provides a poignant account of the need that women feel to protect themselves and their partners from any open identification of wife abuse.

An argument frequently heard is that any physical aggression against a woman by a partner should be regarded as a crime. The two clear goals here are to place an abusive husband in legal custody and provide some safety for the wife. Indeed, some professionals who deal with battered women believe that any physical aggression, whether a slap or a beating, should be handled by the criminal justice system. This specific issue is moot, but the more the problem is treated simply as a criminal act, the more it will remain socially stigmatized.

Failure to Recognize Physical Abuse/Aggression as a Major Problem. When women and men attend marital clinics and physical aggression exists in the relationship, few men or women consider the physical aggression a major problem in the marriage. In a sample of 200 men and women assessed on an initial intake survey of five major marital problems in our university marital clinic, only 6% of the women and 3% of the men reported that physical aggression or physical abuse was a major problem in the marriage

(O'Leary, Vivian, & Malone, 1992). These figures were in stark contrast to the actual prevalence of physical aggression reported by the women in the past year; 54% of the women reported that their husbands engaged in various acts of physical aggression against them.

Professional Reasons

Minimization of Abuse by Medical and Mental Health Personnel. Even when a woman revealed to a mental health professional that her partner was physically abusive, the problem was often seen as the woman's problem (Snell, Rosenwald, & Robey, 1964). According to Snell et al. (1964), abused women were diagnosed as having masochistic personalities until the diagnosis was dropped in DSM-IV (1994). In metropolitan hospitals, as many as one third of women seen in emergency rooms were abused though they were rarely treated for the problem (Stark et al., 1981). Fortunately, emergency room physicians are now much more attuned to the diagnosis of physical abuse since the American Medical Association launched a public media campaign (*Time*, March 1992) concerning cases of abuse seen in emergency rooms.

Federal Funding. From the 1960s to the 1990s, the Veteran's Administration and the National Institute of Mental Health were the primary sources of funding for the research and training of psychologists who deal with social and clinical problems. Given that the Veteran's Administration (VA) served primarily men, the large numbers of psychologists funded by the VA clearly saw men more frequently in their training than women. Funding by agencies such as the VA and NIMH was often linked to diagnostic categories such as schizophrenia, depression, and anxiety disorders, and abused women did not fit these categories.

Absence of Assessments and Treatments. Assessment instruments for wife abuse received little attention from psychologists until sociologists Straus, Gelles, and Steinmetz published their book *Behind Closed Doors* in 1980. Not a single article on wife abuse appeared in the *Journal of Consulting and Clinical Psychology* in the 1970s. The journal published the first such article in 1981 (Rosenbaum & O'Leary, 1981). It contained an ad hoc measure of wife abuse. *Behind Closed Doors* and the Conflict Tactics Scale (CTS) used to measure partner abuse in a large nationally representative survey of family violence became important resources for psychologists who needed a measure with reasonable psychometric properties. For a decade or more, the CTS was used in most NIMH-funded research on wife/partner abuse.

In the 1970s and 1980s psychologists focused considerable attention on treatments for anxiety, depression, sexual dysfunctions, and alcoholism. Graduate students naturally gravitated toward these subjects and often conducted research themselves or participated in treatment teams concerned with the efficacy of these interventions. At the same time, there were very few treatment programs for either the victims or the perpetrators in physically abusive relationships. Indeed, the lack of assessments and treatments for wife abuse was a primary reason for the establishment of our NIMH research training grant for pre- and postdoctoral fellows in this area of endeavor.

Lack of Recognized Diagnostic Classification for Abuse. Until the advent of DSM-IV (1994), no diagnostic category officially recognized the problem of wife/partner abuse. As a result, if a physically abused woman came to a psychological or psychiatric clinic, in order to qualify for insurance reimbursement for services she received, she would have to be given some other diagnosis, such as major depressive disorder, post-traumatic stress disorder, or anxiety disorder not otherwise specified. If a man abused his wife and happened to ask for help, he, too, would have to be given a diagnostic label other than physical abuse. The presence of a diagnostic label recognizing physical abuse of partner in DSM-IV (American Psychiatric Association, 1994; see O'Leary & Jacobson, 1997), does not automatically ensure that all insurance companies will provide reimbursement for the services provided, but it is a necessary first step in the reimbursement process.

The lack of a diagnostic category that allows for insurance reimbursement also has clear negative implications for psychologists in private practice and those in hospital and clinical settings. With no monetary incentive to treat abusive men and abused women, new professionals must often do so on a volunteer basis or reduced fee-for-service basis. In short, monetary reinforcement for clinical work in the area has been markedly less than in most other areas.

Lack of Coverage of Spouse Abuse by Marital Therapists and Professional Journals. Physical abuse in marital relationships was neglected by scientists until very recently. Classic texts on marriage (Paolino & McCrady, 1978) and marital therapy (Jacobson & Margolin, 1979) devoted less than 10 pages to the topic of wife abuse. Fortunately, some texts written in the past few years contain entire chapters or sections on marital aggression (e.g., Fincham & Bradbury, 1990; L'Abate, 1994). A search for articles on abuse in the official psychiatric and clinical psychology journals over a 10-year period (1983 to 1993) revealed no articles in *Archives of General Psychiatry* and only 8 articles in the *Journal of Consulting and Clinical Psychology* in the same period. This situation is undoubtedly changing within clinical psychology, and at least a half-dozen specialty journals now publish research on violence exclusively (O'Leary, 1993).

Interim Summary. Until recently, wife/spouse abuse has been largely neglected by psychologists. The reasons range from sociolegal reasons to more pragmatic financial reasons that hampered development of the field. Professionals and patients/clients also denied and minimized the problem of physical abuse. Fortunately, there is evidence that the tide is turning and that violence in general and spousal violence in particular are beginning to receive long-deserved recognition.

Developmental Course of Physical Aggression in Marriage

Partner Aggression over the Life Span: Cross-Sectional Trends

Over the past two decades, prevalence rates of aggression against a partner have been studied in a variety of samples. Straus, Gelles, and Steinmetz (1980) were the first to document strikingly high rates of physical aggression in marriage using a national, random probability sample of over 2,143 married or cohabiting spouses. More recent studies show that physical aggression in dating relationships starts in the teenage years, and, as we will document across age groups, the rates of dating aggression exceed those of married couples. Although this information does not fully account for changes in aggression for specific couples or age cohort effects, it suggests important trends based on age and gender.

Prevalence rates of dating aggression in published studies of high school populations range from 13% to 25% (Bergman, 1992; Henton, Cate, Koval, Lloyd, & Christopher, 1983; Jones, 1987; O'Keefe, Brockopp, & Chew, 1986; Roscoe & Callahan, 1983; Smith & Williams, 1992). Recent results from several surveys in suburban New York high schools (*N*'s across studies range from 253 to 383 students) reveal an even higher point prevalence of dating aggression among high school students than rates observed in general prevalence studies. In three separate surveys, 15% to 65% of students reported physical aggression against a dating partner in the year prior to assessment (Avery-Leaf, Cascardi, & O'Leary, 1994; Cascardi & O'Leary,

1990; Schwartz, O'Leary, & Kendziora, 1996). Across all these surveys, females self-reported engaging in physical aggression more (37% to 65%) than did males (15–39%).

College students also report high rates of dating aggression. Between 20% and 72% of college students experienced physical aggression in at least one dating relationship (Bernard & Bernard, 1983; McKinney, 1986; Makepeace, 1981; Sigelman, Berry, & Wiles, 1984; White & Koss, 1991), and physical aggression occurs in over 20% of students' ongoing relationships (Arias, Samios, & O'Leary, 1987; Riggs, O'Leary, & Breslin, 1990). The large range of estimates of dating aggression may be due to region and sample differences. For example, some of the highest rates of dating aggression in high school students were found at a large, multiethnic high school close to New York City (Avery-Leaf et al., 1994). Thus it appears that prevalence rates of physical aggression against dating partners are highest in urban areas with ethnic diversity. Whether the differential rates are due primarily to economic factors or some other variables is not clear.

Rates of courtship aggression among young adults (aged 18–24) are similar to those reported by college students (Elliot, Huizinga, & Morse, 1986; O'Leary et al., 1989). In a large, nationally representative sample of young married or cohabiting partners, 43% of females and 37% of males reported aggression against a partner in the past year (Elliot et al., 1986). Among couples ($N = 272$) from Onondaga and Suffolk counties in New York State participating in a longitudinal study of early marriage, 44% of females and 31% of males reported engaging in physical aggression toward their partner in the year prior to marriage (O'Leary et al., 1989). More than 90% of these couples were married within six weeks of the initial assessment despite the presence of physical aggression. Over time, the rates of aggression against one's spouse decreased significantly for females, and less so for males. At 30 months after marriage, 32% of females and 25% of males reported aggression in the past year (O'Leary et al., 1989).

Rates of marital aggression appear to decrease over the life span of both sexes. In a national, random probability sample of 2,143 adults (aged 18–50 years) 12.1% of males and 11.6% of females reported aggression against their spouses in the year prior to assessment (Straus et al., 1980). A 1985 replication study of 3,520 married or cohabiting spouses documented similar rates: 11.3% of males and 12.1% of females reported physical aggression against a spouse in the past year (Straus & Gelles, 1986). These rates parallel those found in other surveys of random probability samples of females from various regions in the United States: 10% to 19% (Hornung, McCullough, & Sugimoto, 1981; Nisonoff & Bitman, 1979; Schulman, 1979).

When rates of physical aggression against a spouse for married couples over the age of 30 are considered, the prevalence in the past year for males and females is 5% (Straus & Gelles, 1986). In a study of predictors of physical aggression against a female partner in the military, Pan, Neidig, and O'Leary (1994), found that age was associated with decreases in aggression. More specifically, of 11,870 white men, for every 10-year increase in age, the odds of being severely physically aggressive toward one's wife decreased by 19% (as compared with a nonaggressive man). In sum, cross-sectional data indicate that the rates of physical aggression against a partner decrease markedly as one gets older. While some of these age-related differences could be due to the fact that violent marriages may end more quickly than nonviolent marriages, we found physical aggression declining across a 30-month period in a sample of 272 newly married men and women who were assessed repeatedly (O'Leary et al., 1989).

Although the overall rate of marital aggression decreases across the life span, when specific couples are tracked across time, a significant proportion remain aggressive. Moreover, there is some evidence that aggression worsens across the years for a significant proportion of couples. In the longitudinal study just cited, young men's and women's reports of premarital aggression were significantly associated with their own reports of physical aggression at 18 and 30 months after marriage (O'Leary et al., 1989). Fifty-one percent of the men and 59% of the women who reported physical aggression at premarriage also reported physical aggression at 18 months after marriage. Over the first 3 years of marriage, 25% to 30% of the 272 couples evaluated were stably aggressive (O'Leary et al., 1989). Three other studies also show that approximately 50% of young partners remain physically aggressive across a 2- to 3-year period (Feld & Straus, 1990; O'Leary & Malone, 1992; Mihalic, Elliot, & Menard, 1994). Spousal aggression often starts early in a dating relationship and, for perhaps as many as 25% to 30% of those who report first instances of aggression in early dating relationships, it escalates to more severe forms across time (O'Leary et al., 1989; Roscoe & Benaske, 1985).

Adolescent and Young Samples: Bivariate Associations with Partner Aggression

Correlates of high school and college dating violence have focused on prior experience with aggression in and out of the home, attitudes that justify the use of dating violence, verbal aggression, dominance-oriented problem-solving strategies, sex-role socialization, and enactment of behaviors to control one's partner (e.g., Avery-Leaf et al., 1994; Bird, Stith, & Schladale, 1991; Bookwala, Frieze, Smith, & Ryan, 1992; Henton et al., 1983; Riggs, 1990; Riggs & O'Leary, 1996; Schwartz et al., 1996; Smith & Williams, 1992; Tontodonato & Crew, 1992).

In a study of 1,353 high school students in rural North Dakota, students raised in abusive homes were significantly more likely to report dating violence than those not raised in such homes (Smith & Williams, 1992). On the other hand, Schwartz et al. (1996) did not find such an association in a sample of approximately 250 high school students. This inconsistency may be due to the statistical association documented in the larger sample, even though the magnitude of the association was small.

A history of physical victimization in childhood (defined as being hit by a parent), witnessing parental violence, a personal history of dating aggression (Malone et al., 1989; Riggs & O'Leary, 1996), and a personal history of aggression with peers have also been associated with dating aggression in college students and early married individuals (Gwartney-Gibbs, Stockard, & Bohmer, 1987; Riggs, O'Leary, & Breslin, 1990). Past experiences with aggression in the family of origin or with peers may prompt individuals to use aggression as a means of interacting with intimates; such aggression may be viewed as normative and result in accepting attitudes toward the use of aggression.

Attitudes justifying the use of relationship aggression have been strongly correlated with males' use of dating violence in high school and college samples and inconsistently associated with females' use of such violence (Avery-Leaf et al., 1994; Cate et al., 1982; Riggs, 1990). Cate et al. (1982) reported that the use of physical aggression was associated with attitudes justifying courtship violence in aggressive males and females. Using path analysis, Riggs (1990) found that attitudes accepting physical aggression as a means of conflict resolution had a direct effect on physical aggression in intimate relations for male and female college students. Bookwala et al. (1992) and Tontodonato and Crew (1992) both found justification of physical aggression was a significant risk factor for male aggression in a college sample, but it was not predictive of physical aggression by females.

In recent data from high school students (Cano et al., in press), the correlation between males' dating aggression and attitudes justifying the use of such aggression ($r = .49$) was quite strong. On the other hand, the same correlation was nonsignificant for females ($r = .03$). Schwartz et al. (1997) also found very strong associations between justification of physical aggression and males' reports of physical aggression ($r = .72$) in a large ($N = 253$) high school sample. As in Cano et al. (in press), there was no association between females' justification of physical aggression and their reports of physical aggression against a partner.

The significant association between the justification of violence and use of aggression for males and not for females in some studies points to a link between a males' beliefs of entitlement and aggression. Justification of aggression on the part of some males may stem from the process of sex-role socialization whereby men learn to use physical aggression as a means to dominate and/or control their partners (see Birns, Cascardi, & Meyer, 1994). As noted earlier, such a link between entitlement and aggression has not emerged consistently for females. Female aggression may be less motivated by entitlement (or a desire to control another) and is more likely related to emotional arousal tied to jealousy (Campbell, 1993; Riggs & O'Leary, 1996).

Sex-role socialization is often viewed as a key feature of development related to males' entitlement, as is females' deference and subsequent victimization. However, researchers have failed to demonstrate a consistent pattern between sex-role stereotypes and relationship aggression. Several investigators have proposed that men who fit traditional sex-role stereotypes become abusers and traditional women become victims (Currie, 1983; Gelles, 1974; Pagelow, 1981). Sigelman et al. (1984) found more traditional attitudes toward women's roles in a college sample of male aggressors. Thompson (1991) found that a more masculine and less feminine gender orientation predicted courtship aggression for both males and females. However, others have found no relationship between courtship aggression and attitudes toward women's societal roles (Bernard & Bernard, 1983). Interviews by Follingstad, Rutledge, Polek, and McNeill-Hawkins (1988) with 48 female college students revealed that those who experienced repeated violence tended to have more traditional sex-role attitudes. Results on sex roles and the use of violence are mixed (Sugarman & Hotaling, 1989) and likely hinge on perceptions of one's role as primary aggressor or victim, repetition of violence, and intensity of the relationship. That is, if violence is repeated and severe, if the male views his role as the primary aggressor, and if the female views herself as the primary victim, then the endorsement of traditional sex roles is more likely to be high than if the violence is episodic, occurs at low levels, and both male and female view their roles as aggressors. Furthermore, findings from clinical interviews with partners who participated in the longitudinal study of early marriage described earlier indicate that some young men from very traditional backgrounds with respect to sex roles also believe that violence against women is never justified under any circumstances. Thus justification or acceptance of violence as a legitimate form of conflict resolution would appear to interact with traditional sex-role orientations, relationship characteristics, and background factors as well.

There is considerable evidence to suggest that relationship-specific situational factors may be strong correlates of physical aggression as well. Verbal aggression has been repeatedly associated with physical aggression in research with young couples and is posited to precede the use of physical aggression (Comins, 1984; Murphy & O'Leary, 1989; O'Leary, Malone, & Tyree, 1994). Relationship and problem-solving skill deficits or the use of violence as a method of negotiation have also been highlighted as important correlates of courtship aggression (Bird et al., 1991). Bird et al. found that negative affect (insulting, disagreeable attitude), domineering negotiation style, confrontational coping (blame), and limited advice-seeking from friends and family successfully discriminated nonviolent and violent college students. In addition to an insulting, disagreeable negotiation style, verbal aggression has been found to predict the first episode of physical aggression among young, newly married couples (Murphy & O'Leary, 1989). In a recent study of high school students (Avery-Leaf et al., 1994), the association between one's negotiation style and physical aggression was accounted for by the frequency of verbal aggression. Moreover, the association between verbal and physical aggression was .59 for males and .73 for females. Such results argue for interventions with teens aimed at changing their verbal interaction styles as a means of preventing physical aggression between partners.

Models of Courtship Aggression

A background-situational model of courtship aggression grounded in social-learning and conflict theories has been constructed to integrate many of the bivariate relationships reported in the preceding section (Riggs & O'Leary, 1989). According to this model, background factors (interparental aggression, child abuse, prior aggressive behavior, acceptance of interpersonal violence) and situational factors (drinking, relationship problems) that increase conflict within the relationship function in tandem to increase the probability of specific aggressive incidents. At the most general level, background factors increase the tendency of an individual to behave aggressively and the level of conflict within a relationship increases the probability of aggression in a specific situation.

Riggs and O'Leary (1996) tested this model on a sample of 345 college undergraduates (232 females and 113 males) using structural equation modeling. Results indicated that, for men and women, a more accepting attitude toward dating aggression and past aggressive behavior were important background factors in the prediction of dating aggression. For women, aggression in the family increased both acceptance of aggression and the previous use of aggression. For men, aggression in the family had little or no effect on either aggressive behavior or attitudes.

Malamuth, Sockloskie, Koss, and Tanaka (1991) proposed an integrated theoretical model of sexual and nonsexual aggression by college student males. Their model emphasized childhood experience with sexual abuse, general delinquent inclinations, sexual precociousness and promiscuity, attitudes supporting violence against women, and power and hostility motives. Their model rests on the supposition that a violent home environment increases involvement in delinquency and fosters hostile attitudes toward women. Such hostility and peer experiences increase both sexual and nonsexual aggression against women. The results of their structural equation modeling with 2,652 male college students emphasize the importance of hostility and social isolation in the prediction of nonsexual violence against women.

Another multivariate investigation of dating aggression in college students found that justification for dating aggression on the basis of humiliation predicted the use of physical aggression by both males and females, whereas justification on the basis of self-defense did not. Justification on the basis of humiliation reflected items such as "being made to feel stupid" and "makes me feel like a fool in front of his family and friends." The self-defense scale included being hit or threatened with a weapon. As aptly indicated by the authors, one reason that justification may not have correlated with the use of physical aggression could have been that such justification is so common that it may not be a feature that differentiates those who use physical aggression from those who do not. This study highlights the issue of assessment of attitudes justifying violence as a predictor of use of physical aggression. In short, a major problem in assessing attitudes toward violence in intimate relationships is that most men and women do not justify such aggression, and floor effects are a problem of this measurement.

In addition to justification, family of origin abuse of different types was also associated with physical aggression for both males and females (Foo & Margolin, 1995). Furthermore, this dating aggression study was the first to make comparisons across Caucasian and Asian groups. There were no differences in the rates of reported aggression in these two groups, but Asians were more likely to rate humiliation as a justification for dating aggression. In part because of the small number of Asian males (N = 23) and females (N = 40), none of the correlations of the predictors and dating aggression were significant for either gender, even though the correlation between alcohol use and aggression was .37 for males and .30 for women. In both cases, however, the correlation of alcohol use and physical aggression was the highest correlation reported.

Community and Marital Clinic Samples

Bivariate Associations with Marital Aggression

Community and clinic samples of married or cohabiting spouses have highlighted similar correlates and predictors of physical aggression. The primary focus of these controlled studies has been individual and relationship characteristics. At the individual level, they have examined experiences with aggression in the family of origin, personality styles, and alcohol abuse (Arias, 1984; Malone, Tyree, & O'Leary, 1989; O'Leary, Malone, & Tyree, 1994; Straus et al., 1980; Straus & Gelles, 1992). Relationship characteristics such as communication patterns, problem-solving strategies, verbal aggression, and marital conflict have been used to discriminate aggressive from nonaggressive couples (Dutton & Browning, 1988; Holtzworth-Munroe & Anglin, 1991; Margolin, John, & Gleberman, 1988; Murphy & O'Leary, 1989; O'Leary, et al., 1989; Rosenbaum & Golash, 1987; Vivian & O'Leary, 1987; Vivian, Mayer, Sandeen, & O'Leary, 1988; Vivian, Smith, Mayer, Sandeen, & O'Leary, 1987).

Individual Characteristics. Aggressive males have been characterized as having experienced abuse as a child, witnessed parental violence, having aggressive and impulsive personality styles, and having experienced low self-esteem and alcohol-abuse problems at higher levels than nonaggressive males (Arias, 1984; Arias & O'Leary, 1988; Sugarman & Hotaling, 1986; Neidig, 1986). In a longitudinal analysis of aggressive wives, Malone et al. (1989) found that witnessing parental violence and experiencing aggression as a child predicted females' use of aggression against a partner; this effect was mediated by an aggressive personality style.

Although there is convincing support for an association between violence in the family of origin and enactment of physical aggression against a partner, limited support has been demonstrated for the link between violence in the family of origin and *victimization* by a male partner. In a reanalysis of the National Family Violence Survey data on over 5,000 spouses, Sugarman and Hotaling (1986) found no support for the association of witnessing or experiencing parental violence and victimization by a male partner. Malone and Tyree (1991) also found that experiencing or witnessing violence in one's family of origin was predictive of female aggression but not of their victimization. Thus experience with violence in the family of origin appears to be associated only with aggression against a partner. Perhaps growing up in a violent family makes one less likely to tolerate being a victim of physical aggression.

Relationship Characteristics. As noted earlier, among high school and college students there is a strong association between verbal aggression and physical aggression, and in early marriage verbal aggression against a spouse has been found to predict the first instances of physical aggression (Murphy & O'Leary, 1989). In addition, decreases in marital satisfaction are associated with repeated physical aggression against a spouse (O'Leary et al., 1989). In samples of spouses seeking treatment for marital difficulties, those who report aggression in marriage report lower rates of marital satisfaction than nonaggressive spouses also seeking marital treatment (Cascardi, Langhinrichsen, & Vivian, 1992; O'Leary & Curley, 1986; Rosenbaum & O'Leary, 1981).

Several researchers have attempted to identify unique patterns of communication and problem solving that give rise to aggression during conflict situations. In these studies, couples were observed for 15 minutes while they discussed a problem area in their relationship. In general, aggressive couples displayed significant difficulties in communication compared with nonaggressive couples (Margolin et al., 1988; Vivian & O'Leary, 1987; Vivian et al., 1987; Vivian et al., 1988). Specifically, aggressive couples have been found to express more anger toward each other during problem solving and to engage in higher levels of negative reciprocity (i.e., the anger of one spouse increases the likelihood the other spouse will also respond with anger) than nonaggressive spouses. Although both males and females who report aggression display this pattern of behavior during conflict, there is some evidence that males' negative affect and anger serve a more coercive function than that of females. That is, males' use of negative affect and anger functions to control the outcome of the conflictual discussion.

Longitudinal Models of Aggression in Early Marriage

Although there is evidence to support individual and relationship differences between aggressive and nonaggressive spouses, the multivariate, interactive influences of these factors have only recently received attention.

Moreover, only one study to date has examined the influence of back-ground, personality, and relationship characteristics as predictors of physi-cal aggression against a spouse in a prospective, longitudinal study across the first 3 years of marriage. O'Leary, Malone, and Tyree (1994) used path analysis to examine the influences of aggression in one's family of origin, personality characteristics (aggressiveness, impulsivity, and defendence [a readiness to defend oneself, suspicion of others, and a tendency to be eas-ily offended]), marital discord, and psychological aggression on physical aggression at 30 months after marriage. For females, violence against peers or parents had a direct effect on their physical aggression. In addition, fe-males' impulsivity had a direct effect on their level of marital discord, and discord had a direct effect on physical aggression. These paths accounted for 30% of the variance in wives' physical aggression. For males, parental violence had a direct effect on their use of marital aggression. Marital dis-cord and psychological aggression also significantly influenced their use of physical aggression. However, these factors explained only 17% of the vari-ance in husbands' aggression.

This path analysis indicates that impulsive women who are distressed by their relationship may be more likely to use aggression against their part-ners during discordant interactions. And, as Campbell (1993) suggests, women's aggression may be perceived as a challenge to men's power, which increases the likelihood of physical aggression by men. This cycle may es-calate the intensity and severity of physical aggression across time. As a re-sult, males' use of power and intimidation would be expected to increase (Walker, 1979, 1984). These psychological aggression and control tactics would be expected to have an adverse effect on women's self-esteem and general well-being (Follingstad et al., 1990).

Although there is unambiguous evidence that the experience of aggres-sion is far more negative physically and psychologically for females than males (see Cascardi et al., 1992; Schwartz, 1987; Stets & Straus, 1990), some females initiate aggression against their partners (Straus & Gelles, 1992) and others deny any serious negative impact of their own aggression (O'Leary, Vivian, & Malone, 1992). Ability to discriminate those couples most at risk for severe wife abuse where the female is undeniably and sys-tematically terrorized by her spouse from those who appear to engage in reciprocal aggression arising from dysfunctional interactions will not only quell contentious debate (cf. O'Leary, 1993) but will help us to theorize and intervene in meaningful, gender-sensitive ways. To this end, developmen-tal models of aggression in marriage will make it possible to use longitudi-nal examinations of the shift in power within marital relationships to identify those most at risk for severe violence sooner and with greater accuracy than current empirical results permit.

Attachment Models and Physical Aggression

Since the mid-1980s research on attachment-related phenomena in adults has increased greatly. Some of this research has revolved around community samples and some around clinical samples. For the most part, the work has been guided by Bowlby's (1988) ideas that early parent–child relationships serve as prototypes for later relationships. According to Bowlby, from repeated interactions with a primary caregiver, the child eventually abstracts a set of expectations and postulates about how close relationships operate and how they are used in ordinary and emergency situations. This set of expectations, beliefs, or "working models" of attachment are held to govern affect, behavior, and cognition in attachment relationships throughout one's life. A number of methods have been developed to assess individual differences in attachment representations or styles (for a review, see Crowell & Treboux, 1995).

Attachment theory is beginning to be applied to the understanding of domestic violence (for a review, see Rathus, 1994), and hence empirical studies are relatively few. Using a self-report measure of attachment style, Babcock, Jacobson, and Gottman (1992) found that physically violent husbands were less secure, more anxious/ambivalent, and reported more care seeking than nondistressed, nonviolent, and happy nonviolent husbands. Using the Adult Attachment Interview (AAI), an assessment of individual differences in attachment representations, Holtzworth-Munroe and Hutchinson (1992) found that violent men were more often classified as insecure than nonviolent men. Furthermore, in a sample of battered men, 80% of the men had insecure attachment patterns as assessed by self-report measures (Dutton, Saunders, Starzomski, & Bartholomew, 1994). Likewise, 94 percent of a sample of battered women assessed with the AAI were classified as having insecure attachments (Sullivan-Hanson, 1990). In a normative sample of engaged couples, there was an association between adult attachment status of women and their partners' aggression. Insecure women were found to report more verbal and physical aggression of their partner (O'Connor, Pan, Waters, & Posada, 1995). Interestingly, there was no association of attachment of men and their aggression. Moreover, premarital insecurity predicted reports of partner's physical aggression 18 months later (Gao, Treboux, Owens, Pan, & Crowell, 1995).

Although attachment theory offers a promising approach to understanding marital aggression, further research needs to delineate the mechanisms linking attachment and aggression in adulthood. Clearly, not all controlled research on domestic violence supports the position that men who engage in repeated physical aggression against their wives have attachment problems that differ from other men (Rathus, 1994). In addition, it remains to be seen how an individual's attachment relationship with one's parents compares with variables that are more proximal to the physical aggression, such as interaction styles with an intimate partner. Nonetheless, there is considerable evidence to substantiate many of the predictions about insecure attachment and aggression (Crowell & Treboux, 1995).

Shelter and Court-Mandated Samples: Bivariate Associations with Severe Wife Abuse

Physically abusive men in batterer treatment programs have been found to display higher rates of personality disorders, alcohol abuse, lower self-esteem, higher levels of depression, are more generally violent, are more likely to be unemployed or report lower incomes, and are more likely to have witnessed more and/or experienced more violence in the family of origin than nonphysically abusive men (Gondolf, 1988; Hamberger & Hastings, 1986, 1988; Murphy, Meyer, & O'Leary, 1994; Rosenbaum & O'Leary, 1981). O'Leary (1993) posits a continuum of violence such that those enacting the most serious forms of aggression (e.g., punching, beating) are more likely to show signs of personality disorders, emotional lability, and poor self-esteem. What seems clear in both the conceptual and empirical literatures is that level of personality disturbance and general psychopathology do indeed increase as the level of violence increases.

Another interesting shift that occurs when the violence under investigation is quite severe is that the gender disparity in regard to impact, injury, and circumstance exceeds that of marital clinic and community samples. Where there has been controversy over the findings from community samples in which males and females self-report aggressive behaviors at roughly equivalent rates, when the samples are drawn from individuals involved in the criminal justice, medical, or community-based domestic violence agencies, victim and perpetrator are delineated clearly. One could argue that this is merely an artifact of the systems in which those individuals are served. That is, domestic violence agencies operate within a specific philosophical framework; and our criminal justice system is designed to assign blame to one party. However, findings that women self-identifying as victims of domestic violence suffer depression, post-traumatic stress disorder, immense fear, and substantial restrictions on or access to money, friends, family, and so forth (Cascardi & O'Leary, 1992; Gleason, 1993; Tolman, 1989; Walker, 1979, 1984) imposed by their partners suggests the gender disparity is more than a system artifact.

Models of Severe Wife Abuse

Stith and Farley (1993) evaluated a cross-sectional model of male spousal violence "based on social learning theory and previous research" (p. 183). The subjects in this study were 39 men in male violence programs and 52 men in alcoholism programs. This study indicated that severe violence was significantly predicted by approval of male violence and sex-role egalitarianism. These two variables had direct effects on marital violence. The model accounted for 19% of the variance in severe violence. Indirect effects of marital violence, self-esteem, marital stress, and level of alcoholism were also noted.

Though it did not employ a shelter or treatment sample, another multi-variate analysis of severe wife abuse was conducted by Pan et al. (1994). They found that self-reports of having an alcohol or drug problem were more likely among men who reported engaging in severe wife abuse than those who engaged in mild forms of physical aggression. For example, the use of drugs did not predict mild physical aggression; however, it increased the odds of severe physical aggression by 121%.

Recommendations for Understanding Marital Aggression in a Developmental Context

A developmental perspective toward spousal abuse raises more questions than it answers. The literature reviewed in this chapter concerned high school and college students, young adults from the community, couples seeking marital treatment who report aggression, and those involved in the courts or community-based domestic violence agencies. Interestingly, younger populations drawn from the community appear to show less disparity between males and females with respect to the impact and correlates of physical aggression. In clinic samples, the gender disparity becomes more apparent, particularly as the aggression becomes more severe. It is essential for research to identify *how* power distributions within intimate relationships shift over time, and how these shifts correlate with increases or decreases in physical aggression. It is also important to determine *who* terminates relationships marked by aggression in high school, college, and early marriage. Furthermore, it is necessary to predict who will stop engaging in physical aggression and who will not supplant the physical aggression with more subtle forms of coercion.

Biological Models of Physical Aggression in Marriage

There has been strong resistance to the study and portrayal of aggression as behavior with biological causes. The resistance to biological models of human aggression comes in part from minority groups, especially blacks, because physical aggression, particularly lethal aggression, is disproportionately high among blacks. More specifically, from 1976 to 1985 blacks accounted for 45.4% of all spouse homicide victims (Mercy & Saltzman, 1989). In fact, Ronald Walters, chairman of the political science department at Howard University, became an adviser to the National Committee Against the Federal Violence Initiative (Stone, 1992). Their function was to be a watchdog committee and try to minimize any stigma that could result from empirical associations of race and aggression, especially biological factors and aggression. Feminist writers and proponents are another source of resistance to biological explanations of physical aggression. This resistance to biological explanations stems in part from the concern that if the cause were indeed biological, the explanation would simply be seen as an excuse for the behavior. This concern was obvious in the consideration of the proposed DSM-IV diagnosis, Partner Abuse, and in related abuse diagnoses. Partly as a result, the diagnoses are a V code (Other Conditions That May Be Focus of Clinical Attention).

The debate over the role of biological factors in aggressive behavior will undoubtedly continue, as is clear from the furor over seminars about biological causes of aggression at the 1993 meeting of the Association for the Advancement of Science (Mann, 1994). At this meeting (reported by Mann, 1994), Raine, Brennan, and Mednick presented data showing that the combination of birth complications and parental rejection was associated with high levels of violent criminality in a sample of 4,269 consecutive males born in Copenhagen. Interestingly, neither variable itself was associated with high levels of violent criminal behavior, but together they were strongly associated with such behavior. An alternative panel at the same meeting, which included individuals such as Peter Breggin from the Center for the Study of Child Psychiatry, argued that the "Violence Initiative" of several federal agencies was basically a pretext for oppressing members of the black population by searching for biological causes of behavior that would in turn justify giving drugs to black children. In a related vein, the president-elect of the Behavior Genetics Association of the United States resigned to protest a speech by psychologist Glayde Whitney that called for studies to determine whether some of the discrepant contribution to crime by blacks in the United States has genetic roots (*Science,* 1995, Vol. 270, p. 1125). Despite the controversy, some important research has been done on the role of biological factors in aggressive behavior, though little of it has been tied directly to spouse abuse.

Brain Injury

Brain injury has been shown to be higher in men who injure their partners than those who do not (Rosenbaum & Hoge, 1989; Rosenbaum et al., 1994). In one study, 61% of 39 battering men attending a treatment program for domestic violent offenders had significant head injury (Rosenbaum & Hoge, 1989). In a follow-up study conducted with neurological assessors unaware of the status of the men being evaluated (Rosenbaum et al., 1994), men who physically abused their spouses were compared with men who were recruited for (1) marital discord and nonviolence and (2) marital satisfaction and nonviolence. Fifty-three percent of the batterers, 25% of the discordant nonviolent, and 16% of the satisfied nonviolent men had histories of significant, closed head injuries. Furthermore, regression analyses indicated that a history of significant head injury increased the likelihood of marital aggression more than sixfold.

Testosterone

Blood analyses reveal that testosterone is 10 times higher in males than females. Because testosterone accounts for a number of male characteristics such as deepening of the voice and growth of body hair, it is natural to expect testosterone to cause or be correlated with aggression in men. However, reviews of this research indicate that the relationship between testosterone and aggression is weak and only suggestive of a relationship (Baron & Richardson, 1994).

In one of the largest studies of testosterone and antisocial behavior, Dabbs and Morris (1990) examined the records of 4,462 male military veterans. The average age of the veterans was 37, and they were representative of the U.S. population in terms of race, education, income, and occupation. The investigators compared the behavior of the men who scored in the upper 10% of the distribution of testosterone with all other males. Testosterone was associated with a variety of antisocial behaviors such as childhood delinquency and marijuana use. In addition, the men with the high testosterone levels had records of more adult delinquent acts (including assaultive marital or relationship problems, job trouble, violence, and negligence toward children and more unauthorized leaves from the military). When analyses were conducted separately for high and low SES (education and income), it was found that the risk for engaging in a wide variety of antisocial behaviors held strongly for the low SES groups but not for the high SES groups. Thus it appears that testosterone interacts with social class variables to place one at greater risk for varied antisocial behavior. Physical aggression against a female partner was not measured separately in this study, and therefore one must be careful in applying the results to wife abuse. It should also be noted that with large samples such as these (4,462), it is possible to get highly significant results when the correlation between two variables are small. In this particular case, the correlation (Phi) estimated from the published tables between testosterone and adult delinquency in the lower SES group (where the association was significant) was approximately .15.

In another study assessing the association between testosterone and aggression, Olweus (1987) randomly sampled a ninth-grade male student population in a suburb of Stockholm. He found a significant association between testosterone and self-reported levels of verbal (.38) and physical (.36) aggression. Olweus noted that the correlations with testosterone were highest with the physical aggression items that measured response to provocation and frustration. He therefore argued that testosterone has a direct effect on provoked physical aggression and an indirect effect on unprovoked physical aggression. In addition, path analyses showed that testosterone had a direct effect on provoked aggressive behavior. Moreover, its effects were not substantially reduced when other variables were controlled, such as mother's negativism, mother's permission for aggression, and the boy's temperament. Again, as in the aforementioned Dabbs and Morris study, there was no direct assessment of physical aggression against a female (dating partner). However, the results have implications for such aggression because aggression against adult partners and aggression in general are correlated.

In reviewing assessments of the relationship between circulating testosterone and self-reports of physical aggression, Gladue (1994) found that numerous studies report weak yet significant correlations between these two variables. An association between circulating testosterone and aggression using experimental manipulations provided for an assessment of both aggression and competitiveness. Competitiveness per se was not associated with circulating testosterone but defeating an opponent with skill was. Defeating an opponent by chance was not.

In summary, both correlational and experimental studies have revealed a small but significant association between testosterone and self-reported physical aggression in males. At the same time, the literature indicates that criminal populations arrested for assault versus those arrested for other crimes have not shown associations between the testosterone and physical aggression (see Baron & Richardson, 1994). Thus the conclusions one reaches about testosterone and aggression depend upon the type of research used to assess the association.

Physiological Reactivity

Physiological reactivity of physically abusive men was studied by Jacobson (1994) and Jacobson et al. (1995). Overall, physically abusive men do not differ physiologically from maritally discordant nonabusive men. However, about 20% of physically abusive men had heart rates that *declined* while in a heated discussion with their partner about a marital problem. To Jacobson et al. (1995), these men were like well-toned athletes who were unaffected by the heat of the moment. The authors also thought that they were probably unamenable to treatment and similar to psychopaths in their physiological responding. Such work is proactive and challenging, but it needs to be replicated by other investigators. Moreover, because there are so few variables that are reliably predictive of treatment responsivity of any kind, it remains to be seen whether such physiological reactivity is indicative of failures to respond to treatment. It is also important to know to what extent the decline in physiological responsivity was associated with frequency and severity of physical aggression. In any case, the work is noteworthy and deserves attention. As O'Leary (1993) and Holtzworth-Munroe and Stuart (1994) noted, all aggression is certainly not alike, and categorization is necessary for the field to proceed. Thus calls for typologies of physical aggression are now being issued from several quarters.

Evolutionary Analyses

Some attention has also been given to an evolutionary analysis of aggressive behavior (e.g., Archer, 1994; Daly & Wilson, 1988). The most noted analyses of spouse abuse by those interested in this approach are those of Daly and Wilson (1988), who studied homicide statistics. Their basic premise is that men and women attempt to maximize their gene potential ("self-interests conflict because of rivalry for representation in future gene pools"). They found that men and women kill their stepchildren more frequently than they kill their own children. They also report that men kill their estranged wives more often than estranged wives kill their husbands because of the coercive tactic of proprietary men. Daly and Wilson (1988) concluded that jealousy was the leading motive in spousal homicide. Data on murder of wives is consistent with the evolutionary view that males are interested in protecting their own gene pool from being "mixed" with that of others. That is, "If I can't have her, nobody else can."

While the data on homicide are consistent with an evolutionary view, other interpretations also fit these data. First, marital discord has been found to correlate highly with severe spouse abuse. Alcohol and drug abuse is also significantly correlated with severe spouse abuse (Pan et al., 1994), as is lower socioeconomic background (Straus et al., 1980). Evolutionary interpretations provide an alternative view of homicide data to the often discussed sociological/psychological views. It remains to be seen whether the evolutionary views can elucidate factors that might help in the amelioration of the problem and whether the evolutionary conceptualizations can be linked to cognitive psychological data. It is possible that the current situation of almost completely independent theoretical bases could be brought into closer focus if variables such as jealousy or some cognitive or affective variables were assessed and theoretically related to variables about preservation of the gene pool.

Aggression Gene

The search for the causes of aggressive behavior in our genes has been going on for some time. According to animal behaviorists Huntingtonford and Turner (1987), some differences in aggressive behavior can be ascribed to genetic differences. They add, however, that the role of genes is small compared with that of the environment. Basically, two lines of inquiry have been followed in addressing this question of the inheritance of aggressive behavior. First, one can look at similarities in the aggressive behavior of relatives in the general population. Second, one can look at highly aggressive people to determine whether they have a genetic defect.

Twin studies indicate that there are inherited differences in personality traits such as impulsivity and fearlessness that may influence how and whether aggression is expressed. Moreover, such twin studies have been interpreted as providing strong evidence of genetic influences on personality formation (Plomin, 1990). In no case, however, have the twin studies assessed aggressive behavior per se. However, twin studies in the United States and Canada provide strong evidence for genetic influences on self-reported aggressive personality styles (Rushton et al., 1986; Tellegen et al., 1988).

The search for a specific gene that may cause aggressive behavior has been made more likely by new genetic marking techniques. The search along these lines by a Dutch research team was described in *Science* by Morell (1993) and was the subject of a *Time* essay, "Born to Raise Hell?" (Overbye, 1994). A clinical geneticist in Holland, Brunner, reported that in 1978 a woman came to his office asking for help with a problem in her family. The woman told Brunner that many of the men in her family had been prone to aggressive outbursts that had no apparent provocation. According to family records, 14 male relatives had displayed unusually aggressive behavior. One raped a sister and later attacked a warden of the mental institution with a pitchfork; another threatened his sister with a knife to get her to undress; and a third attempted to run over his employer with a car. All the aggressive male relatives were mildly retarded (IQ about 85). In contrast, none of the women in the family were prone to aggressive outbursts, and none were mentally retarded. This pattern suggested to Brunner that the aggressive disorder was caused by a recessive gene on the X or female chromosome. The reasoning is as follows: because men have only one X chromosome, they develop the symptoms in question if they inherit the bad gene. Women, on the other hand, are protected because their second chromosome carries a good copy of the gene. The search for the gene aberration led nowhere for 10 years, but with the development of information markers, Brunner and his colleagues were able to search for the X chromosome. They identified the MAO gene region as the likely site for the cause of the aggressive behavior in this family. There are two sites for monoamine oxidase enzymes, and both are located on the X chromosome near each other (MAOA and MAOB). However, urine analyses revealed that the affected men secreted more than average levels of chemicals that the monoamine oxidase chemically devour. Basically, it appears that the MAOA is at fault, since the MAOB and the chemicals with which it interacts were normal.

Whenever a result like this is heralded in the press, many often generalize to the population at large. While the results may hold promise for the aggression-prone members of this Dutch family, it must be remembered that the suspected mutation has only been found in one family. Moreover, as pointed out by Morell (1993), even if found in other families, its expression might be modified by social, genetic, and cultural factors. In other words, it is not cause for a screening of monoamine oxidase deficiencies – as some did for the XYY defect.

Summary

Mental health professionals and academic researchers paid little attention to wife abuse until the 1980s. This topic only began to appear with any regularity in psychological and psychiatric journals in the mid-1980s. Then in the early 1990s, several federal agencies planned initiatives to address needed research on wife abuse. The Center for Disease Control and NIMH have both launched studies that address partner abuse and the prevention of injury to women.

We examined the developmental course of spouse abuse from several perspectives. Rates of physical aggression against an intimate partner start at low levels in early high school and then increase to a high during the intense dating periods when partners are between 18 and 24. This result holds for men and women. For total populations, the rate of such aggression decreases across the life span. Unfortunately, it is not known which individuals in dating and early marriage continue to increase in aggression across time. However, a family history of violence, male's attitudes approving of violence, and a history of aggression with peers are repeatedly associated with the use of physical aggression. Contrary to many researcher's predictions, traditional sex-role stereotypes have not been reliably associated with young male's use of physical aggression against a partner. Prediction of sexual aggression against a female dating partner appears to be influenced by a violent home environment, delinquency, and hostility. In long-term dating relations and in marriage, relationship discord becomes a very salient predictor of physical aggression, which then operates over and above the aforementioned factors in predicting aggression. Physically abusive men seeking treatment or in treatment programs have higher rates of psychopathology, more violence in their family of origin, and lower self-esteem. Moreover, the level of fear and intimidation reported by women married to men who repeatedly use strong physical force against them suggests qualitative differences between such men and young married men who use lower levels of physical aggression.

There is no single predominant theoretical conceptualization of physical aggression against a partner. At the same time, the feminist position that male's use of power and control are central has been very influential, especially in treatment settings. Variants of learning models have repeatedly shown that men's observation of violence in the family of origin is a correlate or a direct path to physical aggression against an intimate partner. Dyadic models of marital interaction have shown that psychological aggression and marital discord are predictors of physical aggression. Finally, extremes in personality style or psychopathology of one or both of the partners are also associated with physical aggression.

There has been strong political resistance to biological models of wife abuse, and they have just begun to receive attention. Brain injury is disproportionately high in samples of men who abuse their wives. Testosterone is associated with general physical aggression in males, and there is suggestive evidence that it may be associated with wife abuse. Some abusive men have physiological patterns that resemble those of psychopaths; that is, they decrease their physiological activity during conflict. The search for a gene that controls aggressive behavior persists, and the MAO gene region on the X chromosome appears to be one possible site of the cause of aggressive behavior of some extremely aggressive individuals.

There is no single cause of aggressive behavior. Although psychological and biological models have received attention here, sociological and cultural models also have their place as poverty and cultural attitudes are certainly related to family violence. A developmental analysis of physical aggression against an intimate partner, however, reveals one clear fact, namely, that such aggression decreases markedly with age. Any future theoretical analyses will have to address this issue. Unlike the statements of many professionals who treat victims of physically abusive men, we now know that physical aggression does not always escalate. In many men, aggression decreases and eventually stops. The challenge is to be able to successfully predict those who stop being physically aggressive and those whose aggression escalates across time.

References

American Psychiatric Association. (1994). *Diagnostic and statistical manual of mental disorders* (4th ed., rev.). Washington, DC: Author.

Archer, J. (1994, June). *What can ethology offer the study of human aggression?* Paper presented at the World Meeting: International Society for Research on Aggression. Delray, FL.

Arias, I. (1984). *A social learning explanation of the intergenerational transmission of physical aggression in intimate heterosexual relationships.* Unpublished doctoral dissertation, State University of New York at Stony Brook.

Arias, I., & O'Leary, K. D. (1988). Cognitive-behavioral treatment of physical aggression in marriage. In N. Epstein, S. E. Schlesinger, & W. Dryden (Eds.), *Cognitive-behavioral therapy with families* (pp. 118–150). New York: Brunner/Mazel.

Arias, I., Samios, M., & O'Leary, K. D. (1987). Prevalence and correlates of physical aggression during courtship. *Journal of Interpersonal Violence, 2,* 82–90.

Avery-Leaf, S., Cascardi, M., & O'Leary, K. D. (1994, August). *Modifying attitudes to decrease dating violence: Efficacy of a dating violence prevention program.* Presented at the annual conference of the American Psychological Association, Los Angeles.

Babcock, J., Jacobson, N., & Gottman, J. (1992, November). *Insecure attachment among batterers and victims: Using attachment theory to organize patterns of emotion and behavior.* In C. Murphy (Chair), Attachment theory and marital violence: Integrating cognitive, behavioral, and affective processes. Association for Advancement of Behavior Therapy, Boston.

Baron, R. J., & Richardson, D. R. (1994). *Human aggression,* (2nd ed.). New York: Plenum.

Bergman, L. (1992). Dating violence among high school students. *Social Work, 37,* 21–27.

Bernard, M. L., & Bernard, J. L. (1983). Violent intimacy: The family as a model for lover relationships. *Family Relations, 32,* 283–291.

Bird, G. W., Stith, S. M., & Schladale, J. (1991). Psychological resources, coping strategies, and negotiation styles as discriminators of violence in dating relationships. *Family Relations, 40,* 45–50.

Birns, B., Cascardi, M., & Meyer, S. L. (1994). Sex role socialization: Developmental influences on wife abuse. *American Journal of Orthopsychiatry, 64*(1), 50–59.

Bookwala, J., Frieze, I. H., Smith, C., & Ryan, K. (1992). Predictors of dating violence: A multivariate analysis. *Violence and Victims, 7,* 297–311.

Bowlby, J. (1988). *A secure base: Parent-child attachment and healthy human development.* New York: Basic Books.

Campbell, A. (1993). *Men, women, and aggression.* New York: Basic Books.

Cano, A., Avery-Leaf, S., Cascardi, M., & O'Leary, K. D. (in press). Dating violence in two high schools: Discriminating variables. *Journal of Primary Prevention.*

Cascardi, M., Langhinrichsen, J., & Vivian, D. (1992). Marital aggression, impact, injury, and health correlates for husbands and wives. *Archives of Internal Medicine, 152,* 1178–1184.

Cascardi, M., & O'Leary, K. D. (1990). *Dating violence in high school: Prevalence and attributions.* Unpublished manuscript. State University of New York at Stony Brook.

Cascardi, M., & O'Leary, K. D. (1992). Depressive symptomatology, self-esteem, and self-blame in battered women. *Journal of Family Violence, 7*(4), 249–259.

Cate, R. M., Henton, J. M., Koval, J., Christopher, F. S., & Lloyd, S. (1982). Premarital abuse: A social psychological perspective. *Journal of Family Issues, 3,* 79–90.

Comins, C. A. (1984). *Courtship violence: A recent study and its implications for future research.* Paper presented at the Second Annual Conference for Family Violence Researchers, Durham, NH.

Cronkite, K. (1994). *On the edge of darkness.* New York: Doubleday.

Crowell, J. A., & Treboux, D. (1995). A review of adult attachment measures: Implications for theory and research. *Social Development, 4,* 294–327.

Currie, D. W. (1983). A Toronto model. *Social Work With Groups, 6,* 179–188.

Dabbs, J. M., & Morris, R. (1990). Testosterone, social class, and antisocial behavior in a sample of 4,462 men. *Psychological Science, 1,* 209–211.

Daly, M., & Wilson, M. (1988). Evolutionary social psychology and family homicide. *Science, 242,* 519–524.

Dobash, R. E., & Dobash, R. (1979). *Violence against wives.* New York: Free Press.

Dutton, D. G., & Browning, J. J. (1988). Power struggles and intimacy anxieties as causative factors of wife assault. In G. W. Russell (Ed.), *Violence in intimate relationships* (pp. 163–176). New York: PMA.

Dutton, D. G., Saunders, K., Starzomski, A., & Bartholomew, K. (1994). Intimacy anger and insecure attachment as precursors of abuse in intimate relationships. *Journal of Applied Social Psychology, 24,* 1367–1386.

Elliot, D. S., Huizinga, D., & Morse, B. J. (1986). Self-reported violent offending: A descriptive analysis of juvenile violent offenders and their offending careers. *Journal of Interpersonal Violence, 4,* 472–514.

Fedders, C., & Elliot, L. (1987). *Shattered dreams.* New York: Harper & Row.

Feld, S. L., & Straus, M. A. (1990). Escalation and desistance from wife assault in marriage. In M. A. Straus & R. J. Gelles (Eds.), *Physical violence in American families* (pp. 489–503). New Brunswick, NJ: Transaction.

Fincham, F. D., & Bradbury, T. N. (1990). *The psychology of marriage: Basic issues and applications.* New York: Guilford.

Follingstad, D. R., Rutledge, L. L., Polek, D. S., & McNeill-Hawkins, K. (1988). Factors associated with patterns of dating violence toward college women. *Journal of Family Violence, 3,* 169–182.

Follingstad, D. R., Rutledge, L. L., Berg, B. J., Hause, E. S., & Polek, D. S. (1990). The role of emotional abuse in physically abusive relationships. *Journal of Family Violence, 5,* 81–95.

Foo, L., & Margolin, G. (1995). A multivariate investigation of dating aggression. *Journal of Family Violence, 10,* 351–377.

Gao, Y., Treboux, D., Owens, G., Pan, H., & Crowell, J. (1995). *Working models of adult relationships: Foundation in childhood, fine tuning in marriage.* Poster presented at the biennial meeting of the Society for Research in Child Development, Indianapolis, IN.

Gelles, R. J. (1974). *The violent home: A study of physical aggression between husbands and wives.* Beverly Hills, CA: Sage.

Gladue, B. A. (July, 1994). *Hormones, aggression, and competition in men and women.* Paper presented at the Eleventh World Meeting: International Society for Research on Aggression. Delray, FL.

Gleason, W. J. (1993). Mental disorders in battered women: An empirical study. *Violence and Victims, 8,* 53–68.

Gondolf, E. F. (1988). Who are those guys? A typology of men who batter. *Violence and Victims, 3,* 187–203.

Gwartney-Gibbs, P. A., Stockard, J., & Bohmer, S. (1987). Learning courtship aggression: The influence of parents, peers, and personal experiences. *Family Relations, 36,* 276–282.

Hamberger, L. K., & Hastings, J. E. (1986). Personality correlates of men who abuse their partners: A cross validation study. *Journal of Family Violence, 1,* 323–341.

Hamberger, L. K., & Hastings, J. E. (1988). Skills training for the treatment of spouse abusers: An outcome study. *Journal of Family Violence, 3,* 121–130.

Henton, J., Cate, R., Koval, J., Lloyd, S., & Christopher, F. S. (1983). Romance and violence in dating relationships. *Journal of Family Issues, 4,* 467–482.

Holtzworth-Munroe, A., & Anglin, K. (1991). The competency of responses given by maritally violent versus nonviolent men to problematic situations. *Violence and Victims, 6,* 257–269.

Holtzworth-Munroe, A., & Hutchinson, G. (1992, November). *Attachment styles and cognitive prototypes of relationships among maritally violent men.* Poster presented at the Association for Advancement of Behavior Therapy, New York, NY.

Holtzworth-Munroe, A., & Stuart, G. L. (1994). Typologies of male batterers: Three subtypes and the differences among them. *Psychological Bulletin, 116,* 476–497.

Hornung, C. A., McCullough, B. C., & Sugimoto, T. (1981). Status relationships in marriage: Risk factors in spouse abuse. *Journal of Marriage and the Family, 43,* 675–692.

Huntingtonford, F., & Turner, A. (1987). *Animal conflict.* Chapman & Hall, New York.

Jacobson, N. S. (1994, June 22). Standard therapies may help only impulsive spouse abuse. *New York Times,* Health, C11.

Jacobson, N. S., Gottman, J. M., Waltz, J., Rushe, R., Babcock, J., & Holtzworth-Munroe, A. (1994). Affect, verbal content, and psychophysiology in the arguments of couples with a violent husband. *Journal of Consulting and Clinical Psychology, 62,* 982–988.

Jacobson, N. S., & Margolin, G. (1979). *Marital therapy.* New York: Brunner/Mazel.

Jones, L. E. (1987). *School curriculum project evaluation report.* Minnesota Coalition for Battered Women, Minneapolis, MN.

L'Abate, L. (1994). *Handbook of developmental family psychology and psychopathology.* New York: Wiley.

McKinney, K. (1986). Perceptions of courtship violence: Gender difference and involvement. *Free Inquiry in Creative Sociology, 14,* 61–66.

Makepeace, J. M. (1981). Courtship violence among college students. *Family Relations, 30,* 97–102.

Malamuth, N. M., Sockloskie, R. J., Koss, M. P., & Tanaka, J. S. (1991). Characteristics of aggressors against women: Testing a model using a national sample of college students. *Journal of Consulting and Clinical Psychology, 59,* 670–681.

Malone, J., & Tyree, A. (1991, August). *Cycle of violence explanations of marital aggression and victimization.* Paper presented to the 86th meeting of the American Sociological Association, Cincinnati, OH.

Malone, J., Tyree, A., & O'Leary, K. D. (1989). Generalization and containment: Different effects of past aggression for wives and husbands. *Journal of Marriage and the Family, 51,* 687–697.

Mann, C. C. (1994). War of words continues in violence research. *Science, 263,* 1375.

Margolin, G., John, R. S., & Gleberman, L. (1988). Affective responses to conflictual discussion in violent and non-violent couples. *Journal of Consulting and Clinical Psychology, 56,* 24–33.

Matthews, W. J. (1984). Violence in college couples. *College Student Journal, 18,* 150–158.

Mercy, J. A., & Saltzman, L. E. (1989). Fatal violence among spouses in the United States. *American Journal of Public Health, 79,* 595–599.

Mihalic, S. W., Elliot, D. S., & Menard, S. (1994). Continuities in marital violence. *Journal of Family Violence, 9,* 195–225.

Morell, V. (1993). Evidence found for a possible "aggression gene." *Science, 269,* 1722–1723.

Murphy, C. M., Meyer, S., & O'Leary, K. D. (1994). Dependency characteristics of partner assaultative men. *Journal of Abnormal Psychology, 103,* 729–735.

Murphy, C. M., & O'Leary, K. D. (1989). Psychological aggression predicts physical aggression in early marriage. *Journal of Clinical and Consulting Psychology, 57,* 579–582.

Neidig, P. (1986). *Spouse abuse issues and attitudes: A guide for family advocacy public information presentations in the military.* Beaufort, SC: Behavioral Sciences Associates.

Nisonoff, L., & Bitman, I. (1979). Spouse abuse: Incidence and relationship to selected demographic variables. *Victimology, 4,* 131–139.

O'Connor, E., Pan, H., Waters, E., & Posada, G. (1995). *Attachment classification, romantic jealousy, and aggression in couples.* Paper presented at the biennial meeting of the Society for Research in Child Development, Indianapolis, IN.

O'Keefe, N. K., Brockopp, K., & Chew, E. (1986). Teen dating violence. *Social Work, 31,* 465–468.

O'Leary, K. D. (1993). Through a psychological lens: Personality traits, personality disorders, and levels of violence. In R. J. Gelles & D. R. Loseke, (Eds.). *Current controversies on family violence* (pp. 7–30). Newbury Park, CA: Sage.

O'Leary, K. D., Barling, J., Arias, I., Rosenbaum, A., Malone, J., & Tyree, A. (1989). Prevalence and stability of physical aggression between spouses: A longitudinal analysis. *Journal of Consulting and Clinical Psychology, 57,* 263–268.

O'Leary, K. D., & Curley, A. D. (1986). Assertion and family violence: Correlates of spouse abuse. *Journal of Marital and Family Therapy, 12,* 281–289.

O'Leary, K. D., & Jacobson, N. S. (1997). *Partner relational problems with physical abuse: DSM IV literature summary* (pp. 673–692). American Psychiatric Association: Washington, DC.

O'Leary, K. D., & Malone, J. (1992). *Stability of physical aggression in young married couples.* Unpublished manuscript. State University of New York at Stony Brook.

O'Leary, K. D., Malone, J., & Tyree, A. (1994). Physical aggression in early marriage: Pre-relationship and relationship effects. *Journal of Consulting and Clinical Psychology, 62,* 594–602.

O'Leary, K. D., Vivian, D., & Malone, J. (1992). Assessment of physical aggression in marriage: The need for a multimodal method. *Behavioral Assessment, 14,* 5–14.

Olweus, D. (1987). Testosterone and adrenaline: Aggressive antisocial behavior in normal adolescent males. In S. A. Mednick, T. E. Moffitt, & S. A. Sacks (Eds.), *The causes of crime: New biological approaches* (pp. 263–282). New York: Cambridge University Press.

Overbye, D. (Feb. 21, 1994). Born to raise hell? *Time.*

Pagelow, M. D. (1981). *Woman battering: Victims and their experiences.* Beverly Hills, CA.: Sage.

Pagelow, M. D. (1984). *Family violence.* New York: Praeger.

Pan, H. S., Neidig, P. H., & O'Leary, K. D. (1994). Predicting mild and severe husband to wife physical aggression. *Journal of Consulting and Clinical Psychology, 62,* 975–981.

Paolino, T. J., & McCrady, B. S. (1978). *Marriage and marital therapy: Psychoanalytic, behavioral, and systems theory perspectives.* New York: Brunner/Mazel.

Pleck, E. (1987). *Domestic tyranny: The making of American social policy against family violence from colonial times to the present.* New York: Oxford University Press.

Plomin, R. (1990). The role of inheritance in behavior. *Science, 248,* 183–188.

Rathus, J. (1994). *Attachment, coercive control, and wife abuse.* Unpublished doctoral dissertation. The University of New York at Stony Brook.

Riggs, D. S. (1990). *Tests of a theoretical model of self-reported courtship aggression.* Unpublished doctoral dissertation. The University of New York at Stony Brook.

Riggs, D. S., & O'Leary, K. D. (1989). The development of a model of courtship aggression. In M. A. Pirog-Good & J. E. Stets (Eds.), *Violence in dating relationships: Emerging social issues* (pp. 53–71). New York: Praeger.

Riggs, D. S., & O'Leary, K. D. (1996). Aggression between heterosexual dating partners. *Journal of Interpersonal Violence, 11,* 519–540.

Riggs, D. S., O'Leary, K. D., & Breslin, F. C. (1990). Multiple correlates of physical aggression in dating couples. *Journal of Interpersonal Violence, 5,* 61–73.

Roscoe, B., & Benaske, N. (1985). Courtship violence experienced by abused wives: Similarities in patterns of abuse. *Family Relations, 34,* 419–424.

Roscoe, B., & Callahan, J. E. (1983). Adolescent's self-report of violence in families and dating relationships. *Adolescence, 10,* 545–553.

Rosenbaum, A., & Hoge, S. K. (1989). Head injury and marital aggression. *American Journal of Psychiatry, 146,* 1048–1051.

Rosenbaum, A., Hoge, S. K., Adelman, S. A., Warnken, W. J., Fletcher, K. E., & Kane, R. (1994). Head injury in partner abusive men. *Journal of Consulting and Clinical Psychology, 62,* 1187–1193.

Rosenbaum, A., & Golash, L. (1987). *Communication and aggression in beginning marriages.* Unpublished manuscript, University of Massachusetts Medical Center, Worcester, MA.

Rosenbaum, A., & O'Leary, K. D. (1981). Marital violence: Characteristics of abusive couples. *Journal of Consulting and Clinical Psychology, 49,* 63–71.

Rushton, J. P., Fulker, D. W., Neale, M. C., Nias, D. K. B., & Eysenck, H. J. (1986). Altruism and aggression: The heritability of individual differences. *Journal of Personality and Social Psychology, 50*(6), 1192–1198.

Schulman, M. (1979). *A survey of spousal violence against women in Kentucky.* (Study No. 792701 for the Kentucky Commission on Women.) Washington, DC: U.S. Department of Justice, Law Enforcement Assistance Administration.

Schwartz, M. D. (1987). Gender and injury in spousal assault. *Sociological Focus, 20,* 61–75.

Schwartz, M., O'Leary, S. G., & Kendziora, K. T. (1997). *Dating aggression among high school students.* Unpublished manuscript, The University of New York at Stony Brook.

Sigelman, C. K., Berry, C. J., & Wiles, K. (1984). Violence in college students' dating relationships. *Journal of Applied Social Psychology, 14,* 530–548.

Smith, J. P., & Williams, J. (1992). From abusive household to dating violence. *Journal of Family Violence, 7,* 153–165.

Snell, E. J., Rosenwald, R. J., & Robey, A. (1964). The wife beater's wife. *Archives of General Psychiatry, 11,* 107–112.

Stark, E., Flitcraft, A., Zuckerman, D., Grey, A., Robinson, J., & Frazier, W. (1981). *Wife abuse in the medical setting: An introduction for health personnel.* Monograph 7, Office of Domestic Violence, Washington, DC.

Stets, J. E., & Straus, M. A. (1990). *Gender differences in reporting marital violence and its medical and psychological consequences.* In M. A. Straus and R. J. Gelles (Eds.), *Physical violence in American families* (pp. 151–165). New Brunswick, NJ: Transaction.

Stith, S. M., & Farley, S. C. (1993). A predictive model of male spousal violence. *Journal of Family Violence, 8,* 183–201.

Stone, R. (1992). HHHS "violence initiative" caught in a crossfire: Race and public policy. *Science, 258,* 212–213.

Straus, M. A., & Gelles, R. J. (1986). Societal change and change in family violence from 1975 to 1985 as revealed by two national surveys. *Journal of Marriage and the Family, 48,* 465–479.

Straus, M. A., & Gelles, R. J. (1992). *Physical violence in American families: Risk factors and adaptations to violence in 8,145 families.* New Brunswick, NJ: Transaction.

Straus, M. A., Gelles, R. J., & Steinmetz, S. K. (1980). *Behind closed doors: Violence in the American family,* Garden City, NY: Anchor Books/Doubleday.

Sugarman, D. B., & Hotaling, G. T. (1986). *Violent males in intimate relationships: An analysis of risk factors.* Paper presented at the Eastern Psychological Association Meetings, New York, NY.

Sugarman, D. B., & Hotaling, G. T. (1989). Dating violence: Prevalence, context and risk markers. In M. A. Pirog-Good & J. E. Stets (Eds.), *Violence in dating relationships: Emerging social issues* (pp. 3–32). New York: Praeger.

Sullivan-Hanson, J. (1990). *The early attachment and current affectional bonds of battered women: Implications for the impact of spouse abuse on children.* Unpublished doctoral dissertation. University of Virginia.

Tellegen, A., Lykken, D. T., Bourchard, T. J., Wilcox, K. J., Rich, S., & Segal, N. L. (1988). Personality similarity in twins reared apart and together. *Journal of Personality and Social Psychology, 54*(6), 1031–1039.

Thompson, E. H. (1991). The maleness of violence in dating relationships: An appraisal of stereotypes. *Sex Roles, 24,* 261–278.

Tolman, R. (1989). The development of a measure of psychological maltreatment of women by their male partners. *Violence and Victims, 7,* 159–177.

Tontodonato, P., & Crew, B. K. (1992). Dating violence, social learning theory, and gender: A multivariate analysis. *Violence and Victims, 7,* 3–14.

Vivian, D., Mayer, F. J., Sandeen, E., & O'Leary, K. D. (1988). *Longitudinal assessment of the role of communication skills in interspousal aggression.* Paper presented at the Behavior Therapy World Congress, University of Edinburgh.

Vivian, D., & O'Leary, K. D. (1987). *Communication patterns in physically aggressive engaged partners.* Paper presented at the Third National Family Violence Research Conference, University of New Hampshire, Durham, NH.

Vivian, D., Smith, D. A., Mayer, F., Sandeen, E., & O'Leary, K. D. (1987). *Problem-solving skills and emotional styles in physically aggressive couples.* Paper presented at the 21st Annual Convention of the Association for Advancement of Behavior Therapy, Boston.

Walker, L. (1979). *The battered woman.* New York: Harper & Row.

Walker, L. (1984). *The battered woman syndrome.* New York: Springer.

White, J. W., & Koss, M. P. (1991). Courtship violence: Incidence in a national sample of higher education students. *Violence and Victims, 6,* 247–256.

PART II

Invited Commentaries

12　On Intervention and Relationship Events: A Marital Therapist Looks at Longitudinal Research on Marriage

Andrew Christensen

Most, if not all, investigators of marriage assume that their work may have implications for clinical practice. Some may even use these implications as part of the justification for their work. I approach this commentary initially from the perspective of a clinician asking about these implications. What can the clinician learn from longitudinal research on marriage? How might longitudinal research have greater applicability to the clinician?

Although my initial comments focus on the clinical implications of the findings here, I would argue that basic research does *not* need to have applied implications in order to be justifiable or important. Greater knowledge about marriage is important for its own sake. Furthermore, this greater knowledge will ultimately, even if it does not immediately, assist our efforts to promote human well-being in marriage. Too great an effort to make research relevant to clinical practice may even bias research. For example, Bradbury, Cohan, and Karney (this volume) argue that a desire to be clinically relevant made researchers ignore predictors of marital discord that are relatively un-changeable. So my conclusions about the clinical implications of the present research may not necessarily address the overall importance of the research to a science of marriage or, more broadly, to a science of close relationships. After discussing clinical implications of this research, however, I will dis-cuss some of my broader reactions to this work. My comments are organized around a few assertions about the current research that I believe are justified. First, I focus on longitudinal research as it relates to intervention.

Intervention

Longitudinal Research Offers Much to the Clinician – Maybe Too Much

The literature on longitudinal research on marriage has provided evidence that a large number of variables are predictors of marital discord and/or marital breakup. In their review of longitudinal research on marriage, Karney and Bradbury (1995) found that over 200 independent variables were investigated as possible predictors of marital satisfaction and stability; many of them turned out to have a relationship with marital outcome. This book also provides data on a diverse set of empirically supported predictor variables. I have grouped these variables in the following categories, on the basis of the categories that the authors themselves used and what seemed to me intuitively reasonable categories. In each category, I provide a few specific examples of actual variables used in these studies.

a. Personality variables such as neuroticism, femininity, masculinity, and expressiveness.
b. Communication variables such as extent of conflict, emotional invalidation, anger expression, disengagement, and accommodation to partner.
c. Attitudes and beliefs such as sex-role traditionalism, sexual conservatism, romanticism, religiosity, and dysfunctional beliefs.
d. Perceptions of self, such as views of one's own physical attractiveness, one's desirability as a partner, and satisfaction with self.
e. Similarities, differences, and incompatibilities such as a similar desire not to be single, differences on expressivity, and incompatibilities in leisure interests and role preferences.
f. Level of interdependence such as preference not to be single, extrinsic motives for being married, faith in marriage, and autonomy.
g. Intimacy and commitment such as love toward partner and commitment to partner.
h. Social network variables such as parental approval, living at home during college, partner liking friends, and social support.
i. Specific important classes of behavior, such as positive sexual interaction, drinking alcohol, and physical aggression.
j. Background variables such as socioeconomic status, race, and presence of children at the time of marriage.

This is an impressive list of empirically documented predictor variables. Although the variables studied in this book are undoubtedly not an exhaustive list of predictor variables of marital discord and instability, I would be surprised if these variables or ones similar to them are not a substantial part of the final predictor story.

For the clinician, this is, on the one hand, an optimistic list. Most of the variables, except for the background variables, are potentially alterable. Some of the variables, such as those in category e (similarities, differences, and incompatibilities) and some social network and interdependence variables, might require intervention well before marriage (e.g., helping potential spouses with the selection process). However, intervention in many of the variables could happen at any time (e.g., one could teach communication skills before partners have met their mate, before they marry, or after).

On the other hand, this list is distressing for the clinician for several reasons. First, it is far too long. Designing an intervention to change any variable in the list is a challenge (e.g., designing an intervention to change attitudes to marriage). Designing an intervention to incorporate a large number of these variables is indeed daunting. Second, we do not know which of the variables are causes of marital discord and which are only predictors of marital discord because they are correlated with the causes. For example, let us assume a simple model that posits neuroticism is the cause of marital discord. Therefore, communication would be a predictor of marital discord because neurotics do not communicate well, and incompatibility would be a predictor of marital discord because neurotics are bad at mate selection. If this model were correct, and we chose to intervene by training communication skills and assisting partners with mate selection, our intervention might be weak at best because we did not intervene at the causal culprit – neuroticism.

It is likely that in a complicated human relationship such as marriage there is no single cause of discord or breakup but rather a multitude of complex, interconnected causes. A third concern for the clinician is that we do not yet know which are the most important predictors in this complex web and, more important, which are the leading causes.

Clearly, questions about the central causes of marital discord and divorce are of paramount concern to basic researchers of marriage, as well as to clinicians. However, clinicians have additional concerns beyond those that may occupy the attention of basic researchers.

Determining the Causes of Marital Satisfaction and Stability Is Only Part of the Clinical Problem

When basic researchers of marriage finally discover the causes and consequences of marital satisfaction and stability, they might well consider their job done and close up their labs. Those discoveries, as important as they are, only mark the beginning for the clinician. Consider, for example, AIDS research. We know that the HIV virus causes AIDS, and we know how that virus is transmitted. Comparable knowledge about marital satisfaction and stability are a long way away. Yet this knowledge about AIDS has been only the beginning of the battle for clinicians who want to prevent the transmission of the AIDS virus. What kinds of intervention campaigns are necessary for what kinds of people (gays, heterosexuals, teens)? For example, is it more effective to advocate abstinence for teenagers or condom use? Is public education enough, or do you need skills training in how to say no to sex and how to insist that your partner wear a condom? What about drug users? Do you educate them, give them skills training, or just provide them with clean needles? Those who want to prevent AIDS must face these diverse and important questions even when the knowledge of causality is definitive.

For another example that is closer to home, consider cognitive factors, particularly attributions, as a cause of marital distress. Extensive research has shown that attributions are cross-sectionally related to marital discord, and additional evidence indicates that attributions are longitudinally associated with marital discord (for a review, see Bradbury & Fincham, 1990). There is even an experimental study on the manipulation of attributions that suggests attributions influence negative behavior (Fincham & Bradbury, 1988). On the basis of this literature, one could easily argue that targeting marital cognitions should enhance marital intervention. This argument gains even greater strength when one considers that in the therapy literature cognitive approaches have been used successfully in altering depression (e.g., Robinson, Berman, & Neimeyer, 1990) and panic (e.g., Barlow, Craske, Cerny, & Klosko, 1989). Thus the use of cognitive techniques to alter marital discord seems an idea whose time has come. Seven studies have now examined cognitive approaches to marital therapy and compared them to traditional behavioral couples therapy, which emphasizes behavioral but not cognitive change (for a review, see Baucom, Epstein, & Rankin, 1995). Whether cognitive therapy is used alone or in combination with traditional behavioral couples therapy, it performs as well as, but no better than, traditional behavioral couples therapy. These studies do not mean that a cognitive therapy component, perhaps devised or implemented differently, might provide added power for couples, or at least some portion of couples. However, the studies do illustrate that the movement from basic research to applied clinical intervention is not a simple or easy one. This brings us to our next point.

The Best Way to Learn About Intervention Is to Do It

One could make a compelling, logical argument that we should hold off on marital intervention and prevention until basic research has provided us with more information about the causes of marital discord. Are we not intervening blindly, and perhaps futilely, if we do not know the causal roots of marital discord and instability?

The history of medical research suggests that this argument is fundamentally flawed. Effective medical interventions have been developed to ameliorate human disease and suffering in the absence of much understanding of the causal processes of disease. For example, cancer treatments based on surgery, radiation, and drugs have been used effectively even with limited understanding of the causes of cancer. Likewise, prevention programs based on early detection of tumors have been effective in the absence of knowledge about what gives rise to these tumors.

More relevant to the topic at hand, behavioral marital therapy was developed in the late 1960s and 1970s with only a limited understanding of the causes of marital satisfaction and stability. Yet extensive research has shown that this treatment assists a majority of couples, with about 50% achieving a clinically significant improvement that has enabled them to join the ranks of the happily married at the end of treatment (Jacobson & Addis, 1993). Although there is ample room for improvement in this therapy (Christensen, Jacobson, & Babcock, 1995), particularly since some couples relapse over follow-up periods (Jacobson & Addis, 1993), the results to date are no small feat. In addition, the Premarital Relationship Enhancement Program (PREP) developed by Markman and his colleagues (Markman, Renick, Floyd, Stanley, & Clements, 1993), which was similarly based on limited data on the causes of marital discord, has shown that premarital training in communication and conflict resolution can have positive effects on couples years later. Like behavioral marital therapy, there are limitations to PREP and its documented impact (see Bradbury et al., this volume), yet it remains an important accomplishment in the prevention of marital discord.

Thus behavioral marital therapy and PREP were based loosely on an inadequate basic science of marital discord and divorce, yet each provided effective treatment or prevention. Furthermore, the research on these treatments has increased our knowledge of intervention. For example, we know what components of behavioral marital therapy are most effective (Jacobson, 1984) and we know what kinds of couples respond to this treatment (Jacobson, Follette, & Pagel, 1986). Furthermore, treatment research has had considerable influence on basic research by focusing such research on particular theories, variables, and assessment procedures.

On the basis of the field's experience with intervention, I would encourage longitudinal investigators of marriage to consider incorporating an intervention protocol in their design (for an example, see Lindahl, Clements,

& Markman, this volume). This will certainly add to the work and complexity of their study. Furthermore, it will have some methodological consequences. Those subjects who are treated are different than those who are not treated, and so it limits the number of subjects available for longitudinal analyses that examine the naturalistic course of marriage. However, one can limit the effort, complexity, and methodological problems by randomly selecting only a relatively small subset of couples for intervention. The payoff is that the research will be more relevant to intervention efforts. It may offer answers not only to the question of what are important variables to change but also to the equally important question of how does one change those variables.

If You Want to Know How Something Works, Try to Change It

I remember from a philosophy of science course long ago that three conditions were necessary to establish a causal relationship between two variables: (a) covariation between the variables, (b) the temporal precedence of the putative cause (causes must always precede effects), and (c) factor isolation (the cause must be distinguished from possible other variables with which it is correlated). Cross-sectional studies can typically only demonstrate covariation between variables; longitudinal studies have the advantage of demonstrating temporal precedence as well. Thus longitudinal research can determine the direction of causality between two variables. If we find in longitudinal research that marital satisfaction drops *after* the birth of the first child, we can rule out the possibility that a drop in marital satisfaction caused the couple to have a child (e.g., the couple decides that having a child would bring them together and overcome their drop in marital satisfaction). (For a discussion of research on marital satisfaction and the transition to parenthood, see Lindahl et al., this volume.)

However, longitudinal research is plagued by the third variable problem – the possibility that variables other than those being examined are accounting for the phenomena of interest. Despite advances in multivariate analyses, we still cannot extract causation from correlation, even from correlations among diverse variables collected over multiple time points.

The experiment has a well-deserved place at the top of design strategies because one can conclude causation from experiments. Possible experimentation related to the causes of marital discord and divorce are limited because of ethical concerns. We can do brief, temporary deceptions of couples that induce brief periods of stress (e.g., Fincham & Bradbury, 1988), but we cannot expose couples to serious and extended stressors that might alter their chances of success in marriage. Nor can we mate particular individuals to examine mate selection hypotheses. However, we can expose couples to experimental interventions designed to improve their satisfaction or increase their stability. If the studies are properly conducted and the interventions are successful, we can conclude that the interventions determined the improvement.

The interpretative step from successful intervention to etiological causation is a tricky one. Because an intervention was successful does not mean that the absence of intervention caused the problem. Nor does it mean that the variable being dealt with in the intervention was the causal problem. For example, surgical removal of a tumor can cure a cancer but, obviously, the lack of surgery or lack of tumor removal does not cause cancer. A diet rich in fruits and vegetables may prevent certain cancers, but these cancers may be caused by environmental toxins (e.g., radiation and smoking). Thus substances in fruits and vegetables may minimize the effects of cancer caused by radiation, but we cannot conclude that a shortage of these substances is a cause of cancer. In each of these examples, evidence of successful intervention hones in on the causal processes of cancer (e.g., that cancerous processes can be stopped with the removal of the tumor, that certain substances will counteract cancer). Thus intervention studies can be an important aid in our search for the causes of disorder. If you want to know how something works, try to change it.

Relationship Events

Being a clinician inevitably focuses one on important relationship events. When couples come in for treatment, they typically have specific events at the top of their mind. These may be dramatic incidents such as an affair or violent conflict, or they may be mundane but nonetheless painful events – her criticism of his parenting, his withdrawal of affection from her. Even if they come in with complaints that they have "grown apart" or "lost their interest in each other," it often does not take much to uncover specific incidents that in their minds have led to their current state. For example, recently a couple came to see me with vague complaints about the loss of closeness between them, but it was not long before each could recount specific incidents that had distanced them, such as the wife's distress about the way her husband had reacted when her mother died.

It is not just my clinical experience that brings me to focus on events. A number of other clinical and social psychologists and I (Kelley et al., 1983) concluded that close relationships could best be conceptualized as consisting, in essence, of interconnected events between the participants in that relationship. Obviously, the sheer quantity of events that transpire in most close relationships make it difficult to study these events in any detail. However, even everyday events can be sampled. And important or critical events can be examined in more detail. My remaining comments dwell on the inclusion of events in longitudinal research.

Events May Be More Important Than Time in Longitudinal Research on Marriage

The longitudinal research described in this book, and perhaps most longitudinal research on marriages, is what I call "time-based longitudinal research." Participants are observed over time, and they are assessed at temporally defined intervals (e.g., at yearly intervals or 6-month intervals). This approach assumes that the mere passage of time exerts or influences change in the process under investigation. This assumption is incontestable in the study of child development, an area in which there is perhaps the most longitudinal research in psychology. Children show enormous changes in cognitive, affective, and social behavior over time despite enormous variation in environmental circumstances. Barring serious injury, illness, or environmental insult, a child of 2 is dramatically different from a child of 1 simply because of time-based maturational processes.

The assumption of time-based processes is not so easy to defend in the study of marriage. Although there may be some time-based processes (e.g., a decrease in marital satisfaction over time since the wedding (see Huston & Houts, Kurdek, and Lindahl et al., this volume), events may determine much more variance than the passage of time itself. Are all couples who have been married 2 years more alike than all couples who have just had their first child, even though they have been married from, say, 1 to 10 years? Are all couples who have been married 25 years more alike than all couples who are having their last child leave home, even though they have been married from 20 to 30 years? It is clearly an empirical question, but my guess is that there is greater similarity across marriages because of similarity of experience rather than similarity in length of time married.

I would suggest that longitudinal researchers consider what I call "event-based longitudinal research" – the study of marriages over time but with assessments based on events in the marriage rather than time since the marriage. The most obvious events on which to base assessments would be those having to do with children. Lindahl et al. (this volume) are interested in studying the impact of children on the marriage, but they note that their research was limited because their assessments, which were based on time, occurred randomly with respect to the birth of the child, sometimes occurring within weeks of the birth to as long as a year from the birth. Taking an event-based longitudinal approach would solve this problem, but it would require close and regular contact with couples to know when the wife became pregnant, perhaps even when the couple was trying to get pregnant.

Event-based longitudinal assessments could be targeted not only to the appearance and development of children. If one were studying external stress and marriage, it is possible through close contact with couples to learn of stressors before they occur (e.g., an impending job loss, a move, a decision for one or the other spouse to go back to work or to retire) or soon after they occur (e.g., the death of a parent, an accident or injury). I would suggest that assessments timed around these stressors would provide greater information about their impact than time-based longitudinal research that simply followed the clock.

My suggestions for event-based longitudinal research are not without problems. They require, as I have indicated, close contact with couples to know when events are happening. They also may introduce methodological problems. For example, if focused on children, couples who had several children might be the subject of more frequent assessments than those who had fewer children. However, I believe these problems are solvable. My primary belief is that the course of marriage is determined more by the events that couples create and events that happen to them than by the simple passage of time. Furthermore, these events do not follow the calendar or the clock. Perhaps neither should our assessments.

Marriage Is Just an Event, Albeit an Important One: Much Happens Before Marriage

There is perhaps a tendency among the public at large and longitudinal researchers to see marriage as a beginning point. Legally, it is a beginning point. Couples are not married until the wedding takes place. Longitudinal researchers typically start their assessment clocks on the wedding date rather than at the couples' first meeting, their first date, or the point at which they started living together. However, several chapters in this book have demonstrated that destructive patterns develop premaritally. Noller and Feeney provide evidence that problematic patterns of interaction develop before marriage. Leonard and Roberts report that over a third of their large sample of couples were aggressive prior to marriage, and O'Leary and Cascardi also report high levels of premarital aggression. Huston and Houts provide strong support for a "perpetual problems model" in which problems surface during courtship and persist through early marriage. In addition, their discussions, and that by Hill and Peplau have shown that premarital variables can predict marital outcomes. Clearly, marriage is not the beginning point when it comes to processes related to its outcome.

From a longitudinal research perspective, it may make most sense to look at marriage as an event, which, like other events in the relationship, has causes and consequences. Certainly, marriage is an important event in a couple's life and there may be features about the wedding, such as a high level of satisfaction, that make it a good starting point for longitudinal research (see Bradbury et al.'s remarks in this volume). However, the impact of marriage on a relationship is likely to differ for couples. For example, in Chapter 5, Veroff, Douvan, Orbuch, and Acitelli used premarital parenthood, cohabitation prior to marriage, and household income as control variables because these variables differed across their samples of white and black couples. It occurs to me that premarital cohabitation and premarital parenthood are also likely to affect the impact of marriage on a couple. It seems intuitively likely that in relationships in which couples are already living together and already dealing with children, the event of marriage may have less of an impact than for couples who are not cohabiting and are childless.

Current Longitudinal Research Primarily Measures Spouses'
Global Impressions of Their Relationships and Brief Laboratory
Samples of Their Interaction: It Tells Us Little About the Critical
Events of Marriage

As both a clinician and a scientist, I would like to find answers to the following kinds of questions. What kind of events lead to disaffection, separation, and divorce? Do dramatic events mark turning points in the relationship, such as an affair, a violent episode, an explosive and humiliating argument? Certainly, some couples experience these kinds of dramatic events, but others must face a less dramatic, but nonetheless painful, series of daily tensions and disappointments. How do couples with the more dramatic events differ from those with chronic marital stress? How do couples try to recover from these hurtful events? What are the key events that typically divide couples? How do stressful events divide some couples and bring others closer together? How do friends and family become involved in the unraveling of a marriage? When is their impact positive and when is it negative? What role do children play in their parents' struggles and in their parents' decision to try again or to give up?

I think current longitudinal research is unable to answer these kinds of questions very well. Most of the research reported in this book deals with self-report measures of broad constructs, such as relationship satisfaction, commitment, trust, equity, love, personality, social support, and beliefs and attitudes toward self, other, children, and family life. A less common but still widely used method is having couples interact in the laboratory, usually about an area of disagreement, and later coding or rating videotapes of these interaction samples. I have used, and will probably continue to use, both of these kinds of measures, and I think they are important to the field. However, I think they are unable to tell us much about the critical events in couples' lives. For example, ratings of trust and commitment do not tell us how wives handle contact with old boyfriends or how husbands react to exciting stories from their single friends. Coded interaction in the laboratory may provide us some insight into how couples discuss problems, but these discussions are in my view fundamentally different from critical incidents of conflict. An important conflict event in a couple's life is likely to (a) be initiated by a provocative stimulus (not by a neutral experimenter's instruction), (b) last longer (or much shorter) than the 10–15 minutes allotted to those discussions in research, and (c) escalate beyond what couples are willing to demonstrate in public for a camera. Thus, although the coded laboratory interaction is useful in measuring interaction processes, it does not tell us about crucial conflicts, in which one partner does or says something that the other finds difficult or impossible to forget or forgive and that may therefore alter the course of marriage.

I think the questions I have posed can only be answered by focusing on critical events. Because these critical events typically do not occur in front of us, they will need to be assessed through self-report, preferably from both spouses independently. Ideally, these events are assessed individually, rather than having spouses aggregate many incidents to provide a global rating of, for example, the extent to which their parents are involved in their conflicts, the extent to which they have dramatic incidents, and so forth. Ideally, these incidents should be assessed soon after they occur.

The assessment of critical events poses many methodological and practical challenges and problems. First, how are they best assessed? Diaries are one possibility, but as Tallman, Burke, and Gecas (this volume) note, they provide rich data but place a burden on the couples. As of yet, these authors do not report data from their diaries. Huston and Houts (this volume) report data from telephone interviews that assessed events. However, for their purposes, they report frequency measures of negative acts and positive acts. The content, processes, and impact of these events are not analyzed here.

Ideally, one wants to assess important events that mark turning points in the relationship or illustrate fundamental relationship processes. There is a danger of casting a net that includes too many events and thus includes many unimportant events alongside a few important ones. How can one code individual incidents into categories that allow for revealing quantitative analyses? How does one know which incidents are important? It is beyond the scope of this chapter to delve into these questions; furthermore, I do not pretend to have the answers to all these issues. However, I think the field could profit from an emphasis on marital events, because they are the stuff of relationships. But there is another reason as well.

Focusing on Events Can Help Us Avoid an Old Problem in Psychology: Demonstrating That a Construct Correlates with Itself and Its Close Relatives

Marital researchers have expressed appropriate concern when two variables under study share item overlap. For example, Rusbult, Bissonnette, Arriaga, and Cox (this volume) excluded conflict items from the Dyadic Adjustment Scale because of their concern that these items might overlap with items on their measures of interdependence, which they hypothesize were related to dyadic adjustment. Obviously, if there is item overlap between two measures, we are likely to find a correlation, which suggests a tautological finding rather than a substantive one.

Even without specific item overlap, *construct overlap* can make a connection between two variables difficult to interpret. Consider the notion that personality, particularly neuroticism, is related to marital satisfaction. Leonard and Roberts (this volume) define neuroticism as a "propensity to experience negative affect," a perfectly reasonable definition of the construct. Various measures of neuroticism presumably measure this tendency. It would be interesting to know whether a propensity toward negative affect prior to ever meeting one's spouse predicts maladjustment with that partner. However, for obvious practical reasons, we do not have that data. So at best we have data on a propensity toward negative affect when there is already a relationship between the partners. Therefore, the measure of propensity toward negative affect includes the tendency to experience negative affect toward the partner. If we find a connection between the two variables of neuroticism and marital satisfaction, our finding consists of the following: those who have a propensity to experience negative affect, including negative affect toward their partner and their relationship with their partner, are more likely to experience their relationship with this partner negatively. The conceptual overlap between the constructs makes the finding almost tautological.

In principle, we could try to correct this problem by assessing propensity to experience negative affect for all aspects of life except for partner. Then we would have a finding that the tendency to experience negative affect in other aspects of life besides the marriage is related to the tendency to experience negative affect in the marriage. Conceptually, this is an improvement, but practically it would be difficult for individuals to rate themselves on a broad construct but exclude their marital experiences from that construct. Likewise, it would be difficult for friends and family members who know the individuals well to rate them on a broad construct but exclude their marital experiences.

Empirically, we could try to circumvent this problem if we were able to show that neuroticism was uncorrelated with relationship satisfaction at one time point (e.g., at the wedding or soon after) but it predicted dissatisfaction later in the marriage. This finding would put us on more solid ground, but a remaining issue for me would be the meaning of neuroticism (tendency to experience negative affect) and its overlap with marital satisfaction (a measure of affect toward the marriage). I think measures of neuroticism may assess a tendency to experience negative affect through exposure over time. For example, we do not assume, and neuroticism measures do not require, that individuals high in neuroticism never experience positive affect about, say, a new job or a new friend or a new spouse. Neuroticism measures assess general tendencies rather than initial reactions. Presumably, those people high in neuroticism who have a new job or new friend or new spouse act and think in ways that over time generate negative affect for themselves (and those around them). So if our measures of neuroticism assess a tendency to experience negative affect with greater exposure toward situations and people, then the finding of greater negative affect toward a partner over time would be expected for individuals high in neuroticism. This same thinking would lead one to predict that neuroticism is uncorrelated with job satisfaction at the beginning of a new job, but that it predicts later job dissatisfaction and termination.

A more subtle version of the problem of conceptual overlap has to do with the *implicative meaning* of relationship terms. I borrow this concept of implicative meaning from the classic text on personality assessment by Wiggins (1973). Personality researches have investigated the extent to which personality descriptors that are not synonyms may imply each other. For example, to what extent does complaining imply resentfulness? Researchers have examined this question by asking subjects to rate the similarity between trait descriptors or by giving them trait pairs of the following format: "Given that a person is immodest, how likely is it that he is also religious?" (Wiggins, 1973, p. 336). Research using this approach has shown that the implicative meaning of traits can be judged with considerable consistency. In a similar vein, Wiggins discusses research in which complete strangers were asked to rate each other and the results revealed an external structure (relationship between traits) similar to that found when close acquaintances rated each other. These two sets of studies raised the possibility that some trait-rating studies were reflecting only the implicative meaning of the traits. Perhaps traits at times existed in the raters' heads rather than in the people being rated.

I believe these issues of implicative meaning are relevant to marital research. If we find that global measures of marriage are related, we must ask ourselves whether some of the obtained relationships reflect the implicative meaning of our concepts. Perhaps people who rate themselves as satisfied also rate themselves as trusting in part because the one concept implies the other.

When we study events, we generally avoid these problems. Certainly, various biases may operate when clients report on events in their relationships. However, the implicative meaning of terms is more likely to affect broad ratings than reports of specific incidents. For example, the mere fact of reporting oneself as being in a satisfied marriage is more likely to affect a broad rating of trust in one's partner than it is to affect the report of an argument over the partner being flirtatious with others.

Conclusion

The role of a commentator is not unlike that of a clinician. You listen to (or read) some information and than provide counsel – encouraging this, suggesting that. All of this can be done without having to engage in the difficult task of actually following through with directions or suggestions!

One piece of conventional wisdom in counseling is that you focus on strengths as well as weaknesses. It is probably good wisdom for commentators as well. I realize that my commentary has been short on the strengths in the available research. However, that is not because there are few strengths in the current body of literature. In fact, in reading the preceding chapters, I was surprised and pleased to see how much longitudinal research there is on marriage and the level of sophistication it has achieved. These discussions show that the field has heeded the call for longitudinal research and has made an auspicious beginning in our understanding of how relationships change over time.

Another piece of conventional wisdom in counseling is that the more experienced you are, the less advice you actually give. You learn that people often are unwilling or unable to follow advice, or if they do, they follow it only temporarily. You learn that people are more motivated when they reach their own discoveries. So you try to create a setting in which they can find their own way and hope that when they discover it, they will be more motivated to implement it. I am unsure whether there is some analogous wisdom in providing commentary. If so, I have *not* followed it. I have made a number of what may be controversial suggestions for how the field should proceed. Even if no one follows the advice, I hope it generates some thought and discussion.

A clinician (and perhaps a commentator) does not want to focus only on problems. Ideally, a clinician should work to enhance the relationship. A commentator might also be concerned with enhancing the work of the field. In this regard, I think that a focus on intervention and events can make longitudinal research more interesting at an individual data level. Intervention, as well as events, gets one into the nitty gritty of marriage. I have hardly ever found a questionnaire, particularly one that contains broad ratings, interesting in and of itself. These measures are only interesting in the aggregate, when subjected to data analyses. However, I have almost always found behavioral events to be interesting at the individual level. When couples provide a sample of their interaction, or describe a recent conflict, or discuss the history of their relationship, I find myself invariably interested in this snapshot of their life. Beyond what it can do for the field, a focus on events and intervention may make work more interesting for researchers.

References

Barlow, D. H., Craske, M. G., Cerny, J. A., & Klosko, J. S. (1989). Behavioral treatment of panic disorder. *Behavior Therapy, 20,* 261–282.

Baucom, D. H., Epstein, N. E., & Rankin, L. A. (1995). Cognitive aspects of cognitive-behavioral marital therapy. In N. S. Jacobson & A. S. Gurman (Eds.), *Clinical handbook of couples therapy* (pp. 65–90). New York: Guilford.

Bradbury, T. N., & Fincham, F. D. (1990). Attributions in marriage: Review and critique. *Psychological Bulletin, 107,* 3–33.

Christensen, A., Jacobson, N. S., & Babcock, J. C. (1995). Integrative behavioral couple therapy. In N. S. Jacobson & A. S. Gurman (Eds.), *Clinical handbook of couples therapy* (pp. 31–64). New York: Guilford.

Fincham, F. D., & Bradbury, T. N. (1988). The impact of attributions in marriage: An experimental analysis. *Journal of Social and Clinical Psychology 7,* 147–162.

Jacobson, N. S. (1984). A component analysis of behavioral marital therapy: The relative effectiveness of behavior exchange and problem solving training. *Journal of Consulting and Clinical Psychology, 52,* 295–305.

Jacobson, N. S., & Addis, M. E. (1993). Research on couples and couple therapy: What do we know? Where are we going? *Journal of Consulting and Clinical Psychology, 61,* 85–93.

Jacobson, N. S., Follette, W. C., & Pagel, M. (1986). Predicting who will benefit from behavioral marital therapy. *Journal of Consulting and Clinical Psychology, 54,* 518–522.

Karney, B. R., & Bardbury, T. N. (1995). The longitudinal course of marital quality and stability: A review of theory, method, and research. *Psychological Bulletin, 118,* 3–34.

Kelley, H. H., Berscheid, E., Christensen, A., Harvey, J. H., Huston, T. L., Levinger, G., McClintock, E., Peplau, L. A., & Peterson, D. R. (1983). *Close relationships.* San Francisco: W. H. Freeman.

Markman, H. J., Renick, M. J., Floyd, F. J., Stanley, S. M., & Clements, M. (1993). Preventing marital distress through communication and conflict management training: A 4- and 5-year follow-up. *Journal of Consulting and Clinical Psychology, 61,* 70–77.

Robinson, L. A., Berman, J. S., & Neimeyer, R. A. (1990). Psychotherapy for the treatment of depression: A comprehensive review of controlled outcome research. *Psychological Bulletin, 108,* 30–49.

Wiggins, J. S. (1973). *Personality and prediction: Principles of personality assessment.* Reading, MA: Addison-Wesley.

13   A Developmentalist's Perspective on Marital Change

Ross D. Parke

A developmental perspective on marriage and marital dysfunction is a welcome advance for the field. Tracing the pattern of change over the course of a marital career is one of the great intellectual puzzles for scholars, clinicians, and couples themselves. One of the goals of this commentary is to place the study of marriage in a life span developmental perspective in order to broaden the scope of the inquiry and provide an overarching framework for considering the longitudinal study of marriage.

A Life Span Developmental Perspective

Several tenets of a life span view merit attention. First, the focus on normative and nonnormative events is of relevance to the study of marriage. Second, this viewpoint emphasizes multiple developmental trajectories. Although the individual development of adults (and children) within a family is important, these can only be understood with reference to other aspects of development, such as the developmental pathway followed by larger units such as the husband–wife dyad or the parent–child dyad, as well as the family unit itself (Parke, 1988; Sigel & Parke, 1987). Moreover, it is argued that the concept of multiple developmental trajectories not only recognizes that individuals, dyads, and family units may follow disparate developmental pathways but that it is necessary to acknowledge the interplay among these different trajectories in order to understand the longitudinal course of marital relationships.

Preparation of this chapter was supported in part by NICHD grant R01 HD32391. Thanks to Tracy Bunker for typing the manuscript.

Individual Adult Development

Although developmental psychologists have traditionally focused on the developmental pathways followed by individual children, in recent years increased attention has been directed to changes in individuals across adulthood. As Erikson (1982) reminded us, development does not cease in childhood but instead is a life-long process. Adults' reactions to marriage over time change as a function of the development of the individual partners. As Rusbult and colleagues note (this volume), several theoretical orientations to marriage have emphasized the role of individual-level factors in marital development, including the attachment (Hazan & Shaver, 1994) and evolutionary-biological (Buss & Schmitt, 1993; Daly & Wilson, 1988) approaches. However, these approaches do not give much attention to the *developmental changes* in individual partners over time. Individual adult development can be viewed from two perspectives: developmental status and cultural agenda. First, adults' cognitive, social, emotional, and biological capabilities will determine the level and quality of their understanding of marital events, as well as the type of intrapersonal resources and coping strategies available to deal with the vicissitudes of a changing relationship. We are only beginning to describe and understand the normative changes that occur in functioning across different developmental domains in young and middle adulthood (Schaie & Willis, 1991). In part, this may reflect the assumption that these types of developmental changes are less important in the young and middle adult periods but assume increasing significance during later periods. However, it is unlikely that developmental status, alone, in terms of cognitive, physical, and socioemotional functioning – even in older populations – is a useful predictor of individual contributions to marital trajectories. Instead, a sociocultural agenda needs to be considered as well, one that focuses on the location of adults along a variety of educational, occupational, and social-relational dimensions. Moreover, individuals may or may not be in harmony concerning the timing of transitions associated with these dimensions. To take one example, consider the case of work. The increased rate of maternal employment and the move toward greater wage equity across males and females has transformed the nature of husband–wife relationships. Women who stay home but desire to be employed outside the home are more depressed than women who are not employed outside the home but are satisfied with this homemaker role (Hock & DeMers, 1990). The implications of this situation for the marriage are clearly detrimental (Conger & Elder, 1994). Or consider the case of educational attainment. When one individual continues to gain advanced educational credentials while the spouse trails in terms of educational attainment, this dysynchrony in the individual educational trajectories of the individuals may create strain on the marital relationship. The individual trajectories of husbands and wives may vary and hence may put greater or lesser strain on the couples' relationship.

Individual Development of the Child

Since most marriages involve children, the individual developmental changes that children undergo need to be considered as well. Again, two perspectives are useful: a developmental status perspective, in which children's cognitive, social, and biological functioning is considered, and a cultural agenda perspective that determines the timing of the child's entry into various social settings such as the transition to elementary school, junior high school, or college. Often these two perspectives interact in determining children's reactions to family events. Children who are experiencing puberty at the same time that another transition is occurring (e.g., the transition to junior high school) respond very differently from children who are responding to only a single transition (Simmons & Blyth, 1987). Moreover, recent research suggests that children of different ages respond very differently to interadult conflict (Cummings & Davies, 1994).

My proposition is that the longitudinal study of marriage needs to address how the child's developmental status interacts with the developmental position of the marital partners. Earlier research on divorce has indicated marital breakup is not independent of the child's development. For example, divorce or separation is more likely to occur when the child (or children) have completed high school than at earlier points in the child's development (Hetherington, Stanley-Hagan, & Anderson, 1989).

Beyond Individual Trajectories: The Dyad and Family as Developmental Units of Analysis

Students of marital relationships have long recognized the marital dyad as a unit of analysis, although different theoretical orientations place differing emphasis on the dyadic level of analysis. In the current volume, Rusbult and her colleagues' interdependence theory (this volume) offers a clearer commitment to dyadic-level processes than several other approaches, such as social learning, attachment, or evolutionary-biological approaches. Similarly, Kurdek, in his call for a relational dialectic perspective (this volume), recognizes the importance of a dyadic focus. However, less attention has been given to the developmental trajectory followed by the dyad and the determinants of this trajectory. Changes in the marital dyad are obviously related to the changes that ensue in the individual adult partner or individual child but are not derivable from a separate examination of either of them. This volume is testimony to the progress that is being made in filling this void. According to a life-course viewpoint, however, the marital dyad does not operate independently. Models that limit examination of marital relationships to either individuals or dyads are inadequate for the full appreciation of the causes and consequences of changes in marital functioning across time (Hinde & Stevenson-Hinde, 1988; Parke, 1988; Parke, Power, & Gottman, 1979). Couples with children exist in a larger family context, just as couples – regardless of whether they have children – are located in networks of extended family and kin. Many studies (for reviews, see Parke, 1995, 1996; Parke & Tinsley, 1987) document that the quality of the husband–wife relationship is linked to the quality of parenting. Men's quality of parenting is especially affected by the nature of the spousal relationship. This argues that other dyads, particularly the parent–child dyad, need to be considered as well. Moreover, mother–child and father–child dyads may follow independent developmental courses that merit examination. There is substantial documentation that the quality of the relationships between parents and children is, in part, determined by the quality of the marital relationship (Katz & Gottman, 1994). Less is known about the reverse issue, namely the impact of the nature of the parent–child relationship on marital quality, stability, and satisfaction. From a life span perspective, documentation of shifts in the nature of triadic or tetradic interaction patterns across time would be of interest in order to determine how alliances and factions alter the developmental course of marital relationships.

Finally, families as units change across development and respond to change as units. Little is known about the ways in which different types of family units relate to the marital unit. Several theorists (Reiss, 1981; Boss, 1983; Sameroff, 1994) have offered useful typologies of families as units of analysis. Reiss (1981), for example has described a variety of family paradigms that describe a set of enduring assumptions about the social world shared by all family members. Differences in paradigms, in turn, are related to the extent to which families seek outside help for their problems or to their views of the social world as ordered or chaotic. Virtually no data are available concerning how marital functioning is differently linked to variations in family paradigms. This area is clearly ripe for future research.

Normative and Nonnormative Transitions

A life-course perspective underscores the importance of distinguishing normative and nonnormative transitions. Normative transitions that affect marriage include such events as the birth of a baby, reentry into the workplace, entry of children into day-care or school contexts. There has been an extensive literature on the impact of these transitions on shifts in marital relationships. Studies by Cowan and Cowan (1992) and Belsky and Pensky (1988) illustrate the impact of the transition to parenthood on the marital relationship. In contrast to traditional views that families follow a scripted and stage-like course (e.g., Waller, 1938; Hill & Rodgers, 1964), a life course view recognizes that the *timing* of occurrence of these normative events can dramatically alter the impact of these transitions (Elder, 1984). The timing of marriage itself as well as the timing of the onset of parenthood can alter the course of marital relationships, as Lindahl and her colleagues have shown (this volume). As the literature on adolescent marriage indicates, these unions are less likely to be stable than later-timed marriages (Furstenberg, Brooks-Gunn, & Chase-Lansdale, 1989). Timing is important in less extreme cases as well. As Hill and Peplau illustrate in their comparisons on early- and late-timed marriages (this volume), where all couples were beyond their teen years, the correlates of marital stability and satisfaction are quite distinct for these two groups. The timing of entry into marriage is a major factor that merits consideration in our studies of marital stability. Similarly, early- and late-timed parenthood has very different implications for role distributions between couples. As Daniels and Weingarten (1982) have found, late-timed parents are more likely to share household and child care responsibilities more equally. Moreover, early- and late-timed parents follow different work trajectories. Late-timed mothers are more likely to follow a simultaneous pattern of parenting and working, while early-timed parents follow a sequential pattern of parenting followed by a return to work. The implications of these different patterns on marital relationships over time merit examination. Similarly, the impact of children's normative transitions on marital stability merit attention. The transition to school may alter wives' work patterns, which, in turn, may alter the nature of the marital relationship. Or the transition to puberty, to junior high school, or college represents potential emotional and financial stressors that may have an impact on the marriage. Similarly, "leaving the nest" may be either an opportunity for closeness or a catalyst for problems in differing types of marriages.

Not only do families follow idiosyncratic patterns of timing of entry into various normative transitions, but a life course view underscores the importance of nonnormative transitions as well. The impact of nonnormative transitions such as unemployment on marital relationships has a long history. Elder's classic work on the impact of the Great Depression on family functioning (Elder, 1974) illustrated how nonnormative events can alter marital stability and satisfaction. Strong marriages at the onset of economic adversity were more likely to survive than weak ones. Similarly, Conger and Elder's (1994) recent work on the impact of the Midwest farm crisis on marriage is a further illustration of what unanticipated and nonscripted events can do to the course of marital functioning. More work needs to be done on how these events play out across time in marriages at differing stages of development. Are newlyweds more vulnerable to nonnormative stressful events than longer-term marriages? Do marriages respond to all types of nonnormative events in similar ways? A number of theorists have provided useful dimensional analysis of stressful events and distinguished such dimensions as predictability, intensity, duration, and controllability (Moos & Schaefer, 1986; Parke & Beitel, 1988). A wide variety of stressful events, such as the birth of a preterm baby, residential mobility, and death of a family member, merits consideration. Do they yield similar or different effects on marital relationships? A better understanding of how couples cope with different types of stressful events will provide a richer understanding of the determinants of the developmental course of marriage. In this volume, Tallman and his colleagues offer a promising theoretical framework for incorporating these events into our theories of marital functioning.

Little attention has been paid to the role of child-centered nonnormative transitions or unexpected life events on marital relationships. The onset of drug or alcohol use, school failure, and childhood accidents are all nonnormative events that bear scrutiny for their impact on marriage. In recent years, an increasing number of adult children have been returning home. What impact does this unexpected event have on the marital relationship? This set of questions is of theoretical interest because it reminds us of the potential impact of child events on marriage as well as vice versa. Clearly, there are bidirectional effects across generations that may be exaggerated by these types of transitions.

Finally, the interplay between normative and nonnormative transitions needs more attention. Do couples react differently when normative and nonnormative events co-occur? For example, the cumulative impact of several sources of stressful change such as birth of an infant and job loss is not well understood.

How does a focus on transitions affect the longitudinal study of marriage? This perspective has major implications for such studies in that it helps investigators select appropriate time points for follow-up evaluations in their design of a longitudinal project. Time alone is a poor basis for selecting retest points in a study. Although age may be of some value for children, adult age per se is unlikely to be a helpful guideline. Instead, a focus on normative and nonnormative transitions provides a more useful set of guidelines for selecting time points for a follow-up (Fine & Kurdek, 1994; Parke, 1994). As noted earlier, however, transitions may occur at different points for children and adults, and transitions may affect different units of analysis such as individuals, dyads, or families differently.

While the focus on transitions as an organizer for longitudinal work is well understood and generally accepted, the related issue concerning what point after the transition to report the effects is less clear. What are the meaningful break points for reporting follow-up effects? In the final analysis, we need a better set of theories about the temporal course of change in marital relationships that can provide guidelines for investigators about the most appropriate time points that are likely to be sensitive to the earlier event. The studies in this volume are a first step in providing some empirical guideposts for future investigators. Real progress awaits better theories to integrate the descriptive data.

Variations in Marital Relationships

Historical Continuity

One of the lessons of this volume is that greater attention needs to be given to issues of generalizability. A life course view reminds us that the historical context needs to be considered in our studies of social relationships, including marriage. The assumption here is that it is inappropriate to try to account for changes in marital relationships by the same set of processes in different historical periods. Unfortunately, we still know relatively little about the nature of this historical variation. Historical analyses can serve several functions. First, history can provide unique opportunities to assess the generalizability of our explanatory principles in different historical periods. Historical variations such as war, famine, or economic depression represent important and powerful natural experiments that permit opportunities for theory and model testing, often under conditions that are much more drastic than developmental researchers could either ethically or practically engineer or produce in either the laboratory or the field. Elder's (1974) exploration of the effect of economic depression on family functioning and life-course development of children is a classic example of this approach. Current work (Conger & Elder, 1994) in which similar issues of the impact of economic hardship are being addressed provides a unique opportunity to assess the historical boundedness of the family–employment relationships. An interesting and profitable enterprise would be to investigate how historical shifts in family organization, in turn, alter marital relationships. During wartime, for example, the increased degree of husband–wife separation accompanied by a higher percentage of mothers in the workplace and children in day care provides unique opportunities to assess marital relationships in different time periods. Cross-time comparisons between earlier periods and the present era, in which women's outside employment is high, would provide interesting insights concerning how the historical period conditioned marital relationships and how the impact of women's work on marriage has changed.

Cultural Continuity

Just as history provides us with naturally occurring variations, cross-cultural contexts provide opportunities for exploring the boundary conditions of our theories. More and more social scientists are recognizing that culture shapes the nature, timing, and rate of developmental change in close relationships such as marriage. This recognition is part of our shift away from endorsement of a positivistic assumption that psychological laws of development are applicable universally. At a minimum, the necessity of examining the assumption of universality by replicating findings in other cultural contexts is increasingly common, while in stronger form it is assumed that culture organizes behavioral patterns in fundamentally unique ways (see Rogoff, 1990). Both cross-cultural variations and intracultural differences in our own society need to be considered (Parke & Buriel, 1997).

Variations in family organization and structure that are evident in different societies represent one point of departure. Do extended family arrangements produce types and qualities of marital relationships that differ from nuclear family types? Different role arrangements for household members provide opportunities to examine variations in how those variations alter marital relationships. To take another example, attitudes toward maternal employment, as Chase-Lansdale (1994) notes, vary across ethnic lines, with African-American women being more accepting than Euro-American females of extra-familial employment. As Veroff and his colleagues (chapter 5, this volume) have found for African-American husbands, equity, being higher in role sharing, and being a parent are especially associated with marital well-being. This "androgynous gender role orientation," to use Veroff's term, represents an interesting parallel to earlier work that African-American boys and girls are treated more equally in terms of gender roles during childhood than Euro-American white children (Allen & Majidi-Abi, 1989). Perhaps there is cross-generational continuity in their orientation toward role sharing that is not specifically gender-based. A final illustration of the need to consider ethnicity comes from Leonard and Roberts (this volume). They found that couples with one minority partner are more likely to experience marital disruptions – perhaps because they have failed to gain acceptance from the culture or perhaps because individuals of different ethnic backgrounds bring differing expectations to the marriage. In turn, these differences in attitude may alter the impact of these experiences on families – women as well as their children. Cross-cultural and within-culture comparisons offer important opportunities to test the generalizability of our prior findings concerning the developmental course of marriage.

Intervention: Moving Beyond the Couple

Intervention efforts can be undertaken for several reasons. Although the goal is generally to improve the health of the marital unit, another central reason for interventions is to provide a test of a theoretical position. Several examples of this strategy are provided in the present volume (e.g., Lindahl, Clements, & Markman, and Bradbury, Cohan, & Karney, this volume). However, other issues, too, can be usefully addressed by an intervention approach. First, this is a useful strategy for examining how changes in marriage can modify other family relationships such as parent–child relationships. This is a beginning step in unraveling the direction of influence issue, in particular to see how shifts in marital functioning can alter other relationships within the family setting. It simply requires that another set of measures of family relationships such as parent–child or sib–sib relationships be secured, in addition to the outcomes centered on the couple. Second, to address the impact of the child or the parent–child dyad on marital relationships, the child or the parent–child unit could be used as the target of intervention. In turn, the effects of this treatment on subsequent marital functioning could be assessed. Third, a wider variety of contexts need to be targeted for intervention purposes. Although clinical contexts have been utilized frequently, as Crouter (1994) notes, the impact of interventions at the work site on marital functioning have been relatively infrequent. These represent interesting opportunities for future research in light of Repetti's (1989) work linking work-related stress and subsequent marital functioning.

Marriages Do Not Exist in a Vacuum

Under the influential writings of Bronfenbrenner (1979, 1989) researchers have begun to recognize the embeddedness of families in a variety of social settings. As Bradbury et al., Tallman, Burke, and Gecas and others note in this volume, researchers in the marital field are beginning to appreciate the importance of this characterization for understanding marital stability and change. Bronfenbrenner's characterization of four spheres or levels of social context continues to be a convenient taxonomy for organizing research findings. These levels include the *microsystem,* which refers to factors that have a direct impact on the child (e.g., family, peer group). In fact, as a field we have made considerable progress in describing microsystems such as the family (Dunn, 1985; Parke & O'Neil, 1997). Moreover, progress is being made in describing different types of marriage and the impact of these types on children's social relationships (Katz & Gottman, 1994; Grych & Fincham, 1990). In short, we are making considerable progress in expanding our understanding of the relationships within the family that are critical for understanding children's development. A second level – the *mesosystem* – refers to the combined impact of multiple systems (impact of peers, schools, extended families) or the influences among microsystems, whereby marital interaction and/or disruption influences the child's adaptation to the peer group or classroom or the individual adults functioning in the workplace (Hetherington, 1989). The *exosystem* refers to those settings that influence an individual's development but in which the individual does not directly participate or play a direct role. As Crouter (1994) shows, parents' workplaces are a prime example of a setting that has a profound impact on children and spouses, even though children's or spouses' involvement and participation are minimal. Other examples of the exosystem might include the local school board, the zoning commission, or a school class attended by an older sibling. Finally, both mesosystems and exosystems are embedded in a set of ideological and institutional patterns of a particular culture or subculture, as well as historical eras. This has been labeled the *chronosystem.*

Traditionally, research has been skewed toward understanding the microsystem to a large degree, with a primary focus on how factors within the family context influence marital outcomes. However, one of the lessons of this volume is our movement toward understanding other levels of analyses. For example, much of the work can be characterized as operating at the mesosystem level, in which the interface between microsystems is explored. Examples include the chapters by Bradbury et al. (this volume) on the relationship between adaptation in the workplace and the marriage. Illustrations of the exosystem level of analysis are offered by Crouter (1994) and Repetti (1989) in their explorations of the ways in which family and workplace interact to alter marital and parent–child functioning.

Toward Intergenerational Models

This volume pays a surprising lack of attention to the developmental antecedents of marital stability. While some contributors allude to these issues (e.g., O'Leary & Cascardi, this volume), the impact of earlier family relationships, either the parent–child relationship or the child's recollections of his or her parents' own marital relationship, on current marital functioning deserves more attention. Recent studies of attachment theory (Hazan & Shaver, 1994) as a model for describing adult close relationships, including marriage, are beginning to address this issue. Similarly, recent studies of the impact of recalled parent–child attachment relationship on current parental functioning are relevant (Main, Kaplan, & Cassidy, 1985; Cowan, Cohn, Cowan, & Pearson, 1996). Less is known about the impact of adult recollections of the quality of their parents' marital relationship on their own functioning in the marital role. Do children develop separate "cognitive working models" of parent–child relationships and of marital relationships? Is there differential predictability from a general working model versus working models that are specific to different types of relationships? How do individuals in a marital relationship with different working models reconcile their two views of the nature of social relationships? Some evidence (Rutter & Rutter, 1983) suggests that a spouse with a healthy family-of-origin history can help modify the unhealthy working models of a spouse, but the conditions that facilitate this kind of protective process remain unspecified. These types of questions underscore a broadened view of development, namely, the need to consider not only developmental aspects of the marriage, but the developmental histories of the partners in the relationship.

Part of the difficulty in appreciating the value of this expanded developmental perspective is that the study of marital relationships has been largely influenced by a Lewinian situational orientation that stresses current rather than historical processes in accounting for marital effects. One of the challenges for a fully mature developmental theory of marital relationships is to integrate concurrent influences and prior developmental histories into our models.

Integrating Short-Term and Long-Term Change

One of the challenges for all developmental analyses concerns the problem of integrating short-term fluctuations in marital functioning into long-term patterns. Marital relationships fluctuate in response to a series of daily life events such as hassles (Lazarus, 1991). For example, as Repetti (1989) has shown, stressful changes in the workplace can negatively affect short-term shifts in the patterns of marital functioning. These studies are valuable for tracing the routine variability in marital relationships. Over short periods of time, these changes can in turn be instructive for beginning to delineate the processes by which short-term fluctuations translate into more stable and long-term changes in the marital relationship. Process-oriented studies of marriage (e.g., by Gottman, Fincham, Bradbury, & Markman), which focus on specific mechanisms such as emotional reciprocity, or cognitive attributions provide us with hypotheses concerning how short-term changes translate into stable patterns. Short-term longitudinal studies that combine frequent measurement with accompanying assessment of specific theoretically derived processes may begin to answer this vexing question. The Gottman–Levenson (1992) cascade model is a step in this direction, except that it focuses on stages or states, rather than the processes that lead to different stages of dissatisfaction. This argument has both design and methodological implications, namely that we need more intensive process-oriented studies of short-term changes if we are going to go beyond description of long-term changes in marriage.

Are the Processes Unique to Marriage?

One of the advantages of being an outsider to the marital relationships arena is that one has an opportunity to discover parallels with processes in other forms of relationship. From the perspective of a student of parent–child relationships, many of the findings are not surprising. The emphasis on the central role of negative affect that has a long-standing status in this field (e.g., Gottman, 1979; Huston & Houts, Noller & Feeney, and Lindahl et al., this volume) is being discovered in other forms of close relationships as well. There is considerable evidence that high negativity, especially reciprocal negative affect, is characteristic of poor parent–child relationships (Boyum & Parke, 1995; MacDonald & Parke, 1984; Patterson, 1982). As in the case of marital relationships, it is not the absence of negative affect and conflict that distinguishes well-adjusted and poorly adjusted parent–child dyads, but rather their ability to effectively manage negative affect in the relationship. Similarly, adult and child friendships tend to show similar processes in operation (Matthews, 1986; Newcomb & Bagwell, 1995). Finally, Lindahl and her colleagues' finding that poor negative conflict-resolution strategies were predictive of children's negative escalation with peers is a further illustration of potentially parallel processes across relationships. A major task for future students of close personal relationships is to determine what processes are unique to marriage and which ones are common properties of a variety of close relationships. Recent work on the role of attachment (Hazan & Shaver, 1994) is moving in that direction, but work that focuses more specifically on the underlying processes in different kinds of social relationships is clearly needed to adequately evaluate this question.

Toward Multiple Methods

One of the interesting advances in the social sciences over the past decade is the proliferation of methods. Instead of relying on a single strategy, such as observational approaches, the field has recognized the importance of a range of verbal reports, especially cognitive constructions of the meaning of events and of the relationship itself. Several chapters illustrate this embrace of multiple methods (e.g., by Bradbury et al., Hill & Peplau, Noller & Feeney). Similarly, tracking the daily fluctuations in marriage is still an underdeveloped task, but Noller and Feeney's use of diaries is a step in this direction. Larson and Richards's (1994) successful use of beepers to monitor changes in interaction patterns and affect is another promising strategy that could be employed to track changes in marital interactions. Finally, the role of ethnographic techniques in the study of marriage would allow a fuller appreciation of how daily fluctuations in the lives of a couple influence their levels of marital satisfaction.

Conclusion

In conclusion, the developmental course of marriage may be better understood by casting the issues in a life-course framework. As this volume indicates, the study of marital change is itself developing and clearly emerging out of a childhood phase toward a more mature level of both theory and measurement. The trajectory clearly seems promising for the emergence of a healthy adult phase in our search that will help us understand how marriages develop and change.

References

Allen, L., & Majidi-Abi, S. (1989). Black American children. In J. T. Gibbs & L. N. Huang (Eds.), *Children of color.* San Francisco, CA: Jossey Bass.

Belsky, J., & Pensky, E. (1988). Marital change across the transition to parenthood. In R. Palkowitz & M. B. Sussman (Eds.), *Transitions to parenthood* (pp. 133–156). New York: Hawthorne.

Boss, P. G. (1983). The marital relationship: Boundaries and ambiguities. In H. I. McCubbin & C. R. Figley (Eds.), *Stress and the family* (Vol. 1, pp. 26–40). New York: Brunner/Mazel.

Boyum, L., & Parke, R. D. (1995). Family emotional expressiveness and children's social competence. *Journal of Marriage and Family, 57,* 593–608.

Bronfenbrenner, U. (1979). *The ecology of human development.* Cambridge, MA: Harvard University Press.

Bronfenbrenner, U. (1989). Ecological systems theory. In R. Vasta (Ed.), *Annals of child development* (Vol. 6, pp. 187–250). Greenwich, CT: JAI Press.

Buss, D., & Schmitt, D. P. (1993). Sexual strategies theory: An evolutionary perspective on human mating. *Psychological Bulletin, 100,* 204–232.

Chase-Lansdale, L. (1994). Families and maternal employment during infancy: New linkages. In R. D. Parke & S. Kellam (Eds.), *Exploring family relationships with other social contexts* (pp. 25–48). Hillsdale, NJ: Lawrence Erlbaum.

Conger, R., & Elder, G. (1994). *Families in troubled times: Adapting to change in rural America.* New York: Aldine.

Cowan, C. P., & Cowan, P. A. (1992). *When partners become parents.* New York: Basic Books.

Cowan, P. A., Cohn, D. A., Cowan, C. P., & Pearson, J. L. (1996). Parents' attachment histories and children's externalizing and internalizing behavior: Exploring family systems models of linkage. *Journal of Consulting and Clinical Psychology, 64,* 1–11.

Crouter, A. C. (1994). Processes linking families and work: Implications for behavior and development in both settings. In R. D. Parke & S. Kellam (Eds.), *Exploring family relationships with other social contexts,* (pp. 9–28). Hillsdale, NJ: Lawrence Erlbaum.

Cummings, E. M., & Davies, P. (1994). *Children and marital conflict.* New York: Guilford.

Daly, M., & Wilson, M. (1988). Evolutionary social psychology and family homicide. *Science, 242,* 519–524.

Daniels, P., & Weingarten, K. (1981). *Sooner or later: The timing of parenthood in adult lives.* New York: Norton.

Dunn, J. (1985). *Sisters and brothers.* Cambridge, MA: Harvard University Press.

Elder, G. (1974). *Children of the Great Depression.* Chicago, IL: University of Chicago Press.

Elder, G. (1984). Families, kin and the life course: A sociological perspective. In

R. D. Parke (Ed.), *Review of child development research: Vol. 7. The family* (pp. 80–136). Chicago: University of Chicago Press.

Erikson, E. (1982). *The life cycle completed: A review.* New York: Norton.

Fine, M. A., & Kurdek, L. A. (1994). Publishing multiple journal articles from a single data set: Issues and recommendations. *Journal of Family Psychology, 8,* 371–379.

Furstenberg, F. F., Brooks-Gunn, J., & Chase-Lansdale, L. (1989). Teenaged pregnancy and childbearing. *American Psychologist, 44,* 313–320.

Gottman, J. M. (1979). *Marital interaction: Experimental investigations.* New York: Academic Press.

Gottman, J. M., & Levenson, R. (1992). Marital processes predictive of later dissolution: Behavior, physiology and health. *Journal of Personality and Social Psychology, 63,* 221–233.

Grych, J. H., & Fincham, F. D. (1990). Marital conflict and children's adjustment: A cognitive-contextual framework. *Psychological Bulletin, 108,* 267–290.

Hazan, C., & Shaver, P. R. (1994). Attachment as an organizational framework for research on close relationships. *Psychological Inquiry, 5,* 1–22.

Hetherington, E. M. (1989). Coping with family transitions: Winners, losers and survivors. *Child Development, 60,* 1–14.

Hetherington, E. M., Stanley-Hagan, M. S., & Anderson, E. R. (1989). Divorce: A child's perspective. *American Psychologist, 44,* 303–312.

Hill, R., & Rodgers, R. H. (1964). The developmental approach. In H. T. Christensen (Ed.), *Handbook of marriage and the family.* Chicago, IL: Rand McNally.

Hinde, R. A., & Stevenson-Hinde, J. (Eds.). (1988). *Relationships within families.* New York: Oxford University Press.

Hock, E., & DeMers, D. K. (1990). Depression in mothers of infants: The role of maternal employment. *Developmental Psychology, 26,* 285–291.

Katz, L. F., & Gottman, J. M. (1994). Patterns of marital interaction and children's emotional development. In R. D. Parke & S. Kellam (Eds.), *Exploring family relationships with other contexts* (pp. 49–74). Hillsdale, NJ: Lawrence Erlbaum.

Larson, R., & Richards, M. (1994). *Divergent realities.* New York: Basic Books.

Lazarus, R. S. (1991). *Emotion and adaptation.* New York: Oxford.

MacDonald, K., & Parke, R. D. (1984). Bridging the gap: Parent–child play and peer interactive competence. *Child Development, 55,* 1265–1277.

Main, M., Kaplan, N., & Cassidy, J. (1985). Security in infancy, childhood and adulthood; A move to the level of representation. In I. Bretherton & E. Waters (Eds.), Growing points in attachment theory and research. *Monographs of the Society for Research in Child Development, 50,* 1–2, Serial No. 209.

Matthews, S. H. (1986). *Friendships through the life course.* Newbury Park, CA: Sage.

Moos, R. H., & Schaefer, J. A. (1986). Life transitions and crises: A conceptual overview. In R. H. Moos (Ed.), *Coping with life crises: An integrated approach* (pp. 3–28). New York: Plenum Press.

Newcomb, A. F., & Bagwell, C. L. (1995). Children's friendship relations: A meta-analytic review. *Psychological Bulletin, 117,* 306–347.

Parke, R. D. (1988). Families in life span perspective: A multi-level developmental approach. In E. M. Hetherington, R. M. Lerner, & M. Perlmutter (Eds.), *Child development in life span perspective* (pp. 159–190). Hillsdale, NJ: Lawrence Erlbaum.

Parke, R. D. (1994). Multiple publications from a single data set – A challenge for researchers and editors: Comment on Fine and Kurdek (1994). *Journal of Family Psychology, 8,* 384–386.

Parke, R. D. (1995). Fathers and families. In M. Bornstein (Ed.), *Handbook of parenting* (pp. 27–64). Hillsdale, NJ: Lawrence Erlbaum.

Parke, R. D. (1996). *Fatherhood.* Cambridge, MA: Harvard University Press.

Parke, R. D., & Beitel, A. (1988). Disappointment: When things go wrong in the transition to parenthood. *Marriage & Family Review, 12,* 221–265.

Parke, R. D., & O'Neil, R. (1997). The influence of significant others on learning about relationships. In *Handbook of personal relationships* (2nd ed., pp. 29–59). New York: Wiley.

Parke, R. D., Power, T. G., & Gottman, J. M. (1979). Conceptualizing and quantifying influence patterns in the family triad. In M. E. Lamb, S. Suomi, & G. Stephenson (Eds.), *Social interaction analyses: methodological issues* (p. 488). Madison: University of Wisconsin Press.

Parke, R. D., & Buriel, R. (1997). Socialization in the family: Ethnic and ecological perspectives. In N. Eisenberg (vol. ed.), *Handbook of child psychology.* New York: Wiley.

Parke, R. D., & Tinsley, B. J. (1987). Family interaction in infancy. In J. D. Osofsky (Ed.), *Handbook of infant development* (2nd ed., pp. 579–641). New York: Wiley.

Patterson, G. R. (1982). *A social learning approach: Coercive family processes.* Eugene, OR: Castilla.

Reiss, D. (1981). *The family's construction of reality.* Cambridge, MA: Harvard University Press.

Repetti, R. L. (1989). Effects of daily work load on subsequent behavior during marital interaction: The roles of social withdrawal and spouse support. *Journal of Personality and Social Psychology, 57,* 651–659.

Rogoff, R. (1990). *Apprenticeship in thinking.* New York: Oxford University Press.

Rutter, M., & Rutter, M. (1983). *Developing minds.* New York: Basic Books.

Sameroff, A. (1994). Developmental systems and family functioning. In R. D. Parke & S. Kellam (Eds.), *Exploring family relationships with other social contexts* (pp. 199–214). Hillsdale, NJ: Lawrence Erlbaum.

Schaie, K. W., & Willis, S. L. (1991). *Adult development and aging.* New York: Harper-Collins.

Sigel, I., & Parke, R. D. (1987). Conceptual models of family interaction. *Journal of Applied Developmental Psychology, 8,* 123–137.

Simmons, R., & Blyth, D. (1987). *Moving into adolescence: The impact of pubertal change and school context.* Hawthorne, NY: Aldine.

Waller, W. (1938). *The family: A dynamic interpretation.* New York: Dryden.

14 Couples, Gender, and Time: Comments on Method

David A. Kenny

The difficulties of conducting research in the social sciences are compounded when one studies longitudinal married couples. To begin with, married couples are not randomly paired. They are similar to one another on a host of variables. Second, there are all sorts of missing data. One or both members do not show up for one of the sessions; if enough time passes about half the couples will separate. Third, the partners influence each other. Fourth, the meaning of variables changes over the course of the relationship. Despite these and many other difficulties, many researchers still attempt to study marriage over time.

This chapter provides a checklist of things I would like to see in the analysis of longitudinal data on heterosexual couples, with particular emphasis on effects involving couples, gender, and time. I indicate how these three types of effects were treated in the seven empirical chapters in this volume that report on the same variables assessed at least twice. Because I am simply trying to illustrate how these effects have been handled and how they might be handled differently in the future, I discuss only the major analyses, in these chapters; basically, I concentrate on analyses presented in tables and figures. I recognize that many of the analyses that I will recommend have been conducted by these investigators with these data but are presented elsewhere. Moreover, in some instances, we really do not yet know how to do the sorts of analyses I am recommending, and in this sense my checklist presents more of an idealized list than a practical list. Finally, given my role of critic, I am forced to point out the practices that I see as less than optimal. Despite my criticisms, I was most impressed by the care and intelligence of this group of researchers.

Before beginning, I am happy to report that no study in this volume com-

The research was supported in part by grants from the National Science Foundation (DBS-9307949) and the National Institute of Mental Health (RO1-MH51964). I want to thank Thomas Bradbury and Cynthia Mohr for several helpful suggestions.

410

mitted the following very common error in couples' research. Suppose that a researcher wants to look at the effect of the one spouse on his or her partner's cigarette smoking. One member of the couple, *the smoker,* is denoted as the subject, and his or her responses are treated as the dependent variable. The other member is called *the influence agent,* and his or her response becomes the independent variable. So, for instance, the effect of the influence agent's attitude is used to predict the subject's attitude. The error in this type of analysis is that it fails to acknowledge that influence flows in both directions. It is a mistake to assume that only one person influences the other in relationships. A related error may arise when an investigator realizes that there is bidirectional influence and so in a cross-sectional study uses the husband's attitude to predict the wife's attitude, and vice versa. The error here is that multiple regression cannot be used to estimate bidirectional influence.

Couple Effects

It takes two people to make a marriage, and there are some statistical analyses that capitalize on this fact. This section considers three types of couple effects.

Agreement

The basic type of couple effect is the extent to which members of a couple agree or are similar to each other. For instance, do members of a couple agree with each other about how satisfied they are? Agreement in married couples can be measured by simply correlating their two responses. As can be seen in Table 14.1, several studies in this volume examined whether there is any agreement in couples. Huston and Houts (this volume) found little or no similarity between the personalities of husbands and wives. By contrast, Rusbult, Bissonette, Arriaga, and Cox (this volume) found varying levels of agreement for the different variables reported in Table 14.1.

One reason for looking at agreement is that it affects the choice of the unit of analysis. If there is no agreement, then the person, not the couple, can be used as the unit of analysis. If there is agreement, then the couple must be the unit of analysis (however, see Kenny, 1995a). Generally, marital data show some agreement, and the safe course of action is to treat the couple as the unit.

Sometimes investigators are disappointed about the level of agreement between husbands and wives. For instance, they find a .3 correlation, and

Table 14.1. *Couple effects*

Author[a]	Agreement	Couple-level effects	Partner effects
Noller	No	No	No
Leonard	No	Yes	No
Rusbult	Yes	Yes	No
Huston	Yes	No	Yes
Veroff	No	No	Yes
Kurdek	No	No	Yes
Lindahl	No	No	No

[a]The studies, denoted by first author, are listed in the order of the chapters.

they state that only 9 percent of the variance is shared. In interpreting agreement correlations, one should adopt the standards that Cohen (1988) has set for small (.1), medium (.3), and large (.5) correlations. Moreover, an agreement correlation itself represents the amount of variance that is shared between husband and wife, and so it makes no sense to square the correlation because it is already a variance measure. If one views a latent variable as causing the responses of both persons, the size of the path from this latent variable is the square root of the agreement correlation. So a .3 agreement correlation represents a .55 path from some common factor to both members of the couple. Thus it makes more sense to square root, not square, an agreement correlation. Investigators should be proud of, not embarrassed by, their .3 agreement correlations.

Couple-Level Effects

If couples respond very similarly on a variable, then the variable may not reflect on them as individuals but rather on them as a couple. The appropriate level of generalization is the couple, and conclusions refer to the couple. The couple becomes the unit of measurement as well as the unit of analysis.

The simple way to estimate couple-level effects is to average the scores of the two persons and treat the couple as the unit of analysis. A more complicated, but more appropriate, method of estimation is to treat the husband and the wife as two indicators of a latent variable. Variance not explained by the latent factor is called uniqueness. It would then be assumed that the uniqueness from the husband would be correlated across measures as well as uniqueness from the wife. In essence, the model is like a multitrait-multimethod matrix in which the traits are variables and the methods are the husband and the wife.

The estimation of couple-level effects is very rarely attempted in this volume. Leonard and Roberts (this volume) perform a couple analysis, but they do it on only the dependent variable. One interesting twist in some of their analyses is that they do not average the two scores, but, because of reporting bias, they take the larger score. In some of their analyses, Rusbult, Bissonnette, Arriaga, and Cox (this volume) treat the couple as the unit. By and large, however, they treat the couple as a nuisance variable and remove all of its variance. As I discuss later in this chapter, I think that this approach is too conservative.

There may be a greater yield if couple-level analyses were undertaken. In research in person perception (Kenny, 1995b), it has been found that consensual perceptions have much more validity than do idiosyncratic perceptions. Rusbult et al.'s results (this volume) support this view. Couple-level results are generally stronger than individual-level results.

Partner Effects

In studying a person's responses, it is only natural to think that characteristics of that person would be important. In a couple study, however, there are two persons in the relationship, and we should consider the effect of the other. So when we regress wife commitment on satisfaction, we should always consider using husband satisfaction to predict wife commitment. Many studies in this volume use partner as well as self when computing correlations and regressions. Partner effects and couple-level effects are two alternative models of explaining couple agreement (Kenny, 1996). Which model should be used depends on past research and theory.

The estimation of partner effects can be difficult when dyads cannot be distinguished (Kenny, 1996; Kraemer & Jacklin, 1979), but for married couples it is relatively easy. The structural equation approach that is developed in subsequent sections can be used to estimate partner effects. Kashy and Snyder (1995) nicely illustrate the estimation of partner effects in couples' research.

Gender Effects

Mean Difference

The first and most obvious thing to do with gender is to test whether the means are significantly different. As seen in Table 14.2, many studies in this volume present means separately for each gender. Often, however, there is

Table 14.2. *Gender effects*

Author[a]	Mean difference	Moderation	Pooling
Noller	Yes	Yes	No
Leonard	No	Yes	No
Rusbult	No	No	Yes
Huston	No	Yes	No
Veroff	Yes	Yes	No
Kurdek	Yes	Yes	No
Lindahl	Yes	No	No

[a]The studies, denoted by first author, are listed in the order of the chapters.

no indication about whether the gender difference is statistically significant or not. I worry that it has become almost obligatory in this literature to present results separately for the genders, even if there are no gender differences. If the means are to be tested, the appropriate test is a matched pairs *t* test or an equivalent multivariate test (Kenny, 1988).

Moderation

A second thing to do with gender is to compute relationships within gender. In essence, gender may moderate a relationship. The moderation can be the usual type or actor moderation. For example, satisfaction affects commitment more for males than for females. It can also be a partner effect: The effect of the male on the female is greater than the effect of the female on the male. Considered below is the simpler actor moderation.

Testing the statistical significance of moderation in couples is not very straightforward, and, as far as I can tell, none of the investigators *statistically* evaluated any gender moderators. They followed the practice of testing whether a relationship was statistically significant for each gender and often found that it was significant in one gender but not the other. However, statistical logic does not follow ordinary logic. Probably, most of the moderator effects found in this volume are not significant. This failure to test gender moderators gives us the mistaken view that gender is very important in this area.

A little thought reveals why the investigators did not conduct tests of significance. Because the males and females are from the same marriages, the correlations and regression coefficients are themselves correlated. Most of the standard tests of the difference between correlations and regression coefficients require independence and so are inappropriate. Thus the failure to test for moderation reveals the sophistication of this group of researchers in that they did not inappropriately apply improper tests. In the next section, I describe a procedure that can be used to pool results across genders. That procedure can also be used to test for the moderating effect of gender.

Pooling

Many studies in this volume have very small samples. For instance, Noller and Feeney (this volume) have only 33 couples. If effects were the same for both men and women, then the precision of estimates could be enhanced by pooling results across the genders. Pooling requires assuming that the strength of the association is the same for both men and women. Thus, before pooling there should be a test of moderation.

The easiest way to pool is to treat the person as the unit of analysis and to compute correlations and regression coefficients ignoring the couple. If there were gender differences in the means, gender would be controlled. Although this technique provides unbiased estimates of effects, the significance tests would be biased. Rusbult et al. (this volume) perform such an analysis and do acknowledge the bias in the significance testing. Corrections to the significance testing have been proposed (Kenny, 1995a), but they are relatively complicated and novel. If it can be shown that scores on the dependent variable are relatively uncorrelated, which may be true for some outcomes (e.g., nonverbal skill) but not others (e.g., satisfaction), then it is perfectly permissible to use the person as the unit of analysis.

The second and probably best way to pool across gender is to use the structural equation modeling approach (e.g., LISREL, EQS, and CALIS). For this application, the purpose is not, as it usually is, to estimate latent variables, but rather to force equality of paths. The couple is the unit of analysis, the covariance matrix is analyzed, and the paths are estimated for both males and females (as well as the partner effects from male to female and from female to male). With this approach, one can force paths to be equal and so can test whether the paths are different for males and females. Although this approach is not used in any of these chapters, it has been used by Murray, Holmes, and Griffin (1996) and by Bui, Peplau, and Hill (1996). Interestingly, both investigations found that results varied little for men and for women. It is hoped that structural equation modeling will be increasingly used for this purpose.

Rusbult et al. (this volume) present an innovative way to pool across the two members of the dyad. Although I am critical of their approach, I agree with the idea behind it, namely, that it is necessary to pool across males and females. In essence, their technique treats the person as the unit of analysis but removes all of the variation due to the couple. I worry that by removing the variance due to the couple, the most important variation may have been dropped. As stated earlier, the variance that is shared is likely to be more valid than the variance that is not. Moreover, as Rusbult et al. (this volume) admit, their method removes about 70 percent of the variance. When variance due to the couple is removed, the results are much weaker. The couple may have been "thrown out" when the data were given a "statistical bath." The Rusbult et al. method also pools over time, and this aspect of it will be discussed later in this chapter.

Marriage researchers should not automatically assume that there are gender differences in effects (i.e., moderation). Given that prior research has indicated that there are not gender effects, it seems more sensible to start with the null hypothesis that there are no gender differences and to pool results across gender.

The focus in the book is on heterosexual couples. One might wonder if the problems of analysis would be easier or more difficult if the couples were gay and lesbian. Actually, the analysis is often much more difficult for gay and lesbian couples because members in such couples cannot be distinguished. To measure agreement, for instance, one must use an intraclass correlation instead of an ordinary correlation (Griffin & Gonzalez, 1995; Kenny, 1988).

Time Effects

Research textbooks discuss the importance of longitudinal data, but researchers often fail to exploit the full utility of such a design. Four issues in longitudinal data analysis are presented here.

Stability

One thing that can be done is to estimate the stability of the variable across time. As discussed by Huston and Houts (this volume), stability has two dimensions. First, the group mean can be stable, as is discussed in the section on trajectories. Second, people can change in relation to each other. These two types of stability are theoretically independent, and so stability in the means does not necessarily imply stability in persons or couples.

As seen in Table 14.3, stability is rarely measured. By looking at the stability correlations, one can determine whether there is much change in the

Table 14.3. *Time effects*

Author[a]	Stabilities	Lagged effects	Trajectories	Pooling
Noller	No	Yes[b]	Yes[c]	No
Leonard	No	Yes	Yes	No
Rusbult	Yes	Yes[b]	No	Yes
Huston	Yes	Yes[b]	Yes[c]	No
Veroff	No	Yes	No	No
Kurdek	No	Yes	Yes	Yes
Lindahl	No	No	Yes[c]	No

[a]The studies, denoted by first author, are listed in the order of the chapters.
[b]No control for prior standing.
[c]Group only.

variable of interest. Many chapters discuss stability, but few of them look at stability correlations.

A test-retest or stability correlation can be low for two reasons. Either there is a lack of stability in the underlying construct, or there is unreliability in its measurement. If there are at least three waves of data, one can separate the instability and the unreliability explanations (Kenny & Campbell, 1989). To do this, one must assume an autoregressive model in which the true score at one time is affected by the true score at the previous time.

Using the data in Table 3.1 of this volume, we find the stability correlation between adjacent waves for commitment is about .83 and the reliability is about .90. If there are four or more waves of data, a much more complicated model, the trait-state-error model (Kenny & Zautra, 1995), can be estimated. In this model, there are three sources of variance. First, there is *trait* variance, which means the sources of variance do not change over time. Second, there is *state* variance; that is, the sources of variance have some but not perfect stability. Third, there is *error* variance, which means the sources of variance have no stability. This analysis requires very large sample sizes and makes strong assumptions about the stationarity of effects. It may not be appropriate during the early years of marriage, when relationships are changing.

Lagged Effects

With longitudinal data, lagged effects can be estimated. For instance, one can evaluate whether, as according to Rusbult (1983), satisfaction leads to changes in commitment. In measuring a lagged effect, initial standing should be controlled. So in measuring the effect of satisfaction on later commitment, a prior measure of commitment must be controlled. Leonard and Roberts (this volume) show how results may differ between controlling and not controlling for prior level of marital satisfaction.

How to control for prior standing is a matter of some debate. Typically, prior standing is controlled by just entering it into the regression equation as another predictor. Alternatively, it is subtracted from the score and so the dependent variable becomes a change score. Ever since Lord's work (1967), it has been recognized that two different approaches generally yield different answers. Most researchers control by the regression adjustment, but the use of change scores is making a comeback (Wainer, 1991).

Trajectories

The third thing to do with data collected over time is to estimate trajectories or growth curves. In this context, many of the scores decline over time and so the term's trajectory seems more appropriate than the more commonly used term-of-growth curve. Trajectories can be estimated in two principal ways. First trajectories can be estimated as a function of time. The simplest such measure is one in which a variable changes linearly with respect to time. For instance, satisfaction might be shown to decline half a unit for every year of marriage. Second, trajectories can be treated as empirically derived. For instance, McArdle and Epstein (1987) described a way to use means across time as a prototype and then allow for variation in this prototype. Another version of this model is profile analysis, in which couples with different patterns are placed into different groups. This section presents only the models in which trajectories are assumed to be a function of time.

Many chapters report the trajectory of the group. That is, they report the means of the sample at each time, usually separately for males and females. Only Kurdek (Chapter 6) attempted to fit a function to the time points. In testing whether the means differ across three or more time points, the appropriate test is a multivariate analysis of variance, as done by Lindahl, Clements, and Markman (this volume) and Kurdek (this volume).

Only Kurdek (Chapter 6) has estimated different trajectories for the person and used them in subsequent analyses, something that is suggested by Bradbury, Cohan, and Karney (this volume). Interestingly, Kurdek found that some results were stronger when he analyzed trajectories as opposed to the level of the response.

If the time period is short and there are very few time points, linear or quadratic trends are a reasonable approach to modeling growth. But if there are many points, more complicated but more realistic models of growth should be used because linear and quadratic trends make the unreasonable assumption that in the long run a variable heads for infinity.

Consider a possible alternative to linear change: an S-shaped model for changes in satisfaction. For a person or a couple, there are an upper and a lower limit, S_U and S_L. As the name suggests, the relationship between satisfaction and time is S-shaped. There is an initial honeymoon period during which satisfaction remains very near S_U. Next is a transitional period during which there is a rather abrupt decline in satisfaction. It is perhaps during this period that the couple is most at risk for dissolution. In the final stage, the satisfaction is relatively stable and asymptotes at S_L. For such a model there would be four parameters, two being S_U and S_L. The other two are T_M, the point in time at which the person or couple is halfway between S_U and S_L, and R, the rate of decline in satisfaction during the transitional period. Eyeballing the data from Lindahl, Clements, and Markman (this volume) and from Kurdek (this volume), the typical value for T_M is about a year and half after marriage. It might well be that R is the most important factor that predicts relationship difficulties that will occur near the point T_M.

Advantages of growth-curve modeling over more traditional statistical modeling are that data need not be gathered at all time points for all couples and that the intervals need not be the same for all couples. Growth-curve modeling is very different in conceptualization from the autoregressive models that have been used to measure stability. Growth-curve models are deterministic, whereas autoregressive models are stochastic (for an application of growth-curve models to the study of couples, consult Raudenbush, Brennan, & Barnett, 1995).

Pooling

When there are more than two waves of data, lagged effects can be estimated repeatedly. With three waves, for instance, the lagged effect of withdrawal on satisfaction can be estimated twice, from wave one to wave two and from wave two to wave three. If there are many waves, the pooling can be accomplished by pooled time-series analysis, as was done by Bolger, DeLongis, Kessler, and Schilling (1989). Kurdek (this volume) estimated linear growth curves for two variables and correlated growth curves. In essence, this approach involves pooling results over time. If there are few waves, structural equation modeling can be used to pool results across time. It could even be modified to allow effects to increase or decrease gradually over time.

The Rusbult et al. (this volume) procedure pools across time. The problem with the approach is that it assumes that couple effects are invariant across time. If there is autoregressive change, for instance, their method is likely to introduce nonindependence. Again their technique tries to do the right thing, pool across results over time, but I worry about how it is done.

Missing Data and Attrition

I want to echo a concern of Bradbury, Cohan, and Karney (Chapter 9) that missing data and sample attrition present serious problems in the analysis of this type of data. Many studies in this volume use only about half the data they have gathered. Consider the study by Lindahl, Clements, and Markman (this volume). They started with 90 couples, but their analysis is based on only 36 couples. They looked only at cases in which both members of the couple had complete data at both waves. They and other investigators are forced to throw away much data, which is inherently wasteful.

Even more problematic, the discarded data represent those couples that are most interesting, that is, those with the greatest marital dysfunction. Many chapters present means over time of marital satisfaction or quality. If the missing couples had been included, the decline in satisfaction would likely have been even steeper. Moreover, because outcome variables are likely truncated because of attrition, the effects of causal variables may be seriously distorted. Most of the distortion is likely underestimation, but overestimation may also occur.

Recently, there have been considerable advances in the estimation (or according to current jargon "imputing") of missing values. Traditionally, techniques for estimating missing data start with the assumption that the missing cases are random items. However, this assumption is violated in marriages because we know that the missing cases are not random. There are some methods that do not require *random* missing data (Muthen, Kaplan, & Hollis, 1987) but they are fairly complicated. Some methods treat the data as if they were censored. In this approach, distributions are assumed to be truncated, and so explicitly this method treats the missing data as nonrandom. However, the method requires very strong assumptions about the shape of the distribution. I wish that I could offer a complete solution here, but I cannot. Currently, we cannot compute the effect that missing data have on the conclusions in our research. Concerted work in this area is essential.

Conclusion

This chapter has two themes. The first is that structural equation modeling might be considered in confirmatory analyses of this type of data. The technique can be used to estimate partner effects, to test for gender moderation, and to pool results across males and females. Some studies measured many variables, and so these analyses were exploratory in that many variables were entered into the regression analyses. For such analyses, structural equation modeling may be impractical. But for a confirmatory analysis, structural equation modeling should be considered. The second theme is that more formal models of change are needed. Two possibilities are the autoregressive models of stochastic change or the growth-curve models of deterministic change.

Relationships are much more difficult to study than are individuals. But individuals are fundamentally a fiction of perception and experience. What we call an individual is really a complex composite of relationships. Persons have meaning only in relationships. This may seem a radical proposition, but a parallel assumption is accepted in contemporary physics. Modern physics has all but abandoned the concept of physical objects. Although our experience suggests that we live in a world of physical objects, it is a world not of objects but of relationships or interactions. While reductionism can be a dangerous practice, it just stands to reason that for the more complex and interesting science of human beings, persons exist only in interactions with others.

References

Bolger, N., DeLongis, A., Kessler, R. C., & Schilling, E. A. (1989). Effects of daily stress on negative mood. *Journal of Personality and Social Psychology, 57,* 808–818.

Bui, K-V. T., Peplau, L. A., & Hill, C. T. (1996). Testing Rusbult's model of relationship commitment and stability in a 15-year study of heterosexual couples. *Personality and Social Psychology Bulletin, 22,* 1244–1257.

Cohen, J. (1988). *Statistical power analysis for the behavioral sciences* (2nd ed.). Hillsdale, NJ: Lawrence Erlbaum.

Griffin, D., & Gonzalez, R. (1995). Correlational analysis of dyad-level data in the exchangeable case. *Psychological Bulletin, 118,* 430–439.

Kashy, D. A., & Snyder, D. K. (1995). Measurement and data analytic issues in couples research. *Psychological Assessment, 7,* 338–348.

Kenny, D. A. (1988). The analysis of data from two-person relationships. In S. Duck (Ed.), *Handbook of interpersonal relations* (pp. 57–77). London: Wiley.

Kenny, D. A. (1995a). The effect of nonindependence on significance testing in dyadic research. *Personal Relationships, 2,* 67–75.

Kenny, D. A. (1995b). *Interpersonal perception: A social relations analysis.* New York: Guilford.

Kenny, D. A. (1996). Models of nonindependence in dyadic research. *Journal of Social and Personal Relationships, 13,* 279–294.

Kenny, D. A., & Campbell, D. T. (1989). On the measurement of stability in overtime data. *Journal of Personality, 57,* 445–481.

Kenny, D. A., & Zautra, A. (1995). The trait-state-error model for multiwave data. *Journal of Consulting and Clinical Psychology, 63,* 52–59.

Kraemer, H. C., & Jacklin, C. N. (1979). Statistical analysis of dyadic social behavior. *Psychological Bulletin, 86,* 217–224.

Lord, F. M. (1967). A paradox in the interpretation of group comparison. *Psychological Bulletin, 68,* 304–305.

McArdle, J. J., & Epstein, D. (1987). Latent growth curves within developmental structural equation models. *Child Development, 58,* 110–133.

Murray, S. L., Holmes, J. G., & Griffin, D. W. (1996). The self-fulfilling nature of positive illusions in romantic relationships: Love is not blind, but prescient. *Journal of Personality and Social Psychology, 71,* 1155–1180.

Muthen, B., Kaplan, D., & Hollis, M. (1987). On structural equation modeling with data that are not missing completely at random. *Psychometrika, 52,* 431–462.

Raudenbush, S. W., Brennan, R. T., & Barnett, R. C. (1995). A multivariate hierarchical model for studying psychological change within married couples. *Journal of Family Psychology, 9,* 161–174.

Rusbult, C. E. (1983). A longitudinal test of the investment model: The development (and deterioration) of satisfaction and commitment in heterosexual involvements. *Journal of Personality and Social Psychology, 45,* 101–117.

Wainer, H. (1991). Adjusting for differential base rates: Lord's paradox again. *Psychological Bulletin, 109,* 147–151.

15 On the Etiology of Marital Decay and Its Consequences: Comments from a Clinical Psychologist

John M. Gottman

Every researcher in our field should buy and study this book. It is a compendium of the best research on the longitudinal course of early marriage, and it is particularly timely because this research is now at an exciting phase: Specific models are being developed to address the etiology of marital deterioration. In my commentary I offer my thoughts on those concepts and ideas represented in this book that seem to have the greatest potential to advance our understanding of how marriages succeed and fail.

Half of all divorces occur in the first seven years of marriage, and Kurdek's chapter lends support to other work that demonstrates that the stresses of the early years of marriage are related to the transition to parenthood. However, Noller and Feeney's chapter raises questions about whether this decay is a function of processes already operating in the relationship at or before the time of marriage. Their results are reminiscent of those reported by Jay Belsky and by Philip and Carolyn Pape Cowan on the transition toward parenthood. This volume presents research that takes us back earlier than the last trimester of pregnancy, and the mystery of the etiology of marital decay is laid out very well here.

Leonard and Roberts's chapter on marital aggression, marital quality, and marital stability in the first year of marriage presents their findings from the Buffalo Newlywed Study, in which aggression and alcohol use are linked to marital deterioration. The importance of this project stems, in part, from the fact that alcoholics have separation and divorce rates eight times greater than the rate in the general population. This chapter represents an attempt to integrate personality measures with marital deterioration; this is an old theme in the field, but it is now being revisited with new vitality.

In their chapter, Rusbult, Bissonette, Arriaga, and Cox write about what may be a critical buffer to marital deterioration in the first few years of marriage. They refer to this process as "accommodation," and I believe that the goal of their work – to understand how, why, and when these processes are activated – is particularly promising.

423

Huston and Houts introduce a marvelously compelling term when they refer to "the psychological infrastructure" of courtship and marriage. As with the development of a community, they suggest that this infrastructure forms the basis of lasting commitment in a marriage. I especially like their ideas of similarity of interests and marital role preferences that then either build over time or fail to do so to create their effects on the marital dyad. These concepts provide a more dynamic picture for me of the unfolding of the marriage than do the personality constructs with which they no doubt interact. This chapter presents evidence that love, affection, and marital satisfaction decline significantly over the first two years of marriage as ambivalence increases and as conflict remains stable and high. Moreover, these authors find more support for a "perpetual problems" model than for a "disillusionment model" of marital breakdown. The data do suggest that conflict erodes feelings of love. It is very interesting that again – and it is an old story in the literature – what matters about personality in marriage is not just the traits of a given spouse but how those traits are perceived by the partner.

Veroff, Douvan, Orbuch, and Acitelli's chapter on happiness in stable marriages is highly commendable on methodological grounds because it reports data from African-American marriages, it employs three useful conceptual frameworks, and it provides information about gender role expectations, affective balance in marriage, and the balance between individual and relational gratification. It is an admirable approach, and I am particularly intrigued by the finding that what has a critical effect on wives is the *husband's* lack of understanding. Our own data from a study of divorce prediction among newlyweds similarly suggest that a key predictor of divorce is the husband's refusal to accept influence from his wife. The amount of "cognitive space" he has for his spouse and the marriage and the degree of fondness and admiration the husband has for the wife are also predictive of marital deterioration.

Kurdek's chapter is noteworthy for its recruitment methodology and for the persistence that he used in following these couples. His work is also valuable in that he pits different explanatory models against one another in highly informative ways. What is most helpful in his conclusions is his challenge to communication-oriented interventions, which by and large have ignored realistic and unrealistic expectations about marriage, as well as normative changes in relationships, normal levels of unrest, and fluctuations in interdependence.

Lindahl, Clements, and Markman's chapter is particularly noteworthy for its use of a multimethod approach rather than relying solely on self-report measures; the heavy reliance on self-report instruments is an unfortunate characteristic of most research on marriage and the family. In their sample, Lindahl and her colleagues found the expected deterioration in marital satisfaction along with a 20% divorce rate; they could discriminate these couples post-hoc using data collected early in marriage with about 80% accuracy. In contrast to other work (e.g., see Kurdek, this volume), they did not find a drop in marital satisfaction associated with the birth of a first child. An added advantage of this work is that the children were studied in an intensive fashion. Doing so enabled them to find, for example, that the infant's attachment security was predicted, albeit to a marginal degree, by the premarital satisfaction of mothers, and that the mothers' (but not the fathers') premarital interaction variables accounted significantly for variation in young children's self-esteem. For the transition to parenthood, however, both mothers' and fathers' data were predictive. Interaction continues to be predictive of child outcomes in their data.

Hill and Peplau's report is distinguished by the fact that marital outcomes are linked to data collected during the dating stage. They report on the 15-year longitudinal follow-up of 231 college-aged dating couples who were first contacted in 1972. Sixty-seven percent of the couples had broken up before marriage, and the remaining third went on to marry. The results of this study are complex and fascinating – particularly the high degree of prediction that was obtained for later relationship outcomes – and I think more work of this sort is needed to understand the full course of relationship development.

The Bradbury, Cohan, and Karney chapter is a methodological critique of the longitudinal research literature. It raises many important challenges in the field, including the undue emphasis on conflict and its resolution in the social learning framework, a lack of attention to the external stressors that couples face, and a lack of attention to individual differences. Bradbury et al. propose a fascinating alternative to the social learning approach with their model of adaptive processes, stressful events, and their provocative concept of "enduring vulnerabilities."

The chapter by Tallman, Burke, and Gecas presents a useful review of the literature, as well as their plans for eventually analyzing their data using a comprehensive four-phase model of socialization into marital roles. Unlike a good deal of prior research on marriage, in which the sociological and psychological approaches have often remained separate, the promise of this study is in the merging of traditional sociological concepts with observational data on marital interaction.

O'Leary and Cascardi discuss the fact that the marital area has, until recently, neglected the problem of physical aggression. These authors then discuss the developmental course of physical aggression in marriage and provide a useful analysis of this emerging literature. There is clearly evidence of high rates of physical aggression in married or cohabiting partners. The chapter by O'Leary and Cascardi explores the roots of this aggression (e.g., being raised in an abusive home, having a personal history of aggression with peers) and reviews a developmental path-analytic model in which impulsive women distressed by their marriage are more likely to be aggressive with their partners. This, in turn, may feed into power issues for men. This model is also likely to prove useful in developing models of relationship deterioration.

Collectively, these chapters present a wealth of ideas that should guide researchers in the field for some years to come. Are there other ideas or themes that I would like to see developed or emphasized more strongly? I believe that a multimethod perspective will be particularly important in future longitudinal research on marriage. The issue of common method variance is rarely addressed, and, though most of the present chapters acknowledge the importance of collecting data across measurement systems, the problem remains in more subtle forms in our field. As a result, it is sometimes quite difficult to say whether one variable actually predicts another or whether their association is an artifact of common method variance. (G.R. Patterson has called this the problem of "glop.") Path models are elegant until one requires the criterion of what used to be called "validity," and then the path models tend to fall apart. One example may clarify this. Neuroticism, which is presumably a measure of personality, correlates with marital dissatisfaction. However, a huge component of neuroticism involves the self-report of varieties of distress or non-well-being, and this is precisely what marital satisfaction measures as well. It is well known that marital satisfaction is highly correlated with global quality of life measures. I believe it is important for investigators to think critically about this issue and to overcome methodological laziness when they develop and test models of marriage and marital change.

In this volume we have an extremely valuable collection of chapters, one that covers the waterfront of what the best researchers in our field are thinking about with regard to the origins and etiology of marital discord and dissolution. I am confident that this book will be seminal in stimulating sound theoretical work on this vital topic.

16 Problems and Prospects in Longitudinal Research on Marriage: A Sociologist's Perspective

Norval D. Glenn

The recent increase in longitudinal research on marriage in the United States and other modern societies, as exemplified by the work reported in this volume, deserves two cheers.[1] It has provided substantial information about the early years of marriage in a few recent marriage cohorts and has contributed to theoretical refinements and new hypotheses about the sources of marital dysfunction and success. We now know much more than we did just a few years ago about what kinds of marriages tend to fail and what kinds tend to succeed, and we have made at least moderate progress in understanding why.

Since much of the best of the research in this genre is reported in this volume, a balanced evaluation of the book would be a great deal more praise than criticism. However, the authors of the research chapters do an admirable job of pointing out the strengths of their work, thus making my praise of it largely redundant. They do less well in pointing out weaknesses and limitations. Furthermore, there is a good reason why we often use the phrase "constructive criticism" but rarely refer to "constructive praise"; discussion of weaknesses is more likely to contribute to the quality of future work than discussion of strengths. In this commentary, therefore, I first concentrate on what I believe to be wrong with the research and the interpretations of the findings.[2] Then I discuss the future of longitudinal research on marriage, emphasizing how some of the problems this kind of research faces can be at least partly overcome.

Why the Research Deserves No More Than Two Cheers

The Major Problems

Two of my criticisms of the research chapters in this volume are major. First, most of the authors seem to overestimate what can be accomplished with the kinds of panel designs they use, which leads them to make unwarranted conclusions. Second, most of the researchers fail to use fully the information their data collection strategies provide, with the result that their research suffers unnecessarily from a major weakness that also afflicts the much-maligned cross-sectional studies of marital failure and success.

Overestimation of the value of longitudinal research without randomized experimentation is common among researchers in almost all specialties in the social and behavioral sciences, as I have pointed out elsewhere (Glenn, 1989a). The call for longitudinal research has become a cliché, often made in a ritual manner without consideration of exactly what longitudinal designs could contribute to the topic at hand. It is almost routine for authors who report cross-sectional analyses to add to their causal conclusions a caveat to the effect that "we will not know for sure until we have longitudinal data." However, the implication that we would know for sure if we only had longitudinal data is virtually always incorrect. A common assumption seems to be that the advantage of nonexperimental longitudinal research over cross-sectional studies is much greater than the advantage of randomized experimentation over nonexperimental and quasi-experimental longitudinal research, but the ranking of the two advantage gaps is opposite to what is commonly assumed.

Nevertheless, the superiority of longitudinal over cross-sectional designs to study the sources of marital dysfunction can be substantial if all of the information provided by panel studies is fully utilized. Correlational data from cross-sectional studies of intact marriages can lead to patently incorrect conclusions about the bases of marital difficulties, because many of the marriages that have become dysfunctional are no longer intact and thus are not studied (see Glenn, 1990b). Consider, for instance, the case of age at marriage, which bears only a very weak relationship to marital quality in cross-sectional data, even though it is known that marriages in which both spouses are very young are much more likely to go bad than those in which both spouses are in their mid-20s or older at the time of marriage. In this case, the lack of evidence in the cross-sectional data for the apparently strong effects of early marriage is due in large measure to a strong tendency of very young persons quickly to end disappointing marriages.

Any independent variable that affects both marital quality and the tendency to end poor marriages will distort cross-sectional evidence of the effects of the independent variable on marital quality, and there are many such variables, including religiosity, commitment to the institution of marriage, willingness and ability to persevere in the pursuit of goals, and, I suspect, many of the personality variables studied by the research reported in this book. Even if an independent variable that affects marital quality does not affect the tendency to end poor marriages, removal of many of the weakest marriages from the population of intact marriages will attenuate most measures of association between the variable and marital quality by reducing the variance of the latter.

The sample selection bias that results from divorce and separation may even create the appearance of an effect that does not exist or may cause the direction of an effect to be estimated incorrectly. A possible example is the case of belief in marital permanence. Persons who strongly believe that marriage should be for life are likely to work harder than others to maintain their marriages, which should result in a positive effect on the probability of marital success. However, such persons' tendency to remain in unsatisfactory marriages might create a negative cross-sectional association between belief in marital permanence and marital quality.

Superior though they are, longitudinal designs are no panacea for the problems involved in assessing the causes of marital dysfunction. Studies that are not randomized experiments can *never* come close to providing conclusive evidence of cause and effect, and of course for ethical and practical reasons randomized experiments cannot be used to assess the importance of most of the probable sources of marital problems.[3]

Suppose that Variable X measured in the first wave of a panel study predicts Variable Y measured in a later wave when the first-wave values of Y and other obviously important control variables are held constant. Does that mean that X affects Y? Not necessarily. It is possible, and sometimes probable, that a third variable, Z, affects both X and Y but with a longer causal lag for the effect on Y than for that on X. Similarly, if the first-wave Variable X values do not predict the later-wave Variable Y values when first-wave Y values and all other obviously important control variables are held constant, does that mean that X does not affect Y, assuming a lack of measurement and sampling error? Not necessarily, because all of the effect of X on Y may have occurred before the first wave. If, however, first-wave values of X and Y are uncorrelated, does that mean that X does not affect Y? Again, not necessarily, because there may be a suppressor variable not included in the analysis – that is, a variable that affects X and Y in such a way as to mask evidence of a causal relationship between them.

I could continue, but these examples suffice to illustrate that the relationships between variables found by multiple-wave panel studies are, in common with relationships found by cross-sectional studies, always subject to more than one interpretation. Only one interpretation may seem reasonable, in view of theory and what is known from other sources about the

phenomena being studied, but one can never know for sure that the interpretation is correct.

Clearly, all causal conclusions from the results of longitudinal studies of
marriage should, in common with virtually all causal conclusions based on
social and behavioral research, be stated tentatively. Authors should keep in
mind the distinction between causal inference and causal discovery and recognize that they can do only the former (for an elaboration of this point, see
Glenn, 1989b).

Chapter 4 of this volume, by Huston and Houts, is almost a model for the
properly cautious and tentative statement of causal conclusions, and Chapter 6, by Kurek, mentions only predictions and associations and avoids even
tentative explicit causal conclusions, which perhaps is being too cautious.
Each of the other research chapters contains at least one untentative, and
thus unwarranted, assertion of causation, though most of the chapters are
appropriately tentative in some of their discussion of possible effects. The
worst offenders in the improper use of causal language are Veroff, Douvan,
Orbuch, and Acitelli (this volume) and Hill and Peplau (this volume). For
instance, the authors of Chapter 8 assert that "religious similarity did affect
the likelihood of divorce" and say that differences among the respondents
in their adherence to traditional beliefs about love, sex, gender roles, and religion "affected the outcomes of their relationships." Confident assertions
of no effects based on a lack of statistically significant associations are ar-
guably even more inappropriate than confident positive causal conclusions,
yet Hill and Peplau conclude that "future oriented beliefs about children had
no impact on respondents' dating relationships or likelihood of marrying
their college partner." Unwarranted statements about causation also appear
frequently in the literature reviews in some of the chapters, where they perhaps reflect the causal language used in the publications reviewed. For
instance, Lindahl, Clements, and Markman (this volume) write that self-
concept "has been found to be highly influenced by parental factors in early
development" and that "direct exposure to marital conflict has been found
to be detrimental to child development." Of course, these effects were not
"found" but were only "inferred" or "estimated," and the estimates may be
incorrect owing to measurement, sampling, and/or specification errors.

Many longitudinal studies, including most of those included in this volume, fail to exploit fully the advantages of the design. If, for instance, the
only data analyzed from a panel study are those from marriages that remained intact through the different waves, sample-selection bias of the same
kind that afflicts cross-sectional studies is likely to distort estimates of the
effects of the independent variables. As in the case of a cross-sectional de-

sign, many if not most of the marriages that have suffered the most negative effects will not be studied, and thus evidence for the effects will be
weakened and may not appear at all. Or, effects that do not exist in the real
world may be thought to exist.

Veroff, Douvan, Orbuch, and Acitelli (this volume) provide a salient example of this problem. The researchers restrict their analysis to marriages
that remained intact for 4 years and in which the spouses never reported considering divorce, the purpose being to identify bases of marital quality
within this restricted group. The apparent assumption is that even though
the findings cannot be generalized beyond this subset of marriages, they are
a sound basis for inferring causation within the subset.

That assumption is incorrect. Relationships between variables within a
nonclosed population can result from movement of individuals out of the
population as well as from causal processes, or movement out of the population can attenuate, erase, or even reverse relationships that would exist if
the movement had not occurred. This can happen when an independent variable or one of its close correlates appreciably affects the probability of leaving or staying in the population.

Consider one of the researchers' counterintuitive findings, namely, that
the more the husbands change their self-perceptions toward the ideals their
wives set for them, the less satisfying the marriages are (except for black
husbands). A possible explanation for this finding not mentioned by the authors is that often the accommodation of the husband failed to improve the
marriage, or failed to improve it very much, but prevented the couple from
contemplating divorce. Perhaps wives tend to be reluctant to think about divorcing husbands who are obviously trying to improve the relationship. For
husbands, some other variable, such as belief in marital permanence, might
account for both the accommodation and the failure to consider divorce. In
either case, the accommodation would not have contributed to the poor marital quality. Rather, the accommodation and/or a correlate of it would have
kept the marriage from moving out of the subset of marriages studied, thus
contributing to an association of accommodation with poor marital quality.
Some of the other counterintuitive findings of this study could have similar
explanations. The researchers apparently have the data needed to test such
explanations, but they do not use them in the study reported. Therefore, their
research suffers from the same major weakness that afflicts cross-sectional
studies of marital quality.

Some of the other authors of the research chapters do better. For instance,
Hill and Peplau use both marital stability/instability and measures of marital
quality as outcome variables. Most of the researchers, however, make little

use of information on the characteristics of couples who divorced during the course of the panel studies and on the timing of the divorces.

Relatively Minor Problems

The remaining weaknesses I detect in the research chapters are less important than the two discussed above. The first one I address occurs in a minority of the studies, and the second one does not cast serious doubt on the validity of any of the conclusions. My comments on the two additional alleged weaknesses I discuss may reflect differences in disciplinary perspectives more than anything else.

A few of the studies reported in this volume (e.g., those by Huston & Houts, Kurdek, and Hill & Peplau) estimate the effects on dependent variables of differences between spouses. Like most other researchers who have attempted to estimate the effects of spousal differences, all of these authors fail to take into account what is often called the "identification problem," which arises when three variables need to be included as independent or control variables in an analysis and when any one is a linear function of the other two. (The classic treatment of the identification problem is in a series of articles by H. M. Blalock, Jr.; see, e.g., Blalock, 1966, 1967.) This problem occurs in cohort analysis, in which the variables are age, period, and cohort; in mobility effects research, in which the variables are origin, destination, and the distance moved; and in research to assess the effects of spousal differences or similarities, in which the variables are husband's characteristics, wife's characteristics, and the difference between the two. All three variables cannot simply be included as independent or predictor variables in a regression or similar analysis, because there is extreme collinearity – the multiple correlation of any two of the variables with the third is unity. In other words, when two are held constant, the variance of the third is zero. If the researcher tries to include all three variables in the analysis, the regression or similar program will not run.

In such a case, there is no way to estimate the linear effects on any dependent variable of any of the three variables, unless it is reasonable to assume that at least one of the variables has no effect. In other words, the linear effects of the three variables are confounded with one another so that they cannot be separated statistically. However, if one can reasonably assume, or has evidence that, one of the variables has no effect, then it can be omitted from the analysis, and the effects of the other two can be estimated in a straightforward manner. Furthermore, because a *nonlinear* effect of any one of the variables will be reflected as an interaction between the other two, the presence of such an interaction can be interpreted as tentative evidence for a nonlinear effect of the first variable. For instance, a spousal difference effect that is the same regardless of the direction of the difference is non-linear (and nonmonotonic) and will be reflected as an interaction between husband's characteristics and wife's characteristics (Glenn, 1990a).

Because the authors of chapters of this volume fail to acknowledge the identification problem and do not test for the effects of spousal differences in an appropriate way, their estimates of difference effects should be viewed with more than the usual caution. In some cases (e.g., Huston & Houts's compatibility measures) the assumption that at least one of the defining variables has no effect on the dependent variable is probably reasonable, but the assumption should be made explicit and defended.

Panel studies always involve the possibility of panel conditioning effects, or effects on the subjects from their participation in the research. These effects are of interest for two different reasons, the ethical issue of possible harm to the subjects and the threat to the validity of generalizations made from the research findings. There is evidence that subjects in marital research are more likely to benefit than to be harmed by their participation (e.g., Bradbury, 1994), but of course any kind of effects – harmful, beneficial, or neutral – may distort conclusions drawn from the findings. Ironically, the better the research in most other respects, the greater is the likelihood of important effects on the dependent variables from the research itself. For instance, the more closely spaced and numerous the panel waves, and the more searching and in-depth the data-gathering procedures, the greater is the probability of panel conditioning effects. It is thus not entirely complimentary to say that the effects are probably not a serious problem for most of the research reported in this volume. The possibility of such effects should always be acknowledged and discussed when findings from panel studies are reported, but in this volume only Lindahl, Clements, and Markman give more than incidental attention to the issue. As the several ongoing studies continue through additional waves, the problem of panel conditioning effects may become more serious and thus will deserve greater attention – a topic to which I return in the next section.

From the perspective of a sociologist, the explanatory variables in the panel studies tend to be too predominantly psychological, with too little attention paid to the social and cultural context in which marriages exist. In their attempts to explain marital problems, sociologists tend to turn to such variables as the state of the economy, the sex ratio at different ages, and broad value configurations. To the extent that social and cultural variables have their effects on marriage through such psychological phenomena as commitment to the institution of marriage and perception of alternatives to the current marriage, omission of the variables will not lower the predictive power of causal models. However, such variables are needed for a full understanding, as opposed to merely a statistical explanation, of the development of marital dysfunction, and their neglect handicaps attempts to explain trends, such as the apparent steep increase in marital failure in the United States during the 1960s and 1970s.[4]

Also from the perspective of a sociologist, the contributions to this volume, and the genre of research they represent, exhibit considerable disciplinary insularity. Written by psychologists, persons trained in psychologically oriented family relations departments, and social psychological sociologists, the chapters give scant attention to numerous publications by sociologists, demographers, and economists that may help explain marital dysfunction. For instance, I find in this volume only one reference to the many articles from the multiple-wave longitudinal study of a national sample of married persons conducted by Alan Booth, Jay Edwards, and Booth's former colleagues at the University of Nebraska. Even though that study is of married persons rather than married couples, the analyses of data from it effectively address many issues similar to those treated in this volume. As far as I can tell, there are no citations in this volume of the dozens of publications that report marriage-related research with data from the Panel Study of Income Dynamics or the National Longitudinal Survey of Labor Market Experience.[5] Nor do I recognize in the reference lists any publications that report data from the National Survey of Families and Households. Supplementing the panel data from small and local samples with data from large and representative national samples would obviously be valuable, even though the large-scale surveys generally provide cruder measures of key variables and more superficial information than do the local panel studies. The two kinds of evidence go well together, since each tends to compensate for the weaknesses of the other.

The Future of Longitudinal Marital Research

Lindahl et al. (this volume) express concern about the future of longitudinal research on marriage in view of shrinking federal funding for research. Their concern is well founded, but it seems to me that a great deal can be accomplished at minimal cost with the data already gathered. If, as I maintain, a major weakness of the recent research is a failure to use fully the information provided by longitudinal designs, the yield from continuing analyses of available data should be substantial.

I realize, however, that it is much easier to exhort researchers to more fully utilize information from panel studies of marriage than it is to respond to the exhortation. There are few guidelines as to how the latter can be done, and I have neither the space nor the ability to give all of the needed guidance here. I can only make a few general suggestions.

The condition involved in causal studies conducted with cross-sectional data on intact marriages, or with data on marriages that remain intact during the course of a panel study, is a special case of sample-selection bias, and there is a fairly large literature on statistical corrections for such bias. These corrections are not widely used, partly because many researchers do not know about them, but also because they require either (a) information on the nature and extent of the bias that is rarely available or (b) possibly incorrect assumptions about the bias. However, some of the panel studies of marriage may provide the information that would allow the corrections to be used effectively. Although it is somewhat dated, the best introduction to sample-selection bias is still Berk (1983). Marital researchers who want to consider use of the corrections should consult the *Social Science Citation Index* for recent methodological publications that cite the Berk article.

I prefer simpler solutions, such as construction of indices of marital success that combine measures of marital stability and quality. I have used very simple and crude indices of this kind with cross-sectional data from the General Social Survey, one of which is a dichotomous index that defines an intact marriage reported to be "very happy" as "successful" and a dissolved marriage or an intact one reported to be less than "very happy" as "unsuccessful" (see Figures 16.1 through 16.3).[6] Even this crude index is useful for some purposes, and the researchers represented in this volume should be able to construct more sophisticated indices with their data.

Another option is to do parallel analyses with marital stability and marital quality as outcome variables, as Hill and Peplau do in Chapter 8, but with explicit attention to assessing the effects of sample selection bias. Just taking into account the probable effects of the bias would be an improvement over the usual current practice.

Even if funding for longitudinal studies of marriage remains stable or increases moderately, some hard decisions will have to be made by researchers and the funding agencies about how the limited resources will be distributed. Should all or most of the studies represented in this volume be continued into the middle years of marriage, or should resources be shifted to new studies, either of the early years or the later ones? Consulting a different kind of data – those from repeated cross-sectional surveys – can help to answer this question, and it is for that reason, rather than to illustrate my

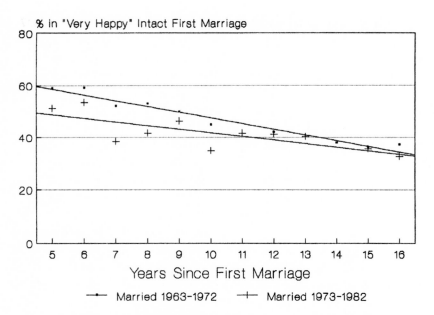

Figure 16.1. Index of marital success, by years since first marriage and marital cohort (linear trend lines). Widowed persons are excluded from base of percentages. "Years Since First Marriage" = midpoint for the cohort.

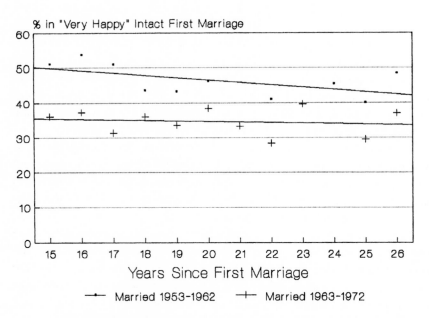

Figure 16.2. Index of marital success, by years since first marriage and marital cohort (linear trend lines). Widowed persons are excluded from base of percentages. "Years Since First Marriage" = midpoint for the cohort.

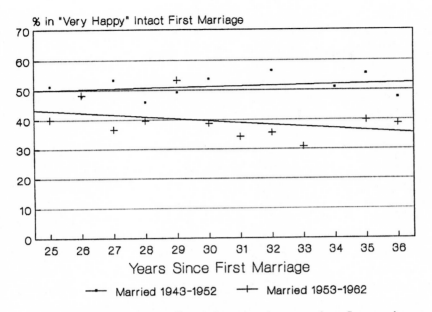

% in "Very Happy" Intact First Marriage

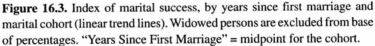

Married 1943–1952   **Married 1953–1962**

Figure 16.3. Index of marital success, by years since first marriage and marital cohort (linear trend lines). Widowed persons are excluded from base of percentages. "Years Since First Marriage" = midpoint for the cohort.

simple and crude measure of marital success, that I present the data in Figures 16.1 through 16.3.

These data from large and representative national samples, like a great deal of similar data, suggest that most marital dysfunction either exists at the beginning of marriages or arises in the first few years. In the marriage cohorts represented in the figures, aggregate-level marital success apparently declined sharply during the first 10 to 15 years and then leveled off or declined more slowly.[7] This pattern suggests that the emphasis of recent longitudinal marital research on the early years is well placed. The data also suggest that the experiences of different marital cohorts are different. Aggregate-level marital success in the 1953–1962 cohort apparently continued to decline through its 3rd decade, whereas both the 1943–1952 and the 1963–1972 cohorts seem to have stabilized at earlier stages. Since the development of marital dysfunction may vary by cohort, and since most of the panel studies have dealt with only a few adjacent cohorts, there is a need for studies of the newer marital cohorts in their early stages.

At least some of the panel studies that have covered the early stages of marriage should be continued into the later stages, but the longer the marriages are studied, the greater is the probability that they will be affected by their participation in the studies. For this reason, later-stage marriages not previously studied should be recruited into supplementary panels. Furthermore, to help estimate panel conditioning effects, new panel studies should add a control or supplementary panel from which data are gathered less frequently than from the main panel, and with less intrusive methods, such as abbreviated questionnaires. A few panel studies of marriage have included control groups, but in this volume I find no use of control-group data to assess panel conditioning effects.

Although longitudinal marital research is valuable, maximum understanding of how dysfunction arises in marriages will not be achieved solely through more and better panel studies. The greatest need now is to integrate information gathered with a variety of methods and from different disciplinary perspectives. Enthusiasm for the kind of research reported in this book could be destructive if it should lead researchers to reject or ignore evidence from longitudinal studies of married persons (rather than couples), cross-sectional surveys with large and representative samples, clinical case studies, and so forth. All of these kinds of studies have limitations and strengths, and though it would be folly to attribute equal value to each one, all can contribute to our understanding of the bases of marital success and failure.

As I see it, the main tasks for those who do longitudinal research on marriage are (1) to become more realistic about what can and cannot be done with panel designs; (2) to devise means to more fully exploit longitudinal data, so that the research will no longer be only marginally better than cross-sectional studies; (3) to deal more effectively with the problem of possible panel conditioning effects; and (4) to become less insular by making greater use of information gathered by other methods and from other disciplinary perspectives. These tasks are only moderately daunting, and thus I judge the prospects for this line of research to be bright. Much has been accomplished in the past decade, and the next few years promise to be even more fruitful.

Notes

1. The term *longitudinal* is sometimes used in a broad sense to include any research design with a temporal dimension, so that repeated cross-sectional, trend and retrospective studies are considered to be kinds of longitudinal research. However, I use the term here in its more restricted sense, to include only studies that gather data from the same units of analysis at two or more points in time.

2. My commentary focuses on the chapters that report longitudinal research rather than on the chapter by Bradbury, Cohan, and Karney, which is an evaluative essay; that by Tallman, Burke, and Gecas, which reports a the-

oretical model and a plan for research; and that by O'Leary and Cascardi, which is a synthetic essay. My failure to comment specifically on these three chapters does not reflect a judgment that they are unimportant, since I regard them as among the most valuable chapters. Rather, evaluating the research chapters and the genre of research they represent is about all that can be accomplished in the space allotted.

3. Of course, randomized experiments do not necessarily provide conclusive evidence of cause and effect either. "True" experiments can fail for a number of reasons, including measurement error and such blunders as misjudging causal lag and thus taking "after" measurements before the effects of the experimental stimulus have had time to occur.

4. Some family social scientists apparently still believe that there was no increase in marital failure, that the increase in divorce merely reflected a decreased willingness of persons to stay in unsatisfactory marriages. A great deal of the available evidence is inconsistent with that view, however, including the data in Figures 16.1 through 16.3. Notice that in each comparison of adjacent marriage cohorts, the older one has the higher estimated marital success.

5. Of course, I do not know the contents of all of the cited publications well enough to be sure that they do not report data from these surveys.

6. The data are weighted by the number of persons in the household aged 18 and older, because the sample is of households rather than of adult individuals and thus the unweighted data overestimate the number of unmarried persons and the extent of marital failure.

7. The leveling off of aggregate-level marital success, as indicated by my crude index, does not mean that many new problems did not arise in the middle-stage marriages. It only means, assuming rough validity of the index, that as some marriages developed new problems, other marriages improved. Since the index could fail to reflect some very important and frequent changes in the marriages, I am by no means arguing that we do not need in-depth studies of middle-stage marriages.

References

Berk, R. A. (1983). An introduction to sample selection bias. *American Sociological Review, 48,* 386–398.

Blalock, H. M., Jr. (1966). The identification problem and theory building: The case of status inconsistency. *American Sociological Review, 31,* 52–61.

Blalock, H. M., Jr. (1967). Status inconsistency, social mobility, status integration and structural effects. *American Sociological Review, 32,* 790–801.

Bradbury, T. N. (1994). Unintended effects of marital research on marital relationships. *Journal of Family Psychology, 8,* 187–201.

Glenn, N. D. (1989a). Some limitations of longitudinal and cohort designs in social and behavioral research. In L. Sechrest, H. Freeman, & A. Mulley (Eds.), *Health services methodology: A focus on AIDS* (pp. 55–62). Bethesda, MD: National Center for Health Services Research and Health Care Technology Assessment.

Glenn, N. D. (1989b). What we know, what we say we know: Discrepancies between warranted and stated conclusions in the social sciences. In H. Eulau (Ed.), *Crossroads of social science: The ICPSR 25th anniversary volume* (pp. 119–140). New York: Agathon Press.

Glenn, N. D. (1990a). The fundamental difference between linear and nonlinear discrepancy effects. *Social Forces, 68,* 621–622.

Glenn, N. D. (1990b). Quantitative research on marital quality in the 1980s: A critical review. *Journal of Marriage and the Family, 52,* 818–831.

17 A Social Psychological View of Marital Dysfunction and Stability

Ellen Berscheid

For those of us who believe that a science of interpersonal relationships is critical to the further development of the social and behavioral sciences as well as to the practice of relationship therapy, the longitudinal expeditions into marital relationships chronicled in this volume make an important contribution. Together with the precious few longitudinal studies of relationships conducted previously, they represent a small island of terra firma in that vast sea of studies that observe behavior at only a single point in time. Such single-shot studies, which have characterized the marital satisfaction and stability literature for many years, have "produced only a modest increment in understanding of the causes and consequences of marital success" (Glenn, 1990, p. 818).

More immediately and personally, these authors' accounts inspire feelings of admiration for those who have undertaken the arduous longitudinal march and returned to tell the tale. Who cannot wince in sympathy with Kurdek's (this volume) aside that he came to dread the publication of yet another set of marriage licenses, signaling the opportunity to recruit additional research participants but also the investment of yet more time and tedium in their pursuit? And who cannot be impressed with the grit required to track down and enlist the further cooperation of couples last seen more than a decade ago (e.g., Hill & Peplau, this volume; Huston & Houts, this volume)? And so who can put this volume down without appreciating why, as Lindahl, Clements, and Markman (this volume) observe, so few young investigators, confronted with the publish-immediately-or-perish pressures of academe as well as ever-diminishing research funds, are electing to take the longitudinal route to furthering our understanding of relationships?

I take it as a given, then, that the contributors to this volume deserve battle ribbons, not kibitzing from spectators however well meaning. Thus the remarks below on the longitudinal quest to better understand the causes and correlates of marital satisfaction and stability, made from a "social psycho-

441

logical perspective," are offered in a humble spirit to future investigators and with gratitude to those who have finished their longitudinal journeys.

The Social Psychological Perspective

In their review of theory, method, and research on the longitudinal course of marital quality and stability, Karney and Bradbury (1995) conclude that the need for theory is especially acute in the study of marriage because "much of the longitudinal work has not been explicitly theoretical in orientation and because subsequent progress in understanding how marriages change is likely to depend heavily on the quality of available models" (p. 4). Improvement of the quality of available models, in turn, depends on understanding the implicit as well as the explicit assumptions underlying the theoretical frameworks currently guiding relationship research.

As Bradbury and his associates observe in their chapter in this volume, many investigators currently examining the longitudinal course of marital dysfunction take a "social learning" approach to the problem. Although similar to the approach social psychologists typically take to relationship phenomena in many of its assumptions, the social learning perspective, especially as it has evolved in marital relationship research, differs from the social psychological perspective in several respects. Several of these differences are sketched below with the aim of illustrating how the social psychological perspective may yield insights into relationship satisfaction and stability that have yet to be explored.

The Social Learning Approach

The social learning theoretical approach originated at Yale in the 1930s when Clark Hull led a graduate seminar in which he attempted to relate his learning theory, formulated largely on the basis of research with laboratory rats, to psychoanalysis, the other major psychological theory at the time (see Miller, 1989). Two students in that seminar, Neal Miller and John Dollard, subsequently applied Hullian theory and its "four fundamentals of learning" (i.e., drive, cue, response, and reward) directly to human behavior. Dollard, Doob, Miller, Mowrer, and Sears's *Frustration and Aggression* (1939), which presented evidence that aggression is an outgrowth of frustration, was followed shortly by Miller and Dollard's *Social Learning and Imitation* (1941), which argued that human "imitative behavior follows the laws of learning and arises under the social conditions which reward it" (1941, p. 12). Bandura (e.g., 1977, 1986) subsequently extended their theory and the concept of imitation, demonstrating in a series of stunning experiments that children could acquire new behaviors simply by watching another person perform them (e.g., Bandura, Ross, & Ross, 1961). Like virtually all learning theories of its vintage, Hullian learning theory was an S–R (stimulus–response) theory; that is, the stimulus situation was taken to be as the experimenter perceived it, ignoring the possibility that the individual whose behavior was to be predicted might interpret that stimulus situation quite differently.

Today, the phrase *social learning theory* encompasses an eclectic collection of principles borrowed from several different learning theories. The basic assumption underlying all learning theories, of course, is that behavior that is rewarded – whether by a pellet delivered to a rat by an experimenter or by a kiss delivered to a wife by a husband – is more likely to be repeated than behavior that is not rewarded. In acknowledging their own debt to social learning theory, Tallman, Burke, and Gecas (this volume) restate social learning theory's basic proposition that people internalize patterns of behavior that have been positively reinforced and avoid behaviors that have been costly or punishing. The theory assumes that an individual's behavior represents a choice between alternative courses of action, a choice that results from the individual's estimates of the likelihood that each action will result in rewarding rather than costly outcomes.

Investigators who take the social learning approach to questions of marital satisfaction and stability thus focus heavily on the rewards and costs partners experience in their interactions with each other. In addition, and perhaps as a residual of the original S–R nature of most learning theories, they highly value direct observation of interaction events in preference to reliance on the partners' self-reports of the rewards and costs they have experienced in interaction. Moreover, it is costs rather than rewards that are of special interest, as reflected in the practice of observing couples interact as they discuss a marital problem (e.g., Noller & Feeney, this volume; Tallman et al., this volume). Observations of the partners' interaction behavior now are often supplemented by partners' self-reports of their affective feelings and/or by physiological measures of emotion because it became clear over the years that observers are poor judges of the extent to which the partners themselves find the interaction rewarding or costly (see Noller & Ruzzene, 1991).

Apart from a focus on spouses' affective responses as they interact, the deductive lines of correspondence between social learning theory and actual research on marital satisfaction and stability are sometimes difficult to trace. But whatever its theoretical source, it appears that many investigators of marital dysfunction subscribe to the thesis that has guided much of Gottman and Levenson's (1988) longitudinal work: "[We] make a case for the hypothesis that marital satisfaction increases or decreases, and that ultimately marriages succeed or fail over time, as a function of how couples handle negative affect" (p. 182). A corollary to this working hypothesis is that improvement of the partners' communication and conflict resolution skills will decrease conflict and negative affect, thereby increasing satisfaction with the relationship, which should promote its stability. This corollary has special appeal because such skill deficiencies are believed to be remediable by the ministrations of a relationship therapist, as Bradbury, Cohan, and Karney (this volume) note. In sum, and as Bradbury et al. (this volume) also conclude, the social-learning approach to marital dysfunction and stability focuses almost exclusively on conflict resolution as the critical behavioral domain within marital relationships.

The Social Psychological Approach

In contrast to the social learning perspective reflected in the learning theories that dominated experimental psychology in the early and midyears of this century, the perspective from which most social psychologists view relationship phenomena is rooted in the approach Kurt Lewin took to predicting behavior. Unlike his learning-theory contemporaries, Lewin was emphasizing that people, if not rats, may perceive and interpret the same stimulus situation very differently, and that it was the individual's cognitive interpretation of the meaning of the stimulus that would influence his or her behavior. Lewin thus put the O (the Organism's cognitive interpretation of the stimulus situation) between the learning theorists' S and R, thereby putting social psychology on a cognitive, or S–O–R, track from its beginning.

In addition, and as important, Lewin rebelled against the "individualistic" approach to behavior that concentrated the search for the causes of differences in individuals' behaviors almost exclusively in differences in the properties of those individuals (e.g., in their different "personalities"). In his Field Theory (see Deutsch, 1954), Lewin proposed that an individual's behavior is a function not only of the properties of the individual but also of the "field" in which the individual is located. His well-known formula, $B = f(P, E)$, simply expressed his view that the properties of the Person interact with the properties of the Environment to influence behavior, with the environment encompassing both the individual's social environment and his or her physical environment.

In addition to being regarded as the founder of experimental social psychology, Lewin is often viewed as the first formal "systems" theorist in psychology because he insisted that the individual and the field in which the individual is located constitute an interdependent system such that a change in the state of one will produce a change in the state of the other. Lewin's stamp on the discipline of social psychology can be seen not only in its traditional focus on the role of cognitive influences on behavior but also in the discipline's emphasis on environmental – or "situational" or "contextual" – determinants of behavior, especially those emanating from the individual's social environment. Social psychologists also, but regrettably less often, attempt to identify how the properties of the environment interact with the properties of the individual to influence behavior (see Snyder & Ickes, 1985).

Lewin's contribution to psychology is not always well understood. In his commentary on Levinger and Huston's analysis of "the social psychology of marriage," for example, the prominent marital researcher, Neil Jacobson, expressed his bewilderment in the following manner:

> I must confess that I have never understood why Lewin was as influential as he was; thus, I have some skepticism about anything that is derived from Lewin's work. According to the authors, the Lewinian framework (and, presumably, the basis for their framework) begins with his notion that "behavior is a function of person and environment." Lewin may have been the first social psychologist to say this, but it is a principle that is so self-evident that it does not seem to be a promising way to begin a conceptual framework designed to take us to places where we have not already been. (1990, p. 272)

Jacobson is to be admired for saying out loud what, no doubt, has puzzled many of his colleagues as well, perhaps as much as the theoretical lines of correspondence between social learning theory and some empirical research on marital dysfunction have puzzled those of us who approach relationships from a different perspective. However, the "self-evident" principle to which Jacobson refers clearly is not evident to everyone, as I discuss shortly.

Social Interdependence Theory

The most influential theory in the social psychological approach to relationship phenomena has been interdependence theory, formulated by Harold Kelley, a student of Kurt Lewin's, and John Thibaut (Thibaut & Kelley, 1959; Kelley & Thibaut, 1978; Kelley, 1979). Often regarded as a "social exchange" theory, interdependence theory shares social learning theory's twin assumptions that behavior will not be repeated unless it is rewarded in some way and that the fundamental internal dynamic of social interaction is the partners' exchange of rewards and costs. Like social learning theory, then, interdependence theory directly focuses on the behavioral options open to the individual at a given time and the rewards (or "goodness of outcomes") the individual expects to receive from the performance of any one of those behaviors. Unlike social learning theory, however, interdependence theory is a "dyadic" theory that addresses the behaviors of both partners in the relationship. It proposes that a partner's behavior in the relationship is a function of the configuration presented by both partners' reward – cost matrices, or the behavioral outcome matrix characteristic of the *relationship* rather than the individual partner's personal payoff matrix alone.

Although interdependence theory is sometimes represented as a theory of rewards and costs, its contribution was not that it emphasized the importance of the reward and cost consequences of social interaction; all social exchange theories (e.g., Homans, 1961) and all learning theories rest on that fundamental assumption. Rather, one of the theory's several contributions to our understanding of relationships has been to identify the possible patterns of the consequences of dyadic interaction, or the ways in which partners may be interdependent with respect to their positive and negative outcomes and thus how they are likely to coordinate their interaction behaviors.

Another contribution of interdependence theory, one that perhaps is most relevant to the aim of understanding marital dysfunction and stability, has been its theoretical decoupling of relationship satisfaction from relationship stability. Many years ago, the great family sociologist Willard Waller (1930/1967) observed anecdotally that the stability of a marriage is not necessarily related to the sweetness of its contents. (For recent evidence pertinent to Waller's observation, see Heaton & Albrecht, 1991; and White & Booth, 1991.) But the assumption that satisfaction with a relationship is the key determinant of its stability remained unexamined until interdependence theory formally addressed the dynamics of "nonvoluntary" relationships, or relationships that people feel compelled to maintain even if they would prefer not to do so.

Separating the question of satisfaction from the question of stability, interdependence theory differentiates between an individual's Comparison Level, or "the standard against which the member [of the relationship] evaluates the 'attractiveness' of the relationship or how satisfactory it is" (Thibaut & Kelley, 1959, p. 21), and the individual's Comparison Level for

Alternatives, or "the standard the member uses in deciding whether to remain in or to leave the relationship" (p. 21). The latter is defined as "the quality of the best of the member's available alternatives . . . [or] the reward-cost positions experienced or believed to exist in the most satisfactory of the other available relationships" (Thibaut & Kelley, 1959, p. 22). When a relationship's goodness-of-outcomes level falls below that available in the best alternative, the theory predicts that the stability of the relationship is threatened regardless of the individual's previous satisfaction with it. Interdependence theory thus views the stability of a relationship not solely as a function of the quality of the interior contents of the relationship but, rather, as a conjoint function of that interior and the relationship's exterior. As a consequence, the theory predicts that even unhappy relationships may be stably maintained and that even satisfying relationships may prove to be unstable if a better alternative presents itself.

As a result of the influence of interdependence theory, most social psychologists who attempt to predict the stability of premarital and marital relationships usually include some assessment of the relationship's social environment, especially along the goodness-of-alternatives dimension that has been shown to help predict premarital relationship stability (e.g., Rusbult, 1983; Simpson, 1987). Recent evidence indicates that the stability of a marital relationship also is likely to be affected by its social environment. South and Lloyd (1995), for example, report that the risk of marital dissolution is highest in geographical areas where the local "marriage market" of potential spouses presents an abundance of alternatives to the present marital relationship. Goodness-of-alternatives thus plays a central role in Rusbult's investment model (see this volume), which has been derived from interdependence theory. Rusbult's inclusion of assessments of this environmental factor, along with Tallman et al.'s (this volume) effort to assess the impact of this and several other environmental factors in their longitudinal study, thus represent an advance in investigations of stability.

Summary

The principal difference between the social psychological approach and the social learning approach, at least as it has been reflected in marital research, lies in the differential importance accorded the nature of the environment in which the relationship is embedded, on the one hand, and the affective quality of the partners' interaction, on the other. Thus what social psychologists will find missing from many longitudinal studies of marital satisfaction and stability is direct attention to the relationship's environmental context, especially its immediate, or proximal, environment (e.g., the social network in which the relationship is embedded).

This lacuna in marital research has been apparent for some time. For example, in his "decade preview" of trends and directions in family research in the 1980s, Berardo concluded: "Research in the sixties and throughout the seventies has been heavily concentrated at the microlevel, with a major focus on the internal transactions between family members. What is needed in the 1980s is a shift to 'the macroenvironment and how it impacts on the . . . microenvironment'" (1980, p. 727). That shift did not occur. It should be acknowledged that although social psychologists tend to be sensitive to the relationship's proximal context, they have directly attended to the more distal cultural and societal influences on relationships no more than other relationship researchers (for a discussion of this point, see Levinger, 1994).

Other differences between the two approaches stem from their differential emphasis on the relationship's interior and exterior. For example, the assumption that the affective quality of interaction microevents is of premier importance in predicting stability implicitly carries with it a number of other assumptions that many who take the social psychological perspective would not endorse. Perhaps the most disconcerting of these implicit assumptions is not that "a spouse is a spouse" (or that "all spouses are created equal," as Bradbury et al., this volume, put it); rather, it is the assumption that "a conflict is a conflict." It is how the conflict is "handled" that appears to be assumed to be critical to satisfaction and stability, whereas the dimensions of the conflict – its roots, its magnitude, its inherent "resolveability" – receive little direct consideration. It is easy to agree that partners equipped with conflict resolution skills ought to be better able to resolve their differences than partners not so equipped. But it is surely true that some couples are more likely than others to encounter conflicts that are inherently difficult to resolve (as viewed by God, Omniscient Jones, or a random sample of marital therapists), and that some couples encounter such problems more frequently and over a longer period of time than other couples do. Attention to the dimensions of the conflict, if not the paths to its resolution as well, inevitably leads to a search for its causes. If a social psychologist were asked to round up the "usual suspects," the relationship's environment would be among the first to enter the paddy wagon. In sum, and from a social psychological perspective, a kiss may be just a kiss and a sigh just a sigh as time goes by in relationships, but not only is an environment not just an environment, a conflict is not just a conflict.

Stability and Temporal Changes
in the Relationship's Environment

Although the social psychological vantage point broadens one's view of relationships to include their immediate environment, it has some blind spots as well. One of the most serious of these has been accurately fingered by Karney and Bradbury (1995) in their evaluation of the several theoretical perspectives currently guiding longitudinal research on marital dysfunction. These critics observe that the social exchange theories, including interdependence theory, lack "a temporal perspective" (p. 5); they do not address the flow of microevents within interaction episodes, except in a very general way, nor do they address the temporal flow of larger events over the course of the relationship. Thus, as Karney and Bradbury observe, the social psychological perspective "does not address how change in marriage comes about" (p. 5).

The temporal deficiency of theories that take a social psychological perspective has not gone unrecognized. Kelley (1995), for example, is extending interdependence theory to better account for the temporal flow of interaction events. With respect to relationship stability specifically, some years ago Berscheid and Campbell (1981) drew upon Levinger's pair cohesiveness model (e.g., 1965, 1991) to provide a theoretical analysis of the temporal interplay between the relationship's exterior and its interior, reasoning that theoretical explanations of dramatic changes in marital stability such as those observed in the past few decades must consider how changes in the relationship's macroenvironment interact over time with the relationship's interior to affect stability (a belief subsequently expressed by other observers as well, such as White, 1990). Berscheid and Lopes (1997) have recently extended and elaborated that analysis, taking their cue from Kelley's (1983) analysis of the concept of relationship commitment.

The Prediction of Relationship Stability

In his analysis of the concept of commitment, Kelley notes that relationship theorists and researchers agree that the concept is intended to account for phenomena associated with relationship stability. To understand and predict relationship stability, he reasons, one must identify the causal conditions that stably support continuation of the relationship. Kelley classifies these conditions into two categories: (a) those responsible for the positive aspects of the relationship as well as the costs that would be incurred upon leaving the relationship, or what he calls the "pros" of the relationship; and (b) those that act to push or draw the individual out of the relationship, which he terms the "cons" of the relationship. Kelley (1983) theorizes that the key feature of these causal conditions for the prediction of stability is the consistency with which, over time and situations, the pros outweigh the cons for each person in the relationship: "If the membership is to be stable, the average degree to which the pros outweigh the cons must be large relative to the variability in this difference" (p. 289).

Kelley's analysis implies that to predict relationship stability, forecasters not only need to identify the causal conditions influencing relationship stability at the present time, but they must also estimate how each of these causal conditions is likely to fluctuate in the future. Because it takes two people to maintain a relationship but only one to dissolve it (for evidence relevant to the "weak link" hypothesis, see Attridge, Berscheid, & Simpson, 1995), such an estimate must be made for each partner individually, because if even one partner's pros dip below that partner's cons, the stability of the relationship is threatened.

The causal conditions responsible for interaction regularities observed in a relationship, including those conditions that constitute the relationship's pros and cons, have been classified into two types (see Kelley et al., 1983): "personal" and "environmental." As the foregoing discussion has highlighted, the influence of environmental causal conditions on stability has been neglected in comparison with the influence of personal causal conditions (e.g., an individual's neuroticism, conflict resolution skills, or his or her relationship satisfaction). According to Bradbury et al. (this volume), the assumption that environmental conditions are usually immutable, or at least difficult to change, may have contributed to this neglect.

Predicting Change in the Relationship's Environment

Berscheid and Lopes (1997) do not endorse the assumption that the social and physical environments in which a relationship is embedded are always immutable or difficult to change. To the contrary, we assume that the relationship's environment is not only likely to change over time, but that it will change in systematic, and thus predictable, ways depending on the type of relationship (e.g., premarital, marital, parental). In order to predict stability, then, it is necessary to forecast (a) how the environmental context of a relationship will change over time, (b) how these changes are likely to influence the quality of the couple's interaction and their satisfaction with it, and (c) how the quality of the partners' interaction may lead one or both partners to actively manipulate the relationship's environmental context in order to enhance or to weaken the relationship's stability.

Berscheid and Lopes's analysis is thus in accord with Bradbury et al.'s (this volume) view that more attention must be paid to the relationship's "ecological niche," as they put it. *Ecological niche* is, in fact, a better term than *environment* for the purposes of Berscheid and Lopes's analysis because it better reflects our emphasis on the interdependence between the relationship's interior and its exterior, as well as our premise that a relationship that thrives in one ecological niche may quickly die if moved to another, and that niches that have proved lethal to many relationships may be healthy for some. But, as previously noted, Berscheid and Lopes do not assume that a relationship's current niche is stable; rather, we assume that its niche is in flux over time, not only as a result of macrosocietal forces exogenous to the relationship (e.g., an economic depression, an AIDS epidemic that decimates the partners' social network) but also as a result of forces endogenous to the relationship – or alterations of the environment that partners themselves make as a direct consequence of their satisfaction with their interaction.

Environmental Interventions by the Partners

The general question of how the quality of the relationship's interior influences the partners' active manipulation of their relationship's exterior encompasses many other questions that have yet to be addressed. For example, information is needed about how and when marital couples attempt to change their relationship's environment with the intent of enhancing (or sometimes deliberately weakening) the relationship's stability. With respect to premarital couples, it is clear that satisfied partners actively make many changes in the relationship's environment in an attempt to ensure the relationship's survival (e.g., change their places of residence to put themselves in closer proximity, which reduces the relationship's interaction costs; give away the cat to which the partner is allergic; eject interfering friends from the social network; sign marital and other legal and financial social contracts whose abrogation will invoke negative sanctions).

In addition to systematic investigation of when these environmental changes actually do occur, and whether the source of the change is exogenous or endogenous to the relationship, it would be useful to know more about partners' awareness of the influence of environmental conditions on their relationship. Social psychological research that documents the prevalence of the "fundamental attribution error" – or the tendency to attribute an individual's behavior to his or her internal dispositions (e.g., personality traits) rather than to forces stemming from the individual's exterior situation – suggests that people often may be unaware of the extent to which environmental conditions are responsible for the quality of their relationship. As Heider (1958) observed long ago, "behavior engulfs the field," and the behavior that is perceptually salient to an individual in a relationship is likely to be the behavior of the partner. As a consequence, people should be more likely to ascribe changes in the interior quality of the relationship to changes in personal causal conditions (e.g., changes in the dispositional attributes of their partner or of themselves) than to changes in environmental causal conditions. Relationship therapists, too, may tend to attribute changes in their clients' interaction quality to changes in personal rather than environmental causal conditions; if so, the focus on personal causal conditions in therapeutic intervention may be a result not only of the assumption that these are more easily changed than environmental conditions, but also of people's tendency to locate the causes of behavior in the individual rather than the environment.

Some evidence that people are less attuned to situational than personal forces influencing their relationships is provided by Kelley, Cunningham, and Braiker-Stambul (see Braiker & Kelley, 1979) who tried hard to persuade partners to frame their relationship problems exclusively at the level of specific behaviors but nevertheless observed a powerful tendency for partners to phrase their problems in terms of their partner's characteristics, dispositions, and attributes (e.g., "He's lazy"). In their own attribution research with marital couples, Bradbury and Fincham (1990), too, comment that distressed couples rarely attribute the partner's behavior to the situation. More definitive information on this point is needed, however. People may be becoming more sensitive to potential environmental threats to their relationships, as suggested by a work and family survey of over 6,000 employees of the Du Pont Company (1995), which revealed that 47% of the women and 41% of the men had told their supervisors that they would not be available for relocation, and many refused to work overtime or to travel extensively as well. It seems unlikely that such relationship-protective behaviors would have been observed just a decade ago.

Knowing which environmental conditions are beneficial to the stability of their relationship is a precondition for the partners to take action to create those conditions; similarly, knowing which environmental conditions are toxic to their relationship, and when they are most likely to be harmful, is a necessary precondition for partners to take effective action to avoid such conditions or to attenuate their effects. Although people may be aware of the influence of some environmental conditions on their relationship, they may be in doubt about the potential influence of others. For example, people often try to forecast whether a geographical change will "cure" conflicts that appear to stem from the close proximity of extended family, or to estimate whether their relationship is too fragile to survive the partners' separation for an extended period of time, or to guess whether inviting a foreign exchange student to reside with them will lower the interior quality of their relationship. Not infrequently, they ask relationship experts for the answers to these questions. What the partners are in effect asking for is an "environmental impact" statement for their relationship. Unfortunately, such requests presuppose a body of relationship knowledge that does not now exist.

Toward Environmental Impact Statements and Environmental Therapy for Relationships

If the Pacific spotted owl and the Mississippi darter fish are entitled by law to environmental impact statements to forecast the impact of certain environmental changes on their well-being and survival, it seems peculiar that the same is not more routine for close interpersonal relationships. It is by now a cliché, of course, to lament the deterioration of family relationships in American society. That decline often has been attributed to a change in personal causal conditions, especially to a change in individuals' values, for example, to their pursuit of happiness in "alternative" life styles or with a succession of relationship partners. But environmental changes that are adversely affecting all interpersonal relationships, not just traditional family relationships, are receiving more attention. In particular, the impact on relationships of changes in the macrosocietal environment – changes that some believe rival those of the industrial revolution in potency – are increasingly being recognized.

One such analysis that has received much media attention has been offered by Cobb, Halstead, and Rowe (1995) who persuasively argue that the gross domestic product (GDP) needs to be replaced as this country's barometer of well-being because it counts as "progress" the monetary products of such events as divorce (e.g., money that changes hands and thereby increases GDP as a result of divorce attorney's fees, real estate sales, multiplication of households, childcare facilities, and health care expenditures). In advocating the use of their own "genuine progress indicator," these economists state that their measure reveals an upward curve from the early 1950s until about 1970 in Americans' quality of life but a gradual decline of roughly 45% since then (e.g., as evidenced by the increasing necessity for people to have two jobs or work longer hours just to stay financially even, thereby losing time to spend in relationships with their families and others).

In sum, evidence supporting social psychological theory is only one reason why increased attention to the relationship's environment is warranted. Just as attention to the physical habitat of humans was neglected until its deterioration became obvious, the apparent deterioration of the habitat of the interpersonal relationship provides another reason why systematic documentation of environmental effects on relationships is desirable. Effective documentation of environmental effects on the survival of relationships that society values at least as much as it does threatened animal species will require longitudinal studies that can clearly trace the interactive effects of the relationship's interior and exterior over time. And that effort must begin with the development of measures that describe a relationship's current ecological niche.

Assessing a Relationship's Ecological Niche

A relationship's ecological niche will be defined by its social physical environment (e.g., one that does or does not contain many good alternatives to the present relationship, geographical proximity to extended family, a residence with only one bathroom for a large family). Although myriad psychological instruments are available to measure the personal dispositions of individuals or to assess interaction quality, virtually no instruments are available to assess the relationship's social and physical environment along dimensions that are likely to forecast the relationship's vulnerability to problems stemming from its environment. Goodness-of-alternative scales constitute one exception. Another is Stanley and Markman's (1992) attempt to assess "social pressure" and "structural investment." We ourselves (Berscheid & Lopes, 1997) also are attempting to develop such measures. In the absence of adequate environmental measures, as well as information about the systematic environmental changes relationships are likely to undergo over time, it is at least encouraging that some investigators are including "life event" inventories in their longitudinal research (e.g., Leonard & Roberts, this volume; Tallman et al., this volume). What is needed, however, is information that would allow the prediction of such life events in advance of their occurrence.

Ecological Niches and Demographic Descriptors

Until adequate measures for assessing a relationship's ecological niche are developed, certain demographic descriptors may provide a rough estimate.

Hill and Peplau's (this volume) relatively affluent and highly educated white couples occupy a very different ecological niche than do Huston and Houts's (this volume) couples with their high school diplomas and working-class backgrounds. Veroff, Douvan, Orbuch, and Acitelli's (this volume) white couples surely occupy a very different ecological niche than their black couples do, and mixed-race couples occupy a different niche still. From these demographic descriptors, a forecast of the number and severity of the problems they are likely to encounter over time might be made. Unfortunately, as Kitson, Babri, and Roach (1985) noted more than a decade ago, "Few efforts have been made to link demographic research to studies of marital complaints and psychological background factors" (p. 279).

In this context, it is especially interesting that Leonard and Roberts (this volume) express respect for the demographic variables that accounted for 10% of the stability variance in their couples, despite the likelihood that their sample was characterized by some restriction in the SES range. These investigators remark that although sociodemographic variables are generally recognized as strong correlates of marital satisfaction and dissolution, they have not received enough attention in longitudinal research investigating marital quality. Veroff and his associates (this volume) corroborate the point when they say that what they can conclude from their own study about the factors that contribute to stability depends upon whether the couple is white or black.

In the past, longitudinal studies were so few and far between that relationship researchers were simply gratified that the investigator had managed to obtain data over time from even a handful of warm bodies; locating the often very small sample demographically in the general population was not of great concern. As more studies are added to the literature, however, the sketchy nature of the demographic information provided about each sample becomes more frustrating. It is often difficult to determine the sample's comparability to other samples, as well as to estimate the dissolution base rates for the segment of the population from which the sample was drawn. Some longitudinal accounts provide only cursory information about the sample, and in other cases important information is provided but it is difficult to interpret. For example, Lindahl, Clements, and Markman (this volume), who provide more information than most, state that the median personal income of their sample at Time 1 was $5,000 to $10,000, and that nine years later it was over $40,000, but how these figures correspond to the median personal income of the population at those times is not clear. One guesses that the sample was below the average at Time 1 but above average at Time 9, their average income having increased more than fourfold in only a decade. (Incidentally, such a rapid increase suggests that many of Lindahl et al.'s couples experienced a dramatic change in their niche over the period of the study.) At a minimum, it seems clear that it will become important for future investigators to develop standard demographic descriptors of their samples as well as information about where that sample is located in the general population. Even better would be the development of ecological niche instruments that directly assess the environmental surround of relationships on a wide variety of dimensions.

A Conclusion

One puts down this anthology of recent longitudinal studies of marital dysfunction and stability with mixed feelings. On the one hand, it is a cause for good cheer that the number of such studies has grown. On the other hand, one thinks about how hard Mother Nature makes relationship researchers work before she grudgingly yields even one of her secrets about relationship dysfunction, as well as how much money she extorts for just one longitudinal peek into the dynamics of marital relationships. And so one inevitably thinks about how much work needs to be done before we will truly understand the course of marital and other kinds of relationships, how few people there are who are both trained and willing to do that work, and how inadequate the resources are to support their efforts. One's thoughts then turn to the American public trying to hold its own against a hostile environmental tide for interpersonal relationships, to the appalling amount of pop psychological pap they are consuming in their efforts to do so, and to the billions they are spending on relationship therapy of various kinds – via private counseling, group relationship enrichment programs and seminars, books and magazines, radio and television programs, audio- and videotapes, and, sometimes, fortune tellers and crystal balls. One cannot help but conclude that if only the tiniest fraction of those billions were used to support the development of the knowledge domain upon which such therapeutic advice presumably depends, the future of a science of relationships would look a good deal brighter.

References

Attridge, M., Berscheid, E., & Simpson, J. A. (1995). Predicting relationship stability from both partners versus one. *Journal of Personality and Social Psychology, 69,* 254–268.

Bandura, A. (1977). *Social learning theory.* Englewood Cliffs, NJ: Prentice-Hall.

Bandura, A. (1986). *Social foundations of thought and action.* Englewood Cliffs, NJ: Prentice-Hall.

Bandura, A., Ross, D., & Ross, S. A. (1961). Transmission of aggression through imitation of aggressive models. *Journal of Abnormal and Social Psychology, 63,* 575–582.

Berardo, F. M. (1980). Decade preview: Some trends and directions for family research and theory in the 1980s. *Journal of Marriage and the Family, 42,* 723–728.

Berscheid, E., & Campbell, B. (1981). The changing longevity of heterosexual close relationships: A commentary and forecast. In M. J. Lerner & S. C. Lerner (Eds.), *The justice motive in social behavior* (pp. 209–234). New York: Plenum.

Berscheid, E., & Lopes, J. (1997). A temporal model of relationship satisfaction and stability. In R. J. Sternberg & M. Hojjat (Eds.), *Satisfaction in close relationships* (pp. 129–159). New York: Guilford.

Bradbury, T. N., & Fincham, F. D. (1990). Attributions in marriage: Review and critique. *Psychological Bulletin, 103,* 3–33.

Braiker, H. B., & Kelley, H. H. (1979). Conflict in the development of close relationships. In R. L. Burgess & T. L. Huston (Eds.), *Social exchange in developing relationships* (pp. 136–168). New York: Academic Press.

Cobb, C., Halstead, T., & Rowe, J. (1995). If the GDP is up, why is America down? *Atlantic Monthly, 276,* 59–78.

Deutsch, M. (1954). Field theory in social psychology. In G. Lindzey (Ed.), *Handbook of social psychology: Theory and method* (Vol. 1, pp. 181–222). Reading, MA: Addison-Wesley.

Dollard, J., Doob, L. W., Miller, N. E.,, Mowrer, O. H., & Sears, R. R. (1939). *Frustration and aggression.* New Haven, CT: Yale University Press.

Glenn, N. D. (1990). Quantitative research on marital quality in the 1980s: A critical review. *Journal of Marriage and the Family, 50,* 317–324.

Gottman, J. M., & Levenson, R. W. (1988). The social psychophysiology of marriage. In P. Noller & M. A. Fitzpatrick (Eds.), *Perspectives on marital interaction* (pp. 182–199). Clevedon, England: Multilingual Matters.

Heaton, T. B., & Albrecht, S. L. (1991). Stable unhappy marriages. *Journal of Marriage and the Family, 50,* 93–98.

Heider, F. (1958). *The psychology of interpersonal relations.* New York: Wiley.

Homans, G. (1961). *Social behavior: Its elementary forms.* New York: Harcourt.

Jacobson, N. S. (1990). Commentary: Contributions from psychology to an understanding of marriage. In F. D. Fincham & T. N. Bradbury (Eds.), *The psychology of marriage: Basic issues and applications* (pp. 258–275). New York: Guilford.

Karney, B. R., & Bradbury, T. N. (1995). The longitudinal course of marital quality and stability: A review of theory, method, and research. *Psychological Bulletin, 118,* 3–34.

Kelley, H. H. (1979). *Personal relationships: Their structures and processes.* New York: Wiley.

Kelley, H. H. (1983). Love and commitment. In H. H. Kelley, E. Berscheid, A. Christensen, J. H. Harvey, T. L. Huston, G. Levinger, E. McClintock, L. A. Peplau, & D. L. Peterson, *Close relationships* (pp. 265–314). New York: Freeman.

Kelley, H. H. (1995, September). *Back to the future: A return to "situation" as the core concept in social psychology.* Paper presented at the meeting of the Society of Experimental Social Psychology, Washington, DC.

Kelley, H. H., Berscheid, E., Christensen, A., Harvey, J. H., Huston, T. L., Levinger, G., McClintock, E., Peplau, L. A., & Peterson, D. R. (1983). *Close relationships.* New York: Freeman.

Kelley, H. H., & Thibaut, J. W. (1978). *Interpersonal relations: A theory of interdependence.* New York: Wiley.

Kitson, G. C., Babri, K. B., & Roach, M. J. (1985). Who divorces and why: A review. *Journal of Family Issues, 6,* 255–293.

Levinger, G. (1965). A social psychological perspective on marital dissolution: An integrative review. *Journal of Marriage and the Family, 27,* 19–29.

Levinger, G. (1991). Commitment vs. cohesiveness: Two complementary perspectives. In W. H. Jones & D. Perlman (Eds.), *Advances in personal relationships* (Vol. 3, pp. 145–150). London: Jessica Kingsley.

Levinger, G. (1994). Figure versus ground: Micro- and macroperspectives on the social psychology of personal relationships. In R. Erber & R. Gilmour (Eds.). *Theoretical frameworks for personal relationships* (pp. 1–28). Hillsdale, NJ: Lawrence Erlbaum.

Many are making work–family tradeoffs. (1995, November 12). *The Minneapolis Star and Tribune* (reprinted from the *New York Times*), p. D3.

Miller, N. E., & Dollard, J. (1941). *Social learning and imitation.* New Haven, CT: Yale University Press.

Miller, P. H. (1989). *Theories of developmental psychology* (2d ed.). New York: Freeman.

Noller, P., & Ruzzene, M. (1991). Communication in marriage: The influence of affect and cognition. In G. J. O. Fletcher & F. D. Fincham (Eds.), *Cognition and close relationships* (pp. 203–234). Hillsdale, NJ: Lawrence Erlbaum.

Rusbult, C. E. (1983). A longitudinal test of the investment model: The development (and deterioration) of satisfaction and commitment in heterosexual involvements. *Journal of Personality and Social Psychology, 45,* 101–117.

Simpson, J. A. (1987). The dissolution of romantic relationships: Factors involved in relationship stability and emotional distress. *Journal of Personality and Social Psychology, 53,* 683–692.

Snyder, M., & Ickes, W. (1985). Personality and social behavior. In G. Lindzey & E. Aronson (Eds.), *Handbook of social psychology* (3d ed., Vol. 2, pp. 833–948). New York: Random House.

South, S. J., & Lloyd, K. M. (1995). Spousal alternatives and marital dissolutions. *American Sociological Review, 60,* 21–35.

Stanley, S. M., & Markman, H. J. (1992). Assessing commitment in personal relationships. *Journal of Marriage and the Family, 54,* 595–608.

Thibaut, J. M., & Kelley, H. H. (1959). *The social psychology of groups.* New York: Wiley.

Waller, W. (1967). *The old love and the new: Divorce and readjustment.* Carbondale, IL: Southern Illinois University Press. (Original work published 1930)

White, L. K. (1990). Determinants of divorce: A review of research in the eighties. *Journal of Marriage and the Family, 52,* 904–912.

White, L. K., & Booth, A. (1991). Divorce over the life course: The role of marital happiness. *Journal of Family Issues, 12,* 5–21.

Author Index

Acitelli, L.K. 168, 386, 400, 424, 430, 431, 455
Addis, M.E. 381
Adelman, S.A. 361
Agnew, C.R. 106
Ahlburg, D.A. 1
Aiken, P.A. 47
Albrecht, S.L. 114, 117, 153, 180, 446
Alexander, J.F. 47, 280
Allen, B.A. 55
Allen, L. 401
Allred, K.D. 47
Amato, P.R. 291, 292
American Psychiatric Association 346
Ames, E.W. 220
Anderson, E.R. 395
Andrews, G. 291
Aneshensel, C.S. 318, 319, 321
Angell, R.C. 318
Anglin, K. 354
Antill, J.K. 47, 119, 123
Antonucci, T.C. 168
Archer, J. 363
Arias, I. 45, 56, 68, 348, 349, 354
Arriaga, X.B. 81, 83, 388, 395, 411, 413, 415, 416, 420, 423
Asher, S.J. 180
Ashmore, R.D. 84
Atkinson, J. 128
Attridge, M. 450
Austin, W.G. 158
Avery-Leaf, S. 347, 348, 350, 352
Axelrod, R. 79, 82

Babcock, J.C. 3, 357, 363, 381
Babri, K.B. 455
Bagi, S. 22
Bagwell, C.L. 405
Bakan, D. 156
Bakeman, R. 2, 331
Baker, L. 55
Baldwin, M.W. 107
Balswick, J. 16

Bandura, A. 316, 327, 442, 443
Banks, D. 209
Barling, J. 45, 56, 68, 348, 349, 354, 355
Barlow, D.H. 380
Barnett, R.C. 304, 419
Baron, R.J. 361, 363
Baron, R.M. 99
Barry, W.A. 2, 15
Bartholomew, K. 357
Bassin, E. 82
Baucom, D.H. 2, 3, 47, 182, 198, 285, 286, 380
Beach, S.R.H. 3
Beitel, A. 398
Bellah, R.N. 154, 326
Belsky, J. 180, 220, 304, 397, 423
Bem, D.J. 123, 130, 132, 291
Bem, S. 186
Benaske, N. 349
Bentler, P.M. 118, 123, 183, 200, 237
Berardo, F.M. 448
Berg, B.J. 356
Berg, J.H. 245
Bergman, L. 347
Berk, R.A. 435
Berley, R.A. 2
Berman, J.S. 380
Bernard, J. 114, 117, 175
Bernard, J.L. 47, 348, 351
Bernard, M.L. 47, 348, 351
Bernard, S.L. 47
Berry, C.J. 348, 351
Berscheid, E. 245, 383, 449, 450, 451, 454
Bielby, D.D. 312, 320
Billings, A. 77
Birchler, G.R. 77
Bird, G.W. 350, 352
Birns, B. 351
Bissonnette, V.L. 87, 387, 395, 411, 413, 415, 416, 420, 423
Bitman, I. 348
Blais, M.R. 182
Blalock, H.M. Jr. 432

461

Blane, H.T. 47, 59
Blau, P.M. 249, 253
Bloom, B.L. 180
Blumberg, S.L. 206
Blyth, D. 395
Bohmer, S. 350
Boles, A.J. 180, 183, 220
Bolger, N. 290, 319, 419
Bonnell, D. 18, 23
Bookwala, J. 350
Booth, A. 182, 185, 434, 446
Boss, P.G. 44, 396
Bouchard, T.J. 365
Boucher, C. 182
Bowers, P.M. 59
Bowlby, J. 357
Boye-Beaman, J. 47
Boyum, L. 404
Bradburn, N. 155, 156
Bradbury, T.N. 3, 4, 5, 47, 63, 118, 119, 129,
    182, 196, 199, 205, 219, 229, 237, 239,
    279, 280, 282, 283, 284, 286, 287, 289,
    292, 293, 296, 298, 300, 301, 304, 305,
    312, 314, 330, 337, 347, 377, 378, 380,
    381, 382, 386, 401, 402, 404, 405, 418,
    420, 425, 433, 438, 442, 444, 448, 449,
    451, 452
Braiker, H.B. 124, 125, 127, 128, 131, 134,
    452
Brant, D. 302
Breggin, P. 360
Brennan, P.L. 46
Brennan, R.T. 304, 419
Breslin, F.C. 348, 350
Brines, J. 322
Brockopp, K. 347
Bromet, E.J. 46
Bronfenbrenner, U. 402
Brooks-Gunn, J. 397
Browning, J.J. 354
Bryk, A.S. 184, 199, 304
Buehlman, K.T. 271, 313
Bugaighis, M.A. 199
Bui, K.-V.T. 272, 275, 415
Bumpass, L.L. 1, 335
Burger, A.L. 119
Burgess, E.W. 114, 116, 118, 237, 244, 248,
    253, 256, 264
Buriel, R. 400
Burke, P.J. 47, 320, 327, 387, 398, 402, 425,
    438, 443, 447, 454
Burns, A. 46
Buss, D.M. 107, 118, 266, 394
Buttenwieser, P. 117
Buunk, B.P. 75, 81, 105, 153, 196, 199, 245,
    249
Byron, Lord 130

Cahalan, D. 54
Cahn, D. 14
Cahn, T.S. 47
Callahan, J.E. 347
Callan, V.J. 24, 36
Campbell, A. 125, 129, 351, 356
Campbell, B. 245, 449
Campbell, D.T. 417
Campbell, S.M. 119, 284
Canary, D.J. 180
Cano, A. 350
Carnelley, K.B. 326
Carson, R.C. 136
Carter, E.A. 44
Cascardi, M. 347, 348, 350, 351, 352, 355,
    356, 359, 385, 403, 425, 426, 439
Caspi, A. 123, 130, 132, 291, 318
Cassidy, J. 403
Cate, R.M. 12, 121, 126, 246, 248, 251, 347, 350
Cattell, R.B. 122, 124
Center for Human Resource Research 241
Cerny, J.A. 380
Chadiha, L. 156
Chase-Lansdale, L. 397, 400
Cherlin, A.J. 281, 297
Chew, E. 347
Chi, S.K. 337
Chodorow, N. 154
Christensen, A. 3, 15, 20, 63, 183, 381, 383,
    450
Christopher, F.S. 347, 350
Cisin, I.H. 54
Clark, L.A. 117, 118, 123, 284
Clarke, S.C. 180
Clements, M.L. 206, 207, 214, 220, 286, 287,
    381, 382, 384, 397, 401, 404, 405, 419,
    420, 424, 425, 430, 433, 434, 441, 455
Cloven, D.H. 14
Cobb, C. 453
Cochran, S.D. 182, 187
Cohan, C.L. 282, 283, 298, 377, 381, 386,
    401, 402, 405, 418, 420, 425, 438, 442,
    444, 448, 451
Cohen, J. 93, 411, 412
Cohen, P. 93
Cohen, S. 55
Cole, C.L. 47, 212, 321
Comins, C.A. 352
Comrey, A.L. 118
Congdon, R.T. 199
Conger, K.J. 312, 318
Conger, R.E. 2, 147, 312, 318, 394, 398, 400
Conley, J.J. 3, 47, 118, 123, 182, 238, 248,
    283, 291
Converse, P. 125, 129
Coopersmith, S. 222
Copeland, J. 199

Costa, P.T. Jr. 55, 123, 186
Costanzo, P.R. 13, 301
Coverman, S. 322
Covey, S.L. 221
Cowan, C.P. 180, 183, 219, 220, 397, 403, 423
Cowan, P.A. 180, 183, 219, 220, 397, 403, 423
Cox, C.L. 81, 83, 388, 395, 411, 413, 415,
    416, 420, 423
Cox, M. 224
Cox, R. 224
Coysh, W.S. 180, 183, 219, 220
Crane, R. 55
Craske, M.G. 380
Crew, B.K. 350
Crockenberg, S. 221
Crohan, S.E. 53, 119, 153, 158, 169, 181
Cronkite, K. 344
Cross, C.E. 312, 318
Crossley, H.M. 54
Crouter, A.C. 122, 129, 401, 402, 403
Crowell, J.A. 357, 358
Cuber, J.F. 152, 153
Cummings, E.M. 395
Curley, A.D. 355
Currie, D.W. 351
Curtis-Boles, H. 180, 183, 219, 220
Cutrona, C.E. 289

Dabbs, J.M. 361, 362
Daly, M. 363, 394
Damon, W. 223
Daniels, P. 397
Davidson, B.J. 16
Davies, P. 395
Davila, J. 298
Davis, M.H. 47
Day, N.L. 46
De La Ronde, C. 114
De Vita, C.J. 1
Dean, D.G. 47
Deane, K.E. 209, 222
Dehue, F.M.J. 80
DeLongis, A. 290, 419
DeMers, D.K. 394
Derogatis, L. 186
Deutsch, M. 444
Dickson-Markman, F. 15, 31, 36, 206
Dillman, D.A. 86
Dindia, K. 180
Dobash, R.E. 45, 343
Dobash, R.P. 45, 343
Dollard, J. 442
Doob, L.W. 442
Douvan, E. 1, 152, 154, 156, 157, 158, 162,
    314, 386, 400, 424, 430, 431, 455
Downey, G. 318
Drigotas, S.M. 81, 83

Dunn, A. 223, 402
Durbin, R.G. 119, 123
Dutton, D.G. 354, 357

Easterbrooks, M.A. 221, 222, 224
Eber, H.W. 122, 124
Edwards, J.N. 182, 185, 434
Eidelson, R.J. 186
Eisen, M. 223
Elder, G.H. Jr. 147, 291, 312, 318, 394, 397,
    398, 399, 400
Elliot, D.S. 348, 349
Elliot, L. 344
Emde, R. 222
Emerson, R.M. 329
Emery, R.E. 221, 224
Epstein, D. 418
Epstein, N. 2, 3, 182, 186, 198, 285, 380
Erikson, E. 394
Estaugh, V. 46
Eysenck, H.J. 365

Falbo, T. 20
Farley, S.C. 359
Fedders, C. 344
Feeney, J.A. 18, 23, 26, 36, 404, 405, 415,
    423, 443
Feld, S.L. 349
Felmlee, D. 82, 261
Ferguson, L.W. 117
Filsinger, E.E. 239, 285
Fincham, F.D. 2, 3, 63, 107, 118, 119, 129,
    182, 199, 221, 224, 237, 280, 284, 286,
    300, 337, 347, 380, 382, 402, 404, 452
Fine, M.A. 399
Finn, J. 47
Fisher, H. 5
Fitzgerald, N. 126
Fitzpatrick, J.A. 119, 123
Fitzpatrick, M.A. 11, 14, 15, 22
Fletcher, G.J.O. 3, 107
Fletcher, K.E. 361
Flitcraft, A. 345
Floyd, F.J. 44, 206, 207, 211, 286, 287, 381
Folger, J.P. 77
Follette, W.C. 77, 381
Follingstad, D.R. 351, 356
Foo, L. 353
Forgatch, M.S. 331
Foster, C.A. 106
Fowers, B.J. 238, 258, 271
Franz, C.E. 163, 291
Frazier, W. 345
Frederickson, C.G. 290
Frieband, D. 163
Frieze, I.H. 350
Fulker, D.W. 365
Furstenberg, F.F. 397

Gangestad, S.W. 81
Gao, Y. 357
Garcia, S. 87
Garmezy, N. 318
Garrett, E. 180, 183, 219, 220
Gecas, V. 324, 325, 326, 327, 387, 398, 402, 425, 438, 443, 447, 454
Geis, G. 119
Gelles, R.J. 45, 46, 345, 347, 348, 349, 351, 354, 356, 364
Gerson, K. 312
Giles-Sims, J. 182
Gilligan, C. 154
Gladue, B.A. 362
Gleason, W.J. 359
Gleberman, L. 58, 354, 355
Glenn, N.D. 297, 337, 428, 430, 433, 441
Golash, L. 354
Goldberg, W.A. 221, 224
Gondolf, E.F. 358
Gondoli, D.M. 59
Gonzalez, R. 416
Gotlib, I.H. 220, 290
Gottman, J.M. 2, 3, 12, 13, 15, 25, 27, 29, 44, 63, 65, 68, 77, 84, 87, 107, 152, 198, 199, 208, 209, 210, 212, 221, 224, 237, 271, 279, 285, 289, 291, 300, 301, 312, 313, 316, 319, 331, 334, 337, 338, 357, 363, 396, 402, 404, 444
Gray, L.N. 328, 329, 337
Green, J.A. 200
Greenberg, L.S. 3
Greenshaft, J.L. 77
Greenstein, T.N. 182, 291
Grey, A. 345
Griffin, D.W. 415, 416
Griffin, W.A. 291
Grych, J.H. 221, 402
Gunn, L.K. 75
Guthrie, D.M. 17
Gwartney-Gibbs, P.A. 350

Haas, S.D. 87
Hackel, L.S. 180, 197, 198
Hahlweg, K. 180, 181, 183, 195, 198, 199, 206, 208, 286, 287
Halstead, T. 453
Halverson, C. 16
Hamberger, L.K. 47, 358
Harmer, S.L. 238
Harroff, P.B. 152, 153
Hart, D. 223
Harter, S. 209, 222, 223
Harvey, J.H. 383, 450
Hastings, J.E. 47, 358
Hatch, R.C. 199
Hatchett, S. 152, 156, 157, 314

Hause, E.S. 356
Hazan, C. 107, 394, 403, 405
Heaton, T.B. 114, 117, 119, 153, 180, 446
Heavey, C.L. 15, 63
Heider, F. 452
Helmreich, R.L. 56, 119, 123, 124
Heming, G. 180, 183, 219, 220
Hendrick, S.S. 16
Henton, J.M. 347, 350
Hernandez, D.J. 180
Hertel, R.K. 2, 15
Hetherington, E.M. 224, 395, 402
Heyman, R.E. 2, 289, 300
Hill, C.T. 119, 240, 241, 256, 258, 266, 272, 274, 275, 386, 405, 415, 425, 430, 432, 435, 441, 455
Hill, R. 319, 397
Hilton, M.E. 46
Hinde, R.A. 279, 396
Hirschman, A.O. 75
Hixon, J.G. 114
Hock, E. 394
Hoffman, J.A. 2
Hoge, S.K. 361
Hollis, M. 420
Holman, T.B. 238
Holmes, J.G. 82, 116, 182, 187, 197, 415
Holtzworth-Munroe, A. 280, 290, 354, 357, 363
Homans, G. 446
Hops, H. 2
Hornung, C.A. 348
Horwitz, A.V. 46
Hotaling, G.T. 351, 354
Houseknecht, S.K. 219, 337
Houts, R.N. 120, 123, 129, 384, 385, 387, 404, 416, 424, 430, 432, 433, 441, 455
Howes, P. 221
Huck, S. 312, 318
Huizinga, D. 348
Hull, C. 442
Huntingtonford, F. 364
Huston, T.L. 11, 12, 13, 17, 27, 57, 84, 114, 116, 119, 120, 121, 122, 123, 124, 125, 126, 127, 128, 129, 132, 139, 180, 182, 183, 246, 248, 251, 261, 383, 384, 385, 387, 404, 412, 414, 416, 417, 424, 430, 432, 433, 441, 445, 450, 455
Hutchinson, G. 357

Ibsen, H. 117
Ickes, W. 87, 445
IPAT Staff 123
Iwaniszek, J. 77

Jacklin, C.N. 413
Jacobs, G. 55
Jacobson, N.S. 2, 3, 13, 77, 119, 280, 282,

283, 288, 290, 300, 346, 357, 363, 381, 445
Jameson, P. 280
Janoff-Bulman, R. 326
Jarrett, J.E. 318
John, O. 123
John, R.S. 58, 354, 355
Johnson, D.J. 77, 81, 82, 83, 84, 106
Johnson, E. 55
Johnson, M.D. 298
Johnson, M.P. 261
Johnson, S.M. 3
Johnson, W.B. 117
Jones, L.E. 347
Jones, R.R. 2
Joreskog, K.G. 200
Jouriles, E.N. 224
Julien, D. 209, 210

Kadushin, F.S. 220
Kahn, M. 15
Kamarck, T. 55
Kane, R. 361
Kaplan, D. 420
Kaplan, N. 403
Karney, B.R. 3, 4, 5, 118, 196, 205, 239, 279, 280, 284, 287, 289, 292, 293, 296, 298, 301, 304, 305, 312, 330, 377, 378, 381, 386, 401, 402, 405, 418, 420, 425, 438, 442, 444, 448, 449, 451
Kashy, D. 413
Katz, L.F. 210, 221, 224, 271, 313, 396, 402
Kaufman-Kantor, K.G. 46
Keith, B. 291, 292
Kelley, H.H. 74, 79, 82, 107, 119, 124, 125, 127, 128, 131, 134, 153, 383, 445, 446, 447, 449, 450, 452
Kelly, C. 3, 12, 246, 248, 251
Kelly, E.L. 47, 118, 123, 182, 238, 248, 283, 291
Kelvin, P. 318
Kendziora, K.T. 348, 350
Kenny, D.A. 99, 411, 413, 414, 415, 416, 417
Kerckhoff, A.C. 119
Kessler, R.C. 290, 291, 319, 320, 321, 419
King, C.E. 3
Kirchler, E. 16
Kitson, G.C. 152, 298, 455
Klosko, J.S. 380
Knight, J. 55
Knox, D. 208
Kochman, T. 168
Koerner, K. 280
Koss, M.P. 348, 353
Kovacs, L. 180, 181, 195
Koval, J. 347, 350
Kraemer, H.C. 413

Krokoff, L.J. 12, 13, 29, 63, 77, 87, 152, 285, 291, 300, 301
Kulka, R.A. 1, 154, 158, 162
Kurdek, L.A. 47, 119, 182, 184, 198, 199, 237, 266, 271, 304, 384, 395, 399, 412, 414, 417, 418, 419, 424, 425, 432, 441

L'Abate, L. 347
Lamke, L.K. 119, 123
Lang, M.E. 220
Langhinrichsen, J. 355, 356
Laplante, B. 184
Larsen, A.S. 183, 312, 313, 238, 251, 258, 271
Larson, R. 405
Law, H. 118
Layne, C. 63
Lazarus, R.S. 404
Leber, D. 169
Lefcourt, H.M. 53
Leik, R.K. 328, 329, 337
Leonard, K.E. 46, 47, 55, 57, 59, 62, 385, 401, 412, 413, 414, 417, 418, 423, 454, 455
Lerma, M. 81
Leslie, L.A. 261
Levenson, R.W. 2, 3, 15, 68, 152, 279, 289, 300, 313, 319, 331, 404, 444
Levinger, G. 119, 123, 152, 245, 383, 445, 448, 449, 450
Lewin, K. 444, 445
Lewis, H.C. 206, 286
Lewis, R.A. 212, 321
Liebrand, W.B.G. 80
Liem, G.R. 318
Liem, J.H. 318
Liker, J.K. 312, 318
Lindahl, K.L. 205, 209, 210, 224, 381, 382, 384, 397, 401, 404, 405, 412, 414, 417, 419, 420, 424, 425, 430, 433, 434, 441, 455
Lipkus, I. 80, 82, 87, 114, 119
Lloyd, K.M. 447
Lloyd, S. 121, 347, 350
Locke, H.J. 53, 129, 208, 287
Longstreth, M. 80
Lopes, J. 449, 450, 451, 454
Lord, F.M. 418
Lorence, J. 321
Lorenz, F.O. 312, 318
Lund, M. 82
Lussier, Y. 184
Lykken, D.T. 365

McCall, G.J. 320
McCardle, J.J. 418
McClelland, D.C. 291
McCleod, J.D. 318, 320, 321, 325
McClintock, C.G. 80
McClintock, E. 383, 450
McCrady, B.S. 46, 346

McCrae, R.R. 55, 123, 186
McCullough, B.C. 348
MacDermid, S.M. 180, 182, 183
McDonald, D.W. 77
MacDonald, K. 404
McGoldrick, M. 44
McGonagle, K.A. 291
McHale, S. 122, 128, 129, 180, 182, 183
McKinney, K. 348
McLaughlin, I.G. 57
McNeill-Hawkins, K. 351
McQuinn, R.D. 245
McRae, J.A. Jr. 320, 321
Madsen, R. 154, 326
Main, M. 403
Maiuro, R.D. 47
Majidi-Abi, S. 401
Makepeace, J.M. 348
Malamuth, N. 353
Malley, J.C. 156
Malone, J. 45, 56, 68, 345, 348, 349, 350, 352,
    354, 355, 356
Mann, C.C. 360
Marco, C.A. 291
Margolin, G. 2, 55, 58, 77, 84, 280, 282, 283,
    346, 353, 354, 355
Markman, H.J. 3, 11, 12, 13, 16, 31, 36, 44,
    63, 77, 84, 180, 181, 183, 195, 198, 199,
    205, 206, 207, 208, 209, 210, 211, 214,
    220, 221, 223, 224, 239, 286, 287, 381,
    382, 384, 397, 401, 404, 405, 419, 420,
    424, 425, 430, 433, 434, 441, 454, 455
Marks, E. 55
Marotz-Baden, R. 324, 326, 327
Martin, T.K. 114, 117
Maslow, A. 155
Matthews, S.H. 405
Mayer, F.J. 354, 355
Meens, L.D. 199
Melby, J. 312, 318
Menaghan, E.G. 318, 320
Menard, S. 349
Mercy, J.A. 360
Mermelstein, R. 55
Meyer, S.L. 351, 358
Mihalic, S.W. 349
Miller, B.A. 59
Miller, G. 327
Miller, N. 442
Miller, N.B. 220
Miller, P.H. 442
Miller, R.S. 53
Mirowski, J. 326
Mitchell, C. 219, 229
Molm, L. 329
Monroe, S.M. 294
Montemayor, R. 223

Montgomery, B.M. 16, 197
Moorman, J.E. 180
Moos, R.H. 46, 398
Morell, V. 365
Morgan, S.P. 181
Morris, R. 361, 362
Morrow, G.D. 77, 82, 84, 106
Morse, B.J. 348
Mortimer, J. 321
Mowrer, O.H. 442
Murphy, C.M. 352, 354, 355, 358
Murray, S.L. 116, 415
Musten, A.S. 318
Muthen, B. 420

National Center for Health Statistics, 180, 298
Neale, M.C. 365
Neidig, P. 46, 349, 354, 359, 364
Neimeyer, R.A. 380
Nelson, G.M. 3
Nesselroade, J.R. 126
Newcomb, A.F. 405
Newcomb, M.D. 118, 123, 183, 237
Nezlek, J. 23
Nias, D.K.B. 365
Nisonoff, L. 348
Nochajski, T.J. 59
Noller, P. 11, 14, 15, 17, 18, 20, 22, 23, 26, 27,
    36, 118, 404, 405, 412, 414, 415, 417,
    423, 443
Norton, R. 19
Notarius, C.I. 77, 84, 205, 208, 209, 210, 211

Oathout, H.A. 47
Obiorah, F.C. 199
O'Connor, E. 357
Oggins, J. 169
O'Keefe, J.L. 47
O'Keefe, N.K. 347
Olds, J. 155
O'Leary, K.D. 2, 3, 11, 12, 13, 20, 45, 46, 56,
    57, 63, 68, 224, 280, 285, 300, 345, 346,
    347, 348, 349, 350, 351, 352, 354, 355,
    356, 358, 359, 363, 364, 385, 403, 425,
    426, 439
O'Leary, S.G. 348
Olson, D.H. 183, 211, 238, 239, 246, 248,
    251, 258, 271, 312, 313
Olweus, D. 362
O'Neil, R. 402
Orbuch, T. 159, 386, 400, 424, 430, 431, 455
Ortega, R. 156
Osborne, L.N. 224
Overbye, D. 365
Owens, G. 357

Paff-Bergen, L.A. 199
Pagel, M. 381

Pagelow, M.D. 343, 351
Pan, H.S. 46, 349, 357, 359, 364
Paolino, T.J. 346
Parke, R.D. 393, 396, 398, 399, 400, 402, 404
Parkinson, D.N. 46
Pasch, L. 282, 289
Patterson, G.R. 2, 14, 107, 313, 317, 318, 331, 404, 426
Pearlin, L.I. 318
Pearson, J.L. 403
Pelligrini, D.P. 210
Pensky, E. 397
Peplau, L.A. 20, 119, 182, 187, 240, 241, 256, 258, 266, 272, 274, 275, 383, 386, 405, 415, 425, 430, 432, 435, 441, 450, 455
Peterson, D.L. 383, 450
Peterson, D.M. 31, 32
Pfiffner, L.J. 224
Pierce, G.R. 186
Pike, R. 209
Pillemer, K. 44
Pindas, P. 324, 326, 327
Pirog-Good, M.A. 47
Pleck, E. 343
Pleck, J.H. 321
Plomin, R. 364
Polek, D.S. 351, 356
Polonko, K.A. 152
Poole, M.S. 77
Pope, M.K. 47
Porterfield, A.L. 15, 27
Posada, G. 357
Poulton, R.G. 291
Power, C. 46
Power, T.G. 396
Pratt, E. 119

Radloff, L.S. 55
Rands, M. 119, 123
Rankin, L.A. 380
Raschke, H.J. 181, 182, 196, 266
Rathus, J. 357, 358
Raudenbush, S.W. 184, 199, 304, 419
Raush, H.L. 2, 15
Reid, J.B. 2
Reis, H. 16
Reiss, D. 396
Reiss, I.L. 337
Reitzes, D. 320
Rempel, J.K. 182, 187, 197
Renick, M.J. 206, 207, 286, 287
Repetti, R.L. 290, 401, 403, 404
Rich, S. 365
Richards, M. 405
Richardson, D.R. 361, 363
Riggs, D.S. 348, 350, 351, 352
Rindfuss, R.R. 181

Roach, M.J. 455
Roberts, L.J. 55, 62, 385, 401, 413, 418, 423, 454, 455
Robey, A. 345
Robins, E.R. 17, 120, 122, 123, 128, 129
Robinson, E.A. 3, 282, 283
Robinson, J.P. 322, 345
Robinson, L.A. 380
Rodgers, R.H. 397
Rodgers, W.L. 125, 129
Rogoff, R. 400
Rogosa, D. 302
Roloff, M. 14
Roscoe, B. 347, 349
Rosenbaum, A. 56, 68, 345, 348, 349, 354, 355, 358, 361
Rosenfeld, S. 319, 321
Rosenwald, R.J. 345
Ross, D. 443
Ross, G.E. 326
Ross, S.A. 443
Rovine, M. 180, 220, 304
Rowe, J. 453
Roy, A.K. 291
Roy, M. 46
Rubin, L. 154
Rubin, M.E. 209
Rubin, Z. 119, 219, 229, 240, 241, 245, 246, 256, 258, 266
Ruble, D. N. 180, 197, 198
Rusbult, C.E. 3, 75, 77, 80, 81, 82, 83, 84, 87, 105, 106, 114, 119, 153, 181, 196, 198, 199, 245, 249, 387, 395, 411, 412, 413, 414, 415, 416, 417, 420, 423, 447
Rushe, R. 363
Rushton, J.P. 365
Russell, S. 55
Rutledge, L.L. 351, 356
Rutter, M. 403
Ruvolo, A. 159
Ruzzene, M. 27, 443
Ryan, C.M. 46
Ryan, K. 350
Ryder, R.G. 211
Ryff, C.C. 152

Sabatelli, R.M. 249
Sabourin, S. 182, 184
Sackett, G.P. 331
Saltzman, L.E. 360
Sameroff, A. 396
Samios, M. 348
Sandeen, E. 354, 355
Sanders, K.J.D. 47
Santa-Barbara, J. 53
Sarason, B.R. 186
Sarason, I.G. 186

Saunders, K. 357
Schaefer, J.A. 398
Schaie, K.W. 394
Schilling, E.A. 291, 419
Schladale, J. 350, 352
Schmaling, K.B. 290
Schmitt, D.P. 107, 394
Schmitt, J.P. 47, 182
Schulman, M. 348
Schumm, W.R. 199
Schwartz, M.D. 348, 350, 356
Sears, R.R. 442
Seff, M.A. 325
Segal, N.L. 365
Seltzer, M. 199
Senchak, M. 47, 55, 57, 59
Serpe, R.T. 320
Shanahan, M.J. 318, 325
Shaver, P.R. 16, 107, 394, 403, 405
Shearin, E.N. 186
Shehan, C.L. 249
Shenk, J.L. 183
Shickmanter, B.K. 298
Sigel, I. 393
Sigelman, C.K. 348, 351
Sillars, A.L. 14
Simmons, J.L. 320
Simmons, R. 395
Simons, A.D. 294
Simons, R.L. 312, 318
Simpson, J.A. 81, 82, 245, 447, 450
Skinner, H.A. 53, 55
Slovik, L.F. 80, 82, 87, 114, 119
Smith, C. 350
Smith, D.A. 11, 12, 13, 20, 57, 63, 285, 300, 354, 355
Smith, J.P. 347, 350
Smith, T.W. 47
Snell, E.J. 345
Snyder, D.K. 413
Snyder, M. 445
Sockloskie, R.J. 353
Sollie, D.L. 119, 123
Sorbom, D. 200
South, S.J. 447
Spanier, G.B. 19, 88, 129, 184, 212, 321
Spence, J.T. 56, 119, 123, 124
Spielberger, C.R. 55
Sprecher, S. 82, 261
Spring, B. 294
Stafford, M.C. 328, 337
Stahelski, A.J. 79
Stanley, S.M. 44, 206, 207, 214, 286, 287, 381, 454
Stanley-Hagan, M.S. 395
Stapp, J. 56, 119, 123, 124
Stark, E. 345

Starzomski, A. 357
Steiger, J.H. 147
Steinberger, J.L. 298
Steinhauer, P.D. 53
Steinmetz, S.K. 45, 345, 347, 348, 354, 364
Stets, J.E. 47, 356
Stevenson-Hinde, J. 396
Stinson, L.L. 87
Stith, S.M. 350, 352, 359
Stockard, J. 350
Stone, R. 360
Storaasli, R.D. 44, 206, 207, 286, 287
Straus, M.A. 44, 45, 46, 54, 56, 57, 58, 208, 345, 347, 348, 349, 354, 356, 364
Stryker, S. 320
Stuart, G.L. 363
Stuart, R.B. 2, 280
Sugarman, D.B. 351, 354
Sugimoto, T. 348
Suhr, J.A. 298
Suitor, J.J. 44
Sullaway, M. 3, 20
Sullivan, K.T. 118, 298
Sullivan, R. 154
Sullivan, W.M. 326
Sullivan-Hanson, J. 357
Suls, J. 291
Supancic, M. 337
Surra, C.A. 80, 114, 119, 126
Sussman, M.B. 298
Sutherland, L. 156
Swain, M.A. 2, 15
Swann, W.B. Jr. 114, 327
Sweet, J.A. 335
Swidler, A. 154, 326

Tallman, I. 324, 326, 327, 328, 329, 337, 387, 398, 402, 425, 438, 443, 447, 454
Tanaka, J.S. 353
Tannen, D. 24
Tatsuoka, M.M. 122, 124
Teachman, J.D. 152
Tellegen, A. 318, 365
Tepperman, L. 312
Terman, L.M. 117
Thibaut, J.W. 74, 107, 445, 446, 447
Thoits, P. 320
Thoma, S.J. 239, 285
Thompson, E.H. 351
Thompson, L. 196
Tinsley, B.J. 396
Tipton, A. 154
Tipton, S.M. 326
Tolman, R. 359
Tontodonato, P. 350
Treboux, D. 357, 358
Turkewitz, H. 280

Turner, A. 364
Turner, R.H. 312
Tyree, A. 45, 56, 68, 348, 349, 350, 352, 354, 355, 356

U.S. Bureau of the Census 1

Vallerand, R.J. 182
Van Lange, P.A.M. 80, 81, 83
Van Lear, C.A. 326
Vangelisti, A. 11, 12, 13, 27, 57, 124, 125, 128, 129
Vanzetti, N. 208, 209
Vega, W.A. 155
Verette, J. 80, 81, 82, 87, 114, 119
Veroff, J. 1, 53, 152, 153, 154, 156, 157, 158, 159, 162, 163, 169, 181, 314, 386, 400, 412, 414, 417, 424, 430, 431, 455
Vincent, J.P. 77
Vitiliano, P.P. 47
Vivian, D. 11, 12, 13, 20, 57, 63, 285, 300, 345, 354, 355, 356

Wagner, B.C. 47
Wainer, H. 418
Walker, A.J. 196
Walker, L. 356, 359
Wallace, K.M. 53, 129, 208, 287
Wallace, P.M. 220
Waller, W. 114, 116, 117, 130, 131, 136, 142, 145, 397, 446
Wallin, P. 114, 116, 118, 237, 244, 248, 253, 256, 264
Walters, R. 360
Waltz, J. 363
Wampold, B.E. 77, 84
Warnken, W.J. 361
Waters, E. 209, 222, 357
Watson, D. 117, 118, 123, 284
Weinberger, J. 291
Weingarten, K. 397
Weisberg, J. 14
Weiss, R.L. 2, 37, 77, 105, 280, 288, 289, 300
Westberry, L. 55
Wethington, E. 290, 319
Wheeler, L. 23

Whiffen, V.E. 290
Whitbeck, L.B. 312, 318
White, A. 14, 15, 20
White, H.R. 46
White, J.W. 348
White, L. 14, 27
White, L.K. 46, 68, 249, 266, 446, 449
White, S.W. 180
Whitney, G. 361
Whitney, G.A. 80, 82, 87, 114, 119
Whyte, K.M. 239, 246, 258
Wieselquist, J. 106
Wiggins, J.S. 389
Wilcox, K.J. 365
Wildschut, R.T. 81
Wiles, K. 348, 351
Wilkie, C.F. 220
Willard, S. 240
Willett, J.B. 304
Williams, G.K. 298
Williams, J. 347, 350
Willis, S.L. 394
Wilsnack, R.W. 62
Wilsnack, S.C. 62
Wilson, B.F. 180
Wilson, D.P. 117
Wilson, M. 363, 394
Wilson, S.J. 312
Winke, J. 14, 15
Witcher, B.S. 81, 83
Woody, E.Z. 13, 301
Wright, J. 184
Wright, R. 220
Wylie, R. 222

Yoppi, B. 209
Young, A. 163
Yovetich, N.A. 80, 81, 106

Zanna, M. 182, 187, 197
Zautra, A. 417
Zeehandelaar, R.B. 298
Zegree, J.B. 47
Zembrodt, I.M. 75, 77
Zimowski, M. 302
Zubin, J. 294
Zuckerman, D. 345

Subject Index

Accommodation, 66, 74, 84, 159, 423
  and commitment, 109
  definition, 77
  determinants and consequences, 80
  ideal and actual self and spouse, 159
  model, 114
Affectional expression, 124, 128
Affective affirmation, 169
Affective balance, 155
Agency/communion dialectic, 156, 197
Aggression, 45, 168, 343, 426
  and alcohol, 46, 59, 423
  and attachment, 357
  attitudes justifying, 350
  biological models, 360
  and brain injury, 361
  changes over the lifespan, 348
  in dating relationships, 347
  developmental course, 347
  diagnosis by physicians, 345
  as a DSM-IV diagnosis, 346
  feminist models, 360, 366
  and negative affect in interaction, 355
  and personality disorders, 358
  predictors, 57
  prevalence, 44, 56, 345
  reasons for neglect of area, 343
  reciprocal aggression, 356
  recognition by spouses as a problem in marriage, 344
  socialization factors, 351
  stability of, 349
  and testosterone, 361
  typologies, 363
  verbal aggression, 352
Alcohol Dependency Scale, 55
Alcohol use
  and aggression, 46, 59
  marriage as drinking partnership, 62
  measurement, 54
  potential pathways, 59
  prevalence, 46

Ambivalence, 128
  and conflict, 134
Attachment, 107, 182, 186, 206, 403, 425
  and aggression, 357
Attachment Behavior Q-Set, 209
Attributions, 108, 118, 198, 380
  fundamental attribution error, 451
Autonomy, 182, 186

Bem Sex Role Inventory, 186
Boston Couples Study, 240
Buffalo Newlywed Study, 45

Center for Epidemiological Studies Depression Inventory, 55
Change (also see Stability)
  culture as contributing factor, 400
  defined as trajectories, 189, 302, 418
  growth-curve analysis, 304
  intraindividual, 184
  methods for assessing, 300
  residualized change, 301
  short-term and long-term, 404
Children (also see Parenthood), 209
  conduct disorder, 221
  expectations, 254, 273
  individual development of, 395
  mother–father–child interaction, 210
  parent–child interaction, 210, 221, 396
  peer relations, 206, 210
  self-esteem, 425
Cognitive variables (also see Attributions)
  expectancies, 154, 198, 317
  selective perception, 198
Cohabitation, 116, 157, 246, 249, 335
Commitment, 75, 82, 109, 116, 152, 154, 199, 316, 378
  asymmetry in, 321
  definition, 82
  development in courtship, 126
  hesitancy to commit, 127
  turbulence, 127

Communication, 14, 16, 121, 206, 238, 378
  change over time, 11, 212
  conceptualized as adaptive processes, 288, 290
  destructive patterns, 39
  diary studies, 15, 17, 22, 35, 314, 334
  and femininity, 119
  marital problems, 208, 335
  and marital satisfaction, 2, 24, 37, 322, 331
  nonverbal behavior, 210
  perceptions, 22
  predicted by earlier satisfaction, 13, 30
  premarital, 12, 239, 385
  skills, xiii, 209
Communication Patterns Questionnaire, 17, 20
Companionateness, 163
Compatibility, 114, 121, 123, 378
  theories, 143
Competence in marriage, 169
Conflict
  anger expression, 55, 66, 283
  avoidance, 14, 21, 55
  in black community, 168
  child's exposure to, 224
  coding, 20, 87, 209, 210
  coercion, 14, 21
  constructive style, 163
  constructive versus destructive acts, 77
  demand/withdraw pattern, 15
  domineering behavior, 59
  early years of marriage, 44
  engagement versus disengagement, 13
  escalation, 209
  long-term effects, 12, 13
  and marital satisfaction, 13, 14, 16, 62
  negative affect, 12, 205, 206, 209, 331
  negative reciprocity, 77
  negativity, 124, 127, 128
  perceived harm to relationship, 251
  premarital, 251
  problem-solving, 55, 199, 327
  resolution, 199
  responses, 14, 75
  sadness, 283
  and social support, 282, 289
  strategies, 21
  tasks, 211
  undue emphasis on, 281
Conflict Inventory, 55
Conflict Tactics Scale, 54, 345
Conversational patterns, 27
Correlations
  comparing strength, 147
  inadequacy, 67
Couples Interaction Scoring System, 210

Courtship, 116, 121, 237
  aggression in, 347, 352
  problems in, 249
  romanticism, 256
  satisfaction, 242
  trajectory of, 126
  transition to marriage, 237
Cross-sectional research
  limitations, 3
Cultural change, xv

Dating relationships (*see* Courtship)
Denver Family Development Project, 205
Depression, 221, 283
Discriminant analysis, 214, 238, 271
Disillusionment model, 114, 145
Dissolution (*see* Marital instability)
Divorce (*see* Marital instability)
Dyadic Adjustment Scale, 17, 19, 88, 184
Dyadic data, 410, 412, 413
Dyadic interaction paradigm, 87

Early versus late nesters, 273
Early Years of Marriage Study, 157
Economic hardship, 318
Enduring vulnerabilities, 288, 425
Equity, 160, 326
Exit-Voice-Loyalty-Neglect typology, 75, 76

Faith, 182, 187, 196
Family Assessment Measure, 53
Family socialization, 316, 324
  family of origin, 324
Field theory, 444

Gender
  identity, 154
  and norms for marital functioning, 176
  testing gender effects, 413

Help-seeking, 1
Hierarchical linear models, 199, 304, 418
Household work, 119, 322

Individual differences (*see* Personality)
Interactional Dimensions Coding System, 209
Interdependence theory, 74, 78, 79, 107, 182, 249, 445
Intergenerational models, 318, 403
Interview data, 51, 122, 126, 157, 314, 333
  via telephone, 122, 128
Intimacy, 245, 272
Investment model, 82, 447

Kansas Marital Satisfaction Scale, 199

Lagged effects, 417
Leisure activities, 119, 123, 163
Life events (*see* Stress)

Liking Scale, 246
Longitudinal research on marriage
  attrition, 420
  clinical relevance, 377
  compared to cross-sectional studies, xiii
  dependent variable, xv
  failure to study relationship events in, 383
  funding, 230, 434
  historical trends, 3
  individual adult development and, 394
  life span developmental approach, 393
  limitations of two-wave designs, 300, 302
  links to prevention, 285
  literature addressing, 279
  measurement decay, 199, 229, 242
  null model tests in, 284
  overestimation of the value of, 428
  sampling, 297, 298
  scarcity, 180, 441
  scientific costs, 5
  tedious nature, 198
  third variable problems, 382, 429
  time-based versus event-based, 384
  unintended effects, 229, 314, 334, 433
Love, 127, 248, 272
  and conflict, 134
  and long-term outcomes, 245
Love Scale, 246

Macromotives, 82
Marital Adjustment Test, 53, 208, 287
Marital Agendas Protocol, 208
Marital Communication Inventory, 17, 22
Marital dissatisfaction
  onset versus continuing course, 5
  as risk factor for psychopathology, 221
Marital instability, 46, 57, 108, 180, 199, 238,
    316, 431
  cascade model, 68, 404
  and cohabitation, 249
  prediction, 63, 198, 313, 424
Marital interaction (*see* Communication; Con-
    flict; Support in marriage)
Marital outcomes
  cohort effects, 437
  premarital predictors, 240, 425
Marital quality (*see* Marital satisfaction)
Marital role preferences, 123
Marital satisfaction
  and alcohol use, 46
  changes, 19, 56, 60, 89, 131, 181, 195, 212
  measurement issues, 19, 63, 129
  parental models, 238, 326
  and similarity, 119
  social construction, 154
Marital therapy, xiii
  behavioral marital therapy, 2, 207, 380

cognitive-behavioral marital therapy, 3, 285,
    380
  emotionally focused marital therapy, 3
  integrative couples therapy, 3
Marriage statistics
  divorce rate, 1, 281, 291
  marriage rate, 1
  peak period for divorce, 5, 298
  remarriage, 180
Mate selection, 119, 237
Miller Social Intimacy Scale, 53
Mindreading, 186
Motives
  intrinsic and extrinsic, 182, 186

National Longitudinal Survey of Labor Mar-
    ket Experience, 434
National Survey of Families and Households,
    434
Negative Affectivity (*see* Personality)
Negativity (*see* Conflict)
Neuroticism (*see* Personality)
Newlywed marriage
  challenging tasks, 44
  as developmental period, 44
Nonindependence of multiple observations, 93
Nonverbal accuracy
  development, 15
  and marital satisfaction, 15
  standard content paradigm, 21

PAIR Project, 121
Panel Study of Income Dynamics, 434
Parenthood
  parent–child relationships, 205
  parental status, 160
  premarital, 53, 157
  stepchildren, 181, 182
  transition to, 145, 180, 183, 199, 206, 218,
    423
Perceived control, 169
Perceived Stress Scale, 55
Perpetual problems model, 114
Personal Attributes Questionnaire, 56
Personality, 45, 47, 55, 114, 121, 182, 283,
    378
  abrasiveness, 163
  agreeableness, 118, 163
  anxiety, 122, 162
  as cause of marital distress, 117
  contrariness, 129
  divorce-prone, 182
  expressiveness, 119, 122, 182, 186
  femininity, 47, 56, 119, 283
  impulsivity, 238, 283
  intergenerational transmission, 318
  interpersonal theories, 136
  masculinity, 47, 56, 283

neuroticism, 47, 55, 117, 118, 182, 238, 283
responsiveness, 129
zest, xiii, 156, 162
Pictorial Scale of Perceived Competence and Social Acceptance for Young Children, 209
Power
  and aggression, 359
  in decision-making, 160
  power/dependence balance, 328, 329
Premarital pregnancy, 53, 157, 184
Premarital sexual activity, 238
PREPARE, 238
Prevention, xv, 5, 45, 181, 197, 206, 280
  empirically based approach, 286
  normalizing decreases in satisfaction, 198
Prevention and Relationship Enhancement Program, 206, 207, 286, 381
Problem-solving versus coping, 328
Psychoanalytic theory, 155

Quality Marriage Index, 17, 19

Race and ethnicity, 51, 65, 155, 157, 325, 401
  conflict style, 168
  and norms for marital functioning, 176
Rapid Couples Interaction Scoring System, 87, 331
Recruitment, 18, 48, 85, 184, 207, 227, 240, 298
  response rate, 50, 85, 184, 241
  retention, 228
Relationship beliefs, 182, 186, 238
Relationship Beliefs Inventory, 186
Relationship maintenance, 124, 127, 196
Relationship Problem Inventory, 208
Religion, 238, 258, 264
Remarriage, 180
Response biases, 299
Roles
  role expectations, 316, 333
  role identities, 317, 320, 333
  role negotiations, 316, 324, 327, 330
  role sharing orientation, 159
  role structure, 333
  social roles, 317

Sample size, 228
Sampling biases, 50, 188, 298, 420, 429, 435
Selection biases, 48
Self-disclosure, 246
Self-efficacy, 327
Self-esteem, 206, 333
  and aggression, 358
Self-evaluations, 259, 378
Sentiment override, 37, 105

Sex role traditionalism, 258, 273
Sexual interaction, 163, 246
Sexual restraint, 248, 256
Similarity of spouses, 119, 182, 266, 378, 411
Sleeper effects, 272
Social exchange theory
  alternatives, 252, 272, 447
  relative involvement, 253
  rewards and costs, 249, 272
Social learning theory, 107, 155, 280, 316, 442
  limitations, 281
Social networks, 261, 378
Social Support (*see* Support in marriage)
Sociodemographic factors, 45, 154, 181, 253, 264, 325, 333, 378, 453, 455
  income, 157
  insufficient attention given, 62
  sociocultural agenda, 394
  women in labor force, 312, 320
Socioemotional behavior, 121, 124
Spielberger Trait Anger Scale, 55
Spillover effects, 319
Spouse abuse (*see* Aggression)
Stability, 89, 416
  of aggression, 349
  of communication behaviors, 12
  distinguished from satisfaction, 153, 446
  of satisfaction, 56
  types of, 130
Stable marriages, 152
  definition, 158
Stress, 147, 282, 288, 316, 318, 332, 386
  and marital interaction, 290
  normative and nonnormative, 397
  relationship environments, 450, 454
  stress-related hormones, 319
Support in marriage, 21, 31, 163, 182, 186, 209, 282, 289, 321
Survey of Relationship Values, 187
Symptom Checklist 90-R, 185
System for Coding Affect Regulation in the Family, 210

Trust, 106

Understanding, 169
Unique variance approach, 67
University of North Carolina Marriage Study, 85

Vulnerability-Stress-Adaptation Model of Marital Outcomes, 293

Work
  expectations for combining marriage and career, 254, 272, 321
  job achievement, 160

Printed in the United States
58757LVS00003B/1-24